EDUCATIONAL PSYCHOLOGY

IN THEORY AND PRACTICE

SECOND EDITION

James W. Vander Zanden
Ohio State University

Ann J. Pace
University of Missouri - Kansas City

RANDOM HOUSE

NEW YORK

Second Edition

98765432

Copyright © 1980, 1984 by Random House, Inc.

Library of Congress Cataloging in Publication Data

Vander Zanden, James Wilfrid.
  Educational psychology.

  Bibliography: p.
  Includes indexes.
  1. Educational psychology.   2. Learning, Psychology of.
3. Classroom management.   4. Educational tests and measurements.   I. Pace, Ann, 1936–   . II. Title.
LB1051.V326   1983   370.15   83-13896
ISBN 0-394-33546-5

Manufactured in the United States of America

Except where noted, all photographs by Patrick Reddy

Cover and Interior design: Karin Kincheloe
Cover art: Caroline S. Portny

TO THE INSTRUCTOR

Writing an educational psychology textbook is a serious undertaking because the book provides teachers-to-be with their first introduction to the field. A great deal depends on the nature of their early impressions and experiences. Consequently, it is essential that we seize on the initial eagerness that so many students bring to our classes and channel their enthusiasm in the development of genuine professional competence and commitment.

An educational psychology textbook is a serious undertaking for another reason. We *know* that good teachers *do* matter. Indeed, we aim to be such teachers ourselves and to inspire our students to become capable, resourceful, and self-actualized men and women. For its part, the public has increasingly come to demand of us even higher standards of educational performance as well as improvement in the quality of our schools.

The first edition of *Educational Psychology: In Theory and Practice* aimed for a combination of strengths—both a firm grounding in basic material *and* the application of this material within the classroom experience. Fortunately, this approach was well received. In this new edition Professor Ann Pace of the University of Missouri - Kansas City has joined the venture. Together with her skills and insights and the feedback provided by users, the second edition builds on and strengthens the integration of theory with practice.

The following features characterize the second edition.

A Solid Foundation in Fundamentals. Good classroom practice is founded on a solid knowledge of learning processes and instructional strategies. Consequently we have carefully surveyed the research literature in psychology and education to identify instructional approaches, techniques, and tools with demonstrated effectiveness. We seek to provide a firm theoretical undergirding so that teachers-to-be can grasp the principles behind various classroom practices. In this manner they can gain the freedom and competence to depart from particular practices and formulate new ones when doing so becomes necessary. Classroom teaching is a complex undertaking that does not lend itself to a set of recipes that will apply to all situations and problems. In fact, teaching derives its professional status from its theoretical body of knowledge. Without such knowledge, teachers become merely technicians. Although technicians have skills, they have little theoretical understanding of what it is that they are doing.

Classroom Applications. We recognize the teachers-to-be, by virtue of their inexperience, are legitimately concerned with their ability to handle typical classroom situations during their first year or so of teaching. Fortunately, through the years experienced classroom teachers have written about their problems and strategies in the *Instructor*, a national magazine for teachers. We have gleaned twenty-five of the most pertinent of these articles from issues of the past fifteen years and incorporated them as boxed inserts within the appropriate sections of the text. In this manner we seek to bring the full drama, color, and richness of the classroom experience to bear for teachers-to-be. From these selections they can acquire a ''hands-on'' grasp for key principles and strategies.

Contemporary Issues. In addition to the boxed inserts from the *Instructor*, the text contains other boxed inserts that provide an in-depth examination of topical issues. The focus is on contemporary matters that affect the schools or educational psychology as a discipline. For example, Chapter 2 contains the boxed inserts ''Teachers and the Abused Child,'' ''Combatting Sexism in the Classrooms,'' and ''A Classroom Exercise in Prejudice.''

Exercises. Professor Philip Langer of the University of Colorado has prepared end-of-chapter exercises for students. These activities consist of review questions, questions requiring the application of principles and concepts, and projects. They provide students with opportunities to explore classroom situations and to identify important themes in a chapter.

Photographs. In keeping with the classroom emphasis of the text, the text contains over 120 photographs showing actual classroom situations with students and teachers. The majority of them were taken in a variety of schools in Ohio and Kentucky by professional photographer Patrick Reddy.

Organization of the Text. We have reordered much of the material and the chapters in the second edition so as to match the sequence used by most instructors. However, there is no one ''right'' way

to teach educational psychology, and the material that is presented can be adapted to an instructor's teaching objectives. In sum, users of this text should feel free to make it serve their own particular purposes.

Pedagogical Aids. To assist the student in mastering the material, we have used a number of pedagogical aids:

- *To the student:* This section precedes the text itself and introduces students to the philosophy and organization of the book, explaining how best to study and benefit from the material presented.
- *Chapter outlines:* Each chapter begins with an outline of the sections of the chapter, which allows students to review the material to be covered at a glance.
- *Chapter previews:* Each chapter also opens with a brief discussion of the material that is to follow, providing students with a clear introduction and questions to consider as they study the chapter.
- *Chapter summaries:* A numbered summary at the end of each chapter recapitulates the central points. This feature allows students to review what they have read in a systematic manner.
- *Chapter glossaries:* At the end of each chapter there is a glossary that defines all the major terms that appear in the chapter. Thus, students have a convenient vehicle by which to look up and review key concepts.
- *Glossary:* At the end of the text, glossary terms are listed together with the chapter in which the concept is defined and discussed.
- *Appendix:* At the end of the text is an appendix that covers the major statistical concepts and operations commonly needed by the classroom teacher. It can also serve as a handy reference source for the student in the years ahead.

This text has benefitted from the kind and talented help of a number of people in the Random

House College Division. We are indebted to Judith Rothman, acquisitions editor; Leslie Carr, developmental editor; Laurel Miller and Marion Corkett, project editors; Karin Kincheloe and Barbara Grodsky, designers; Brian Hogley and Linda Goldfarb, production supervisors; and R. Lynn Goldberg, photo editor.

We have also received a good many helpful suggestions from our reviewers: Theodore Bayer, SUNY Albany; Nancy Hoar, Western New England College; Pat Jones, San Francisco State University; Bill D. Lamkin, Baylor University; Philip Langer, University of Colorado; John T. Lloyd, Washington State University; Beatrice Moosally, Mankato State University; Jeannette Roberts, Miami University; and Ronald W. Zellner, University of Northern Colorado.

James W. Vander Zanden
Ann J. Pace

TO THE STUDENT

Welcome to educational psychology, the study of learning and teaching. In this textbook we have two primary goals. First, we seek to pass along to you some of what educational psychologists have discovered about the process of learning and about various instructional strategies. Second, we want to assist you in applying these principles to deal effectively with life in the classroom.

Incorporated in the main text are a number of features that we hope will help you to learn the material and make practical use of it. If you take advantage of these aids, you will get more out of the book and find it a beneficial tool. They include the following:

Organization. The opening chapter introduces you to the field of educational psychology. The book is then divided into three parts: the learner, learning, and teaching. The first part—the learner—focuses on what students bring with them as individuals to the classroom situation. The second part—learning—examines those processes by which relatively permanent changes occur in a person's behavior as the result of experience. The final part—teaching—considers those activities and strategies that promote learning, especially in classroom settings.

Chapter Outlines and Previews. Each chapter opens with a "bird's-eye" view of what lies ahead

of you. Educational psychologists find that procedures that make the organization of material more obvious facilitate the learning of the material.

Definitions. Educational psychology, like other academic disciplines, employs a variety of technical terms as part of its professional language. Words, especially everyday words that refer to behavior, vibrate with many overtones and even double and triple meanings. Hence a professional language is a definite asset in scientific work, for it provides a more precise and condensed form of communication. We have employed a two-tier system in the use of technical terms. Those concepts that typically assume top priority within the field of educational psychology appear in bold type. Somewhat less critical but nonetheless significant terms are in italics.

Chapter Summaries. At the end of each chapter we have provided a summary that repeats the main points of the chapter in the form of numbered paragraphs. The summary should help you mentally to rehearse what you have learned and hence facilitate the retention process. The summary should also prove of help in reviewing the material for examinations.

Chapter and Book Glossaries. At the end of each chapter we have placed all the first-tier, or bold-type, terms and definitions that we introduced in the chapter. As a further aid to your study, at the end of the text we have listed all the glossary terms and definitions together with the chapter in which the concept is defined and discussed. We did not include italicized words in the glossaries because we wish to avoid a dictionary mentality. Instead we focus on those strategies that are useful in promoting classroom learning.

Boxed Inserts. Scattered throughout the chapters are boxed inserts, many of which present articles from the *Instructor,* a national magazine for teachers. In these selections classroom teachers share with you their experiences, problems, and educational strategies. Other boxed inserts deal with contemporary issues that affect the schools and education. These are designed to provide you with in-depth information on matters that you will encounter as professional teachers.

Exercises. At the end of each chapter a number of exercises have been prepared for your use. These activities are designed to give you opportunities for analyzing classroom situations and to assist you in identifying the important themes of the chapter.

We wish you well on your journey in educational psychology. You will have the opportunity to learn more about yourself and about the teaching experience. You are proceeding down the road of a very demanding yet exceedingly rewarding profession.

James W. Vander Zanden
Ann J. Pace

CONTENTS

EDUCATIONAL PSYCHOLOGY

IN THEORY
AND PRACTICE

**SECOND
EDITION**

CHAPTER OUTLINE

1

INTRODUCTION

CHAPTER PREVIEW

This first chapter has several purposes. One is to examine the discipline of educational psychology and to explore how knowledge of teaching-learning processes and theories can lead to sound recommendations for effective classroom instruction. Another is to describe how the enterprise of education is organized administratively at federal, state, local, and school levels. Additionally, the overriding objectives of education in Western society are reviewed. A major goal of this chapter is to examine what it is like to be a teacher in today's society: Teachers' role perceptions and career expectations; the rewards and satisfactions teachers derive from teaching, as well as their frustrations; and the differential distribution of men and women across various teaching and administrative positions are examined.

The outline gives an overview of the organization and content of this introductory chapter. In addition, the following questions should alert you to its underlying concerns and encourage you to think about the implications of the information presented. By keeping these questions in mind as you read, and then reflecting on them, you should be able to relate the material covered to your personal concerns about teaching. The questions should also provide a conceptual framework for helping you integrate the facts and issues discussed:

■ How can knowledge of the learner, learning, and teaching help the teacher become a more effective professional educator?
■ How do various groups and levels of government share responsibility for the administration of public education in the United States and Canada?
■ How do the broad objectives of education affect educational practice?
■ How do teachers conceive of their role and why do teachers' views of teaching differ widely?
■ What satisfactions do teachers typically derive from teaching and what factors affect teachers' morale and physical and emotional well-being?

You want to be a teacher—a good teacher. You are looking forward to the day when you will have your own classroom and a group of students. You yourself have been a student for much of your life. You have had inspiring teachers who have turned you on to learning and to science, history, or some other subject matter. And you have also had teachers whom you considered "disasters." You are determined to be as successful as your inspiring teachers. Your future students, their parents, and the community at large also want you to succeed. This text is designed to help you to become a teacher—a good teacher. (See the boxed insert on page 5.)

THE NATURE OF EDUCATIONAL PSYCHOLOGY

We have entered an age in which education is not just a luxury permitting some men an advantage over others. It has become a necessity without which a person is defenseless in this complex, industrialized society. . . . We have truly entered the century of the educated man.

LYNDON B. JOHNSON
Commencement Address, Tufts University, June 9, 1963

Schools came into existence several thousand years ago as instruments to train a select few for leadership and key professions. A hundred or so years ago, public schools were introduced in Western societies to teach people the three Rs, thereby providing them with the literacy required in an industrial-urban age. At the present time, a third educational revolution is taking place as nations come to view education as an indispensable weapon for national survival. Perhaps not surprisingly, a rapid expansion of educational enrollments has occurred in the vast majority of the nations of the world, especially the Third World, since 1950 (Meyer et al., 1977).

The Boundaries of Educational Psychology

Education is a human activity. It implies a formal, intentional, systematic transmission of knowledge and skills. The focus of education is upon the learner and the teacher and the interaction that takes place between them. It is also the focus of **educational psychology**, an academic discipline that studies the learning-teaching process. Thus,

EDUCATIONAL PSYCHOLOGY
Educational psychology is primarily concerned with the dual processes of teaching and learning.

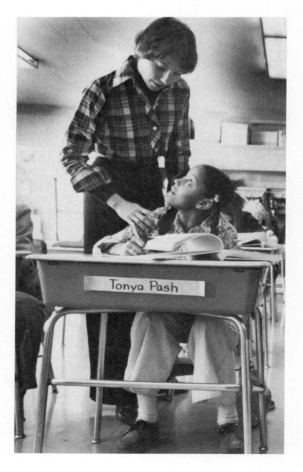

Tonya Pash

ESPECIALLY FOR STUDENT TEACHERS

JUNE MARIE SCHASRE

Second-Grade Teacher, Buffalo, New York

Are you prepared to become a dedicated and enthusiastic teacher? It takes a lot of time and effort—more than the ordinary individual may be willing to give. Start evaluating yourself. Look at your strengths and weaknesses objectively; then use this checklist to rate your "Effective Teacher Potential."

- Do you care about children? Do you enjoy working with them? Can you see each child as an individual? Can you be a wise, supportive friend to each?
- Are you preparing a resource file? If you haven't already, now is a good time to start. You'll have a head start on your first days as a beginning teacher. Include pictures, documents, brochures, journal clippings, notebooks, and other references.
- Do you want to continue studying new approaches in your field? This may mean taking in-service courses, working for a higher degree, or reading as many professional publications as possible. And don't forget how much you can learn from fellow teachers and your students.
- Do you look forward to active participation in board meetings, faculty discussions, PTA events, and extracurricular student activities?
- Have you considered the challenge and interest of a potential position more than the salary, fringe benefits, or "easy" working conditions?
- Can you accept criticism from your critic teacher or supervisor now? Or do you feel you are being unfairly judged? Are you willing to change your viewpoint in favor of one that might present a more effective solution?
- Are you able to cope with emergencies and drastic changes in routine?
- Do you work well with your fellow students? Not all schools will be progressive to the point of having team teaching, of course. However, all good schools consist of a team of teachers working together for a common purpose—quality education. Will you be able to cooperate effectively with colleagues when you launch your teaching career?
- Are you diplomatic enough to converse objectively, yet sincerely, when confronted with excited parents? Do you display maturity in your judgment and discretion in your remarks?
- Do you constantly evaluate the effectiveness of your methods and procedures, explore alternate solutions, and recognize your weaknesses as well as your strengths?

If you can honestly answer YES to these questions (at least most of them), you have an excellent chance of becoming an outstanding teacher.

Keep the above checklist for future use. If you note any weak points now, prepare yourself for the challenge of strengthening them. Be willing to change now *and* in the future, for you will be working in an ever-changing atmosphere. Your world will consist simultaneously of revolutionary innovations and accepted conventions. Prepare for them.

Source: June Marie Schasre, "Especially for Student Teachers," *Instructor*, 81 (April 1972):17.

educational psychology is concerned with understanding and facilitating instructional practice.

Educational psychology is a multidisciplinary field that represents the intersection of two separate areas of study—psychology and education. As such, it involves both the study of behavior and the process of education. Psychologists have traditionally directed their energies toward an understanding of the nature and process of learning in a relatively abstract sense. In contrast, educators have been chiefly interested in identifying and implementing the most effective instructional strategies for children. The one discipline has focused primarily upon the behavior of the learner; the other upon the behavior of the teacher.

Educational psychologists draw upon the basic knowledge of both psychology and education. Further, they undertake independent research dealing with the learning-teaching process. However, it should be stressed that, at best, academic disciplines are only loosely defined areas. In practice, the borderlines are so vague that researchers give little thought to whether they are ''invading'' another discipline's field of study. Far from being undesirable, such overlap can contribute a freshness of approach and provide a stimulus to the advancement of the frontiers of knowledge. Although some scholars take the position that they ''own'' a particular content area, most scientists welcome aid and collaboration from any qualified person, whether that person is in the same or another discipline.

Knowledge and Application

Educational psychology is concerned both with the *creation* of a body of knowledge directly relevant to the educational process and the *application* of this knowledge to effective classroom instruction. In other words, it involves both knowledge *production* and knowledge *utilization*. Each dimension is linked to the other, strengthening and reinforcing it. By way of analogy, surgeons are not expected to undertake a gall bladder operation without a basic knowledge of the body's anatomy and physiology. Nor should we expect teachers to undertake classroom instruction without knowledge of what goes on within the learner and between learner and teacher. Further, we do not expect prospective physicians to instruct themselves in the application of surgical principles. Neither should we expect teachers to enter classroom settings without appropriate instructional concepts and techniques. In this sense, knowledge of production and knowledge of utilization complement and supplement one another.

Traditionally, educational psychologists have been interested in both theories of learning and theories of instruction (Bruner, 1966). Theories of learning are *descriptive*. They are explanatory, telling us the conditions under which individuals acquire knowledge and skills. Theories of instruction are *prescriptive*, providing us with procedures and practical application in a classroom context. Their usefulness depends on establishing the rules so that knowledge and skills can be transmitted effectively from teacher to learner. The emphasis of a theory of instruction is on the experiences that predispose a pupil toward learning, the ways a body of knowledge should be structured, and the sequences that present material most effectively (Kane and Marsh, 1980).

In some areas a close linkage exists between theories of learning and theories of instruction. For instance, the instructional strategy of mastery learning (students master one unit before proceeding to the next unit in an educational sequence) is consistent with many of the principles of learning derived from both behavioral and cognitive theories (see Chapters 5, 6, and 14). The same holds true of classroom management techniques involving principles of behavior modification (see Chapters 5 and 16). If we focus only on prescriptions for instruction, we would neglect the contributions that theories of learning can make to theories of instruction.

The relationship between a theory of learning

and a theory of instruction is not always direct or readily apparent. Nevertheless, teachers can better understand why some strategies work and others fail because of their acquaintance with basic learning principles. These principles permit teachers to analyze a situation by pointing out where to look and what to expect (Hilgard and Bower, 1975).

Educational psychology is premised on the assumption that effective instructional strategies, techniques, and tools can be identified and made available to teachers. James J. Gallagher makes the point in these terms:

> Is teaching an art? Indeed it is. Perhaps too much of one. Surgery was once too much an art and many people died as a result. Cooking is an art, and while few people die of it these days, drugstores do a thriving business in remedies for misbegotten creative culinary efforts. For when a set of skills is in a developmental stage where people say, "It is an art," they mean several things. First, that there are only a very few persons who have the skills that can identify them as highly effective practitioners, as "artists." Second, even these artists cannot give a systematic account of how they practice their art, and they are reduced to modeling their performance for those who would learn from them. But it is hard to imitate the true artist, and his genius too often dies with him. . . .
>
> Those interested in the improvement of education and teaching would like to remove some of the mystery of the art of effective teaching through systematic study. [1970:30]

Educational psychologists search for a scientific basis for teacher education and for improving teacher effectiveness. The teacher-to-be should not have to rediscover the "tools of the trade." With appropriate knowledge and skills, each generation of teachers can benefit from the discoveries and inventions of its predecessors. In this fashion, each generation of teachers can rise from the shoulders—and the achievements—of the previous generation.

The purpose of courses in educational psychology is not simply to train individuals to teach but to provide them with a theoretical background that they can apply in their teaching and in their daily lives. By having a firm grasp of the theory behind particular practices, the professional gains the freedom and competence to depart from such practices and to formulate new ones when necessary. Indeed, one hallmark of a profession is its particular body of theoretical knowledge that is useful in assisting clients who come to the professional for help. Without such knowledge, the teacher becomes merely a technician (Williams, Neff, and Finkelstein, 1981; Little, 1982). Although technicians have skills, they have little theoretical understanding of what it is that they are doing. They may be well equipped to perform the skill, but they lack the insight to know how to alter their performance purposefully to meet changed circumstances (Samuels and Terry, 1977). Without appropriate theoretical background, there is little to distinguish a teacher from a teacher-aide or some other professional.

EDUCATIONAL ORGANIZATION AND OBJECTIVES

The school is a social organization that brings together the activities of a good many people, all of whom, in theory at least, direct their activities toward instructing the young. The integration of these activities within a larger whole gives rise to a unique institution. As such, schools are organizations where the central task is to process people rather than material objects. In contrast to organizations like General Motors, where the emphasis is on assembling raw materials, schools deal with people, who are neither passive nor available in uniform lots (Parelius and Parelius, 1978). Schools are therefore social systems—in many respects small communities—having their own characteristics and functions.

SCHOOLS AS COMPLEX ORGANIZATIONS
Schools are large-scale social organizations that integrate a great many activities
and people.

Organizational Structure

Like many other complex organizations, schools do not exist in isolation. They are tightly interlocked with other institutions. At the very top of this organizational arrangement is the federal government, which through various agencies, including the Department of Education and the federal court system, profoundly influences educational life. Consider, for example, the recent programs dealing with handicapped children and court rulings in school desegregation cases. Below the federal level is the state level. State educational authorities provide encompassing standards and regulations, like those setting the number of days in a school year, and they allocate state monies for specified programs. Finally, there are local boards of education and the individual schools.

Within the United States and Canada, there is a tradition of local control of education. In the United States, there are more than 20,000 local school districts, each governed by a separate school board. A board is composed of lay members from the local community (either appointed or elected) who are responsible for the schools' fiscal and other policies. The board of education generally appoints, assigns, and dismisses principals, teachers, and other school personnel; decides curricular and extracurricular programs; determines the type of school organization; secures school sites and approves building construction; determines special services, including health, guidance, vocational training, and the like; approves operational budgets; and recommends local tax levies for the financial support of the schools.

The superintendent is the top school administrator in a district. The superintendent makes policy decisions in consultation with the school board and is responsible for implementing these decisions. The next level in the chain of command is the school principal. The principal's duties encompass the general management of the school and the instructional program. Although principals are expected to be master teachers who supervise the instructional program, most of their time and energy is devoted to other tasks only remotely related to teaching (Swift, 1974). For the principal, the school is less a problem of education than of logistics—buildings, books, grounds, supplies, maintenance personnel, secretaries, teachers, and students. The principal must also manage relations between inside groups (teachers and students) and relations with outside groups (superiors in "central office" and parents).

In some instances, there may be an assistant principal below the principal (especially at the secondary school level). Below the principal, the structure usually branches off in two directions, one for the teachers and students and another for noninstructional staff (maintenance personnel, the dietitian, cooks, secretaries, and others). Teachers are the immediate day-by-day link between the larger system and individual students. Thus, the school system is characterized by a *chain of command*, a network of positions functionally interrelated for the purpose of accomplishing educational objectives. It is a hierarchical arrangement in which the pyramiding order is based upon division of function and authority.

Objectives of Education

Whenever we do anything about education, we are forced up against the ultimate definitions, the ultimate questions: "What are we? What are we to do with our lives?"

G. B. LEONARD
Education and Ecstasy, 1968

Within Western nations education is commonly viewed as having four broad objectives. First, there are those objectives that pertain to a child's acquisition of basic literacy skills and a general education. A major priority of modern societies is that children achieve competency in the three Rs and develop a fund of basic concepts and information. Such skills and knowledge dominate contemporary life and are prerequisites for adequate functioning within an urban-industrial world.

Second, there are those objectives that concern the individual's ability to respect and get along with other people and to understand and practice the ideals associated with good citizenship. Above all, humans are social beings and live their lives in a social environment. The school provides a major vehicle for preparing students for social and civic responsibilities so that they may be full and active partners in the larger human enterprise.

Third, there are those objectives that deal with an individual's own health and well-being. The school is given the task of promoting sound health habits and an appreciation for effective physical fitness. Further, the school can assist students to become total, complete persons, capable of finding the promise of self-realization and fulfillment in their lives. School can also assist students to appreciate beauty in the world and to cultivate those interests and skills necessary for the productive use of leisure time. Gilbert Highet writes:

> Many theorists have written about education as if it were chiefly intended to teach young people to live in society. Of course that is one of its purposes. . . . Yet it is clear, when we look at young men and women, that they also need to be taught how to live with themselves. Many of the most important things in life happen to us in solitude. Intellectual discoveries, powerful emotional experiences, enlargements of the soul, come more commonly to a man or a woman alone in a quiet room or sitting in the heart of wild nature, than in the restless and noisy and often thoughtless group. [1976:43–44]

Fourth, there are those objectives that involve preparing a pupil for family living and for an appropriate occupational role. The school can help a student to develop the attitudes and awareness

PREPARING INDIVIDUALS FOR THE LARGER HUMAN ENTERPRISE
One set of educational goals focuses on the ability of individuals to function successfully within group contexts.

that are necessary for successful living in a family group. And the school can assist the student in acquiring self-understanding and developing self-direction in identifying individual occupational abilities and skills. By the same token, the school affords an individual opportunities for gaining the knowledge and skills required for gainful employment. Finally, the school has the responsibility for promoting an understanding of what it means to be a good manager of money, property, and resources.

THE ROLE OF TEACHER

The way to become an effective *teacher* is to become an effective *person!*
DOUGLAS J. STANWYCK
''Teaching for Personal Growth and Awareness,'' 1977

There are within the United States 2.2 million public school teachers, making teaching by far the nation's largest profession (Bureau of the Census data). Of these, 1.2 million teach at the elementary level and 1 million at the junior- and senior-high level. In addition, there are 226,000 nonpublic school teachers (150,000 at the elementary level; 96,000 at the secondary level). Another 138,000 individuals are principals and supervisors. The overwhelming majority of teachers have at least a bachelor's degree and more than 40 percent have a master's degree or more.

Elements of the Role

All the world's a stage,
And all the men and women merely players.
They have their exits and their entrances;
And one man in his time plays many parts . . .

WILLIAM SHAKESPEARE
As You Like It

As we go about our everyday activities, we encounter people in a variety of roles—neighbor, pedestrian, shopper, physician, meter reader, baseball player, mother, drug addict, elderly woman, and so on. A **role** is a set of expectations that defines the appropriate behavior for a particular category of individuals. It specifies who does what, when, and where (Vander Zanden, 1984). By virtue of roles we can collapse or telescope a large number of behaviors into manageable bundles (Goffman, 1959). We know what we can expect of others, and they know what they can expect of us.

It is usually assumed that there is considerable uniformity in the definitions setting forth the role expectations of teachers. Sociologist Ronald J. Pellegrin (1976) tested this assumption as part of the larger Organizational Attributes Project funded by the federal government (undertaken by the Center for the Advanced Study of Educational Administration at the University of Oregon between 1967 and 1970). Elementary teachers in eighteen schools in the Midwest, East, and Northeast completed a job description in which they identified and described the main sets of tasks or dimensions of their work. The task areas and the proportion

of all job-related tasks falling into each category were as follows: instructional activities, 25.0 percent; management, 19.7 percent; planning, 16.5 percent; evaluation, 14.1 percent; supervision-discipline, 10.1 percent; special instruction, 4.5 percent; public relations, 3.4 percent; meetings, 3.3 percent; professional development, 1.7 percent; and miscellaneous or other tasks, 1.7 percent.

Overall, Pellegrin found a good deal of uniformity in the task distributions of teachers from one region or school district to another. However, considerable variation existed from one school to another *within* a district. For example, in one school district the percentage of all tasks listed that fell into the instructional category was 45.3 in one school and 17.2 in another. All of this led Pellegrin to conclude that considerable variation occurs among teachers in how they conceive of their teaching tasks. Little agreement existed among teachers, even among those in the same school, as to what the main dimensions of the job were. Nor was there high consensus concerning the importance of a given task or the amount of time to be devoted to it.

Pellegrin concluded:

> A task to which one teacher devotes considerable time and energy may be virtually ignored by another teacher whose official position in the division of labor is virtually identical to that of the first. To the extent that teachers engage in common activities, the commonality apparently grows largely out of the general expectation that each will teach students and that they will all deal with like content and use similar materials. In any case, behavioral uniformities do not arise from common conceptualizations of their roles as teachers. There is simply too much variation in task performance and emphasis for these conceptualizations to provide a great deal of commonality of behavior. [1976:366]

In sum, Pellegrin found considerable variation from teacher to teacher in both task identification and performance.

MULTIPLE DIMENSIONS OF THE TEACHER'S ROLE

The role of teacher is diverse and has many requirements beyond actual classroom instruction.

As Pellegrin's research suggests, the role of a teacher does not exist in a social vacuum. It is bound within a network of other roles. Consequently, the nature of this network has important implications for what teachers do and do not do. This point is highlighted when the school is examined as a workplace (Little, 1982). Prevailing norms and patterns of interaction among teachers have a powerful influence upon staff development and improvement in teaching. Teacher "learning on the job" is highest in those schools characterized by "close" faculties who routinely "work" together. In these settings, teachers come to view themselves as colleagues. Collegial expectations within the work setting encourage teachers to discuss their teaching with one another, to plan together, to experiment with new programs, and to cooperate in the implementation of various school programs.

Teaching: Profession or Job?

What nobler employment, or more valuable to the state, than that of the man [person] who instructs the rising generation?

CICERO
De divinatione, II, 78 B.C.

Considerable debate surrounds the issue of whether teachers are or should be professionals. Teacher organizations have long campaigned for official public recognition of teachers as professionals, a legal status comparable to that accorded physicians, lawyers, and accountants. Many believe that professionalism would promote higher standards and over time would result in better teachers. Professionalization would also promote an improvement in teachers' occupational prestige and remuneration. According to the National Education Association (NEA), fourteen states have already granted professional status to teachers (Goldman, 1978). However, local school boards have vigorously opposed the licensing of teachers, fearing it would decrease their authority while increasing that of teachers (as recognized specialists, teachers would make many of the educational decisions now reserved for school board members).

The criteria or qualifications for the label "professional" are not a settled matter among sociologists, educators, or the public (Ornstein, 1981). According to Ronald G. Corwin, an educational sociologist, a *profession* "is an organized work group that has a legal monopoly to establish procedures for recruiting and policing members and for maximum control over a body of theoretical knowledge which is applied towards the solution of problems" (1970:3).

In order for an occupation to be recognized as a profession, it is generally thought that at the very minimum it must have a strong and unique base of expert knowledge. The Commission on Education for the Profession of Teaching of the AACTE (American Association of Colleges for Teacher Education) stresses the importance of a knowledge base or "professional culture," holding that "to fail to develop principles, concepts, and theories, and to validate practice is to restrict the occupation [of teaching] to the level of a craft . . ." (Howsam et al., 1976:11). The commission notes that, without a shared, systematic, and scientific knowledge base for instructional decisions, "teachers remain forever captives of limited personal experience, whether their teachers' or their own" (1976:81).

A broad spectrum of commentators on American education have argued that although there are large numbers of courses and textbooks dealing with teaching methods, the actual knowledge base upon which these depend is weak (Parelius and Parelius, 1978). The sociologist Dan C. Lortie argues:

> Special schooling for teachers is neither intellectually nor organizationally as complex as that found in the established professions. The study of medicine and engineering is rooted in science; law and divinity can point to generations of scholars who have contributed to their development. Neither holds for education, for specialized study of the subject has a short history and an erratic connection with the mainstream of intellectual development in modern society. . . . Nor do we find an equivalent to the centuries of

TEACHER ORGANIZATIONS

The two principal teacher organizations are the National Education Association (NEA) and the American Federation of Teachers (AFT). The former has about 1.4 million members; the latter, approximately 450,000. Until the late 1960s, the NEA largely confined its activities to the improvement of the professional status of teachers. It sought to raise the quality of teacher training, to foster standards of professional ethics, and to build public respect for teachers. It saw teachers and members of boards of education as public servants who shared a common concern for both the welfare of students and the community. As such, the NEA did not view the two parties as adversaries divided by a conflict of interests in the manner of corporations and blue-collar workers. Indeed, the NEA opposed work stoppages and attempted to maintain a politically neutral course in election campaigns.

All of this changed in the late 1960s and early 1970s, in part influenced by the political turbulence and activism of the period. The emphasis placed upon "social harmony" that had pervaded the post-World War II period gave way to a "confrontation" ethos. The militancy of blacks, women, and antiwar advocates had a profound impact upon the educational community and the NEA. In response to the changing times, the NEA redefined the strike as an appropriate weapon for advancing teacher interests and increasingly assumed a political posture in lobbying for legislation that is favorable to teachers and supporting sympathetic political candidates.

The AFT, a union from the beginning, has also benefited from the new spirit, more than doubling its membership in the decade since 1970. It has viewed the relationship between school boards and teachers as that of an employer and employee. As such, it has pressed hard for improvements in salary, benefits, and working conditions. Nor has the AFT shunned a political role. Since the orientation, goals, and activities of the NEA and AFT have substantially converged over the past decade, suggestions for them to merge are increasingly heard.

---

codified experience encountered in law, engineering, medicine, divinity, architecture, and accountancy; no way has been found to record and crystallize teaching for the benefit of beginners. [1975:58]

Another sociologist, Richard L. Simpson, while concluding that education is not a profession, nonetheless emphasizes that teaching "offers opportunities for professionalism among individual teachers if they are professionally inclined" (1969:xiii). He attributes the failure of education to attain professional status to the fact that it is a predominantly feminine occupation. Simpson says that "the primacy of family rather than work role orientations among women keeps them from being professional in outlook or behavior" (1969:xii). Moreover, he concludes that teaching is just a job for many teachers, "something they do to earn money or fill time but to which they have little intrinsic professional commitment" (1969:9).

Many educators agree with Simpson that teachers have had difficulty winning professional recognition because of their occupation's identification as a feminine career. However, they vigorously dispute Simpson's argument that teachers lack a professional outlook or commitment. They believe such statements are insulting and perpetuate sexist myths. The clear implication of such reasoning is that women are by nature suited only for domestic roles. Further, it denies women the right accorded men of integrating and combining both career and family roles and finding meaning from and commitment to both work and home. Sexism, these educators say, has victimized teachers and their profession.

Educators also dispute charges that their discipline lacks a knowledge base. Readers of this text can judge for themselves the extent to which the field relies on scientific theories and research. Moreover, simply because a field borrows findings and insights from other disciplines in no way diminishes its authoritative foundations. Medicine, often taken to be the epitome of a profession, is essentially an "applied" science. It offers no apologies when it draws upon the findings of physiology, anatomy, chemistry, biochemistry, physics, and other "pure" sciences for various practices and treatments. Viewed from this perspective, physicians, lawyers, accountants, and engineers (individuals in traditionally "male" occupations) have had the clout to effect and guarantee public definitions of their work as "professional." Until relatively recently, teachers have been less able to translate their preferences—their will—into the reality of human life by virtue of their more limited power resources. In keeping with this view, one sociological authority on professions and professionalism, Magali Sarfatti Larson (1977), suggests that the necessary key to professional status is the ability of a group to translate one order of scarce social resources—special knowledge and skills—into another—social and economic rewards.

There are also those educators who reject the physician-lawyer model of a profession as an appropriate way for structuring teaching. Robert J. Nash and Edward R. Ducharme argue:

Teachers, after all, have no oath to swear to as do doctors, no comparable rite of passage such as passing the bar exams, no long-enforced study to encode the ravings of 19th century seers. . . . Joseph Conrad, in his novel *Lord Jim*, may have better described this aspect of professionalism with his "one of us" phrase, a phrase richly suggestive of some mythic past that produced

some kind of wisdom and skill. We wonder, do teachers really need that? If an appeal to an at-best myth-saturated professionalism is what we need for better self-concept, for better delivery of the services and skills we have, then maybe we are asking the wrong questions. If teachers should be seeking professionalism similar to that currently exemplified by some of the other professions, then maybe what is needed is a fraternity/sorority, a lapel button or two, some songs, and a necktie and scarf. [1975:362–363]

Nash and Ducharme call instead for an alternative structuring of a profession, one that emphasizes idealistic components of service as opposed to one that stresses the internal status and the material needs of the professional group.

The Choice of Teaching as a Career

Within complex modern societies like the United States, there is a complex division of labor and thousands of occupations. For the most part, these positions are not inherited but are open to individuals based on choice and talent. Societal survival requires that people be routed into various kinds of work and that they perform the tasks associated with these roles. In a real sense, occupations compete for members as individuals choose among alternative lines of work. Since occupations differ in their advantages and disadvantages and people differ in their dispositions and personal circumstances, an occupation attracts some people while repelling others (Lortie, 1975).

Attractions

Lortie (1975) interviewed a sample of teachers in five towns in the Boston metropolitan area. In these interviews teachers were asked to describe the attractions they saw in teaching. Lortie was able to compare his results with an earlier survey conducted by the National Education Association. Although no one reward was cited by a majority

NOTES FROM THE DIARY OF A STUDENT TEACHER

WAYNE O'BRIEN

It was my very first day as a student teacher. A classful of five- and six-year-olds poured in from every direction. What seemed like eternal hours of education classes, trial lesson plans, and textbook study were whirling in my head. This was the moment my training had prepared me for!

There were kids all over. I was surrounded and panic-stricken. Beating a hasty retreat to the

Source: Condensed from Wayne O'Brien, "Notes from the Diary of a Student Teacher," *Instructor,* 88 (October 1978):118–124.

teachers' lounge seemed the only logical alternative. But my supervising teachers would have frowned on that so I stuck it out in the front lines, praying for divine guidance all the while.

Since I had no training in the foreign language spoken by first graders, communication was a problem. They do not always say what they mean. I learned this while sitting with a woeful little boy who wailed, "Wanna go home! Want my momma!" A tide of tears ebbed and flowed; so I put a hand on his head. This brought another flow, but with it came an under-

standing twinkle from under a puffy red eyelid as he put his head on my lap. The crying continued, so I stepped into the principal's office for suggestions. He looked at the wet spot on my trousers where Kevin's nose had rested, smiled, and then said, "Did he go to kindergarten here?" The boy was still sobbing when I returned. When I asked where he had gone to kindergarten, the tears stopped. Thank heaven for a knowing principal! We talked about kindergarten and his kindergarten teacher, with only an occasional tear. He, in his way, was telling me that

of the teachers in either study, a "desire to work with people" was a common theme. Over the past thirty-five years J. Marc Jantzen (1947, 1959, 1981) has polled students in teacher education classes at three California colleges. Students have consistently selected an "interest in dealing with children" as the primary reason for their entering teaching. Unlike nursing and social work, teaching offers a unique opportunity to work with a wide range of children and youth who are healthy and for the most part free from serious problems.

The opportunity to perform an important service for the community was mentioned by 17 percent of the teachers in Lortie's sample and 28 percent in the National Education Association study. A number of teachers also mentioned that they had "liked" school as youngsters and wished to continue their association with schools. Some said that they had school-linked interests that they could not engage in outside educational institutions. For example, a teacher might be attracted to a hard-to-market subject like a foreign language, have an

first grade was different and scary—he didn't really want to go home, he wanted help with this new experience. We returned to work, hand in hand, with an understanding born of a mutual need.

I was fortunate to be placed as a student teacher in a progressive school where the kids are expected, and helped, to take some of the responsibility for their own education and actions. That afternoon a boy pulled on a girl's pink and white homemade beaded necklace—sending beads shooting in every direction. The girl dissolved into mournful tears, clutching a small part of the necklace still intact. The boy stared at his hands in shocked disbelief. There was no question about what had happened and who was at fault. The question was, where do we go from here? Again, my body told me to head at full speed out the door but I stayed and faced the music. Amazingly, they settled the problem themselves, after a tearful discussion and a few suggestions from the teacher who refereed.

Questions were seldom answered outright, rather they were turned back to the student with a "What do you think?" or "What might happen if . . . ?" reply. The students were thus encouraged to find answers on their own, ask a friend for help, or try every alternative they might devise to find an answer. It was exciting to see how these minor frustrations increased children's thinking and problem-solving abilities, except when it happened to me. I asked a tiny elf of a boy where the teacher kept the broom. He drew himself up to his full 3'10" height and replied "Well, where do you think it might be kept?"

I was especially thankful on one particular day for our policy of not answering questions outright. It was my last day at school, and from the air of excitement, secretive looks, hushed whispers, and being told that a certain part of the room was off limits to me, I discovered that a party had been planned in my honor. By answering direct questions indirectly, I narrowly avoided letting everyone know that the party wasn't totally a surprise.

Two first graders greeted me carrying a tagboard apple nearly as large as themselves. On it was a full-color self-portrait of all 50 kids along with their autographs. A leaf drawn at the top bore a message.

The party began and through teary eyes I tried to look cheerful. I snapped pictures like a tourist, sang songs, accepted artwork gifts, received hand-printed good-bye messages, and had a great time.

Sooner than I expected the school day ended. One little girl asked me to bend down, planted a Kool-Aid kiss on my cheek, and asked, "Mr. O'Brien, do you have to leave?" As she raced out the door, I told her I'd be back.

affection for music, or be interested in sports but lack the necessary ability for a career as a full-time professional in one of these areas.

Few teachers listed material rewards as attractions to teaching. Material benefits were mentioned by only 6 percent of those in Lortie's sample. It may be that social expectations reduce teachers' readiness to include material benefits among the field's attractions. Since many people consider teaching to be an occupation with dedicated personnel, teachers may hesitate to discuss financial matters. Support for this interpretation is found in Lortie's "projective" questions. When asked to cite the factors they believed motivated *other* teachers, 37 percent of the teachers listed money; 34 percent security; and 12 percent prestige.

Ease of Entry

In comparison with many other professions, teaching is relatively easy to enter (Falk, Falkowski, and Lyson, 1981). This ease of entry has been facilitated by the wide accessibility of colleges offering teacher education programs and non-elitist admission standards (Lortie, 1975). Although the number of years spent in training has increased, many teachers begin their careers after acquiring a B.A. degree in education. For those individuals who have already completed college in another program, it is relatively easy to acquire the necessary courses and become qualified to teach by attending night classes and summer school. In contrast, it is more difficult to gain entry into certain other programs like medical school that often require a prerequisite core of foundation courses. Nor is the financial investment necessary to become a teacher as great as that encountered in many other professions (Parelius and Parelius, 1978).

Some individuals enter teaching after having considered an alternative occupation. In his Boston-area study, Lortie (1975) found that this held true for approximately three-quarters of the teachers. Indeed, at least a third had preferred another line of work but decided upon teaching when their plans had fallen through. The major obstacle most frequently reported was financial; the teachers had lacked the funds to secure the training necessary for entry into their first-choice occupation. Although a second occupational choice, many of these individuals brought to teaching above-average educational qualifications. In this respect, teaching has an enviable competitive position; its accessibility allowed the entry of able young people who might otherwise never have gone to college to become teachers.

Career Patterns

Professionals are expected to have a strong commitment to life-long careers in their chosen work. Much of the literature on education stresses the failure of teachers to live up to this ideal (Parelius and Parelius, 1978). Yet, here again sexism has intervened to victimize women and the teaching profession.

During the colonial period and until the Civil War, teaching was primarily a male occupation. In about 1850, women began replacing men in elementary teaching, in part because the salaries and working conditions were deemed unrewarding for men (Lortie, 1969). By the end of the nineteenth century, rapid population growth, large-scale immigration, and the enactment of compulsory school attendance laws provided teaching opportunities for many thousands of women. Indeed, teaching was one of the few career alternatives open to women.

Until relatively recently, the notion was prevalent that women who remained unmarried and childless were "defective" and "unfeminine." Simultaneously, cultural tradition required that women who married had to relinquish their teaching careers. Consequently, women found themselves in a no-win situation. If they left teaching after a few years for the traditional roles of homemaker and mother, they were said to be unprofessional and lacking career commitment. If they remained unmarried and childless, continuing their teaching careers, they were stigmatized as "old maids" and unfavorably stereotyped.

According to another popular stereotype, the typical woman teacher accepts her first teaching position after receiving the bachelor's degree, teaches for several years, resigns her position to bear and rear children, and then may or may not return to teaching ten or fifteen years later when her children are in school. Yet, this pattern does not typify the experience of the vast majority of female teachers.

Surveys of teachers by the National Education Association (1972) in 1966 and again in 1971 revealed that the percentage of women who had interrupted their careers for marriage or full-time homemaking declined from 17 to 10 percent. More recent research shows that the retention rates of male and female teachers are now virtually the same. For instance, of all new teachers entering St. Louis area school systems in 1968, 60.5 percent of the men and 66.1 percent of the women remained after one year, 52.5 percent of the men and 47.1

percent of the women after three years, and 42.2 percent of the men and 30.7 percent of the women after eight years. However, by 1973, 81.5 percent of the new male teachers and 84.6 percent of the new female teachers remained after one year and 64.0 percent of the men and 65.0 percent of the women after three years (Mark and Anderson, 1978).

A study by the Bureau of Labor Statistics (1976) shows that public school teachers lead the nation in moonlighting. Of the total American labor force, 3.9 million (4.5 percent) hold two or more jobs. Of males in the multiple-job category, 18 percent are public school teachers, more than any other job classification. Female teachers also lead all categories with a 5.2 percent moonlighting rate. Individuals are most likely to get a second job to meet expenses (30 percent), although 20 percent say they chose to moonlight because they like the work. Further, some teachers take nonschool-related jobs during the summer months.

Gender-Related Differences in Teacher Placement

Important gender-related differences characterize the placement of teachers. Some two-thirds of elementary and secondary school teachers are women. Whereas 42 percent of all male teachers are found at the senior-high level, this is true of only 18 percent of the female teachers. In contrast, one-fourth of the men and two-thirds of the women teach at the elementary school level.

GENDER AND TEACHER PLACEMENT
Male teachers tend to be concentrated in the secondary schools and female teachers in the elementary schools.

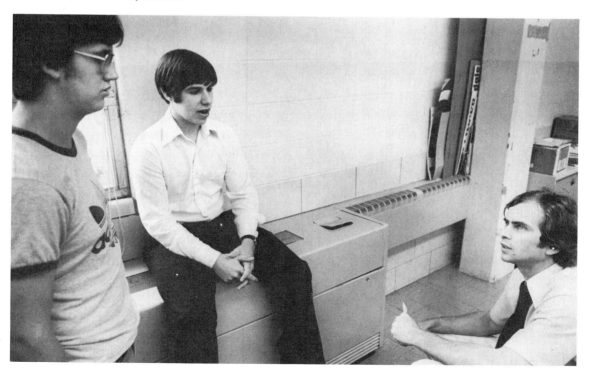

TEACHER JOB INTERVIEWS

Sooner or later a prospective teacher confronts the task of applying for a teaching position. The candidate is usually asked to complete an application form. The personnel officer of the school district reviews and evaluates the applications and schedules personal interviews with selected applicants. In a sense, the application form may be considered a "written" interview that may or may not lead to a face-to-face interview. Hence, in a competitive job market, teachers are required to "merchandize" themselves and their skills.

Teacher application forms typically ask candidates for information regarding their personal history, educational background, and work and teaching experience. Applicants are also expected to provide the names of three or four individuals who can supply professional references. Frequently, the application form contains a number of open-ended questions such as the following:

- What are your reasons for wanting to teach?
- Please describe your teaching style. How would you usually function in the teaching role on a day-to-day basis?
- What should be the nature of the relationship between students and teachers?
- What are the most important things you want to know about your students?
- What are your reasons for seeking a position with our school system?

Candidates can expect to be asked similar questions in face-to-face interviews.

What do administrators look for in a candidate? A survey of 104 Ohio central office administrators and junior- and senior-high-school principals revealed the following (Johnson, 1976). In terms of personal characteristics, the vast majority mentioned physical appearance, personal neatness, and emotional balance. Also high on their lists were good verbal skills, command of the English language, a strong work ethic, and confidence and enthusiasm. Over

Even more striking, males dominate as school administrators and superintendents. According to the National Education Association, in 1928 some 55 percent of elementary school principals were women. By 1980, this figure had fallen to 20 percent (Dullea, 1975; Lyman and Speizer, 1980). Moreover, less than 2 percent of secondary school principals were women (a decline from 6 percent in 1950) and less than 1 percent of school superintendents were women. Further, men outnumber women nearly nine to one on school boards. Overall, women have steadily lost ground in educational administration over the past seventy years (Sadker, 1975; Bach, 1976; Adkison, 1981).

This pattern of male concentration in administration is mirrored by the proportions of male-female enrollment in various areas of specialization. In 1973, females earned 25 percent of all doctoral degrees awarded in education. But whereas women earned 55 percent of doctoral degrees in elementary education, they earned only 9 percent of the doctorates in educational administration (Vetter and Babco, 1975). Moreover, a survey of the future educational plans and leadership aspirations of prospective teachers in a college of education at a large state university revealed that over 15 percent more men than women would be willing to accept the position of a school principal.

80 percent expressed a preference for persons between ages twenty and twenty-five, and over 60 percent preferred to hire a single person. Among the letters of reference, the administrators valued most highly those written by the applicant's cooperating teacher, the student's college supervisor, and the building principal at the school where the candidate did student teaching. The Ohio administrators also stressed that applicants should be clear about their professional goals and be able to provide for individual differences in their classes.

Prospective candidates can prepare for interviews by familiarizing themselves with the job description a school district usually publishes prior to the application process (Mahoney, 1978). Then, in the course of the interview, the candidate should try to match his or her experiences with those expectations (the candidate is usually interviewed by the di-

rector of personnel and the building principal). Common questions include: What do you see as your duties? How would you carry them out? What do you see as your major problems? How would you deal with them? What would you do in a situation in which a number of your students are in conflict? How would you deal with a parent who complains that his or her youngster is not learning anything in school? What areas of expertise do you have? Questions should be answered directly and simply. Further, the candidate should attempt to provide specific answers that involve both his or her past experiences and knowledge of the new job.

Over the past several years a new selection and evaluation device has come into use in a growing number of districts (especially in large metropolitan areas), the Teacher Perceiver Interview (TPI). The TPI consists of sixty open-ended interview questions. The

responses are scored as correct or incorrect, so that a candidate's total score can range from 0 to 60. The interviews are audio-taped. They then are scored locally or by raters employed by the Selection Incorporated Academies in Lincoln, Nebraska.

TPI questions are distributed over twelve areas including mission, empathy, individualized perception, listening, and innovation. The system favors an individual who can articulate why teaching was selected over other vocations, perceive situations from the student's perspective, individualize instruction, and employ creative teaching approaches. School administrators have been attracted to TPI as a selection device by virtue of its low cost, ease of administration, consistency across situations, and purported objectivity and validity. Critics, however, charge that TPI fails to meet minimal requirements for instrument validity (Haefele, 1978).

About 50 percent of the women said they would accept leadership roles in county educational organizations, but only about 20 percent would do so at the state or national level. In contrast, approximately 40 percent of the men said they would accept leadership roles at all three levels in professional organizations (McMillin, 1975).

Women have been victimized by discrimination. Research suggests that male superintendents are unlikely to hire women as administrators (Weber, Feldman, and Poling, 1981). The fact that women principals are older and more experienced than men when assuming their first administrative position also reveals discrimination. Sixty-five per-

cent of the men responding to a survey undertaken by the National Association of Elementary School Principals received appointments as principals before age thirty-five; 25 percent of the women were appointed before age thirty-five (Pharis and Zachariya, 1979). It appears that a good many women lower their occupational expectations in keeping with the employment opportunities available to them in a sexist labor market (Wirtenberg et al., 1981). Further, some of these women may internalize the concept that high-level leadership roles are for men and not for women. These circumstances are unfortunate since a mounting body of research reveals that women generally have a better record as elementary school principals than men do (Adkison, 1981).

Neal Gross and Anne E. Trask (1976) undertook a study of 189 big-city elementary schools, focusing on sex as a factor in administrative competence. Compared with the male principals, the women principals showed greater concern with individual differences in pupils, the social and emotional development of pupils, and efforts to help deviant pupils. On the average, the learning was higher in the schools administered by women. Further, the women had equally high standards for academic performance, exhibited equal ability to maintain student discipline, and achieved equal levels of staff morale. Overall, the women were more interested in instruction and enjoyed it more than did the men. In contrast, the men derived more satisfaction from the management of routine administrative affairs. Gross and Trask credit the superior performance of female principals to the fact that they had about three times as much teaching experience as the men. In their sample, one-third of the male principals, as compared to only 3 percent of the female principals, had no elementary teaching experience at all.

Other research tends to confirm these findings. Norma Hare (1966) found that female principals are more democratic and more concerned with the objectives of teaching, with pupil participation, and with the evaluation of learning than male

WOMEN IN ADMINISTRATIVE POSTS
Only 20 percent of elementary school principals and less than 2 percent of secondary school principals are women. Over the last seventy years, women have steadily lost ground in educational administration.

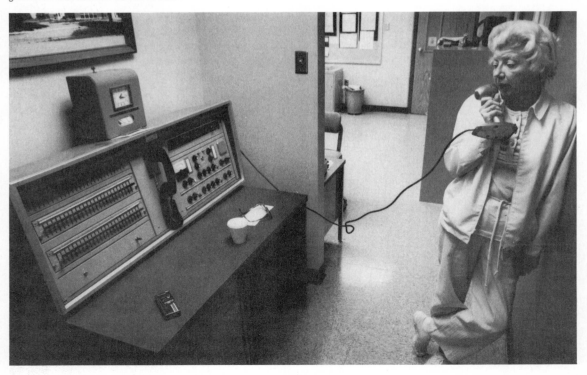

principals. John K. Hemphill, Daniel E. Griffiths, and Norman Frederikson (1962) concluded from their research that female principals are superior to male principals in their ability to work with teachers and the community. Further, they were more concerned with objectives, possessed greater knowledge about teaching methods and techniques, and were able to gain more positive reactions from teachers and superiors.

THE HUMAN CONTEXT

We commonly identify work with an individual's means for earning a living. But work is more than simply a response to economic necessity. A consistent research finding is that the vast majority of men (upwards of 80 percent) would continue to work even if they inherited enough money to live comfortably (Morse and Weiss, 1955; Tausky, 1969; Kaplan and Tausky, 1972). This is not to deny that monetary payoff is a major source of work motivation. However, people also work because they enjoy it, gain a sense of self-respect, achieve a feeling of self-actualization and self-fulfillment, wish to have established social relationships with others, and want to keep busy (Kaplan, 1977). Even money has meaning beyond what it can immediately purchase; its acquisition represents achievement, success, safety, public recognition, and power. And the fact that someone will pay us for our work is an indication that what we do is needed by others—that we matter.

How we earn our living has vast consequences

INTERPERSONAL REWARDS IN TEACHING
As in any other occupation, work-related friendships are an important aspect of teaching.

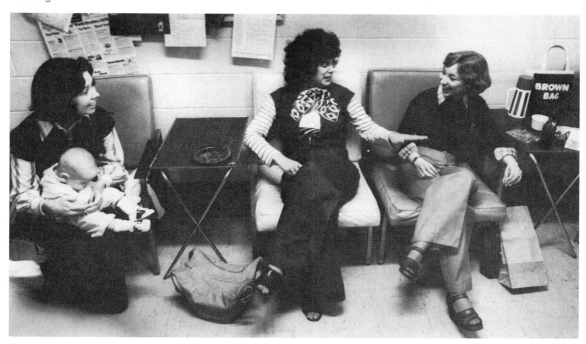

for other facets of our lives. It influences our life-chances—the typical probability that we will have access to a given level of goods and services, external conditions of life, and subjective satisfactions or frustrations. Thus, our work plays a major part in determining such diverse aspects of our lives as the neighborhood in which we live, our access to various leisure-time activities, and our mental and physical health.

Rewards in Teaching

A teacher affects eternity; he can never tell where his influence stops.

> HENRY ADAMS
> *The Education of Henry Adams,* 1907

As is true of any occupation or career, teachers differ in the satisfactions they derive from their work. Yet the findings of three recent polls suggest that most teachers are pleased with their profession. Of more than 10,000 teachers responding to a 1981 poll by the *Instructor* (a teachers' magazine), 97 percent said yes to the question, "Do you like teaching?" Ninety-three percent planned to continue teaching, and 66 percent thought enough of the profession to recommend it to students. A survey of teachers undertaken by researchers at the University of California, Los Angeles, found that 78.3 percent of the teachers agreed with the statement, "I usually look forward to each working day at this school" (Bentzen, Williams, and Heckman, 1980). And 68.7 percent said that if they had to do it over again, they would choose education as a profession. Finally, Earl W. Harmer (1979) polled teachers who were at least fifty years of age. Seventy-eight percent said that they were satisfied to have chosen teaching as a life career. Eighty-three percent enjoyed teaching and 79 percent felt respected at school.

In his study of Boston-area teachers, Lortie (1975) found that single women tended to put more into their work than married women did. However, single women were less satisfied with teaching than were married women. Further, younger men—many of whom were striving for promotions to administration—reported lower satisfaction scores than did older men (the lowest satisfaction scores occurred among young men who did not know as yet whether they would be promoted).

When Lortie asked the teachers about the "costs" associated with being teachers, 53 percent of the married women *denied* that they lost anything by choosing to teach. Only 26 percent of the single female teachers made a similar denial. Whereas 59 percent of the men mentioned inadequate income as a cost, only 4 percent of the women mentioned low salaries. The cost most frequently cited by single women was the isolation involved in teaching. Single young women emphasized that teaching is a poor base from which to meet people, including eligible men. They felt that the social life of the teacher is constricted.

The common denominator that brings most people to work is pay (Fein, 1976). This also holds for teachers. But relative to many other professions, teaching does not afford many opportunities for achieving great fame or personal wealth. In many respects the status of the young tenured teacher is not substantially different from that of the more highly experienced old-timer. Opportunities for an improvement in status are primarily limited to increased seniority and additional course-taking, or leaving classroom teaching to go into full-time administration.

As part of his study of the teaching profession, Lortie (1975) questioned teachers in Dade County, Florida, about the rewards associated with teaching. These teachers considered psychological rewards to be their major source of satisfaction—76.5 percent chose psychological rewards compared to 11.9 percent mentioning extrinsic rewards (for instance, salary and prestige) and 11.7 percent ancillary rewards (for example, job security, holidays, and vacations). Among the psychological rewards commonly cited by teachers was the sense of having "reached" students and having participated in their intellectual and social growth. Of interest, many teachers in the Lortie study emphasized the satisfactions associated with transmitting

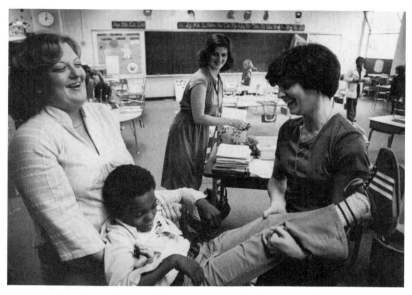

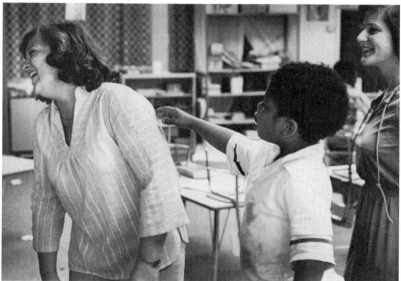

**PSYCHOLOGICAL REWARDS
IN TEACHING**
Teachers consider psychological
rewards to be their major source
of work satisfaction.

moral standards and good citizenship practices, what they viewed as character formation. And many mentioned a particularly satisfying case in which they were able to contribute to the normal functioning of what had been a ''problematic'' and ''difficult'' youngster. Thus, many teachers seem to feel that teaching affords them the opportunity not only to make a meaningful contribution to others but also to achieve a sense of their own self-actualization.

Teacher Morale

Morale is the extent to which individuals experience a sense of general well-being and satisfaction with their job situation (Mathis, 1959; Coughlan, 1970). Sociologists find that a good predictor of strong work attachment and high morale is an occupation with high prestige (Blauner, 1969; Dubin, Hedley, and Taveggia, 1976). Donald J. Treiman (1977), a sociologist, has developed an occupational prestige scale that goes from 0 to 100. He finds that teachers are ranked high in the prestige hierarchy at 64. In comparison, physicians and university professors are at 78; lawyers, 71; business executives, 71; professional nurses, 54; real estate agents, 49; key punch operators, 45; receptionists, 38; and taxi drivers, 28.

Control also represents an important component in work satisfaction (Israel, 1971; Kohn and Schooler, 1973; Form, 1975). Sociologists find that the greater an individual's control over time, physical movement, and pace of work, the greater the job satisfaction and the higher the morale. At first sight, it may appear that teachers enjoy little autonomy in their work. Schoolwide decisions are largely the province of the principal, and individual teachers have few opportunities for determining policy directly. Yet, within the classroom itself, teachers have considerable control over the instructional context.

A substantial majority of the teachers surveyed as part of the Organizational Attributes Project believed that they exercised "considerable control" over their work situation (Pellegrin, 1976). Although a school system is a large-scale bureaucratic organization, many of its policies and procedures are only irregularly and partially enforced. In contrast to many other types of organizations, schools feature a relatively high proportion of low-constraint decisions and a wide range of tolerated possibilities (Lortie, 1969). For the most part, the administrative personnel spend most of their time dealing with such matters as building maintenance, finances, routine duties, and public relations. Rarely

do principals devote much energy to instructional matters, leaving teachers pretty much to their own devices (Charters, 1962; Meyer and Cohen, 1970; Pellegrin, 1976).

Teachers studied in the Organizational Attributes Project were asked to identify the strongest constraints that impeded them in their instructional activities. Substantial proportions of teachers (listed in order of choice) mentioned lack of time, the difficulty or complexity of instructional tasks, conflicts between duties, lack of resources, and the responses of students. Only infrequently did teachers cite the reactions of parents, official school district policies, reactions of the principal, or the actions of central office personnel (Pellegrin, 1976).

The fact that each school is largely a distinct entity and each classroom a self-contained organizational unit gives teachers broad discretionary powers. Indeed, Lortie concludes: "Indications are that that which is most central and unique to schools—instruction—is least controlled by specific and literally enforced rules and regulations" (1969:14). Teachers prize this element of individual autonomy (Jackson, 1968). "Freedom from interference" is a vital component of teacher ideology. Although teachers may relinquish control over the affairs of the school as a whole, they appear more concerned about their autonomy in the classroom than they are about any other educational matter (Carson, Goldhammer, and Pellegrin, 1967).

Over and above the morale problems confronted by their colleagues, first-year teachers encounter a number of special problems (Gaede, 1978). They must establish a favorable reputation among students, other teachers, and administrators; they must organize and prepare lessons for courses they never taught before; and they must adapt to an entirely new professional role. In many ways they find their first year to be one of disillusionment. The term "reality shock" has been applied in various professions to describe the feelings experienced by many neophytes when they graduate from their academic training programs and confront the "real world."

Whereas education majors compare themselves with other student teachers and college students, first-year teachers compare their knowledge and performance with that of their more experienced colleagues and find themselves wanting. Further, they often find unanticipated gaps in their professional competencies, areas they did not recognize during their preservice training as having importance for them. Although students can gain some experience as preservice teachers, they still operate in the *student role*. The student teacher has a wealth of resources upon which to draw and is expected to exhibit various shortcomings and limitations. In contrast, beginning teachers often complain of the failure of school administrators to provide them with support; they feel that all too often they are simply thrown into full teaching responsibilities to sink or swim on their own merits.

The Health of Teachers

An appropriate concern of any occupation or profession is the health of its members. Over the past decade, increasing attention has been drawn to the close ties that exist between people's work and their health. This has been dramatically highlighted in the case of coal miners who have contracted black lung disease, shipyard workers who are more vulnerable to lung cancer by having inhaled asbestos particles, workers in the petroleum industry who have significantly higher rates of cancer of the respiratory system than the general population, and pregnant nurses working in operating rooms who have a high incidence of spontaneous miscarriages due to their exposure to anesthetic gases (Vander Zanden, 1984).

No comprehensive, well-conceived study is currently available on the health of teachers. At best, we can only piece together information from a number of polls that employed less than adequate sampling procedures. One of these was undertaken by the *Instructor* (Landsmann, 1978). With the cooperation of the American School Health Association (ASHA), the magazine published a questionnaire in its September 1976 issue to which 9,000 teachers responded.

The teachers in the *Instructor* poll had missed an average of 4.5 days of work during the previous school year because of illness. Only 27 percent indicated that they had a chronic health problem, 7 percent that they ever had psychiatric treatment, and 40 percent that they were currently taking prescription drugs. Seventy-eight percent of the teachers rated their health as good to excellent.

Of the teachers responding to the poll, 84 percent said that health hazards existed in teaching. The questions that elicited open-ended answers identified stress as the most common problem. The teachers reported that tension and pressure arose from large class sizes, the lack of teaching materials, an increase in recent years in discipline problems, more public pressures on teachers, and schedules that permit few or no breaks.

Some teachers cited the current trend to make the schools (and hence the teachers) the major problem-solving agents of society as a factor contributing to increasing stress. One Syracuse teacher observed:

> We're asked to assume broader roles, yet we are more and more criticized by the public. Areas once covered by the family and church (such as sex education and moral education) are now plopped on the teacher's lap. We're even administering breakfast programs. The same parents who are demanding that we go back to the basics (reading and math) also want us to teach their children discipline, to teach them right from wrong. It's no wonder more and more experienced teachers are leaving the profession. To do all these things without support is demoralizing. [Landsmann, 1978:49]

Another major area of health concern was weight, diet, and exercise. Lunch was a particular source of frustration. Only 25 percent buy lunch in the school cafeteria, while the others bring their own or skip lunch. Still another concern was the physical environment of the school, some one-third indicating that it affected their health negatively. Most commonly teachers complained about the temperature in the classrooms.

Overall, many of the teachers believed that the principals could do much to improve the health of teachers. Only 39 percent said that their principals

FIRST-WEEK SURVIVAL KIT FOR A BRAND-NEW TEACHER

MAY RICHSTONE

Public School 196 Annex,
Forest Hills, New York

You're a new teacher! You're enthusiastic about teaching! You've got lots of ideas! But you've also got problems, little ones, mostly concerned with pupil attitude and behavior. What to do? These survival hints, compiled by experienced classroom teachers, will help you through that first week and month.

- *Hang on to your sense of proportion.* Be ready to minimize Johnny's mischievous tendencies. Watch out for your own overreactions. Some problems are fostered, if not created, by your insecurity.
- *Try for understanding.* What's prompting George's behavior pattern? More important than concern for each incident should be your concern for George himself. Seek out his previous teacher, call in a parent, and give each one a thoughtful listening-to. Create some chances to listen to George, too.
- *Never say fail.* Sylvia may seem incorrigibly devoted to her bad habits, but never write off your effect on her as failure. Keep in mind two words, "As yet." You haven't been able to prove to her, as yet, that you're on her side and that some helpful changes are imperative, but keep thinking, keep experimenting, keep reassuring her that together you'll succeed.
- *Speak privately of private matters.* Without a word, you can signal a rendezvous to Karen at the doorway. Here you can, while respecting her dignity, indicate the need for wiser behavior in a hurry. A friendly word, a friendly pat, a bit of physical activity—Karen can use all three.
- *Write encouraging notes.* "You've been doing so well lately, I'm proud of you. Keep it up!" Such a note on Peter's desk might very well evoke an affirmative nod and a more serious attitude (if only briefly). At some moment in the day, there is something good to say about each child.
- *Remove the child briefly.* Momentum is sometimes Tony's problem. Almost always a change of climate helps him. With the administration's sanction and a colleague who cares, you might park him plus an assignment in another classroom for half an hour. Let him return with a friendly nod, no comment.
- *Save your breath.* Has a long lecture ever helped a child? If you were Scott, would a barrage of words tempt you to wear a halo? Four firm, serious words, "That's wrong. Stop it!" are probably better than four hundred and easier on both of you.

Source: May Richstone, "First-Week Survival Kit for a Brand-New Teacher," *Instructor,* 81 (August/September 1971):80.

- *Criticize the act, not the child.* Charles, who has a tendency to dawdle, is not a dawdler—not at punch ball. Dawn did some tampering with the truth. This does not make her a liar. Teachers should remember that the label belongs on the act, not on the child.
- *Evoke the weight of the pen.* Dissension in the classroom is an important part of the learning process. Getting along with others isn't automatic, but wrangling is not part of any curriculum area. So when two children would rather fight than switch to math, a solution is a sheet of paper to each child and the request, "Write down just what happened to help me understand it better. You're both too excited now to make it clear to me." In the act of writing, the children's strong feelings are dissipated. Very often, too, the mere assignment of writing makes children realize that the incident isn't worth the effort of putting it on paper. In any case, the teacher has taken seriously what was important to the children, without letting it usurp class time.
- *Preparation and pace pre-* clude many problems. As children are winding up one activity, they can be advised of the next one. Teachers learn to plan enough work for the more capable scholars and a modicum of indulgence for the slower ones. The sky will not fall, the halls of education will not crumble, if Tommy doesn't do as many division examples as the others.
- *Invest in a timer.* "Let's finish before the timer rings" suggests a happy competition. It's the timer ticking away those precious minutes, not the tiresome voice of the teacher.
- *Vary the activities.* All sedentary work makes for restless pupils. Let the timer sound at the end of five minutes of freedom, its gentle ring being the signal, "Back to seats and back to work."
- *Stroll to the trouble spots in advance.* Your physical presence at various parts of the room reinforces better behavior. As you move toward Cynthia's desk, you're a comfort to her and a source of strength *before* she tears up her spelling paper.
- *Experiment with a buddy sys-* tem. Plan on clubs where better students can work with slower ones on reading, math, spelling. The fewer children who fall behind, the fewer classroom problems. There are good feelings engendered. Everybody benefits as children help one another and learn from one another.
- *Giving up may be a good idea.* You try to motivate, to relate what you're about to teach to the child's experience and interest. But sometimes, in the middle of a lesson, you realize that it hasn't been done and can't be done, now. There's nothing wrong in asking, "How many would like to stop this lesson this very minute?" What eager hands go up!
- *Make a home visit.* The child on home territory may be a revelation. One teacher with a particularly recalcitrant scholar reported that on the day following a visit in the boy's home, he warned his cronies, "She visits!"
- *One final reminder.* Enjoy the children as a class, appreciate each child as an individual. Children will respond and try to please you.

helped them to stay mentally and physically healthy. Principals, they believed, could create a supportive environment in working with children, parents, and central office personnel and could provide them with more positive reinforcement.

A poll of Chicago teachers suggests that many large-city teachers find teaching tense work (*Wall Street Journal,* April 4, 1978). Some 56 percent of 5,000 teachers responding to the poll said they suffered physical ailments because of job pressure, and 26 percent blamed job pressure for mental ailments. However, the teachers say that teaching itself is the least stressful thing. It is such things as discipline problems and lack of supplies that most distress them.

In order to determine the real seriousness of stress, Fred C. Feitler and Edward Tokar (1982) collected data from more than 3,300 public school teachers. Only 16 percent of the teachers responded that their "job environments" were either "very stressful" or "extremely stressful." The vast majority, 76 percent, rated their jobs as being either "moderately stressful" or "mildly stressful," and 7 percent said their jobs were "not stressful at all." When asked the number one source of job-related stress, 58 percent replied "individual pupils who continually misbehave." The responses suggested that teacher stress is more often produced by one or two students who chronically misbehave than by widespread student behavior problems. Nineteen percent of high-school teachers reported high levels of stress on the job; this compared to 16 percent for junior high and 13 percent for elementary school teachers. Of interest, teachers in the thirty-one to forty-four age range reported higher levels of stress than teachers either under thirty or forty-five years and older.

A teacher's health is a community concern, since it is linked to his or her classroom performance. The influence of the teacher and the school is far-reaching, second in importance only to the home in the development of a child's personality. Although the evidence that maladjusted teachers always have a negative effect on their pupils is far from conclusive, it seems reasonable to assume that their mental health status has an influence, good or bad, on the intellectual, social, and emotional development of their pupils. All of us find that excessive stress and fatigue has consequences for our work. Teachers are obviously no exception.

It is reassuring that the mental health of teachers is at least equal to, and perhaps even superior to, that of the general public (Hicks, 1934; Bentz, Hollister, and Edgerton, 1971). Further, it appears that the stresses and tensions of teaching do not often lead to complete mental breakdown, although they may aggravate certain emotional disabilities (Tanner and Lindgren, 1971).

CHAPTER SUMMARY

1. Educational psychology is a multidisciplinary field that represents the intersection of two separate areas of study—psychology and education. As such, it involves both the study of behavior and the process of education. Psychologists have traditionally directed their energies toward an understanding of the nature and process of learning in a relatively abstract sense. In contrast, educators have been chiefly interested in identifying and implementing the most effective instructional strategies for children.

2. Educational psychology is concerned both with the creation of a body of knowledge directly relevant to the educational process and the application of this knowledge to effective classroom instruction. In other words, it involves both knowledge production and knowledge utilization. Each dimension is linked to the other, strengthening and reinforcing it.

3. Each school district is governed by a separate school board. The superintendent is the top school administrator in a district. The next level in the chain of command is the school principal. Teachers are the immediate day-by-day link between the larger system and the individual students.

4. Within Western nations, education is commonly viewed as having four broad objectives: those that pertain to a child's acquisition of basic literacy skills and a general education; those that concern an individual's ability to respect and get along with other people and to understand and practice the ideals associated with good citizenship; those having to do with an individual's own health and well-being; those that have to do with preparing a pupil for family living and for an appropriate occupational role.

5. Considerable variation occurs among teachers in how they conceive of their teaching tasks. Little agreement exists among teachers, even among those in the same school, as to what the main dimensions of the job are. Teachers spend about one-quarter to one-third of their time in instructional activity. Other responsibilities consume the greater proportion of their time.

6. In order for a profession to be recognized as a profession, it is generally thought that at the very minimum it must have a strong and unique base of expert knowledge. A broad spectrum of commentators on American education have argued that although there are large numbers of courses and textbooks dealing with teaching methods, the actual knowledge base upon which these depend is weak. Educators dispute this charge. They point out that simply because a field borrows findings and insights from other disciplines in no way diminishes its authoritative foundations.

7. Many individuals enter teaching because of a desire to work with people. The opportunity to perform an important service for the community is another frequently mentioned attraction. Few teachers list material rewards as attractions to teaching.

8. In comparison with many other professions, teaching is relatively easy to enter. This has been facilitated by the wide accessibility of colleges offering teacher education programs and non-elitist admission standards.

9. Professionals are expected to have a strong commitment to life-long careers in their chosen work. Much of the literature on education stresses the failure of teachers to live up to this ideal. Sexism has contributed to this state of affairs. Women traditionally found themselves in a no-win situation. If they left teaching after a few years for the roles of homemaker and mother, they were said to be unprofessional and lacking career commitment. If they remained unmarried and childless, continuing their teaching careers, they were stigmatized as "old maids" and unfavorably stereotyped.

10. Important gender-related differences characterize the placement of teachers. Whereas 42 percent of all male teachers are found at the senior-high level, this is true of only 18 percent of the female teachers. Further, males dominate as school administrators and superintendents. Overall, women have steadily lost ground in educational administration over the past seventy years.

11. As is true of any occupation or career, teachers differ in the satisfaction they derive from their work. On the whole, however, most teachers appear pleased with their profession. Teachers report that their major sources of satisfaction are psychological rewards. A psychological reward commonly cited by teachers is the sense of having "reached" students and of participating in their intellectual and social growth.

12. Sociologists find that a good predictor of strong work attachment and high morale is an occupation with high prestige and one that allows individuals control over their work situations. In both respects, teaching ranks high. Teaching ranks among the top third of occupations in prestige. And on the whole, teachers believe they exercise considerable control over their work situation.

13. Teachers generally report that stress is the primary health hazard of the occupation. They indicate that tension arises from large class sizes, the lack of teaching materials, an increase in discipline problems in recent years, more public pressures on teachers, and schedules that permit few or no breaks. However, it is reassuring that the mental health of teachers is at least equal to, and perhaps even superior to, that of the general public.

CHAPTER GLOSSARY

educational psychology An academic discipline that studies the learning-teaching process.

morale The extent to which individuals experience a sense of general well-being and satisfaction with their job situation.

role A set of expectations that defines the appropriate behavior for a particular category of individuals.

EXERCISES

Review Questions

1. Following Bruner's classification, descriptive is to prescriptive as
   a. theory is to application
   b. production is to utilization
   c. creation is to application
   d. a, b, and c are true
   e. b and c are true

2. The major purpose of a course in educational psychology should be to
   a. teach students the technical skills necessary for effective teaching
   b. demonstrate that teaching is primarily an art that cannot be taught
   c. provide students with a theoretical background that they can use in making decisions in their teaching
   d. provide students with a set of prescriptions that will remove much of the uncertainty surrounding teaching decisions

3. The major difference between an organization such as General Motors and a school is that schools

   a. are nonhierarchical
   b. lack division by function
   c. process people rather than products
   d. a, b, and c are true
   e. b and c are true

4. In his study on the role expectations of teachers, Pellegrin determined that
   a. teachers spend more time in classroom management than any other task area
   b. there is more variance within as compared to between school districts as to task distribution
   c. nationally, teachers in the Northeast have distinctly different role expectations
   d. there is more variance between school districts as to task distribution
   e. a and d are true

5. The critical issue as to whether education is or will become a profession appears to be a function of
   a. the increasing unionism among teachers
   b. a lack of a uniform licensing exam
   c. the depth and breadth of the existing knowledge base
   d. a, b, and c are true

6. According to Lortie and also the NEA studies, the most prevalent reason given by individuals for choosing teaching is
   a. desire to work with children
   b. inability to find work in field of first choice
   c. ease of entry
   d. security
   e. a and d are true

7. Current surveys have shown that
   a. the current retention rates for men and women are about equal
   b. relatively few teachers ''moonlight''
   c. percentagewise, there are significantly fewer male elementary school principals now than in 1928
   d. a and c are true

8. Which of the following is more likely to be true in a building administered by a male principal?

   a. greater concern for individual differences
   b. higher pupil achievement
   c. greater previous classroom experience as compared to female administrators
   d. more emphasis on routine administration
   e. b and d are true

9. The factor that contributes most significantly to the classroom teacher's morale is

   a. lack of administrative responsibilities
   b. relative simplicity of instructional tasks
   c. classroom autonomy
   d. differences among pupils

10. The factor most cited by teachers as contributing to health problems is

   a. lack of exercise
   b. administrative management behaviors
   c. restrictions on parental expectations concerning school
   d. classroom-related stress

Answers

1. d (See p. 6)
2. c (See p. 7)
3. c (See p. 7)
4. b (See p. 11)
5. c (See pp. 13–15)
6. a (See pp. 15–17)
7. a (See p. 18)
8. d (See p. 22)
9. c (See pp. 26–27)
10. d (See pp. 27, 30)

Applying Principles and Concepts

1. An educational psychology professor is delivering his usual opening remarks to students in his class. Underline those parts of the following passage with which the text *does not* agree.

First of all, let me assure you that the relationship between theory and private practice is obvious and direct. By emphasizing theory you will achieve greater insight into your own practices and will be in a better position to analyze success and failure. Indeed, it has been my observation that success in teaching is dependent entirely on recognizing that it is not an art but an exact science.

2. The following are some of the goals for the elementary grades developed by a local school district. Check those that reflect any of the four broad educational objectives commonly held in modern democratic societies.

_____ a. Students will appreciate the importance of keeping physically fit and will develop skills they can use to engage in enjoyable and beneficial physical activities.

_____ b. Students will be able to identify various occupations found in contemporary communities and have some understanding of the educational requirements and skills needed for them.

_____ c. Students will recognize that the needs of an orderly society take precedence over the rights of individuals and that individual goals and aspirations should be adjusted to the greater social good.

_____ d. Students will acquire a sufficient command of oral and written language so that they can read with understanding at a fourth-grade level, at least, and communicate their ideas effectively to others.

_____ e. Students will have begun to develop a coherent set of moral principles that are consistent with the values of the local community and that can guide their future educational decisions.

3. You have heard the following comments in a teachers' lounge in a typical elementary school. Check any that research would support as typical.

_____ a. "It seems I spend about a fourth of my time actually teaching."

_____ b. "I must spend half my time between school meetings and taking courses."

_____ c. "I'll bet there are other schools in the district where teachers have more time for planning."

_____ d. "There's so little time in the day for tutoring."

_____ e. "I wish I could spend as much time planning and testing as I do teaching."

4. The local school superintendent is interviewing a prospective teacher for his district. Which of these statements by the candidate might help his or her chances?

_____ a. "One of the reasons I want to teach is a chance to use my major in German."

_____ b. "I work hard, and I expect my students to do the same."

_____ c. "I just can't be certain how I'll handle that kind of troublemaker; it all depends."

_____ d. "I'd rather not ask for letters of reference from my cooperating teacher. He was unfair."

_____ e. "My philosophy of education is pretty complicated. It will take a while to explain."

5. Assume you have conducted a poll among your local high-school teachers. Check those responses that can be substantiated by research.

_____ a. Female, married, tenured, 30: "I am glad I went into teaching. I would do it again."

_____ b. Male, single, untenured, 28: "My take-home pay is too low; the men complain more than the women."

_____ c. Female, single, untenured, 22: "It's a great place to meet eligible men."

_____ d. Male, married, tenured, 45: "After all these years, I guess my greatest reward is knowing when I have succeeded."

_____ e. Male, married, tenured, 35: "Freedom—in the classroom I can pretty much do as I please."

6. An experienced teacher is making some general observations to a first-year teacher. Check those statements that the author or research suggests may have some basis in fact.

_____ a. "Let's face it, you're not a student anymore. There's no place to hide."

_____ b. "I think the first year of teaching brings the greatest satisfaction. It's all so new."

_____ c. "Planning for the first year is always more difficult."

_____ d. "Kids usually are more sympathetic with a new teacher."

_____ e. "Don't worry; there will always be someone around to help you if you get in trouble."

Answers

1. Underline "relationship between theory and practice is obvious and direct," "it is not an art but an exact science." (See pp. 6–7)
2. a, b, d (See pp. 9–10)
3. a, c, d (See pp. 11, 13)
4. a, b (See pp. 20–21)
5. a, b, d, e (See pp. 24–25)
6. a, c (See pp. 26–27)

Project 1

OBJECTIVE: To gain some insight into the uses of educational psychology in the classroom.

PROCEDURE: Visit one or more teachers (at any level) who have been teaching less than five years. If you do not have access to teachers, choose peers who have had some student teaching. Use the following questions as the basis for your interview:

1. How long have you been (student) teaching?

2. Looking back over that period of time, would you say what you learned in educational psychology has become more useful, less useful, or about equally useful in terms of your teaching?

3. What areas of educational psychology have been the most immediate and practical use to you? The least?

4. If you could restructure the educational psychology course you took, what would you add? Remove? Why?

5. Is there anything else you would like to add?

ANALYSIS: The questions are designed to give you some insight into the ways you should perceive the value of the content of your course. The answers to Question 3 can and should be used by you to seek additional learning beyond that required by the course. You may also want to discuss the implications of Questions 2 and 4 in class.

Project 2

OBJECTIVE: To assess prospective teachers' attitudes toward unionism.

PROCEDURE: This project should be carried out with peers in your class or other educational courses. We suggest you interview at least three or four. You may want to make a copy of p. 14 of the textbook in case the answer to Question 1 is "Don't know enough" or "undecided" or the teacher is uncertain about Question 2. The following questions might be used:

1. Do you favor teacher unions?

2. Are you aware of the NEA and AFT and the differences between them? (Show p. 14 if the subject is uncertain.)

3. What do you think are some of the advantages and disadvantages of teachers' joining unions?

4. Have you heard much about unionism in your education classes? From your cooperating teachers? What feelings do you get from these sources?

5. Which of the two kinds of unions described would you join? Why?

ANALYSIS:

1. Compile the answers from all subjects, and see if a composite answer emerges. Determine whether or not significant prounion or antiunion thinking emerges.

2. On the basis of the answers given, determine the salient reasons for the stands taken. Are they personal or part of professional training (college faculty, cooperating teachers, and so on)?

PART ONE

THE
LEARNER

CHAPTER OUTLINE

2

DEVELOPMENT DURING INFANCY AND CHILDHOOD

CHAPTER PREVIEW

By the time children enter school, they have lived some of the most important years of their lives. The experiences of the next few years also significantly affect their later development, as well as the attitudes and actions they display in school. These early periods of development—infancy and childhood—are the focus of this chapter. In particular, attention is paid to the importance of children's interactions with parents and other caretakers and to the child's developing sense of gender and racial identity.

Other aspects of development, such as cognitive and language development, are treated in subsequent chapters in this text (Chapters 6 and 9, respectively). Development during adolescence is the topic of Chapter 3. Appreciating the significance of the factors treated here helps provide the necessary context for viewing students within the relative isolation of the school setting.

As you read, keep the following questions in mind:

- How do experiences during the prenatal period affect children's development after birth?
- What kinds of relationships with others do children experience in their early years and how do these influence their personality and behavior?
- Several aspects of family life— whether parents are strict or more lenient, whether one or both parents are at home, whether the mother works or not—can affect the growing child. How do these factors influence children's development?
- How do children come to think of themselves as either boys or girls and to exhibit gender-specific attitudes and behaviors?
- How do children in multiethnic societies acquire awareness of and attitudes toward different racial groups?

Human development is the process by which individuals change and grow while remaining in some respects the same. It encompasses the orderly and sequential changes that occur as we move across the life span from conception to death. Indeed, development meets us at every turn. Consider that within a mere 600 days the newborn becomes a walking, talking, and socially functioning child. And at puberty youth undergo a marked spurt in size and acquire various secondary sexual characteristics. Such developmental changes have profound implications for teachers and the schools. They provide the contextual framework within which education occurs. In all realms—mental, emotional, motor, and social—children's developmental capabilities both set broad limits to and open vast possibilities for learning experiences.

PRENATAL DEVELOPMENT

Between conception and birth, the human organism grows from a single cell to a mass of about seven pounds containing some 200 billion cells. Of the **prenatal period**—the time elapsing between conception and birth which normally averages about 266 days—the physical anthropologist Ashley Montagu says:

> Never again in his life, in so brief a period will this human being grow so rapidly or so much, or develop in so many directions, as he does between conception and birth. . . . During this critical period, the development of the human body exhibits the most perfect timing and the most elaborate correlations that we ever display in our entire lives. The building and launching of a satellite, involving thousands of people and hundreds of electronic devices, is not nearly so complex an operation as the building and launching of a human being. [1964:20–21]

The prenatal period is commonly divided into three stages. The first, the *germinal period*, extends from conception to the end of the second week; the second, the *embryonic period*, from the end of the second week to the end of the eighth week; and the third, the *fetal period*, from the end of the eighth week until birth. During the germinal period, the *zygote* (the fertilized egg) begins its growth and establishes a linkage with the support system of the mother. The embryonic period is characterized by rapid growth, the establishment of a placental relationship with the mother, the early structural appearance of all the chief organs, and the development, in form at least, of a recognizable human body. During the fetal period, the differentiation of the major organ systems continues, and the organs themselves become capable of assuming their specialized functions.

Environmental influences operate upon the developing human being during all phases of the prenatal period. The zygote undergoes a hazardous week-long journey down the oviduct (the Fallopian tube) and around the uterus, experiencing a highly variable and chemically active medium. Upon implanting itself in the uterus, the embryo becomes vulnerable to maternal disease, malnutrition, and biochemical influences.

The thalidomide tragedy in the 1960s highlighted the potential dangers of drugs and chemical agents to pregnant women. Thousands of European women who took thalidomide (a tranquilizer) during the embryonic period of their pregnancies gave birth to children with malformed limbs. Medical authorities include tobacco smoking and alcohol usage in the drug category. Expectant mothers who are chronic smokers are twice as likely to give birth to premature infants as are nonsmokers (Simpson, 1957; Peterson, Morese, and Kaltreider, 1965). And recently, the Food and Drug Administration has warned pregnant women that those women who drink as little as one ounce of alcohol twice a week show a sizable increase of risk for spontaneous abortion. One ounce of alcohol is the amount contained in two glasses of wine. Further, women who drink an ounce of alcohol a day bear significantly smaller babies. Two drinks of hard liquor a day can cause the *fetal alcohol syndrome,* associated with growth retardation, congenital eye and ear problems, heart defects, extra digits, and disturbed sleep patterns in the newborn (Greenberg, 1981).

Nutritional deficiencies in the expectant mothers, especially severe ones, affect prenatal development. Poorly nourished mothers run a greater risk than do well-nourished mothers of spontaneous abortions and premature births. Further, newborns of poorly nourished women are more likely to be underweight at birth, to die in infancy, or to suffer rickets, physical and neural defects, and some types of mental retardation. These difficulties are most prevalent among American Indian, black, Chicano, and Puerto Rican children, whose mothers are more likely to be undernourished than the mothers of white children.

INFANCY

The first two years of life are termed **infancy.** Few characteristics of the period are more striking than children's relentless pursuit of competence. They expend an enormous amount of energy initiating behaviors by which they interact with their environment. In the process they expand and perfect a vast range of capabilities. At the same time, the important people in their lives are placing greater demands upon them to develop new controls over their activities, to master toilet training, and to eat and sleep at scheduled times.

Physical Growth

In general, the growth of children is a very regular, orderly process. Nonetheless, it is unevenly distributed over the first twenty years of life. From birth until age four or five, the rate of growth in height declines rapidly. Indeed, about twice as much growth occurs between the ages of one and three as between the ages of three and five. After age five, the rate of growth is practically

constant up to the beginning of the adolescent growth spurt. At puberty there is again a marked acceleration in growth (Tanner, 1978).

The typical girl is slightly shorter than the typical boy at all ages until adolescence. However, at about the age of eleven the girl temporarily shoots ahead, since her adolescent spurt occurs two years earlier than that of the boy. At around age fourteen she is surpassed again in height by the typical boy, whose adolescent spurt is well underway, whereas that of the girl is nearly completed (Tanner, 1978). Further, relative to other children of their age group, broadly built children tend to grow faster than average, while slenderly built children grow more slowly than average (Bayley, 1935).

A particularly striking characteristic of growth is its "self-stabilizing" or "target-seeking" quality. James M. Tanner, a noted authority on the subject of growth in children, says:

> Children, no less than rockets, have their trajectories, governed by the control systems of their genetical constitution and powered by energy absorbed from the natural environment. Deflect the child from its growth trajectory by acute malnutrition or illness, and a restoring force develops so that as soon as the missing food is supplied or the illness terminated the child catches up toward its original curve. When it gets there, it slows down again to adjust its path onto the old trajectory once more. [1970:125]

Accordingly, children exhibit a compensatory property of "making up" for arrested growth when conditions return to normal.

Different parts of the body grow at different rates. The internal organs, including the kidneys, liver, spleen, lungs, and stomach, keep pace with the growth of the skeletal system. These systems undergo the same two growth spurts in infancy and adolescence. In contrast, the nervous system develops more rapidly than the other systems so that it is largely completed by four years of age. At birth the brain is about 25 percent of its adult weight; at six months, nearly 50 percent; at two-and-a-half years, 75 percent; at five years, 90

PRINCIPLES OF DEVELOPMENT

Development follows two patterns, the cephalocaudal principle and the proximodistal principle. The *cephalocaudal principle* involves development that proceeds from the head to the feet. Improvements in structure and function come first in the infant's head region, then in the trunk, and finally in the leg region. In newborns the head makes up about one-fourth of the body as opposed to about one-tenth to one-twelfth of the body among adults. From birth to adulthood the head doubles in size, the trunk trebles, the arms and hands quadruple in length, and the legs and feet grow fivefold (Bayley, 1935, 1956).

Motor development also follows this principle. Infants first learn to control the muscles of the head and neck, next their arms and

FIGURE 2.1 GROWTH OF DIFFERENT SYSTEMS

The curves show the percent of the total growth attained by the typical individual by the age of twenty. Size at age twenty is represented by 100 on the vertical scale. The lymphoid system includes the thymus and lymph nodes. The brain and head include the skull, brain, and the spinal cord. The curve labeled "general" entails the skeletal system, lungs, kidneys, and digestive organs. Finally, the reproductive system covers testes, ovaries, the prostate, seminal vesicles, and oviducts. *(Source: Richard E. Scammon, "The Measurement of the Body in Childhood," in J. A. Harris, C. M. Jackson, D. G. Paterson, and R. E. Scammon, eds.,* The Measurement of Man *[Minneapolis: University of Minnesota Press, 1930], Figure 73, p. 193. By permission.)*

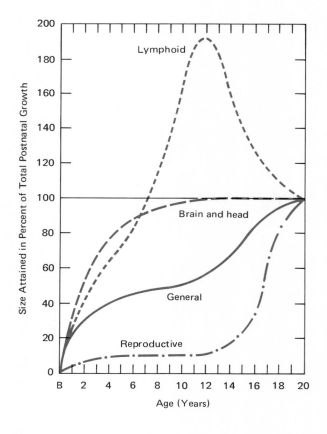

abdomen, and finally their legs. When babies first begin crawling, they propel themselves with the upper part of their bodies while dragging their legs passively behind them. Likewise, infants learn to hold their heads up before they sit, and they learn to sit before they walk.

The *proximodistal principle* entails development that proceeds from near to far, outward from the central axis of the body toward the extremities. Initially, infants have to move their heads and trunks if they are to orient their hands when grasping an object. Only later do they become capable of employing their arms and legs independently, and it takes them still longer to make refined movements with their wrists and fingers. On the whole, large-muscle control precedes fine-muscle control. Kindergarten and first-grade teachers commonly find that children are somewhat more adept at activities such as jumping, climbing, and running, which involve the use of large muscles, than at activities like drawing and writing, which involve smaller muscles.

percent; and at ten years, 95 percent (Tanner, 1970; 1978). (See Figure 2.1.)

Lymphoid tissue (the thymus and lymph nodes) shows a different growth curve from other tissue systems (see Figure 2.1). At twelve years of age it is more than double the level it will reach in adulthood. After age twelve, the system declines until maturity. The reproductive system exhibits a totally different pattern. It grows very slowly until puberty, then accelerates, and finally levels off at maturity.

Attachment Behaviors

It is an elemental fact that humans are social beings who exist in group settings. The developmental psychologist Harriet L. Rheingold observes, "The human infant is born into a social environment; he can remain alive only in a social environment; and from birth he takes his place in that environment . . ." (1969:781). In sum, humanness is a social product.

One of the earliest expressions that infants give of a social orientation is attachment behavior. **Attachment** is an affectional tie that individuals form between themselves and another person that binds them together in space and endures over time (Ainsworth and Bell, 1970). It finds expression in behaviors that promote proximity and contact. Infants demonstrate attachment through following, clinging, and signaling (smiling, crying, and calling). As such they show that specific people are important, satisfying, and rewarding to them.

H. Rudolph Schaffer and Peggy E. Emerson (1964a) studied the development of attachment behaviors in sixty Scottish infants. They identified three stages in the children's social responsiveness. During the first stage, which occurred during the first two months after birth, the infants were aroused by *all* parts of their environment. It seemed to make little difference if the source of stimulation were human or nonhuman. Around the third month, they entered the second stage in which they became responsive to human beings as a general class of stimuli. Attachment was *indiscriminate;* they would protest the withdrawal of any person's attention, familiar or strange. At about seven months of age, they began showing *specific* attachment. This marked the beginning of the third stage. The infants would display a preference for a particular person, and during the next three to four months would make progressively greater effort to be near this person.

The ages at which children moved from one

ATTACHMENT BEHAVIORS
By about seven months of age, most infants show a preference for particular individuals. Attachment behaviors are manifested in activities that promote proximity and contact.

The Significance of Early Social Experience

In the orphanage, children become sad and many of them die of sadness.

From the diary of a
Spanish Bishop, 1760

Children reared in orphanages, foundling homes, and other institutional settings do not flourish as well as do children reared by their parents in a home environment. For instance, in 1915 James H. M. Knox, Jr., of the Johns Hopkins Hospital, reported that in spite of adequate physical care, 90 percent of the infants in Baltimore-area orphanages and foundling homes died within a year of admission (Gardner, 1972). During the 1930s and 1940s, the term **maternal deprivation** came to be applied to the problems of homeless and neglected children. The concept implies that the absence of normal mothering can result in psychological damage and physical deterioration in infants and children.

René Spitz (1945, 1946), an Austrian psychoanalytic physician, launched the first large-scale study of infants raised in an institutional setting. He compared infants being reared in a foundling home with those being reared in a prison nursery. The babies in the foundling home were provided with good physical care, but the overworked nursing personnel gave them little or no individual contact and attention. The babies in the prison nursery were with their own mothers most of the time and hence received individual care and love. Despite impeccable hygiene, the foundling-home infants were especially susceptible to infection and illness, and over a third of them died in the two-year period of the study. Further, the babies revealed severe mental and motor retardation. By contrast, the infants reared by their own mothers made considerably better progress by all standards of development. Other studies of infants raised in foundling homes have likewise reported the retarding effects of institutional life (Goldfarb, 1945, 1947, 1949; Dennis, 1973).

stage to the next varied considerably. One of the babies in the Schaffer and Emerson study gave evidence of specific attachment at twenty-two weeks. Two others, however, did not show attachment until they were a year old. Children of different cultures also exhibit differences in ages at which they display specific attachment. Mary D. S. Ainsworth (1967) found that infants in the African nation of Uganda showed specific attachment at about six months of age, a good month earlier than the children in the Scottish sample. In addition, Barry M. Lester and his associates (1974) reported that separation protest occurs earlier among infants in Guatemala than among those in the United States.

More recently the foundling-home research has been widely criticized for faulty design and interpretation (Casler, 1961; Biehler, 1976). Samuel R. Pinneau (1955) has shown that much of the serious decline that Spitz observed in the Austrian foundling homes had occurred even before the children had been separated from their mothers. Moreover, in all studies of foundling-home children, some infants had been adopted or placed in foster homes. It is conceivable that the children who went unadopted or unplaced were viewed as less desirable, and hence they constituted an unrepresentative sample.

Despite the limitations of the foundling-home research, there is still ample evidence that extreme deprivation in early life can retard development and distort the personality (Davis, 1947; Rutter, 1974; Langmeier and Matějček, 1974). Further, researchers have demonstrated that physical contact and sensory stimulation can improve the overall functioning of children in institutionalized environments (Rheingold, 1961; Skeels, 1966; White, 1969; Saltz, 1973). Apparently, even small amounts of extra handling can have a significant influence, at least over the short term. Children also differ; some show greater vulnerability to deprivation experiences than do others.

Psychologists disagree as to the source of the disabilities that children experience under circumstances of extreme deprivation. Some point to the lack of "mother love" and others to the lack of sensory stimulation. Psychologists influenced by the Freudian psychoanalytic tradition argue that it is the lack of intimate interpersonal relationships that is responsible for the impairment observed in institutionalized settings (Ainsworth, 1962). Others like Lawrence Casler (1961, 1967) challenge the view that a warm, affectionate relationship with the mother is essential for healthy development. Casler says that the crucial factors are the degree of sensory stimulation and the range of experiences provided the child.

In some respects the issue is a pseudocontroversy. The underlying feelings of warmth or aversion that mothers experience toward their infants are communicated through their behavior, for example, whether or not they talk to their babies, touch and caress them, hold them, carry them about, and otherwise provide them with sensory stimulation and varied experiences.

Recently, Susan Curtiss (1977) has stirred new interest in deprivation cases with her report on Genie. Genie was discovered at the age of thirteen after having experienced a childhood of severe and unusual deprivation and abuse. From the age of twenty months, she had been locked in a small room by her father and rarely saw anyone. When she came to public attention at thirteen years of age, Genie was a malformed, incontinent, unsocialized, and malnourished child. On various maturity and attainment tests she scored as normal one-year-old children score.

From the time of Genie's discovery, a program was designed to rehabilitate and educate her. Psycholinguists at UCLA undertook to train Genie in language usage. At first she spoke only in one-word utterances in the manner that toddlers do when they first begin talking. In time Genie progressed to two-word and three-word language strings. But unlike normal children, Genie never acquired the ability to ask questions and her understanding of grammar remains limited. Four years after she began stringing words together, her speech continued to be slow and resembled a garbled telegram.

Psychologists are not certain why Genie has failed to learn the kind of grammatical principles that underlie human language and communication (Pines, 1981). Her deficiencies do not appear to be inborn. Nor can her difficulties be attributed to a lack of accomplished teachers. Since discovery and until age twenty, she enjoyed an enriched environment and competent speech therapists. In 1978, Genie's mother became her legal guardian and filed suit against a number of UCLA researchers for subjecting Genie to "unreasonable and outrageous" testing, not for treatment, but to exploit Genie for personal and economic benefits. Since then, research on Genie's development has been halted. One hypothesis advanced to explain Genie's

TEACHERS AND THE ABUSED CHILD

Officials of the U.S. Department of Health, Education, and Welfare estimate that more than 1 million children in the United States suffer abuse or neglect each year. Of these, 100,000 to 200,000 are physically attacked, 60,000 to 100,000 are sexually abused, and the remainder are neglected. Every year some 2,000 children die under circumstances that suggest maltreatment. Research sponsored by the National Institute of Mental Health suggests that these figures may even be too low. From interviews with 2,143 married couples representing a demographic cross section of American families, sociologists at three eastern universities estimate that parents kick, punch, or bite as many as 1.7 million children a year; beat up 460,000 to 750,000 more; and attack 46,000 others with knives or guns (*New York Times,* March 20, 1977:6E).

Child abuse is a catchall term referring to physical, emotional, social, or sexual mistreatment inflicted upon a child by an adult caretaker. Physicians term severe injuries associated with physical abuse the *battered child syndrome* (abrasions, lacerations, burns, fractures, concussions, hemorrhages, and bruises caused by a caretaker's hitting, yanking, shaking, kicking, chok-

ing, burning, or throwing a child around). Many psychologists have implicated childhood abuse in later adult problems. For instance, Lee Harvey Oswald and Sirhan Sirhan (the assassins of John F. Kennedy and Robert Kennedy) were abused as children.

Child abuse is found among families from all social, religious, economic, and racial backgrounds. However, divorce, separation, and unstable marriages, as well as minor criminal offenses, tend to be more characteristic of families in which child abuse occurs. Other factors that tend to be associated with child abuse are social and economic stress, lack of family roots in the community, lack of immediate support from extended families, social isolation, high mobility, and unemployment (Spinetta and Rigler, 1975; Steinberg, Catalano, and Dooley, 1981; Cicchetti and Rizley, 1981). However, these factors are neither sufficient nor necessary causes for child abuse, since the great majority of parents who are experiencing social and economic difficulties do not abuse their children.

Although it is difficult to generalize about parents who abuse their children, they do tend to have some characteristics in common. They frequently lack self-esteem,

are emotionally immature and self-centered, and feel incompetent as parents. They are unrealistic in their expectations, demanding that their child behave like an adult. When the child "crosses" the parent by acting "childish," the parent sees it as merely being vindictive:

> Henry J., in speaking of his sixteen-month-old son, Johnny, said, "He knows what I mean and understands it when I say 'come here.' If he doesn't come immediately, I go and give him a gentle tug on the ear to remind him of what he's supposed to do." In the hospital it was found that Johnny's ear was lacerated and partially torn away from his head. [Steele and Pollock, 1977:96]

An abusive parent also commonly looks to the child to fulfill parental needs for comfort and love, and when the child fails the parent, as he or she inevitably must, the parent strikes out against the child in anger:

> Kathy made this poignant statement: "I have never felt really loved all my life. When the baby was born, I thought he would love me: but when he cried all the time, it meant he didn't love me, so I hit him." Kenny, age three weeks, was hospitalized with bilateral sub-

dural hematomas [severe bruises]. [Steele and Pollock, 1977:96]

Abusive parents often possess an intense fear of spoiling their children and hold a strong belief in the effectiveness of corporal punishment. Such parents are themselves likely to have been abused when they were children and to have been raised in the same authoritarian style that they recreate with their own children. Indeed, it appears that the pattern of abuse is unwittingly transmitted from parent to child, generation after generation (Spinetta and Rigler, 1975; Steele and Pollock, 1977; Kempe and Kempe, 1978).

On the whole, however, not more than 10 percent of abusing parents show severe psychotic tendencies or other signs of serious psychiatric disorders. In these latter cases it is usually advisable that the child be removed from the home. Psychiatrists estimate that the other 90 percent of abusing parents are readily treatable if they receive competent counseling (Helfer and Kempe, 1977).

Abused children also tend to have some characteristics in common. Premature babies are more subject to abuse than full-term babies. The same holds true of colicky babies. Similarly, hyperactive or withdrawn children are more often the targets of abuse. Overall, a child whom an abuse-prone parent views as being "strange," "different," or "handicapped" is more at risk than are other children in the family (Soeffing, 1975; Brenton, 1977).

Since teachers are the only adults outside the family whom many children see with any consistency, they are in an excellent position to detect signs of child abuse and neglect and, by reporting them to the proper authorities, to begin the process of remediation. Indeed, teachers are required by law to report child abuse and neglect in forty-one states and the District of Columbia. Further, recognizing the fear that many people have over the possibility of legal action against them should their reports prove erroneous, most states have enacted legislation providing legal immunity for mandated, good-faith reports.

Many schools and school systems have a basic policy regarding the reporting of abuse and neglect cases. The most logical place for the teacher to begin is usually the principal (although in some school districts teachers are required to funnel their reports through the guidance counselor or the school nurse). Another avenue of assistance is the social agency in the area that normally handles such cases. However, teachers should not contact the parents on their own initiative.

The American Humane Association has published a list of signs teachers should look for as possible tipoffs of child abuse and neglect. Among these are the following:

- Does the child have bruises, welts, and contusions?
- Does the child complain of beatings or maltreatment?
- Does the child frequently arrive early to school and stay late (the child may be seeking an escape from home)?
- Is the child frequently absent or late?
- Is the child aggressive, disruptive, destructive, shy, withdrawn, passive, or overly compliant?
- Is the child inadequately dressed for the weather, unkempt, dirty, undernourished, tired, in need of medical attention, or frequently injured?

Parental attitudes can also be symptomatic of child abuse or neglect:

- Are parents aggressive or abusive when asked about problems concerning the child?
- Are parents apathetic or unresponsive?
- Is parental behavior bizarre or strange?
- Do parents show little concern about their child or little interest in the child's activities?
- Do the parents fail to participate in school activities or allow the child to participate?

Additional material and pamphlets on child abuse and neglect can be secured by writing the American Humane Association, Children's Division, P.O. Box 1266, Denver, Colorado 80220; the National Center on Child Abuse and Neglect, U.S. Children's Bureau, P.O. Box 1182, Washington, D.C. 20013; Child Abuse Project, Educational Commission of the States, 1860 Lincoln Street, Denver, Colorado 80203; National Center for the Prevention and Treatment of Child Abuse and Neglect, 1205 Oneida Street, Denver, Colorado 80220.

language deficits is that there are critical periods in the development of language capabilities that cannot be successfully bridged once children enter puberty.

The Two-Way Street of Parent-Child Interaction

Of men and women he [the infant] makes fathers and mothers.

HARRIET L. RHEINGOLD
"Infancy," 1968

Psychologists and educators have long accepted, and with good evidence, that parents have a profound impact in shaping their children's personalities and behaviors. What has often been overlooked is that the influence also runs the other way. Children act upon their parents and, in turn, influence the kind of treatment that they receive (Sameroff, 1975; Gewirtz and Boyd, 1976; Segal and Yahraes, 1978; Martin, 1981). The characteristics of the child—intensity of response, cuddliness, and temperament—elicit quite different responses and behaviors from adults (Osofsky and Danzger, 1974; Marcus, 1975; Lytton, 1980).

One especially striking difference among newborns has to do with their responses to cuddling. Schaffer and Emerson (1964b) studied the reactions of thirty-seven newborns to physical contact and found that the babies could be classed as *cuddlers* or *noncuddlers*. Mothers of cuddlers described their babies in these terms: "He snuggles into you," "She cuddles you back," and "He'd let me cuddle him for hours." Mothers of noncuddlers said their babies objected when they held them on their laps, pressed them against their shoulders, or gave them skin-to-skin contact such as kissing or cheek stroking: "He won't allow it—he fights to get away," "Try and snuggle him against you and he'll kick and thrash, and if you persist he'll begin to cry," and "She struggles, squirms, and whimpers when you try to hold her close."

Alexander Thomas and Stella Chess (1977) have similarly found in their studies of more than 200 children that infants show a distinct individuality in temperament that is independent of their parents' handling or personality styles. Some infants they term *difficult babies*. These youngsters wail and cry a good deal, have violent tantrums, spit out new foods, scream and twist when their faces are washed, eat and sleep in irregular patterns, are not easy to pacify, and seem to sap even a generous supply of parental patience and emotional strength. Other infants are *slow-to-warm-up babies*. They tend to have low activity levels, adapt very slowly, withdraw readily, seem somewhat disposed to be negative, and show wariness in new situations. Still other infants are termed *easy babies*. Easy babies respond positively to new situations, adapt quickly to new foods and people, are generally cheerful, and display regular patterns of eating, sleeping, and eliminating. About 10 percent of all infants are difficult babies, 15 percent are slow-to-warm-up babies, 40 percent are easy babies, and the remaining 35 percent show a mixture of characteristics.

Each type of child can have considerable influence on parental behavior and, in turn, on the course of the child's own subsequent development. We do not have to be around infants very long before we appreciate the fact that we experience different feelings about babies who wail and fuss no matter what we do to calm them and babies who quickly and cheerfully respond to our soothing efforts. As a consequence, both the caretaker and the child become caught up in an interacting spiral. Mothers of children with difficult temperaments tend to look at them less, stay away from them more, and play with them less.

It appears that the mothers become "turned off" by their difficult children and provide them with less stimulation and caretaking. It is hardly surprising that these youngsters tend to be less competent than other children when they are two and three years of age. And being less competent, they are less likely to receive positive feedback as to their worth, reinforcing a vicious circle that tends to lock the children within the "difficult" category

(Ainsworth and Bell, 1969; Bell and Harper, 1977; Segal and Yahraes, 1978). Further, difficult and unsoothable babies are overrepresented among abused children (Korner, 1979). Constant fussing, colicky fretfulness, highly irritating crying, and other exasperating behaviors provoke violence in some parents. Indeed, some battered children continue to be abused in a succession of foster homes where no other child had been abused previously. Unhappily, some children seem to convert otherwise "normal" parents into "abnormal" ones. The behavior of the children simply exceeds their parents' coping capabilities.

CHILDHOOD

Childhood is the period in the human life span between two years of age and puberty. During this time, children appreciably enlarge their repertoire of behaviors. As a consequence, they become progressively integrated within the larger context of group life. Schooling plays an important part in this process, whereby children take on the ideas and sentiments of their culture, and whereby society perpetuates itself from one generation to the next. When children attend school, they are outside the home and their immediate neighborhoods for several hours a day. In this new setting teachers become a major source of influence.

Child-Rearing Practices and Techniques

Both the lay public and behavioral scientists have been interested in the effects various child-rearing practices have in shaping a child's personality and behavior. Underlying this interest has been the implicit assumption that all parental actions, whether intentional or not, play a part in fashioning a child's social and emotional development. Two basic psychological traditions have

promoted this emphasis (Skolnick, 1978). The first has derived from the psychoanalytic formulations of Sigmund Freud (1856–1939). The second has had its roots in the ideas of early behaviorists like John B. Watson (1878–1958).

It was Freud's view that what happens to an individual later in life is merely a ripple on the surface of a personality structure that is fashioned during the child's first five or six years. According to the psychoanalytic school of thought, breast feeding, a prolonged period of nursing, gradual weaning, a self-demand nursing schedule, easy as well as late bladder and bowel training, and frequent mothering promote the growth of emotionally healthy personalities. Children are viewed as vulnerable and sensitive beings, easily damaged by traumatic events and emotional stress.

Watson's behavioristic model of child rearing presented the image of a malleable child whom parents could shape however they might wish. He clearly stated his extreme environmentalist position in this famous passage:

> I should like to go one step further now and say, give me a dozen infants, well-formed, and my own specified world to bring them up in and I'll guarantee to take any one at random and train him to be any type of specialist I might select— doctor, lawyer, artist, merchant-chief, and yes, even beggar-man and thief, regardless of his talents, penchants, tendencies, abilities, vocations, and the race of his ancestors. [1924:104]

As viewed by Watson, children require stern parents. By placing children on a strict schedule, parents could eradicate bad habits in eating, sleeping, and crying and thus fend off possible permanent maladjustments in character.

Despite their differences, both the psychoanalytic and behavioral models grant parents an omnipotent role in child development (Skolnick, 1978). Both approaches emphasize that only by doing the right things at the right times can parents ensure that their children will turn out happy, successful, and free of mental frailties. Further, whether explicitly stated or not, it is assumed that if somehow children turn out socially maladjusted and beleaguered with emotional problems, then the parents have only themselves to blame.

Increasingly, social and behavioral scientists are coming to recognize that children are neither as vulnerable nor as malleable as they may once have believed them to be. Research by Jerome Kagan and other developmental psychologists has shown that most children are resilient and show amazing adaptive abilities (Kagan, Kearsley, and Zelazo, 1978). Other research has demonstrated that the factors stressed in the psychoanalytic literature, including those associated with bladder and bowel training, are not related to later personality characteristics (Sewell and Mussen, 1952; Behrens, 1954; Schaffer and Emerson, 1964a). Likewise, a longitudinal study carried out by M. I. Heinstein (1963) revealed no significant differences in the later behavior of bottle-fed and breast-fed babies.

All of this is not to suggest that parents have little influence on their children's development. But although *influencing* it, they do not *control* it. Arlene Skolnick, a research psychologist, observes:

> Most child-care advice assumes that if the parents administer the proper prescriptions, the child will develop as planned. It places exaggerated faith not only in the perfectibility of the children and their parents, but in the infallibility of the particular child-rearing technique as well. But increasing evidence suggests that parents simply do not have that much control over their children's development; too many other factors are influencing it. [1978:56]

Based on their studies of difficult, slow-to-warm-up, and easy babies, Thomas, Chess, and their associates similarly conclude that children are so different that, "There can be no universally valid set of rules that will work equally well for all children everywhere" (1963:85). Parents with difficult children often experience guilt and anxiety, wondering, "What are we doing wrong?" These researchers have a reassuring word for such parents:

> The knowledge that certain characteristics of their child's development are not primarily due to parental malfunctioning has proven helpful to many parents. Mothers of problem children often develop guilt feelings because they assume that they are solely responsible for their children's emotional difficulties. This feeling of guilt may be accompanied by anxiety, defensiveness, increased pressures on the children, and even hostility toward them for "exposing" the mother's inadequacy by their disturbed behavior. When parents learn that their role in shaping of their child is not an omnipotent one, guilt feelings may lessen, hostility and pressures may tend to disappear, and positive restructuring of the parent-child interaction can become possible. [1963:94]

There are many ways in which parents influence their children's development. One recurrent finding by developmental psychologists is that the warmth of the parent-child relationship is important (Sears, Maccoby, and Levin, 1957; Becker, 1964; McClelland et al., 1978). Parents display warmth toward their children through affectionate, accepting, approving, understanding, and child-centered behaviors. When disciplining their children, parents who are warm tend to employ frequent explanations and to use words of encouragement and praise; only infrequently do they resort to physical punishment.

Another key aspect of the home atmosphere has to do with parental restrictiveness in such areas as sex play, modesty, table manners, toilet training, neatness, orderliness, care of household furniture, noise, and aggression toward others (Sears, Maccoby, and Levin, 1957; Becker, 1964; Lewis, 1981). For the most part, research suggests that highly restrictive parenting fosters dependency and interferes with independence training (Maccoby and Masters, 1970). But as Wesley C. Becker notes in his review of the research on parenting, it is difficult to come up with a "perfect" all-purpose set of parental guidelines:

> The consensus of the research suggests that both restrictiveness and permissiveness entail certain risks. Restrictiveness, while fostering well-controlled, socialized behavior, tends also to lead to fearful, dependent, and submissive behaviors, a dulling of intellectual striving and inhibited hostility. Permissiveness on the other hand, while

fostering outgoing, sociable assertive behaviors and intellectual striving, tends also to lead to less persistence and increased aggressiveness. [1964:197]

Overall, researchers are finding confirmation of the common-sense observation that the way parents *feel* about their children has a major impact upon the children's social and emotional development. In the early 1950s, Robert Sears and his associates (1957) interviewed a sample of mothers of kindergartners as to their child-rearing practices. Twenty-five years later, David C. McClelland and his colleagues (1978) did a follow-up study of the children, now adults. They found that when parents, especially mothers, really loved their children (they demonstrated affection for the children and enjoyed playing with them), the sons and daughters were likely to achieve high levels of social and moral maturity. In contrast, adult maturity had little to do with the duration of breast feeding, the age and severity of toilet training, or strictness about bedtimes. Even the mother's anxiety about whether she was doing a good job neither hurt nor helped her children. The researchers concluded that parents promote moral and social maturity in later life by loving their children, enjoying them, and wanting them around.

Different Family Patterns

A good many Americans still think of the typical family as a social unit in which the husband is the only breadwinner, the wife is a homemaker who is not part of the labor force, and there are minor children. Yet, this does not represent the typical American family of the 1970s and still less the 1980s. Even in 1975, only 7 out of 100 American families fitted this description (*New York Times,* March 8, 1977). Indeed, American families show such a wide range of differing patterns that it is doubtful that there is such a thing as the "typical" family. Accordingly, the classroom teacher encounters children with quite different home experiences. Let us consider a number of these.

Birth Order

Were children to come from families with essentially identical structures, they still would have somewhat different family experiences. Developmental psychologists find that the number, sex, and spacing of siblings (their birth order) have major consequences for a child's development and socialization. An only child, an oldest child, a middle child, and a youngest child all seem to experience a somewhat different world, because of the somewhat different networks of key relationships and roles that encompass their lives.

First-born children appear to be fortune's favorites. They are overrepresented in college populations (Altus, 1965), at the higher IQ levels (Zajonc, 1976; Steelman and Mercy, 1980), among National Merit and Rhodes Scholars, in *Who's Who in America,* and among American presidents (52 percent). One explanation for the differences between first-born and later-born children is that parents typically attach greater importance to their

BIRTH ORDER POSITIONS

The number, sex, and spacing of siblings creates somewhat different relationships and roles for each child in a family.

first child. They tend to show them more affection, provide them with greater caretaking interactions, and hold higher expectations for them. Another explanation is that first-borns play a parent-surrogate role with their younger siblings, a ''helper'' role that appears to be instrumental in the development of verbal and cognitive skills.

Single-Parent Families

Over the past twenty years, single-parent families have increased seven times more rapidly than the traditional two-parent family. Two out of every five children now live in a single-parent home for at least part of their childhood. Most children in single-parent homes are reared by their mothers; less than 9 percent are raised by their fathers. Single-parent homes are produced by divorce, desertion, marital separation, death, unmarried parenthood, and in some cases by adoption.

The major cause of single-parent families within the United States is divorce. E. Mavis Hetherington, Martha Cox, and Roger Cox (1976, 1977) undertook a two-year study in which they matched one preschool child in a divorced family with a child in an intact family on the basis of age, sex, birth-order position, and the age and education of the parents. In all, forty-eight divorced couples were paired with forty-eight intact families. The researchers found that the interaction patterns between divorced parents and their children differed significantly from those in the intact families:

> Divorced parents make fewer maturity demands of their children, communicate less well with their children, tend to be less affectionate with their children and show marked inconsistency in

WORKING WITH PARENTS

LANA McWILLIAMS AND PERRY McWILLIAMS

The following are games that can help develop skills in visual and auditory discrimination, alphabetizing, vocabulary, writing, reading, and so on. They were specifically designed to be played while traveling in a car, but they can easily be adapted to other

Source: Lana McWilliams and Perry McWilliams, "Working with Parents," *Instructor*, 89 (March 1980):57–58.

empty-time situations such as waiting to see the doctor or riding in an elevator. The materials needed are readily available and purposely selected to be unlike typical school materials.

PERCEPTUAL SKILLS
- Pretend you are a police officer and the next car that passes belongs to robbers who have just held up a bank. Study the license plate letters and numbers until the car is out of sight. Wait five seconds and repeat the letters and numbers.
- Choose several travel folders (obtained from state welcome centers, motels, and service stations) or objects from the glove compartment or litter bag. Allow children several seconds to study them. Then, while they

discipline and lack of control over their children in comparison to parents in intact families. Poor parenting seems most marked, particularly for divorced mothers, one year after divorce, which seems to be a peak of stress in parent-child relations. [Many of the mothers referred to their relationship with their child one year after divorce as involving "declared war" and a "struggle for survival."] Two years following the divorce, mothers are demanding more . . . [independent and] mature behavior of their children, communicate better and use more explanation and reasoning, are more nurturant and consistent and are better able to control their children than they were the year before. A similar pattern is occurring for divorced fathers in maturity demands, communication and consistency, but they are becoming less nurturant and more detached from their children. [1976:424]

Accordingly, many single-parent families have a difficult period of readjustment following the divorce. However, the situation generally improves during the second year.

The literature is contradictory on the effects of parental separation on children. A number of studies report a higher proportion of delinquent, aggressive, and antisocial behavior among children of divorce (Glueck and Glueck, 1950; McDermott, 1970; Morrison, 1970). And a recent study by B. Frank Brown (1980) found that children from one-parent families cause a disproportionate share of discipline problems in schools and fare worse academically than their peers from two-parent homes. Children from single-parent homes are three times more likely to be suspended from school than those with two parents living at home and twice as likely to drop out of school. And

---

cover their eyes, remove one of the objects. Let children guess which one was removed. Variation: Display several folders or objects in a row, allow players several seconds to study them, then mix them up, and let children put the objects back in their original order.
■ Designate one person to be "it." "It" begins play by saying, "Ritha, Ritha, Marie, I see something you don't see." The other persons try to guess. The one who guesses first gets to be "it." Variations: Provide clues. For example, "Ritha, Ritha, Marie, I see something you don't see and it rhymes with _____," or "its color is _____," or "it starts like _____."
■ Choose a color. All players look for something of that color. The first person to point out five things chooses the next color.

■ Using travel folders, newspaper, or other printed material, cut or tear pages apart. Put them back together using cues such as color, letter size, or shapes.
■ Using travel folders, discuss the main attraction of each. Mix them up, then let players identify the attractions.
■ Choose several travel folders, line them up, and take turns

(continued)

Working with Parents (*continued*)

finding certain things. For example, "I see a wooden table. Can you find it?"

- Have someone choose a word and whisper it from person to person. The last person says aloud what he or she heard. (The final word is often quite different from the original word.)
- Let one player choose a word. The next player must choose a word that rhymes with it. Play continues until no more rhyming words can be given.
- Listen to songs on the radio and list or name all the rhyming words.
- Using travel folders, put in one stack all those folders that are primarily yellow, those that are primarily red, and so on.
- Using main headings in travel folders, assign each child a "trouble" letter and have them find all the words that begin with their letter or contain their letter.

ALPHABETIZING

- Look out the window until someone spots an object that begins with the letter *a*. This game can be played with everyone looking for the same letter, or with each person taking turns with successive letters. Then proceed through the alphabet.
- The first player begins this game by saying, "My name is Annie, I'm going to Alabama and I'm taking an *a*pple." The next player uses *b* and says, "My name is *B*ob, I'm going to *B*uffalo, and I'm taking a *b*anana," and so on through the alphabet.
- Take turns describing the people in a town you have just passed through. Use adjectives beginning with *a* until everyone has had a turn, then use words beginning with *b*, and proceed through the alphabet. For example, the first player might say, "The people in this town are *a*ppealing," and the second person might say, "The people in this town are *a*wful." Variation: Player one says, "I looked out the window and I saw an *a*ngry *a*ntelope." Player two says, "I looked out the window and I saw a *b*ig *b*ull."
- The first player says, "If I had a million dollars, I would buy an *a*pricot." The second player repeats the first player's object and adds a second that begins with *b*, and so on. For example, "If I had a million dollars, I would buy an *a*pricot and a *b*anana."

ANALYSIS SKILLS

- Choose a consonant, consonant blend, or consonant digraph. Each person thinks of a word that begins with the specified sound until no more words can be supplied. Choose another sound and continue.
- The first player says a word. The next player says a word that begins as the first person's word ends. Example: jum*p*—*p*arro*t*—*t*e*n*—*n*ut, and so on. Variation: Use names of states. Example: Texa*s*, *S*outh Da*k*ota, and so on.
- Look at pictures contained in travel folders or magazines. Write the beginning letter on every object your child can identify.
- Have one person call out a word and the other players clap out the number of syllables it contains.

youngsters from two-parent homes are four times more likely to be high achievers than are youngsters from one-parent homes.

However, a number of researchers question the assumption that divorce produces children with negative behavior (Nye, 1957; Raschke and Raschke, 1979). They find that children from divorced homes often show no more, and sometimes less, delinquent behavior and fewer adjustment problems than children from unhappy intact homes do. Many professionals believe that the behavior problems of some children who have divorced parents stem

VOCABULARY DEVELOPMENT

- Select a state from a passing license plate. Make as many words from the letters in that state's name as possible until a new state's license plate passes by. Begin again with that new state.
- List all the adjectives, nouns, and verbs from signs that you pass. One person may be assigned verbs; another, adjectives.
- Select a word and write it down. Give clues about the word until someone guesses it. The person who guesses correctly then chooses a word and play continues.

COMPREHENSION SKILLS

- Read a sign along the highway. Count to ten. Then have your child recall the main idea and supporting details contained in the sign.
- Using travel folders, classify each according to specified criteria. Example: Classify all drive-through tours, all-day tours, all within one city, all within one state.
- Select one person to be "it." This person makes up a question and the other players must raise their hands if they know the answer. The first player to raise his hand (or clap) gets the first chance to answer. If he is correct, he may ask the next question; if not, someone else gets a chance and becomes "it." Example: What were the seven dwarfs' names?
- Select a key word and ask players to supply related words until no more can be added. The last person to supply a word becomes "it" and calls another key word. Example: Car—wheel, mirror, gas, engine, and so on.
- The first player selects a category, the second player a letter of the alphabet, the third player must supply something that fits in the category and starts with the letter. For example: The category is animals and the letter is *h*. The answer may be hen, horse, hare, and so on.

LANGUAGE STIMULATION AND EXPANSION

- The first player begins a story and each player adds a part, until the story reaches the last player. He provides an ending.
- Choose a nursery rhyme that everyone knows. Tell it in everyday language with contemporary characters, but keep the original plot. The first person to correctly identify it gets to make up the next modern nursery rhyme.
- Take turns describing the things you see while looking at the clouds or stars.
- Choose an object or animal and pretend to be that thing. What would it say? How would it feel? What would it do?
- Choose a problem or make up a situation and decide how this problem could be solved. Example: What if we ran out of gas now? What if we had a flat tire and found the spare was also flat?
- Fill a paper bag with small objects. Have your child reach in, feel an object, describe it, and then guess what it is.

WRITING AND SPELLING

- Make a list of things to look for on the trip. Check them off as they are found.
- Have your child keep a trip diary describing interesting sights you have passed along the way.
- Keep a list of all the state license plates seen during one day or throughout the trip.

not directly from the disruption of family bonds but from the difficulties in interpersonal relations with which the disruption is associated (Rutter, 1974). They note that divorce may reduce the amount of friction and unhappiness that a child experiences; consequently divorce can lead to better behavioral adjustments. Much research suggests that it is the *quality* of children's relationships with their parents that matters more than the fact of divorce (Hammond, 1979; Hess and Camara, 1979; Santrock and Warshak, 1979). Nonetheless, adjustment to divorce can take a long time. Judith

S. Wallerstein and Joan B. Kelly (1980), in a study of sixty families five years after divorce, found 34 percent of the children happy and thriving, 29 percent doing reasonably well, and 37 percent depressed and wistfully looking backward to the predivorce family.

Divorce and single-parent arrangements have important implications for teachers (Hammond, 1979). Teachers need to become more aware of their choice of words, examples, and attitudes when discussing families with their pupils. They should guard against depicting all families as being composed of a mother, a father, and children. A recent survey of 1,200 single parents in forty-seven states suggests that the schools continue to stigmatize children from single-parent families (Collins, 1981). Nearly half of the parents indicated that they had had the experience of hearing school personnel use ''broken home'' and other pejorative terms in referring to single-parent families. More than 40 percent said that their children's schools planned social activities for only the mother or father to attend with their children (for instance, ''Breakfast with Dad''), and 64 percent indicated that their children had been asked to make gifts in school for the absent mother or father. And more than 45 percent of the parents felt that teachers and principals assumed that any problems their children might have were related to their single-parent status. Teachers should be alert so that negative views and stereotyping do not become a self-fulfilling prophecy for children from single-parent homes. And they need to exercise care that they not communicate messages to their students that single-parent youngsters are not as good as children from two-parent homes.

Working Mothers

The increasing labor force participation of women is one of the most significant transformations of the American social structure to occur since World War II. Women now account for nearly half of the national labor force. Further, in 1980, 64.3 percent of women with children six to seventeen years of age and 42 percent of women with children under six years of age were in the labor force (O'Connell, Orr, and Lueck, 1982).

The Department of Labor reported that in 1977, 62 percent of children aged three to thirteen with working mothers received child care only from their parents (*American Demographics*, 1981). Many of these children are left alone for at least part of the day. They are termed ''latchkey'' children because many of them carry their housekey on a chain around the neck. Lynette Long, a psychologist from Baltimore's Loyola College, interviewed a number of middle- and lower-middle-class latchkey children in the District of Columbia

WORKING MOTHERS
Children whose mothers work outside the home find that the workplace clock is not calibrated with that of the school.

area (*Columbus Dispatch*, March 25, 1981). She found that most of the children are alone about three hours. They are under strict orders not to leave the home and not to allow anyone into the home. About one-third of the children had very high fears (most commonly associated with people breaking in). They typically spent their time watching television.

In addition to the health and safety problems associated with young children being left home alone, some psychologists and laypeople have expressed concern about the loss to children in terms of supervision, love, and cognitive enrichment when both parents work. There are those who claim that maternal employment contributes to juvenile delinquency. Yet, in a classic study of lower-class boys, Sheldon and Eleanor Glueck (1957) found that sons of regularly employed mothers were no more likely to be delinquent than sons of nonemployed mothers. However, inadequate supervision does appear to be implicated in delinquency, whatever the mother's employment status (Hoffman, 1974).

Whether or not a mother has a job outside the home seems in its own right to have only a limited impact on her children's development (Etaugh, 1980; Schachter, 1981). Other factors, such as the nature of the employment, family circumstances, and the attitude the mother holds toward her various roles, assume greater importance than her actual employment status. Lois W. Hoffman and F. Ivan Nye (1974), a psychologist and sociologist respectively, have made a survey of the research dealing with working mothers. They conclude that the working mother who obtains personal satisfaction from employment, who does not feel excessive guilt, and who has adequate household arrangements is likely to perform as well as or better than the nonworking mother.

Flora F. Cherry and Ethel L. Eaton (1977) studied 200 low-income families to determine the possible harmful outcomes associated with a mother's working during her child's first three years of life. When the children were eight years old, the children of mothers who had worked were compared on various physical (growth and weight) and cognitive (IQ and reading, arithmetic, and spelling achievement) levels with children of mothers who had not worked. In all respects, the children of workers performed as well as those of nonworkers.

A working mother provides a somewhat different role model for her children than does a nonworking mother. As a consequence, the sons and daughters of employed mothers tend to have less traditional sex-role concepts, more approval of working mothers, and a higher evaluation of female competence (Hoffman and Nye, 1974; Gold and Andres, 1978a, 1978b; Stevens and Boyd, 1980).

Gender Identification

What are little boys made of? What are little boys made of? Frogs and snails, and puppy dogs' tails, that's what little boys are made of. What are little girls made of? What are little girls made of? Sugar and spice and all that is nice, and that's what little girls are made of.

J. O. HALLIWELL
Nursery Rhymes of England, 1844

Of considerable interest to psychologists and educators is the process by which children acquire their gender identifications. Apparently all societies have seized upon the anatomical differences between men and women to assign *gender roles*. Gender roles are sets of cultural expectations that define the ways in which the members of each sex should behave. Societies vary in the types of activities they assign to men and women (Murdock, 1935). Nonetheless, most people evolve gender identities that are reasonably consistent with the gender-role standards prevalent in their society. **Gender identities** are the conceptions that people have of themselves as being male or female.

Hormonal and Social Influences

Until recently, it was assumed that our sex and hence our gender identity are determined at conception. The XY combination of chromosomes was thought to lead in a rather straightforward way

COMBATING SEXISM IN THE CLASSROOMS

Teachers are in a unique position to counteract sex-role stereotypes and practices among their students. As the old system of male and female roles has been rendered increasingly obsolete by social and technological changes, the schools have a responsibility to prepare children for egalitarian roles and relationships. This is not to deny that considerable sexism still remains in the schools. For instance, girls start off speaking, reading, and counting sooner than boys, but by high school a different pattern emerges, and the performance of girls declines relative to that of boys. Nonetheless, there are many things that teachers can do to combat sexism within their classrooms. Among these are the following:

- Rather than grouping children into "boys on one side" and "girls on the other side," a variety of other grouping techniques can be employed. Children can be divided on the basis of whether their birthdays come on even or odd numbered days, whether they live on a street going east and west or north and south, whether they prefer popcorn or ice cream, and so on. In this manner, they can be encouraged to make friends and feel comfortable working and playing with individuals of both sexes (Nilsen, 1977).
- Many traditional nursery, kindergarten, and first-grade classrooms separate quiet academic and play-house activities on one side of the room and activities involving building blocks, trucks, and tools on the other side of the room. These areas can be combined to break down the invisible barriers between "girl" and "boy" activities. It should be remembered that a good many more Americans live in homes in which pliers are kept in the kitchen drawer than in homes containing a separate workroom (Nilsen, 1977; Bossert, 1981).
- Avoid traditional classroom divisions of labor, such as having girls serve the cookies and punch during school parties, while boys move the furniture and carry the books.
- Encourage parents to dress their children in clothing that facilitates activity and is not delicate or frilly.
- Provide pictures in the classroom showing female judges, police officers, and aviators and male nurses, teachers, and child caretakers.
- Avoid reinforcing sex-typed behaviors. For instance, do not follow the conventional practice of commenting upon how "cute" a girl looks in particular clothes or of feeling a boy's muscles and telling him how strong he is.
- Avoid sexist books and teaching materials (Scott, 1980). For instance, of those books winning the Caldecott Medal (an award provided by the Children's Service Committee of the American Library Association for the most distinguished picture books), between 1953 and 1971 there was a ratio of eleven pictures of males for every one picture of a female. In the sample of Caldecott winners and runners-up between 1967 and 1971, only two of the eighteen books contained stories about females. Further denigrating quotes are common throughout children's literature (Sadker, 1975). For instance:

"Aw, you're just a dumb girl," sneered Scooter. "Yes, a dumb girl," echoed Robert.
Beverly Cleary, *Henry Huggins,* 1950

"I don't know anything about him," snapped Mary. "I know

fireman (fire fighter), housewife (homemaker), layman (layperson), mankind (human beings), manpower (work force), middleman (intermediary), workmanlike (businesslike), and salesman (salesperson) (Scott, 1980).

- Involve both mothers and fathers in school projects and programs. In sending notes home asking for help with such things as bake sales or field trips, address the note to both parents, unless the child comes from a single-parent home. Further, refer to parents on take-home sheets listing students and their parents as *Ethel and Ray Jones* rather than *Mr. and Mrs. Ray Jones.* And inaugurate a program of *room parents* instead of *room mothers* (Nilsen, 1977).

It should be emphasized that sometimes equal treatment is not equal treatment. To compensate for past sex-role stereotyped training, girls may require more encouragement in some areas and boys in others. Allowing children to choose their activities "freely" often results in the passive acceptance of the status quo (Chasen, 1974; Bossert, 1981).

you don't," Basil answered. "You don't know anything. Girls never do. . . ."

Frances Hodgson Burnett, *The Secret Garden,* 1938

- Avoid sexist language, for example, airline stewardess (flight attendant), businessman (business executive), chairman (chairperson), coed (student),

to manhood and the XX combination to woman-hood. However, the research of John Money and his colleagues at Johns Hopkins University has shown that the labeling of a baby at birth as a boy or a girl and the stylized socialization that then ensues play as much a part in a person's gender identification as the biological fact (Money and Ehrhardt, 1972; Money and Tucker, 1975; Ehrhardt and Meyer-Bahlburg, 1981). Money says:

> Sex differences programmed to take place after birth become incorporated into the body quite as firmly and indelibly as do those that take place before birth. Differentiation of gender identity/role . . . becomes programmed into the central nervous system as firmly as if it were genetically determined, though, in fact, it is a product of social interaction. [1977:31]

Money's case studies are highlighted by a case involving an identical-twin boy whose penis was inadvertently cauterized during circumcision. Early in his life, the child's parents opted for surgical reconstruction to make him a female, and the child is progressing well, having developed a female gender identification. By the time the twins reached four years of age, there was no mistaking which of the children was the girl and which the boy. At five the girl preferred dresses to pants, enjoyed wearing hair ribbons, bracelets, and frilly blouses, headed her Christmas list with dolls and a doll carriage, and unlike her brother, was neat and dainty.

Other cases involve *hermaphrodites*, individuals who have the reproductive organs of both sexes. By virtue of prenatal detours at critical junctures, individuals may develop both male and female internal reproductive organs or external reproductive organs that are so ambiguous that the persons appear to be one sex at birth only to find at puberty that they are the other. In one of Money's cases, a genetic female labeled a "male" at birth learned at puberty, when breasts began to develop, that he harbored female sex organs. He demanded and received medical assistance that enabled him to marry and, save for reproduction, live an impeccably male life.

The part that the sex hormones play in the development of psychological characteristics is the source of considerable controversy and debate. The various endocrine glands secrete *hormones*—special chemical messengers—that are carried by the bloodstream to every part of the body. Among the most important are testosterone (a male hormone) and progesterone and estrogen (female hormones). The difference between the sexes, hormonally, is in the ratio of these three hormones, not in whether they are present or absent.

Over the past fifteen years, experimental studies with rats, guinea pigs, and monkeys have revealed that their brains contain sensitive tissues that have a bisexual potential. During the prenatal period, these tissues become "imprinted" and subsequently serve to stimulate either masculine or feminine mating behavior at puberty. Apparently testosterone suppresses the "female" pattern so that "male" neural tissues become organized in programming later male sexual responses. If testosterone is absent, the sensitive brain areas differentiate as "female." It is as if some inner behavioral dial is set at "male" or "female" during the prenatal period (Gerall, 1973; Scharf, 1976).

The situation with humans is less clear. Money and his associates have found that girls whose mothers had undergone hormonal treatment during pregnancy or who themselves had metabolic disorders resulting in high levels of male hormones during the prenatal period are physically more energetic and less interested in playing with dolls than most girls (Money and Ehrhardt, 1972; Ehrhardt and Meyer-Bahlburg, 1981). Erotically, however, they do not as a general rule turn to lesbianism. They are slower in reaching the romantic stage, but they do reach it. Money credits these behavioral differences to prenatal hormonal influences upon the brain. Other psychologists disagree and suggest that these girls were treated differently by their parents and were unsure of their role as mothers due to certain biological problems (for instance, in some cases they experienced a delay of menses) (Quadagno, Briscoe, and Quadagno, 1977).

Recently the psycho-endocrinologist June Reinisch found evidence to buttress the hormonal argument (Brody, 1981; Rubin, Reinisch, and Haskett, 1981). She studied seventeen girls and eight boys whose mothers had been treated with synthetic progestins to prevent miscarriages. She compared these children with their unexposed siblings by giving each child a standard aggression test in which they responded to six conflict situations that provided for four possible responses: physical aggression, verbal aggression, withdrawal, or nonaggressive coping (for instance, appealing to a higher authority). Significant differences existed between the two groups of children. Progestin-exposed males scored twice as high in physical aggression as did their unexposed brothers, and twelve of the seventeen females scored higher than their unexposed sisters.

The research by Money and Reinisch does not mean that environment is unimportant in shaping gender identities and behaviors. Rather hormones merely seem to "flavor" individuals for various kinds of gender behavior. Apparently, hormones predispose an individual to learn a particular social role. The hormonal action does not compel the individual to learn the role; it simply makes it easier to acquire certain behaviors (Gelman, 1981).

FATHERS AND SEX-TYPING
Developmental psychologists find that fathers play a critical part in pressing their children toward culturally sex-appropriate behaviors.

Social-Learning Theory

Some psychologists stress the part that learning plays in the process by which children acquire knowledge about sex roles and come to invest themselves emotionally in their sex roles. Termed *social-learning* theorists, these psychologists say that children are essentially neutral at birth and that the biological differences between the sexes are insufficient to account for later differences in gender identities. Selective reinforcement and imitation are viewed as the principal means by which children acquire a gender identity (see Chapter 5). Most commonly children are rewarded for modeling the behavior of individuals of the same sex. Boys and girls are actively rewarded and praised by adults and their peers for what are generally seen as sex-appropriate behaviors, and they are ridiculed and punished for behaviors deemed inappropriate to their sex.

Many studies reveal that parents treat boys and girls differently (Maccoby and Jacklin, 1974; Baumrind, 1980; White and Brinkerhoff, 1981). One pervasive finding is that mothers and fathers seek to elicit gross motor behavior more in their sons than in their daughters (they play more roughly and vigorously with baby boys). They also permit their sons to roam over a wider area of the community without special permission than they do their daughters. Another difference in socialization patterns has to do with the kinds of toys given to children. Most commonly parents give boys playthings that represent the world of work (trucks, tools, and building equipment), whereas they provide girls with playthings of the home-maker and mother roles (dolls, dishes, and miniature household appliances). Although the sex typing of playthings has diminished through the influence of the women's liberation movement, recent parent-interview and home-observation studies show that the general pattern still holds.

The psychologist Albert Bandura (1971, 1973b) provides an additional dimension to social-learning theory. He notes that children do not simply do what they see other people doing. They also learn by observing the behavior of others, although they themselves may not immediately act in the same manner. According to Bandura, children mentally encode the behavior they watch and in this fashion build up a large repertoire of potential behaviors. However, children do not enact the behaviors they observe unless they believe it will have a positive outcome for them.

Bandura (1965) has experimentally shown that boys and girls learn aggressive acts equally well from watching an adult behave in an aggressive and destructive manner. Nonetheless, boys are more likely to translate this knowledge into overt action in their own play behaviors. Thus, Bandura believes that boys and girls learn essentially the same information, but, by virtue of their different socializing experiences, differ in the extent to which they activate particular kinds of behavior.

Cognitive-Developmental Theory

The psychologist Lawrence Kohlberg (Kohlberg, 1966; Kohlberg and Ullian, 1974) has proposed a theory that stresses the significance of cognitive growth in the organization of various gender-related behaviors. He says that children first learn to *label* themselves as males or females and then attempt to acquire and master the behaviors that fit their gender category. In Kohlberg's view, children form a stereotyped conception of maleness and femaleness based on a relatively limited set of highly visible traits like hairstyle, clothes, stature, and occupation. This image is oversimplified, exaggerated, and cartoonlike (Meyer,

1980; Martin and Halverson, 1981). Children in turn select and cultivate behaviors that are consistent with their gender concepts, a process of *self-socialization.*

Kohlberg differentiates between his approach and social-learning theory in these terms. According to the social-learning model, the following sequence occurs: "I want rewards; I am rewarded for doing boy things; therefore I want to be a boy." In contrast, Kohlberg believes that the sequence goes like this: "I am a boy; therefore I want to do boy things; therefore the opportunity to do boy things (and to gain approval for doing them) is rewarding" (1966:89).

Apparently, children of two and three years of age possess substantial knowledge of the gender-role stereotypes prevailing in the adult culture (Thompson, 1975). Of interest, girls of this age tend to ascribe positive characteristics to their own sex and negative characteristics to males, while boys do the reverse (Kuhn, Nash, and Brucken, 1978). However, full knowledge about gender-role stereotypes is not learned until age seven, and some aspects may await age twelve and beyond (Williams, Bennett, and Best, 1975; Best et al., 1977). Further, based upon his research, Money concludes that if hermaphrodites are to be switched in gender role, it must take place before they are two-and-a-half years of age. By this time, children have come to categorize themselves as male or female, and any later change in their gender-role assignment usually results in inadequate sex typing and poor psychological adjustment (Money and Ehrhardt, 1972).

Synthesis

Both the social-learning and cognitive-developmental theories contribute to our understanding of the process by which children acquire their gender identities. Janet Shibley Hyde and B. G. Rosenberg point out:

Social learning theory is important in its emphasis on the social and cultural components of sex-role development—the importance of society in shaping sex-typed behaviors. . . . Social learning investigators have . . . contributed some very impressive laboratory demonstrations of the power of reinforcements in shaping children's behavior, in particular sex-typed behaviors. Social learning theory also highlights the importance of imitation in the acquisition of sex roles. . . . Finally, cognitive-developmental theory emphasizes that sex-role learning is a part of the rational learning process of childhood. . . . Children actively seek to acquire sex roles. [1976:48–50]

The processes described by both theories occur simultaneously over a substantial period of time and serve to supplement and complement each other.

Racial Awareness and Prejudice

The development of children's ethnic and intergroup attitudes is a lengthy and complex process. The early stages appear to be dependent upon perceptual and cognitive processes. Before children acquire specific beliefs about particular groups, they must be aware of physical differences among people and come to categorize individuals with regard to relevant physical cues (Katz, 1973). Research shows that children as young as three can correctly identify racial differences between blacks and whites. By the age of five, most children can make such identifications accurately (Goodman, 1952; Porter, 1971; Katz, 1976; Williams and Morland, 1976).

Research by Phyllis A. Katz and her associates (1975) suggests that during the preschool period, white children attend less to distinguishing characteristics among blacks than among whites. For

RACIAL AWARENESS
By the time children enter school, they can correctly identify racial differences between blacks and whites. During middle childhood they develop increasing awareness of racial cues.

A CLASSROOM EXERCISE IN PREJUDICE

In 1968, Jane Elliott, a third-grade teacher at Community Elementary School in Riceville, Iowa, came up with an imaginative and arresting method for teaching her white students about prejudice. Triggered by the tragic news of the assassination of Rev. Martin Luther King, Jr., Elliott decided to impose a system of discrimination in her classroom so that her pupils might gain empathic insight into the experience. She began by "explaining" that brown-eyed children were superior to blue-eyed children. Not only were they "cleaner," but they were innately "more civilized" and "smarter." She then separated the students into brown-eyed and blue-eyed groups and told the children that the brown-eyed children were worthy of more rights and privileges. The blue-eyed children were informed that they could no longer play on the big playground equipment at recess and could only play with brown-eyed children if they were invited.

The children learned their new roles quickly:

> One lovely and brilliant blue-eyed girl, among the most popular children in the class, almost disintegrated under the pressure. She walked in a slouch, became suddenly awkward, tripped twice over things, did poorly in her work. At recess, walking disconsolate across the playground, she was struck across the back by the deliberately outstretched arm of a brown-eyed girl who the day before had been her best friend. [Peters, 1971:24]

Elliott observed:

> All of the children enjoyed being considered superior, and the feeling that they were had ob-viously pushed them to do better work than they had ever done before. But some of them took a savage delight in keeping the members of the "inferior" group in their place, in asserting their "superiority" in particularly nasty ways. . . . I was wholly unprepared for their lack of compassion for people they normally considered their best friends [Peters, 1971:37]

The next day Elliott reversed the roles. Again, the children behaved socially and academically in ways keeping with their new "superior" or "inferior" roles. After the experience, Elliott had every child write about how it felt to be discriminated against. She concluded that the technique offered a means by which she could teach her students about the injustice of discrimination and communicate the arbitrariness and unfairness of the practice.

instance, the presence of eyeglasses or a smile on black faces is a less important differentiating feature than the same cue is for white faces. During middle childhood, white children appear to explore racial cues actively and to attend more closely to a wide range of individual differences among both whites and blacks. However, as the children move into adolescence, they again give less attention to individual differences among blacks, suggesting that their attitudes are becoming more firmly established.

Over the past fifteen years, the psychologist John E. Williams and his associates have studied racial awareness and attitudes in children (Williams and Stabler, 1973; Williams and Morland, 1976). They have found that both black and white children show a preference for the color white over the color black, although this is less true for black than for white children. Williams speculates that such preferences reflect the experiences of both black and white children with light and darkness. Human beings, he says, require reasonably high levels of illumination to interact effectively with their environment. Consequently, they find darkness inherently aversive. Williams believes that this predisposition readily translates into a preference for the color white over the color black. *Cultural symbolism* (the cultural equating of ''white'' with purity, virginity, virtue, beneficence, and God and ''black'' with filthiness, sin, baseness, evil, and the devil) confirms and reinforces children's initial feeling that white is good and black is bad. The practice of color coding racial groups as ''whites'' and ''blacks'' encourages children to generalize color meanings to racial groups so that a pro–Euro-American and anti–Afro-American bias emerges in children of both races.

Williams and his associates claim that a pro-white bias prevails among both black and white preschoolers and persists into the early school years. Further, black preschoolers show a white racial preference in their choice of playmates. But when black children enter integrated public schools, they shift to a black racial preference. It should be stressed, however, that much of this research was undertaken before the full impact of the Black Power movement (with its strong emphasis on black standards of beauty and black cultural heritage) was felt in black communities.

These studies, while telling us about children's *attitudes,* provide us with little information about the specific interracial *actions* of children. It is doubtful that children, especially those in the early grades, show coherent, consistent *prejudice*—a system of negative conceptions, feelings, and action orientations toward the members of a particular religious, racial, or nationality group. Much research shows that how people *act* in an interracial situation bears little or no relation to how they feel or what they think (Wicker, 1969; Vander Zanden, 1983). The *social setting* in which people find themselves does much to determine whether individuals will act in a racist or egalitarian manner.

CHAPTER SUMMARY

1. Human development is the process by which individuals change and grow while remaining in some respects the same. It encompasses the orderly and sequential changes that occur as we move across the life span from conception to death.
2. The prenatal period is divided into three stages. The first, the germinal period, extends from conception to the end of the second week; the second, the embryonic period, extends from the end of the second week to the end of the eighth week; and the third, the fetal period, extends from the end of the eighth week until birth.
3. In general, the growth of children is a regular process and takes place in an orderly fashion. Nonetheless, it is unevenly distributed over the first twenty years of life. From birth until age four or five, the rate of growth in height declines rapidly. After age five, the rate of growth is practically constant up to the beginning of the adolescent growth spurt. At puberty there is again a marked acceleration of growth.
4. In infants one of the earliest expressions of social orientation is attachment behavior, which manifests itself in behaviors that promote proximity and contact. Initially, children are aroused by all parts of their environment. About the third month, however, they become responsive to human beings as a general class of stimuli. Still later, about the seventh month, infants display a preference for a particular person.
5. Children reared in orphanages, foundling homes, and other institutional settings do not flourish as well as do children reared by their parents in a home environment. Evidence suggests that extreme deprivation in early life can retard development and distort the personality.
6. Psychologists and educators have long accepted, and with good evidence, that parents have a profound impact in shaping their children's personalities and behaviors. What has often been overlooked is that the influence also runs the other

way. Children act upon their parents and, in turn, influence the kind of treatment that they receive.

7. Social and behavioral scientists are coming to recognize that children are neither as vulnerable nor as malleable as they may once have believed them to be. Most children are resilient and show amazing adapting abilities.

8. Researchers are finding confirmation of the common-sense observation that the way parents *feel* about their children has a major impact upon the children's social and emotional development.

9. American families show such a wide range of differing patterns that it is doubtful that there is such a thing as the "typical" family. Accordingly, the classroom teacher encounters children with highly different home experiences. Developmental psychologists find that the number, sex, and spacing of siblings (their birth order) have major consequences for a child's development and socialization. Further, an increasing number of children are coming from single-parent homes and from homes where the mother works.

10. Until relatively recently, it was assumed that our sex and hence our gender identity were determined at conception. More recent research shows that the labeling of a baby at birth as a boy or a girl and the stylized socialization that then ensues play as much a part in a person's gender identification as the biological fact of anatomy.

11. Social-learning theorists say that children acquire their gender identities through the processes of selective reinforcement and imitation. Cognitive-developmental theorists say that children first learn to label themselves as males or females and then attempt to acquire and master the behaviors that fit their gender category. Many psychologists believe that the processes described by both theories occur simultaneously over a substantial period of time and serve to supplement and complement each other.

12. The development of children's ethnic and intergroup attitudes is a lengthy and complex process. The early stages appear to be dependent upon perceptual and cognitive processes. Before children acquire specific beliefs about particular groups, they must be aware of physical differences among people and come to categorize individuals with regard to relevant physical cues.

CHAPTER GLOSSARY

attachment An affectional tie that individuals form between themselves and another specific person that binds them together in space and endures over time.

child abuse A catchall term referring to physical, emotional, social, or sexual mistreatment inflicted upon a child by an adult caretaker.

childhood The period in the human life span between two years of age and puberty.

gender identities The conceptions that people have of themselves as being male or female.

human development The process by which individuals change and grow while remaining in some respects the same. It encompasses the orderly and sequential changes that occur as organisms move across the life span from conception to death.

infancy The first two years of human life.

maternal deprivation The notion that the absence of normal mothering can result in psychological damage and physical deterioration in infants and children.

prenatal period The time elapsing between conception and birth and normally averaging about 266 days in humans.

EXERCISES

Review Questions

1. The prenatal stage in which all the chief organs are formed is the

a. germinal
b. embryonic
c. fetal
d. neonatal

2. The fetal alcohol syndrome includes all but which of the following defects?

   a. growth retardation
   b. mental retardation
   c. heart defects
   d. disturbed sleep patterns

3. The body system that shows a decrease in size proportionate to the rest of the body as the individual approaches adolescence is the

   a. general
   b. reproductive
   c. brain and head
   d. lymphoid

4. The Schaffer and Emerson study on infant attachment revealed that

   a. children showed remarkable consistency moving from stage to stage
   b. from birth, children were more sensitive to human stimulation
   c. on the average, specific attachment did not occur until after the sixth month of life
   d. a and c are true

5. Parents who abuse their children frequently display

   a. social and economic stress
   b. social isolation
   c. unrealistic expectations concerning the child
   d. a, b, and c are true
   e. b and c are true

6. The Thomas and Chess study on infant temperament leads to which of the following conclusions?

   a. Infant temperament is clearly related to early parental handling.

b. The most common type of temperament category is the ''easy'' baby.
   c. Mothers can be ''turned off'' by temperamentally difficult children.
   d. a, b, and c are true
   e. b and c are true

7. Contemporary views of parenthood differ from those of Watson and Freud in that

   a. parents are not considered omnipotent
   b. parental attitudes appear to be more critical than specific child-rearing practices
   c. individual differences among children are not as extensive as once thought
   d. a, b, and c are true
   e. a and b are true

8. Single-parent homes and working mothers are two of the more recent significant changes in the American family pattern. As far as the children are concerned, which of the following is true?

   a. Children of divorced parents are not invariably more likely to become delinquent.
   b. Schools generally have recognized and accepted the changing patterns of family life.
   c. Maternal attitudes toward work are not as critical as the simple fact she is working.
   d. a and b are true

9. The text argues that the single most important conclusion we can draw from studies of hormonal influence on gender is that

   a. the impact of hormones on gender is about equivalent in animals
   b. hormones can emphasize a same-sex related behavior
   c. hormones seem to predispose individuals toward social roles
   d. a and c are true

10. Research in racial discrimination among young children has established that

a. most children can make accurate racial identifications by the age of five
b. white preschool children and adolescents attend less to distinguishing characteristics among blacks than those in middle childhood
c. both black and white children seem to show a preference for the white color
d. a, b, and c are true
e. a and c are true

Answers

1. b (See p. 40)
2. b (See pp. 40–41)
3. d (See pp. 42–43)
4. c (See pp. 43–44)
5. d (See pp. 46–47)
6. e (See pp. 48–49)
7. e (See pp. 49–50)
8. a (See pp. 52–57)
9. c (See pp. 57, 60–61)
10. d (See pp. 63–65)

Applying Principles and Concepts

1. Assume that you are in a position to interview parents about problems displayed by their children in class. Indicate by checkmarks those traits listed below that you think would involve the prenatal period.

_____ a. Undersized physically
_____ b. Socially aggressive
_____ c. Impaired hearing
_____ d. Mental retardation
_____ e. Poor academic motivation

2. Here is a case history of a child suspected to be the victim of child abuse. Underline the key words or phrases potentially suggesting abuse.

John is an eight-year-old boy, somewhat small for his age. Academically he's about average, although frequent absences are probably hurting him. He can be overly aggressive toward others, especially

when hurt. Ms. Jones (his teacher) reports that she has written home on several occasions about John's coming to school ill-prepared for the weather and that the parents have been very abusive toward her about these concerns.

3. A case history has been prepared for a child in your class. Included is a number of references to certain kinds of parental activities. Next to each activity indicate by a check whether a follower of Freud or Watson would regard it as significant. (It is possible for both to agree.) If neither would consider the phrase significant, leave it blank.

Parental Activity	Freud	Watson
a. Degree of maternal contact and interaction	_____	_____
b. Consistency of parental disciplining	_____	_____
c. Age of weaning	_____	_____
d. Type of feeding schedule in infancy	_____	_____

4. Lisa and Shauna, both aged ten years old, come from single-parent families. Lisa's parents were divorced (D), after years of quarreling. She lives with her mother, who has been separated less than a year. Shauna's mother has been working (W) since Shauna has been in school. She likes her job, needs the money, and has a housekeeper to take care of Shauna when she gets home. On the basis of the research available, indicate by a D and/or a W in the space provided whether or not the home situation is likely to adversely affect the behavior described.

_____ a. Relationships with adults
_____ b. Feelings of dependency
_____ c. Self-concept
_____ d. Physical growth
_____ e. Academic performance

5. There are three theories of gender identification. Under "Parental Remark" there are a number of statements that reflect one theory or the other. Next to each statement place a checkmark in the appropriate theory column.

Parental Remark	Hormonal	Social-Learning	Cognitive-Developmental
a. "That's being a man, son, boys don't cry."	_____	_____	_____
b. "My, Jennifer, that dress looks so cute on you."	_____	_____	_____
c. "Boys and girls shouldn't both have long hair."	_____	_____	_____
d. "Lisa, you help your mother cook the food; Tom and I will build the fire."	_____	_____	_____
e. "Women will never take to sports like men; they aren't naturally aggressive enough."	_____	_____	_____

Answers

1. a, c, d (See pp. 40–41)
2. Underline "frequent absences," "overly aggressive," "ill-prepared for the weather," and "parents have been very abusive." (See pp. 46–47)
3. a, Freud; b, Watson; c, Freud; d, Freud and Watson (See p. 49)
4. a, D; b, D; c, D; d, blank; e, D (See pp. 52–57)
5. a, social-learning; b, social-learning; c, cognitive; d, social-learning; e, hormonal (See pp. 57, 60–62)

Project

OBJECTIVE: To find incidents of sexism in school textbooks and the classroom.

PROCEDURE: This analysis can be carried out at any grade level. The project should include both curriculum materials and classroom activities. If public school texts aren't available, library books can be used.

1. Content may include literature, social studies, or science. The following indices are suggested:
   a. Of a dozen pictures chosen at random, how many are exclusively either male or female?
   b. Take ten pages at random and count the number of times reference is made to a male ("he" or "him") and to a female ("she" or "her").
   c. Take another ten pages at random, and look for examples of masculine and feminine achievement and dominance. Are the areas of achievement and dominance stereotyped?
2. Observe some classroom interaction (or use your own experience in public school) and look for incidents like the following:
   a. Activities pitting boys against girls
   b. Separation of play activities
   c. Stereotyped sexual references to physical abilities and aptitudes

ANALYSIS:
1. In Questions 1a and 1b, dominance is measured by the ratio of males to females in pictures and by the ratio of male references to female references, respectively. For Question 1c, stereotyping is measured by the ratio of the number of males associated with achievement and dominance to the number of females with the same associations. How many areas of stereotyping did you find?
2. How many incidents did you observe or could recall? Were girls or boys more often the target? Discuss your findings with teachers and students (if they are old enough). Ask whether they think that sexism as they have experienced it is increasing, decreasing, or remaining about the same.

CHAPTER OUTLINE

3

DEVELOPMENT DURING ADOLESCENCE

CHAPTER PREVIEW

Perhaps no period of development has received so much attention in popular fiction and in the media as the topic of this chapter—adolescence. This apparent fascination with the teen years may reflect the puzzling nature of this transitional period between childhood and full assumption of adult roles. Teachers of adolescents should have a good understanding of the concerns facing students of this age in order to deal intelligently with them.

The outline highlights the issues addressed in this chapter, which center around adolescents' relationships with peers and parents, their developing sexuality, and their future goals. Special attention is given to some of the problems encountered by teenagers today, such as drug and alcohol abuse and high rates of unemployment.

Questions to consider as you read are these:

- Why has adolescence typically been viewed as a time of turbulence, and does evidence support this conception?
- What picture is presented by recent research of teenagers' relationships with their parents and peers?
- How has the pattern of sexual behavior during adolescence changed during the past twenty years?
- What are some of the difficulties involved in trying to deal with problems like teenage drug abuse, alcohol abuse, and school-related delinquency?

Adolescence is that phase of the life span that lies between childhood and adulthood. During this period, the individual undergoes changes in growth and development that have profound consequences. For the first time in their lives young people find themselves equal to adults in size and strength. Simultaneously, the reproductive system, which grows very slowly until adolescence, accelerates in development. Adolescence also marks a period in which youth are progressively inducted into adult roles. For young people this means a time of achieving independence from their immediate families, deciding on future alternatives, and establishing a stable identity.

PUBERTY

Puberty is the term applied to the period in the life cycle when sexual and reproductive maturation occurs. Girls typically enter puberty about two years earlier than boys. At about age twelve in girls and age fourteen in boys, a rapid increase in height and weight takes place. For a year or more, the growth rate doubles and is termed the **adolescent growth spurt.** Over a two-year period, girls gain about six to seven inches and boys gain about eight to nine inches in height (see Figure 3.1).

Girls also begin their sexual development earlier than boys. About ten years of age, their breasts begin increasing in size as a result of the proliferation of glandular cells and the formation of fatty and connective tissue. *Menarche*—the first menstrual period—takes place later in puberty, usually following the peak of the growth spurt. Over the past 100 years, the average age of menarche in industrialized nations has shown a steady decline. However, the trend seems to have ended, stabilizing at about 12.8 years of age.

The first indication of puberty in boys begins about twelve years of age with an acceleration in the growth of the testes and scrotum. Between thirteen and sixteen years of age, the testes and scrotum continue growing, the penis lengthens and thickens, and the voice begins to change as the larynx enlarges and the vocal folds double in length. Some two years following the first appearance of pubic hair, facial and body hair typically begin to appear. Around fourteen years of age, the prostate gland is producing fluid that can be ejaculated during orgasm (mature sperm are generally not present until about a year later).

Children show considerable variation in growth and sexual maturation. Some children do not begin their growth spurt and the development of secondary sexual characteristics until other children have virtually completed these stages (Tanner, 1978). Because of their different rates of maturation, some adolescents enjoy an advantage with respect to various cultural ideals associated with height, strength, physical attractiveness, and athletic prowess. Consequently, young people can receive markedly different feedback concerning their worth and desirability. Any difference from the peer group in growth and development tends to pose difficulties for the adolescent. This is most notable when it places the individual at a physical disadvantage or in a position of unfavorable contrast to peers.

Adolescents often feel troubled about the size and shape of their faces and bodies. A large proportion want to change their weight, believing themselves to be either "too thin" or "too heavy." Concern and anxiety about their complexions, especially acne, are common. Besides skin problems, adolescents often feel self-conscious about irregular teeth, orthodontic braces, and glasses.

PSYCHOLOGICAL DEVELOPMENT

Erik Erikson (1968), a neo-Freudian psychoanalyst, has popularized the notion that the chief psychological task confronting the adolescent is the development of a stable identity. **Identity** refers to an individual's sense of placement within

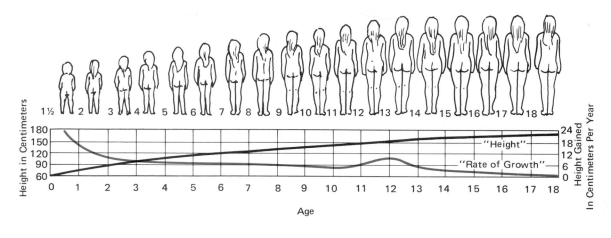

Females

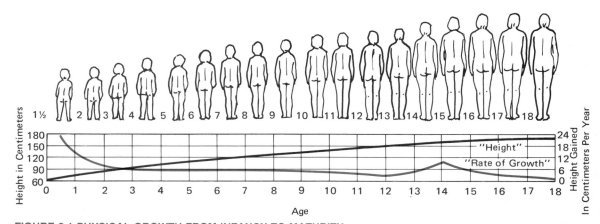

Males

FIGURE 3.1 PHYSICAL GROWTH FROM INFANCY TO MATURITY

The figure depicts the changes in body form and the increases in height that occur
between infancy and adulthood among girls and boys. The height curve (black) is an
average for children in North America and Western Europe. The figure also shows the
rate of growth (color), the increment of height that is gained from one age to the next.
Note the sharp peak in the rate of growth at puberty, and note that this peak is
achieved two years earlier in girls than in boys. *(Source: Adapted from "Growing Up"
by James M. Tanner. Copyright © September 1973 by Scientific American, Inc. All
rights reserved.)*

ERIKSON'S PSYCHOSOCIAL STAGES OF DEVELOPMENT

Erik Erikson describes a progression of psychosocial stages in which individuals confront unique developmental tasks as they pass through life. Each stage poses its own crisis that individuals must confront. The crisis is not so much a catastrophe as a turning point, a period of increased vulnerability and heightened potential. Should a crisis not be successfully resolved, the rest of development is adversely altered, and individuals are thought to be hindered in dealing effectively with later crises. Erikson's psychosocial stages of development are as follows:

- *Trust versus mistrust* (birth to one year): Erikson views human life as a social enterprise involving linkages and interactions among people. This requires that children come to trust other people. Infants whose needs are met and who are cuddled, fondled, and shown affection develop a sense of the world as a safe and dependable place. Infants who experience the world about them as chaotic, unpredictable, and rejecting do not trust their environment.
- *Autonomy versus shame and doubt* (two to three years): As children acquire new skills, like crawling, walking, climbing, and exploring, they confront a new dilemma: whether or not to assert their will. When parents are patient, cooperative, and encouraging, children evolve a sense of competence and independence. But children who are restricted or overprotected come to experience excessive shame and self-doubt, instead.
- *Initiative versus guilt* (four to five years): New horizons open to children with the expansion of their motor and mental abilities. Parents who give their children ample freedom and

the world—the meaning that one attaches to oneself as reflected in the answers one provides to the questions "Who am I?" and "Who am I to be?"

Erikson divides the developmental sequence over the life span into eight major psychosocial stages (see the boxed insert above). Each stage poses a somewhat different issue or turning point when development must move in either a positive or negative direction. The focus of each stage is upon a major task in ego- or self-development. Erikson's fifth stage, which covers the period of adolescence, revolves around the individual's search for identity.

Development of Self-Concepts

Erikson says that the adolescent, like a trapeze artist, must release his or her hold on childhood and reach in midair for a firm grasp on adulthood. He believes that the search for identity becomes particularly acute during adolescence. Not only do individuals undergo rapid physical changes, they must also confront many imminent adult decisions and tasks. Occupational decisions need to be made, moral values have to be decided upon, and sexual and friendship choices must be determined. Si-

opportunity to cultivate new interests and abilities promote self-reliance and initiative in their children. Where parents curtail freedom, children come to view themselves as inept intruders in an adult world.

■ *Industry versus inferiority* (six to eleven years): During the elementary school years, children move out from their homes into the larger world and become concerned with how things work and how they are made. They gain a sense of industry by winning recognition for their accomplishments. In contrast, children who are rebuffed and ignored by parents and teachers acquire a sense of inadequacy and inferiority.

■ *Identity versus role confusion* (twelve to eighteen years): According to Erikson, adolescents confront an identity crisis. They must come to grips with the questions "Who am I?" and "Who am I to be?" They try on a variety of roles as they come to terms with romantic involvements, vocational choices, and adult statuses. Should adolescents fail to arrive at a consistent, coherent, and integrated identity, they confront identity diffusion or the development of a negative self-image.

■ *Intimacy versus isolation* (young adulthood): Successful living involves the ability to reach out and make contact with other people and in so doing to enter into intimate relationships and friendships. Yet, some individuals find that close involvement leads them to painful rejection, and hence they opt for more shallow relationships. Their lives come to be characterized by withdrawal and isolation.

■ *Generativity versus stagnation* (middle adulthood): Erikson considers generativity to be a reaching out beyond one's own immediate concerns to experience concern for the welfare of society and future generations. This entails the development of an element of selflessness as opposed to a self-centered preoccupation with one's own self and interests.

■ *Integrity versus despair* (old age): As individuals confront the fact that they do not have many years of life remaining, they tend to take stock of themselves and the years that have gone before. Some people feel satisfied with their accomplishments, while others experience despair (a sense that time is now too short to start another and more successful life).

multaneously, adolescents must achieve emancipation from adult authority.

According to Erikson, adolescents must synthesize a variety of new roles in order to come to terms with themselves and the world about them. This dictates that they "try on" various roles, ideologies, and commitments. But in "trying on" various roles and exploring new self-definitions, many adolescents are left with blurred self-conceptions, a condition Erikson terms *role confusion*. Individuals are bewildered about who they are, where they belong, and where they are going. Erikson says that a certain amount of role confusion is an inevitable accompaniment to adolescence. Indeed, to "find" oneself too soon, he argues, is to run the risk of inadequately exploring alternative roles and foreclosing many of life's possibilities.

All of this means, in Erikson's view, that adolescence is a time when individuals are often at sea with themselves and others. This ambiguity and lack of stable anchorage lead many adolescents to overcommit themselves to cliques, allegiances, loves, and social causes:

> To keep themselves together they temporarily overidentify with the heroes of cliques and crowds

DEVELOPING SELF-IDENTITIES
According to Erik Erikson, adolescence confronts young people with the need to develop and clarify their identities. As he views the process, a certain amount of role confusion and turmoil is inevitable.

to the point of an apparently complete loss of individuality. Yet in this stage not even "falling in love" is entirely, or even primarily, a sexual matter. To a considerable extent adolescent love is an attempt to arrive at a definition of one's identity by projecting one's diffused self-image on another and by seeing it thus reflected and gradually clarified. . . . Young people can become remarkably clannish, intolerant, and cruel in their

exclusion of others who are "different," in skin color or cultural background, in tastes and gifts, and often in entirely petty aspects of dress and gesture arbitrarily selected as the signs of an in-grouper or out-grouper. [1968:132]

Erikson's view of adolescence has gained much popular acceptance. However, considerable uncertainty prevails among psychologists as to the real nature of the "adolescent identity crisis" and how serious it is. Unquestionably some individuals in Western societies undergo changes in their self-conceptions during adolescence (Waterman, Geary, and Waterman, 1974). But while psychiatrists and clinical psychologists do encounter a small minority of youths who present themselves at clinics and consultation centers because they are experiencing disturbances in their self-concepts, it is becoming clear that most adolescents do not experience anything approaching an identity "crisis." Indeed, a mounting body of literature suggests that considerable stability and consistency characterize the adolescent years (Nawas, 1971; Monge, 1973). Studies that follow up children across time typically do not reveal a discontinuity between childhood and adolescent self-concepts and attitudes. The adolescent self-concept evolves through continual and gradual growth based both upon social circumstances and emergent cognitive competencies and skills (Prawat, Jones, and Hampton, 1979; Dusek and Flaherty, 1981).

The Notion of Storm and Stress

The phrase "storm and stress" has long been employed as a description of adolescence (Coleman, 1978). Many early Greek writers depicted adolescence as a time of emotional upheaval, and the idea was further championed by the German philosopher-psychologists of the nineteenth century. In the United States, G. Stanley Hall, a major figure in early American psychology, popularized the view in his 1904 classic, *Adolescence*. He wrote:

> The teens are emotionally unstable and pathic. It is a natural impulse to experience hot and perfervid psychic states, and it is characterized by emotionalism. We see here the instability and fluctuations now so characteristic. [1904, Vol. II: 74–75]

In turn, the psychoanalysts took up the notion of emotional turmoil and maladjustment during adolescence. Anna Freud (1936, 1958), the daughter of Sigmund Freud and an accomplished psychoanalyst in her own right, argued that the psychological defenses developed in childhood are not capable of dealing with the upsurge of instincts that engulf the individual at puberty. Indeed, she went so far as to assert, "The upholding of a steady equilibrium during the adolescent process is itself abnormal" (1958:275).

Sociologists point out that Western societies make the transition from childhood to adulthood quite difficult (Dragastin and Elder, 1975; Sebald, 1977). As they enter their teens, boys and girls are expected to stop being children, yet they are not expected to be adults. The role expectations provided them are contradictory. They are repeatedly told that they are no longer children. Nonetheless, they continue to be treated like dependents, economically supported by their parents and often stereotyped by adults as untrustworthy and irresponsible. Many non-Western societies ease the transition by providing *puberty rites*—initiation ceremonies that symbolically mark the passage from childhood to adulthood.

Not all social and behavioral scientists agree that adolescence in Western societies is a period of turmoil and conflict. The psychologist Albert Bandura (1964) says that the storm-and-stress portrait of adolescence is merely a stereotyped image derived from a small proportion of adolescents who appear in psychiatric clinics and juvenile probation programs. He claims that the "stormy-decade myth" is due more to cultural expectations

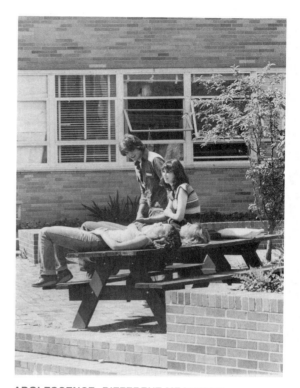

ADOLESCENCE: DIFFERENT MEANINGS
Adolescence is not necessarily a period of storm and stress. It has different meanings for different individuals. Accordingly, there are multiple roads to adulthood.

and the representations of youth in the mass media than to actual fact. Based upon his study of a sample of sixty-one middle-class adolescent boys, Daniel Offer (Offer, 1969; Offer and Offer, 1975) reached a similar conclusion. He found that most of the boys were happy, responsible, and well adjusted. Adolescent "disturbance" appeared to be limited mostly to "bickering" with parents.

All of this suggests that adolescence is not one experience but many experiences. It has different meanings to different people and proves there are multiple roads to adulthood. This, hence, accounts for the diversity of experiences encountered by individuals of different cultures and even among individuals of the same culture during the course of puberty.

The Generation Gap

As already pointed out, research has shown that the full-blown storm-and-stress syndrome of adolescence is relatively infrequent. Much the same case is true for the "generation gap." The idea is prevalent that considerable mutual antagonism, misunderstanding, and separation prevail between young people and adults. However, psychologists and sociologists find little support for the view.

One survey undertaken in the early 1970s, when the generation gap was supposedly at its peak, revealed that nearly 90 percent of the adolescents in the United States (youth between thirteen and nineteen years of age) had "a lot of respect" for their parents as people (Sorensen, 1973). Moreover, 75 percent of the boys and 85 percent of the girls agreed with the statement, "I have a lot of respect for my parents' ideas and opinions." Only 21 percent of the young people said that they lacked strong affection for their parents, and only 6 percent felt, "My parents don't really like me."

In 1980 the Gallup Youth Survey found that 60 percent of teenagers said that they got along very well and 37 percent claimed they got on fairly well with their parents (Gallup, 1980a). Only 3 percent indicated that did not get along very well. Questioned about parental strictness, 82 percent perceived their parents' disciplinary efforts as "about right," whereas 11 percent said their parents were too strict and 7 percent claimed they were not strict enough.

The concept of the generation gap vastly oversimplifies the relationship between young people and their parents. It assumes that attachment to the peer group precludes attachment to the adult group. Yet research shows that both the peer group and the family are anchors in the lives of most teenagers (Biddle, Bank, and Marlin, 1980; Davies and Kandel, 1981; Wright and Keple, 1981).

Further, no behavior comes under the exclusive dominance of a particular generation, although the relative influence of peers and parents differs with the issue involved. When the issues have to do with immediate gratification, such as marijuana use, smoking, drinking, and academic cheating, or peripheral matters, such as musical tastes, personal adornment, and entertainment idols, teenagers tend to be most responsive to the preferences of their peer groups. But when the issues involve future life goals, fundamental behavior codes, and core values, adolescents tend to be most responsive to the parental generation.

It is also easy to overlook the fact that the beliefs and values of adolescents are similar to those of adults. A large proportion of young people see no reason to distinguish between the value systems of their parents and those of their friends (Larson, 1972). For instance, surveys reveal that adolescents tend to be in considerable agreement with both their parents and their friends regarding educational plans (Kandel and Lesser, 1972; Davies and Kandel, 1981). Thus, conflict is often minimal, since peer group values are likely to be extensions of parental values. Teenagers commonly feel most comfortable within peer groupings that adopt values similar to those prevailing in their home environment (Offer and Offer, 1975). In sum, little support is found for the "hydraulic" view that the greater the influence of the one generation, the less the influence of the other. In critical areas, interactions with peers serve to support the values of the parents.

HETEROSEXUAL DEVELOPMENT

Among the major adjustments adolescents must make are those having to do with their developing sexuality. Hormonally induced changes and social pressures compel teenagers to begin coping with their sexual impulses. This process requires that they integrate their sexuality with other aspects of their developing sense of self and with their ongoing network of social relationships.

The Course of Heterosexual Interest

Children in the early elementary school years tend to select for friends and playmates individuals who are of the same sex as themselves. The prevalence of this childhood sex cleavage led Sigmund Freud to conclude that the preadolescent years represent a kind of developmental plateau in which sexual impulses are repressed. However, research has cast doubt on Freud's formulation. Carlfred B. Broderick and George P. Rowe (1968), studying a sample of 1,029 Pennsylvania school-children between ten and twelve years of age, concluded that preadolescents show the developing roots of adult heterosexual interests and activities.

Of the children in the Pennsylvania sample, 84 percent of the girls and 62 percent of the boys said that they expected to get married; 71 percent of the girls indicated that they had a boyfriend, and 56 percent of the boys that they had a girlfriend; and 51 percent of the girls and 47 percent of the boys claimed to have been in love.

Broderick and Rowe suggest that children typically pass through a number of phases in the course of heterosexual social development. First, preschool children gain an awareness of marriage as involving a relationship between a man and a woman who feel attraction for one another. Second, and somewhat later, children define marriage as an attractive and desirable prospect in their own imagined future. Third, children single out some member of the opposite sex of particular interest to them and then place this person in the category of "boyfriend" or "girlfriend." As yet, however, the boyfriend-girlfriend relationship is nonreciprocal, and the object of affection is usually unaware of his or her status.

Having been "in love" seems to prepare children for the fourth phase, one in which they come to appreciate the desirability of engaging in an activity with a member of the opposite sex, such as going bowling together. And fifth, having thought about the possibility of companionship with a member of the opposite sex, they are likely to go out on a "date." The Pennsylvania research suggests that even though same-sex friendships predominate among children of ten and eleven years of age, they show a steady and progressive development of cross-sex interests as they move toward puberty.

Sexual Behavior in Adolescence

First sexual intercourse is one of the most important events in a young person's life cycle. Among the meanings attached to sexual intercourse are a declaration of independence and autonomy from parents, an affirmation of sexual identity, and a statement of capacity for interpersonal intimacy (Jessor and Jessor, 1975). It is significant, therefore, that substantial changes have occurred over the past twenty years in American attitudes toward sexual activity. Certainly greater openness and permissiveness have come to prevail regarding premarital sex, homosexuality, extramarital sex, and a variety of specific sexual practices. Nudity and sex in the movies have acquired wide acceptance. And college students who cohabit or sleep together hardly raise an administrative eyebrow on the majority of campuses.

This century has witnessed *two* periods of very rapid change in sexual attitudes and behavior (Reiss, 1976). The first occurred about the time of World War I and the second during the Vietnam War years. Before 1915, some 75 percent of all first-time brides were virgins, a figure that dropped to 50 percent by 1920. This decrease in virginity was largely associated with the increasing proportion of women who had premarital relations with their future husbands.

Between 1920 and 1965, little overall change occurred in *actual* sexual behavior. Although the incidence of premarital relations did not increase, attitudes did become more permissive in the post–

HETEROSEXUAL DEVELOPMENT

Among the adjustments confronting adolescents are those associated with their developing sexuality. They must integrate their sexuality with their self-conceptions and their network of friendships.

World War II period. Perhaps not surprisingly, a 1978 Gallup poll revealed that among adolescents between thirteen and fifteen years of age, only 25 percent of the boys and 39 percent of the girls believed premarital sex to be "wrong" (Gallup, 1978a).

However, it was not until the mid-1960s that dramatic changes again occurred in sexual behavior. This liberalization was associated with the beginning of sexual experimentation at an earlier age. The result was that more adolescents are now sexually experienced than was the case in earlier generations.

Recent studies of adolescent behavior may overstate the incidence of premarital intercourse. One observer has commented, "Today's adolescent has not had as much sex as he says he has, while a generation ago he probably had more sex than he admitted to" (Godenne, 1974:67). Nonetheless, all evidence points to the fact that a growing proportion of teenagers are sexually active and are beginning their sexual activity at earlier ages. National surveys reported that 49.8 percent of single female teenagers had experienced intercourse in 1979 compared with 43.4 percent in 1976 and 30.4 percent in 1971. Much of the increase is attributable to white women, 46.6 percent of whom said that they had had premarital intercourse, up from 38.3 percent in 1976 and 26.4 percent in 1971. Of black women, 66.2 percent were sexually active in 1979 compared to 66.4 percent in 1976 and 53.7 percent in 1971 (Zelnik and Kantner, 1980). In contrast, less than 20 percent of the women in their mother's generation had engaged in sexual intercourse prior to turning twenty years of age (Kinsey et al., 1953).

For the most part teenage sexual activity is sporadic. The 1979 survey found that about half of the sexually experienced teenagers had not had intercourse in the month prior to the survey. However, with increasing sexual experience, teenagers are also contracting veneral diseases in growing numbers. Teenagers aged fifteen through nineteen are three times more likely to contract gonorrhea than people over twenty; the risk of syphilis is 61 percent greater for teenagers.

Some clinical psychologists, psychiatrists, and physicians express concern about these sexual trends. They fear that many teenagers are being forced into sexual behavior for which they are socially and emotionally unprepared. Richard V. Lee says:

> The new sexual morality has replaced Victorian prudery with an equally pernicious dictatorship of the erotic. There is no room in this mythology for the adolescent who doesn't want to be a sexual participant. This is hardly a permissive society. One needs only to glance through magazines and their advertisements to see what is valued and who is of value. Certainly not modesty, virginity, virgins, or the so-called sexual failures—the kids who didn't like their first sexual experience, the boys who worry about homosexuality, the girls who get pregnant. [1977:12]

For some youths sex has become a duty and orgasm some sort of merit badge. Lee asserts that too often neither are regarded as a pleasure but rather an obligation, creating an inverted puritanism.

It is important to stress, however, that recent changes in patterns of sexual behavior do not amount to a breakdown in morality. If anything, young people appear to be quite concerned about the moral aspects of sexual behavior. Many young people judge the acceptability of sexual relations in terms of a couple's emotional involvement. Sexual intercourse is viewed as morally permissible as long as the couple are engaged or feel love or strong affection for each other (Reiss, 1976). One survey revealed that 72 percent of American teenagers agree with this statement: "When it comes to morality in sex, the important thing is the way people treat each other, not the things they do together" (Sorensen, 1973). For the most part, young people do not regard the new morality as license for promiscuous thrill seeking.

Teenage Pregnancy

In 1978 there were 1,142,000 pregnancies and 554,000 births among teenagers (Brozan, 1981). Seventeen percent of the women conceived after marriage. Thirty-eight percent of the pregnancies were terminated by abortion; somewhat over 20 percent were miscarried; and 22 percent resulted in out-of-wedlock births. Teenage mothers, half of whom are unmarried, are raising 1.3 million children. With the waning of the stigma attached to illegitimacy, about 93 percent of unwed teenage mothers keep their babies.

The incidence of teenage pregnancy has sharply increased over the past century. A contributing factor has been the drop in the age of puberty. In 1840, the average woman in Western societies menstruated for the first time at age seventeen. As noted earlier in the chapter, menarche now occurs at about 12.8 years of age. Thus, the age of first possible pregnancy has appreciably declined over the past one hundred years.

Teenagers who become pregnant prior to eighteen years of age have a higher maternal death rate and a considerably higher risk of miscarriage, prematurity, and complications than do women in their early twenties. Teenage mothers are also much more likely to drop out of school than their peers. Between one-half and three-quarters of girls who become pregnant in high school never graduate, and less than half have any work experience. Further, the younger a girl is when her first child is born, the more likely she is to wind up in poverty and on welfare. In New York City, only 50 percent manage to secure even temporary employment during their first four years of motherhood, and nine out of ten land on public assistance rolls.

Some teenagers try to cope by marrying before the baby is born. However, one out of five teenagers who marry after becoming pregnant breaks up within a year, one-third within two years, and three out of five within six years. Inept parenting, child neglect, and child abuse are also more frequent among teenage parents.

Some 59 percent of teenagers believe that contraceptives should be made available to people their age. Only 27 percent are opposed (Gallup, 1978b). However, of sexually active teenagers under fifteen years of age, only 7 percent are receiving contraceptive services. Overall, the level and consistency of contraceptive use increased among teenagers during the 1970s. In 1979, seven in ten teenagers said they had taken precautions at the last instance of intercourse, compared with five in ten in 1971 and six in ten in 1976 (Zelnick and Kantner, 1980). Some 27 percent of the sexually active teenagers reported in 1979 that they had never used a birth control method. Teenagers who use contraceptive devices commonly wait until they have been sexually active about nine months before beginning usage.

General nervousness about the pill has contributed to its decline as the first choice among contraceptive methods. Between 1976 and 1979, teenage contraceptive users who said pills were their most recent birth control method fell from 53 percent to 51 percent among blacks and from 46 percent to 38 percent among whites. Condom use remained steady. However, teenagers relying on withdrawal increased from 7 percent to 8 percent of blacks and from 17 percent to 21 percent of whites (Zelnick and Kantner, 1980).

A number of factors account for the failure of more teenagers to use birth control:

- Considerable ignorance prevails among teenagers regarding sexual functioning and reproduction. For instance, the explanation is frequently voiced by teenagers that they have sex too "infrequently" or that they have intercourse at the "safe" time of the month (despite the fact that only 41 percent of teenagers can identify the time of the menstrual cycle when pregnancy is most likely to occur).
- Many teenagers believe that contraception interferes with sexual spontaneity and pleasure.
- Some teenagers have ambivalent feelings regarding sex. As a consequence, they deny to themselves and others that they intend to have sexual relations.
- A large number of teenagers believe that "pregnancy will happen to others but won't happen to me."
- One-fourth of teenage mothers apparently had

SEX EDUCATION

It is estimated that fewer than 43 percent of American teenagers are being provided with sex education in the schools. Of those receiving sex education, 72 percent indicate that their course included material on birth control. The overwhelming majority of young people who have a class in sex education say the course has been either "very helpful" (36 percent) or "fairly helpful" (46 percent). More girls than boys and more younger than older teenagers label the course helpful (Gallup, 1978c).

Sex education is not new. In the 1960s programs were instituted in many parts of the United States. First-graders planted seeds, fourth-graders raised gerbils, junior-high-school students studied the human reproductive system, and high-school students discussed what makes for a good marriage and a good parent. Sex education programs are incorporated in various parts of the school curriculum. Some are found in biology, while others are taught under other headings like family life or health education.

Considerable controversy surrounds sex education. Many believe it should be confined to a description of reproductive anatomy and physiology. Others see it as a vehicle for combating social problems like sexually transmitted diseases, illegitimacy, and unhappy marriages. Still others would like it to free young people from a rigid Victorian sexual morality so that sex will be more relaxed and fun (Powledge, 1977; Brick, 1981; Rienzo, 1981). Unhappily, teachers all too often find themselves embroiled in controversy, since one or another group finds their approach to sex education unsatisfactory or distasteful.

---

wanted to become pregnant. For some troubled teenagers, a baby seems to offer a purpose in life and someone who will love them.

- Some teenagers voiced medical or moral objections to contraceptives.

SELECTION OF A VOCATION

Adolescence is the threshold of adulthood, a bridge between childhood and adult roles. A critical and central aspect of adult life is the assumption of a vocational identity and position. In Western nations, the jobs people hold largely dictate their life-styles and the relationships they have with others in their communities. Jobs link people within the larger social network and give them a purpose in life.

Apparently, the process by which young people enter the world of occupations is only partially based on accurate information and rational choice (DeFleur and Menke, 1975). Based upon a survey of research in this area, the sociologist Wilbert E. Moore concludes:

> Moving toward an adult occupation consists of a complex mixture of narrowing the range of choices (or having them narrowed by poor educational performance) . . . [and] exploration of alternatives by use of information, misinformation, and sheer chance. The availability of reliable information is very uneven. [1969:872]

During middle childhood, children's knowledge about the labor market rises sharply. It levels off into a plateau during the high-school years but rises sharply again as adolescents look for jobs and enter the labor force. Preadolescent children seem to increase their occupational knowledge on a continuous basis much like they expand their general knowledge about the world. Surprisingly, high-school students have relatively little additional access to realistic occupational information. Further, the youth subculture has typically assigned low priorities to achievement in school and preparation for work roles. However, this picture changes as young people graduate and must begin coping with the realities of occupational life (DeFleur and Menke, 1975).

Some young people are better informed than others regarding occupational roles and opportunities. A consistent research finding is that the amount and accuracy of occupational knowledge is greater among students with higher grade-point averages. Likewise, the children of white-collar workers are better informed than the children of service and blue-collar workers (U.S. Department of Labor, *Career Thresholds,* 1970).

Some young people postpone entry into adult occupational roles through college attendance. Within the United States, 43.9 percent of the youth go to college. In Canada the proportion is higher: 49.8 percent. In West Germany and France, which have more elitist systems of higher education, the figures are 15.8 percent and 26.4 percent, respectively (Farnsworth, 1976).

Many teenagers are introduced to work experience while still in high school (Cole, 1980). In 1940, 4 percent of sixteen-year-old males and 1 percent of similarly aged females attended school and worked part time. Forty years later an estimated 50 percent of high-school juniors and seniors and 30 percent of all ninth- and tenth-graders worked at some time during the school year. Many laypeople assume that one of the benefits of working is that young people get on-the-job training. Although in point of fact most teenagers secure little training that is technically useful, they nonetheless do gain practical knowledge about how the business world functions, how to find and hold a job, and how to manage money. Most generally, working teenagers find employment in the fields of food

HIGH-SCHOOL VOCATIONAL TRAINING PROGRAMS
Most school systems offer some type of vocational education. This district provides a program in automobile repair.

service, retail sales and cashiering, manual labor, clerical work, and cleaning.

Work compels young people to deal with competing demands on their time (Cole, 1980). Overall, compared with their nonworking classmates, teenagers who work feel less involved in school, are absent more frequently, and do not enjoy school as much. Working teenagers often complain that school does not permit them to do those things that they feel they do best. Workers typically have lower grade-point averages than do nonworkers. More workers report that their grades fell than improved after they began working. However, it

CAREER EDUCATION

There is no satisfaction in life that equals that of work well done. Of all the things that satisfy human cravings, work is the largest. You cannot eat eight hours a day, you cannot make love eight hours a day, you cannot fish eight hours a day—not every day unless that is your livelihood. Work is a satisfaction that no one else can give you—and no one can take away.
Elliot Richardson

Career education has been one of the major educational movements of the past decade. It has been defined as "preparation for all meaningful and productive activity, at work or at leisure, whether paid or volunteer, as employee or employer, in private business or in the public sector, or in the family" (Hoyt et al., 1972:2). Most state departments of education have appointed career education coordinators, and many states have mandated career education in their educational legislation. These developments have been a response to the widely voiced claim that students leave school with little knowledge about or explicit training for jobs.

Career education is not the same thing as vocational education. The U.S. Office of Education makes the following distinctions between the two:

- Vocational education concerns itself primarily with a particular *segment* of students at the secondary and postsecondary, subbaccalaureate degree level. Career education concerns itself with *all* students at *all* levels of education.
- Vocational education's primary concern is the world of paid employment. Career education is concerned with both paid employment and unpaid work—including volunteerism, work of the homemaker, and work done as part of productive use of leisure time.
- Vocational education places a primary substantive emphasis on specific job skills. Career education adds to this a substantive emphasis on adaptability skills required to help students cope with change.
- Vocational education is rooted in the philosophy of vocationalism. Career education seeks to fuse the philosophy of vocationalism with the philosophy of humanism.
- Vocational education is carried out primarily through the teaching-learning process. Career education seeks to fuse the teaching-learning process with the career development process.
- Vocational education seeks to emphasize education, as preparation for work, by adding new kinds of programs to the curriculum. Career education seeks to emphasize education, as preparation for work, by adding an emphasis on internal changes in the professional commitments of all educators in ways that will encourage them to stress such emphasis in all classrooms. (Office of Career Education, 1976)

Career education stresses career awareness among students and vocational appreciation of all school curricula. It seeks to help individuals find purpose and meaning in their lives. It aims to make students knowledgeable about available jobs and the skills they demand while simultaneously providing students with a set of marketable job skills by the time they leave the formal educational system (either in high school or college).

In the elementary grades, this requires exposing students to the kinds of work available to adults and fostering an appreciation of work. Later, in grades seven through ten, students receive more specific exposure to "career clusters" (groups of occupations) and begin to make tentative choices about the cluster in which they wish to specialize. The last two grades of high school are then devoted to specialized training in the cluster chosen earlier (for some students this entails a college preparatory program).

is not the fact of working but rather the number of hours worked that seems to affect schooling. Typically, tenth-graders experience a drop in grades when they work more than fourteen hours a week; eleventh-graders appear, on the average, to be able to work up to twenty hours a week before their grades are affected.

SPECIAL CONCERNS

Any number of young people encounter difficulties of one sort or another. These problems have many negative consequences for the adolescents in their daily lives. The problems are also a concern to teachers and school authorities, since they have implications for the educational process and for the effective functioning of the schools.

Drug Abuse

We hear a good deal nowadays about drugs. The word, however, is imprecise. If we view a drug as any chemical, then everything that we ingest is technically a drug. Accordingly, a drug is arbitrarily defined as a chemical that has some extraordinary effect beyond the life-sustaining functions associated with food and drink. A drug may heal, put to sleep, relax, elate, inebriate, result in a mystical experience, and so on.

Drug abuse refers to the excessive or compulsive use of chemical agents to an extent that they interfere with health, social, or vocational functioning, or the functioning of the rest of society. The vast majority of American school systems encounter drug abuse problems, especially those in urban settings. For instance, in New York City chronic drug abusers account for 70 percent of the 100,000 junior- and senior-high-school students who are regularly absent (approximately 500,000 seventh- through twelfth-graders are enrolled in the city's schools). Compared with students who

regularly attend school, chronic truants abuse heroin, tranquilizers, and cocaine four times more often; PCP (phencyclidine, commonly known as "Angel Dust"), hallucinogens, inhalants, and stimulants three times more frequently; and marijuana and sedatives twice as frequently (testimony before the House Select Committee on Narcotics Abuse and Control, August 30, 1978).

In 1981 the University of Michigan's Institute for Social Research surveyed 17,000 seniors in a representative sample of public and private high schools (Reinhold, 1982). Two-thirds of the seniors said they had tried at least one illicit drug during the previous year. One in fourteen indicated that they smoked marijuana daily (down from one in nine in 1978). Twenty-five percent reported having used amphetamines in the previous twelve months, and 16.5 percent had tried cocaine. However, 60 percent said they believed that regular marijuana users faced a "great risk" of harming themselves. Nearly half opposed even occasional use of marijuana. Similarly, a 1980 Gallup Youth Survey found that four out of every ten teenagers perceive marijuana smoking as a very big problem in their schools (Gallup, 1980b).

By 1973 public concern with drug abuse led over twenty-four states to require drug education in the public schools. The purpose of drug education was threefold: (1) to increase knowledge about drugs, (2) to promote healthy attitudes toward the use of drugs, and (3) to decrease drug abuse behavior among young people. The results of the programs have been disappointing (Horan, 1974; Stuart, 1974; Bard, 1975). Indeed, there appears to be a direct relationship between knowledge about drugs and decisions to use drugs. Research has shown that the more information youths have on drugs, the more likely they are to hold favorable attitudes toward the use of drugs and the more probable it is that they will engage in drug abuse behavior.

Various explanations have been offered for the failure of drug education programs. A Ford Foundation (1972) report said the programs were "neither realistic nor frank." The programs tended to

MARIJUANA USE
National surveys show that about 7 percent of high-school seniors smoke marijuana every day.

be "one-shot" undertakings and to propagandize. Ill-founded statements, sensationalism, and scare techniques often had a boomerang effect. For instance, the message of many programs was "prevention": "Stay away from *all* drugs and you'll live a healthier life." The approach was dishonest and students knew it. Failing to differentiate between marijuana and heroin is comparable to lumping together aspirin and antibiotics as "medicine." Despite benevolent intentions, many drug educators created an enormous credibility gap that some students partially filled through their own experimentation. Further, some of the films

used in connection with the programs offered virtual how-to-do-it kits on techniques to shoot heroin, sniff glue, and down goofballs.

Other shortcomings were also associated with early drug education programs. They failed to address the very important part that the recreational use of illegal drugs has played in many adolescent peer groups. Generally speaking, adolescents who use illegal drugs move in peer groups in which drugs are not only approved but also have an important part in day-to-day interactions (Kandel, 1974; Thomas, Petersen, and Zingraff, 1975). Nor did the programs address the use of psychoactive agents (such as tranquilizers, barbiturates, and stimulants) by the students' parents. Many students see their parents using these drugs, and as a consequence they begin taking mood-changing drugs themselves. An effective program for dealing with drug abuse must see the problem from a societywide perspective and not simply as a problem of young people.

Alcohol Abuse

Among Americans, adolescents and adults alike, alcohol is the most frequently abused drug. According to the federal government's National Institute on Alcohol Abuse and Alcoholism, by the time they reach twelfth grade, more than half of the nation's young people drink alcohol at least once a week. Nearly half of all teenagers who drink say they have been intoxicated at least once (compared with only 19 percent a decade ago). Five percent admit to drunkenness once a week or more often; 12 percent drink to intoxication at least once a month; and 34 percent say their habit has created problems with friends, school, or police. The average amount of alcohol consumed by young people doubled in ten years to the equivalent of four twelve-ounce cans of beer a week (beer is the favorite alcoholic beverage of teenagers). On the whole young people who drink alcoholic beverages tend to hang out with other young people who drink. And teenagers whose parents drink are almost twice as likely to drink as are teenagers whose parents are teetotalers (Gallup, 1980c).

Drinking among teenagers has created serious problems on the highways. Exceedingly conservative government estimates indicate that 4,000 drinking drivers fifteen through twenty years of age were involved in 1977 in fatal motor vehicle accidents in which nearly 5,000 people died. An additional 40,000 were disfigured. In 1976, nearly 113,000 young people under twenty-one (including 50 children ten years of age or younger) were arrested for driving under the influence of alcohol. In the same year, 206,607 young people under twenty-one were arrested for violation of liquor laws, and nearly 145,000 (including 240 children ten and younger) were picked up on charges of drunkenness.

Most states require some instruction in public schools about alcohol use and alcoholism. The current approach is generally different from old-style techniques that tended to be unrealistic and frightening. Today, most instruction is low-key and designed to show young people not only the consequences of drinking but also why many are drawn to it. Nonetheless, some psychologists and sociologists believe that the problem will persist as long as the larger society views alcohol as a convenient solution to tension, a necessary component within social gatherings, and an acceptable substance that falls outside of the "drug" category.

Adolescent Suicide

Within Western societies suicide is virtually an unmentionable; it is considered a dirty word. The act violates most basic tenets of Western belief. Many religions condemn suicide as a sin, and it is a crime in some nations. The suicide rate among young people has more than doubled within the United States over the past decade (Holinger, 1980). The actual number of suicides is generally believed to be considerably higher than what is reported in government statistics. Many suicides are disguised by family members, often with physicians' cooperation, as deaths attributable to other causes. Many more young people attempt suicide than succeed. The ratio for adolescents has been estimated by some to be 120 to 1; by others, more conservatively, as 20 to 1 (the adult ratio is approximately 8 to 1).

Today suicide ranks as the second or third leading cause of death among young people in virtually every industrialized nation in the world. Male students are three times more likely than females to commit suicide. However, fewer males than females attempt suicide. Males are more successful since they are more likely to use violent methods—shooting, hanging, or jumping from heights. Females are more likely to employ overdoses of drugs.

Suicides rarely occur without warning. Teachers are often in a unique position to notice behavior changes that may signal that an adolescent is a high-risk candidate for suicide. These include the following:

- A dramatic shift in the quality of school work.
- Social behavior changes, including excessive use of drugs or alcohol.
- Changes in daily behavior and living patterns, such as extreme fatigue, boredom, decreased appetite, preoccupation, and inability to concentrate.
- Open signs of mental illness, such as hallucinations and delusions.
- Giving away prized possessions.
- Any type of serious sleep disturbance—nightmares, difficulty in falling asleep, and early-morning awakening.
- A preoccupation with thoughts and signs of death, reflected in such statements as, "Oh, I don't care. I won't be around anyway to find out what happens"; "I would like to sleep forever and never wake up"; "Sometimes I would just like to take a gun and blow off my head . . . but I'm only joking"; "How many aspirin does it take to kill yourself?"

Teachers should trust their own judgments and their own subjective feelings in assessing a potentially suicidal person. If they believe someone is in danger of suicide, they should act on their beliefs. Teachers are well advised not to let others mislead them into ignoring suicidal signals.

In most cases teachers are not trained in suicide prevention. Indeed, teachers should not act as therapists, although they can provide emotional support for young people undergoing therapy. Most importantly, teachers can put the troubled adolescent in touch with agencies and specialists. One program that has emerged over the past decade is the *crisis hotline*. Hotlines are staffed by volunteers who have been screened psychologically and trained to respond to emergency calls. Their job is to listen, to buy time, and to refer callers to the appropriate counselor, psychologist, or psychiatrist. It is important to emphasize that teachers should not moralize or preach to the student, since doing so may block further communication.

School-Related Delinquency

School-related delinquency is a major concern of parents, teachers, and students alike. During the 1970s, vandalism and violence surfaced as a major problem in many school districts. However, evidence from a number of studies and official sources indicates that acts of violence and property destruction in schools increased throughout the 1960s and into the early 1970s but has leveled off after that. A survey undertaken by the federal government's National Institute of Education (1977) provides estimates of the problem's dimensions:

- Eleven percent of secondary school students in the United States have something worth more than $1 stolen from them in a month. Most of the reported thefts involve small amounts of money, sweaters, books, notebooks, or other property commonly found in lockers. Only one-fifth of the reported thefts involve money or property worth $10 or more.
- An estimated 1.3 percent of secondary school students report that they are attacked at school in a typical one-month period. The proportion of junior-high-school students reporting attacks

is about twice as great as that of senior-high students (2.1 percent compared with 1 percent). About two-fifths of the reported attacks result in some injury, but only 4 percent involve injuries serious enough to require medical attention.

- In a typical month, an estimated 12 percent of the teachers in secondary schools have something worth more than $1 stolen from them.
- About one-half of 1 percent of secondary teachers are physically attacked at school in a month's time. Nearly one-fifth of the attacks require medical attention.
- A school's risk of experiencing some vandalism in a month is greater than one in four. The average cost of an act of vandalism is $81. In addition, one in ten schools is broken into, at an average cost per burglary of $183. Schools are about five times as likely to be burglarized as commercial establishments, which have the highest burglary rates reported in the National Crime Survey.
- For property offenses, the risks to schools do not differ much throughout metropolitan areas. In fact, the per capita cost of school crime is higher in the suburbs than in the cities.
- The risks of personal violence increase with the size of the community. Overall, the risks of all types of school offenses are smallest in rural areas.
- The risks of being a victim of either attack or robbery in secondary schools decline steadily as grade level increases. Seventh-graders are most likely to be attacked or robbed and twelfth-graders are least so.
- The crime rate and the presence or absence of fighting gangs in the school's attendance areas affect its violence. The more crime and violence students are exposed to outside school, the greater the problems in the school.
- Academic competition seems to decrease a school's risk of violence while increasing the amount of vandalism. The data suggest that violent students are more likely to be those who have given up on school, do not care about grades, find the courses irrelevant, and feel that

nothing they do makes any difference. Vandalism, in contrast, is more likely to occur in schools where students consider grades and leadership positions important and where students rebel against the unfair use of grades for disciplinary purposes.

- A firm, fair, and consistent system for running a school seems to be a key factor in reducing violence. Where the rules are known, and where they are firmly and fairly enforced, less violence occurs.
- The leadership role of the principal appears to be a critical factor. Visibility and availability to students and staff are characteristics of the principals in schools that have made a dramatic turnaround from periods of violence.
- Very few schools (1 percent) have regular police stationed in them, but the proportion is much higher in big-city secondary schools (15 percent). School security officers are more widely used. They are present during the day in half of the junior highs and two-thirds of the senior highs in large cities.

A poll by the National Education Association of a selected sample of its members revealed that in the 1976–77 school year, 3.1 percent of teachers viewed student violence as a major problem; 24.4 percent, a minor problem; and 71.1 percent, not a problem (NEA Research, 1978). Three percent said that they had been physically attacked. Eight percent reported that their personal property had been maliciously damaged. Secondary teachers (12.0 percent) experienced a greater incidence of such episodes than did elementary teachers (5.2 percent).

SCHOOL VANDALISM
Preventing damage to schools and the costs of repairing them amount to more than $600 million a year, about as much as the schools spend on textbooks.

Students also express concern about the behavior of their classmates. A 1980 Gallup poll found that 64 percent of teenagers believed classroom disturbances to be a "very big" or "fairly big" problem (Gallup, 1980b). Fifty-one percent assigned similar problem status to personal theft, 46 percent to vandalism, and 33 percent to fighting.

School Dropouts

The dropout rate among high-school students within the United States is relatively high. One method for determining high-school dropout rates is to compare the number of graduates with the ninth-grade enrollment four years earlier. For reasons that are not entirely clear, the dropout rate varies considerably from city to city: Chicago and St. Louis, 52 percent; Detroit, 51 percent; New York, 49 percent; Baltimore, 45 percent; Cleveland, Philadelphia, and Washington, D.C., 40 percent; Milwaukee, 34 percent; Dallas and Houston, 33 percent; Phoenix, 31 percent; Los Angeles, 30 percent; San Diego, 29 percent; Denver, 9.9 percent; and Kansas City, 6.3 percent.

A recent report prepared for the U.S. Department of Labor (Rumberger, 1981) notes that in the United States in 1900, the percentage of fourteen- to seventeen-year-olds enrolled in high school was 11 percent. This rate increased steadily over the decades, reaching 94 percent in 1978. But the trend now seems to be reversing. Data in California reveal that the state dropout rate ranges from 13 percent among fourteen-year-olds to 30 percent among seventeen-year-olds, and is increasing. Many females drop out because of pregnancy. Males get bored with classes and leave to search for jobs. Foreign-born students become discouraged because of various language problems. And many students encounter difficulties with teachers or classmates.

School difficulties, both educational and social, are prominent elements in the history of most dropouts. Lucius Cervantes (1965) has done a comparative study of high-school graduates and dropouts. This research revealed that dropouts tend to share a number of characteristics: Many had failed at least one grade; by seventh grade they were two years behind their classmates in reading and arithmetic; their attendance record was poor; often they were "underachievers"; they had changed schools frequently; many had behavior problems or were troubled emotionally; and they tended to resent authority. Overall, evidence suggests that academic difficulties become cumulative, showing a gradual rise over the elementary school years and reaching a high point in the ninth and tenth grades (Fitzsimmons et al., 1969).

Pupils who have difficulties with academic work and who view their assignments as incomprehensible and irrelevant tend to find school frustrating and disheartening. A good many youth fail to see any "payoff" associated with school attendance and continued effort. Psychologist Jerome Kagan notes:

> There is no reason for a student to work for A's in his courses if he has decided to ignore college and anticipates feeling no pain upon a rejected application. If prestige is empty and elitism wicked it is easy to forget about grades, for students of every age view the grade as a good conduct medal to be used in parades or to gain entry into hallowed halls, rather than as a confidential report on the state of their expertise. [1972:99]

Accordingly, many teenagers, especially those in big-city ghettos, regard school as irrelevant to their personal, social, and vocational needs.

Teenage Unemployment

Securing work has become increasingly difficult for American young people since the 1950s (Ginzberg, 1980). Over the past decade, the unemployment rate among white teenagers periodically reached the 20 percent level. However, the rate of unemployment among black youth consistently ran about double the white rate. In some areas, such as Oakland, California, the unemployment rate of black young people has been as high as 70 percent.

The proportion of young blacks out of work has been increasing steadily through periods of both prosperity and recession. A number of factors have contributed to this problem:

- The number of blacks seeking jobs has grown more rapidly than the number of white job seekers and faster than the rate of new jobs being created.
- New jobs are increasingly located in the suburbs, away from the central cities where most blacks live.
- Young blacks are being squeezed by the changing economy and job market, which increasingly put a high premium on good education, skill, and experience.

CHAPTER SUMMARY

1. Girls typically enter puberty about two years earlier than boys do. At about age twelve in girls and age fourteen in boys a rapid increase in height and weight takes place. Girls also begin their sexual development earlier than boys. Children show considerable variation in growth and sexual maturation.

2. Erik Erikson, a neo-Freudian psychoanalyst, has popularized the notion that the chief psychological task confronting the adolescent is the development of a stable identity. Not only do individuals undergo rapid physical changes, they must also confront many imminent adult decisions and tasks.

3. Considerable uncertainty prevails among psychologists as to the real nature of the "adolescent identity crisis" and how serious it is. There seems to be little question that many individuals in Western societies undergo changes in their self-conceptions during adolescence. Yet, considerable stability and consistency also exist during the adolescent years.

4. The phrase "storm and stress" has long been employed as a description of adolescence.

5. Adolescence is not one experience but many experiences. It has different meanings to different people and hence offers multiple roads to adulthood. Considerable diversity exists among cultures and even among individuals in the same culture.

6. Research has shown that the full-blown storm-and-stress syndrome of adolescence is relatively infrequent. Much the same is true for the "generation gap."

7. Among the major adjustments adolescents must make are those having to do with their developing sexuality. A study involving Pennsylvania schoolchildren reveals that even though same-sex friendships predominate among children of ten and eleven years of age, they show a steady and progressive development of cross-sex interests as they move toward puberty.

8. Evidence points to the fact that a growing proportion of teenagers are sexually active and that they are beginning their sexual activity at earlier ages. However, for the most part, teenage sexual activity is sporadic.

9. The incidence of teenage pregnancy has sharply increased over the past century. A contributing factor has been the drop in the age of puberty. Teenagers who become pregnant prior to eighteen years of age have a higher maternal death rate and a considerably higher risk of miscarriage, prematurity, and complications than do women in their early twenties.

10. Adolescence is the threshold of adulthood, a bridge between childhood and adult roles. A critical and central aspect of adult life is the assumption of a vocational identity and position. Apparently, the process by which young people enter the world of occupational life is only partially based on accurate information and rational choice.

11. The vast majority of American school systems, especially those in urban settings, encounter drug abuse problems. The results of drug education programs have been disappointing. Research has shown that the more information youths have on drugs, the more likely they are to hold favorable

attitudes toward the use of drugs and the more probable it is that they will engage in drug abuse behavior.

12. Among Americans, adolescents and adults alike, alcohol is the most frequently abused drug. Five percent of teenagers admit to drunkenness once a week or more often; 12 percent drink to intoxication at least once a month; and 34 percent say their habit has created problems with friends, school, or police.

13. Suicide ranks as the second or third leading cause of death among young people in virtually every industrialized nation in the world. Suicides rarely occur without warning. Teachers are often in a unique position to notice behavior changes that may signal that an adolescent is a high-risk candidate for suicide.

14. School-related delinquency is a major concern of parents, teachers, and students alike. During the 1970s, vandalism and violence surfaced as a major problem in many school districts. It appears to have leveled off in recent years, however, after an increase throughout the 1960s and early 1970s.

15. The dropout rate among high-school students within the United States is relatively high. One method for determining high-school dropout rates is to compare the number of graduates with the ninth-grade enrollment four years earlier. For reasons that are not entirely clear, the dropout rate varies considerably from city to city. The percentage of fourteen- to seventeen-years-olds enrolled in high school increased steadily over the previous eight decades, but now the trend seems to be reversing.

CHAPTER GLOSSARY

adolescence The phase of the life span that lies between childhood and adulthood.

adolescent growth spurt A period that begins at about the age of twelve in girls and fourteen in

boys when they undergo a rapid increase in height and weight.

drug abuse The excessive or compulsive use of chemical agents to an extent that they interfere with health, social, or vocational functioning.

identity An individual's sense of placement within the world; the meaning that one attaches to oneself as reflected in the answers one provides to the questions "Who am I?" and "Who am I to be?"

puberty The term applied to the period in the life cycle when sexual and reproductive maturation occurs.

EXERCISES

Review Questions

1. Which statement about puberty is true?
   a. Girls typically mature about two years earlier than boys.
   b. The average age of the first menses is still showing a marked decline.
   c. Although children may show a marked difference in onset of puberty, once started, timing and rate appear fairly consistent between individuals.
   d. a and c are true
   e. b and c are true

2. Which of the following individuals accepts a storm-and-stress view of adolescent development?
   a. Hall
   b. A. Freud
   c. Offer
   d. a and b are true

3. Research on the "generation gap" seems to indicate that

a. the majority of contemporary adolescents show a great deal of respect for their parents
b. the typical adolescent gets along well with parents
c. on issues involving future life goals the peer group is most influential
d. a and b are true
e. a, b, and c are true

4. As compared to twenty years ago, contemporary sexual behavior

a. is more liberal regarding premarital and extramarital sex
b. involves about the same incidence of veneral disease
c. indicates teenagers now tend to separate sex from morality
d. a and c are true
e. b and c are true

5. Given the increase in teenage pregnancy, which of these statements about the teenage use of contraceptives is true?

a. The level of use of contraceptives has generally remained constant during the 1970s.
b. Teenagers who use contraceptives tend to delay first usage.
c. The use of the pill has increased significantly among teenagers because of availability.
d. a and b are true
e. b and c are true

6. Adolescent choice of a vocation is influenced by the fact that

a. consideration of a vocation does not begin till early adolescence
b. students with higher grade-point averages tend to have more and better occupational knowledge
c. there has really been no increase in the last several decades in the percentages of high-school juniors and seniors working during the school year
d. a and c are true

7. By definition, which would be considered a drug?

a. alcohol
b. tobacco
c. LSD
d. a and c are true
e. a, b, and c are true

8. In a typical junior- and senior-high-school setting, the teacher will encounter the probability that

a. chronic truants use drugs more heavily
b. the incidence of marijuana has increased dramatically in the last year or two
c. only a small percentage of teenagers see any wrong in the use of drugs such as marijuana
d. a and b are true
e. b and c are true

9. Failures in drug education programs have been attributed to

a. significance of parental modeling in use of psychoactive drugs
b. programs that did not discriminate among drugs as to harmfulness
c. peer group pressures that were not fully recognized
d. a, b, and c are true
e. b and c are true

10. The literature on alcohol reveals that

a. it is the most frequently abused drug among adolescents as well as adults
b. drunk driving among teenagers is not yet considered a serious problem
c. adolescent use of alcohol does not appear related to parental drinking patterns
d. a and b are true
e. a, b, and c are true

Answers

1. a (See p. 72)
2. d (See pp. 76–78)
3. d (See p. 78)
4. a (See pp. 79–80)
5. b (See pp. 82–83)
6. b (See pp. 83–86)
7. e (See p. 86)
8. a (See pp. 86–87)
9. d (See pp. 86–87)
10. a (See pp. 87–88)

Applying Principles and Concepts

1. Erik Erikson has defined the identity crisis as the major psychological problem of adolescence. Check those adolescent behaviors below that represent the search for self, an attempt to solve the problem of identity.

_____ a. John is working at McDonald's to earn extra money.
_____ b. Mary is seriously questioning her religious beliefs.
_____ c. Tom is very concerned about his weight.
_____ d. Elizabeth just frets constantly over her braces.
_____ e. Jennifer desperately wants to join a high-school sorority.

2. A father has kept a record of remarks made by his nineteen-year-old daughter from her early childhood on. Rank these remarks in order of increasing age of occurrence, marking the earliest as #1.

_____ a. "A group of us boys and girls are going swimming."
_____ b. "Daddy and Mommy like each other."
_____ c. "Bob has asked me for a date."
_____ d. "I like John."
_____ e. "I want to get married when I get older."

3. A pregnant teenager has sought out the school counselor for advice. Underline those passages in her narrative that can be supported by research data.

Why did it happen to me? I thought I knew when it would be safe. I'm sure my boyfriend will marry me and we'll finish school together. He says we can make it if he gets a part-time job.

4. A high-school teacher has been keeping anecdotal records on a male student whom he considers to be deeply troubled. Place a check before those observations that reflect a potential suicide pattern.

_____ a. Seems to be doing less and less academically since the term began, and he was such a good student
_____ b. Is putting on a lot of weight
_____ c. Has been very depressed lately
_____ d. Is starting to drink
_____ e. Frequently late to school in the morning; he says he's oversleeping

5. If you taught in a typical junior high school, what kinds of delinquency could you expect? Check each statement that is true.

_____ a. There is more violence in our junior high as compared to the senior high.
_____ b. Most of our teachers fear physical violence.
_____ c. If we were in a rural area, we would get less violence between students.
_____ d. The gangs in our school avoid in-school violence because they like to settle it outside.
_____ e. I always expect less violence from college-bound students.
_____ f. Making rules for the kids and enforcing them doesn't help; they get mad about them.

Answers

1. b, e (See pp. 74–76)
2. 1, b; 2, e; 3, d; 4, a; 5, c (See p. 79)
3. Underline "Why did it happen to me?" and "I thought I knew when it would be safe." (See pp. 81–83)
4. a, c, d (See pp. 88–89)
5. a, c, e (See pp. 89–91)

Project

OBJECTIVE: To learn about the procedures used in schools to help students with problems of pregnancy, drug abuse, or alcoholism.

PROCEDURE: If you have access, visit a local junior or senior high school, and try to find an administrator or counselor willing to answer the following questions. Otherwise you can conduct a group discussion with peers. In the latter instance, the questions have been rephrased so that the student is talking about their particular school.

For a school visit:

1. How frequent are these problems? How does the school compare to others in the district?
2. What are the kinds of help the school or district can give to these students? Does the district help you determine symptoms?
3. What is the teacher's role in the process?
4. Is there a standardized procedure for handling these cases? Are they unique to this school or districtwide?
5. What kinds of pitfalls should the teacher avoid in handling these problems?

For a peer discussion:

1. How frequent were the problems in your school?
2. What kinds of help could you or your friends get?
3. Were your teachers sympathetic? How did they help?
4. Did you or your friends have to follow regulations to get help?
5. Did the school tend to hassle people with problems? Did teachers get in trouble for trying to help?

ANALYSIS: If you do a school visit, you should determine what differences in approach exist between the school and district. Visiting one or two classroom teachers will help to determine the validity of what you have been told. That is, certain procedures may exist on paper, whereas others are actually used.

If you conduct a group discussion with peers, the discussion should enable you to determine the uniqueness or universality of problems and solutions.

CHAPTER OUTLINE

4

INDIVIDUAL FOUNDATIONS AND DIFFERENCES

CHAPTER PREVIEW

Descriptions of developmental sequences tend to focus on patterns or modes of behavior that are typical of people at a certain age or stage. Though children—or adults—may share characteristics in common with others at a particular phase of the life span, individuals clearly differ from one another in many ways. Several dimensions along which students may differ are discussed in this chapter. Attention is centered, particularly, on factors that are important in school learning, such as differences in measured aptitude or ability and characteristic ways people have of approaching various tasks (''cognitive style''). An understanding of individual differences is crucial for effective classroom instruction. Also important is an appreciation of the extent to which instruction may be able to modify individual characteristics. Thus, this chapter begins with a consideration of the complex issue of the respective roles of heredity and environment in individual development.

Use the following questions to guide your reading and understanding of these concerns:

- In what ways has the nature-nurture or heredity-environment controversy been debated, and why is this issue of continuing interest to educators?
- How have different theorists described intelligence, and why is this concept so difficult to define?
- How is intelligence usually assessed, and what problems are associated with the measurement or testing of this concept?
- How is the heredity-environment issue related to different conceptions of intelligence and to racial differences in intelligence test scores?
- How can differences in students' cognitive styles affect their performance in school, and what possible implications do these differences have for instruction?

Schoolchildren differ. The point seems obvious. Indeed, it is the foundation for various techniques and strategies of individualized instruction (see Chapter 14). For instance, children vary in the amount of time they need to master an instructional unit and in the number of units they are able to handle over a given time (Gettinger and White, 1980). Nonetheless, strong traditions that define children as essentially similar and even inter-changeable prevail in American life. This is most apparent in the school system, probably the most age-graded of our institutions. The schools place six-year-olds in the first grade and eleven-year-olds in the fifth grade, each grade having a distinct but relatively standard curriculum. All first-graders are expected to master certain basic skills related to the three Rs and proceed over the next eleven years in more or less lockstep fashion through the elementary and secondary school levels.

Although the school may be founded upon the principle that various common denominators exist in children's growth and development, the fact of their individual differences always remains. The truth is that all children are alike in some ways and different in others. Their basic components may be similar, but the components fit together in different proportions and combinations. Since children differ, every teacher is compelled by the realities of classroom life to recognize this fact. Children vary by virtue of their differing biologies and their differing social experiences—the subject matter of this chapter.

THE RELATIONSHIP BETWEEN NATURE AND NURTURE

Much of our thinking about education reflects our underlying beliefs about how heredity and environment operate in human behavior. Are human infants genetically prewired with differing types and levels of ability and aptitude? Are they thus locked within predetermined and programmed limits of growth and development by the accidents of their biology? Or are children at birth essentially empty vessels into which society may pour a virtually limitless range of traits and capabilities? These questions have long intrigued humans and are traceable back to the classical Greek era of Plato and Aristotle.

Differing Models

The way a question is asked limits and disposes the ways in which any answer to it—right or wrong—may be given.

SUSANNE K. LANGER
Philosophy in a New Key, 1957

The psychologist Anne Anastasi (1958, 1973) points out that many of the difficulties associated with the nature-nurture controversy derive from the fact that scientists operate from different models or basic assumptions. Various investigators have asked different questions, and as a result, they have come up with different answers. The way we go about phrasing our questions presupposes certain alternatives in how the questions can be answered. When investigators assume that others are trying to answer *their* questions (but in reality are answering their own set of questions), the answers do not fit, and each side believes the other is talking nonsense.

Scientists began by asking *which* factor, heredity or environment, is responsible for some trait like a particular aptitude or personality characteristic. Later they sought to determine *how much* of the observed differences among a population of people with respect to some trait are due to differences in heredity and *how much* to differences in environment. More recently, some scientists like Anastasi have inquired *how* specific hereditary and environmental factors *interact* to shape given outcomes.

The "Which" Question

Scientists no longer ask whether heredity or environment is more important. The "either-or" question raises a hopeless division between the two factors. Carried to its logical conclusion, biologically inborn behavior would be defined as behavior that appears in the absence of environment and learned behavior would be that which does not require an organism. The question would be comparable to asking whether oxygen or hydrogen is more important to water. Obviously, without either oxygen or hydrogen, there could be no water.

The "How Much" Question

As the "which" question fell into disrepute, scientists started asking how much heredity and how much environment are required to produce a particular characteristic. For instance, they asked,

"Does a child's level of intelligence as evidenced by performance on an IQ test depend upon 80 percent heredity and 20 percent environment, 60 percent heredity and 40 percent environment, or some other ratio?"

Answers to the "how much" question are typically sought in family resemblance studies. Probably the best known research approach involves *identical,* or *monozygotic,* twins. Identical twins are formed when, by some accident, a fertilized egg gets split into two parts shortly after conception. Since identical twins develop from the same egg, their genetic endowments are the same. Therefore, any differences between them are presumed to result from environmental influences.

Another approach for assessing family resem-

IDENTICAL TWINS
Researchers have sought answers to the "how much" question in the nature-nurture controversy through the study of identical twins.

blances involves studying adopted children. Some characteristic of the children is compared to the same characteristic in the biological parents and in the foster parents. This allows researchers to weigh the relative impact of the genetic factor and the home environment.

Illustrative of family resemblance research are the landmark studies by John C. Loehlin and Robert C. Nichols (1976) involving nearly 2,500 high-school-aged twins who took the National Merit Scholarship test in 1962 and 1965. The twins also completed a battery of personality, attitude, and interest tests. In addition, their parents answered a comprehensive questionnaire related to the children's infancy and childhood and their family environment. Among the comparisons made by Loehlin and Nichols were the average differences in the characteristics of identical and *fraternal twins* (fraternal twins come from two different eggs fertilized by two different spermatozoa so that the twins are simply siblings who happen to be born at the same time). This research suggests that about half of the variations among people in a broad spectrum of psychological traits are due to genetic factors. Overall, the results of the research seem to be more consistent with the position of middle-of-the-roaders than with that of either fervent hereditarians or environmentalists.

The "How" Question

A number of pyschologists (Anastasi, 1958, 1973; Wohlwill, 1973; Lerner, 1976, 1978) argue that the "how much" question, like the "which" question, leads to no productive end. They say that the "how much" question assumes that heredity and environment are related to each other in such a way that the contribution of one is *added* to the contribution of the other to produce a given behavior. These psychologists dispute this view. Hans G. Furth observes:

> We have been accustomed, if not brainwashed, to look at an organism as one entity and the environment as another, separate entity, and then we ask how these two things get together. However, from a biological viewpoint, these two things

have never been separated at all. Quite the opposite. An organism can exist only insofar at it is related to or corresponds to the environment. [1977:16]

Scientists of this school of thought ask *how* heredity and environment interact to produce behavior. They view the two factors as so intertwined that it is a hopeless task to identify "which" produces a particular behavior or to determine "how much" each contributes. Take the case of diphtheria, an infectious disease affecting the air passages of the throat (Anastasi, 1973). Susceptibility to diphtheria is believed to depend upon a recessive gene and immunity upon a corresponding dominant gene. The disease, however, cannot be contracted in the absence of the diphtheria bacillus.

Among a population, all the members of whom have an inherited susceptibility to the disease, individual differences in the development of diphtheria are entirely attributable to environmental factors (exposure to the bacillus). In contrast, in a population in which all the members are exposed to the bacillus, individual differences in contracting the disease are a function of heredity (the presence or absence of the dominant gene). To the "how much" question ("What proportion of the variance in the incidence of diphtheria is attributable to heredity?"), opposite answers would be obtained in these two populations. Hence, it may not be possible to attach exact percentages to the contributions of heredity and environment. Since heredity and environment interact in a relationship of varying dependence, what appears to be an environmental contribution in one context can be seen as an hereditary contribution in another.

Heredity and Environment in Individual Development

The nature-nurture controversy continues to arouse a good many emotions and passions. Yet, scientists are increasingly asking new questions and turning away from old formulations. We are reminded of

John Dewey's observation, made over a half century ago, about ideas:

> Old ideas give way slowly. . . . The conviction persists—though history shows it to be a hallucination—that all the questions that the human mind has asked are questions that can be answered in terms of the alternatives that the questions themselves present. But in fact intellectual progress usually occurs through sheer abandonment of questions together with both the alternatives they assume. . . . We do not solve them: we get over them. Old questions are solved by disappearing, evaporating, while new questions corresponding to the changed attitude of endeavor and preference take their place. [1909:23]

One of these new lines of scientific inquiry has to do with the actual chain of events through which a particular hereditary or environmental factor influences an individual's behavior. For the most part, it appears that the greater the number of biochemical steps between a particular gene and the final appearance of the trait, the more indirect the hereditary influence and the greater the opportunities for environmental factors to come into play. At one extreme, the link between a gene and a behavior is relatively direct and immediate. This is the case with some hereditary metabolic disorders such as *phenylketonuria (PKU),* a form of mental retardation.

PKU is a disorder that is transmitted genetically according to straightforward Mendelian principles. Children with PKU lack an enzyme needed to metabolize phenylalanine (an amino acid found in protein foods). As a consequence of this metabolic failure, a buildup of substances occurs that is toxic to the nervous system. It has been found that if these infants are placed on a low-phenylalanine diet from their first month through age four, intellectual impairment can often be minimized or even prevented. Note, however, that environmental influences are not entirely absent even in the case of PKU, since the disorder appears only in the presence of a diet containing phenylalanine (admittedly a very common food ingredient).

At the other extreme, there are certain forms of behavior in which hereditary influences are rela-

tively indirect and subtle and where environmental factors play a critical part. Language affords a good illustration. Language is a group product that permits the transfer of information and mental states from one person to another. Language provides a vehicle for both abstract thought and problem solving. Whether we speak English, French, Russian, Hindi, or Gujarati is a function of the social group in which we were reared. Note, however, that language usage presupposes the existence of appropriate hereditary mechanisms. For instance, although chimpanzees reveal remarkable communicative skills, their abilities are not equivalent to human linguistic capabilities (Limber, 1977).

In between these extremes are various intermediate types of nature-nurture interchanges (Plomin, DeFries, and Loehlin, 1977; Scarr et al., 1981). Research by a team of psychologists—Harold D. Grotevant, Sandra Scarr, and Richard A. Weinberg (1977, 1978; Scarr and Weinberg, 1980)—points to how such interactions shape individuals' career interests. The researchers compared the interests of two groups of parents and their teenagers: 109 adoptive families and 114 biologically related families. The two groups of families were similar in education and income. The children and their parents were rated on whether they preferred pursuits that were rugged, investigative, artistic, business oriented, humanistic, or highly structured and repetitive.

Considerable similarity existed between parents and children in biologically related families. But the lack of similarity between adoptive parents and their genetically unrelated children was striking. Even though the children had lived with their adoptive parents since infancy, their interests were no more similar to their foster parents than they would have been to other adults chosen randomly from the population. Furthermore, biological siblings were reasonably similar to each other, while adoptive siblings revealed no overall pattern of similarity.

The findings do not suggest that we inherit genes for rugged, artistic, or humanistic interests. Rather, genes influence our styles for interacting and coping

SIMILARITY IN INTERESTS AMONG GENETICALLY RELATED FAMILY MEMBERS
Some researchers claim that genetic factors influence our styles for interacting with the world. Accordingly, certain activities, hobbies, and occupations tend to "run in" families.

with the world. As such, they predispose us to view certain activities, hobbies, and occupations as attractive. For instance, a very sociable person with a high activity level would likely find a routinized occupation such as that of a keypunch operator highly unsatisfactory. Likewise, a shy and retiring person would probably be uncomfortable selling autos or real estate.

Grotevant and his associates also speculated that another avenue of biological influence on interests, especially during adolescence, has to do with a person's rate of physical maturation. The timing of the adolescent growth spurt is controlled hormonally and, ultimately, genetically. Further, in the case of males, late-maturing boys differ from early-maturing boys in a variety of behaviors and interests (Jones and Bayley, 1950; Mussen and Jones, 1957; Weatherley, 1964). It is conceivable that boys may come to have interests similar to their biological fathers because they both have similar *social* experiences as a result of sharing a similar *biologically* controlled rate of growth.

INTELLIGENCE

Much school-related activity has to do with the three Rs and various content areas like the sciences, history, literature, and civics. Since some students perform better than others at many of these tasks, the assumption has frequently been made that pupils differ in their underlying capabilities. For nearly a century, psychologists have used various labels— such as *intelligence, capacity, aptitude, ability,* and *potential*—to refer to these inferred mental capabilities. Further, many psychologists have assumed that if we ascertain these capabilities by some sort of measuring device (a test, a questionnaire, or a scale), we can make predictions about a student's future performance or behavior.

The Concept of Intelligence

Most of us have a reasonably clear idea about which kinds of behavior we judge to be intelligent. Usually, we conceive of **intelligence** as a person's ability to engage in new behaviors that solve problems without recourse to other people's instructions. As the psychologist Dalbir Bindra notes, we say that people's actions are intelligent "when they are more purposive than haphazard, more intentional than accidental, and more foresightful and innovative than impulsive and stereotyped" (1976:1).

Some psychologists define intelligence as the capacity to learn (profit from experience); others, as the ability to think abstractly; and still others, as the capacity to integrate new experiences and adapt to new situations. Yet another group says that intelligence is whatever is measured by an intelligence test.

The problem all of us encounter in defining intelligence is that we never observe intelligence but only intelligent *behavior*. We *infer* an underlying capacity or trait from what a person says or does and call this intelligence. Some psychologists find parallels between the concept of intelligence and that of electricity, which physicists find equally difficult to define. Ledford J. Bischof points out that intelligence, like electricity, "is measurable, and its effect, but not its properties, can be only imprecisely described" (1976:137).

INTELLIGENCE
For the most part, we conceive of intelligence as a person's general problem-solving ability. Yet psychologists encounter difficulty in defining the term because intelligence cannot be directly observed but only inferred from a person's behavior.

The Structure of Intelligence

Intelligence testing began in earnest with the development of the first individual intelligence test by Alfred Binet (1857–1911) in 1905. Binet, a French psychologist, was interested in measuring intelligence to identify children who required special educational treatment. He arranged the various items in his test scale in order of difficulty and devised a crude scoring system based on the highest item attained. The following are illustrative of the sample of tasks making up the Binet scale for various age groups. With minor modifications, some of the items are included in the latest Stanford-Binet test:

- *Age 3:* Points to nose, eyes, mouth.
- *Age 4:* Names certain familiar objects shown to him or her (key, knife, penny).
- *Age 6:* Repeats sentence of sixteen syllables.
- *Age 8:* Adds up the value of five coins.
- *Age 10:* Names the months of the year in correct order.
- *Age 11:* Defines abstract words (charity, justice, kindness).
- *Age 13:* Rearranges in imagination the relationship of two reversed triangles and draws results.

Binet viewed his own work with considerable caution. Since education could increase "the capacity to learn," he believed that his test scores should not be treated as if they recorded a fixed faculty. "Intellectual qualities," argued Binet, "cannot be measured as linear surfaces are measured" (quoted by Miller, 1981:106). However, Binet did provide for the computation of a single "intelligence" score. It remained for Charles E. Spearman (1863–1945), an English psychologist, to propose that intelligence is basically a general intellectual capacity and that tests can be constructed to provide for a single pooled score across many items (Brody and Brody, 1976).

Spearman (1904, 1927) believed that all tests of intelligence have two components—the "g" factor and the "s" factor. The *"g" factor* is that portion of variance that all tests of intelligence have in common. The portion that is unique or specific to each test is the *"s" factor*.

Spearman argued that since tests of ability correlate positively with one another, all the tests are to some extent measuring "g." Accordingly, he viewed the "g" factor as a basic intellectual power that pervades all of an individual's mental activity. But since a person's performance across various tasks is not perfectly consistent, Spearman identified many specific factors (s_1, s_2, . . . s_n) that pertain to particular types of activity. This approach is known as the **two-factor theory of intelligence.**

In the 1930s and 1940s, Louis L. Thurstone (1887–1955) refined and elaborated Spearman's procedures for factor analysis. He rejected the notion of a general intelligence and focused instead on groups of traits or factors. Each of the traits within a particular group had more in common with other traits within that group than with traits in other groups. Thurstone (1938, 1947) identified seven primary mental abilities: verbal comprehension, word fluency, numerical ability, space visualization, associative memory, perceptual speed, and reasoning. He described an individual's ability in terms of a profile representing the person's scores in these primary areas.

More recently, J. P. Guilford (1967, 1979) has proposed that there are 120 separate types of mental abilities. Designers of intelligence tests have found Guilford's model useful for suggesting types of intelligence that can, in turn, be translated into question items. Guilford begins by distinguishing five types of mental operations: cognition, memory, divergent production (generation of logical alternatives), convergent production (generation of logic-tight conclusions), and evaluation. His second dimension has to do with four content areas in which mental operations are performed: figural, symbolic, semantic, and behavioral. Finally, Guilford identifies six types of products: units, classes, relations, systems, transformations, and implications. The various combinations of operations, contents, and products make up the 120 (5 × 4 × 6) different abilities portrayed in Figure 4.1. Guilford claims that research has empirically demonstrated that at least 82 of the 120 factors actually exist.

Some psychologists make still other distinctions. Raymond B. Cattell (1943, 1971) differentiates between fluid intelligence and crystallized intelligence. **Fluid intelligence** consists of a factor of general brightness or abstract mental efficiency that Cattell considers to be independent of schooling or cultural experience. **Crystallized intelligence** entails knowledge and skills that are acquired through cultural experience. Fluid intelligence is usually measured by performance on nonverbal tests involving figure classification, figural analogies, and number and letter series tests. In contrast,

FIGURE 4.1 GUILFORD'S MODEL OF INTELLECT
J. P. Guilford has formulated a three-dimensional model of intelligence. His dimensions are (1) operations, (2) content, and (3) products. Operations has to do with the kind of performance required of a test-taker. Content refers to the kind of content or material that is involved. Products refers to the kind of outcomes that are produced. In all, there are 120 cubical cells. *(Source: From* The Nature of Human Intelligence *by J. P. Guilford. Copyright © 1967 McGraw-Hill. Used with the permission of McGraw-Hill Book Company.)*

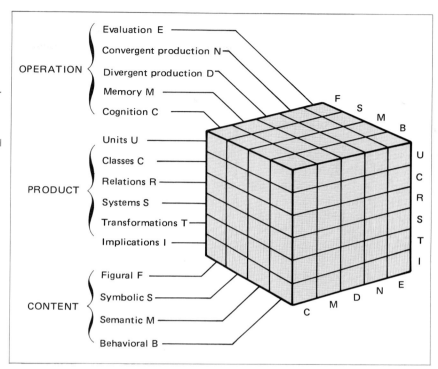

tests of general information, vocabulary, abstruse word analogies, and the mechanics of language are viewed as measures of crystallized intelligence.

Finally, Jean Piaget, a Swiss developmental psychologist, has advanced a radically different view of intelligence (see Chapter 6). Piaget was interested in identifying the stages of development through which children's modes of thinking changed. He insisted that the thought of infants and children was not a miniature version of adult thought. Rather, it passed through qualitatively distinctive and unique sequential periods. Central to Piaget's theory is the notion of *process:* Through new experiences and interactions with the environment, children come to know their world and to modify their understanding of it. In Piaget's view, this dynamic interplay between an individual and the environment is the foundation of intelligence. Since Piaget did not conceive of intelligence in set or fixed terms, he showed little interest in the static

assessment of individual differences in various capacities.

Intelligence Testing

If we define intelligence as a mental capacity, then we must have some basis for inferring that capacity. Psychologists usually surmise an individual's intelligence from that person's performance in a test setting involving various learning or problem-solving tasks. However, intelligence tests do not directly measure a person's learning or problem-solving capacities. Instead, the tests seek to ascertain an individual's performance on a diverse sample of behaviors. As such, tests serve as indicators or signs of a relatively open-ended list of activities (Carroll and Horn, 1981).

The results of a person's performance on an intelligence test are reported as a numerical score termed the *intelligence quotient,* or *IQ.* IQ is a descriptive concept, an expression of a person's performance on some mental measure relative to the average performance of individuals at his or her chronological age. Two of the most widely employed intelligence tests are the Stanford-Binet scales and the intelligence scales prepared by David Wechsler and his associates.

The Stanford-Binet Scales

The current Stanford-Binet tests are lineal descendants of Binet's 1905 scale consisting of thirty short items. In 1908 Binet revised the scale with age standards and in 1911 introduced a number of minor test modifications. Lewis M. Terman and his associates at Stanford University became interested in Binet's work and in 1916 brought out an American version of the test. Over a third of the items were new, while Binet's remaining items were revised and rearranged. In 1937 Terman further revised the tests. The new version consisted of two equivalent forms, L and M. Another version that took the best items from the L and M forms and placed them within a single form (Form L-M) was prepared in 1960. In 1972 new norms were derived for the 1960 tests based on an updated and more representative sample of students, although the test content remained unchanged.

All the revisions of the Stanford-Binet tests have followed essentially the same pattern. A series of tasks are arranged by age level. For instance, the tasks for age six are the following:

- *Vocabulary:* Tells the correct meaning of six or more words from a graded list of forty-five words (words like "tap" and "gown").
- *Differences:* Explains the differences between a series of two things named by the examiner (for instance, a bird and a dog). Needs two out of three for credit.
- *Mutilated pictures:* Tells what part is missing on five cards where a part of an object is absent. Needs four out of five for credit.
- *Number concepts:* Gives examiner the number of blocks requested (out of twelve blocks).

Needs four out of five different combinations for credit.
- *Opposite analogies:* Completes three out of four verbal analogies for credit ("A table is made of wood; a window of ____").
- *Maze tracing:* With a pencil traces the shortest distance between a starting point and stopping point on a maze. Needs two right out of three for credit.

The person who administers the tests starts at a level below the chronological age of the student. The examiner then works downward to lower age levels, should this be necessary, until the student successfully completes all the tasks associated with that age level. This is termed the *basal age.* The tester then proceeds upward until a level is reached where the student fails all the tasks, called the *ceiling age.*

The student's mental age is computed by adding to the basal age appropriate weights for the items answered correctly up to the ceiling age. The mental age is converted to an IQ by means of tables presented in the test manual. The test fixes the *mean* (average) score at 100 with a distribution of 16 points on either side (a standard deviation of 16). This constitutes the range of "normal" intelligence—scores above 116 are considered to be above average, and those below 84 as below average.

The Stanford-Binet test enjoys wide popularity among educators and psychologists. It is frequently used as a tool for predicting students' future scholastic success. The test's most limiting feature is that it is chiefly a measure of verbal ability. It is not designed to differentiate among the various aspects of intelligence.

The Wechsler Scales

The Stanford-Binet scales provide a global sampling of intelligence. In contrast, the tests developed by David Wechsler contain separate verbal and nonverbal components. There are three Wechsler tests: the Wechsler Adult Intelligence Scale (WAIS) for ages sixteen and over; the Wechsler

Intelligence Scale for Children (WISC) for children ages six to sixteen; and the Wechsler Preschool and Primary Scale of Intelligence (WPPSI) for children ages four to six and one-half.

Each test consists of a verbal scale containing six subtests and a performance scale made up of five subtests:

Verbal Tests	*Performance Tests*
1. Information	7. Picture completion
2. Comprehension	8. Picture arrangement
3. Arithmetic	9. Block design
4. Similarities	10. Object assembly
5. Vocabulary	11. Coding or mazes
6. Digit Span	(alternate)
(alternate)	

The items on the Wechsler tests are not organized into age levels, as with the Stanford-Binet. Rather, the items are graded in order of increasing difficulty within each subtest. The final IQ score is made up of discrete verbal and nonverbal performance scales, each of which can be considered apart from the total. Like the Stanford-Binet, the Wechsler scales fit the mean score at 100, but the standard deviation is 15 rather than 16 (rendering 85–115 as the range of "normal" intelligence). Unlike the Stanford-Binet, the Wechsler tests employ a series of point scales (each test item is assigned points for a correct response). The raw score from each test can then be converted to an IQ by using an accompanying test manual.

The strength of the various Wechsler scales derives from the size and representativeness of the sample populations on which they are based. They are also characterized by the high technical quality of the procedures employed in item construction. The Wechsler scales offer more diagnostic information than do the Stanford-Binet tests by virtue of their separate verbal and performance scores. Because of its demonstrated reliability, educators and psychologists prefer the WAIS to the Stanford-Binet as a measure for individuals sixteen years of age and older (the Stanford-Binet is not designed to test adults). However, its relation to academic

success has not been as clearly established as has that of the Stanford-Binet. Overall, the scores on the Stanford-Binet and Wechsler scales correlate reasonably well (between 0.70 and 0.85).

Uses and Misuses of Intelligence Tests

Intelligence tests are chiefly measures of scholastic aptitude. Most educators and psychologists regard them as reasonably good predictors of academic success. Indeed, a strong relationship between IQ and academic achievement is built into intelligence tests, so that what we have come to mean by intelligence is the probability of acceptable school performance. While errors in prediction are usually not large for groups, it is possible that the use of an IQ test score alone for a single individual may result in a relatively large error in prediction. Further, an individual's IQ, unlike his or her blood type, is not fixed or unchanging. It varies from time to time, even under ideal testing conditions. Plus, it is amenable to modification by environmental interventions.

It is not possible to predict success in all of life's endeavors from a test designed to predict academic success. The more the real-life situation differs from that of the school environment, the less valid the scores from intelligence tests will be in making predictions about an individual's future performance (and thus the less willing we should be to make inferences about a person's intelligence in a nonschool area of functioning). For instance, intelligence tests are not necessarily relevant to various occupations requiring mechanical and artistic talents. Nor are intelligence tests designed to tell us about children's curiosity, their motivation, their personal inner thoughts, their ability to get along with people, or their chances to become active and responsible members of society.

Proponents of intelligence testing say that knowledge of general aptitude scores can assist a teacher in making decisions about the kind and level of material with which to provide each student. They argue that good teaching dictates that teachers design instructional strategies in accordance with the differing aptitudes of their students. When combined with other test results and classroom observations, an IQ score can prove to be a helpful tool. However, it is crucial that teachers recognize that a single IQ score provides, at best, an exceedingly tentative estimate of a student's scholastic aptitude.

Critics of intelligence testing point out that some teachers use low IQ scores as an excuse for not attempting to teach particular students. Unfortunately, there is sometimes truth to this charge. Of course, any tool can be abused. Although IQ scores can assist teachers in developing realistic expectations of students, the scores should not be used to form fatalistic expectations. Teachers should be especially aware that IQ scores are less dependable for some of their students (Gronlund, 1976):

- Those who come from minority group cultural or racial backgrounds.
- Those who find school-related tasks relatively unmotivating.
- Those who are weak in reading skills or have other difficulties with verbal materials.
- Those who have difficulties in emotional adjustment.

IQ scores can also be used in counseling. For instance, a troublesome child, if very bright, may be bored and require greater challenge. Or a child may pose discipline problems because of difficulty in handling a given level of work and may be causing trouble because of frustration. If the child is of average intelligence, the source of the misbehavior may reside in emotional problems. Data from an intelligence test may provide insight in assessing which of the competing hypotheses is most tenable (Mehrens and Lehmann, 1978). Additional consideration will be given to these and related matters in Chapter 18.

Underachiever and Overachiever Labels

One frequently hears teachers, and even parents, making reference to children as "underachievers" or "overachievers." The terms mean that there is a disparity or gap between a child's IQ score and school achievement, with the IQ score serving as a benchmark for assessing school achievement. However, the labels have recently come in for a good deal of criticism. Psychologists Edward Zigler and Penelope K. Trickett observe:

> If a middle-class child does not do very well in school, both the school and the family appear more comfortable if we call the child an underachiever. If an economically disadvantaged child does poorly in school, we are tempted to call him or her stupid, using the school performance itself as the ultimate gauge of a child's intellectual level. This situation becomes even more ridiculous when we use the nonsensical label of overachiever. . . . [We cannot] be very tolerant of a label that essentially asserts that some individuals achieve more than they are capable of achieving. [1978:792]

Other psychologists, while recognizing potential dangers in the use of the terms, nonetheless find them helpful. A gap between a child's IQ score and school achievement, particularly in the case of underachievement, provides a signal to alert the teacher to a potential problem. School or other environmental factors may be interfering with the child's realization of his or her full potential. This situation calls for appropriate diagnosis of the difficulty and the introduction of suitable corrective measures.

Heredity and Environment in Relation to Intelligence

Since psychologists disagree on what intelligence is, how to measure it, and how many intellectual factors there are, it is hardly surprising that they find themselves in disagreement about the relative part that heredity and environment play in producing individual differences in intelligence. Moreover, they differ in how to go about phrasing the nature-nurture question.

As noted earlier in the chapter, the "which" question—"Which is more important in the determination of intelligence, heredity or environment?''—is no longer regarded as an acceptable way to formulate the issue. Accordingly, the ''which'' question came to be replaced by the ''how much'' question—''How much of the total variation in intelligence within a particular population can be attributed to genetic factors and how much to environmental factors?'' Arthur R. Jensen, an educational psychologist at the University of California at Berkeley, has vigorously championed the ''how much'' phrasing of the nature-nurture question.

Like others who approach the issue in terms of ''how much,'' Jensen has sought his answer in family resemblance studies. He points out that as the genetic or biological kinship relationship between two individuals increases (gets closer), the correlation coefficient between their IQ scores also increases (see the Appendix). Table 4.1 provides correlation data between relatives.

If the correlation coefficient is +1.00, the correspondence in IQ scores between pairs of individuals would be perfect (knowing the IQ score of one person would tell us the IQ score of the other). If there is no relationship between the IQ scores of pairs of individuals, the correlation coefficient would be 0.00 (knowing the IQ score of one person would tell us nothing about the IQ score of the other). Hence, the nearer the correlation coefficient is to +1.00, the closer is the overall correspondence of the IQ score of one relative to the IQ score of the other relative.

On the basis of family resemblance studies, Jensen concluded that about 80 percent of the variation in IQ scores in the general population is attributable to genetic differences and 20 percent to environmental differences. However, many other scientists dispute the claim that differences in intelligence are primarily a function of heredity. And a goodly number of scientists also disagree with the phrasing of the nature-nurture question in ''how much'' terms, preferring instead to ask, ''How do heredity and environment interact to affect performance on intelligence tests?''

Some psychologists, termed *environmentalists*, say that mental abilities are learned. They claim that intellect is increased or decreased according to the degree to which an individual is exposed to an enriched or impoverished environment. Leon J. Kamin, a Princeton University psychologist and a leading environmentalist, asserts: ''There exists no data which should lead a prudent man to accept the hypothesis that IQ test scores are in any degree heritable'' (1974:1).

Recently, Reuven Feuerstein, an Israeli psychologist, has emerged as a leading advocate of the environmentalist position (Chance, 1981; Hechinger, 1981). He views intelligence as a soft plastic that can be shaped almost at will. Consequently, Feuerstein insists that teachers should not make rigid assumptions regarding what given children can and cannot learn. At the heart of Feuerstein's approach is active intervention—what he terms ''mediation''—by experienced adults. Feuerstein insists that it is not sufficient for adults, including teachers, to act as mere dispensers of information. Instead, they must explain a stimulus to a child or change the stimulus on the child's behalf. They must select and highlight certain stimuli, repeat others, and screen out still others. In so doing adults assist a child in isolating the significant stimuli in a problem-solving situation; they train the child to identify relevant cues in a situation, to link critical cues to certain others, and to create meaning. In short, Feuerstein believes that the thought processes commonly associated with in-

TABLE 4.1

Median Correlation Coefficients for Intelligence Scores Showing Degree of Similarity Between Performance of Individuals of Varying Degrees of Kinship

Category	Median Coefficient
Foster parent-child	.20
Parent-child	.50
Siblings reared together	.49
Fraternal twins	.55
Identical twins reared apart	.75
Identical twins reared together	.87

Source: Adapted from L. Erlenmeyer-Kimling and L. F. Jervik, ''Genetics and Intelligence: A Review,'' *Science*, 142(1964):1477–1479.

STIMULATING EARLY ENVIRONMENTS
Some psychologists claim that children reared in stimulating home environments enjoy
an advantage in intellectual development.

telligence can be cultivated and nurtured through conscious adult intervention and environmental enrichment.

In support of their position, environmentalists cite data that show that when cultural conditions improve over a period of time, so does the overall intelligence test performance of the population. This is reflected in the improvement in the test scores of American soldiers between World War I and World War II (Tuddenham, 1948). A representative sample of enlisted men from both periods was administered comparable tests. The data revealed that the median performance of the World War II sample fell at the eighty-third percentile of the World War I sample (in other words, 83 percent of the World War I men fell below the median score of the World War II men). It is noteworthy that the educational level of the American population increased by an average of two years over this twenty-five-year interval and that vast changes had occurred in other areas of life (including the introduction of radio and motion pictures).

Some educators like Benjamin S. Bloom claim that teaching requires a commitment to the environmentalist stance:

The psychologist and the geneticist may wish to speculate about how to improve the gene pool—the educator cannot and should not. The educator must be an environmentalist. . . . It is through the environment that he must fashion the educational process. Learning takes place within the child; the educator tries to influence this learning by providing the appropriate environment. If heredity imposes limits—so be it. The educator must work with what is left, whether it be 20 percent of the variance or 50 percent. [1969:421]

To all of this Jensen makes the following responses:

I do believe that educational policy decisions should be based on evidence and the results of continuing research—and not just the evidence which is comfortable to some particular ideological position, but *all* relevant evidence. I submit that the research on the inheritance of mental abilities *is* relevant to understanding educational problems and formulating educational policies. For one thing, it means that we take individual differences more seriously than regarding them as superficial, easily-changed manifestations of environmental differences. [1969b:479]

Clearly these issues remain unresolved and highly controversial.

IQ and Race

Do not obtain your slaves from the Britons, for the Britons are so stupid and so dull that they are not fit to be slaves.

CICERO

The debate surrounding racial differences in intelligence test scores is closely linked with the larger nature-nurture controversy. In 1969 the academic world was rocked by the appearance of a paper by Jensen (1969a) in the prestigious *Harvard Educational Review*. Later issues of the journal carried both rebuttals by prominent psychologists and Jensen's rejoinder. The debate was widely publicized in the press and in *Newsweek*, *Time*, and *U.S. News & World Report*. As John C. Loehlin, Gardner Lindzey, and J. N. Spuhler

point out, when questions regarding race and intelligence are examined in the context of a society ridden with unresolved racial tensions, "It is not surprising that the result should be massive polemic in which personal conviction and emotional commitment often have been more prominent than evidence or careful reasoning" (1975:3).

Jensen (1973a, 1973b, 1980) finds that, on the most commonly used intelligence tests, there is an average 15-point difference in the IQ performance between blacks and whites. He concludes that this difference is attributable more to heredity than to environment:

All the major facts would seem to be comprehended quite well by the hypothesis that something between one-half and three-fourths of the average difference between American Negroes and whites is attributable to genetic factors, and the remainder to environmental factors and their interaction with genetic differences. [1973c:358]

And:

There is a true difference between blacks and whites, and at this time it is impossible to devise a reasonable test of mental abilities which does not show that difference. [Quoted by Sewall and Lee, 1980:59]

Many psychologists challenge Jensen's interpretation regarding the existence of racial differences in intelligence. Some sixty years ago, a number of psychologists had taken a position similar to that of Jensen. During World War I, nearly 2 million American recruits were administered intelligence tests. The results were interpreted as showing that native-born whites were superior to blacks in mental ability. However, in the 1920s, psychologists took a second look at the test scores. It was found that blacks from the South, where economic and educational handicaps were more severe, scored lower than Northern blacks. Of even greater interest, blacks from Pennsylvania, New York, Illinois, and Ohio averaged higher scores than whites from Mississippi, Arkansas, Kentucky, and Georgia. Presumably, the superior environmental opportunities enjoyed by Northern blacks accounted for their superior test performance.

During the 1930s, the psychologist Otto Klineberg (1935) had a sample of New York City children take an IQ test. He found that black children who spent a longer time in New York City tended to have higher scores than black children of more recent residence. These findings challenged the prevailing notion that IQ is a fixed trait unsusceptible to environmental influence. Everett S. Lee (1951), a sociologist, confirmed Klineberg's findings. He analyzed the intelligence test scores of blacks in the Philadelphia school system. There was a steady upward trend in the average IQ scores of black migrants from the South. By the ninth grade, those children who had come in at the first-grade level were less than a point below those blacks born in Philadelphia. More recently, Sandra Scarr and Richard A. Weinberg (1975, 1976) have found that a substantial part of the IQ gap between blacks and whites is closed among black children who are adopted as infants by white middle-class foster parents.

Some psychologists dispute Jensen's claim that intelligence tests are "color-blind" (Garcia, 1981). They assert that the tests reflect white, urban, middle-class culture and linguistic usage. For black ghetto children, standard English vocabulary and middle-class "wisdom" may be relatively unfamiliar. Jensen's critics say that most IQ tests contain a good deal of culturally loaded material, particularly in verbal content like vocabulary (Vander Zanden, 1983). Accordingly, children of different groups may not understand a question in the same way (the same question may not have the identical meaning in all environments). For instance, often black ghetto and Spanish-speaking children are fearful of the testing process and expect to do poorly. They may be insensitive to speed requirements, unfamiliar with the problem contents, and not able to develop spontaneously the most effective strategies (by middle-class standards) to solve the problems. Yet, many of these same children are competent problem solvers in their nonschool environment. They have mastered the skills, knowledge, and strategies necessary to achieve a successful adjustment. Clearly these children do learn and profit from their experiences more than their IQ scores and school achievements reveal (Babad and Budoff, 1974).

DIFFERENCES IN COGNITIVE STYLE

Much thought and energy have been given by psychologists and educators to breaking lockstep practices in education and making allowances for individual differences. Increasingly, they are coming to recognize that the major question confronting education is not finding *the* method or methods that are best for all students. When we ask whether a highly structured classroom is superior to a more informal classroom, whether lecture, recitation, or discussion works best, or whether programmed instruction is preferable to a live teacher, we find that for the mythical statistical *average* student, it makes little difference which alternative is employed. However, when we examine data student by student, we find that some pupils improve, others remain unaffected, and still others regress under particular teaching conditions. The process of averaging the pluses, the minuses, and the nonchangers masks the fact that different strategies work with different students (Cross, 1976; Cronbach and Snow, 1977).

Usually the problem of individual differences has been defined as one of distinguishing between "fast" and "slow" learners as determined by aptitude and achievement tests. But there are other differences among students that are also important, including **cognitive style**. In its broadest sense, cognitive style may be thought of as an individual's typical mode of processing information. It refers to the consistencies in an individual's way of functioning in his or her day-to-day activities, especially when the activities have to do with organizing and categorizing perceptions. Although psychologists have identified any number of cognitive styles, only a few have been extensively researched (Kogan, 1976). Among the latter are field dependence-independence and reflection-impulsivity.

Field Dependence and Field Independence

The field dependence and field independence dimensions have particular interest for educators (Annis, 1979; Linn and Kyllonen, 1981). **Field-independent** people tend to analyze the individual elements making up a task or situation; they focus upon undertakings in an analytical manner, separating items from their backgrounds. In contrast, **field-dependent** people tend to categorize a task or situation in a global way; they focus upon the whole, overlooking the individual elements. Put in colloquial terms, some people tend to be "splitters" while others are "lumpers."

In many learning situations the teaching material lacks a clear, inherent structure. This requires that the learners themselves provide some sort of organization to help them learn. Field-independent people have a greater facility for providing structure to a task or situation than do field-dependent people. Generally, field-dependent students have a greater need for teachers to provide them with external structuring. Overall, field-independent people have greater skills in problem-solving tasks that involve analysis and structuring than do field-dependent people.

It appears that field-dependent people are particularly interested in and selectively attentive to social aspects in the world about them (Witkin and Goodenough, 1977; Witkin et al., 1977). They tend to be people oriented, showing a strong preference for social situations in which they can be with others. These characteristics add up to a set of social attributes and skills that are less evident in field-independent people. As a consequence, field-dependent students tend to be better at learning materials with a social content than are field-independent people.

The different clusters of characteristics found in field-dependent and field-independent people help each group to deal with particular sets of problems or situations. Neither style is inherently good or bad but can be judged only with reference to its adaptiveness in different real-life situations. It is of interest that field-dependent college students tend to major in the humanities, the social sciences, education, social work, and fields that involve a global perspective. In contrast, field-independent students tend to be attracted to mathematics, the natural sciences, engineering, and subjects that require a high level of analytical reasoning (Witkin, 1973). Further, students whose initial college majors are inconsistent with their cognitive styles tend to shift to more compatible majors by college graduation or graduate school (Witkin et al., 1977).

Reflective and Impulsive Styles

One dimension of cognitive style that psychologists have found to be an important determinant of academic progress and success is conceptual tempo. Jerome Kagan (1965) has shown that in various problem situations in which several possible alternatives are available, some children proceed by slow deliberation and make few errors, termed a **reflective style.** Other children test hypotheses quickly and make many errors, termed an **impulsive style.** The reflection-impulsivity dimension is concerned with the degree to which individuals reflect on the validity of their problem solutions under circumstances of high response uncertainty (Kagan and Kogan, 1970). The criteria are response time and accuracy. Researchers estimate that about 30 percent of preschool and elementary school children are impulsive.

Studies show that reflective children tend to perform better than impulsive children on reading tasks (Kagan, 1965), recognition memory tests (Siegel, Kirasic, and Kilburg, 1973), tasks involving reasoning (Kagan, Pearson, and Welch, 1966), and creative projects (Fuqua, Bartsch, and Phye, 1975). Further, impulsivity is found to affect school performance, as shown by the greater impulsivity of children with reading difficulties, learning disabilities, and school failure (Messer, 1976). However, there are a few tasks involving a large number of dimensions in which impulsive children are favored over reflective children (Rollins and Genser, 1977).

INDIVIDUAL DIFFERENCES IN COGNITIVE STYLE
Individuals differ in their typical mode for processing information—called cognitive style. Some students tend to be field-dependent and others field-independent. Further, some individuals proceed by slow deliberation, while others test by hypotheses quickly.

Since successful learning in most classroom settings requires attention to a task and careful consideration of the concepts to be mastered, impulsive children tend to be at a disadvantage. This is especially true of situations in which the correct answer is not immediately obvious or where concentrated attention is required as in beginning reading. Accordingly, educators have been interested in identifying strategies to assist children in altering their conceptual tempo to be able to achieve more effective learning.

The degree to which impulsivity is modifiable is the subject of some controversy (Messer, 1976; Margolis, Brannigan, and Poston, 1977; Isakson and Isakson, 1978). Nonetheless, it appears that the most effective means for aiding impulsives to be more attentive, contemplative, and accurate is to teach them the scanning methods employed by reflectives. The children are taught various search strategies by the use of materials that stress attention and the analysis of visual stimuli through the comparison of component parts. Simultaneously, the children are asked to speak aloud to themselves certain scanning instructions (for instance, "I have to look carefully at this one, then this one"). In contrast, strategies that merely have children delay their response have typically not been sufficient to help impulsive children to become reliably more reflective.

Matching Instructional Practice to Cognitive Style

Educators have shown considerable interest in finding applications for knowledge regarding cognitive styles in the classroom. The foremost question is whether matching instructional practice to

LEARNING STYLES AND TEACHING STYLES

Educators are paying increased attention to learning styles and teaching styles. *Style* refers to a pervasive quality in a person's behavior, a component that persists even when the content changes (Fischer and Fischer, 1979). People of all ages and intellectual capacities learn in ways that differ dramatically (Dunn and Dunn, 1979). Some require virtually complete silence in their environment when they are concentrating; others can "block out" extraneous sound; and still others need background sound when they are studying (they invariably turn on the radio or phonograph whenever they are attempting to learn something). Some students work and learn best alone and are distracted by other people; others achieve best in group settings with a large element of peer interaction. Some individuals appear to learn and remember best what they hear (an estimated 20 to 30 percent of school-age children are predominantly auditory); others are primarily visual (perhaps 40 percent); still others are either tactual/kinesthetic, visual/kinesthetic, or some combination of these senses (an estimated 30 to 40 percent).

What is sometimes overlooked is that teachers also have their preferred style of teaching (Fischer and Fischer, 1979). Indeed, what goes on in most classrooms depends more on the cognitive styles of teachers than on those of the students. Some teachers are primarily task oriented, prescribing the materials to be learned and demanding specific types of performance from the students. Others are group oriented, encouraging cooperative activities among classmates. Still others are child centered, allowing students considerable leeway in what they choose to do. These and other variations add up to enormous differences among teachers in both classroom orientation and practice.

Some educators, like Richard L. Turner (1979), dean of the University of Colorado's School of Education, point out that school organizations have traditionally made little effort to match the styles of learners to the styles of teachers. Turner says that this has been a positive strength. Over long periods of time students are exposed to many different teachers and teaching styles. Students encounter some teaching styles to which they can readily adapt and some with which they must struggle.

Other educators believe that teachers should do more to match instructional resources to student characteristics. They say teachers should expand their modes of operation to help students who have not responded to their prevalent strategies (Dunn and Dunn, 1979). For instance, teachers who prefer whole-class lectures and discussions can supplement their teaching methods with other techniques. Small groups can be formed for students who like to work with their peers. Self-motivated and persistent students who prefer working alone can be permitted to do so.

Although it is easy to suggest that teachers and students should be matched, most educators recognize there are dangers and limitations to such an approach. Learning style and teaching style characteristics do not necessarily cluster into neat packages. Neither students nor teachers are consistently one way or another. And most teachers can become effective with most students and simultaneously promote a humanistic classroom atmosphere.

cognitive style makes for better student learning (Saracho and Dayton, 1980). Some argue that ideally teachers should gear the schooling environment to each child's unique learning needs and preferences. They say that to do otherwise is to risk placing a student in a hostile environment that breeds frustration, hostility, and low motivation and, in the long run, impairs effective learning. These educators buttress their arguments with research that suggests that teachers tend to be more effective with students who match their cognitive style (DiStefano, 1970; Packer and Bain, 1978).

Other educators take a more cautious view. They question whether matching instruction to students' cognitive styles is desirable. These educators suggest that under some circumstances students should be exposed to a *challenge match,* one in which they find themselves in an uncongenial context so that they are compelled to deal with their area of weakness and gain appropriate coping mechanisms. For instance, field-dependent students favor material that is informational in content, while field-independent students prefer material that is theoretical and abstract (Witkin et al., 1977). Clearly, real-life situations confront individuals with circumstances requiring both kinds of responses. Hence, these educators say it would be a disservice to students to provide them with only those forms of instruction that are congenial with their cognitive style.

Further, it has been noted that field-independent students tend to have greater difficulty with social situations than do field-dependent students. This may require a *remedial match,* in which field-independent students are assisted in developing interpersonal skills. Other situations may call for a *compensatory match,* in which pupils are encouraged to counterbalance deficiencies in one skill by using other skills in which they are more proficient. Under these circumstances, a deficiency is left untouched, but its negative effects are circumvented. Thus, impulsive children may be encouraged to employ particular scanning or search strategies to compensate for their underlying impulsive tendencies.

Still another approach involves a *capitalization match,* in which pupils are encouraged to develop their strengths. It exploits a student's strong points. For instance, field-dependent students may be encouraged to major in those academic areas that take a global approach and field-independent students in areas requiring a high level of analytical reasoning. All of this highlights the fact that care must be exercised in deciding about the desirability of given matching strategies (see Chapter 17). Any strategy should be tentative, monitored, and verified in the course of ongoing interaction with the student.

CHAPTER SUMMARY

1. Many of the difficulties associated with the nature-nurture controversy derive from the fact that scientists operate from different models or basic assumptions. Various investigators have asked different questions and as a result have come up with different answers. The way we go about phrasing our questions presupposes certain alternatives in how the questions can be answered.

2. Scientists began by asking which factor, heredity or environment, was responsible for some trait, like a particular aptitude or personality characteristic. Later, they sought to determine how much of the observed differences among a population of people with respect to some trait are due to differences in heredity and how much to differences in environment. More recently, some scientists have inquired as to how specific hereditary and environmental factors interact to shape given outcomes.

3. Some psychologists define intelligence as the capacity to learn (profit from experience); others, as the ability to think abstractly; and still others, as the capability of integrating new experiences and adapting to new situations. And then there are those who say intelligence is whatever is measured

by an intelligence test. The problem all of us encounter in defining the term is that we never observe intelligence but only intelligent behavior. We infer an underlying capacity or trait from what a person says or does and call this intelligence.

4. Intelligence testing began in earnest with the development of the first individual intelligence test by Alfred Binet in 1905. However, it remained for Charles Spearman to propose that intelligence is largely a general intellectual capacity and that tests can be constructed to provide for a single pooled score across many items. Louis L. Thurstone refined and elaborated Spearman's procedures for analyzing specific factors that pertain to particular types of activity. He rejected the notion of general intelligence and instead focused upon groups of traits or factors. More recently, J. P. Guilford has proposed that there are 120 separate types of mental abilities.

5. Some psychologists make additional distinctions regarding intelligence. Raymond B. Cattell differentiates between fluid intelligence and crystallized intelligence. Fluid intelligence consists of a factor of general brightness or abstract mental efficiency that Cattell considers to be independent of schooling or cultural experience. Crystallized intelligence entails knowledge and skills that are acquired through cultural experience.

6. Psychologists usually surmise an individual's intelligence from the person's performance in a test setting involving various learning or problem-solving tasks. Intelligence tests seek to ascertain an individual's performance on a diverse sample of behaviors. As such, they serve as indicators or signs of a relatively open-ended list of activities.

7. Two of the most widely employed intelligence tests are the Stanford-Binet scales and the intelligence scales prepared by David Wechsler and his associates. In the Stanford-Binet tests, a series of tasks are arranged by age levels. They provide a global sampling of intelligence. In contrast, the tests developed by Wechsler contain separate verbal and nonverbal components. The items on the Wechsler tests are not organized into age levels, as with the Stanford-Binet. Rather, the items are graded in order of increasing difficulty within each subtest.

8. It is not possible to predict success in all of life's endeavors from a test designed primarily to predict academic success. The more the real-life situation differs from that of the school environment, the less valid the scores from intelligence tests will be in making predictions about an individual's future performance (and thus the less willing we should be to make inferences about the person's intelligence in a nonschool area of functioning).

9. Although IQ scores can assist teachers in developing realistic expectations of students, the scores should not be used to form fatalistic expectations. Teachers should be especially aware that IQ scores are less dependable for some of their students: those who come from minority group backgrounds, those who find school-related tasks relatively unmotivating, those who are weak in reading skills, and those who have problems in emotional adjustment.

10. Since psychologists disagree on what intelligence is, how to measure it, and how many intellectual factors there are, it is hardly surprising that they find themselves in disagreement about the relative part that heredity and environment play in producing individual differences in intelligence. Moreover, they differ in how to go about phrasing the nature-nurture question.

11. The debate surrounding racial differences in intelligence test scores is closely linked with the larger nature-nurture controversy. Jensen suggests that the average differences in IQ scores between blacks and whites may be attributable more to heredity than to environment. Many psychologists dispute this view. They assert that intelligence tests reflect white, urban, middle-class culture and linguistic usage.

12. Usually the problem of individual differences has been defined as one of distinguishing between ''fast'' and ''slow'' learners as determined by aptitude and achievement tests. But there are other differences among students that are also important. One group of individual differences distinguishable

from the IQ factor is cognitive style. Although psychologists have identified any number of cognitive styles, only a few have been extensively researched. Among these are field dependence-independence and reflection-impulsivity.

13. Field-independent people tend to analyze the individual elements making up a task or situation. They focus upon undertakings in an analytical manner, separating items from their backgrounds. In contrast, field-dependent people tend to categorize a task or situation in a global way. They focus upon the whole, overlooking the individual elements.

14. In various problem situations in which several possible alternatives are available, some children proceed by slow deliberation and make few errors. This is termed a reflective style. Other children test hypotheses quickly and make many errors. This is termed an impulsive style. The reflection-impulsivity dimension is concerned with the degree to which individuals reflect on the validity of their problem solutions under circumstances of high response uncertainty.

CHAPTER GLOSSARY

cognitive style   An individual's typical mode of processing information; the consistencies in an individual's ways of functioning in his or her day-to-day activities, especially relative to organizing and categorizing perceptions.

crystallized intelligence   Knowledge and skills acquired through cultural experience. Tests of general information, vocabulary, abstruse word analogies, and the mechanics of language are viewed as measures of crystallized intelligence.

field dependence   A cognitive style characterized by the tendency to categorize a task or situation in a global way. Individuals who are field-depend-

ent focus upon the whole, overlooking the individual elements.

field independence   A cognitive style characterized by the tendency to analyze the individual elements making up a task or situation. Individuals who are field-independent focus upon undertakings in an analytical manner, separating items from their backgrounds.

fluid intelligence   A factor of general brightness or abstract mental efficiency that is thought to be independent of schooling or cultural experience.

impulsive style   A cognitive style in which individuals test hypotheses quickly and make many errors.

intelligence   A person's ability to engage in new behaviors that solve problems without recourse to other people's instructions.

reflective style   A cognitive style in which individuals proceed by slow deliberation and make few errors.

two-factor theory of intelligence   An approach that views intelligence as consisting of two components: (1) a general or ''g'' factor that is employed for abstract reasoning and problem solving, and (2) special or ''s'' factors that are peculiar to given tasks.

EXERCISES

Review Questions

1. The set of behaviors assumed to have the most clearly established genetic relationship is
   a. intelligence test performance
   b. effects of PKU
   c. personality
   d. language skills

2. Binet's major contribution to intelligence testing was that

a. his instrument was the first intelligence test ever devised
b. the test was designed to identify a special group of students
c. the test provided a single intelligence test score
d. a and c are true
e. b and c are true

3. Which individual comes closest to the belief that intelligence is a single unitary trait?

a. Thurstone
b. Spearman
c. Cattell
d. Piaget

4. Which of the following items is *not* a component in Guilford's model of intelligence?

a. mental operations
b. content areas
c. "s" factors
d. products

5. Piaget differs from most other theoreticians regarding intelligence because he

a. claimed intelligence did not exist
b. insisted intelligence could not be measured
c. viewed intelligence in terms of process
d. was a strict environmentalist

6. Which of these statements about the Stanford-Binet test is true?

a. The items with which the examiner begins testing are generally those assigned for that child's age.
b. The ceiling age is the level at which the child fails the majority of items.
c. The child's IQ is derived by converting the mental age to a scale with a mean of 100 and a standard deviation of 16 points.
d. a, b, and c are true

7. What do the WAIS, the WISC, and the WPPSI have in common?

a. The tests yield both a verbal and nonverbal score.
b. Test items are organized by age levels.
c. The Wechsler scales usually provide more diagnostic information than the Stanford-Binet.
d. a, b, and c are true
e. a and c are true

8. Which of the following statements about IQ tests is false?

a. There is a strong relationship between IQ and school performance.
b. IQ scores can be used to predict performance in a wide variety of nonacademic situations.
c. IQ scores do not change.
d. Student emotional and motivational problems do not affect test performance.
e. b, c, and d are false

9. The cognitive styles of the more successful college student are likely to be

a. field-independent, impulsive
b. field-dependent, reflective
c. field-dependent, impulsive
d. field-independent, reflective

10. An impulsive child with specific learning problems is placed with a teacher who has a history of success in overcoming these problems. This would be an example of a

a. challenge match
b. remedial match
c. compensatory match
d. capitalization match

Answers

1. b (See p. 103)   6. c (See p. 108)
2. e (See pp. 105–106) 7. e (See pp. 108–109)
3. b (See p. 106)   8. e (See pp. 109–110)
4. c (See p. 106)   9. d (See pp. 115–116)
5. c (See p. 107)   10. b (See pp. 116, 118)

Applying Principles and Concepts

1. Suppose you have been presented with data on three pairs of children: Although the sets are unidentified, you know one consists of identical twins, another of same-sex fraternal twins, and the third of same-sex children drawn at random from their own age group.

Following is a list of traits. For each pair indicate whether the children are likely to be very similar (V), moderately similar (M), or unalike (U) with respect to each trait.

Trait	Pairs		
	Identical	Fraternal	Random
a. Height and weight	_____	_____	_____
b. Susceptibility to diphtheria	_____	_____	_____
c. Interest in hobbies	_____	_____	_____
d. Language acquisition	_____	_____	_____

2. Teachers usually react to certain pupil behaviors as indicators of intelligence. Place a checkmark in Column 1 for those behaviors that, if the child deviates markedly from the average, are likely to lead to a more favorable or negative estimate of intelligence. Place a checkmark in Column 2 if the ability can be tested *directly* by the Stanford-Binet.

	Column 1	Column 2
a. Verbal ability	_____	_____
b. Social ability	_____	_____
c. Scholastic achievement	_____	_____
d. Cognitive style	_____	_____
e. Motor dexterity	_____	_____

3. You have the Stanford-Binet IQ scores for four eleven-year-old children from different family backgrounds. Using the following chart, indicate in Column 1 whether the child is classified as above average (AA), average (A), or below average (BA) in intelligence. In Column 2 place a checkmark if you suspect that the score may not adequately reflect the child's intelligence.

	Column 1	Column 2
a. Mexican-American, migrant workers—90	_____	_____
b. White, reading disability—80	_____	_____
c. Black, professional parents—135	_____	_____
d. White, blue-collar workers—110	_____	_____

4. A local school board is caught up in a busing situation. A parent who is adamantly opposed makes the following remarks. Underline those that can be substantiated by research.

> Jensen has found that on most of the commonly used IQ tests, blacks average about 15 points less than whites. These widely used tests are clearly free of cultural bias. Most psychologists accept these findings as evidence of the fact that IQ is an inherited trait. Regardless of where they come from or what they do, blacks score lower than whites. Improvements in education have had little impact on blacks' intelligence test performance.

5. In your school you have the following students who have the relationships indicated. Rank from 1 (highest) to 4 (lowest) the similarity in intelligence test scores that might be expected.

Children	Relationship	*Rank*
a. Tom and Bill (age 12)	Fraternal twins	_____
b. Norma and Ann (ages 15 and 17, respectively)	Sisters	_____
c. John and Betty (age 10)	Brother and stepsister	_____
d. Jenna and Amanda (age 13)	Identical twins	_____

6. As a high-school counselor interested in learning styles, you have to help students decide on academic careers in college. You have field dependence-independence and reflective-impulse scores on five students. In Column 1 their chosen academic fields are listed. In Column 2 indicate with "yes" or "no" whether or not the student has made an appropriate choice, assuming you are emphasizing a capitalization match.

Student	Column 1: Academic Area	Column 2: Decision
a. Dependent-reflective	History	_____
b. Dependent-impulsive	Math	_____
c. Independent-reflective	Physics	_____
d. Independent-reflective	Sociology	_____
e. Dependent-reflective	English	_____

Answers

1. a, Identical (V), Fraternal (M), Random (U); b, Identical (V), Fraternal (M), Random (U); c, Identical (V or M), Fraternal (V or M), Random (U); d, Identical (V or M), Fraternal (M or U), Random (U) (See pp. 101–104)
2. a, Column 1—check, Column 2—check; b, Column 1—no check, Column 2—no check; c, Column 1—check, Column 2—no check (the Stanford-Binet does not directly measure achievement); d, Column 1—check (but impulsive children sometimes are penalized on estimates of intelligence because achievement tends to be lower), Column 2—no check; e, Column 1—no check, Column 2—no check (See pp. 104–108)
3. a, Column 1—A, Column 2—check; b, Column 1—BA, Column 2—check; c, Column 1—AA, Column 2—no check; d, Column 1—A, Column 2—no check (but depends on ambitions of parents; general statement cannot be made for this group) (See pp. 109–114)
4. Underline "Jensen has found that on most of the commonly used IQ tests, blacks average about 15 points lower than whites." (See pp. 113–114)
5. a, 2; b, 3; c, 4; d, 1 (See pp. 110–112)
6. a, yes; b, no; c, yes; d, no; e, yes (See pp. 114–116, 118)

Project

OBJECTIVE: To explore the kinds of student behaviors a teacher uses to estimate a child's intelligence. The project can be conducted either in a school or with peers.

PROCEDURE:

In a school:

1. Visit one or two elementary school classrooms. Ask the teacher what kinds of behavior (aside from IQ testing) he or she uses to gain estimates of a child's intelligence.
2a. Put these behaviors in a list. Visit two other teachers (or parents), and ask them to rank on a 5-point scale (5 = very important to 1 = unimportant) how much these traits influence their judgment of a child's intelligence.
2b. Then ask each teacher to think of one pupil whom he or she considers very bright and one who is slow. Have the teacher go through your list and indicate those behaviors in which the child deviates markedly positively (+) or negatively (−) from the norm. *Do not let the teacher see his or her previous rankings of importance.*

With peers:

1. Conduct a discussion with your peers. Ask them what kinds of behavior (aside from IQ tests) they use to estimate another individual's intelligence.
2. Ask each individual to rank his or her behaviors on a sheet.
3. Collect the behavior rankings and assemble a complete list of behaviors and relative importance.

ANALYSIS: In a school project, if the teachers are consistent, behaviors scaled 4 or 5 should be those marked by a + or − . If this is indeed the case, then the teachers are consistent in their observations. If not, then ask the teachers what other kinds of pupil behaviors they use in their assessments.

In a project with peers, the behaviors and rankings should provide an estimate of the kinds of observations (and biases) others are likely to have. Discuss the implications for minority students and other nontraditional groups.

PART
TWO

LEARNING

CHAPTER OUTLINE

5

CONDITIONING AND OBSERVATIONAL LEARNING

CHAPTER PREVIEW

The preceding three chapters have focused on characteristics of the *learner*. In the next several chapters, attention is shifted to *learning,* to the process of acquiring new behaviors, skills, or ideas through experience with the world, whether in school or out. Several theories have been offered to explain or describe how learning occurs. This chapter discusses three learning theories associated with the concept of behavorism. Two of these are conditioning theories—classical conditioning and operant conditioning. The third, a more recently developed theory, examines observational or social learning. Major components of these theories are listed in the chapter outline. The principles underlying these theories can help teachers understand how their actions affect students' behavior, and vice versa.

Consider the following questions as you read:

■ What are the differences between classical and operant conditioning?
■ How can operant conditioning be used to modify students' classroom behavior?

■ How are the principles of reinforcement and punishment different? Which do you think would be more effective in the classroom? Why?
■ How does observational learning differ from conditioning?
■ What are some implications of observational learning for educational practice?

Learning is a fundamental process within our lives. It allows us to adapt to our environment by building on previous experience. As we interact with others and the world about us, we acquire knowledge that enables us to modify our behavior. Through our successes and failures in coping with our life circumstances, we derive an accumulating body of information that serves to guide our decisions and our actions.

Psychologists have traditionally defined learning in terms of three criteria. First, there must be some *change* in behavior. Second, this change must be relatively *stable*. And third, the change must result from *experience* (Stallings, 1973; Hall, 1976). In brief, **learning** is a relatively permanent change in behavior or capability that results from experience. It is a process that we infer from the relatively stable changes that occur in an individual's behavior through interaction with the environment. Hence, learning is a special kind of change in behavior. It does not include those changes having to do with growth processes or with temporary conditions such as fatigue or the influence of drugs.

Both psychologists and educators are concerned with learning. Psychologists are primarily interested in determining how people *learn*. Educators direct their energies toward finding efficient ways of *teaching* them (Zimmerman and Kleefeld, 1977). Although learning and teaching are different processes, they are nonetheless sufficiently related so that educators can benefit from knowing how children learn.

Theories of learning fall into three broad categories: conditioning theories, observational (imitation) theories, and cognitive theories. These conceptions of the learning process have value for organizing educators' ideas about teaching. The theories highlight the kinds of influence that teachers can exert in facilitating learning. They can (1) condition students; (2) provide a model for imitation by students; and (3) change the cognitive structure by which students think about their en-

LEARNING
Learning is said to occur when a relatively permanent change in behavior results from experience.

vironment (Gage, 1972). This chapter will deal with the first and second types. The next chapter will examine the third type of learning.

CLASSICAL CONDITIONING

The basic condition for the formation of a conditioned reflex is, generally speaking, a single or repeated coincidence of an indifferent stimulus with the unconditioned one. The formation of the reflex is quickest and meets with least difficulties when the first stimulus directly precedes the second.

IVAN PAVLOV
Big Medical Encyclopedia, 1934

During this century a number of ideas, termed **behaviorism,** have dominated much of psychological thinking and educational practice. Viewed from a behaviorist perspective, learning results primarily from some external happening. Behaviorism focuses on the activities of humans—their "doings and sayings," in brief, on how people *behave.* Traditionally, behaviorists have segmented *behavior* into units called **responses** and divided the *environment* into units called **stimuli.** Behaviorist theory emphasizes two types of learning: (1) classical, or respondent, conditioning and (2) operant, or instrumental, conditioning. Let us consider each in turn.

The Experiments of Ivan Pavlov

Classical conditioning is based upon the work of Ivan Pavlov (1849–1936), a Russian physiologist. Pavlov had gained international renown and a Nobel Prize earlier in his career for his work dealing with the role gastric juices play in digestion. In this research, Pavlov measured the secretions produced in the stomachs of dogs by meat powder. In the course of this work, he noticed that when he began working with a dog, the dog would salivate only when food was placed in its mouth. But with the passage of time, the dog's mouth would water *before* it tasted the food. Moreover, the mere sight of the food or the sound of the experimenter's footsteps would cause salivation.

Pavlov became intrigued by the anticipatory flow of saliva in the dogs, a phenomenon he called "psychic secretion." Against the advice of some of his colleagues, he shifted the focus of his research so as to delve into this puzzling matter. He saw the study of "psychic secretions" as a powerful and objective means for investigating the mechanisms by which organisms adapt to their environment. Pavlov devised a series of experiments in which he rang a bell just before feeding a dog. After doing this on a number of occasions, the dog's mouth would water at the sound of the bell even though food did not follow.

In his experiments, Pavlov dealt with a behavior that is biologically preprogrammed within a dog through genetic inheritance: the salivation reflex. The reflex is an involuntary and unlearned response that is automatically activated by a particular stimulus, the presence of food in the mouth. By pairing the sound of the bell with food, Pavlov established a *new* relationship or connection between a stimulus (the sound of the bell) and a response (salivation) that had not previously existed. This phenomenon is termed **classical conditioning**—a process of stimulus substitution in which a new, previously neutral stimulus is substituted for the stimulus that naturally elicits the response.

Pavlov's experiments resulted in a number of concepts being utilized to describe classical conditioning:

- **Unconditioned stimulus (UCS):** The stimulus that naturally elicits a particular response. In Pavlov's experiment, the unconditioned stimulus was the presence of food in the dog's mouth.
- **Unconditioned response (UCR):** The unlearned, biologically preprogrammed reaction evoked by an unconditioned stimulus—salivation in Pavlov's experiment.
- **Conditioned stimulus (CS):** A previously neutral stimulus that acquires the property of elic-

NEUTRAL STIMULI

Most stimuli are neutral. Children learn positive or negative responses on the basis of their conditioning experiences. Hence, this child does not find a jack-o-lantern frightening.

iting a particular response through being paired during training with an unconditioned stimulus. Pavlov employed a bell as the conditioned stimulus in his experiment.

- **Conditioned response (CR):** A response aroused by some stimulus other than the one that naturally produces it. After a number of pairings

with the unconditioned stimulus, the conditioned stimulus elicits a response similar to that evoked by the unconditioned stimulus—salivation in the case of Pavlov's dogs. (See Figure 5.1.)

The "Little Albert" Study

In 1920, John B. Watson and Rosalie Rayner reported on a study they had conducted demonstrating that humans can learn through classical conditioning. They succeeded in experimentally producing a fear reaction in "Little Albert":

> This infant was reared almost from birth in a hospital environment; his mother was a wet nurse in the Harriet Lane Home for Invalid Children. Albert's life was normal: he was healthy from birth and one of the best developed youngsters ever brought to the hospital. . . . At approximately nine months of age we ran him through the emotional tests that have become part of our regular routine in determining whether fear reactions can be called out by other stimuli than sharp noises and the sudden removal of support. . . . The infant was confronted . . . with a white rat, a rabbit, a dog, a monkey, with masks with and without hair, cotton wool, burning newspapers, etc. . . . At no time did this infant ever show fear in any situation. [1920:1–2]

The researchers did find, however, that when Watson would hit a steel bar with a hammer behind Albert, the child would exhibit a fear reflex: Albert would startle, check his breathing, and cry. Thus, for their experiment, Watson and Rayner decided to employ a loud noise as the unconditioned stimulus and the fear reaction as the unconditioned response.

Two months later, when Albert was eleven months of age, Watson again presented him with a white rat (the neutral stimulus that was to become the conditioned stimulus). Once more Albert showed no fear and reached for the animal. But this time, whenever Albert reached for the rat, Watson would

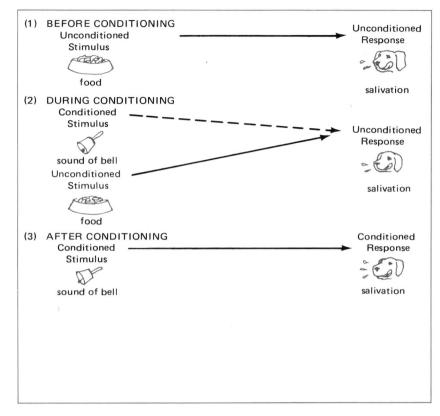

(1) BEFORE CONDITIONING
Unconditioned
Stimulus

food

Unconditioned
Response

salivation

(2) DURING CONDITIONING
Conditioned
Stimulus

sound of bell
Unconditioned
Stimulus

food

Unconditioned
Response

salivation

(3) AFTER CONDITIONING
Conditioned
Stimulus

sound of bell

Conditioned
Response

salivation

FIGURE 5.1 CLASSICAL CONDITIONING PROCEDURES
An unconditioned stimulus, such as food, is provided the dog, causing a reflex reaction, such as salivating (unconditioned response). A neutral (conditioned) stimulus, one that does not produce an unconditioned response (such as the sound of a bell), is presented to the dog *prior* to the presentation of the unconditioned stimulus: neutral (conditioned) stimulus → unconditioned stimulus → response. After the conditioned stimulus and the unconditioned stimulus have been paired a number of times, the conditioned stimulus becomes capable of eliciting the response in the absence of the unconditioned stimulus, and the dog will salivate. The previously unconditioned response becomes a conditioned response linked to the conditioned stimulus.

strike a steel bar with a hammer immediately behind the child's head. At such times, Albert would display a marked fear reflex. After only five trials pairing the noise and the rat, Albert would show fear when exposed to the rat alone. He would cry, bury his face in a mattress, and crawl away rapidly. Further, his fear of the rat generalized to other furry objects and animals such as a sealskin fur coat, cotton wool, a Santa Claus mask, a dog, and Watson's hairy head. Retests on subsequent occasions showed that the fear reactions persisted. It should be emphasized that such a study would now be viewed as highly unethical and in direct violation of the standards of the American Psychological Association.

Classical Conditioning in the Classroom

Many of the emotional responses that children show in school settings are learned through conditioning (Ringness, 1976). Kindergarten youngsters who are met during the first week of school by a teacher who greets them individually by name, gives every child a friendly smile and a warm embrace, and provides each with a positive comment may eagerly come to anticipate school on subsequent mornings. The greetings, smiles, embraces, and comments function as the unconditioned stimulus. The children's pleasant emotional feelings are the unconditioned response. The classroom setting, the previously neutral stimulus, then comes to be associated with the unconditioned stimulus and elicits similar pleasant feelings.

Following are listed three illustrations of situations that could be explained by the principles of conditioning. In each case try to identify the unconditioned stimulus, the conditioned stimulus, the unconditioned response, and the conditioned response:

■ A capable student develops intense nausea associated with fear when confronted with a test situation. Two years earlier, when a second-grader, the girl had a teacher who kept in from recess those students who did poorly on an assignment and assigned them extra studying.

■ A boy of small size and slender build has developed anxiety about physical education from being compelled to compete against stronger and bigger boys.

■ A fifth-grader has developed stage fright when asked to give a presentation before the class as a result of being laughed at on earlier occasions when reading orally before his reading group.

In these illustrations, being held in from recess, bigger children, and the laughter of the reading group may be interpreted as the unconditioned stimulus. The nausea, anxiety, and fright can be

FASHIONING EMOTIONAL RESPONSES TOWARD THE SCHOOL SETTING
How teachers meet their students during the first few days of the new school year sets the tone for how students will feel about their school experience during the weeks and months ahead.

interpreted as the unconditioned response. The previously neutral test situation, physical education, and class presentation (the conditioned stimulus) are associated with the unconditioned stimulus and come to elicit nausea, anxiety, and stage fright (the conditioned response).

One way teachers can assist students to deal with these types of difficulties is to have them engage in the situations, as opposed to avoiding them, and while doing so to provide the children with pleasant stimuli. Thomas A. Ringness (1976:455) cites the following techniques that he has employed among junior- and senior-high-school students:

> 1. For test anxiety, such prior activities as teaching how to take tests, dry runs on practice tests, careful explanations of what tests would be like, study hints, and the use of many small tests rather than a few important ones.
> 2. For stage fright, gradual entry into the situation, such as having band students (who freeze at the thought of playing a solo) first play as members of a small combo; later as a quartet, trio, or duet; and finally all alone.
> 3. For biology students who fear snakes, the use of fearless students as models in picking up harmless snakes, with discussions of how the snake might feel . . . , and gradual movement toward picking him up by feeling his dry skin as others hold him.

If teachers are aware of conditioning processes, they may employ them in assisting their students. If they are doubtful or unsuccessful, they should obtain the aid of the school psychologist or guidance counselor.

OPERANT CONDITIONING

Any act which in a given situation produces satisfaction becomes associated with that situation so that when the situation recurs the act is more likely than before to recur also.

EDWARD L. THORNDIKE
The Elements of Psychology, 1907

Classical conditioning depends on the prior existence of a reflex that can be mustered in the service of a new stimulus. Dogs automatically salivate when food is placed in their mouths. Accordingly, Pavlov was able to effect a connection between the sound of a bell and salivation. But the conditioning of reflexes does not take us very far in training a dog or any other organism. Usually, we lack some preexisting unconditioned stimulus with which we can link a new stimulus. Thus, much behavior is not acquired through classical conditioning.

The Nature of Operant Conditioning

What alternative mechanism exists for conditioning organisms? Consider how we teach a dog to "beg." With one hand we press the dog steadily and firmly down by its haunches into a sitting position; simultaneously, we lift the dog's paws off the floor by pulling upwards on its collar. We then reward the dog with a morsel of food. This procedure entails first getting the dog to *enact* the behavior as well as we can and then rewarding it with food; the food *follows* the response. But in classical conditioning of the sort undertaken by Pavlov, the food comes *before* the response.

In teaching a dog to beg we employ **operant conditioning**—a type of learning in which the *consequences* of a behavior alter the strength of that behavior. We term *operants* those behaviors that are susceptible to control by changing the effects that follow them; they are responses that "operate" (act) upon the environment and generate consequences. Hence, when a hungry dog engages in behavior that *produces* food, the behavior is strengthened by this consequence and therefore is more likely to recur (Skinner, 1974). This is not true with classical conditioning, since it is the food that *produces* the behavior of salivation.

In sum, classical conditioning derives from preexisting reflexes; operant conditioning does not.

In classical conditioning a stimulus is said to *elicit* the response, whereas in operant conditioning the response is *emitted*. In classical conditioning the response probability is determined by antecedents; in operant conditioning it is determined by consequences (see Table 5.1).

The Work of Thorndike and Skinner

Edward L. Thorndike (1874–1949), a pioneer American psychologist, is usually credited with developing many of the experimental procedures that are used in studying operant conditioning. He would place a hungry cat in a specially designed "puzzle box." When the cat accidentally tugged at a loop of string suspended inside the box, the door opened, allowing the animal to escape and secure a piece of fish. After several trials, a cat would progressively reduce the time needed to escape, evidence that "trial-and-error" learning had occurred. From this research, Thorndike formulated the *Law of Effect:* The strength of a stimulus-response connection is increased when the response is followed by a satisfying state of affairs.

B. F. Skinner (born 1904) deserves credit for building upon Thorndike's formulations and de-

veloping even more sophisticated experimental procedures. In a survey conducted in 1967 among heads of college psychology departments, Skinner was selected as the most influential American psychologist of the twentieth century (Myers, 1970). Over the past forty years, college students enrolled in psychology courses have become familiar with Skinner's famous experimental chamber termed a "Skinner box." It is a direct descendant of the puzzle box used by Thorndike.

The Skinner box provides a soundproof enclosure that isolates the subject—a rat, mouse, or pigeon—from distracting outside stimuli. When the subject presses a lever or pecks a key (a disk) in an accidental or exploratory fashion, a food pellet is released (simultaneously, a counting device also electrically records the learning event). In the course of its random activity, the subject sooner or later again activates the feeder mechanism. As this process is repeated over time, the subject "learns" to press the lever or peck the key in order to receive the reward. Skinner's ideas and research have provided the basis for the programmed instruction movement and for behavior modification procedures, topics to be considered in later chapters.

However, we need to exercise caution in carrying over findings regarding the behavior of pigeons (or other organisms) to that of human beings

TABLE 5.1

Comparison of Classical and Operant Conditioning

Characteristic	Classical Conditioning	Operant Conditioning
Stimulus-response sequence	The stimulus precedes the response.	The response occurs prior to the effect (reward).
Role of stimulus	The response is elicited.	The response is emitted.
Specificity of the stimulus	A specific stimulus results in a particular response.	No specific stimulus produces a particular response.
Process	One stimulus substitutes for another.	A substitution in stimuli does not take place.
Content	Emotions such as fears are primarily involved.	Goal-seeking activity is primarily involved.

BEHAVIORS OF THE OPERANT VARIETY
Among the behaviors teachers wish to establish among their students is the practice of raising their hands and waiting to be called on before speaking aloud. This type of behavior is illustrative of operant conditioning.

(Locurto, Terrace, and Gibbon, 1981). For instance, pecking is peculiar to pigeons (and other birds) in feeding situations. An organism's biology (through preprogramming) contributes to how and what it learns. Thus psychologists are increasingly coming to discover that biology has been contributing all along to studies that were presumed to have eliminated biology as a significant factor (Schwartz, 1981). Psychologists term this phenomenon *autoshaping,* for automatic shaping.

Nonetheless, despite this reservation, educational psychologists have found the concept of operant conditioning a useful analytical tool. Donald L. MacMillan points out that most of the behavior that teachers want to modify in students is of the operant variety. In other words, the acts are emitted by children rather than being elicited by stimuli in the classroom. Among the problems encountered by teachers that are susceptible to modification by operant conditioning are the following: (1) How can I assist children to stop emitting a particular behavior? (2) How can I assist children to emit a new behavior that they as yet have not evidenced? and (3) How can I assist children to emit a particular behavior (for instance, a reading skill) more frequently? The boxed insert on pages 136–137 contains examples of the use of operant conditioning in the classroom.

OPERANT CONDITIONING CAN WORK

RAYMOND BOTTOM

Administrative Assistant for Elementary Education
in the Monroe Public Schools, Michigan

In the great search to find ways to motivate and teach children, educators often reject the theory of operant conditioning. They feel that giving a material reward to reinforce a positive response is merely bribing the child. But this attitude leads them to turn their backs on a psychologically sound approach for increasing achievement motivation. Nowhere is the value of operant conditioning seen more clearly than in working with so-called disadvantaged children—children whom teachers label "unreachable."

Operant conditioning has been put into action in Lincoln School, Monroe, Michigan. One example is sixth-grade teacher Walter Grams's "Cloud Nine vs. Doghouse" project.

"An inordinate amount of time," he says, "was being taken up with matters of discipline. I was looking for something that would reward positive performance and at the same time allow each student to

Source: Raymond Bottom, "Operant Conditioning Can Work," *Instructor,* 81 (February 1972):128F–134.

assume responsibility for his own behavior."

Mr. Grams's system works in this manner: The children and the teacher agree upon a list of positive behavior characteristics and performance criteria in subject areas that will gain the youngsters points in "Cloud Nine." A corresponding list of negative behavior characteristics and poor performance standards—for both quantity and quality—will give them points in the "Doghouse." At the beginning of the school year, each student is given a certain number of points in "Cloud Nine." From that point, he accumulates more points in "Cloud Nine," or loses them to the "Doghouse." At the end of each week, students with a point total equal to or larger than their starting number in "Cloud Nine" receive a small reward such as a pencil, eraser, or candy bar. At the end of the month, the boy and the girl with the highest number of points each receive a "major" prize of a model airplane, paint set, or similar item, and the "game" starts all over.

"I don't believe the total cost of

the prizes for the year exceeded twenty dollars," Mr. Grams said, "but it saved me untold hours of instruction time that otherwise would have gone into classroom control."

The time given to discipline with disadvantaged pupils is a factor no teacher can afford to ignore. A colleague of Mr. Grams feels that one of the greatest crimes perpetrated by teachers in schools serving the disadvantaged is the disproportionate time they spend on class discipline. "While they scold or spend time with their problem cases, the rest of the kids sit idle, either enjoying the show or building greater resentments and hostilities toward teachers."

Another weekly feature of Mr. Grams's project is that children each earn time in a "private corner." While the student is in the private corner he can do as he wishes, as long as it doesn't infringe on the rights of others. "After a while," Mr. Grams says, "the private corner was more popular than any other reward."

Several colleagues of Walter

Grams tried their own versions of operant conditioning. A second-grade teacher was highly successful in math and spelling through the use of performance contracts. Each week a contract was signed by both teacher and student, specifying how many problems would be done, or how many words would be spelled, at an 85 percent mastery level. Paper money was given for successful daily performances. At the end of the week the money was exchanged for marbles and balloons.

"The change was amazing," the teacher said. "Children who hadn't finished three pages of math a week were suddenly doing three or four pages a day.

"I think the early grades are the place to start," she added. "The kids are still enthusiastic about small rewards. When they find they can succeed, the paper money and prizes become less important than doing good work."

A fifth-grade teacher, capitalizing on his students' interest in space exploration, contracted for "moon dust," which could be exchanged, when a pint container was filled, for inexpensive models, pictures, toys, or books relating to space.

A teaspoonful of "moon dust" (gathered from the teacher's garden) was given for each assignment completed at an 80 percent mastery level. Each month those students successfully filling a container were inducted into the "Space Explorers Club" and their pictures placed on a moon suspended from the room ceiling.

Filled containers were labeled and kept on a shelf. Thus, children had concrete evidence of what they had accomplished, and the added incentive of seeing how many containers they could fill in a year.

"The moon dust became so important," the teacher said, "that the children carried it home at the end of the year as a prized possession."

On the basis of successful application by various teachers in Lincoln School, it was decided to use performance contracts in a summer program with 288 disadvantaged children, grades three to seven, in the areas of math and reading.

A cardboard coin was given for each page of math and each reading worksheet successfully completed by a student. The standards of performance were worked out between the teacher and student, to allow for individual differences. Each Friday the tokens were exchanged for a choice of various five-cent items. At the program's conclusion, all points earned by each student were tallied and the top point gainer in each group of six was awarded a "major" prize, valued at less than a dollar.

The teachers were uniform in their praise of the results.

"I've taught in summer school for five years," one teacher remarked, "and I've never seen kids work so hard and attend so well."

A seventh-grade teacher observed: "This is a good thing because it allows the students to share in decision making and assume personal responsibility for their own efforts. My students kept a daily progress chart which soon became their major concern."

His observation was substantiated by a sixth-grade teacher's evaluation. "Letting these students help set goals is essential if you want their cooperation. They aren't going to accept everything a teacher says just because he thinks it's important. One boy asked me: 'Why do we have to do these problems?' So I told him. He said, 'You're the first teacher that ever explained why.' "

Some other representative comments were:

"One caution: Don't set the standards too low. They'll fool you with what they can do when a reward is waiting."

"Operant conditioning," points out a veteran teacher, "is not a panacea for all these youngsters' learning problems. But it does encourage them to try, and that's an important step."

BASIC CONCEPTS AND PROCESSES OF CONDITIONING

Operant conditioning involves a variety of processes. These include reinforcement, shaping, extinction, stimulus generalization, and stimulus discrimination. In the typical classroom, they come together to weave a complex and integrated totality that constitutes learning. Some of the processes, particularly extinction, stimulus generalization, and stimulus discrimination, also occur within classical conditioning.

Reinforcement

When a bit of behavior is followed by a certain kind of consequence, it is more likely to occur again, and a consequence having this effect is called a reinforcer.

B. F. SKINNER
Beyond Freedom and Dignity, 1971

Reinforcement plays a critical role in conditioning an organism. The term refers to any event that strengthens the probability of a particular response. Two centuries ago Benjamin Franklin recognized the usefulness of reinforcement procedures for modifying behavior. A minister on a ship complained to Franklin that the sailors rarely attended prayer meetings. Franklin suggested that the minister take charge of passing out the daily ration of rum and that the brew be dispensed immediately after the prayers. The minister took Franklin's advice and "never were prayers more generally and more punctually attended" (Franklin, 1969).

Most teachers and parents are aware that rewarding a child for a behavior reinforces that behavior. Usually overlooked, however, is that a *chance,* or unplanned occurrence following a response, may also strengthen the response, often with undesirable consequences. For example, in nursery school a teacher may observe a little boy screaming, throwing himself down, and banging his head against the floor. Alarmed, the teacher may rush over to the child, pick him up, utter soothing words, and affectionately ask the child not to carry on in the same way in the future. It should not come as a surprise to us if the child later repeats the behavior; the response of screaming and banging his head was reinforced by attention, affection, and physical contact. The teacher overlooked the effect of his or her behavior. Parents do much the same thing when they give attention to children only when they whine or provoke attention through antisocial behavior (Hall and Lindzey, 1970; Budd, Green, and Baer, 1976).

Psychologists distinguish between the principle of reinforcement and the principle of punishment (Skinner, 1953; Craighead, Kazdin, and Mahoney, 1976). The **principle of reinforcement** refers to an *increase* in the frequency of a response when it is followed by a contingent or associated stimulus. The **principle of punishment** refers to a *decrease* in the frequency of a response when it is followed by a contingent or associated stimulus. As portrayed in Figure 5.2, there are two types of reinforcement and two types of punishment.

Students often confuse the *principle* of reinforcement with the *stimulus* (the event) that follows a behavior, termed either a *positive reinforcer* or a *negative reinforcer*. The principle of reinforcement entails an increase in the frequency of a response when either a positive reinforcer is applied or a negative reinforcer is withdrawn. The principle of punishment involves a decrease in the frequency of a response when either a positive reinforcer is withdrawn or a negative reinforcer is applied.

Positive Reinforcers

A **positive reinforcer** is a stimulus that, when applied following a behavior, strengthens the probability of the behavior's future occurrence. Something (food, water, personal contact, or the like) is *added* to the situation. Positive reinforcers play a prominent and varied role in education. Indeed,

STIMULUS	APPLIED	TERMINATED
POSITIVE REINFORCER	POSITIVE REINFORCEMENT An increase occurs in the frequency of a response.	PUNISHMENT BY REMOVAL A decrease occurs in the frequency of a response.
NEGATIVE REINFORCER	PUNISHMENT BY APPLICATION A decrease occurs in the frequency of a response.	NEGATIVE REINFORCEMENT An increase occurs in the frequency of a response.

FIGURE 5.2 STIMULUS-RESPONSE RELATIONSHIPS
Positive reinforcement entails the application of a positive reinforcer and results in a response occurring more often. *Negative reinforcement* involves the withdrawal of a negative reinforcer and results in an increase in the incidence of a response. *Punishment by removal* entails the withdrawal of a positive reinforcer and results in a response occurring less often. *Punishment by application* involves the adding of a negative reinforcer and results in a decrease in the incidence of a response.

IMPROVING INTERGROUP RELATIONS
Positive reinforcers can be a powerful tool in effecting better intergroup relations among children of different racial groups.

teachers can consciously employ positive reinforcers to realize a wide variety of goals. Consider by way of illustration the following example (Hauserman, Walen, and Behling, 1973).

A first-grade teacher found that in her class of twenty white students and five black students, the black children were consistently isolated from the white children in social activities. To encourage integrated interaction, the teacher decided that some prompting mechanism was necessary:

> For four consecutive school days as children lined up in their room before walking to the cafeteria, the teacher announced a game whereby children would eat lunch with a "new friend." She produced a hat containing pairs of children's names. The teacher encouraged all children "to sit in the cafeteria and to eat with your new friend." Each black pupil was paired with a white child and consistent cliques of white pupils were mixed and paired with other white pupils. [1973:195]

The teacher made no reference to race but rather centered her remarks about "new friends."

When the children were seated in the cafeteria and eating their lunches, the teacher went to each table and noted: "Good! I'm glad you are sitting with your new friend." She then provided each child with a pink ticket shaped in the form of an oak leaf and said, "This is for sitting with a new friend today. Later on, at recess, you give me your pink tag, and I will give you something good to eat." When the thirty-minute lunch period was nearly ended, the teacher gave each child who had remained together with a "new friend" a second ticket entitling the child to an additional treat.

The experimental conditions were extended for an additional nine days. However, the teacher no longer used the names-in-the-hat technique. She simply encouraged the children to "sit and eat with friends" and continued the procedure of reinforcing the "new friend" behavior with oak leaf tickets and treats. As a consequence of the reinforcement program, interracial behavior in free-time play tripled during the experimental period.

Negative Reinforcers

A **negative reinforcer** is a stimulus that, when *removed* following a behavior, strengthens the probability of its future occurrence. Something (a loud noise, a blinding light, extreme heat or cold, an electric shock, or the like) is *removed* from the situation. For instance, taking two aspirin to relieve a headache is negatively reinforced by the termination of pain. Psychologists distinguish between reinforcers according to whether their presentation or removal strengthens a preceding behavior. In the case of a negative reinforcer, the organism learns something in order to *escape* some consequence (Hilgard and Bower, 1975).

Punishment

Whereas reinforcement (both positive and negative) involves the strengthening of a response, punishment is designed to *weaken* a response. In reinforcement, the frequency of the response increases; in **punishment,** it decreases. Within the United States, people tend to place a good deal of faith in the effectiveness of punishment. They spank their children, fine or imprison lawbreakers, and withhold the salaries of malingering employees. Nonetheless, considerable controversy exists among psychologists and educators regarding the effectiveness and ethics of punishment, matters that will be considered at length in Chapter 16.

Students often confuse punishment with negative reinforcement. Both concepts are defined solely in terms of the *effect* they have upon behavior. Hence, punishment produces a *reduction* in the frequency of a response, whereas negative reinforcement results in an *increase* in the incidence of a response. Punishment is of two types: punishment by *application* and punishment by *removal*. Punishment by application involves bringing an aversive stimulus (negative reinforcer) to bear following a response, for instance, a spanking. Punishment by removal entails bringing about a loss of a positive reinforcer, for instance, losing privileges, having a driver's license revoked, and being fined money

A CLASSROOM EPISODE: REINFORCEMENT AND PUNISHMENT

TRANSCRIPT

Mr. Larson was teaching a seventh-grade biology class about the circulatory system. On his desk was a plastic model of a heart. He removed the aorta from the model, held it up before the class, and said, "Who can tell me what this is?" Bret's hand darted up, and Mr. Larson nodded toward him. Bret responded, "The aorta." Mr. Larson smiled at Bret, walked over to his desk, and handed Bret the plastic piece representing the aorta. "Do you think you can place the aorta back in its proper position?" Bret replaced the aorta. Mr. Larson muttered, "Good! Good job!" while patting Bret on the shoulder.

Out of the corner of his eye, Mr. Larson detected Marie with her head down on her desk and her eyes closed. Without uttering a word, he picked up a yardstick, walked over to Marie's desk, and whacked the ruler forcefully upon it. The impact produced a loud sound. Marie jerked her head upward, displaying a startled and frightened expression. Since Marie subsequently maintained attention, Mr. Larson did not use the ruler this way again.

Mr. Larson walked over to the blackboard. With his back turned to the class, he wrote on the board with a piece of chalk, "aorta." While his back was turned, Peter threw a spitball at Mike. Mike ducked and "fell" seat-first upon the floor. He flashed a big grin and his classmates laughed.

Mr. Larson quickly walked over to Mike and violently yanked him upward by the arm into a standing position.

With a firm grasp on Mike's arm, Mr. Larson marched Mike off to the lab supply room. Angrily he said, "Stay in there until you can behave yourself!"

SIMPLIFIED INTERPRETATION

The principle of reinforcement: Bret's behavior was being strengthened by the *application* of positive reinforcers: a smile, special attention, verbal praise, and physical contact.

The principle of reinforcement: Marie's attentive behavior was *strengthened* by the removal of a negative reinforcer: a loud sound.

The principle of reinforcement: Mike perceived his misbehavior as rewarded by his classmates' attention (a positive reinforcer).

The principle of punishment: By the *application* of punishment, Mr. Larson hoped to decrease Mike's misbehavior.

The principle of punishment: By the *removal* of a positive reinforcer (being with his classmates), Mr. Larson hoped to decrease Mike's misbehavior (note that Mike received conflicting messages from his classmates and Mr. Larson).

for misbehavior (Craighead, Kazdin, and Mahoney, 1976).

One technique widely employed by American teachers that involves the removal of positive reinforcers is the *time-out procedure*. It is an approach in which inappropriate behavior is followed by a brief period of social isolation. The social isolation is designed to deprive the child of people and objects of interest. Usually, the child is sent to the hall or an unoccupied room. However, teachers should be aware of the ethical and practical problems inherent in the use of this procedure. Probably its most serious drawback is that it removes the child from contact with the positive reinforcements in the classroom that build desirable social and academic repertoires (Doleys et al., 1976; Plummer, Baer, and LeBlanc, 1977; Gast and Nelson, 1977). Further, in some instances social isolation may be welcomed by the student as an opportunity to escape from unpleasant classroom situations; in this case it functions as a positive reinforcer for deviant behavior (Solnick, Rincover, and Peterson, 1977).

Schedules of Reinforcement

Reinforcement in everyday life is not always consistent or continuous. Nonetheless, learning occurs and we continue behavior, even when a

SELF-REINFORCING ACTIVITIES
Many activities are self-reinforcing by virtue of the rewards associated with the activities themselves.

response is only intermittently reinforced. Skinner (1953:99) observes:

> We do not always find good ice or snow when we go skating or skiing. . . . We do not always get a good meal in a particular restaurant because cooks are not always predictable. We do not always get an answer when we telephone a friend because the friend is not always at home. . . . The reinforcements characteristic of industry and education are almost always intermittent because it is not feasible to control behavior by reinforcing every response.

Accordingly, psychologists distinguish among differing patterns, or *schedules,* of reinforcement.

In *continuous reinforcement,* each performance of a behavior is followed by a reinforcer, whereas in *intermittent reinforcement,* a reinforcer only follows a response occasionally. Researchers find that continuous reinforcement is most effective in the early stages of learning, since it produces change in behavior quickly. However, intermittent reinforcement is usually preferable for response maintenance, since it renders a behavior more resistant to erosion than does continuous reinforcement (Humphreys, 1939; Skinner, 1953; Haaf and Smith, 1976). The boxed insert on pages 144–145 discusses four types of intermittent reinforcement schedules.

Shaping

Very often we cannot find an already existing response in a subject's repertoire of behavior that totally represents the behavior we would like to reinforce. The desired behavior may involve a complex array of elements that seldom, if ever, is spontaneously emitted in the proper sequence by the organism. For instance, Skinner wished his experimental pigeons to move about in a perfect figure eight. But such behavior did not exist in the birds' repertoire. Accordingly, Skinner instituted a procedure known as **shaping.** A desired behavior

is broken down into successive steps that are taught one by one. Each step is reinforced until it is mastered, and then the subject proceeds to the next step. In this fashion, the new behavior is gradually learned as the organism comes closer and closer to the final approximation of the behavioral goal (Stolz, Wienckowski, and Brown, 1975).

In order to teach a pigeon to move in a perfect figure eight, Skinner would carefully watch a hungry pigeon strut about. When the bird made a slight clockwise turn, he would instantly reward it with a food pellet. Again the bird would strut about, and, in due course, would make another clockwise turn. Skinner would repeat the reward. He found that by reinforcing positions successively closer to a circle he could get a pigeon to make a full circle in about two to three minutes. Next, Skinner would reinforce the bird only when it would move in the opposite direction after making a full circle. Other steps closer to the final goal would be sequentially reinforced. By means of this procedure, Skinner was able to condition a pigeon to do a perfect figure eight in ten to fifteen minutes.

Teachers can also shape their students' behavior by controlling feedback and knowledge of results (Davis, Alexander, and Yelon, 1974). As teachers employ shaping procedures over time, they generally find that they become more skilled at it. Initially, many teachers find that they either proceed too rapidly or too slowly. If they move too quickly in narrowing the range of responses that they wish to reinforce, the behavior that has already been shaped begins to extinguish. If they proceed too slowly, the students tend to "fix" at a particular stage, and the training takes excessively long to complete.

MacMillan (1973) stresses that teachers should move in small steps toward their goal rather than taking an "all-or-none" approach in their rewarding procedures. The child who has difficulty remaining seated for two minutes cannot be expected to become a model student overnight and sit quietly for forty-five minutes. Once a desired behavior has largely stabilized, the teacher needs to move on to

RATIO AND TIME-INTERVAL SCHEDULES

Different schedules of intermittent reinforcement tend to represent variations on two basic patterns. First, reinforcers may be delivered on the basis of the prior emission of a certain number of responses, termed a *ratio schedule*. Second, the reinforcers may be provided on the basis of the passage of time, called a *time-interval schedule*. Ratio schedules tend to produce high response rates, whereas time-interval schedules maintain high levels of consistency.

Each of these two types of schedules may be either *fixed* (unvarying) or *variable* (continually changing). Combining these bases of classification provides four kinds of schedules: fixed-ratio, fixed-interval, variable-ratio, and variable-interval (see Figure 5.A).

FIXED-RATIO (FR) SCHEDULE

In a **fixed-ratio schedule,** the individual is reinforced after a specific number of responses. For instance, a reinforcer may be provided after every fifth or every eighth or every twenty-fifth re-sponse. Piecework arrangements among migrant farm laborers illustrate fixed-ratio schedules. Workers are paid a certain sum for picking a specific number of boxes of fruit. Teachers employ a fixed-ratio schedule when they tell their students, "When you have completed the first seven problems, you may go out for recess."

FIXED-INTERVAL (FI) SCHEDULE

On a **fixed-interval schedule,** a specific period of time must elapse after a reinforcer is delivered before another can be secured. Thus, on a fixed-interval schedule operating on a five-minute frequency, individuals cannot receive a reinforcer more often than every five minutes no matter how many responses they make. If a response is delayed longer than five minutes, the reinforcer is correspondingly postponed.

If the subject's responses are recorded cumulatively on a graph, a fixed-interval schedule produces a *scallop* effect. At the beginning of the time interval, individuals respond slowly and, in some instances, not at all. As the end of the time period approaches, they gradually increase their speed of responding in anticipation of the reinforcer.

Students' studying behavior sometimes follows this pattern:

Suppose a given class has a midterm and a final exam. These exams represent reinforcing events (positive or negative, depending upon how you look at them). Many students do very little studying as the semester begins. As the midterm approaches studying behavior picks up until, just before the exam, it reaches a high rate. After the exam it drops to zero and remains there only to accelerate again as the final approaches. Obviously, not all students study in this manner, and, obviously, not all materials are handled in this fashion (for example, students may be less likely to "scallop" their reading assignments than they are the memorization of lecture notes). But there is an interesting, and quite striking, correspondence between the effects of FI schedules and the

a closer approximation of the terminal goal (no longer reinforcing the old response). Shaping, then, is a "sliding-scale" process in which the standards for reward continually but gradually shift toward more accomplished performance.

Extinction

Extinction refers to a decrease in a response that results from its repeated failure to find reinforcement. But it is not simply a synonym for the

effects of our traditional examination patterns. [Houston, 1976:154]

VARIABLE-RATIO (VR) SCHEDULE

With the **variable-ratio schedule,** individuals receive a reinforcer after a different number of responses on different occasions (usually varying around an average). Proprietors of gambling casinos employ the schedule with considerable success. Slot machines, roulette wheels, and dice games pay off after an irregular number of responses. Gamblers never know if they will win on the next play, but over an extended series of plays, there is generally a certain proportion of wins. In this manner the gambler becomes "hooked." In school settings, variable-ratio schedules are encountered in such activities as teaching children to shoot baskets (points are commonly awarded for every shot successfully made).

VARIABLE-INTERVAL (VI) SCHEDULE

In the **variable-interval schedule,** reinforcement occurs after a given period of time that differs from one reinforcement to the next. For instance, in fishing we drop our line in the water, periodically check our lines, and for the most part wait for a fish to bite (the reinforcing event). Richard W. Saudargas, Charles H. Madsen, Jr., and John W. Scott (1977) found in their study with a class of twenty-six third-graders that variable-interval feedback was more successful than fixed-interval feedback in getting students to complete assignments. During fixed-interval home reporting, each student was given a report to take home every Friday that told the parent the quantity and quality of work completed by the child during the week. During the subsequent variable-interval procedure, seven to nine students were randomly selected each day to receive the same report.

Unhappily, much misbehavior is maintained on a variable-interval schedule. When a teacher manages to ignore certain behavior repeatedly in hopes of extinguishing it but in a moment of weakness succumbs, the variable-interval reinforcement serves to strengthen the response and make it even less susceptible to extinction (Bijou and Baer, 1961).

FIGURE 5.A SCHEDULES OF REINFORCEMENT

The *fixed-ratio schedule* requires the same number of responses for each reinforcing episode. The *variable-ratio schedule* delivers reinforcement on the basis of a changing number of responses (usually varying around an established average). The *fixed-interval schedule* necessitates the same elapsed time period from one reinforcing episode to another. The *variable-interval schedule* provides reinforcement over a continually changing period of time.

	RATIO (number)	INTERVAL (time)
FIXED	Fixed–Ratio (FR)	Fixed–Interval (FI)
VARIABLE	Variable–Ratio (VR)	Variable–Interval (VI)

reduction of a response. Other procedures like punishment also reduce a behavior. Bear in mind that punishment involves a decrease in a response that follows from the application or removal of a stimulus. Extinction occurs, however, precisely because a response is *not* followed by some associated environmental event (Craighead, Kazdin, and Mahoney, 1976). We usually do not keep on doing something that does not work. Indeed, extinction allows us to eliminate behavior that no longer produces positive outcomes or avoids negative consequences. Thus, we discard excess behavioral baggage that otherwise might clutter our lives and have maladaptive implications for us.

Teachers employ extinction procedures when they ignore students who do not raise their hands or otherwise speak out of turn. There are, however, a number of limitations to the approach. For one thing, extinction works gradually. It is not always possible to ignore the disruptive behavior of children. Frequently, the very behaviors that have become established through intermittent schedules are the most resistant to extinction. Another consideration is that initially extinction often results in an increase in the behavior the teacher is attempting to reduce and only later does the behavior begin to decrease (Amsel, 1967; Clarizio, 1976). Children frequently ''test the system'' to see if the teacher is really going to ignore the disruptive behavior (Drabman, Jarvie, and Archbold, 1976). Hence, extinction procedures require considerable patience and perseverance on the part of the teacher, since the behavior must be ignored *every time* it occurs (Bellack and Hersen, 1977).

Stimulus Generalization

If we are to adapt to the people and world about us, it is essential that we engage in the right behavior at the right time. This often requires that we apply a response learned with respect to one stimulus to other similar stimuli, a process termed **stimulus generalization.** For instance, we may have learned to stop when we encounter a particular traffic sign at the intersection near our elementary school. In turn, we came to recognize that we are to stop when we come across somewhat similar traffic signs at other intersections. Racial prejudice is another illustration of stimulus generalization. Attitudinal and emotional responses that we have come to connect with one, or perhaps a few individuals, are generalized to other people whom we perceive as being similar (Houston, 1976).

In a well-known experiment, Norman Guttman and Harry I. Kalish (1956) used a variable-interval schedule to train pigeons to peck at a disk for a grain pellet. The disk was illuminated with a yellow-green light. When the pecking response was established, the researchers tested the effects of other colors. Sometimes the test light was blue, other times orange, and so on. The color on the disk would skip randomly up and down the color spectrum (the wavelengths that are experienced as different colors). The closer the color was to the yellow-green color, the more times the pigeons would peck at it. This is termed the *stimulus-generalization gradient*.

The experiment demonstrated two things about stimulus generalization. First, the effectiveness of conditioning is not limited to the stimulus that was originally employed in the conditioning. And second, the ability of a stimulus to elicit a conditioned response decreases as the stimulus becomes less similar to the one employed in the original conditioning (Hulse, Deese, and Egeth, 1975).

Teachers are well aware that their students are more likely to attend to academic tasks and engage in less disruptive behavior when they are present in the classroom than when they are absent from it. When they are in the classroom, teachers directly monitor the children's behavior and dispense both positive and negative reinforcers. David Marholin II and Warren M. Steinman (1977) investigated how teachers might best generalize the effects associated with their classroom presence to situations in which they were absent. The researchers distinguished between on-task behavior and the rate and accuracy of academic performance. On-task behavior included getting out appropriate materials, looking at books, working problems, turning to the appropriate assignment, waiting with hand raised, and so on. The rate of academic performance involved the number of math problems the student attempted; accuracy entailed the percentage of problems correctly answered.

In the first phase of the study, two observers recorded the behavior and academic performance of eight fifth- and sixth-grade children with behavior problems in a classroom setting. During this baseline period, the children's behavior was not reinforced by the teacher. In the second and fourth phases of the study, the teacher reinforced only on-task behavior. In the third and fifth phases, she reinforced only the rate and accuracy of academic performance. The teacher was absent for a portion of the class session every day in each of the five phases of the study. In the teacher's absence, on-task behavior declined and disruption increased, regardless of the reinforcement condition in operation. The teacher's absence also resulted in fewer problems attempted and decreased accuracy.

The researchers found, however, that when the teacher reinforced the students for academic accuracy and rate of output, they were less disruptive and more productive in her absence than under on-task reinforcement. For instance, there were decreases of 54 and 79 percent in student work output in the teacher's absence, when on-task behavior was reinforced (the second and fourth phases, respectively). This compared with decreases of 17 and 12 percent when she reinforced accuracy and rate (the third and fifth phases, respectively). Marholin and Steinman concluded that by providing reinforcement for the products of a child's classroom activities (academic achievement) rather than for some aspect of task orientation or appropriate social behavior, the child becomes less dependent upon a teacher's continual surveillance. In sum, the responses that are acquired in a teacher's presence are more likely to generalize to the teacher's absence where academic performance is reinforced than where on-task behavior is reinforced.

Stimulus Discrimination

In carrying out our life activities, it is not only necessary that we recognize some stimuli as being similar; it is also necessary that we be able to distinguish among stimuli. Only by differentiating between relevant and irrelevant stimuli are we able to attune our behavior to the demands of a particular situation. The ability of an organism to respond to relevant information and ignore irrelevant information from the environment is termed **stimulus discrimination.** Whereas stimulus generalization

involves reaction to similarity, stimulus discrimination entails reaction to difference (Hilgard, Atkinson, and Atkinson, 1975).

Psychologists have investigated discrimination learning in experimental settings with a variety of animals. For instance, a hungry rat is confronted with two doors on hinged flaps. One door provides access to food while the other door is locked. The door containing the food is decorated with a triangle and the locked door with a circle. In the course of its random activity, the rat collides with the door containing the triangle and secures access to the food. Soon the rat learns to differentiate between a door with a triangle and a door with a circle, regardless of which door is placed to the left or to the right.

The experimenter then temporarily confounds the rat by reversing the clue—the door with the triangle is locked while the door with the circle gains the rat entry to the food. In a very short time the rat changes its responses and makes use of the door with the circle. Should the experimenter persist in changing the "rules of the game" as soon as the rat has settled on one habitual response, the rat quickly discovers the underlying regularity. It switches to the opposite response as soon as it receives a clue (one "mistake") that the situation has been reversed.

Many psychologists interpret this research as revealing that the rat has engaged in discrimination learning and has come to pay attention to the difference that is significant. Once the rat identifies the relevant clue—attends to the decoration on the door rather than to the side the open door is on or was on the previous time—the rest is easy. In brief, both rats and humans have to learn which differences are relevant and which are irrelevant (Smith, 1975).

OBSERVATIONAL LEARNING

As humans we are social beings, and we have mutual and reciprocal influences on one anothers' attitudes, feelings, and actions. We observe the

OBSERVATIONAL LEARNING
Many classroom activities involving the use of visual aids are premised on the principle of observational learning.

behavior of others, and we learn from it. From an educational point of view, this is of crucial importance, since teaching is primarily a social process. If we learned solely by direct experience—by the reinforcing or punishing consequences of our behavior—most of us would not survive to adulthood. What if we had to rely upon direct conditioning to learn how to cross busy intersections? Most of us would already be traffic fatalities. With direct reinforcement as our only method of learning, it is doubtful that we could ever become adept at playing football, driving a car, solving mathematical problems, cooking meals, or even brushing our teeth. The principles of classical and operant conditioning do not explain how a child can learn

a completely new response from watching another person perform the behavior. Children would already need to have the same responses in their behavioral repertoire as the model before their responses could be reinforced (Zimmerman, 1977).

We can avoid tedious, costly, trial-and-error experimentation by reenacting a behavior we see performed by socially competent models. Thus, humans are heir to a cultural tradition that eventually becomes a social legacy. Each generation can rise from the "achievement shoulders" of the preceding generation. By watching others, we learn new responses without first having to experience the response ourselves. This process is termed **observational learning** (also **social learning**).

Although observational learning has been known throughout the ages, it is only in the past several decades that psychologists have directly addressed themselves to its study.

Effects of Modeling on the Observer

Albert Bandura (1969, 1977), a psychologist whose research has greatly contributed to our understanding of observational learning, suggests that modeling can influence the observer in three different ways: learning new responses, inhibition and disinhibition, and facilitation.

Learning New Responses

We can acquire new patterns of behavior by watching the performance of others. When a model exhibits a novel response that we have not yet learned to make, we may try to imitate that response. A child may observe a parent standing on a kitchen chair to reach objects on a high shelf. The child, in turn, may use the chair to reach otherwise inaccessible objects on the kitchen counter. Teachers employ the technique when they use a blackboard to demonstrate how to solve a particular type of mathematical problem.

Models need not be presented in real-life forms to be effective. Symbolic or pictorial presentations—through newspapers, books, movies, and television—function as important model sources. Children, for instance, are as likely to imitate aggressive behavior if they witness it in a movie or in an animated cartoon as they are if they witness it in a real-life situation (Bandura, Ross, and Ross, 1963).

Inhibition and Disinhibition

By observing the behavior of others, we may come to *inhibit* or avoid a particular action. This is especially true if we observe others experiencing negative consequences when they engage in a behavior. Teachers often punish one child in the presence of others to achieve a "spillover" effect— other children are deterred by what they witness. Likewise, the folklore of a people, various parables and fables, often provide a symbolic modeling of vicarious punishment through oral or written accounts. The expulsion of Adam and Eve from the Garden of Eden is meant to inhibit people from engaging in religiously prohibited behavior (Zimmerman and Ghozeil, 1974).

It is also possible to *disinhibit* certain actions by observing a model. Children who witness other children successfully violating school rules are more likely to follow suit. If one child gets away with running down the hall, especially if the floors are slippery enough to permit sliding, others quickly imitate the behavior. Should the child receive additional rewards, such as being the first to reach the playground and gain access to the kickball, the effect is enhanced (Zimmerman, 1977). By the same token, many types of fear can be reduced by exposing children to a model who fearlessly approaches and deals with a feared stimulus, such as a dog (Bandura and Menlove, 1968).

Facilitation

Often, we have certain responses in our repertoire that we do not use. When we see others engaging in a behavior that we have but do not use, we recall the behavior and may apply it to the same situation. Thus, modeling can *facilitate* our responding in ways in which we might not otherwise.

Facilitation is not the same as disinhibition. Disinhibition occurs only if a behavior has been inhibited, as in the case of punishment. Facilitation occurs when a response that we were unlikely to make becomes more probable (Zimmerman and Ghozeil, 1974; Zimmerman and Koussa, 1979). For instance, children may know how to smoke a cigarette but never have done so. But when another child lights up, the others may join in the behavior.

Critics of contemporary television programming

point to studies that demonstrate that programs that display violence facilitate violent responses in children. Television viewing may also add certain kinds of violent actions to children's behavioral repertoires; later, when confronted by comparable circumstances, the children recall the responses and, in turn, translate them into their own overt actions (see the boxed insert on pages 152–153).

Observational Learning in Educational Practice

Much evidence suggests that modeling is more economical as a teaching-learning technique than either classical or operant conditioning. This is particularly true where novel responses or complex skills are involved. Teachers find observation and imitation a particularly useful approach for teaching a wide variety of skills including adding a column of numbers, throwing a basketball, and playing the violin.

Teachers also influence students by the behaviors that they themselves model: altruism or selfishness, cleanliness or slovenliness, racial equality or racial bigotry, self-discipline or disorganization, and so on (Bandura and Mischel, 1965; Muuss, 1976). Take the matter of *altruistic behavior*—action that is carried out to benefit another person without any expectation of external reward. This behavior plays a critical part in group life, particularly small, intimate groups like our immediate family, our companions and friends, and our daily associates. Research suggests that the altruistic responses of students are influenced more by what the teacher *does* than by what the teacher *says* (White, 1967; Gagné and Middlebrooks, 1977).

A study by Elizabeth Midlarsky, James H. Bryan, and Philip Brickman (1973) also revealed that adult action speaks louder than adult words. Indeed, adult hypocrisy may boomerang. In their research, Midlarsky and her associates employed a sample of seventy-two sixth-grade girls. Each

girl played an individual game with an adult model in which both realized winnings from a pinball machine (unknown to the girls, the machine was rigged to provide more winning than losing scores). When the model completed her game, she told each child:

> Now it is your turn. But before you begin, let me remind you about the poor children [a cannister for poor children stood nearby]. Please think about them as you are playing and about how very much they would love to receive the prizes that these chips can buy. It would make them very happy to get toys and candy—because it is so easy for a needy child to feel really forgotten. Let us let them know that we remember them. [1973:323]

Even though the adult preached altruism and praised the child when the child dropped a chip into the cannister, she contradicted her own words by keeping her winnings. As the study then went on to prove, the child was less likely to be charitable on subsequent occasions than in situations where the hypocritical adult had not praised the child. Hence, a selfish-acting but generous-speaking model serves to discourage charitable behavior by approving it but not acting on it.

Many educators have stressed the need for children to learn by doing. However, some educational authorities have gone even further and have insisted that children must directly perform an operation themselves before any real learning can occur. Although few would dispute the notion that personal experience can facilitate task learning, modeling research has convincingly demonstrated that children can learn new responses simply by observing another perform a task.

Indeed, under some circumstances, overt performance can interfere with learning (Zimmerman, 1977). Psychologists Ted L. Rosenthal and Barry J. Zimmerman (1973) compared observational learning procedures to direct guidance of a child's action in learning a complex skill involving dial-reading. In the guided practice procedure, third-

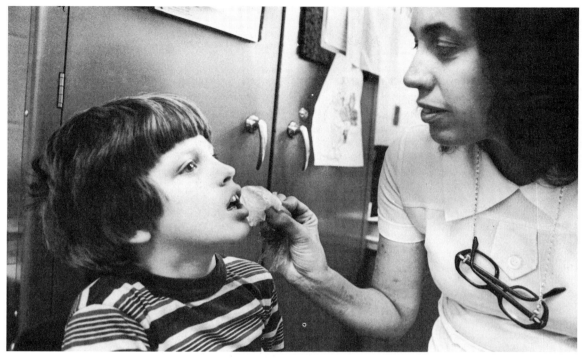

ALTRUISM
Helping responses among students are influenced more by what school personnel do than by what they say.

and fifth-grade children had their hands guided by the experimenter and hence never had occasion to do the operation erroneously. In the modeling procedure, the children simply observed the experimenter carrying out the task.

Both procedures created significant learning. But the modeling procedure was nearly two times more effective than the direct guidance procedure. Although involving children in motor operations often assists them in learning unfamiliar tasks, teachers must be cautious about generalizing the principle to all situations, especially those involving the learning of abstract rules. However, where the motor component is primary, as in swimming and other athletic areas, learning does require a high degree of overt performance.

CHAPTER SUMMARY

1. Theories of learning fall into three broad categories: conditioning theories, observational (imitation) theories, and cognitive theories. The theories highlight the kinds of influence that teachers can exert in facilitating learning. They can condition students, provide a model for imitation by students, and change the cognitive structure by which students think about their environment.

2. Classical conditioning is based upon the work of Ivan Pavlov. It involves a process of stimulus substitution in which a new, previously neutral stimulus is substituted for the stimulus that naturally

MEDIA VIOLENCE

Throughout history, most societies have provided their children with fictional materials containing a good many violent happenings. For instance, fairy tales tell about fire-breathing dragons and dangerous giants. Hence, children are not generally isolated from knowledge regarding violence. However, today children are provided with an additional dimension of violence—television programs that visually depict human beings engaged in violent activities with which children can readily identify (Gentry, 1974).

Research by Albert Bandura (1965) and his associates points to the powerful impact that observing aggression has on children. In one experiment, the researcher had nursery school children individually observe a five-minute movie on a television set. In the movie, a man—"Rocky"—walked up to an inflated, adult-sized toy clown and ordered it to clear the way. After glaring at the noncompliant doll, Rocky struck it with a mallet, punched it in the nose, and threw rubber balls at it. Each aggressive act was accompanied by some comment such as "Pow, right in the nose, boom, boom."

Each child was then shown one of three conclusions to the movie. One group of children saw the model rewarded for his behavior. Another adult made an appearance, informed Rocky that he was a "strong champion," and provided him with a soft drink and candy.

A second group of children observed Rocky punished. The second adult called Rocky a "big bully" and spanked him with a rolled-up magazine.

A third group was shown only the first part of the movie. The second adult did not appear, and the model's behavior had no consequences associated with it.

Immediately following the movie, the children were taken to a playroom (the room was equipped with a one-way mirror through which, unknown to the child, researchers in an adjoining room could record and rate the child's behavior at five-second intervals for ten minutes). The playroom contained dart guns, plastic farm animals, a doll family, and other toys. Children who had witnessed the model being rewarded for his behavior or as suffering no negative consequences displayed more aggressive behavior than did children who observed Rocky punished. This was particularly true of the boys (see Figure 5.B).

In the next phase of the experiment, the researcher entered the room with booklets of sticker pictures and an assortment of juices in a colorful juice-dispensing fountain. The child was offered a sticker and a small amount of juice for each physical or verbal response correctly imitated from the movie. The experimenter gave the children such instructions as,

"Show me what Rocky did in the TV program" and "Tell me what Rocky said." Bandura assumed that the number of different responses that a child could imitate under this positive-incentive condition would provide a relatively accurate index of learning.

Figure 5.B contains the mean (average) number of responses exhibited by the children under the different conditions. The introduction of the positive incentives (the stickers and juice) in the second phase of the experiment eliminated the differences that were found between the three groups during the first phase. Moreover, the initially large difference between boys and girls in the display of aggression largely disappeared.

Bandura's study demonstrated that children who saw the model punished engaged in less aggressive behavior than did the children in the other conditions. This was most noticeable for the girls. Nonetheless, these children were able to reconstruct the model's aggressive responses when they were encouraged to do so. Although the children differed in their *performance* of the observed acts during the initial phase of the study, the follow-up phase revealed that all groups had *learned* an equivalent amount of information from viewing the movie. Bandura warns that even when aggression is punished, children may still learn new forms of ag-

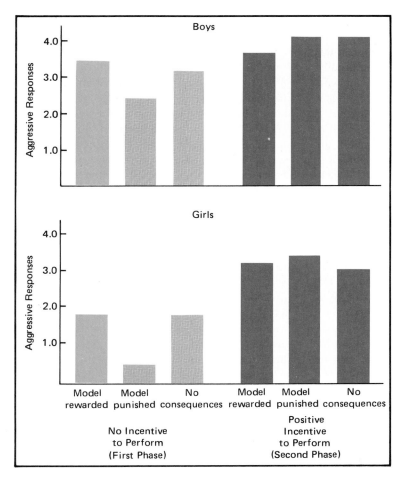

Boys

Girls

Model rewarded   Model punished   No consequences   Model rewarded   Model punished   No consequences

No Incentive
to Perform
(First Phase)

Positive
Incentive
to Perform
(Second Phase)

FIGURE 5.B AVERAGE NUMBER OF AGGRESSIVE RESPONSES PRODUCED BY THE CHILDREN
The figure shows the mean number of imitative aggressive acts that the children displayed in each of the three treatment conditions during the no-incentive and positive-incentive phases of the experiment. *(Source: Adapted from Albert Bandura, "Influence of Models' Reinforcement Contingencies on the Acquisition of Imitative Responses,"* Journal of Personality and Social Psychology, *1 [1965]:592.)*

gressive behavior. Those who witness violence may later reenact the aggressive actions when the situation suits them.

An accumulating body of research by Bandura and others suggests that all three modeling effects reside in the exposure of violence on television (Liebert and Baron, 1972; Bandura, 1973b; Andison, 1977; Withey and Abeles, 1980). First, individuals learn new ways of aggressing from viewing violent scenes. Second, their inhibitions against antisocial acts are lowered and, in some cases, eradicated. And finally, exposure to violent episodes facilitates similar behaviors by affecting the willingness of observers to imitate these actions.

elicits the response. After a conditioned stimulus and an unconditioned stimulus have been paired a number of times, the conditioned stimulus becomes capable of eliciting the response in the absence of the unconditioned stimulus.

3. Classical conditioning depends upon the prior existence of a reflex that can be mustered in the service of a new stimulus. However, we usually lack some preexisting unconditioned stimulus with which we can link a new stimulus. Accordingly, we may wish to employ operant conditioning, a type of learning in which the consequences of a behavior alter the strength of that behavior. In contrast with classical conditioning in which a stimulus is said to elicit a response, in operant conditioning the response is emitted.

4. Psychologists distinguish between the principle of reinforcement and the principle of punishment. The principle of reinforcement refers to an *increase* in the frequency of a response when it is followed by a contingent or associated stimulus. The principle of punishment refers to a *decrease* in the frequency of a response when it is followed by a contingent or associated stimulus.

5. Students often confuse the principle of reinforcement with the stimulus (the event) that follows a behavior, termed either a positive reinforcer or a negative reinforcer. The principle of reinforcement entails an *increase* in the frequency of a response when either a positive reinforcer is applied or a negative reinforcer is withdrawn. The principle of punishment involves a *decrease* in the frequency of a response when either a positive reinforcer is withdrawn or a negative reinforcer is applied.

6. Psychologists distinguish among differing patterns or schedules of reinforcement. In continuous reinforcement each performance of a behavior is followed by a reinforcer, whereas in intermittent reinforcement a reinforcer only occasionally follows a response. Psychologists differentiate between four main kinds of schedules: fixed-ratio, fixed-interval, variable-ratio, and variable-interval.

7. Very often we cannot find an already existing response in a subject's repertoire of behavior that totally represents the behavior we would like to reinforce. Under these circumstances a procedure known as *shaping* may be employed. Each step is reinforced until it is mastered, and then the subject proceeds to the next step.

8. Extinction refers to a decrease in a response that results from its repeated failure to find reinforcement. It is not, however, simply a synonym for the reduction of a response. Other procedures like punishment also reduce a behavior. Extinction occurs because a response is *not* followed by some associated environmental event.

9. If we are to adapt to the people and world about us, it is essential that we engage in the right behavior at the right time. This often requires that we apply a response learned with respect to one stimulus to other similar stimuli, a process termed *stimulus generalization.*

10. Whereas stimulus generalization involves reaction to similarity, stimulus discrimination entails reaction to difference. In carrying out our life activities, it is necessary that we be able to distinguish among stimuli.

11. As humans we are social beings, and we have mutual and reciprocal influences on one anothers' attitudes, feelings, and actions. We observe the behavior of others, and we learn from it. From an educational point of view, this is of crucial importance, since teaching is primarily a social process. We can avoid tedious, costly, trial-and-error experimentation by reenacting the behavior performed by socially competent models.

12. Modeling can influence the observer in three different ways. First, we can acquire new patterns of behavior by watching the performance of others. Second, by observing the behavior of others, we may come to inhibit or disinhibit a particular action. And third, modeling can facilitate our response to behaviors by showing us new options.

13. Teachers find observation and imitation to be particularly useful approaches for teaching novel responses and complex skills. Teachers also influence students by the behaviors that they themselves model. Altruistic behavior provides a good illustration.

CHAPTER GLOSSARY

behaviorism The view that psychology should concern itself with external, observable events and that a functional relationship exists between a particular stimulus and a particular response.

classical conditioning A process of stimulus substitution in which a new, previously neutral stimulus is substituted for the stimulus that naturally elicits the response.

conditioned response (CR) A response aroused by some stimulus other than the one that naturally produces it.

conditioned stimulus (CS) A previously neutral stimulus that acquires the property of eliciting a particular response through being paired during training with an unconditioned stimulus.

extinction A decrease in a response that results from its repeated failure to find reinforcement.

fixed-interval (FI) schedule A schedule of reinforcement in which a specific period of time must elapse after a reinforcer has been delivered before another can be secured.

fixed-ratio (FR) schedule A schedule of reinforcement in which the individual is reinforced after a specific number of responses.

learning A relatively permanent change in behavior that results from experience.

negative reinforcer A stimulus that, when removed following a behavior, strengthens the probability of its future occurrence.

observational learning (also termed **social learning**) The process through which, by watching others, we learn new responses without first having to experience the response ourselves.

operant conditioning A type of learning in which the consequences of a behavior alter the strength of that behavior.

positive reinforcer A stimulus that, when applied following a behavior, strengthens the probability of the behavior's future occurrence.

principle of punishment A decrease in the frequency of a behavior when it is followed by a contingent or associated stimulus.

principle of reinforcement An increase in the frequency of a behavior when it is followed by a contingent or associated stimulus.

punishment Any consequence of behavior that has the effect of decreasing the probability of the response.

reinforcement Any event that strengthens the probability of a particular response.

responses Behavior segmented into units.

shaping The process of breaking down a desired behavior into successive steps that are taught one by one.

stimuli The environment segmented into units.

stimulus discrimination The ability of an organism to respond to relevant information and ignore irrelevant information from the environment.

stimulus generalization The ability to apply a learned response with respect to one stimulus to other similar stimuli.

system A complex arrangement or structure made up of interdependent but semiautonomous parts.

unconditioned response (UCR) The unlearned, biologically preprogrammed reaction evoked by an unconditioned stimulus.

unconditioned stimulus (UCS) The stimulus that naturally elicits a particular response.

variable-interval (VI) schedule A schedule of reinforcement in which reinforcement occurs after a given period of time that differs from one reinforcement to the next.

variable-ratio (VR) schedule A schedule of reinforcement in which individuals receive a rein-forcer after a different number of responses on different occasions (usually varying around an average).

EXERCISES

Review Questions

1. According to the text, which criterion is *not* generally included in most definitions of learning?
   a. maturation
   b. stability
   c. change
   d. experience

2. In classical conditioning, the initial UCS-UCR response is characterized as
   a. behavioral
   b. intuitive
   c. reflexive
   d. thoughtful

3. Which of the following might be considered a classically conditioned behavior?
   a. answering "four" when the teacher asks, "What is two to the second power?"
   b. placing silverware properly on the table
   c. getting anxious before a test
   d. mowing the lawn
   e. a and b are true

4. Ringness would consider as acceptable such teacher practices as
   a. giving as few tests as possible if students show great test anxiety
   b. having students start as members of a small combo if they are fearful of performing solo in the school orchestra
   c. having students pick up small harmless snakes first if they are fearful of snakes
   d. b and c are true

5. When comparing classical and operant conditioning we find that
   a. in classical conditioning the response is elicited; in operant conditioning the response is emitted
   b. in both classical and operant conditioning a specific simulus produces a specific response
   c. in classical conditioning the stimulus precedes the response; in operant conditioning the response occurs prior to the rewarding stimulus
   d. a, b, and c are true
   e. a and c are true

6. It has been observed that many compulsively neat people are so in order to avoid the appearance of disorder. This would suggest that the underlying mechanism is
   a. positive reinforcement
   b. negative reinforcement
   c. punishment by application
   d. punishment by removal

7. If we wished to teach and maintain a new skill as efficiently as possible, research suggests that we
   a. go from an intermittent to a continuous reinforcement schedule
   b. go from a continuous to an intermittent reinforcement schedule
   c. stay with an initial continuous reinforcement schedule
   d. stay with an initial intermittent reinforcement schedule

8. The game of "you're getting warmer" best typifies
   a. extinction
   b. shaping

c. generalization
d. spontaneous recovery

9. A teacher first rewards a student for every fifth math problem completed, and then makes the reward contigent on doing twenty minutes of math work. The teacher is proceeding from a

a. fixed-ratio to a variable-ratio schedule
b. fixed-interval to a fixed-ratio schedule
c. variable-ratio to a variable-interval schedule
d. fixed-ratio to a fixed-interval schedule

10. According to Bandura, children who behave in a certain manner because they have seen others ''get away with it'' are probably demonstrating

a. inhibition
b. disinhibition
c. facilitation
d. learning new responses

Answers

1. a (See p. 128)
2. c (See p. 129)
3. c (See pp. 131–133)
4. b (See p. 133)
5. e (See pp. 133–134)

6. b (See p. 140)
7. b (See p. 143)
8. b (See pp. 143–144)
9. d (See pp. 144–145)
10. b (See p. 149)

Applying Principles and Concepts

1. Jonathan has a real problem with tests. Facing an exam, he becomes quite anxious, which hurts his performance. His concerned teacher notices that Jonathan loves to chew gum, which he does in a relaxed manner. She decides to let him chew gum during exams to help him calm down. From the following list select the CS, UCS, CR, and UCR of the conditioning process. (Hint: An answer may be used more than once.)

_____ a. Test
_____ b. Gum
_____ c. Anxiety
_____ d. Teacher
_____ e. Relaxed feeling

2. Classify the following as positive reinforcement (PR), negative reinforcement (NR), punishment by application (PA), punishment by withdrawal (PW), or extinction (E).

a. A teacher gets red in the face screaming at his students, who make even more noise.
b. A girl tries to break off a relationship with a boy by insulting him every time he speaks.
c. The student stops working on a difficult assignment to talk to his girl friend.
d. The mother tells her son that because of his behavior he'll not be able to watch his favorite TV show.
e. The parent ignores a child's temper tantrum.

3. Indicate whether the following is an example of a fixed-ratio (FR), variable-ratio (VR), fixed-interval (FI), or variable-interval schedule (VI).

a. The persistence of an insurance salesperson
b. A ''pop'' or surprise quiz
c. Christmas shopping
d. A subcontractor who gets paid when the job is done

4. A mother watches her two-year-old walk up to a Saint Bernard and say ''woof.'' The child most likely is exhibiting

_____ a. Generalization
_____ b. Discrimination
_____ c. Shaping
_____ d. Extinction

5. The same child as in Question 4 does not say ''woof'' to a cat. A good guess as to the attribute of the cat to which the child is responding is

_____ a. Fur
_____ b. Four legs
_____ c. Size
_____ d. Color

6. In the space provided before each behavior, indicate whether it is likely to have occurred as a result of modeling (M) or reinforcement (R).

_____ a. Laura, a six-year-old, holds up her hand to traffic crossing the street.

_____ b. Albert, a ten-year-old, rushes to the head of the cafeteria line so that he can finish early and play.

_____ c. Ellen, a twelve-year-old, tries to fix her hair just like her favorite television actress.

_____ d. Billy, a nine-year-old, wants to be known as "the fastest gun in the West."

7. A television producer has just given his evidence before a congressional committee concerned with violence on television. Underline those parts of his testimony on modeling of aggression that could be supported by Bandura and others.

> While it is true there is a lot of violence on TV, we make it clear to viewers that the villain is punished. Even if the child remembers the specific acts of violence, I am sure that he is also aware of the differences between violence for good and bad ends. Frankly, it is my opinion that kids are becoming blasé about the whole thing.

Answers

1. a, CS; b, UCS; c, CR, UCR; e, CR, UCR (See pp. 129–130)
2. a, PR; b, PA; c, NR; d, PW; e, E (See pp. 138–140)
3. a, VR; b, VI; c, FI; d, FR (See pp. 144–145)
4. b (See pp. 143–147)
5. c (See pp. 146–147)
6. a, M; b, R; c, M; d, M (See pp. 149–150)
7. Underline "there is a lot of violence on TV" and "the child remembers the specific acts." (See pp. 152–153)

Project

OBJECTIVE: To manipulate the frequency of a child's response through positive reinforcement and extinction.

PROCEDURE: Visit an elementary school classroom (preferably), and ask the teacher to participate in increasing the frequency of a desired response or decreasing the occurrence of an undesirable response in one child. For the purposes of this project do not try to do both simultaneously. Each phase will take about two weeks.

Positive Reinforcement

1. Decide in advance with the teacher which response he or she would like to see increased in a specific child. It may be paying attention, sitting in the seat, working at the assigned task, or the like. Select a behavior that is initially low in that child.
2. Pick a forty-minute period during the day in which to carry out the project. It will help if that period is given to the same type of activity each day. The behavior can be measured either by frequency or duration, depending on which seems more appropriate. For example, cooperating with another child or raising one's hand would be measured by frequency, whereas work at a task would be measured by duration.
3. Sit in the back of the room, and ask the teacher to conduct class as usual. Observe the child during the period and count frequencies or make time estimates of the targeted behavior. At the end of the period summarize the data in a graph:

Indicate on the ordinate (vertical dimension) the total frequency (or time) above Day 1 on the abscissa (horizontal dimension). If the child raised his or her hand five times your graph will look like this:

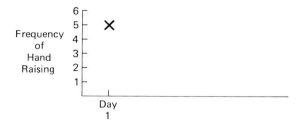

4. For the next several days (at least three and possibly four) keep a daily record. On the same graph put the results, connecting them with a line. This curve represents the baseline period:

5. For the treatment phase, ask the teacher to praise the child each time he or she makes the appropriate response. If you are using a duration measure, tell the teacher to praise the child during the response (for example, while he or she is working on task). Do not overdo the latter! Once

or twice even during several minutes is enough. Record the data on the graph for the next several days (at least four). Connect the data points. You may draw a vertical line to separate the two phases. (See the graph in the section on analysis.)

Extinction

1. Decide in advance which behavior you want to reduce in frequency. It could be calling out, getting out of the seat, or the like. It may be impossible to ignore physical aggression toward another child, so do not use that. This behavior can also be measured in terms of frequency of duration. Select a behavior that is initially high.

2. Carry out the collection of baseline data as for positive reinforcement.

3. When the treatment phase begins, ask the teacher to ignore completely the targeted behavior. Record the next four or five days. Follow the same graphing procedures as for positive reinforcement.

ANALYSIS:

Positive Reinforcement

Here at the end of the treatment phase your graph might look like the one at the bottom of this page.

If your experiment has been successful, the treatment curve will be higher on the average than the baseline curve. If it is not, then it is conceivable

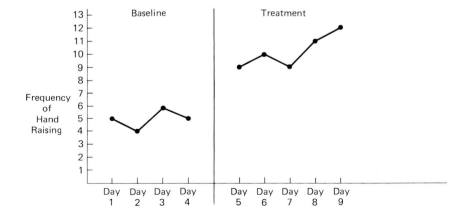

that praise did not function as a reinforcer or that other factors (for example, peer approval) intervened. Talk the possibilities over with the teacher.

Extinction

Suppose you had selected "calling out" as the behavior to be extinguished. If you were successful, your graph should look like the one below.

Success in this case means a *decrease* in the behavior. However a common occurrence is that at the start of extinction the response may *temporarily* increase. Failure may reflect the teacher's inconsistent application of extinction principles, peer reinforcement, and so on. Again you may want to discuss your results with the teacher.

You may also want to try these procedures several times, using negative reinforcement and punishment. The latter two have sometimes had emotional after-effects, however.

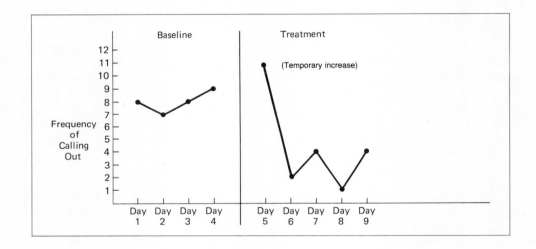

CHAPTER OUTLINE

162

6

COGNITIVE LEARNING

CHAPTER PREVIEW

Cognitive theories of learning are the topic of Chapter 6. They differ from the theories discussed previously in that they emphasize the mental processes by which people make sense of the world and derive new meaning and understanding from their experiences. Perhaps you wondered at the absence of such words as "thinking" and "knowing" in the last chapter; the reason is that the theories described there deal with observable behaviors rather than mental activity. A central focus of this chapter is the cognitive developmental theory of Jean Piaget, who spent more than half a century investigating the development of logical thinking. The ideas of two other psychologists who have been concerned with the relationship between cognitive processes and educational practice—Jerome Bruner and David Ausubel—are also examined, with particular attention given to their advocacy, respectively, of discovery and expository learning.

Questions to guide your reading of this chapter are:

- What are the essential features of Piaget's theory of cognitive development?
- What recommendations for educational practice may reasonably be drawn from Piagetian theory?
- How does Bruner's theory differ from Piaget's?
- What are the characteristics of discovery learning, and what are some of the problems associated with this method?
- How does expository or reception learning contrast with discovery learning? When might each approach, or a variation of it, be useful?

Man is obviously made to think. It is his whole dignity and his whole merit.

PASCAL
Pensées

Conditioning and observational learning are two forms of learning. A third is cognitive learning. Broadly considered, **cognition** refers to the process of thinking and knowing. It involves our reception of raw sensory information and our transformation, elaboration, storage, recovery, and use of this information (Neisser, 1967, 1976). Theories of cognition seek to account for how human beings get information through contact with the environment and how they mentally manipulate this information. Psychologists who stress cognitive processes view people as intervening in the course of human affairs with conscious deliberation. They portray human beings as capable of making rational decisions in that the decisions are based on available information and an ability to process the information intelligently. Mental activity ''makes something'' out of perceptions, and this something is meaningful and organized. Thus, cognitive psychologists are interested in how people use information from their environment and their memories to make decisions about what to say and do.

THE THEORY OF JEAN PIAGET

Man's mind stretched to a new idea never goes back to its original dimensions.

OLIVER WENDELL HOLMES

Over the past two decades, psychologists and educators have shown an increasing interest in cognitive processes. Perhaps no individual has contributed more to this interest than Jean Piaget (1896–1980), a Swiss developmental psychologist. For fifty years, Piaget investigated the development of cognitive processes as they unfold in children from birth through the various stages of infancy, childhood, and adolescence.

Piaget's technique for observing, recording, and understanding the way a child thinks was literally to imagine himself in the child's mind. He tried to see the world through the eyes of children and to experience the logic of the assumptions they have regarding it. Whereas psychologists usually employ large samples of subjects and complicated statistical procedures, Piaget concentrated on the intensive study of small samples and rarely computed even the simplest statistic. Indeed, many of his most valuable insights were derived from observing his own three children.

Structure of Thought

When Piaget undertook his research with children in the 1920s, most psychologists assumed that children thought and reasoned in essentially the same way as adults did. Piaget quickly challenged this notion. He forcefully argued that in their intellectual activity children are not miniature adults; instead, they think in a qualitatively unique and distinctive manner. Hence, when children say that the sun follows them about when they go for a walk, that the name of the moon is the moon, and that dreams come through the window, they are not ''illogical''; rather, children are operating from a different mental framework or set of rules for interpreting the world.

According to Piaget, the child—like the adult—is an active knower. Both actively select and interpret environmental information rather than register it passively. Piaget says that the human mind builds cognitive structures that take external sensory input and interpret, transform, and organize it. Like an artist's painting, such mental portrayals are not a simple copy of life; they are a construction of life that is fashioned by the unique combination of what individuals take from their experiences and what they add or subtract from them.

Children's mental reality is qualitatively different from that of adults, since their means for constructing reality out of experience are less adequate than those fashioned by adults. According to Piaget, children progressively construct and

THE CHILD AS AN ACTIVE KNOWER
Piaget said that the child is involved in continuing interaction with
the environment, and this interaction leads to new perceptions of
the world and to new cognitive structures.

reconstruct their sense of reality until it approxi-
mates that of adults. Thus, less adaptive ideas have
to be given up for more adaptive ones, and vague
ideas have to be transformed into higher level
conceptions, eventually resulting in the capacity
for abstract and logical thought (Elkind, 1975,
1976; Flavell, 1977).

Interactionism

Piaget views the individual and the environment
as engaged in continuing interaction that leads to
new perceptions of the world and new organizations
of knowledge. A new experience interacts with
the previously existing cognitive structure, thereby
altering the structure and making it more adequate.
This modified structure, in turn, influences the
individual's new perceptions. These new perceptions are then incorporated into a more complex
structure. In this manner, experience modifies
structure, and structure modifies experience (Cross,
1976).

Thus individuals, in interacting with their environment, ensure their own development. By
acting on the environment, they cause the environment to change. In turn, individuals must
themselves change if they are to adapt to the
modified conditions. Accordingly, people are shaped
and altered by the consequences of their own
actions. Cognitive structures arise through this
process of continual transformation. Individuals
literally change themselves by acting.

Piaget viewed intellectual development as the
product of adaptation:

> Intelligence is an adaptation. . . . Life is a con-
> tinuous creation of increasingly complex forms
> and a progressive balancing of these forms with
> the environment. [1952:3]

According to Piaget, at birth infants begin their
lives with simple reflexes. With advancing age,
they gradually modify their repertoire of behaviors
to meet various environmental demands. In the
course of interacting with their environment during
play and other activities, children construct a series

of mental schemes—concepts or models—for coping with their world. **Schemes** is the term that Piaget employed for thinking structures that people evolve for dealing with specific kinds of situations in their environment. They are the cognitive capacity that underlies and makes possible organized or structured patterns of behavior. Knowledge, then, is a system of transformations (schemes) that become progressively adequate when judged against the dictates of the individual's environment (Piaget, 1970).

According to Piaget, adaptation consists of two complementary processes: assimilation and accommodation. **Assimilation** is the process of taking in new information and interpreting it in such a manner that the information conforms to a currently held scheme. Piaget says that children typically stretch an existing scheme as far as possible to fit new observations. However, their experiences confront them periodically with the inadequacy of their current adaptations; some of their observations simply do not fit their present schemes. This produces disequilibrium or imbalance. Consequently, children must restructure or reorganize their view of the world to make it accord with their new experiences. Thus, they find that they must invent increasingly better schemes to portray their world more adequately. **Accommodation** is the process of changing a scheme to make it a better match to the world of reality. In sum, assimilation entails incorporating new experiences within old ones, while accommodation involves modifying old thinking structures so that they fit new experiences.

Assimilation and accommodation are bipolar processes that involve the individual in a search for a better state of **equilibrium**—a balance among contending forces (Piaget, 1977). When equilibrium exists, assimilation again operates in terms of the new scheme that the child arrives at through accommodation. But assimilation builds new pressures for the structuring of a new cognitive model to fit reality better. Thus, Piaget saw cognitive development as characterized by alternating states of equilibrium and disequilibrium. Each stage in development consists of particular sets of schemes that are in a relative state of temporary equilibrium at some point in the life span.

By way of illustration, Piaget asked a child if she had a bad dream. Susie, aged four, replied by telling about her dream involving a giant:

> "Yes, I was scared, my tummy was shaking, and I cried and told my mommy about the giant." Asked, "Was it a real giant or was it just pretend? Did the giant just seem to be there, or was it really there?" she answers, "It was really there but it left when I woke up. I saw its footprint on the floor." [Kohlberg and Gilligan, 1971:1057]

Piaget did not consider Susie's response the product of a wild imagination. It represents a particular stage in development in which the child fails to distinguish between dreams and real happenings. Around five years of age, Susie will come to recognize that dreams are not real events. For instance, she may observe that a "footprint" is in fact not on her floor. This assimilation of new information will cause her to question her existing scheme and will contribute to cognitive disequilibrium. Through accommodation she will modify her current thinking structure to fit the new experience. She will then formulate a new scheme to establish a new level of equilibrium. Not untypically, a child of Susie's age will evolve a scheme in which dreams are interpreted as imaginary happenings but happenings that can nonetheless be seen by other people.

The processes of assimilation and accommodation continue to operate in dynamic interplay through additional steps. Soon after Susie recognizes that dreams are not real events, she will discover that other people do not know about the content of her dreams. This realization will lead her to fashion a new scheme to incorporate this information. In still a later step, she will conceive of dreams as internal but nevertheless material events. Finally, when she is between six and eight years of age, Susie will become aware that dreams are nonmaterial happenings—thoughts—that transpire in her mind.

Developmental Sequence

Piaget argued that intelligence and thought progress through four major stages or periods. His **stage** concept implies that the course of development is divided into steplike levels, with changes in behavior occurring from one phase to the next. Each stage represents a break with a previous mode of thinking; each new cognitive structure constitutes a distinctly new integration of an underlying thought organization. This change in quality or kind occurs because the building blocks of the preceding period become linked with new elements, creating a new thinking structure.

In each period children not only construct new notions of time, volume, number, weight, length, and the like; they also discard some of their old ideas while finding new relationships between older concepts and new ones. In this sense, children do not start each stage from scratch but rise from the achievement level of the previous stage. Piaget claims that although the ages at which the stages appear vary among children, the *sequence* in which the stages occur is the same.

Sensorimotor Stage

The *sensorimotor stage* (birth to two years) begins with the infant's genetically given reflexes and ends with the appearance of language and other symbolic ways of representing experience. Piaget termed the period "sensorimotor" because the chief developmental tasks confronting the infant revolve around the coordination of motor activities with sensory inputs (perceptions). During this period, babies achieve the ability to guide their grasping and walking by visual, auditory, and tactual cues. And they learn that their hand is a part of themselves, whereas their bed is not.

One of the chief accomplishments of the sensorimotor stage is children's mastery of the notion of **object permanence:** They come to view a thing as having a reality of its own that extends beyond their immediate perception of it. Piaget observed that when a baby of four or five months is playing with a toy and the toy rolls out of sight behind another object, the infant does not look for it, even though it remains within reach. For the child, "out of sight" is literally "out of mind." Between six and nine months of age, children grasp the principle of object permanence and will retrieve an object. This is a critical ability, since the capacity to distinguish between objects or experiences is a prerequisite to making generalizations and inferences about them.

Preoperational Stage

According to Piaget, infants are limited to the immediate here-and-now. They know food to the extent that they can eat it and manipulate it with their fingers; however, they cannot conceive of it apart from these activities. Infants have a mental picture of food only insofar as actual sensory input reveals the existence of the food. When the sensory input ceases, so does its mental representation. Hence, infants are unable to form a mental image of food "in their heads" in the absence of the actual visual display.

The principal achievement of the *preoperational period* (from two to seven years) is children's developing capacity to represent the world *internally* to themselves through the use of symbols. **Symbols** are things that stand for something else. They are the mechanisms that free children from the rigid boundaries of the here-and-now. By employing symbols, children are able to represent not only present events but past and future ones. Most particularly, the symbolic representations provided by developing language skills enable children to encode experiences by assigning names to them. Language, then, facilitates thought and problem-solving activities.

Stage of Concrete Operations

The hallmark of the *stage of concrete operations*—which coincides roughly with the elementary school years (when the child is from seven to eleven years old)—is the unfreezing of the rigidities of preoperational thought, allowing children to solve conservation problems. **Conservation** involves the recognition that the quantity or amount of something stays the same despite changes in shape or position. This implies that in their minds children become capable of compensating for external changes in objects by various mental operations (see Figure 6.1).

Perhaps an illustration by Piaget will help clarify the matter:

> Children see water in various forms every day. They see water in glasses from which they drink; they see water in bottles that they tip. Moreover, they see water running in bathtubs and lakes and rivers. In all cases, the water is horizontal. So the notion that water is horizontal should be a basic permanent notion.
>
> In some research we did many years ago, we asked the child [of under eight or nine years of age] to predict what would happen to the water

inside a bottle if we tipped it. The child was unable to see the water inside the bottle because it was covered. He was asked to draw a picture of the water inside the bottle when it was tipped. . . . He always draws the line parallel to the bottom of the bottle as it is when the bottle is upright. [1977:4]

Piaget further found that if the cover is taken off the bottle and children are given a chance to compare the bottle with their drawing, they say, "Yes, that's just the way I drew it. Just like my drawing" (1977:4).

Piaget suggested that the reason that young children are unable to "see" that the line of the water is horizontal results from a preoperational cognitive structure. He maintained that the conservation of a substance is the product of reasoning, not perception (1977:6). Preoperational children fix ("center") their attention upon *either* the width

FIGURE 6.1 THE CONSERVATION OF QUANTITY
When we show children of about five or six years of age two identical glasses A and B that contain an equivalent amount of water, the children will acknowledge that the glasses have the "same to drink." If we then pour the water from one of the glasses (A) into a taller and narrower glass (C), the water reaches a higher level. We next ask the children whether there is the same amount of water in the two differently shaped glasses (B and C). Most children under six respond that the tall, narrow glass (C) has more water. Since the children "center" on height and ignore width, they cannot deal with this transformation. In the stage of concrete operations they come to recognize that the amount of water is the same, regardless of the differences in the shapes of the containers. Piaget referred to this ability as the "conservation of quantity," an ability that children acquire between six and eight years of age.

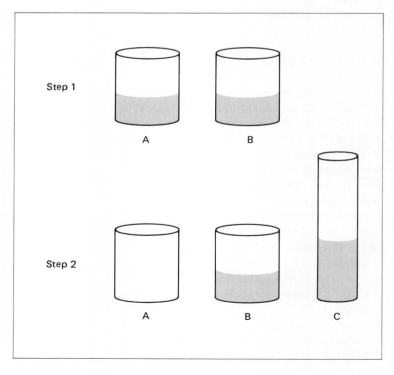

A CONSERVATION EXPERIMENT
(*left*) Place two balls containing the same amount of clay before a four-year-old child and ask if the balls are the same size. Invariably, the child responds affirmatively. (*center*) As the child watches, roll one of the balls into a long, sausagelike shape and again ask the child if the two objects are the same size. (*right*) The child will now assert that one of the clay objects is larger than the other. In this case, the child has claimed that the sausage-shaped clay is larger than the clay ball. Not until the child is several years older will he or she recognize that the two different shapes contain the same quantity of clay—the principle of the conservation of quantity.

or the height of the container and ignore the other dimension. In contrast, concrete operational children *decenter* (they focus simultaneously upon both width and height). Further, concrete operational children also attend to *transformations*—to the gradual shift in the height or width of the fluid in a container as the liquid is poured from it. Thus, during the period of concrete operations, children achieve the capacity for handling relations and classes; they can deal with two or more judgments at the same time.

Stage of Formal Operations

Piaget termed the *stage of formal operations* (from age eleven on) the final and highest level in the development of intelligence from infancy to adulthood. Two major features characterize this mode of thought that typically emerges during adolescence (Looft, 1971). First, adolescents gain the ability to think about their own thought proc-

esses; they are able to deal efficiently with the complex problems involved in reasoning. Second, they become capable of imagining the various possibilities that are contained within a situation; they can generate mentally all possible outcomes of an event and critically evaluate each of them. Hence, adolescents achieve the capacity of thinking in *logical* and *abstract* terms.

Concrete operational children are limited to dealing with tangible problems. They have difficulty comprehending hypothetical situations. For example, an adolescent will accept and think about the following problem: "All three-legged snakes are purple; I am hiding a three-legged snake; guess its color" (Kagan, 1972:92). Most children in elementary school will become confused by the initial premise and insist that snakes are not purple. Adolescents have learned to free themselves from physical "givens" and to deal with hypothetical possibilities. It is this type of thought that is involved in scientific problem solving.

Evaluation

Piaget's works are difficult to understand. He wrote in a highly technical manner and employed an elaborate and at times confusing terminology. Nonetheless, his contributions are recognized as substantial, and along with Sigmund Freud, he is considered to be a giant of twentieth-century psychology. For the most part, American researchers have confirmed that children pass through the broad sequential stages in thought that Piaget described. However, the prevailing opinion among many American educators and psychologists is that Piaget's methods of study tended to underestimate children's cognitive capabilities and the age at which they are acquired (Brainerd, 1977, 1979; Gelman, 1978; Breslow, 1981). Considerable controversy also surrounds Piaget's view that special training has little or no effect in accelerating children's progress through various cognitive stages, a matter that will be considered later in this chapter.

There are likewise those who point out that Piaget neglected some areas of human cognition (Gardner, 1976). Although Piaget had a good deal to say about the development of mathematical and scientific thinking, he provided us with little insight about thinking that involves literature, art, and music. And in his zeal to capture the operations of the mind, Piaget neglected the affective realm of feelings and emotions. We gain little information from Piaget's work regarding children's fears, anxieties, peak experiences, hopes, and aspirations. Nonetheless, it is important to note that we would not know as much as we do concerning the development of children's thought and problem-solving processes without the monumental contributions of Piaget.

Applications to Teaching

As Piaget (1970b) himself emphasized, educators should be exceedingly cautious in moving from theory to practice. While theory frequently provides a rich lode for the mining of ideas about educational practice, the value of such applications must be *demonstrated* by research and not assumed. For his part, Piaget believed that traditional education focuses too much on the technology of teaching and too little upon an understanding of the stages of child development. From Piaget's suggestions and the ideas of other psychologists and educators, it is possible to extract some of the educational implications of cognitive developmental theory (Elkind, 1976; Duckworth, 1979; Kuhn, 1979; Webb, 1980).

First, teaching strategies and materials should be consistent with a child's stage of development because:

> . . . the child can receive valuable information via language or via education directed by an adult only if he is in a state where he can understand the information. That is, to receive the information he must have a structure which enables him to assimilate this information. [Piaget, 1964:13]

Teachers should ask themselves: "What is going on in the heads of the students who are listening to me? What frames of reference and problem-solving processes are they employing?" Educators need to encourage students to change their mental structures so that their thinking and reasoning processes can become more powerful and adaptive. In sum, students have to take responsibility for their own learning, and this cannot be achieved if students simply memorize factual information (Jacobson, 1980). Children take in only as much as suits them, and they remain disdainfully ignorant of everything that exceeds their mental level (Piaget, 1963). Viewed from a Piagetian perspective, much of the education that goes on in children occurs independently of formal education; children are the principal agents in their own education and mental development.

Thus it is not sufficient that teachers provide children with a correct verbal explanation. For instance, math curricula often take for granted the logical abilities of children and presume that only the specifics of mathematical concepts or facts need be learned. But simply because a particular curriculum is coherent to adult mathematicians

PIAGET'S DEVELOPMENTAL THEORY
The late Swiss psychologist Jean Piaget is here seen (upper left) watching children at
play in a park. Much of Piaget's developmental theory was based on his careful
naturalistic observation of children. *(Yves De Braine/Black Star)*

does not necessarily make it coherent to elementary school children (O'Brien, 1973). Likewise, first- and second-grade teachers would be well advised to avoid materials that require an understanding of classification at the concrete operational level. The children may learn to repeat a phrase involving logical structures ("I live in Columbus, Ohio; Columbus is a city in Ohio"), but they are unlikely to comprehend the concept (Metz, 1978). Further, Piaget said that eoncepts such as social justice, humanity, and social values are on the level of formal operations and hence are inaccessible to elementary school children because the children still employ concrete operational thought (Inhelder and Piaget, 1958).

A second implication of Piagetian concepts is that those responsible for curriculum construction should base the sequence of expected learnings on the sequences discovered by developmental researchers. Ideally, the introduction of programs within and between grade levels should occur in terms of the readiness state of students and the inherent logic of the subject matter. At present, however, the bridge between the theory of cognitive development and the aims of curriculum planners still remains fairly obscure.

A third implication for educators follows from Piaget's (1970b) view that an "active" classroom is the best classroom. Telling children information may possibly result in their remembering given facts and even regurgitating them on command. But this does not guarantee that children have mastered the information or acquired new knowledge. For instance, sixth-grade children have been shown to be capable of describing complicated physical phenomena by correctly using textbook terms. But when asked to explain the information in their own words, they reveal incredible ignorance and little understanding (Joyce, 1966). Practical situations that correspond closely to children's natural activity provide the best kind of learning situations (Duckworth, 1979). According to Piagetian educators, teachers can best help children by providing them with a cognitively rich environment. Teachers need not specifically organize content for children because children "organize things for themselves" as they seek to make sense out of the world (Kamii and DeVries, 1978). Each child structures each learning situation in terms of his or her own schemes. Consequently, it is unlikely that two students will derive the same meaning or benefit from a given experience (Webb, 1980).

In sum, Piagetian theory suggests that children need to be actively involved in the learning process. Through a constant exchange—indeed confrontation—with their social and physical environments, children assimilate knowledge and make the necessary accommodations to this new knowledge:

> Good pedagogy must involve presenting the child with situations in which he himself experiments, in the broadest sense of that term—trying things out to see what happens, manipulating things, manipulating symbols, posing questions and seeking his own answers, reconciling what he finds one time with what he finds at another, comparing his findings with those of other children. [Duckworth, 1964:2]

The content of education is geared to the stages of development in which children build, decompose, and recombine concepts at more adequate adjustmental levels. Such sequences of instruction do not aim to force new cognitive structures on children but to provide the atmosphere in which optimal growth can occur. Hence, the emphasis of Piagetian education falls on facilitating the development of more adequate schemes rather than on acquiring facts. And learning is viewed as an active restructuring of thought rather than an increase in content. Piagetians believe that education then

becomes germane to real children living their lives in a real world.

The Readiness Controversy

Piaget's discoveries were largely ignored by American psychologists prior to 1960. However, during the 1960s and 1970s this situation changed, and Piaget's theoretical framework won considerable acclaim. But with acclaim has also come controversy. Indeed, a number of early American followers of Piaget have become disenchanted with Piaget's stages of development. One of these is John H. Flavell (1978, 1982). He writes:

> Piaget's stage model is proving increasingly less credible to developmentalists and less useful to educators. There is reason to doubt whether "stages" of the broad, Piagetian "period" variety (e.g., the concrete-operation period) will figure prominently in future theorizing about cognitive development. However much we may wish it were otherwise, human cognitive growth may simply be too contingent, multiform, and heterogeneous—too variegated in developmental mechanisms, routes, and rates—to be accurately characterizable by any stage theory of the Piagetian kind. [1978:187]

Nonetheless, other developmental psychologists find that Piaget's model is sound. They believe that whatever revisions are made will most likely be in terms of the framework that Piaget outlined and the questions he posed.

One exceedingly controversial issue has been Piaget's notion that "teaching children concepts that they have not attained in their spontaneous development . . . is completely useless" (1970a:30). As noted earlier in the chapter, Piaget emphasized that cognitive development proceeds through a fixed sequence of steps. Thus, development is said to control when and how learning processes operate. Educators and psychologists who share Piaget's view hold that children should be allowed to become ready for school and for particular materials at their own pace. Seen from this perspective, readiness comes as a healthy child grows

READINESS CONTROVERSY
Psychologists such as Jerome S. Bruner believe that children's cognitive development can be accelerated through an enriched environment. This four-year-old child from an advantaged background can correctly match his fingers with the number of arranged objects.

and matures: "Time is the answer—not special drills or special practice" (Hymes, 1958:10).

Other psychologists and educators reject Piaget's arguments and insist that schools can and should teach readiness rather than wait for it (Clarizio, 1977). They believe that providing children with an enriched environment can produce substantial benefits. For example, the psychologist Jerome S. Bruner asserts that "any subject can be taught effectively in some intellectually honest form to any child at any stage of development" (1960:33). And he continues to defend his position: "I have a lot of scars from controversies over that dictum. But there has not been one single shred of evidence that goes counter to it" (1970:30).

Over the past twenty years, the principle of conservation has been the fundamental concept in Piaget's theory and has been subjected to the greatest scrutiny. As pointed out earlier in the chapter, Piaget argued that young children are incapable of understanding that when water is poured out of a full glass and into a wider glass that the water fills only part way, the amount of water remains unchanged. Piaget attributed this inability to the deficiency of young children's cognitive structure. He adamantly insisted that one cannot teach young children the principle of conservation. Rather, knowledge of conservation can only be gained when all the prior components of that knowledge are present and properly developed in children.

During the 1960s, many attempts were made to train young children in conservation. Most researchers had little success in teaching conservation skills (Smedslund, 1961; Flavell, 1963; Kuhn, 1974). However, Robert M. Gagné (1968) performed a task analysis of Piaget's test for the conservation of liquid quantity. He suggests that the task requires a variety of cognitive skills and information that is not necessarily related to conservation. For instance, children must know that containers vary in three dimensions. They also need to recognize how these dimensions are interrelated so that changes in one or more dimensions affect the container's volume and hence the level of the liquid. These matters, Gagné says, involve knowledge and not simply logic; as such, he argues that conservation concepts can be taught.

Gagné proposes that educators should teach each skill involved in a task in its sequential order. Hence, if one wishes children to learn the principle involved in conserving quantity, it is necessary to break a conservation task down into its underlying components and to teach each skill in turn; doing so requires providing children with a set of subordinate and prerequisite concepts that are organized to produce cumulative learning (each element building upon the others in a progressive fashion). More recently, psychologists like Barry J. Zimmerman (1977, 1978) have followed this procedure. They have employed observation learning methods and have successfully taught conservation principles to young children.

Many educators see dangers in extreme formulations of both the natural-readiness and the accelerated-readiness positions. Natural-readiness views can become a vehicle for justifying decisions to terminate or delay instruction of a child who displays difficulty in mastering complex skills in mathematics or reading (Zimmerman, 1977). These conceptions can foster defeatism and pessimism that, in turn, breed self-fulfilling prophecies.

Teachers must remind themselves that children come from varied family backgrounds. As a result, some have a learning history that has provided them with learning capabilities that are well matched to the typical school environment. Children from other kinds of backgrounds lack many of these capabilities when they enter school (Glaser, 1973). Teachers must not allow themselves to become complacent with these latter children; a ''wait and see'' approach can easily degenerate into one of ''doing nothing.''

Dangers also lie in certain accelerated-readiness programs. Not only does premature practice waste the time and energy of both teachers and students, but more importantly, students can lose interest and develop negative attitudes toward learning. Those children who cannot keep pace find themselves judged unfavorably by their teachers, parents, and peers, often with damaging consequences for their self-conceptions and self-esteem. Students who experience continual frustration and repeated failure—who are ''intellectually burned''—tend to search for ways to escape from the school setting, since they find it unpleasant and aversive (Clarizio, 1977).

THE APPROACHES OF BRUNER AND AUSUBEL

Piaget's theory has had a considerable impact on educational psychology. Two other psychologists have likewise made major contributions to our understanding of cognitive processes and their relation to education: Jerome S. Bruner and David P. Ausubel. The approaches of Piaget, Bruner, and Ausubel are similar in their recognition that adaptation to an external reality plays a major role in development. The three theories also postulate the existence of an internal structure that affects whether and how various aspects of knowledge are acquired. However, each theory provides varying explanations for exactly what it is that develops in cognition and what mechanisms are involved in developmental processes. Moreover, each theorist offers a somewhat unique view of what constitutes the best educational practice. Piaget espoused an ''activity school.'' Bruner advocates practices that encourage students to ''discover'' certain truths through their own self-directed activities. In contrast, Ausubel assigns a considerably greater role than either Piaget or Ausubel to ''expository'' teaching, in which the instructor directly tells students the required concepts and principles (Lawton, Saunders, and Muhs, 1980).

The Theory of Jerome S. Bruner

Jerome S. Bruner (born 1915) was one of the first American psychologists to appreciate the importance of Piaget's contributions. Bruner is a distinguished psychologist in his own right, a past president of the American Psychological Association, and a recipient of its Distinguished Scientific Award. Although influenced by Piaget in his early thinking about education, Bruner moved away from strict Piagetian formulations and developed an approach that became characteristically his own. This change in direction was influenced by Bruner's research, which convinced him that Piaget's stage theory is structurally too rigid and fails to give sufficient attention to the media by which children represent their experience.

Modes of Representing the World

Bruner's approach is both cognitive and developmental. He emphasizes that the chief goal of education is to promote the general understanding of the structure of a subject. This requires that children recognize the ways in which a subject fits together and how other things are meaningfully related to it. Thus, Bruner stresses the importance of teaching global concepts and integrating principles (Bruner, 1960).

The developmental aspect of Bruner's theory lies in his interest in the ways human beings represent their experience of the world:

> There are striking changes in emphasis that occur with the development of representation. At first the child's world is known to him principally by the habitual actions he uses for coping with it. In time there is added a technique of representation through imagery that is relatively free of action. Gradually there is added a new and powerful method of translating action and image into language, providing still a third system of representation. Each of the three modes of representation—enactive, ikonic, and symbolic—has its unique way of representing events. Each places a pow-

MODES OF REPRESENTING THE WORLD

According to Jerome S. Bruner, cognitive development is associated with shifts in children's favored modes for representing the world. Mental images and pictures play an especially important part in the representative process of preschool and kindergarten youngsters.

erful impress on the mental life of human beings at different ages, and their interplay persists as one of the major features of adult intellectual life. [Bruner, Olver, and Greenfield, 1966:1]

Hence, in Bruner's view, human beings "know" something in three ways: through doing it—*enactive;* through a picture or image of it—*ikonic;* and through some socially standardized means such as language—*symbolic*. Take, for example, our "knowing" a knot. We can know it by the actual physical operations involved in tying it; we can have a mental image of a knot as an object on the order of a pretzel or a mental "motion picture" of the knot being formed; and we can represent a knot linguistically by combining four alphabetical letters, k-n-o-t, or by linking together utterances in sentences to describe the process of tying a string (Bruner, Olver, and Greenfield, 1966).

Bruner suggests that cognitive development is centered upon the changes that occur in children's *favored* mode for representing the world. At first, during that period Piaget termed the sensorimotor stage, the representative process is enactive; children come to terms with the world through their motor activities such as crawling and walking. In the preschool and kindergarten years, ikonic representation is preferred (although children are capable of ikonic representation by their first birthday); children employ mental images or pictures that are closely linked to perception. During the middle school years, the emphasis shifts to symbolic representation (although children begin mastering language by their second birthday); children use arbitrary and socially standardized representations of things. These three modes, then, are the ways by which individuals "know" the world.

Instructional Theory

Bruner has not been satisfied with merely *describing* the processes by which children learn or develop. He has shown considerable concern with the problems of education (Bruner, 1966). As such, he has been interested in fashioning an instructional theory that *prescribes* the optimal conditions for facilitating meaningful learning. He seeks to provide rules for the most effective acquisition of some body of knowledge or of a skill. And he aims to provide techniques for measuring educational outcomes. Further, Bruner argues that an instructional theory should be *normative,* setting goals for education and establishing criteria by which success or failure can be judged. For instance, Bruner anticipates that an instructional theory will outline procedures and techniques for teaching mathematics, allowing a teacher to derive specific instructional plans for handling a class in ninth-grade algebra.

Bruner (1966) outlines four features that should be included within a theory of instruction. First, the theory should specify the conditions that predispose individuals toward learning. The formulation should state the experiences that contribute to an individual's desire to learn in general and also to master particular material. Here the emphasis falls on a student's motivation.

Second, Bruner suggests that a theory of instruction should indicate the ways in which a body of knowledge is to be structured so that students can readily learn and use it. If appropriately organized, Bruner (1960, 1966) believes that any idea or problem can be presented in a form that is simple enough for any learner to understand. This does not mean that a seven-year-old can intelligently discuss all the ramifications of Einstein's theory of relativity; however, if properly structured and taught, the child should be able to grasp and explain the principle underlying the theory.

A third ingredient in a theory of instruction is the specification of the most effective sequences by which material is to be presented. This entails effectively ordering information for the learner in terms of its difficulty and logic:

> Instruction consists of leading the learner through a sequence of statements and restatements of a problem or body of knowledge that increase the learner's ability to grasp, transform, and transfer what he is learning. In short, the sequence in

which a learner encounters materials within a domain of knowledge affects the difficulty he will have in achieving mastery. [Bruner, 1966:49]

Finally, Bruner believes that a theory of instruction should specify the nature and pacing of the rewards. Ideally, educators should move from extrinsic to intrinsic rewards—that is, the learner should become progressively less dependent upon a teacher's rewarding behavior and should come to experience inherent psychological satisfaction from the task itself. The optimal timing of rewards also assumes critical importance. For instance, if an outcome is gained too early it stifles further exploration; if too late, the feedback may no longer be helpful. Hence, the teacher's role is one of sensitive tuning.

Discovery Learning

> The goal of education is not to increase the amount of knowledge, but to create the possibilities for a child to invent and discover.
>
> JEAN PIAGET
> *Cognitive Development
> in Children,* 1964

Distinguished educators like Jean Jacques Rousseau (1712–1778). Maria Montessori (1870–1952), and John Dewey (1859–1952) have advocated providing students with opportunities so that they themselves can discover rules and broad principles (Clarizio, Craig, and Mehrens, 1977). More recently, this viewpoint has been espoused by psychologists who emphasize the cognitive aspects of learning like Jean Piaget (1964) and Jerome S. Bruner (1960, 1966). During the 1960s and early 1970s, discovery-learning proponents had a major impact on the revisions that were made in the curricula of the physical and biological sciences, mathematics, and social sciences (see the boxed insert on pages 178–179).

Discovery learning is an umbrella concept that has somewhat different meanings among different groups of educators (Wittrock, 1966; Nuthall and Snook, 1973; Strike, 1975). Broadly defined, **discovery learning** refers to the teaching of principles, rules, and problem solving through minimal teacher guidance and maximal student exploration and trial-and-error learning (Shulman, 1968). Bruner states the matter in these terms:

> To instruct someone in [a] discipline is not a matter of getting him to commit the results to mind; rather, it is to teach him to participate in the process that makes possible the establishment of knowledge. We teach a subject, not to produce little living libraries from that subject, but rather to get a student to think . . . for himself, to consider matters as a historian does, to take part in the process of knowledge getting. Knowing is a process, not a product. [1966:72]

The discovery approach has come to be identified with *inductive* reasoning. Thus, Robert Glaser observes:

> A learning-by-discovery sequence involves induction. This is the procedure of giving exemplars of a more general case which permits the student to induce the proposition involved. [1966:15]

Induction involves "seeing" the general in the particular. For instance, the teacher might ask each child to measure the angles in a number of triangles to see if each can formulate some generalization regarding the sum. Or the teacher might present the students with a number of examples and allow the students to discover the appropriate definition. Such an approach requires rigorous formulation of the materials so that students do not arrive at the wrong definition. For example, a student might make the false discovery that mammals are mother animals if the teacher only provides illustrations of females (Davis, Alexander, and Yelon, 1974).

Bruner (1961) claims four advantages for discovery learning. First, it enhances memory retention, since the students are required to organize information in a meaningful manner. Second, discovery learning increases general intellectual potency by providing students with information

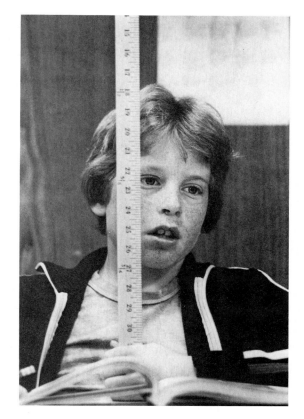

DISCOVERY LEARNING
Discovery learning involves children in the process of acquiring knowledge for themselves.

that is readily available for problem solving. Third, it fosters intrinsic rather than extrinsic motivation by using the satisfactions and rewards inherent within the discovery process. And fourth, discovery learning promotes the acquisition of the attack skills and heuristics of discovery (see the boxed insert on page 180).

In sum, the student is said to acquire from a discovery-learning approach not only the generalization or concept but the process of discovery

CONTROVERSIES SURROUNDING MATHEMATICS CURRICULA

In recent decades, considerable controversy has surrounded the mathematics curricula of the nation's schools. At the present time, the focus of much debate has been the "new math." The heart of current criticism of mathematics programs is embodied in the lament, "The kids don't learn to compute as we used to." Critics seek to document their charges by pointing to the results of Scholastic Aptitude Tests. The median score in mathematics dropped from 502 in 1963 to 467 in 1982 (the maximum score is 800). Many lay the blame for the students' inadequacies on the new math program.

New math encompasses a wide range of innovations for teaching mathematics. In truth, the term is frequently used so broadly that it now has little descriptive value. It has come to mean many different things and is often misunderstood. However, the backbone of the new mathematics movement has been the notion that children should work from the concrete and familiar toward the abstract and unfamiliar (Ballew, 1977). As such, the orientation is largely in keeping with the discovery learning model.

The new math movement received its impetus when the Soviets successfully orbited the first artificial satellite in the fall of 1957. Many Americans were convinced that the Russians were ahead in technology and that something had to be done to protect the nation. Early in 1958, a group of mathematicians who were meeting at the Massachusetts Institute of Technology put together an initial version of the new math. It was an approach that brought some of the sophisticated language of algebra and higher mathematics into the elementary school curriculum.

"Set theory" became a central element in new math programs. The "associative" and "commutative" properties of groups and fields were used to explain the rational and real number systems. Set theory was designed to help teachers make children's work more concrete. When children first come to school, they are already familiar with sets of blocks, sets of dishes, teams of players, boxes of crayons, and so on. Hence,

itself. The process is thought to resemble that involved in problem-solving situations (Nuthall and Snook, 1973). Clearly, this model for learning is quite different from the highly structured and minutely directed model afforded by behavioral psychologists like B. F. Skinner, who favor techniques of programmed instruction.

The benefits claimed for discovery learning are vigorously disputed by the method's critics (Wittrock, 1966; Collinge, 1976). For instance, observational learning theorists like Barry J. Zimmerman (1977) claim that discovery-learning procedures are highly inferior to modeling and explanation techniques. Based on their research, they argue that discovery learning is not suitable for complex tasks in which "guessing" the answer does not make the underlying rule obvious (Zimmerman and Rosenthal, 1972).

Other critics, like Skinner (1968), insist that discovery learning is highly inefficient, since it involves a high degree of trial-and-error responding; students spend a good deal of time solving a trivial problem that a teacher could explain to them in a matter of minutes. It is unreasonable, say these critics, to expect students to rediscover the entire content of culture for themselves. And the critics point to their own research that suggests that discovery methods are not superior to expo-

sets of objects with which children are familiar were introduced to bridge the gap between the concrete world and the world of mathematics (Ballew, 1977).

New math programs marked a departure from the "special techniques approach" that had been introduced in the schools under the influence of behavioral psychologists. Mathematics had been broken down into various types of problems. A special method for performing each type of problem was then taught until it became habitual. For example, if a word problem contained the words "in all," it meant the students were to add. Students would glance through a problem until they encountered "in all," and then they found the sum of the numbers. If they failed to find "in all," there were other catchphrases. And if a catchphrase was absent, they would ask the teacher (Offner, 1978).

Proponents of the "back-to-basics" movement, like Frank E. Armbruster, urge a return to these earlier methods of teaching:

Parents and school-board trustees should examine teaching methods. Many math and other primary-school problems might be reduced by a new emphasis on rote learning. For example, we know how to teach children the multiplication tables, and we know that this knowledge makes long division much easier. Children can and do learn the "times tables" by rote, chanting in unison if necessary. [1977:56]

The controversy regarding the mathematics curriculum is commonly phrased in terms of "new" versus "old" math. If one approach does not achieve the desired results, there are those who believe the "pendulum" must swing back to the other. However, there are educators who see neither method of instruction as particularly successful and who continue the search for still other means (Offner, 1978). Others see a danger in extreme swings between positions, pointing to resulting excesses. Illustrations of such excesses abounded in 1957 when

the new mathematics movement was beginning. One authority wrote in *The Arithmetic Teacher:*

Skills in computation are no longer essential. Calculating machines are available to everyone at prices which are in keeping with their needs. The introduction of the calculating machine has increased rather than lessened the importance of learning arithmetic. The need for extreme skill and speed, however, in obtaining "answers" has disappeared. The demand is now for the understanding of arithmetic, its logical structure, and its practical application. [Schott, 1957:204]

And still others, like the National Council of Supervisors of Mathematics (one of the affiliated groups of the National Council of Teachers of Mathematics), seek to identify the types of skills required for modern living and to formulate programs that facilitate the acquisition of these skills.

sitory methods and in many instances are inferior to them (Anastasiow et al., 1970; Richards and Bolton, 1971; Francis, 1975).

Expository Learning

Discovery learning is often contrasted with **expository learning.** If an inductive approach characterizes the discovery orientation, then a *deductive* approach marks the expository method. In expository teaching, the instructor provides students with the required definitions, principles, and rules. The approach is deductive, since the teacher gen-

erally begins by presenting a concept and then provides examples of it and points out its applications and implications. Take the teacher who wishes to teach his or her students the principle that "the sum of the angles in a triangle equals 180 degrees." The teacher would enunciate the principle and illustrate it with one or more particular triangles drawn on the board. The task would not require any independent discovery on the part of the learners. The principle is presented to them and they are merely required to learn and remember it (Ausubel and Robinson, 1969). Textbooks are also illustrations of the expository method.

David P. Ausubel is one of the principal pro-

DISCOVERY LEARNING

JEROME S. BRUNER

Jerome S. Bruner provides an illustration of the discovery method as shown in Table 6.A. The purpose of the lesson was to teach students that they can reduce a language into types and order:

TABLE 6.A
Learning a Language Through the Discovery Method

First write a sentence on the board. Then get the children to form similar sentences as follows:

The	man	ate	his	lunch.
A	boy	stole	a	bike.
The	dog	chased	my	cat.
My	father	skidded	the	car.
A	wind	blew	his	hat.

At this particular point, we have the children provide other sentences *ad libitum*. And they provide them. Sometimes they are wrong. Usually not. We then shift them to the following puzzle: How is it that one can go from left to right across the sentences in

Source: Jerome S. Bruner, "Some Elements of Discovery," in L. S. Shulman and E. R. Keislar, eds., *Learning by Discovery: A Critical Appraisal* (Chicago: Rand McNally, 1966), pp. 106–107.

practically any row and still come out with a sentence: The boy chased the cat; A father chased a lunch; The man stole my bike; A father stole his hat. Some of the sentences are rather silly, but

clearly sentences. Soon they will say things like, There are five places and you can put lots of things in each place. But which kinds of words will fit into each column? Type and token begin to emerge as ideas. Now we reach a very critical point. Ask, for example, whether they can make up some more columns. One child proposed the following, something that put the class on a new level of attitude toward the use of mind. He said that there is a "zero" column that could contain the word "did." I asked what other

particular words this column could contain. The children said "did," "can," "has." This was the zero column. Then one of the pupils said that this did not quite fit and that you would have to change the word in the third column too but it would not be very much of a change. They were ready and willing now to get into the syntax of the language, to invent it afresh. They talked about the family of words that would fit and that two columns affected the families each could carry. Only then did we introduce some terminology. We talked about type and order, and that in sentences there were words that were types and they appeared in a certain permissible order. One of the children said of types, "They're called parts of speech. A noun, for example, is a 'person, place or thing.' " To produce a pause, we asked about "dying" and "courage." They were quick to grasp the syntactic distinction of "privilege of occurrence" in a certain position, in contrast to the semantic criterion of person, place or thing and found the idea interesting. They soon began on the alternative ways a sentence could be said and have the same meaning. We were soon building up the idea of productivity.

ponents of the expository method (Ausubel and Robinson, 1969; Ausubel, Novak, and Hanesian, 1978). He points out that a concept or principle can become available to us in its final form by either the discovery or reception (expository) routes. Next we must relate this new idea to the knowledge that we already possess. In this second stage, we must consciously act upon the concept or principle in an attempt to remember is so that it will be available to us in the future.

Ausubel says that we undertake to remember something in one of two ways. We may attempt to memorize the idea, without relating it to existing knowledge, a process termed *rote learning*. Or we may seek to retain the idea by relating it to what we already know, thereby "making sense" out of it, a process termed *meaningful learning*. In practice, much learning is neither entirely rote or meaningful but *more or less rote* or *more or less meaningful*.

Ausubel begins his treatment of cognitive learning by distinguishing between reception (expository) and discovery learning on the one hand and rote and meaningful learning on the other. He then

combines each of these dimensions (continua) to arrive at four combinations (see Figure 6.2):

- *Rote discovery learning:* Takes place when learners, having arrived at the concept or principle themselves (typically by trial and error), subsequently commit it to memory without relating it to other knowledge that they possess.
- *Rote reception learning:* Occurs when the teacher presents the concept or principle and the learners merely memorize it.
- *Meaningful discovery learning:* Takes place when learners formulate the concept or principle for themselves and subsequently relate it in some sensible manner to their existing ideas.
- *Meaningful reception learning:* Occurs when the teacher presents a concept or principle in its final form and learners relate it to their existing ideas in some sensible way.

Hence, according to Ausubel, learning tasks can be found that exemplify all combinations of the reception-discovery and rote-meaningful dimensions. He points out that many educators have

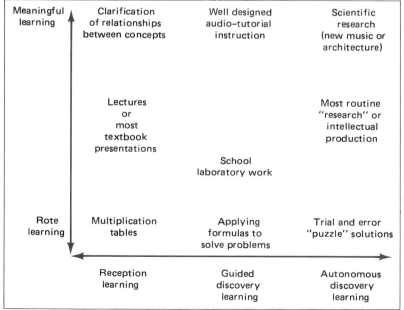

FIGURE 6.2 RECEPTION LEARNING AND DISCOVERY LEARNING
David P. Ausubel distinguishes between reception learning and discovery learning and places them on a separate continuum from role learning and meaningful learning. *(Source: Joseph D. Novak, A Theory of Education [Ithaca, N.Y.: Cornell University Press, 1977], p. 101. Copyright © 1977 by Cornell University. Used by permission of the publisher, Cornell University Press.)*

tended to confuse these dimensions and to assume that all reception (expository) learning must be rote in nature and, conversely, that all discovery learning must be meaningful. His formulations help teachers to recognize that both expository and discovery learning can be either rote or meaningful.

Some educators find it useful to combine principles from both the expository and discovery approaches. For instance, Merlin C. Wittrock (1966) distinguishes between *unguided* discovery and *guided* discovery. In the former case, the teacher provides the students with neither the principle that applies to a problem nor its solution; in the latter, the teacher assists students with recall and application of the principle but not with the solution of the problem. Thus, guided discovery is a form of problem solving that falls in an intermediate area between the extremes of unguided discovery and expository teaching (see Figure 6.2).

Concluding Comment

A clash of doctrines is not a disaster—it is an opportunity.
ALFRED NORTH WHITEHEAD

This and the previous chapter considered three theories or models of learning: conditioning techniques, observational learning, and cognitive learning. Each has its proponents and critics. Nonetheless, the theories are not mutually exclusive; we need not accept one model and reject the others. Models are simply tools—themselves cognitive or mental constructs—that help us to visualize (describe and analyze) something. Any theory has the effect of limiting the viewer's vision by promoting a tunnel perspective. But a good theory also functions like a pair of binoculars and increases the horizon of what is seen. It affords rules of inference through which new relationships can be uncovered and the frontiers of knowledge expanded (Reese and Overton, 1970).

Different tasks call for different models. For some tasks one model or theory may be more fruitful than another. The educational psychologist N. L. Gage notes:

The present stage of development of conditioning and cognitive theory probably makes it desirable to use both approaches in practical school work. For some purposes, the curriculum planner and teacher educator should pay close heed to the importance of reinforcement, to schedules of reinforcement, to the use of appropriate models, to the minimizing of average stimulation, and many other factors emphasized by Skinner and his disciples. For other purposes, or at other stages in the development of practical programs and procedures, it is important for educators to pay heed to the importance of cognitive structure, logical and psychological organization, meaningfulness, context, relevance, and the sequence of ideas. Although scientific consistency and elegance may be sacrificed by practicing this kind of eclecticism, the gains for practical purposes make it worthwhile. [1972:50]

By way of illustration, conditioning techniques can be applied in teaching children multiplication tables and spelling and in managing various disciplinary problems. Observational learning is particularly appropriate for tasks that can be directly imitated and do not involve the grasp of abstract concepts, principles, or relationships. Cognitive approaches are helpful in instructing students in matters that require logical and abstract thought, for instance, the Law of Constant Composition (a chemical compound is always made up of definite proportions by weight of its constituent elements).

CHAPTER SUMMARY

1. Another type of learning involves cognitive processes. Psychologists who stress cognitive learning portray human beings as capable of making rational decisions, in that the decisions are based on available information and an ability to process the information intelligently. Mental activity ''makes something'' out of perceptions, and this something is meaningful and organized.

2. Jean Piaget investigated the development of cognitive processes as they unfold in children from

birth through the various stages of infancy, childhood, and adolescence. He forcefully argued that in their intellectual activity children are not miniature adults; instead, they think in a qualitatively unique and distinctive manner.

3. Piaget viewed the individual and the environment as engaged in continuing interaction that leads to new perceptions of the world and new organizations of knowledge. By acting on the environment, individuals cause the environment to change. In turn, individuals must themselves change if they are to adapt to the modified conditions. Accordingly, people are shaped and altered by the consequences of their own actions.

4. Piaget argued that intelligence and thought develop through four major stages or periods: sensorimotor stage (birth to two years); preoperational stage (two to seven years); stage of concrete operations (seven to eleven years); and stage of formal operations (eleven years and on). He devoted his greatest attention to the stage of concrete operations, in which children acquire the ability to solve conservation problems.

5. Piagetian psychologists and educators believe that teaching strategies and materials should be consistent with a child's stage of development. Further, those responsible for curriculum construction should introduce materials only in terms of the readiness state of students and the inherent logic of the subject matter.

6. Jerome S. Bruner suggests that cognitive development is centered on the changes that occur in children's favored mode for representing the world. At first the representative process is enactive; children come to terms with the world through their motor activities, such as crawling and walking. In the preschool and kindergarten years, ikonic representation is preferred; children employ mental images or pictures that are closely linked to perception. During the middle school years, the emphasis shifts to symbolic representation; children use arbitrary and socially standardized representations of things.

7. Some psychologists and educators emphasize that children should be allowed to become ready for school and for particular materials at their own pace. They believe that teaching children concepts that they have not attained in their natural development is completely useless. Others disagree and insist that schools can and should teach readiness rather than wait for it. Still others see dangers in extreme formulations of either position.

8. Discovery learning has come to be identified with inductive reasoning. It is to be contrasted with expository learning, which involves deductive reasoning. Each method for teaching has its proponents and critics.

CHAPTER GLOSSARY

accommodation A Piagetian concept that refers to the process of changing a scheme to make it a better match to the world of reality.

assimilation A Piagetian concept that refers to the process of taking in new information and interpreting it in such a manner that the information conforms to a currently held scheme.

cognition The process of thinking and knowing; our reception of raw sensory information and our transformation, elaboration, storage, recovery, and use of this information.

conservation The recognition that the quantity or amount of something stays the same despite changes in shape or position.

discovery learning The teaching of principles, rules, and problem solving through minimal teacher guidance and maximal student exploration and trial-and-error learning.

equilibrium A Piagetian concept that refers to a balance among the contending forces of assimilation and accommodation.

expository learning The teaching of principles, rules, and problem solving through maximal teacher guidance and minimal student exploration and trial-and-error learning.

object permanence   The view that a thing has a reality of its own that extends beyond the immediate perception of it.

schemes   The term Piaget employs for thinking structures that people evolve for dealing with specific kinds of situations in their environment.

stage   A concept that implies that the course of development is divided into steplike levels, with clear-cut changes in behavior occurring from one phase to the next.

symbol   Something that stands for something else.

EXERCISES

Review Questions

1. Piaget made a number of assumptions regarding children's thinking, such as
   a. unlike the adult, the child tends to be a passive learner
   b. because of a lack of experience, children's thinking is much more ''illogical'' than that of adults
   c. children's thinking differs qualitatively rather than quantitatively from adults'
   d. a, b, and c are true
   e. b and c are true

2. The process whereby the child interprets new information to make it conform to old ideas is called
   a. accommodation
   b. assimilation
   c. schemes
   d. equilibration

3. Object permanence is an accomplishment of which of Piaget's stages?
   a. sensorimotor
   b. preoperational
   c. concrete
   d. formal operations

4. Representation of the world internally through symbols is accomplished in which of Piaget's stages?
   a. sensorimotor
   b. preoperational
   c. concrete operations
   d. formal operations

5. The ability to analyze one's own thought processes is reached in which of Piaget's stages?
   a. sensorimotor
   b. preoperational
   c. concrete
   d. formal operations

6. Among the criticisms leveled against Piaget is that he
   a. tended to underestimate the age at which children acquired specific cognitive abilities
   b. felt that the child's rate of development through the various stages could not be accelerated
   c. dealt primarily with the content of science and mathematics
   d. a, b, and c are true
   e. b and c are true

7. The arguments heard in the natural versus accelerated ''readiness'' controversy include
   a. accelerated programs may require detailed task analyses that are beyond the ability of many teachers (for example, conservation)
   b. acceleration benefits all children in the program, although in varying amounts
   c. acceleration may prove particularly useful for children entering school with limiting family backgrounds
   d. a, b, and c are true
   e. a and c are true

8. Ikonic representation is the favored mode in
   a. infancy
   b. preschool and kindergarten

c. middle school
d. junior high school

9. From Bruner's point of view, discovery learning has advantages, including that it
   a. requires less need for memory
   b. aids problem solving
   c. enhances intrinsic motivation
   d. a, b, and c are true
   e. b and c are true

10. Compared to discovery learning, expository learning is characterized as
    a. deductive
    b. more teacher structured
    c. receptive
    d. a, b, and c are true
    e. a and c are true

Answers

1. c (See pp. 164–165)
2. b (See p. 166)
3. a (See p. 167)
4. b (See p. 167)
5. d (See p. 169)
6. d (See p. 170)
7. e (See pp. 172–174)
8. b (See p. 175)
9. e (See p. 177)
10. d (See pp. 179, 181)

Applying Principles and Concepts

1. In the space provided before each example, indicate whether it is an example of assimilation (AS) or accommodation (AC).

_____ a. A small child seeing an orange for the first time tries to bounce it.
_____ b. A five-year-old uses a toy clock as a door-stopper.
_____ c. A bigot argues that an intelligent black is an "exception to the rule."
_____ d. A college student tries to reconcile his own views of interpersonal relations with the theories discussed in his psychology textbook.

2. A four-year-old girl has watched her mother prepare a bowl of bread dough. Her mother then proceeds to fill several bread pans, and the girl exclaims, "Where did you get all that extra dough?" According to Piaget, the girl has failed to exhibit which of the following?

_____ a. Sensorimotor development
_____ b. Conservation
_____ c. Symbolic language
_____ d. Transductive reasoning

3. Your local school district has adopted a math curriculum based on the Piagetian model. A description of the new curriculum follows. Underline those passages the text would support.

The new math curriculum carefully sequences all mathematical operations as defined by eminent mathematicians. The logic follows closely the readiness levels universally established by developmental psychologists. Learning is considered to be an active process, following Piaget's strong ideas on teaching. As in any Piagetian model, student attitudes, feelings, and emotions are critical aspects of the program.

4. Consider the problems of a teacher who has been employing a Skinnerian model of teaching and who now wishes to follow Bruner's four-step model of instruction. Which aspect of Bruner's model will provide the most difficulty in transition?

5. A teacher conducting a lesson in electronics makes the following statements. In the space provided before each, indicate whether it represents the enactive (E), ikonic (I), or symbolic (S) mode of thought.

_____ a. " 'Capacitor' is spelled c-a-p-a-c-i-t-o-r."
_____ b. "Trace the main circuit with your finger."
_____ c. "Imagine what would happen if the resistor failed."
_____ d. "What are the notations used for these instruments?"
_____ e. "Explain the major functions of this device."

6. In each instance of learning in the following list, indicate whether Ausubel would define it as rote discovery learning (RDL), rote reception learning (RRL), meaningful reception learning (MRL), or meaningful discovery learning (MDL).

_____ a. Mary, on the way to school for her spelling test, keeps repeating "i before e, except after c."

_____ b. Allan, having learned about pressure-temperature relationships, says to his mother, "Keep the lid on when you cook, Mother; the water will get hotter."

_____ c. Mr. Cloud explains to his friend that, if he depresses his gas pedal for thirty seconds before starting, the car will start under any set of conditions.

_____ d. Laura, a five-year-old, finds that her mother's diamond ring will scratch glass but not the reverse. She finds that the diamond will scratch metal also. "Gosh," she says, "diamonds can scratch anything. They must be harder than anything else; I can cut anything with diamonds."

_____ e. The biology teacher announces that all her students can name the twelve cranial nerves by means of a little phrase. Not only that: her students have now made up phrases to help them with other subjects.

Answers

1. a, AS; b, AC; c, AS; d, AC (See p. 166)
2. b (See pp. 168–169)
3. Underline "learning is considered to be an active process." (See pp. 170–172)
4. Your answer should reflect the Skinnerian emphasis on motivation as environmental manipulation, whereas Bruner's model deals with internal desires. There is also increased emphasis on intrinsic motivation in Bruner's model. Both theories pay close attention to instructional content and sequencing. (See pp. 174–176.) You might want to review the section of Chapter 5 on operant conditioning.
5. a, S; b, E; c, I; d, S; e, S (See p. 175)
6. a, RRL; b, MRL; c, RDL; d, MDL; e, MRL (See pp. 181–182)

Project

OBJECTIVE: To obtain information on the readiness concepts used in local schools.

PROCEDURES: Visit a local elementary school, preferably in grades kindergarten through third grade, and ask the following questions of the teacher.

1. How does the teacher define readiness?
2. What subjects taught in the school use a readiness concept? (This may vary from grade to grade and/or teacher to teacher.)
3. How is a child's level of readiness determined in a given subject area?
4. What differences in readiness exist among children in that grade?
5. Are any attempts made to accelerate readiness? If so, what are some of the procedures?

ANALYSIS: Look over the teacher's remarks and compare them to the text. (See especially pp. 172–174.) In your estimation, does the school adopt a "wait and see" or an "accelerated" approach? What are the implications for teaching the child?

CHAPTER OUTLINE

7

MEMORY

CHAPTER PREVIEW

You are probably most aware of the connection between memory and learning when you are studying for or taking a test. However, for people to make use of anything they have learned, they have to be able to remember it. Memory also assists learning by providing a framework of stored information to which new material can be related. Memory processes and ways in which the remembering of new information might be enhanced are the focuses of this chapter. Theoretical descriptions of information processing and theories of forgetting are discussed. Also examined are strategies that can be used by individuals or the designers of instructional materials to assist the learning and remembering of new facts and ideas. By being aware of the principles and the procedures that can facilitate learning, teachers should be able to make their own instruction more effective.

Remember to look at the outline for a detailed list of the topics to be discussed.

The following questions should help you organize and remember the information covered in this chapter:

- According to the theories of Atkinson and Shiffrin, Craik and Lockhart, how is information stored, retained, and retrieved?
- What implications does the memory research on recall and recognition have for the construction of classroom tests and the interpretation of their results?
- What theories have been proposed to account for forgetting?
- What strategies can students employ to help them remember new information, and are these strategies effective at all grade levels?
- How would you compare the usefulness of adjunct questions and advance organizers for the learning of new information?

We trail behind us, unawareness, the whole of our past; but our memory pours into the present only the odd recollection or two that in some way complete our present situation.

HENRI BERGSON
Creative Evolution, 1911

Twenty-one years ago a man known to researchers as "N.A." was injured when a fencing foil penetrated his nose and stabbed his brain. For the most part he is incapable of forming new, enduring memories. What you and I remember for weeks, N.A. retains for several minutes. He can be taught new skills such as reading mirror-reversed writing. Even though he retains mastery of the skill itself, he forgets how and when he learned it. All events of the past twenty-one years appear lost from the archives of his mind. Unlike N.A. our ability to remember lifts us out of the terrible eternity of moments. Memory allows us to gain a sense of self, to establish enduring bonds with family members and friends, and to acquire and employ a cultural heritage (Greenwald, 1980; Begley, 1981).

In the previous two chapters, we considered learning, the operations whereby we initially attain a potential for a particular behavior. Yet, as the case of N.A. reveals, learning does not get us very far in life unless we form memory units. We must store the learned potential for behavior over time and then be able to retrieve it when we need the information. **Memory** is a broadly defined concept that describes the ability of individuals to recall, recognize, or relearn more rapidly previously practiced behaviors. It provides knowledge about the past that is necessary for the proper understanding of the present.

PHASES IN INFORMATION PROCESSING

When information is remembered, three things occur: (1) **encoding,** the process by which infor-

mation is put into the memory system; (2) **storage,** the process by which information is retained until it is needed; and (3) **retrieval,** the process by which information is regathered when it is needed.

These components are assumed to operate sequentially. Incoming signals are transformed into a "state" where they can be stored. This is termed a **trace.** A trace is a set of information; it is the residue of an event that remains in memory after the event has vanished. When encoded, the trace is placed in storage. Finally, depending on environmental needs, the individual actively searches for stored material.

Encoding

Information processing has been likened to a filing system (Ellis, 1972; Hulse, Deese, and Egeth, 1975; Higbee, 1977). Suppose you are an office clerk, and you have the task of filing a company's correspondence. You have a letter from an important customer suggesting a new product for the company. Under what category are you going to file the letter? If the contents of the letter involve something new, will you decide to create a new category—"product suggestions"—or will you file the letter under the customer's name? The categorizing procedure you employ must be consistent. You cannot file this particular letter under the customer's name and the next similar type of letter under "product suggestions."

Encoding is a process that involves perceiving information, abstracting from it one or more classificatory characteristics, and creating corresponding memory traces for it. As with a filing system, the manner in which we encode information has a profound impact upon our later ability to retrieve it. If we "file" an item haphazardly, we will have difficulty recalling it.

Since the encoding process occurs during the presentation of to-be-remembered material, the distinction between learning and memory research is becoming blurred (Ellis and Hunt, 1977). Indeed,

LEARNING AND MEMORY
Psychologists are finding that the distinction between learning and memory is becoming increasingly blurred. Encoding, or learning information, is part of the process by which to-be-remembered material enters storage so that it can be retrieved later.

Endel Tulving (1968) suggests that learning constitutes an improvement in retention. Thus, according to Tulving, the study of learning is the study of memory.

An accumulating body of research suggests that the encoding process frequently involves the active transformation and alteration of information. Thus, it should not be assumed that encoding is simply a passive process whereby environmental events are mechanically registered upon some sort of memory trace or ''engram.'' The physical-chemical processes that form the basis of learning and memory are still poorly understood (Thompson, 1976). Studies show that we have good retention of the meaning or gist of prose material but poor memory for the specific words (Bartlett, 1932; Ellis and Hunt, 1977). Verbatim recalls are the exception, while the usual mode of recall is the paraphrase. Hence, in information processing, we tend to abstract the general idea from material.

Storage and Retrieval

Although the distinctions among encoding, storage, and retrieval are widely accepted on a theoretical level, psychologists and educators have not reached the point where they can conclusively differentiate among them on an experimental level (Estes, 1976; Houston, 1976; Dempster, 1981). Hence, in practice considerable overlap and interpenetration exist among the components involved in information processing.

From a strictly scientific standpoint, we cannot know that a memory exists unless it can be *used* in some way to affect perception, thinking, or behavior. On logical grounds, however, the distinction between storage and retrieval is clear-cut. We may store information, yet it may not be accessible to us.

By way of illustration, most of us have learned at one time or another the names of the planets surrounding the sun. Try, for instance, recalling the names of all of them. They are very likely ''in there,'' but for a variety of reasons, we may not be able to retrieve the information on demand. In some respects, the retrieval process is comparable to a search through an office filing cabinet. We may first look for a letter under the customer's name, next under ''product suggestions,'' and so on. Similarly, our search for the names of the planets may take several routes. Some of us will initiate the search by starting with the planet nearest the sun and then work outward in space. Others will search for the ''large'' planets and then the ''small'' planets. Still others will employ idiosyncratic features to recall the planets, such as Jupiter has twelve satellites, Saturn has a series of thin, flat rings, Venus is the most brilliant planet, and so on (Houston, 1976).

Memory failure may occur at any phase in information processing. Returning to the illustra-

PROCEDURES FOR STUDYING MEMORY

Psychologists have three major ways to measure memory. They can ask individuals to tell them what they remember on a particular topic—*recall.* They can ask individuals to pick out the material that they remember from a group of items—*recognition.* Or they can compare the amount of time used during original learning and the amount of time required to learn the same material again on a second occasion—*relearning.*

RECALL

Psychologists and educators have long been interested in verbal learning, the type of learning most commonly used in schools (Dempster, 1981). Students are asked such questions as, "Name the original thirteen colonies," or "Name the third president of the United States," or "Recite the multiplication tables by fours." When we talk about remembering something, most of us are making reference to recall.

Psychologists study recall by providing subjects with one or more experimental learning tasks. Among these are free recall, serial learning, and paired-associate learning. *Free recall* is similar to the task you confront when you are asked to name the people who attended your fourth-period class yesterday. In the typical experiment, psychologists present a list of random items (commonly English words) to a subject one item at a time. Later, the subject is asked to recall as many words as possible in any order. The procedure is especially effective in studying how people go about remembering things spontaneously. For instance, subjects often impose some sort of organization on the words. They may recall the nouns referring to places initially, then those nouns making reference to people, and so on. In brief, subjects tend to *cluster* their responses by categories. Free recall allows psychologists to gain a glimpse of the inner mental operations people employ to process various materials and information.

Serial learning is the type of task that confronts us when we are asked to learn the alphabet or memorize a poem. Learning how to put things together in proper serial order is an important psychological process. In generating our current behavior it is not sufficient that we simply remember specific events from the past. We also must know the specific set of relationships that prevails among the events (Hulse and Dorsky, 1977).

In serial learning experiments, psychologists present the subject with a list of words one at a time. The subject is required to learn the list in the order in which the words are presented. In this fashion, each word serves as a cue for the next word. This type of research provides psychologists with insight regarding the process people use to locate information stored in their memories. Psychologists find, for example, that with ordered items, those appearing at the beginning and end are more readily mastered than those in the middle.

We encounter *paired-associate learning* when we mentally link names with faces, students with their grade level, and German words with their English equivalents. In experimental settings psychologists present subjects with a list of pairs, for instance, pairs of objects, pictures, pictures and words, words, or nonsense syllables (*zum-fac, rel-poq,* and *hik-dar*). In later trials, the subject is provided with the first item of the pair (the stimulus) and is asked to produce the associated second item (the response). The procedure is often employed in studying concept formation and problem solving.

RECOGNITION

A second method for investigating memory entails the use of recognition tasks. Psychologists test recognition when the alternatives are made available to the subject; in contrast, they test recall when the alternatives are not made available. In typical recognition experiments, subjects first look at or hear a list of items. They are then tested on them. The experimenter presents each subject with some of the list items along with some items not on the list (these items are termed "distractors"). The subjects are instructed to pick out those items that were on the list and reject those that were not (Klatzky, 1975).

Whereas in a recall test the subject is asked, "What was the item?" on a recognition test the question becomes, "Is this the item?" (Underwood, 1972). For instance, a typical recall question in a school context is, "What is the largest of the fifty states comprising the United States?" It becomes a multiple-choice question when phrased as a recognition task: "Which of the following is the largest of the fifty states comprising the United States? (a) Texas; (b) Alaska; (c) Montana; (d) California."

RECOGNITION VERSUS RECALL

Psychologists have devoted considerable experimental time and energy to the study of recognition and recall. These studies reveal perplexing similarities and dissimilarities between the two that have led psychologists to conflicting interpretations (Brown, 1976). Early

in the study of memory, researchers found that we can generally recognize a good deal more than we can recall (McDougall, 1904). Thus, we sometimes find ourselves admitting to an acquaintance, "Your face is familiar, but I can't remember your name." While remembering the name is usually a recall task, remembering the face is a recognition task (Higbee, 1977).

The superiority of recognition has been interpreted by some psychologists as a function of the strength of the items in memory, termed the *threshold hypothesis.* These psychologists assume that the threshold for recall is higher than that for recognition. According to this view, we should be able to recognize what we recall, since the strength of the memory trace is strong. But where the memory trace is weak, we should be merely capable of recognizing the item.

The difficulty with the threshold hypothesis is that predictions based on it do not necessarily hold in practice. For instance, psychologists present subjects in some experimental settings with a long list of words (Shepard, 1967). Some of the words are common (*child, office, supply*), whereas others are uncommon (*ferule, julep, wattled*). The subjects are then tested for word recognition. Uncommon words are

better *recognized* than common words. But in recall, the outcome is the reverse: common words are better *recalled* than uncommon words (Sumby, 1963; Schulman and Lovelace, 1970; McCormick and Swenson, 1972). If recognition and recall involve the same processes, we should expect to find parallel patterns and operations in both recognition and recall tasks.

In light of these findings, other psychologists suggest a *generation-recognition hypothesis* (Müller, 1913; Kintsch, 1970; Anderson and Bower, 1972). Viewed from this perspective, both recognition and recall share one process in common but differ in that recall requires an additional process. By way of illustration, if we are asked to name the third president of the United States, we are required to search our long-term store (or secondary memory) for the names of early American presidents. Based on the names that we activate mentally (Washington, Adams, Jefferson, Madison, and Monroe), we must decide which individual was the third president. But if we are asked the question in multiple-choice form (a recognition task), we need not retrieve the names of the presidents. We only have to decide which of the listed individuals was the third president. Recognition allows us to avoid the generation
(continued)

PROCEDURES FOR STUDYING MEMORY (*continued*)

phase and the complications (including errors) inherent in this operation. Since the generation phase is bypassed (only the decision aspect is common to both recall and recognition), recognition is better than recall.

Research by Endel Tulving and associates (Tulving and Thomson, 1973; Tulving, 1976; Wiseman and Tulving, 1976; Flexser and Tulving, 1978) points to difficulties with both the threshold and generation-recognition hypotheses. These experiments show that under some circumstances recall is superior to recognition. This could not possibly happen if either the threshold or generation-recognition models were an accurate portrayal of memory processes. The experimental procedures employed by Tulving are complicated and would take us afield were we to detail them here. Suffice it to note that the matter is analogous to a situation in which we fail to recognize the face of our dentist when both of us are on a city bus, although we can mentally picture the dentist's face (recall it) if we are asked to.

Tulving suggests that items are often stored in terms of the context in which they originally occurred and were encoded. If we encoded the face of our dentist within the context of a dental office, the cue (the face) when en-

countered within another context (the bus) will not activate recognition. However, if the cue of our dentist is provided in terms of a dental role in a dental office, we can recall the individual's face with little difficulty. In sum, the *encoding specificity principle* comes into play:

> What is stored is determined by what is perceived and how it is encoded, and what is stored determines what retrieval cues are effective in providing access to what is stored. [Tulving and Thomson, 1973:353]

Admittedly, our knowledge is muddled regarding the relationships between recognition and recall (Houston, 1976; Rabinowitz, Mandler, and Patterson, 1977; Broadbent and Broadbent, 1977). As much as we might like to have definitive answers to various puzzling issues, we will simply have to await the clarification of these matters by future research.

RELEARNING

Another method available to psychologists for investigating memory is the study of relearning. The procedure permits a comparison between the amount of time used during original learning and the amount of time required to learn the same material again on a later occasion. Relearning usually re-

sults in a significant savings in time. For instance, we may find that we can no longer recall a foreign language that we learned earlier in our lives. Nonetheless, we can usually relearn it much more easily and rapidly than had been the case years before.

Some years ago Harold E. Burtt (1941), then a psychologist at Ohio State University, conducted an interesting experiment with his son. Beginning when the boy was fifteen months of age, Burtt read him three twenty-line selections from Greek drama once each day for three months. At the age of eighteen months these selections were discontinued and three others read daily for three months. Burtt continued the procedure until the boy was three years of age.

Burtt retested his son for retention when the boy was eight, fourteen, and eighteen years old. When the boy was eight, it took him 30 percent less time to learn a number of the original passages than it took him to learn comparable new Greek passages. At the age of fourteen, the savings was eight percent. However, at the age of eighteen, there were no savings at all. Except for a few studies such as the one just described, psychologists have not employed relearning extensively in their research Seemingly, this area of study would afford a fertile area for future investigation.

tion of the office filing cabinet, we may receive a letter from a customer. Inadvertently, we may place the letter with trash items that we then discard. Thus, the letter is never encoded, since it is not placed in the filing cabinet. It is *both* unavailable and inaccessible because it was never stored. Or we may place the letter in the filing cabinet but mistakenly put it in the wrong folder. It is now available, although it is inaccessible because it was stored incorrectly. Finally, we may file the letter under the customer's name but later lack the proper cue to activate the category under which we filed it (we may not sharpen the retrieval cue sufficiently so that it can adequately specify the desired event in our memory). Again, the letter is technically available although inaccessible by virtue of a retrieval breakdown.

THEORETICAL APPROACHES

There is no shortage of theoretical approaches for dealing with memory. Over the past decade, however, two theories have commanded particular interest among psychologists and educators, each approach attracting a substantial following. The first is the three-store model formulated by Richard C. Atkinson and Richard M. Shiffrin (1968, 1971; Shiffrin and Atkinson, 1969); the second, a theory identified with Fergus I. M. Craik and Robert S. Lockhart (1972) that focuses on multiple levels of information processing. Let us examine each of these approaches.

The Atkinson-Shiffrin Model

The model of Atkinson and Shiffrin represents memory in terms of three structural components: (1) a sensory register; (2) a short-term store; and (3) a long-term store (see Figure 7.1). These memory stores should not be considered as having a particular physical location in the brain, despite the way they are labeled. They are better viewed

as "aspects" or "operating characteristics" of memory.

The Structures

Incoming information first enters the **sensory register,** where it resides for a fraction of a second, then decays and is lost. Here information is initially processed and selectively passed on to the short-term store. The **short-term store** is our working memory; it receives selected inputs from both the sensory register and the long-term store.

Normally, information in the short-term store

INFORMATION PROCESSING
According to the Atkinson-Shiffrin model of memory, incoming information enters the sensory register, where it is initially processed and selectively passed on to the short-term store. While information resides in the short-term store, portions of it are copied by the long-term store for longer retention.

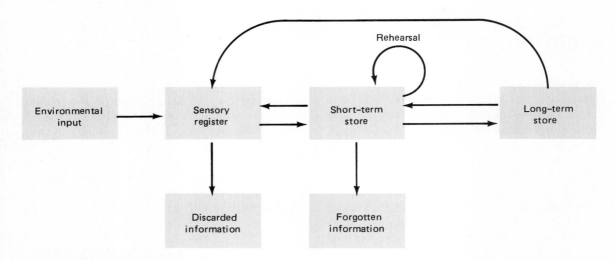

FIGURE 7.1 SIMPLIFIED FLOW CHART OF THE THREE-STORE MODEL
Information flow is represented in terms of three memory stores: the sensory register, the short-term store, and the long-term store. Inputs enter the sensory register where they are selectively passed on to short-term storage. Information in the short-term store may be forgotten or copied by the long-term store. In some instances, individuals rehearse information in order to keep it in active awareness in short-term storage. Complicated feedback operations take place among the three storage components.

decays completely within about thirty seconds (for instance, the telephone number we just looked up in a directory or the name of a person to whom we have just been introduced). By rehearsing information, we can prevent the trace in the short-term store from fading away as long as we desire (for instance, if we wish to retain a telephone number, we repeat it to ourselves at continual intervals). Thus, each decaying trace is "regenerated" or "reset" by rehearsal, at which point it starts decaying again.

While information resides in the short-term store, portions of it are "copied" by the long-term store. The **long-term store** is a fairly permanent repository for information received from the short-term store (for instance our own telephone number, multiplication tables, names of our friends, the location of our home, and so on).

The Short-Term Store

Atkinson and Shiffrin attribute pivotal importance to the short-term store. It acquires its critical function from the fact that it governs the flow of information in the memory system. Of equal importance, it is under our immediate control. By virtue of its latter characteristic, we gain considerable discretion in the learning and memory process. The short-term store provides a working memory in which manipulations of information take place on a temporary basis. It decouples the memory system from the immediate external environment so that the system is not overwhelmed by a continual inflow of large numbers of stimuli. In everyday language we make reference to the short-term store when we say that something is in our "consciousness"—the thoughts and information of which we are currently aware.

The Rehearsal Buffer

The Atkinson-Shiffrin model assumes that in many tasks we employ a **rehearsal buffer.** The rehearsal buffer is the set of memory traces (units of information) that can be maintained in the short-term store. It has a limited capacity and can only hold a fixed number of items at a time. When the buffer is full, the entry of new items causes the items that are already in the buffer to be displaced or "bumped out" (hence the "decay" of items in the short-term store). For instance, if you enter new numbers in the buffer while you are "holding" a telephone number in short-term storage, part of the telephone number will be displaced. The copying of information by the long-term store is thought to be a function of the length of time an item resides in the buffer; the longer the time period, the more rehearsal the item is given, and the more likely it is to transfer to the long-term store.

Control of the System

Atkinson and Shiffrin emphasize that we have a large measure of control over the flow of information among the three storage systems. For instance, we scan information in the sensory register and, with input from the long-term store, selectively introduce information into the short-term store. Thus, if we are talking to someone at a cocktail party and there is a good deal of background conversation in the room, we ignore the drone; but if our name happens to be spoken, we are likely to "hear" it. Accordingly, long-term storage facilitates our identification of items in the sensory register. Again, by way of illustration, if we encounter a brief succession of tones, the long-term store "identifies" them as part of a familiar melody, and the tones are "tagged" or "coded" as such when the string is transferred from the sensory register to the short-term store (Horton and Turnage, 1976).

Links among the Components

Many links exist among the three component units. In retrieval, we search the long-term store by means of one cue and then another until we secure the desired information (as in the filing cabinet illustration in which we conduct a search for a letter under the customer's name, "product suggestions," and other relevant categories until we locate it). As each trace is successively examined, the recovery process determines how much information will be recovered from the trace and placed in short-term storage where we can "consciously" work with it. Simultaneously, the short-term store may contain other information such as the search strategy being employed, salient information recovered previously in the search, long-term storage locations that have already been examined, and some of the links to other traces that have been noted in the search but not yet examined. In this fashion, the short-term store acts as a "window" on the long-term store, allowing us to deal sequentially with a manageable amount of information.

All of this may, at first, seem academic and far removed from the practical day-to-day dictates of classroom experience. Yet, in point of fact it is not all that academic. If we understand how the human memory system operates, we can assist students in cultivating those strategies that will allow them to store and retrieve information more effectively and efficiently, matters that will be considered later in the chapter. Further, this understanding can lead us to have more realistic and reasonable expectations of children and a sympathetic understanding of the difficulties many of them encounter in learning and remembering various materials.

The Craik-Lockhart Model

Craik and Lockhart reinterpret the short- and long-term stores of the Atkinson-Shiffrin model as differences in levels of processing. They view memory as a continuum of processes rather than

TYPES OF MEMORY

Psychologists and educators distinguish between various types of memories. Over the past decade, they have shown particular interest in the distinction between imaginal and verbal memory and between episodic and semantic memory. These classificatory efforts have proven helpful in ordering generalizations about memory and in suggesting new questions for investigation.

IMAGINAL VERSUS VERBAL MEMORY

Various memory researchers have effectively argued that mental imagery is one of the primary means to channel information into the memory (Paivio, 1971; Cooper and Shepard, 1973; Nelson, Reed, and McEvoy, 1977). Indeed, an accumulating body of research reveals that pictures are easier to remember than words. In one study subjects were shown 600 words, 612 sentences, and 612 pictures (Shepard, 1967). Later, they were again provided with many of these items paired with new items. When asked to identify which member of the pair they had seen previously, they correctly recognized 88 percent of the words, 89 percent of the sentences, and 97 percent of the pictures. In another study the researchers showed subjects 2,560 pictures for ten

seconds each. Even when three days had elapsed between learning and again being shown the pictures, the subjects were able to recognize 90 percent of them (Standing, Conezio, and Haber, 1970).

Allan Paivio (1969; Yuille and Paivio, 1969) found that information embodied in concrete words is two or three times easier to learn than information conveyed by abstract words. This appears to be a function of the ability of concrete nouns to produce mental images (for instance, *collie* is more concrete than *dog, dog* is more concrete than *animal,* and *animal* is more concrete than *organism;* accordingly, we find it easier to picture a collie in our minds than we do to picture an organism). The relative concreteness of words—their image-evoking quality—is the most potent determiner of the ability to learn verbal material that has yet been uncovered (Paivio, 1971; Montague and Carter, 1973; Anderson, 1974). What educators have historically attributed to verbal factors like word meaningfulness may in actuality be a product of an imagery effect (visual imagery correlates highly with a word's meaningfulness or the number of associated words it elicits [Paivio, 1971]). To summarize, *imaginability* (the ease with which a visual

image is produced) and concreteness affect our memory for verbal information.

Paivio (1971, 1974) explains these findings by advancing a dual-coding hypothesis. According to his view, information can be coded either in a verbal-sequential store or an imaginal-spatial store (when words are perceived in speech, the sounds occur in sequence, one following the other; in contrast, visual imagery involves information in an area of space and is handled all at once or in a "spatially parallel" manner). Paivio conjectures that abstract words like "democracy" and "truth" are entered as memory traces in the verbal-sequential store. Concrete words like *collie* and *apple* are thought to produce both verbal and visual memory traces. By virtue of this dual representation, concrete words can be recalled better, because they can be retrieved in two ways rather than in only one way (as with the filing cabinet illustration, we are more likely to find a letter if we Xerox it and place the original under the customer's name and the duplicate in another folder under "product suggestions" than if we place it in only one of the folders). Moreover, the imaginal system appears to be more resistant to forgetting than is the verbal system.

The importance of this work lies in its practical applications for teaching (Goldberg, 1974; Levin et al., 1975; Pressley, 1976). It has guided a large number of practical efforts to employ imagery, pictorial representations, and special audiovisual aids in boosting learning in elementary school settings (Hilgard and Bower, 1975). Even children as young as seven years of age can benefit from an instruction to construct a mental image of simple verbal items (Levin et al., 1973).

Joel R. Levin (1973) has shown that some fourth-grade children who possess adequate decoding skills and vocabulary are nonetheless "poor readers" because they fail to employ appropriate organizational strategies for "integrating" material. He finds that these children can improve their reading retention skills if the teacher provides them with visual imagery instructions (they are told to think of a picture in their minds as they read each sentence). Most children, however, do not seem to benefit if they attempt to read and imagine at the same time; rather, the best results are produced if children are told to read a segment of prose and then picture it (Levin and Divine-Hawkins, 1974; Pressley, 1976). All of this suggests that mental imagery training can be easily taught in the classroom and improve children's memory for the material they read.

EPISODIC VERSUS SEMANTIC MEMORY

Tulving (1972) has identified and summarized a distinction now prevalent in memory research between episodic memory and semantic memory. **Episodic memory** refers to information we have about particular *events* that we experienced in the past. **Semantic memory** involves the organized store of knowledge that we have about the world as well as about language and its uses. Episodic memory is an event-knowledge store; semantic memory, a conceptual store.

Episodic memory is illustrated by the recollections we have regarding our meal last evening, our sixteenth birthday, and our first trip to college. It refers to specific events in their temporal and spatial contexts. In contrast, semantic memory refers to such things as the rules of grammar, chemical formulas, rules for addition and multiplication, and knowledge that summer follows spring. In brief, it involves facts that do not depend on a particular time or place but are simply facts (Klatzky, 1975). "The apple I had for lunch yesterday was red" is an example of episodic memory. "Apples are red" is an illustration of semantic memory.

It is convenient to distinguish between episodic and semantic memory, since important differences exist between the two systems (Tulving, 1972). We have ready access to concepts in semantic memory and recall them without apparent search or effort (in speaking, we generally encounter little difficulty in retrieving words and ordering them sequentially in sentences). Further, semantic memory does not register the specific perceptible properties of inputs but only their cognitive referents (the mental constructs of what they represent). Thus, the semantic system (since it contains abstractions and constructions based upon incoming signals) permits the retrieval of information not directly stored in it. This is not true of episodic memory.

Most verbal learning tasks mastered in experimental settings involve the episodic system. The items of a laboratory task involve "episodes" that subject experience to a particular time and context. The researcher does not ask the subject to learn the items as such but rather to remember which words were experienced relative to some specific preceding input (Kausler, 1974). For instance, if I present you with the word *egg* in a list of fifty words, I am not teaching you the word *egg*. Instead, I am teaching you that the word *egg* is currently on your list—a fact that depends on a particular time and situation (Klatzky, 1975).

as a series of discrete stages (with a transfer of information occurring between the stages). Hence, Craik and Lockhart deny that memory is separated into distinct units or stores. They do, however, recognize that different mechanisms underlie memory for recently perceived events and memory for events perceived in the past (Craik and Levy, 1976). Accordingly, they distinguish between *primary memory* (comparable to the short-term store) and *secondary memory* (comparable to the long-term store). The basic distinction is that the emphasis of the Atkinson-Shiffrin model falls on structure, whereas that of Craik and Lockhart falls on process.

The Craik-Lockhart formulation is based on the widely accepted notion that perception involves the rapid analysis of stimuli at a number of levels (Selfridge and Neisser, 1960; Treisman, 1964; Sutherland, 1968). In the initial stages of processing perceptual inputs, stimuli are analyzed in terms of physical or sensory features like lines, angles, brightness, pitch, and loudness. In later stages, they are considered in terms of their meaning. The preliminary information is used to match a stimulus input with stored abstractions or representations from past learning, resulting in pattern recognition. After the incoming stimuli are recognized, they may undergo additional processing (associations may be triggered between the new material and previous experiences). Memory, then, is seen as a series of processing stages involving greater "depth" (cognitive analysis) at each level.

Craik and Lockhart postulate that memory increases as the depth of processing increases. Since we are chiefly concerned with extracting meaning from stimuli, it is to our advantage to store only the products of more sophisticated or deeper cognitive analysis. We have little need to store the products of preliminary analysis, and hence the material is lost. Retention, then, is primarily a function of the depth at which stimuli are processed. In turn, depth of processing is related to the compatibility between the incoming stimuli and the analyzing structures. For instance, stimuli like pictures and printed prose are usually rapidly processed to a deeper level; they are also retained more easily, since they involve stimuli that are generally more meaningful. Other factors also influence the depth of processing. They include the amount of attention devoted to a stimulus and the time available for processing the information.

Each model of memory has a somewhat different focus and is superior to the other for handling certain kinds of scientific evidence. For instance, the Craik and Lockhart approach is capable of explaining why we tend to have greater difficulty recalling material learned by rote than material put in a more meaningful context (meaningful material is processed at a deeper level of cognitive analysis). And the Atkinson-Shiffrin model offers a tidy explanation of why we have difficulty remembering more than a limited number of items at a time (additional items bump the earlier ones out of the rehearsal buffer).

However, neither model offers an explanation that fits all of the existing research data on memory satisfactorily (Baddeley, 1978; Stein, 1978). Future research should assist us in clarifying these matters (Lee and Estes, 1977; Morris, Bransford, and Franks, 1977; Nelson, 1977). Or it may provide a synthesis of the two approaches (Glanzer and Koppenaal, 1977).

FORGETTING

Forgetting has both advantages and disadvantages. If we did not forget, our minds would be cluttered with so many trivial items that we would find it exceedingly difficult to select the useful and relevant items we need for decisions (Higbee, 1977). By the same token, forgetting leads us to lose many useful skills and valuable information. For instance, research reveals that approximately 66 percent of the concepts "learned" in high-school and college courses are forgotten within two years (Pressey, Robinson, and Horrocks, 1959). And even though intellectual skills appear to be

FORGETTING
Although we store countless amounts of information, we also forget a great deal. All too often we forget what we learned in school within a short time after a test and sometimes before the test.

better retained than verbal information, up to 66 percent of the material in first-year algebra (composed mainly of rules or algorithms) is lost after only one year (Layton, 1932).

Although theories of forgetting have been with us since ancient times, we still have a long way to go in understanding the phenomenon. Three theories currently command the greatest interest among psychologists and educators: decay theory, interference theory, and cue-dependent forgetting theory. Each theory has had its vigorous proponents

as well as its critics. Although the thinking of the past seemed to dictate our choosing one of the theories as the single and most powerful cause of forgetting, today it seems that all three of them have some merit (Adams, 1976). This confronts science with the new task of determining the relationships that exist among the three types of processes.

Decay Theory

According to decay theory, deterioration occurs through time in the memory traces of the brain. The approach assumes that learning modifies the central nervous system and that unless information is periodically used (rehearsed), it weakens and eventually is lost. The process is thought to resemble the gradual fading of a photograph over time or the progressive obliteration of the inscription on a tombstone (Hulse, Deese, and Egeth, 1975).

Decay theory lost favor during the 1920s and 1930s when it was shown that the activities that individuals engage in during the retention interval (the period between initial learning and the test of retention) affect memory (McGeoch, 1932). Researchers found that individuals lost a greater amount of information when they were awake than when they were asleep (Jenkins and Dallenbach, 1924). This sleep effect was interpreted as supporting the interference theory of forgetting, since passive decay was presumed to occur as rapidly during sleep as during waking. More recently, a number of psychologists have revived the decay theory for explaining some types of forgetting (Broadbent, 1963; Posner, 1967; Reitman, 1971; Loftus and Loftus, 1980).

Interference Theory

The interference theory holds that a retrieval cue becomes less effective as more and new items come to be classed or categorized in terms of it. Whereas decay theory depicts forgetting as a passive process, interference theory sees it as an active process. Furthermore, whereas decay theory attributes forgetting to a storage failure, interference theory views it as a function of retrieval failure. Most psychologists believe that interference and not decay accounts for much more forgetting. For instance, Bennet B. Murdock, Jr. (1976) suggests that from 85 percent to 98 percent of the variance in forgetting is attributable to interference and the remainder to decay.

Interference theorists propose that two processes are primarily responsible for the detrimental effect that interference has on memory. One mechanism is response competition; the other, unlearning. In *response competition*, recall of an item is blocked by other stored information; the organism has difficulty deciding which of two or more responses

is appropriate. There are two types of response competition: retroactive interference and proactive interference. *Retroactive* interference results when new memories displace older memories (the interference results from the learning coming *between* original learning and the retention list). *Proactive* interference occurs when older memories displace newer memories (the interference is produced by learning that *preceded* the original learning).

Retroactive interference seems obvious to most of us. However, proactive interference is another matter. Benton J. Underwood (1957) demonstrated the importance of proactive interference by providing a to-be-remembered word list to different groups of subjects under various conditions. For instance, he would have the members of one group practice learning a number of word lists before he

INTERFERENCE AND FORGETTING
The interference theory of forgetting says that one reason we forget information is that new memories displace older memories.

provided them with the experimental word list. Another group would not receive any practice but merely learn the to-be-remembered words. He found that one day later the previously trained group remembered only about 25 percent of the experimental word list; in contrast, the subjects without previous training were able to recall 70 percent of this same list. The previously trained individuals performed more poorly because other items they had learned in the practice sessions interfered in some manner with their retention of the items in the experimental word list.

In addition to response competition, interference theorists suggest that *unlearning* also contributes to forgetting (Melton and Irwin, 1940). When individuals undertake the learning of a new list of words, they find that words from earlier lists continue to crop up. But since these old words are now incorrect, they undergo extinction. Although there is some confusion in the current status of interference theory among psychologists, it still remains the most systematic and accepted view of forgetting (Postman and Underwood, 1973; Ellis and Hunt, 1977).

Cue-Dependent Forgetting

Tulving (Tulving and Psotka, 1971; Tulving, 1974) advances a cue-dependent theory of forgetting. He notes that memory is a product of information from two sources: first, the memory trace laid down and retained in an individual's memory store as a result of the original perception of an event; and second, the retrieval cue that involves the information present in an individual's cognitive environment at the time recall occurs. Accordingly, trace information may be *available* in the memory store but be *inaccessible*, because the relevant information is absent from the retrieval environment. Thus, for practical purposes the event is forgotten.

Retrieval information plays the same role in remembering as illumination does in the act of reading a printed page. When the light is turned off, reading becomes impossible. Likewise, remembering is impossible when the appropriate retrieval information is lacking. In contrast, a good retrieval cue functions to narrow the memory domain in which we search for an item.

Olga C. Watkins and Michael J. Watkins (1975) extend Tulving's formulation. They point out that failure to remember material may also result from *cue overload*, a state in which individuals find themselves overwhelmed or engulfed by excessive stimuli. Accordingly, individuals fail to process retrieval information effectively. They are unable to sharpen a retrieval cue sufficiently so that it can adequately specify the desired event in the memory (Craik, 1976).

MNEMONICS

One aspect of memory that is beginning to receive attention is the demonstrated knowledge that we have about memory and the activity of remembering (Cavanaugh and Perlmutter, 1982). Psychologists refer to this knowledge as **meta-memory** to distinguish it from actual memory performance (Flavell and Wellman, 1977; Levin et al., 1977). By the time children enter kindergarten and first grade, they have already developed considerable knowledge regarding the memory process. They have a global awareness that forgetting occurs, that spending more time in inspecting something helps them retain information about it, that it is more difficult to remember many items than a few, and that they can employ retrieval cues, written records, and other people to help them in recalling things. They also understand such terms as *remember, forget*, and *learn* (Kreutzer, Leonard, and Flavell, 1975).

Third- and especially fifth-grade children are even more planful and self-aware than younger children in their approach to remembering information and in retrieving it later. For instance, older children are more likely to recognize that the experiences they have that intervene between learning something and retrieving it affect their recall. They are also more adept at *memory monitoring*—the ability to judge that certain items are or are not retrievable from their memories (Wellman, 1977, 1978). Thus, as children grow older, they become increasingly active and deliberate in their approach to memory tasks (Flavell, 1977).

Effective schooling requires that children develop strategies for comprehending and retaining information. Courses of action that we deliberately instigate for helping us remember things better are termed **mnemonics** (Brown, 1975). There are a variety of mnemonic strategies. Some of these are straightforward; others, exceedingly complex (Young and Gibson, 1966; Higbee, 1977). For the most part, mnemonic systems assist us by imposing meaning and organization on otherwise unrelated items. A number of these strategies are discussed in the following sections (see also the boxed insert on pages 206–207).

Rehearsal

As noted earlier, **rehearsal**—the cycling of information through the memory store—plays an important part in the retention process. Rehearsal strategies vary greatly in complexity and sophistication (Flavell, 1977). Further, individuals show enormous variability in terms of when, what, and how they rehearse for memory tasks (Butterfield, Wambold, and Belmont, 1973).

Age differences also occur. Third-graders rehearse each item as it is presented either singly or in minimal combination with other items; sixth-graders rehearse more actively, with several items being intermixed (Ornstein, Naus, and Liberty, 1975). Peter A. Ornstein, Mary J. Naus, and Barbara P. Stone (1977) find, however, that second-grade children can be instructed to rehearse items together and that this strategy is later maintained in similar learning situations. Other common rehearsal strategies that children come to employ

in the course of their schooling are self-recitation and note-taking.

Visual Imagery

Since the time of classical Greek civilization visual imagery has been recognized as a powerful aid to memory (Yates, 1966). Indeed, many people find that in memorizing a literary selection it is helpful to visualize the events being described. This observation is supported by research (Paivio, 1971; Higbee, 1977, 1979). (See also the boxed insert on pages 206–207.)

Psychologists also find that children's recall from narrative passages is greatly improved if the passages are presented in the company of appropriate visual illustrations (Rohwer and Harris, 1975; Rohwer and Matz, 1975; Pressley, 1977). In contrast, children under eight do not appear to benefit in recall tasks if they are given instructions to generate their *own* mental images to prose (Lesgold et al., 1975; Shimron, 1975). However, by the time they reach the third and fourth grades, children apparently develop the ability to profit from single visual imagery instructions (Guttmann, Levin, and Pressley, 1977). These findings are consistent with those cited earlier in the chapter and point to the value of imagery, pictorial representation, and special audiovisual aids in teaching in primary schools.

Organization

An important tool for learning new information, *organization* involves dividing material into small units and placing these units within appropriate categories. In this fashion, each piece of information fits sensibly with the others. Improved recall is thought to result from organization, since the learner uses category labels as retrieval cues and thus reduces memory overload in recall (Tulving and Pearlstone, 1966).

does for the expert. It facilitates remembering while supplying generative power (Glaser, 1973).

Children younger than the fourth grade generally do not sort information into categories spontaneously. They also produce very little category clustering in output. Yet research reveals that young children can be instructed in sorting skills and that improvements in sorting style accompany significant improvements in recall (Worden, 1975; Bjorklund, Ornstein, and Haig, 1977). Such training involves showing children how to divide prose into meaningful parts, grouping ideas together, and providing headings for each part (Danner, 1976). Further, teachers can expedite children's learning and retention by providing material in a manner that assists children in acquiring optimal and salient schemes for organizing the material at input (Lange and Griffith, 1977).

Note-Taking

The palest ink is better than the best memory.

CHINESE PROVERB

Note-taking combines many of the functions of rehearsal and organization (Bretzing and Kulhavy, 1979). Indeed, some research suggests that the probability of recalling an item that occurs in a person's notes is about seven times that of items not in one's notes (Howe, 1970). Judith L. Fisher and Mary B. Harris (1973), in a study of college students, found that students who take their own notes perform better three weeks later on recall tests than do students who are provided with prepared lecture notes and students who take no notes.

Lecture material appears to be encoded in memory as the information flows from ear to brain to hand to paper. And the external storage of the information later provides valuable aid to review. This later factor may be of even greater significance than the act of note-taking itself (Carter and Van Matre, 1975; Carrier and Titus, 1979; Barnett et al., 1981).

ORGANIZING INFORMATION
Memory bears a resemblance to a library. One reason we can find a book in a library is because the books are organized in a systematic fashion. We would encounter difficulty in locating a book without the card catalog. By organizing information in a meaningful manner when putting it into memory, we can facilitate storage and retrieval. Later, by mentally running through appropriate cues when we require the information, we make the task of retrieval easier.

More than two decades ago, George A. Miller (1956) found that memory is to a large extent a function of the number of things to remember. Accordingly, if information can be chunked or hooked into some meaningful category, it can be retained longer (Hafner, 1977). Organizing material can do for the learner what advanced theory

MNEMONIC TECHNIQUES

Human beings have long been concerned with the practical art of memory. Various stage entertainers have capitalized upon this interest and have advertised themselves as possessing unusual memory powers. Until recently, psychologists ignored the techniques employed by memory performers, since they were thought to practice trickery and deception. Only in the past decade or so have psychologists come to appreciate the value of various memory procedures in simplifying certain memory tasks. Further, such techniques afford many insights into the organization and operation of memory (Norman, 1972). Two of the more useful techniques are the method of loci and the pegword system.

METHOD OF LOCI

The *method of loci,* or the method of places, was employed by orators in classical Greece and Rome to perform what we today would consider prodigious feats of mem-ory (Yates, 1966). It consists of two steps. First, learn in their naturally occurring sequential order some geographical locations with which you are intimately familiar, for instance, the layout of your living quarters, the paths you take between classes, or the floor plans of a building. Second, associate a visual image of the to-be-remembered item with a location in the series; place the items in the order you wish to remember them as you progress along your imaginary walk. In other words, deposit at each location a mental image constructed from the material you wish to memorize. Upon recall, revisit in your mind each place in the house (path or building) in their proper order, retrieving from each the image that you have left there.

By way of illustration, visualize a walk through your home or apartment. You enter the front door, move next through the entryway, then to the living room, to the dining room, to the kitchen, and so on. Use these loci for memorizing a shopping list, for instance, eggs, lettuce, coffee, soap, and milk. Imagine "Humpty Dumpty" blocking the doorway, heads of lettuce rolling down the hallway, a gigantic coffee pot hanging from the ceiling of the living room, soap suds overflowing in the dining room, and a cow sitting at your kitchen table (do not worry if the images are illogical; it may actually help if they are absurd). Later, attempt to recall the items in order by taking an imaginary walk in which you again activate each visual image as you go from one room to the next (see Figure 7.A).

PEGWORD SYSTEM

The *pegword system* was introduced in England in 1879 by John Sambrook. It consists of memorizing a jingle that has the pegs on which you hang the to-be-remembered items by means of imagery. As with the method of loci, the pegword system can be

TABLE 7.A
The Pegword System

Pegword	List Word	Mnemonic Image
one-bun	eggs	a bun eating Humpty Dumpty
two-shoe	lettuce	a head of lettuce growing out of a shoe
three-tree	coffee	coffee pots growing out of tree branches
four-door	soap	soap suds flowing through a doorway
five-hive	milk	milk running from a milk beehive

used to remember shopping lists, errands, sets of facts in educational psychology, historical events, and the like.

First, learn the following jingle:

ONE is a BUN
TWO is a SHOE
THREE is a TREE
FOUR is a DOOR
FIVE is a HIVE
SIX is STICKS

SEVEN is HEAVEN
EIGHT is a GATE
NINE is a LINE
TEN is a HEN

Next, visually associate each item in your shopping list with one of the pegwords as in Table 7.A. To recall the items, you recite the jingle and retrieve the items associated with each pegword.

The method of loci and the pegword system improve memory by a factor of two or three times over normal free recall. They allow you to place the information into storage in an organized and meaningful fashion and then to recall it with explicit retrieval cues. Further, the techniques employ visual imagery. As such, both methods maximize memory by combining a number of potent mnemonic strategies.

FIGURE 7.A THE METHOD OF LOCI
Mentally imagine items from a grocery list placed in sequential locations in your home. Then undertake an imaginary walk in which you retrieve each item in turn from its location as you pass from one room to the next.

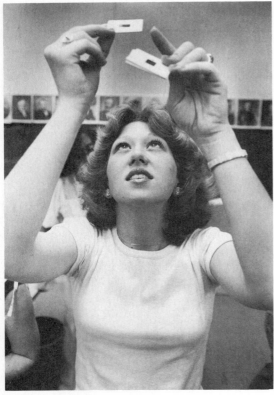

AIDS TO MEMORY
Photographs, pictures, notes, and books function as external mechanisms for storing information and later provide valuable aids to memory recall.

Meaningfulness

Much of the material encountered in school settings can be comprehended by assimilating new information within the context of previously acquired information and cognitive structures. When this happens, the new information is said to be *meaningful*. Teachers can enhance their instructional effectiveness by relating new elements of information to children's existing knowledge (White and Gagné, 1976). For instance, children have been taught basic computer programming concepts by being allowed to control the path of a crawling mechanical turtle by remote commands. And they have learned arithmetic algorithms by moving sticks that could be regrouped and bundled by tens (Mayer, 1976).

Some psychologists believe that if children engage in meaningful activities or experience meaningful events, they will retain the essential features of these activities whether or not a deliberate intention to remember is evoked (Meacham, 1972; Brown, 1975). Soviet psychologists term this "involuntary memory" and suggest that it occurs as children explore and interact with their environment (Smirnov and Zinchenko, 1969).

INSTRUCTIONAL STRATEGIES

Organization is one hallmark of good teaching. The manner in which material is sequenced and arranged has a profound impact on what students learn. Accordingly, various psychologists and educators have reasoned that any procedure that makes the organization of material more obvious and striking should facilitate learning the material. A well-organized "bird's-eye view" of a task is thought to supply students with a useful perspective of what lies ahead. This educational premise has attracted considerable interest over the past fifteen years and has found expression in mathemagenic activities, statements of educational goals, and advance organizers (Hartley and Davies, 1976).

Mathemagenic Activities

Ernst Z. Rothkopf (1970:325) coined the term **mathemagenic behaviors** to describe "behaviors which give birth to learning"—activities on the part of the student that result in the achievement of specified instructional objectives. Rothkopf and his associates have conducted a large number of studies dealing with the learning of prose materials

MATHEMAGENIC ACTIVITIES
Many student manuals or workbooks contain exercises to assist students in recognizing
what material in an accompanying textbook is important and in organizing this material
in a meaningful manner so that it can be assimilated and retained.

(Rothkopf and Bisbicos, 1967; Frase, 1967, 1968; Rothkopf, 1976). They find that testlike questions presented before or after the to-be-learned material function in a mathemagenic manner.

Students who receive questions before reading prose material retain the question-relevant material better than do students who simply read the text without benefit of prequestions. Apparently, readers selectively attend to the information to which the questions have sensitized them. But whereas prequestions facilitate the retention of question-relevant material, they narrow the range of readers' attention and decrease their memory for information not covered by the questions. In contrast, postquestions often facilitate both question-specific and general learning. Postquestions seemingly pro-

mote rehearsal and review of the previously presented material (Wittrock and Lumsdaine, 1977; Rickards, 1979).

Rothkopf's early research with adjunct questions suggested the possibility that learning might also be enhanced by providing learners with a set of educational goals. Instructional objectives can be presented prior to a unit of prose as orienting directions for readers or after a unit of prose as a summary or review. The likelihood that learning will occur in the presence of objectives is greater with shorter passages, fewer objectives, and more specifically phrased statements (Kaplan, 1974). Objectives are thought to lead to the repetition of material (promoting rehearsal), selective attention to the cued information, and increased time spent inspecting a passage for the designated items (Duchastel and Brown, 1974; Kaplan and Simmons, 1974; Mayer, 1980).

As often happens with new ideas in science, initial enthusiastic reports tend to oversell a new procedure. Inevitably, subsequent investigations reveal certain shortcomings with the new approach. And so it has been with instructional questions and educational objectives. Critics point out that the expected benefits do not always result (Ladas, 1973; Rickards, 1977; Sefkow and Myers, 1980). Moreover, there are those who claim that Rothkopf's techniques make learners dependent on artificial aids and impair the development of independent reading skills. A related criticism has been that most adjunct questions and goals are verbatim in nature and useful only for trivial educational objectives (Watts and Anderson, 1971). This has led some psychologists to suggest the use of problem-solving rather than rote-learning questions and statements (Rickards and DiVesta, 1974; Felker and Dapra, 1975).

Advance Organizers

David P. Ausubel (1963, 1968, 1978, 1980) suggests a variation on the theme of mathemagenic activities. In his theory of meaningful verbal learning, Ausubel advocates the use of *advance organizers* to facilitate learning written materials. He argues that learning requires readers to incorporate new ideas within already existing cognitive structures. The process of anchoring ideas within such structures can be expedited by presenting organizing clues. Advance organizers are similar to overviews or reviews except that they are written at "a higher level of abstraction, generality, and inclusiveness than the learning task itself" (Ausubel, 1963:29). Overviews and summaries accomplish their effects through repetition and the omission of selected detail; advance organizers, through providing abstracting and generalizing concepts under which new material can be subsumed (linked

to the broader organizing categories). Hence, advance organizers are designed to provide a conceptual framework that students can use to clarify the task ahead (Mayer, 1979).

Advance organizers are of two types: expository organizers and comparative organizers. *Expository organizers* are employed when the to-be-learned material is unfamiliar. Students are provided with relevant information that will relate the *new* material to already existing knowledge. *Comparative organizers* are used when the new material is *not* entirely novel. They point out ways in which the to-be-learned material is similar to and different from old material (Hartley and Davies, 1976).

Like adjunct questions and statements of educational goals, advance organizers have not entirely lived up to the high expectations they initially engendered (Barnes and Clawson, 1975; Arnold and Brooks, 1976; Lawton and Wanska, 1977; Nugent et al., 1980). Despite the seemingly sound theoretical base provided by Ausubel, some educators complain that Ausubel fails to provide them with a specific way for generating or even recognizing advance organizers.

In their appraisal of the evidence regarding advance organizers, James Hartley and Ivor K. Davies reach the following conclusion:

> Advance organizers would seem to be best reserved for situations requiring some sort of conceptual framework that students can subsequently use to help clarify the task ahead. The subject material should possess a dominant structure that can be readily integrated with the existing knowledge already possessed by the students. Learning tasks should be relatively short in duration. Finally, it is probably best if the students involved—whether adults or children—are of above-average ability, maturity, and sophistication. [1976:259–260]

Perhaps the safest conclusion that can be reached is that advance organizers may enhance relevant learning if they are formulated with care and clarity; if students are aware of them, know how to use them, and employ them; if they are provided in limited number; and if they are inserted with discretion so that they do not break up the continuity of the material (Alexander et al., 1979; Luiten et al., 1980).

CHAPTER SUMMARY

1. When information is remembered, three things occur: encoding, the process by which information is put into the memory system; storage, the process by which information is retained until it is needed; and retrieval, the process by which information is regathered when it is needed. These components are assumed to operate sequentially.

2. Encoding is a process that involves perceiving information, abstracting from it one or more classificatory characteristics, and creating corresponding memory traces for it. An accumulating body of research suggests that the encoding process frequently involves the active transformation and alteration of information.

3. Although the distinctions among encoding, storage, and retrieval are widely accepted on a theoretical level, psychologists and educators have not reached the point where they can conclusively differentiate among them on an experimental level. Hence, in practice, considerable overlap and interpenetration exist among the components involved in information processing.

4. The model of Richard C. Atkinson and Richard M. Shiffrin represents memory in terms of three structural components: a sensory register; a short-term store; and a long-term store. Incoming information first enters the sensory register, where it resides for a fraction of a second, then decays and is lost. The short-term store is our working memory; it receives selected inputs from both the sensory register and the long-term store. The long-term store is a fairly permanent repository for information received from the short-term store.

5. Fergus I. M. Craik and Robert S. Lockhart reinterpret the short- and long-term stores of the Atkinson-Shiffrin model as differences in levels of processing. They view memory as a continuum of processes rather than as a series of discrete stages. Memory is seen as a series of processing stages involving greater ''depth'' (cognitive analysis) at each level.

6. Three theories of forgetting currently dominate the interest of psychologists and educators. According to decay theory, deterioration occurs through time in the memory traces of the brain. Interference theory holds that a retrieval cue becomes less effective as more and new items come to be classed or categorized in terms of it. Finally, the cue-dependent theory of forgetting suggests that trace information may be available in the memory store but be inaccessible because the relevant information is absent from the retrieval environment.

7. Effective schooling requires that children develop strategies for comprehending and retaining information. Courses of action that we deliberately instigate for helping us remember things better are termed mnemonics. There are a number of mnemonic strategies. Among the most effective of these are rehearsal, visual imagining, organizing material, note-taking, and making material meaningful.

8. The manner in which material is sequenced and arranged has a profound impact upon what students learn. Accordingly, psychologists and educators have reasoned that any procedure that makes the organization of material more obvious and striking should facilitate learning the material. This has led to interest in mathemagenic activities such as the use of testlike questions presented before or after the to-be-learned material.

9. David P. Ausubel suggests a variation upon the theme of mathemagenic activities. In his theory of meaningful verbal learning, he advocates the use of advance organizers to facilitate the learning of written materials. Ausubel argues that learning requires readers to incorporate new ideas within already existing cognitive structures. The process of anchoring ideas within such structures can be expedited by presenting organizing clues.

CHAPTER GLOSSARY

encoding   The process by which information is put into the memory system.

episodic memory   The information we have about particular events that we experienced in the past.

long-term store   A fairly permanent repository for information received from the short-term store; the retention of information over an extended period of time.

mathemagenic behaviors   Behaviors that give birth to learning; activities on the part of the student that result in the achievement of specified instructional objectives.

memory   A loosely defined concept that describes the ability of individuals to recall, recognize, or relearn more rapidly previously practiced behaviors.

metamemory   The demonstrated knowledge we have about memory and the activity of remembering.

mnemonics   Courses of action that we deliberately instigate for helping us remember things better.

rehearsal   A process by which we repeat information to ourselves.

rehearsal buffer   The set of memory traces (units of information) that can be maintained in the short-term store.

retrieval   The process by which information is regathered when it is needed.

semantic memory   The organized store of knowledge we have about the world as well as about language and its uses.

sensory register   The store where incoming information initially resides; information remains for a fraction of a second, then decays and is lost.

short-term store   Our working memory; it receives selected inputs from both the sensory register and the long-term store. In everyday language we make reference to the short-term store when we say that something is in our "consciousness."

storage   The process by which information is retained until it is needed.

trace   A set of information; it is the residue of an event that remains in memory after the event has vanished.

EXERCISES

Review Questions

1. According to the filing cabinet analogy, if we *misfile* an item, the error is said to have occurred in which phase?

    a. trace
    b. encoding
    c. storage
    d. retrieval

2. Which one of the following theories explains the superiority of recognition as a memory task over recall as a function of a difference in required tasks?

    a. threshold hypothesis
    b. generation-recognition hypothesis
    c. encoding hypothesis
    d. cue-dependent forgetting hypothesis

3. The amount of information copied by the long-term store is most affected by

    a. perceptual qualities of the item
    b. length of time an item stays in the rehearsal buffer
    c. variations in decay time in the sensory register
    d. storage capacity in the long-term store

4. Which of the following is *not* a characteristic of the short-term store?

   a. conscious
   b. under voluntary control
   c. governs flow of information
   d. no decay under sixty seconds

5. Unlike the Atkinson-Shiffrin model, the Craik-Lockhart model can explain more easily why

   a. meaningful material is recalled more easily
   b. rote material is recalled more easily
   c. functional fixedness exists in problem solving
   d. we can remember only a limited number of items at a time

6. In the cue-dependent theory of forgetting it is assumed that the

   a. memory trace and retrieval cue are synonymous
   b. retrieval cue is part of the perceptual environment
   c. retrieval cue is part of the cognitive environment
   d. memory trace can act as a retrieval cue if necessary

7. In contrasting episodic and semantic memory, Tulving argues that

   a. both episodic and semantic memory depend on specific properties of the percept
   b. semantic memory depends on cognitive referents
   c. episodic memory is generally superior to semantic memory
   d. episodic and semantic memories involve similar levels of processing

8. The mnemonic technique "method of loci" primarily involves which one of the following strategies?

   a. organization
   b. rehearsal
   c. visual imagery
   d. note-taking

9. Which of the following is the most critical element of Rothkopf's definition of mathemagenic behavior? The theory

   a. consists of adjunct question and goals
   b. deals essentially with teacher behavior
   c. is defined in terms of student response
   d. does not necessarily lead to learning

10. Which of the following is synonymous with Ausubel's concept of advanced organizers?

   a. detailed outcome
   b. overview
   c. conceptual framework
   d. summary

Answers

1. c (See pp. 191, 195)
2. b (See pp. 193–194)
3. b (See p. 197)
4. d (See pp. 195–196)
5. a (See pp. 197–200)
6. c (See p. 203)
7. b (See p. 199)
8. c (See p. 206)
9. c (See pp. 208–210)
10. c (See pp. 210–211)

Applying Principles and Concepts

1. Indicate in the space provided whether the test item represents recall (RL) or recognition (RN).

   _____ a. Multiple-choice
   _____ b. Fill-in
   _____ c. Matching
   _____ d. Short answers
   _____ e. Essay
   _____ f. This question

2. A teacher is preparing an astronomy lesson and has listed the following activities. In the space provided after each activity, indicate whether the memory task can be classified as free recall (FR),

serial learning (SL), paired-associate (PA), or recognition (R).

_____ a. Name as many of the planets as possible.

_____ b. List the planets in order from the sun.

_____ c. Tell how many moons each planet has.

_____ d. Identify the planets from pictures shown previously.

3. Which of the following teacher comments are generally compatible with the Atkinson-Shiffrin model of memory?

a. "I try to get students to apply strategies they have used previously."

b. "I avoid overloading the amount of information I give students at any one time."

c. "I use as many examples as I can teaching a concept."

d. "One of my best learning strategies is rehearsal."

4. Indicate in the space provided whether the example of forgetting represents decay (D), proactive interference (PI), retroactive interference (RI), or cue-dependent (CD).

_____ a. The lecturer provided too many examples in making his point.

_____ b. "I can't help you with your math. It's been so long since I studied it."

_____ c. A new high-school basketball coach finds that players just coming into his system remember more easily than those left over from the previous year.

_____ d. "I just can't help you with your history. I thought I remembered what I learned when I was in school, but after reading your assignment I became confused."

5. A social studies teacher has decided to let his high-school history class "act out" a feudal scene in which a vassal swears obedience to his lord.

The class enthusiastically prepares a skit and costumes, and practices until everything is perfect. It is so good that they perform for other classes who observe the play and then discuss its significance.

a. In terms of *viewers,* which type of memory (semantic or episodic) is most likely to be represented seeing the play?

b. In terms of the *participants,* which mnemonic strategies (rehearsal, visual imagery, organization, note-taking, meaningfulness) are likely to be involved?

c. In terms of the *viewers,* which mnemonic strategies are likely to be involved?

6. The following paragraph is taken from a student's description of advance organizers. Underline those passages that the text *cannot* support.

> Ernst Rothkopf coined the term "advance organizers." There are two types—expository and comparative—depending on whether the materials are unfamiliar or familiar respectively. Although they are easy to construct, the research evidence on their effectiveness is not all that clear-cut.

Answers

1. a, RN; b, RL; c, RN; d, RL; e, RL; f, RL (See pp. 192–193)
2. a, FR; b, SL; c, PA; d, R (See pp. 192–193)
3. a, b, c, and d are all compatible (See pp. 195–197)
4. a, CD; b, D, c, PI; d, RI (See pp. 201–203)
5. a, semantic; b, rehearsal, visual imagery, organization, note-taking (possibly), and meaningfulness; c, visual imagery and meaningfulness (organization might be included depending on how the play was structured and presented) (See pp. 199, 204–208)
6. Underline "Ernst Rothkopf coined the term 'advanced organizers' " and "although they are easy to construct." (See pp. 210–211)

Project

OBJECTIVE: To allow you to carry out and analyze an experiment in retroactive inhibition.

PROCEDURES: Procedures have been modified

somewhat to shorten the time spent. We will use paired-associates in this study. You might want to review pp. 192, 201–203. You will use two subjects. The first one is the experimental, and the second is the control. *Read all steps* before you start. To help you with the experiment we have provided you with two lists of paired-associates similar to those used in many experiments. The experimental design is: Experimental subject learns List A and List B, and then tries to recall A. The control first learns List A, then rests, and finally tries to recall List A.

1. Copy each pair of words in each list on 3″ × 5″ index cards. Write only one pair on each card. Since there are twelve pairs per list, you will have twenty-four cards, twelve for each list. We will call these cards the *paired-word* cards. Thus, for List A you will have one card labeled "animal-home," another "house-lord," and so on.

List A	List B
animal-home	animal-history
house-lord	house-law
sugar-kiss	sugar-life
board-knowledge	board-kiss
star-life	star-knowledge
tree-law	tree-love
cat-market	cat-lord
arm-death	arm-home
baby-green	baby-soul
railroad-history	railroad-green
picture-soul	picture-death
valley-love	valley-market

2. Prepare twelve more cards, writing *only* the *first* word for each pair. You will note that Lists A and B have identical first words. Hence you will label one card with the word "animal," another with "house," and so on. These *single-word* cards will be used for both List A and List B.
3. Select a subject. We would recommend any one from elementary grades and older. This first subject will be your experimental subject.
4. Pick up the paired-word cards for List A and

tell the subject, "I am going to show you some cards. On each card is a pair of words. As I show you the card say the word aloud, and try to remember which go together. This is the first list."
5. One at a time, place each List A *paired-word* card face-up before the subject and give him or her up to five seconds to say the pair aloud. Do not let the subject handle the cards, and do not go back and forth in the deck. Once a card is shown, place it face down on the pile. Go through the entire deck three times.
6. Shuffle the deck of *single-word* cards so that the order is *not* the same as the *paired-word* cards (to avoid serial learning). Say to the subject, "I am going to show you just the first word of each pair. You tell me what word was paired with it." Place each *single-word* card one at a time face-up before the subject. Give him or her five seconds to respond. Regardless of what subjects say (or even if they say "I don't know" or don't respond at all) do *not* correct them and/or tell them any answer at any time. As they respond, record the results next to each word in Table 7.1 under Trial 1. Use a system such as 1 equals correct, 2 equals wrong, 3 equals no answer or "don't know."

TABLE 7.1
Recording List-A Answers

List A	Trial 1	Trial 2
animal-home	_____	_____
house-lord	_____	_____
sugar-kiss	_____	_____
board-knowledge	_____	_____
star-life	_____	_____
tree-law	_____	_____
cat-market	_____	_____
arm-death	_____	_____
baby-green	_____	_____
railroad-history	_____	_____
picture-soul	_____	_____
valley-love	_____	_____
Number right	_____	_____

7. Put the number right under the Trial 1 column, but don't tell the subject!
8. Repeat Steps 6 and 7. Tell the subject: "I am going to show you the *single-word* cards again."

Be sure to repeat all activities as before. Remember to shuffle the *single-word* cards before you start the Trial 2 procedure.

9. Repeat Step 7 and record responses under the Trial 2 column.

10. Tally the number right under the Trial 2 column. Generally, there is an increase in the number right from Trial 1.

11. Allow the subject to rest one minute. Do not tell him or her what will happen next.

12. Take the second set of *paired-word* cards (List B) and employ three trials as you did with List A. Again, shuffle the *paired-word* and *single-word* cards between trials. In actuality, you will repeat Steps 4 through 10 with List B, using the same *single-word* cards (which have different associations for List B). Use Table 7.2 to record the answers for Trials 1 and 2. Tell the subject, "This is List 2."

TABLE 7.2
Recording List-B Answers

List B	Trial 1	Trial 2
animal-history	————	————
house-law	————	————
sugar-life	————	————
board-kiss	————	————
star-knowledge	————	————
tree-love	————	————
cat-lord	————	————
arm-home	————	————
baby-soul	————	————
railroad-green	————	————
picture-death	————	————
valley-market	————	————
Number right	————	————

13. Allow the subject to rest two minutes. Tell him or her the experiment isn't quite over yet.

14. This is the Critical Trial. Shuffle the *single-word* cards and ask the subject to recall the pairs for the *first* list. Say, "You have learned two lists of words, I want you now to recall how the words were paired for the *first* list." This is Step 6 again, but this trial is done only once. You're asking the subject to recall List A after having learned List B. Record the results on Table 7.3.

TABLE 7.3
Critical Trial

List A	Critical Trial
animal-home	————
house-lord	————
sugar-kiss	————
board-knowledge	————
star-life	————
tree-law	————
cat-market	————
arm-death	————
baby-green	————
railroad-history	————
picture-soul	————
valley-love	————
Number right	————

15. To show retroactive inhibition (the effect of List B on List A) it will be necessary to use a second subject. Try to get one at approximately the same level of school as the first. He or she will be the control subject. For this subject, go through Step 4 to Step 8. Again, be sure to shuffle the decks each time. In essence, the second subject learns List A as did the first subject. Use Table 7.4 for recording answers.

TABLE 7.4
Second Subject List-A Answers

List A	Trial 1	Trial 2
animal-home	————	————
house-lord	————	————
sugar-kiss	————	————
board-knowledge	————	————
star-life	————	————
tree-law	————	————
cat-market	————	————
arm-death	————	————
baby-green	————	————
railroad-history	————	————
picture-soul	————	————
valley-love	————	————
Number right	————	————

16. Allow the subject to pause for five minutes. This subject does *not* learn List B.

17. Pick up the *single-word* cards, shuffle, and repeat Step 14. Say, "I'd like to try you on the list again." Record the subject responses on Table 7.5.

TABLE 7.5

Critical Trial—Control Subject

List A	Critical Trial
animal-home	_____
house-lord	_____
sugar-kiss	_____
board-knowledge	_____
star-life	_____
tree-law	_____
cat-market	_____
arm-death	_____
baby-green	_____
railroad-history	_____
picture-soul	_____
valley-love	_____
Number right	_____

ANALYSIS: There are several ways to analyze the data. First, to compare the interference effect on List B, contrast the Critical Trial scores for both subjects. Differences in favor of the subject who did *not* take List B show the interference phenomenon. Second, as a further check, compare the Trial 2 scores of the subject who took List B with those of his or her Critical Trial. While some decrease is to be expected (as in the case of the second subject who did not take List B), a sharp drop represents further evidence of interference.

CHAPTER OUTLINE

8

LEARNING GENERALIZABLE SKILLS AND KNOWLEDGE

CHAPTER PREVIEW

Should the primary aim of education be to teach specific facts or information or to help students learn how to learn and become skilled and creative problem solvers? Perhaps these goals are not mutually exclusive, but the question highlights a con-tinuing debate, one that was reflected in the previous discussions of discovery and expository learning. Educators who emphasize the importance of life-long learning urge schools to promote the development of highly generalizable skills and open-ended thinking. Problem solving and creativity, then, are central concerns of this chapter. An important and related issue is that of transfer of learning, which many people view as the principal goal of all education.

Use your problem-solving skills in thinking about these questions:

- How might Gagné's cumulative model of learning be useful in planning instruction?
- What steps are typically involved in the problem-solving process and how could problem solving be used in the classroom?
- What is transfer of learning? Why is it important and how can it be promoted?
- How do schools tend to stifle creativity? How can they foster it, instead?

The human mind is our fundamental resource.

JOHN F. KENNEDY

Life consists of change. We will not live our lives in the world into which we were born, nor shall we die in the world in which we worked in our mature years. The eminent economist, Kenneth Boulding, observes, "The world of today . . . is as different from the world in which I was born as that world was from Julius Caesar's. I was born in the middle of human history, to date, roughly. Almost as much has happened since I was born as happened before" (as quoted by Toffler, 1970:13).

But not only does the world about us change. Over the span of sixty, seventy, or eighty years we, too, undergo dramatic changes as we pass from infancy through childhood, adolescence, adulthood, and old age. Our organism alters with time. So do our roles as we enter school, complete school, get our first job, marry, have children, see our youngest child married, become grandparents, retire, and so on.

Education fails us if it seeks simply to supply us with ready-made solutions to contemporary life circumstances and problems. Indeed, there are many who believe that the first and foremost task of education is to foster highly generalizable skills and knowledge that allow learners to cope effectively with change. According to this view, teaching particular facts and specific content is secondary to equipping students to solve a wide variety of problems. In brief, schools must build youth for the future.

GAGNÉ'S CUMULATIVE MODEL OF LEARNING

The whole art of teaching is only the art of awakening the natural curiosity of young minds for the purpose of satisfying it afterwards.

ANATOLE FRANCE

Robert M. Gagné (1977) has formulated an integrated framework for dealing with various levels of learning. In Gagné's view learning is cumulative. Individuals are portrayed as developing higher-level skills or acquiring more knowledge as they learn capabilities that can be built successively, one on another. Gagné evolved his *cumulative model of learning* in the course of designing more effective educational programs. His interest derived from the work he did as an air force psychologist during World War II. During this period, he was engaged in developing training programs for military personnel (elaborating techniques for teaching someone how to put a radar set in operation or to locate the source of malfunction in complex equipment). Over the past thirty years, his ideas and research have found applications in a variety of areas, particularly in teaching mathematics, language, and science (White, 1973; White and Gagné, 1978).

Types of Learning

In the course of his military experiences, Gagné found that many of the principles contained in traditional theories of learning were seldom useful in bringing about actual training improvement. However, by making adjustments in some of the theoretical formulations, Gagné and his coworkers were able to achieve improved training results. This led Gagné to conclude that there are multiple types of learning. Accordingly, one learning principle is not applicable to all instructional tasks.

Gagné (1977) identifies eight types of learning, arranged as follows in the order of their complexity:

- *Type 1: Signal learning*. This type of learning involves classical conditioning of the sort described by Pavlov. The responses are general and diffuse, occurring involuntarily as learned reactions to certain stimuli that function as signals. For instance, the stimulus (signal), "It is test time," may contribute to the response of fear, failure, and consequent nausea among some students.

- *Type 2: Stimulus-response learning.* Another fundamental kind of learning involves operant conditioning. The learner acquires a precise response that is instrumental in attaining some end or payoff. For instance, the young child learns that saying "wa-wa" results in the parents providing a glass of water. Or the announcement, "Time for reading," results in students preparing to read and the teacher offering them an approving smile (a rewarding experience).

- *Type 3: Chaining.* Chaining is the connection of a set of individual stimulus-response patterns within some particular sequence. This is illustrated by the operations involved in starting an automobile. The person makes a "chain" out of individual links by grouping the events closely together in some order.

- *Type 4: Verbal association.* This form of learning is a type of chaining, but the links are verbal units. A simple verbal link is illustrated by the activity of naming. For instance, the child learns to properly identify an object as a doll and also to say the word "doll." Learning foreign language equivalents of English vocabulary and recalling definitions of words are other illustrations of verbal association.

- *Type 5: Multiple discrimination.* Individuals learn to distinguish between stimuli that might be confused. For instance, we must learn which key fits the front door of our home and which fits the car door. It is necessary to eliminate the "interference" that occurs when we deal with things that are only slightly different. In school, children learn to distinguish among and correctly name different teachers, classmates, flowers, birds, animals, and so on.

- *Type 6: Concept learning.* A concept involves the rules governing the classification of objects or events. In concept learning the individual acquires a common response to a class of stimuli. In educational settings the learner is required to respond to the abstract properties of stimuli, such as shape, color, position, or number (such concepts as a circle and a square, up and down, blue and red, and so on).

- *Type 7: Rule learning.* In this type of learning individuals acquire the ability to relate (in psychological terminology, *chain*) two or more concepts. For example, the statement, "Round things roll," represents the linking of different concepts, *round things* and *roll*. Students demonstrate that they have learned a rule by making correct responses in accordance with a statement. Hence, when provided with an inclined plane and a set of unfamiliar blocks, some of which are round and some not, students should be able to identify the objects that will and will not roll down the incline.

- *Type 8: Problem solving.* Gagné views problem solving as a process by which individuals discover a combination of previously learned rules that they apply to achieve a solution for a novel situation. It is the highest level of learning, involving those activities that we commonly label "thinking." An example is a driver who devises an alternative route to bypass a traffic tie-up or the psychologist who manipulates a number of principles to derive a new theoretical formulation. Good classroom illustrations of problem-solving activities are homework exercises in algebra and geometry. Through problem solving an individual is capable of deriving new ideas independently.

This framework provides a useful set of categories into which learning tasks can be sorted. If we ignore the hierarchical aspect of Gagné's system, most of what commonly goes on in the classroom falls under the last three types of learning—concept learning, rule learning, and problem solving.

Hierarchical Arrangement

The types of learning identified by Gagné are arranged in a hierarchical order so that some are subordinate to and components of more complex types. Thus:

Learning
stimulus-response connections
is prerequisite to learning
chains and
verbal associations
which in turn are prerequisite to learning
discriminations
which must precede the learning of
concepts
which are prerequisite to the learning of
rules
which are required for
problem-solving
[Schramm, 1977:76]

Gagné (1962) began his research on learning hierarchies by attempting to teach seven children how to find formulas for sums of terms in number series. He suggested that this skill could not be acquired unless the pupils possessed certain prerequisite skills. To identify these skills, he asked himself, "What skills must any individual have to attain successful performance on this task?" Through this process of task analysis, he derived a network of component elements. He then taught the skills to the children and observed that they were unable to acquire a skill without also learning all of the skills that were subordinate to it in the hierarchy.

According to Gagné, learning a skill or concept is a hierarchical process in which lower-order elements are gradually integrated to form higher-order ones. Achievement in each type of learning depends on acquiring the preceding one. As a consequence, the teacher needs to consider the relevance of subordinate types of learning when preparing instruction of a higher type. This requires task analysis. Ideally, the teacher should map out the hierarchical structure underlying the educational objective to be attained. The student is then led from the initial or entering position in the hierarchy to the terminal objective, via the intermediate steps indicated by the analysis.

Figure 8.1 shows a learning hierarchy for subtracting whole numbers that resulted from a task analysis. This kind of information provides guidelines for the optimal sequencing of different learn-

ing types and the development of instructional programs that will be most likely to facilitate the respective types of learning.

PROBLEM SOLVING

Thinking is not a heaven-born thing. . . . It is a gift men and women make for themselves. It is earned, and it is earned by effort. There is no effort, to my mind, that is comparable in its qualities, that is so taxing to the individual as to think, to analyze fundamentally.
SUPREME COURT JUSTICE LOUIS D. BRANDEIS

Gagné considers problem solving to be the most complex type of human learning. As noted, he views problem solving as the combination and application of two or more previously acquired rules (principles). As human beings we may be many things. But there is no escaping the fact that above all we are problem solvers. In comparison with many other organisms, we possess relatively little in the way of biologically preprogrammed adaptations to our environment. Indeed, human beings have learned to adjust to geographical and climatic environments ranging from that experienced by Alaskan Eskimos to that of the nomads of the Sahara Desert. Human civilization is a history of problem solving and innovation, from the invention of fire and the wheel to modern space travel.

A **problem** is a stimulus situation for which an organism lacks a ready response (Davis, 1973). In everyday life we encounter problems as situations to which we must respond if we are to function effectively in our environment. Problems may be simple or highly complex, loosely stated or weakly structured, of short duration or extending over prolonged periods of time (Crutchfield, 1969). Usually, a problem solution consists of a new combination or rearrangement of existing ideas. It entails the ability to use previously learned concepts and rules in some combination to achieve some goal (Gagné, 1964).

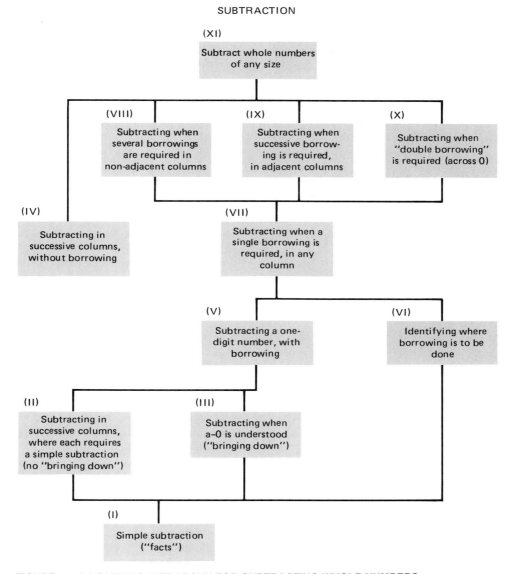

FIGURE 8.1 A LEARNING HIERARCHY FOR SUBTRACTING WHOLE NUMBERS
The figure shows the intellectual skills that are necessary to perform the task of subtracting whole numbers of any size. When students learn the ten prerequisite skills (identified by Roman numerals), they should be able to do subtraction problems. A teacher or preparer of instructional material would design instruction to teach the skills in the order incorporated in the hierarchy. *(Source: From* Principles of Instructional Design *by Robert M. Gagné and Leslie J. Briggs. Copyright © 1974 by Holt, Rinehart and Winston, Inc. Reprinted by permission of Holt, Rinehart and Winston, CBS College Publishing.)*

PROBLEM SOLVING
Problem solving requires that we combine or rearrange existing ideas to achieve some goal.

Steps in Problem Solving

Perhaps the supreme mark of adaptive behavior is an individual's ability to cope with new problems in a flexible and innovative manner. Problem solving, however, is not so much a "happening" as a process. Various psychologists and educators have suggested a number of schemes for depicting the steps or stages in the problem-solving process (Dewey, 1910; Wallas, 1926; Dressel and Mayhew, 1954; D'Zurilla and Goldfried, 1971; Sternberg, 1981b). From these formulations, it is possible to abstract five principal steps:

1. *Sensing a problem:* In the first step, individuals experience some difficulty, strain, or challenge in their lives. But circumstances, no matter how unusual, do not in and of themselves constitute a problem. Rather it is people's definition of some situation as perplexing or stressful that makes it such; they attribute problem status to certain circumstances by assigning a challenging or unfavorable *meaning* to them. This stage is commonly short-circuited or omitted in the typical problem-solving episodes confronting children in classrooms. For instance, a problem in mathematics or science is already provided in a neatly packaged or labeled form (Crutchfield, 1969).

2. *Sharpening the dimensions of a problem:* Usually, in this second step, the difficult or puzzling circumstances are felt to be a "big mess"—a confusing array of facts, difficulties, and gaps in information. At times a search for additional facts is required. In classroom settings this may entail extracting information from children, scrutinizing the textbook for certain facts, searching reference sources for additional data, or even engaging in experimentation (Torrance and Myers, 1972). Thus, individuals become acquainted with the features of a problem, identify its boundaries, distinguish between relevant and irrelevant facts, and order the available information in manageable terms.

Obviously, the larger the knowledge base from which people operate, the more elements there are within their repertoire of responses and the more combinations of old elements or more reapplications of old elements become possible. Problem solving requires that people generate information that they did not have before. Indeed, when we consider intelligence, we typically focus on people's problem-solving abilities. We are interested in their ability to use concepts or form strategies that differ in some respects from those to which they have been accustomed (Sternberg, 1981a). Viewed from this perspective, intelligence consists of a set of developed thinking and learning skills used in problem solving (Sternberg, 1981b).

PROBLEM SOLVING

LOLA MAY AND BARBARA BETHEL

If there is one important mathematical skill children need as they prepare for their future, it is that of problem solving. During the back-to-basics movement, problem solving took a back seat and many teachers still tend to ignore it. But it is the one important skill kids will need to deal with the machines—the calculators and computers—that will make their adult lives more efficient.

With these machines handling the difficult computations, people will be required to ask the correct questions and then understand the solutions to highly sophisticated problems. And to do this, the individual will need a supply of strategies to draw upon that have been acquired through experiences. Our goal then, must be to provide students with thinking experiences, not just computing experiences. Here are some tips that will help you do just that.

1. *Identify the question or questions in a problem:* Understanding what is being asked in a problem is essential to finding the solution. To help students acquire this skill, first have them read a problem silently, then have it read aloud.

Source: Lola May and Barbara Bethel, "Problem Solving," *Instructor,* 90 (April 1981):54–55.

For example: *"Maria has 3 pencils. Sally has 2 pencils. How many more pencils does Maria have than Sally?"* and *"Joe earned $15.50 mowing lawns. He spent $5.75 on a model airplane. How much money does he have left?"*

Wait a few minutes before talking about a problem. Research has shown that if you do so, many of your students will begin to work on a solution among themselves. They will discuss the problem— and they should be allowed to do so.

Then have students restate the problem in their own words, asking them to identify the question that must be answered to solve it. Although the questions may seem obvious to you, not all students will understand them until they are discussed.

Continue this activity with more difficult problems containing two or more questions. For example: *"Sharon had $75. She spent $13.28 and $26.45. How much money does she have left?"* Be sure students understand that questions are often implied rather than asked directly. In the above example, the solution to the question "How much money did Sharon spend altogether?" must be found before the question "How much money does she have left?" can be answered.

2. *Identify the process or operation needed for solving a problem:* If students have trouble with this, try using problems without numbers such as: *"Susie's father earns the same salary each month. How can you find how much he earns for a certain number of weeks?"* (division). *"José bought a baseball, a bat, and a glove. How can you find how much he spent altogether?"* (addition).

3. *Now, help your students examine a problem and make a logical estimate as to what the answer will be:* That way, they'll know when they check their final answer if it makes any sense at all or whether they've gone off in the wrong direction.

4. *In going over the estimation process help students understand that there is not always a single way to solve a problem and that experimentation is essential to good problem solving:* Demonstrate that some problems don't have to be solved through computation alone. For example, many can be effectively solved by constructing a picture or diagram of the problem. This word problem, *"Joe lives 10 miles west of the zoo. Pete lives 7 miles east of the zoo. How far do they live from each other?"* can be illus-

(continued)

PROBLEM SOLVING (continued)

trated with a simple line sketch, with a house drawn in at one end (for Pete), a zoo further along (marked at 7 miles), and a house at the other end (for Joe, and marked 10 miles from the zoo).

5. *Problem-solving skills can be sharpened quickly by creating word problems for a number sentence:* This activity will help focus attention on the problem situation and process for solution. For example, place a number sentence on the chalkboard, such as 9 + 8 = 17. Have students tell or write word problems that could be solved by the number sentence. Here are several possibilities: *"Sam had 9 pencils. His teacher gave him 8 more. How many does he have altogether?"* and *"There are 9 rows of chairs on one side of the auditorium and 8 rows on the other side. How many rows of chairs are there in the auditorium?"*

6. *Identify problems with too much or too little information:* Word problems that contain either unnecessary or insufficient information are difficult or impossible

for children to solve. The following exercise will improve student ability to weed out unnecessary information and to seek out more when it is needed.

Write problems with too much information on the chalkboard. For example: *"Jenny bought a shirt for $8.95 and a purse for $5.79. She gave the clerk $20. How much did she spend?"* Discuss which information in the problem is needed for the solution. Ask a student to put a line through the unnecessary information. The revised problem should read *"Jenny bought a shirt for $8.95 and a purse for $5.79. How much did she spend?"*

Next, write problems containing too little information on the chalkboard. For example: "The trip to San Diego will take the Andersons five hours. About what time will they arrive?" Discuss the given information, the additional information needed, and methods of rewriting the problem so that it can be solved. Have your students add the necessary facts to the problem and then find

the solution. (In this problem, students need to know *when* the Andersons started the trip.)

Obviously, there are countless other problems you can, and should, present to your students—problems that will make them think, not just rely on memorization and computational skills. And there are three important points to always keep in mind: problem-solving activities should start as early as the first grade. This stretching of minds needs to begin that early. Second, convince your students that problem solving is not a clear-cut procedure and solutions are not found instantly. And third, practice . . . practice . . . practice! That is the one sure road to success in this important area.

Problem solving is not just another chapter in your math book. It's the most important skill students can take into the twenty-first century. It involves skills your students will be using the rest of their lives. How well they use them depends on you.

3. *Generating alternative solutions to a problem:* Having defined the problem and identified its dimensions, individuals need to come up with a supply of alternative solutions or promising hypotheses that can be tested. Unhappily, far too little attention tends to be given to the stimulation of ideas at most educational levels. This partly reflects the dictates of the conventional curriculum as well as teaching methods that emphasize the "authority" of established

knowledge (Crutchfield, 1969). However, various strategies are available for encouraging idea generation (see boxed insert on pages 227–228). Generally, successful problem solving is guided by two principles. First, it is *hierarchical;* complex problems need be decomposed into subproblems, until each subproblem becomes solvable. And second, it is governed by *heuristic principles.* Various shortcuts, rules of thumb, and other devices need to be used that

STRATEGIES FOR PROBLEM SOLVING

Educators have long regarded teaching children to think clearly and creatively about ideas and issues as one of their primary goals. Over the past two or three decades, a substantial literature has appeared dealing with conscious methods for producing new idea combinations (Davis, 1976). Two of the most popular of these are brainstorming and synectics.

BRAINSTORMING

Brainstorming is a process by which a great many solutions to a problem are encouraged by deferring judgment and evaluation (Osborn, 1963; Parnes, 1967). The procedure has found wide application in advertising, invention design, journalism, and business. This is hardly surprising, since brainstorming is simple, appealing, fun, and productive.

Brainstorming is based on two principles. The first rests on the assumption that many people find the evaluative process overpowering. As a consequence, they are locked within cut-and-dried patterns of thinking. Their creative thought is deadened by the effects of conformity, reliance on authority, and fear of making errors. In effect, brainstorming encourages people to suspend the process of evaluating ideas in order to allow full play to their imaginations.

The second principle is that the greater the number of ideas generated, the more likely a few of high quality will surface. Generally, people's first ideas are mundane and commonplace. Their more unique and potentially creative ideas occur later. In brief, it is necessary to "get through" safe and conventional ideas to arrive at original ones (Stein, 1975). In classroom settings teachers often employ brainstorming to provide a free and creative atmosphere where students can gain practice in stretching their imaginative capabilities.

These principles result in four essential rules for a brainstorming session. First, criticism is ruled out. Second, freewheeling is welcomed; indeed, the wilder the idea the better, because "it is easier to tame down [an idea] than to think [it] up" (Osborn, 1963:156). Third, quantity is encouraged; the more ideas that are suggested, the greater the probability that an original one will turn up. And fourth, combination and improvement are sought. Participants are encouraged to build on one another's ideas by improving on them or combining them in various ways with other ideas. Of course, the way in which a question is pre-sented to a group influences the answers that evolve. Accordingly, the problem should be stated simply and should focus on a single target.

SYNECTICS

Synectics involves joining together different and apparently unrelated or irrelevant ideas (Gordon, 1961). The approach is based upon metaphorical thinking. Its founder, William J. J. Gordon, points to numerous inventions and discoveries that resulted from someone making nimble, connective leaps from one seemingly unrelated idea to another (Fincher, 1978). This is what the German chemist Friedrich Kekulé von Stradonitz did when he realized that his dream of a snake swallowing its tail held the secret to how rings of carbon atoms are arranged in organic chemistry; what the automotive engineer Charles Duryea was up to when he patterned the spray-injection carburetor after his wife's perfume atomizer; and what Louis Pasteur did when he solved the mystery of wound infection by noting the hidden likeness between it and how grapes ferment when their skins are broken by the wine press.

(continued)

STRATEGIES FOR PROBLEM SOLVING
(*continued*)

Synectics works by making the strange (the problem) familiar. This can be achieved in three ways. In *direct analogy,* knowledge from one field is used in another, and the more distant the knowledge the better. For instance, knowledge regarding how shipworms tunnel into wood serves as an analogy to solve problems in underwater construction. In *personal analogy,* individuals imaginatively identify with something, placing themselves "in their mind's eye in the shoes of the other."

For example, imagining that one is the rope in the Indian rope trick affords a basis for developing a new type of jack. In *fantasy analogy,* individuals create "magical" solutions and then attempt to bring them down to earth by finding ways of making them practical—a notion based on the Freudian idea of wish fulfillment. For instance, someone might invent an airtight zipper for space suits by imagining an insect running up and down the closure manipulating little hatches.

Within the classroom the teacher can employ synectics by making the strange familiar and the familiar strange. In the former case, the teacher facilitates understanding by taking something that is familiar and linking it to a concept that is unfamiliar. In the latter process, the teacher encourages innovation by having the children produce something that is new by taking something that is strange and attempting to link it by analogy to something familiar.

concentrate the search on promising alternatives and enable one to avoid endless blind alleys (Kintsch, 1977).

4. *Evaluating the previously generated alternatives for consequences and relative gains:* This task involves the selection of the most promising ideas. And individuals must select a strategy for sequencing processes and activities in their proper order. Ineffective sequencing results not only in wasted time and effort but in a poor product (Sternberg, 1981b). Thus people must check to determine how consistent the various courses of action are relative to the requirements of the problem. They must weigh evidence to assess what is likely to provide the most successful solution.

5. *Implementing a given course of action and then judging its effectiveness:* As they proceed through a task, individuals must keep track of what they have already done, what they are currently doing, and what remains to be done (Sternberg, 1981b). Putting ideas into practice usually requires making certain changes along the way. The ideas must be reshaped continually to tailor

them to the real-life situation. Should they fail, the entire process of problem solving must be wholly or partly repeated.

These steps in problem solving are essentially the same as those involved in the scientific method. They highlight for us the ingredients involved in problem-solving activities. As such, they provide us with categories or "handles" to describe and analyze thinking, a phenomenon that we never observe but only infer from what people say or do. Perhaps of even greater significance, a study of problem solving helps us to clarify the process and identify that sequence of events that contributes to the successful solution of problems.

Of course, not all problem solving moves through these five steps or phases. Indeed, it is more instructive if we view the steps as *aspects.* Many of the "steps" overlap; people sometimes skip steps; and occasionally they backtrack to earlier steps (Davis, 1973). Hence, the problem-solving process is not a cut-and-dried sequence of phases executed in a rigid fashion. Seldom does the creative thinking of scientists proceed in the exact manner dictated by the venerable doctrine of the

IMPLEMENTING A COURSE OF ACTION
Problem solving entails putting our ideas into practice and
modifying them as necessary to attain our goals.

scientific method. Creative problem solving is
usually a more chaotic and wild process than the
tame and stereotyped "textbook" accounts of
rational scientific thought (Crutchfield, 1969).

Theoretical Approaches

Ideas and theories are like the wings of birds; they allow
man to soar and to climb to the heavens. But facts are
like the atmosphere against which those wings must
beat, and without which the soaring bird will surely
plummet back to earth.

IVAN PAVLOV

Three theoretical approaches have been employed by psychologists and educators to account
for thinking and problem solving. Early behaviorists emphasized stimulus-response associations.
Cognitive theorists have stressed the importance
of insight in problem solving. And a third group
of theorists have employed information-processing
concepts for examining human thinking.

Early Behaviorist Theories

Edward L. Thorndike and B. F. Skinner have
viewed problem solving as an extension of operant
conditioning procedures. As detailed in Chapter 5,
Thorndike conducted his research with cats in
puzzle boxes, and Skinner studied learning among
rats and pigeons by employing the "Skinner box."
Based on this and related research, these traditional
behaviorists conceived of problem solving as a
matter of trial and error, with successful responses
gradually "stamped in" and unsuccessful responses eliminated.

Viewed from this perspective, organisms possess
drives, motives, or desires. They try out various
responses, guiding their behavior as best they can
on the basis of past experience, but they act blindly
if the situation is new. Gradually, they discard
those activities that fail and adopt those that achieve
their ends (Lawther, 1977). Hence, early behaviorists viewed their investigative task as one of
identifying the principles underlying the strengthening and weakening of various responses (Dominowski, 1977).

Cognitive Theories

As discussed in Chapter 6, cognitive psychologists are interested in the inner dynamics of learning
and thinking. An early and famous study dealing
with problem solving from a cognitive perspective
was undertaken by Wolfgang Köhler (1887–1967).
During World War I, Köhler, a German national,
was stranded at the Berlin Anthropoid Station on
Tenerife, one of the Canary Islands off the coast
of Africa. Between 1913 and 1917, he conducted

a series of experiments with a variety of animals, the best known being those involving chimpanzees.

In a number of his experiments, Köhler would place a bunch of bananas outside an ape's cage just beyond the animal's reach. This would pose a problem for the hungry chimp. To reach the banana, the ape would have to use a stick to maneuver the food toward the cage. In another version of the experiment, a banana would be suspended from the ceiling of the cage. Köhler would place boxes in the cage, which, if stacked by the ape to form a platform, would enable the animal to reach the food (Köhler, 1927).

In still another experiment, Sultan, Köhler's most intelligent chimp, was able to join together two bamboo poles to form one long enough to rake in a banana. While playing with the sticks, Sultan happened to insert the end of one into the end of the other. It then "dawned" on the animal that with the elongated stick he could secure the food.

The chimps also evolved on their own various problem-solving activities. One of their fondest amusements was thrusting a pointed stick (that they had sharpened) at chickens. One chimp would bait the hens by dangling a piece of bread through the bars. When a hen approached the bread, his accomplice would spear the unsuspecting victim.

Köhler concluded that such performances by his chimps involved intelligent attempts at problem solving. Confronted by a problem, an ape would frequently "think through" the problem's solution "in its head" before overtly responding. The chimp would seemingly run through a number of "hypotheses" until it would hit on one that appeared workable. When the animal "came to see" the right strategy, *insight* was said to have occurred.

Insight comes suddenly and abruptly. It involves a cognitive leap (a fitting together of ideas that are qualitatively different or of a new kind). The key element in insight is the new organization of the lower level component parts to produce a higher level whole of a different sort. When a principle learned in one context is applied to the solution of another problem, *transposition* is said to have occurred.

One recent version of the cognitive approach is *hypothesis theory* (Tumblin and Gholson, 1981). A problem-solving task presumably encourages a person to entertain various hypotheses for its solution. The individual in turn samples and tests various hypotheses until a solution is achieved. A solution consists of a rule that consistently results in a correct response.

Information-Processing Theories

With the rapid development of computer technology, many psychologists have been attracted to information-processing models for theorizing about human problem solving. Computers have been programmed to play games like chess and checkers, to diagnose medical problems, to navigate spaceships to the moon and distant planets, to solve complex mathematical problems, to design chemical compounds that will match the peculiar dimensions of cancer cells and destroy them, and so on. Many of these activities bear close resemblances to problem solving among human beings.

Computer programs that are designed to mirror human thinking are termed *simulation models*. Researchers break down the problem to be solved by using organized sequences of elementary processes as the building blocks. Generally, they identify the key ingredients in human information processing by having subjects "think aloud" as they solve actual problems. The researchers then prepare a set of computer subprograms, each of which is capable of executing a specialized process that corresponds to one of the hypothesized human processes. For instance, some subprograms may transform or classify input information, others may make comparisons and decisions, and still others may compare calculations against certain solution specifications (Newell and Simon, 1972; Davis, 1973).

The analogy between the computer and the human being does not rest on hardware (computer mechanical components are not viewed as equivalent to brain neurons). Instead, it rests on the *processes* used to reach outcomes. In other words, the investigator formulates a theory about how human beings solve a problem, programs a computer to simulate these theoretical properties, and tests the theory by comparing the computer output with that produced by human beings (Dominowski, 1977).

The first successful attempt to simulate human thinking by means of computers was undertaken by Allen Newell and Herbert A. Simon (1956, 1961). Their program, termed the Logic Theorist, was used to prove the theorems in formal logic derived by Alfred North Whitehead and Bertrand Russell in their famous treatise, *Principia Mathematica* (1925). Whenever the computer proved a theorem, the information was stored in memory along with the original axioms. It was then available for use in proving subsequent theorems, just as Whitehead and Russell had done. The Logic Theorist succeeded in giving adequate proofs for thirty-eight of the fifty-two theorems, and some of the proofs were more ingenious and efficient than those originally proposed by Whitehead and Russell.

The Logic Theorist employed many of the *heuristics* (shortcuts or rules of thumb) used by human beings in their problem-solving activities. For instance, one heuristic it employed was "working backwards." It would begin with the answer and move backward step by step to the initial problem—in the process uncovering the logic involved in the procedure. It would also "make-a-plan" heuristic in which the computer would evolve a problem-attack strategy by solving a similar problem to which the computer already had the solution. Heuristics allowed the computer to reduce the amount of mechanical trial-and-error searching substantially (thus the computer did not blindly search through every possible sequence of logical operations until it "lucked upon" the proof). Such tactics led the Logic Theorist to sudden "insight" into the solution of a problem.

Although the performance of the Logic Theorist is impressive, it is limited to the specific type of problem for which the computer is programmed. It is able to plan chess moves or prove logic theorems, but it cannot do both. This limitation led Newell and Simon (1972) to design a more powerful and sophisticated problem-solving system, the General Problem Solver. It incorporates a large number of strategies and heuristics that are thought to underlie human problem-solving activities. Although the General Problem Solver can design a program for playing chess, prove logic theorems, and compose music, it is hardly an all-purpose system. The General Problem Solver can deal only with well-defined problems in which the goal is described in exactly the same way in all cases. This limits the types of problems it can solve.

Simon and his colleagues have developed another program called BACON, after statesman and thinker Sir Francis Bacon. On its own BACON "discovered" a rule of planetary motion first established by Johannes Kepler in 1609. Further, when it was fed all the facts that were known about chemistry in the year 1800, BACON deduced the principle of atomic weight, a development that took human scientists another fifty years.

The work of information-processing theorists has greatly increased our understanding of a complex human behavior. Yet electronic models do not provide a perfect or even near-perfect analogy to human thinking processes. Human motivation, emotion, language, personality, and experience are all variables that interact in fashioning thought. More specifically, computers can only touch on the fringes of human emotion, an essential ingredient of human intelligence and curiosity. Further, it is exceedingly difficult to simulate the eyes and ears that feed information to the human brain.

Computers do not as yet engage in the crucial step of problem identification. Consequently, they are not adapting organisms as are human beings. Indeed, the operations that computers can perform are a direct function of what they have been programmed to do. The computer programmer can entirely control what is placed in the computer. The problem in the classroom is that students come with events and experiences in their repertoires which the teacher is unaware of, and hence any attempt by the teacher to "program" students with instructional material may backfire (producing unanticipated combinations of information). In sum, the human brain is much more sophisticated, versatile, and complicated than any computer system yet devised.

TRANSFER OF LEARNING

Good instruction leads a student to know more than he has learned; to acquire knowledge, skills, and attitudes that can be carried over for use at other times and in different settings.

STANFORD C. ERICKSEN
Motivation for Learning, 1974

As pointed out earlier in the chapter, learning is a cumulative process, building on itself. The more knowledge and skills we acquire, the more likely it is that our new learning will be influenced and shaped by our past learning. Prior knowledge functions as a point of departure for tackling new tasks. Hence, transfer of learning is a critical aspect of life and a central component in human adaptive capabilities. **Transfer of learning** refers to the influence that prior learning has on performance in a subsequent situation. In brief, we apply knowledge and principles learned in one context to other contexts.

Transfer of learning is the objective of the vast majority of educational endeavors. Accordingly, instruction should be designed to maximize transfer. Indeed, if the learning that occurs in school cannot or does not transfer to other situations, the enterprise is commonly viewed as a waste of time and resources. There are two questions an instructor needs to ask while teaching something to students: (1) Will it transfer? and (2) Have they learned it so that they will remember it and be able to use it later?

In assessing learning transfer, a teacher usually provides students with a situation that requires them to use a particular principle or rule to solve a novel problem (Gagné and White, 1978). In one type of transfer, termed by Gagné *lateral transfer,* students apply knowledge encountered in one situation in new situations. For instance, students are taught to write paragraphs and to use appropriate grammatical constructions in the expectation that

TRANSFER OF LEARNING
A major concern of educators is that the more traditional forms of classroom learning transfer to nonclassroom settings.

they will apply these skills in their subsequent attempts to write prose after they leave the classroom. They are also taught methods for obtaining information for themselves, such as consulting dictionaries and encyclopedias.

A second type of transfer involves combining a previously learned rule with one or more additional rules to find the solution to a problem, termed by Gagné *vertical transfer.* Prior learning at one level in a taxonomy or hierarchy of behaviors influences current learning at a higher level. Take the mattter of teaching students to multiply binomials such as in the problem $(a + b)(a - b)$. Most commonly, students have previously been taught a number of rules, including:

1. The product of two variables with like signs is positive. Hence a × b = ab.

2. The product of two variables with unlike signs is negative. Hence a × −b = −ab.

3. To multiply a polynomial by a monomial, multiply each term of the polynomial by the monomial. Hence (3a + 5b + 6c)(3) = 9a + 15b + 18c.

To solve binomials such as (a + b)(a − b), the students must combine this prior learning with additional rules:

1. The first term of the product is the product of the first terms of the binomials. Therefore a × a = a².

2. The middle term of the product is the sum of the cross products. Hence (b × a) + (a × −b) = ba + −ba = 0.

3. The last term of the product is the product of the last terms of the binomial. Therefore b × −b = −b².

Accordingly, (a + b)(a − b) = a² − b².

Clearly, transfer of learning is a broad topic and one that has many ramifications, and thus consideration of the topic will not be limited to this chapter. Chapter 5 dealt with transfer of learning in the treatment of stimulus generalization. Transfer of learning is also related to memory (the topic of Chapter 7), since initial learning must be retained if it is to affect new learning.

The Nature of Transfer

If transfer of learning did not occur, we would have to start every new undertaking from "scratch." Indeed, by virtue of transfer, we can become progressively more proficient in certain endeavors. For instance, if we master one foreign language like French, we generally find it easier to acquire a second, related language like Spanish. If we grasp the concepts of introductory algebra, we can build upon this understanding to master more advanced principles, and if we learn how to throw a ball through a hoop, we can adapt the procedure to a basketball game.

Schools are premised on the notion that educational experiences will have transfer value for out-of-school tasks and problems. But transfer does not necessarily occur in an automatic fashion. This is reflected in the story of a child who had to stay after school in an attempt to improve his grammar. Upon completing his task, he wrote a note to his teacher (Goodwin and Klausmeier, 1975:428):

Dear teacher:
    I have written "I have gone home" on the chalkboard 100 times, and I have went home.
                Johnny

Teachers need to facilitate transfer of learning by consciously and deliberately building bridges so that skills acquired in one area carry over to other areas (Royer and Cable, 1976).

Transfer effects may be positive, negative, or absent (Gorfein and Viviani, 1978). In *positive transfer,* the practice of one skill facilitates a second; it results in a strengthening of relevant responses. For instance, elementary arithmetic makes it easier for an individual to learn algebra. Learning to make old responses to new stimuli is a basic condition for positive transfer (Ellis, 1972).

In *negative transfer,* the practice of one skill impedes another; it results in a weakening of correct responses or a strengthening of incorrect responses. This is apparent in sports such as basketball and baseball where throwing the ball may initially show negative transfer because of the differences in the size of the ball and the distances the ball is normally thrown. Likewise, playing squash "hurts" a person's tennis game, since tennis requires maintaining a stiff wrist whereas squash requires flexible wrist movements. Generally, negative transfer results when we have to make a new response to an old stimulus situation, particularly if the responses are incompatible or antagonistic (Ellis, 1972). Ideally, teachers seek to arrange classroom materials and procedures in order to achieve positive transfer and avoid negative transfer.

Views of Transfer

Would you have a man reason well, you must use him to it betimes, exercise his mind in observing the connection of ideas and following them in train.

JOHN LOCKE
Conduct of the Understanding, 1709

During the Middle Ages, monks were trained for their priestly and educational functions by means of rigorous schedules of study that involved the mastery of theology, Latin, and Greek. It was widely believed that disciplined study strengthened the mind in much the fashion that exercise increases the power of muscles. Thus, intellectual rigor was thought to improve an individual's ability to think and function. Even as late as the nineteenth century, American schools stressed the importance of students memorizing countless pages of poems and other literary materials to strengthen the mind's faculties. Subjects like Latin and Greek were included in the curriculum because of their ''mental training'' value.

Some ninety years ago, William James (1890), a distinguished American philosopher and psychologist, tested whether mental exercises could improve one's memory. Over an eight-day period, James and his students memorized a number of poems by Victor Hugo. Then each day for thirty-eight days they learned forty lines of Milton's *Paradise Lost.* After this practice period, they again memorized another group of Hugo's poems. James found that despite these efforts, their memory abilities did not improve at all. James concluded that a general transfer from one intellectual activity to another does not occur.

A number of years later, Edward L. Thorndike and Robert S. Woodworth (1901a, 1901b, 1901c), colleagues at Columbia University, conducted a number of studies involving transfer between languages. This research set the ''formal discipline''

theory of the mind into a decline from which it never recovered. Finding that only those aspects of Latin directly related to English (such as word roots) carried across in the learning of languages, Thorndike and Woodworth set forth an *identical elements theory of transfer:* As the number of common elements in two situations increases, the tendency to make similar responses in the two situations also increases. Learning was always specific, never general. According to this view, if you need accounting in your occupation, study the type of accounting you require and not mathematics; if you wish to learn French, do not spend several years concentrating on Latin; and if you wish to solve philosophical problems, do not concern yourself with geometry.

In 1908, C. H. Judd sharply challenged the identical elements theory of Thorndike and Woodworth. In a classic experiment he demonstrated that generalized principles, laws, and specific skills could be transferred from one situation to another. He had two groups of boys throw darts at a small target submerged under water. Prior to the testing, one group of boys was given a theoretical explanation of the principle of refraction—a ray of light bends as it passes obliquely from one medium to another of different density (see the photo on page 235). This theoretical knowledge contributed to a superior performance by one group of boys, since they could take the optical illusion into account and compensate for it when throwing a dart. On the basis of this finding, Judd formulated his *theory of generalized principles,* which involves transfer by generalization.

Teachers can benefit from Judd's finding. In their teaching they need to direct the attention of their students toward the general principles and rules that will help the students recognize the meaning of specific, factual material. This approach also facilitates meaningful as opposed to rote learning and as such contributes to a greater retention of the information and knowledge.

More recently, Harry F. Harlow (1949) has provided laboratory demonstrations of the *learning to learn* phenomenon. Employing both monkeys and

AN APPARENTLY BENT STICK
A ray of light bends as it passes obliquely from one medium to another of different density. This results in an optical illusion. Regardless of how often we have seen straight sticks in water, the stick still appears to be bent at an angle.

children as subjects, Harlow found that individuals improve in their ability to learn new tasks because of their experiences with other similar or related tasks, termed a *learning set*. More specifically, he demonstrated that monkeys and children show the ability to begin at successively higher levels when problems of a like kind are presented to them.

Most of us have encountered confirmation of Harlow's finding in our schooling. For instance, after we practice solving linear equations for several days, we improve our speed and accuracy in solving new and more difficult linear equations. We learn what to attend to and what to ignore in the problems. Thus, we discover *how to attack* similar tasks in an efficient manner—in brief, we learn to learn (Brown, 1982). Teachers can likewise avail themselves of this strategy by carefully planning sequences of study that facilitate the development of their students' creative responses in problem solving.

For the most part, psychologists and educators no longer ask if transfer of learning occurs. Instead, they have come to see their task as one of identifying the *conditions* that influence transfer between tasks. Moreover, most conclude that transfer may take place either by identical elements or by general principles.

CREATIVITY

The shrewd guess, the fertile hypothesis, the courageous leap to a tentative conclusion—these are the most valuable coin of the thinker at work. But in most schools, guessing is heavily penalized and is associated somehow with laziness.

JEROME BRUNER
The Process of Education, 1960

Creativity is commonly viewed as the highest form of mental endeavor and achievement. All living creatures interact with their environment, an adaptive process by which they fit themselves to their surroundings. But human beings are not content merely to adapt themselves to their environment. They also aim to change it, to *create* an environment that better meets and expresses their needs. And in fashioning and changing their world, they also shape and alter themselves (Torrance and Myers, 1972; Gruber, 1981).

The Nature of Creativity

The very essence of the creative is its novelty, and hence we have no standard by which to judge it.

CARL R. ROGERS
On Becoming a Person, 1970

Like intelligence, educators and psychologists find it difficult to define creativity (Klein, 1982). We all use the term. Doubtless we all have a sense of what we mean by it. But when we undertake the task of rigorously defining creativity, we encounter a good many problems. Generally, **creativity** is taken to mean the occurrence of responses that are both new and useful. Yet it is not always easy to specify what is new, since novelty is more

THE MANY FACES OF CREATIVE EXPRESSION
Creativity can be expressed in many different areas of life. It is not limited to those behaviors that have some material end product.

often a question of degree rather than of kind. And what is useful is a matter of subjective appraisal. Indeed, there are those who maintain that creativity is not a name applied to an activity or a process but rather a "medal" we pin on a public product.

Some psychologists suggest that creativity is such a vague term that it should not be used for scientific purposes (Wagner, 1978). Instead, they suggest that educators would be better advised to speak only in terms of divergent and convergent thinking (Guilford, 1959, 1967; Mansfield et al.,

1978). Some tasks require responses that are fluent and flexible, *divergent thinking;* other tasks require responses that are integrative and focused, *convergent thinking.* According to this view, creativity is a particular type of thinking. The distinction can be clarified by citing a number of examples commonly employed in tests of creativity. A task entailing divergent thinking may ask the individual to list as many uses as possible for some common item like a key, shoe, paper cup, or a brick. A task measuring convergent thinking may call on the subject to provide one correct answer to a multiple-choice question or a solution to a problem.

Divergent thinking is considered by some psychologists to be more characteristic of highly creative individuals than those rated less creative (Guilford, 1959, 1967). However, others insist that effective thinking requires the ability to engage in both types of activity, and hence divergent thinking is not necessarily a property distinguishing creative from noncreative endeavors (Wallach, 1970, 1971; Nicholls, 1972; Kogan and Pankove, 1974).

Irving A. Taylor (1975) identifies five types of creativity. *Expressive* creativity involves spontaneity and freedom in some form of activity, such as the musical performance of Louis Armstrong. *Technical* creativity is characterized by proficiency in making a product, such as the talent envidenced by Antonio Stradivari in producing fine violins. *Inventive* creativity entails a display of ingenuity in finding an unusual combination of relationships among materials, such as the inventions of Thomas Edison. *Emergentive* creativity involves the identification of principles or assumptions underlying certain types of artistic expression or scientific knowledge, such as the work of Albert Einstein or Sigmund Freud. *Innovative* creativity is dependent upon the ability to penetrate and understand basic foundational principles already established by others, such as those exemplified by Carl Jung and Alfred Adler in elaborating on Freudian thought.

The Creative Person

To give a fair chance to potential creativity is a matter of life and death for any society. This is all-important, because the outstanding creative ability of a fairly small percentage of the population is mankind's ultimate capital asset.

ARNOLD TOYNBEE
*Is America Neglecting Her Creative
Minority?* 1964

Are some people naturally more creative than others? Or is creativeness a skill that can be learned? One view is that only a few are born with those traits that underlie creative ingenuity; these individuals will be the scientists, artists, and inventors. Another view is that virtually everyone has some creative potential provided that such talents are successfully developed by a stimulating learning environment.

Intelligence and Creativity

The relationship between IQ and creativity has attracted considerable interest and research over the past thirty years. Nonetheless, firm conclusions have remained elusive. This is hardly surprising. Psychologists have had difficulty agreeing on what constitutes intelligence and what constitutes creativity. And there has been the additional problem of finding suitable measures for each. Many creativity tests are so diffuse and global that they fail to distinguish between different talents or types of creativity. Moreover, there has been an absence of independence between some IQ indices and some creativity tests; thus both end up measuring essentially the same attributes (Wallach and Kogan, 1965; Wallach, 1970; Freeman, Butcher, and Christie, 1971).

The well-known study by Jacob W. Getzels and Philip W. Jackson, *Creativity and Intelligence* (1962), has been widely interpreted as demonstrating that creativity counts for much more than high intelligence. The research, however, was severely flawed. It ignored children in the sample who were both highly intelligent and highly creative. Further, all of the subjects were above-average in intelligence. Despite the problems with the Getzels and Jackson research, a variety of other studies have reached essentially the same conclusion. High scores on intelligence tests and high grades in school have a low association with creativity (MacKinnon, 1962; Torrance, 1962; Holland and Nichols, 1964; Holland and Richards, 1965; Wallach and Kogan, 1965).

Probably the safest conclusion to be drawn from the research currently available to us is that an above-average, although not exceptional, level of intelligence is necessary for creative achievement (Nicholls, 1972; MacKinnon, 1975). While high intelligence does not guarantee creative activity, low intelligence militates against it. Further, many factors other than intelligence also influence creativity, including such things as health, motivation, study habits, schooling, and family finances (Telford and Sawrey, 1977).

Some psychologists suggest that there may be a hereditary element in certain creative talents. This seems most probable in the case of mathematics. Observations and surveys reveal that mathematically gifted individuals often exhibit precocity at an early age. Blaise Pascal, Karl Friedrich Gauss, Jakob and Johann Bernoulli, Norbert Wiener, and Charles Fefferman are good illustrations of this. The fact that signs of mathematical talent appeared early in their lives and that some of the mathematicians pursued their mathematical studies and research in spite of parental opposition has led to speculation regarding the role of hereditary determinants in mathematical ability (Aiken, 1973).

Personality Characteristics and Creativity

The most frequently cited research dealing with the characteristics of the creative personality derives from the work of Donald W. MacKinnon (1962, 1975) and his associates at the Institute of Personality Assessment and Research (located on the Berkeley campus of the University of California). The Institute's researchers have focused their attention on highly creative individuals such as architects, writers, mathematicians, and research scientists. By way of illustration, they have found that highly creative architects tend to be individuals who are self-confident, rather low in sociability, dominating in social relationships, free from conventional restraints and inhibitions, flexible, and self-accepting. According to MacKinnon, highly creative persons stress their inventiveness, independence, individuality, insightfulness, versatility, determination, enthusiasm, and industry; in contrast, less creative individuals tend to describe themselves in terms of their good character, concern for others, reliability, dependability, and conventional behavior.

The Institute's researchers (Taylor and Barron, 1963; Barron, 1969) provide a unified picture of the productive scientist as an individual who is challenged by the unknown, by contradictions, and by apparent disorder. Such individuals are somewhat distant and detached in their interpersonal relationships, preferring to deal with things and abstractions rather than with people. They have considerable ego strength, are emotionally stable, resist pressure toward conformity, are self-sufficient and self-directing, have a strong need for independence and autonomy, enjoy abstract thinking, and frequently have strong, forceful personalities. Other research on creative individuals reveals that in their self-ratings and in ratings by others, these adjectives typically appear: creative, independent, uninhibited, iconoclastic, complicated, and asocial (Schaefer, 1969).

Home Background and Creativity

Psychologists and educators have also examined the family backgrounds of creative individuals. One recurrent finding is that creative people do not spend their childhood years basking in parental love and warmth. Instead, rather cool and even detached relationships often prevail between parents and their creative sons and daughters. One speculation is that rejecting parents may inadvertently encourage a rebellious attitude in their children that facilitates independent thinking and action (Siegelman, 1973).

The mothers of creative children, compared to mothers of control group children, show greater self-assurance and initiative, prefer change and unstructured demands, value autonomy, are less sociable and inhibited, are less concerned with creating a favorable impression, and are less nurturant and obligating toward others—traits that suggest that mothers of creative children may be more creative than the general population and promote creativity in their children through the force of their own unstereotyped behavior (Domino, 1970; Getzels and Dillon, 1973). Further, many more creative persons are first-borns than

CONTROVERSY SURROUNDING CREATIVITY
Authorities do not agree on the relative contributions of heredity and environment to creative behavior.

would be expected by chance (Altus, 1965; Zajonc, 1976). And they are more likely to have had a sickly childhood or to have lost a parent at an early age (Roe, 1953; Eisenstadt, 1978).

Despite such findings, there still remains sufficient variation for educators to retain a healthy skepticism as to the predictive value of various family background factors. Both parents and teachers should reserve judgment on which young children will display originality. This will help avoid encouraging self-fulfilling prophecies relative to children's creativity (Aldous, 1973; Suler, 1980).

More recently, a team of University of Chicago educational researchers have looked into the backgrounds of 100 exceptionally talented people between seventeen and thirty-five years of age: concert pianists, Olympic swimmers, tennis players, and research mathematicians (Pines, 1982). These

creative individuals had parents who viewed music, sports, or intellectual activity as a natural part of life. Consequently, their children were immersed in a world of music, sports, or intellect at an early age and learned its "language" easily. Further, the parents believed in the work ethic.

The first teachers of the talented individuals were typically warm and loving persons who made their lessons seem like games and who lavished rewards on their pupils. Often the teacher was not uniquely skilled, usually a neighborhood teacher for the pianists and the father for the mathematicians. However, the instruction was provided on a one-to-one basis and enjoyed parental support and interest. Later, more accomplished teachers during the school years emphasized skill and self-discipline. Here, too, instruction occurred on an individualized basis. Gradually both the children and their parents realized the enormous strides that were being made. In turn they focused even more of their resources on the cultivation of the developing talent. During adolescence the children were provided access to a "master teacher"—an expert who knew how to train top professionals and open the right doors to them. At times the family would travel 2,000 or more miles to find such a mentor.

Typically the swimmers progressed most rapidly, while half of the mathematicians did not know they would become mathematicians until their first year of college. Although all the children were unquestionably more talented than the average, none was a child prodigy. The Chicago researchers had originally expected to find that the talented individuals would have demonstrated some outstanding ability in early childhood and then would have been provided with special attention and instruction. But instead they found that the process seemed to work the other way around. The children blossomed because of the special attention and instruction which they had received.

Creativity in the Classroom

It is not enough to discern a native gift; it must be enticed out again and again. It needs exercise in an atmosphere of approval.

> HUGHES MEARNS
> *Creative Power,* 1929

Few characteristics of young children are more striking than their curiosity. They expend an enormous amount of energy exploring, learning about, and mastering their world (White and Watts, 1973). John Dewey, the famous American educator, noted:

> To children the whole world is new; there is something thrilling to the healthy being in every new contact and it is eagerly sought for, not merely passively awaited and endured. . . . The sum total of these outgoing tendencies constitutes curiosity. It is the basic factor in enlargement of experience and therefore a prime ingredient in the germs that are to be developed into reflective thinking. [1933:44]

Dewey stresses that children's curiosity must be nurtured and cultivated lest it degenerate and evaporate.

Humanistic psychologists like Carl R. Rogers (1959) and Abraham H. Maslow (1968) link creativity with the "fully functioning person" or "self-actualizing individual." Rogers observes:

> The mainspring of creativity appears to be the same tendency which we discover so deeply as the curative force in psychotherapy—man's tendency to actualize himself, to become his potentialities. By this I mean the directional trend which is evident in all organic and human life—the urge to expand, extend, develop, mature—the tendency to express and activate all the capacities of the organism, to the extent that such activation enhances the organism or the self. [1959:72]

Rogers believes that this tendency may be buried under layers of encrusted psychological defenses but that the creative impulse "exists in every individual and awaits only the proper conditions to be released and expressed" (1959:72). Maslow (1968) takes a somewhat similar position, often equating self-actualization (of which creativity is an aspect) with health itself.

Stifling Creative Development

The course of the development of creativity in children is not an easy one (Telford and Sawrey, 1977). Indeed, one of the most persistent and severe indictments of institutionalized education is that it stifles children's curiosity and creative impulses. Many critics, theorists, and practitioners have expressed concern that the schools turn out conformists and stereotyped individuals rather than original and creative thinkers (Rogers, 1959; Silberman, 1970; May, 1975; Landreneau and Halpin, 1978). Fifty years ago, Willard Waller (1932), a sociologist, cogently argued that the reward system of the school fosters "docile assimilation and glib repetition" and discourages "fertile and rebellious creation."

As pointed out by E. Paul Torrance and R. E. Myers, schools are primarily conservative institu-

NATURAL CURIOSITY
Children show a good deal of natural curiosity. Teachers should encourage and nurture children's desire to explore, learn about, and master their world.

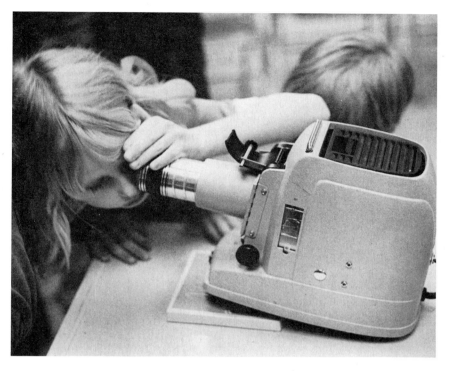

tions by virtue of their culture transmission function:

> Educational institutions exert a conservative pressure upon society because they store the accumulated knowledge of a culture and then they endeavor to transmit as much of this knowledge as they can to young people. Educators come to love this knowledge for its own sake; and they come to love the old ways of transmitting it. But the difficulty for the cause of individualism does not end there—when we encourage the child to think creatively we invite him to challenge society and all of its painfully constructed institutions. [1972:xi]

Torrance (1970, 1972) has been especially concerned about the development of creativity and has studied developmental patterns in elementary schools. He finds that in the early grades creative children often have the reputation among their peers for having silly and unconventional ideas and are seen by their teachers as being haughty

and wild. By the time they reach fourth grade, many creative youngsters learn to keep their ideas to themselves, and hence much of their originality becomes compromised and suppressed. This leads Torrance to conclude:

> In most classrooms, highly creative children are handicapped by their creativeness and are regarded as behavior problems. Frequently, such children are diagnosed as having learning disabilities. For these reasons, I have suggested that highly creative children be designated as a new category of handicapped children in the field of special education. [1972:25]

Research suggests that most teachers are attracted to students who are orderly, passive, and obedient (Silberman, 1969, 1971; Brophy and Good, 1974). Recently, George B. Helton and Thomas D. Oakland (1977) gave questionnaires to fifty-three elementary teachers in ten southwestern schools. The teachers reacted to stories describing children's classroom behavior. Although actual classroom observations would have been preferable, the findings are nonetheless enlightening.

The teachers reported higher feelings of concern for low-ability than for high-ability children and for boys than for girls. When asked about their liking for children with varying abilities and personalities, the teachers indicated they were most attracted to passive conformists and students with above-average ability, especially bright, obedient girls. They were most rejecting of flexible, nonconforming students and those who were independent and assertive. Further, they were unwilling to afford remedial help to these latter groups of students.

Fostering Classroom Creativity

Creativity-oriented educators like Torrance and Sidney Parnes (1971) believe that creativity must not be left to chance. It is not enough that some individuals have a naturally keen eye, a deft hand, or some other outstanding ability. Rather, talent must be actively cultivated and assiduously nurtured. If psychologists and educators asked "How can we encourage creativity?" instead of "How

PROVIDING AN INTERESTING ENVIRONMENT
Teachers can foster creative thinking and originality among children by providing them with an environment that contains examples of creative and original behaviors.

do we identify highly creative individuals?" more might be done to achieve a fuller blossoming of children's creative potential (Crockenberg, 1972; Mansfield et al., 1978).

Rogers (1959) outlines two environmental conditions that are conducive to maximizing people's creative abilities: psychological safety and psychological freedom. *Psychological safety* means that individuals are provided with (1) a sense of their own inherent worth, (2) a climate in which highly judgmental evaluation of them is absent (to minimize threat and a need for defensiveness), and (3) a feeling that they are receiving emphathic understanding (to convince them that teachers appreciate what they are feeling and doing from their own point of view). *Psychological freedom* implies a permissive attitude toward people's symbolic and productive expression, allowing them to think, feel, and be whatever coincides with their inner-most goals.

From the works of Torrance (1968, 1970, 1975; Torrance and Myers, 1972) and other creativity-oriented educators (Barber and Holden, 1977; Klein, 1982), the following tips have been gleaned for fostering creative thinking and originality among children:

- Respect children's right to initiate their own learning efforts.
- Respect children's questions and ideas.
- Respect children's right to reject, after serious consideration, the ideas of adults in favor of their own.
- Take time to plan for imaginative activities.
- Hold freewheeling discussions and brainstorming sessions.
- Share with students one's own activities involving aesthetic and creative expression.

TEACH FOR INQUIRY: ANY DAY, ANY LEVEL, ANY SUBJECT

BEN B. STRASSER
Curriculum and Instruction Consultant
for the Los Angeles County Schools

If learning how to inquire is learning how to learn, then children should have practice in learning how to learn math, science, social studies, art, and so on. Some of the successful subject matter lessons can become inquiry lessons—by making some changes in what the teacher does, what he expects and encourages students to do, and what he hopes to accomplish.

Source: Condensed from Ben B. Strasser, "Teach for Inquiry: Any Day, Any Level, Any Subject," *Instructor*, 82 (March 1973):86–88.

Inquiry lessons are distinguished from noninquiry lessons by four characteristics:

- *The inquiry lesson centers on a problem the students are to solve.* The "problem" may be to seek an explanation or theory, to decide a course of action, to look for a way of working, to make or create something, to learn something, and so on. Or the problem can be a combination of these.
- *The teacher assumes a non-judgmental attitude toward students' ideas, explanations,* theories, or solutions. The major emphasis in teaching for inquiry is to help students expand their repertoire of ways to test the appropriateness of their ideas. If the teacher makes the decision as to which ideas and theories are correct, students will not have the opportunity even to learn that they have the ability to do it for themselves.
- *Students decide how they will test out their ideas.* Learning to inquire means learning to decide what data is needed to test an idea, what action should
(continued)

TEACH FOR INQUIRY
(*continued*)

be taken to find the data, and then what the data means. Students must decide what processes to use, in what situations to use them, and afterwards, whether the processes were or were not effective. The teacher must make it not only possible for students to devise and implement theory-seeking and theory-testing strategies, but also

must make it legitimate for them to do it. He must make them responsible for doing it.

■ *Students discuss the processes and strategies they used.* The teacher encourages students who have worked through a problem to consider how they worked this time, and how the problem-solving strategies might be improved in preparation for the future.

I'm going to describe an early primary lesson in language arts

based on a "Sesame Street" episode. This lesson was chosen because it is brief enough to be easily described and simple enough to highlight the process rather than the lesson content. It demonstrates that inquiry can be done by children on this level, yet the process can also be adapted for any other level or subject.

The purpose of the lesson was to help the children clarify their conceptions of *nearer* and *farther*. A small group was seated in a semicircle around the teacher.

T: Here's what we're going to do today. I'm going to pose a few questions for you. Listen carefully and you'll hear me use the word "nearer" or the word "farther" in each question.

After I pose the question, you will have two jobs. First, see what you think is the correct answer to the question. Some people in the group may think one thing and some people may think another answer is correct. That's OK.

Your second job will be to figure out if your idea is right. Usually, in other kinds of lessons, I have told you if your answers were right or wrong. That will be your job in this lesson. Any questions? OK, let's begin. Here's your first question.

Which is farther from my lips, my toes or my hips?
S: Your toes.
T: OK, all agree? (Teacher pauses, then records the student's response in some appropriate way; for example, he may write the word on a chalkboard, or, for prereaders, circle an appropriate picture on a prepared chart.)

All right, here's the next one.
Which is farther from my hips, my knees or my lips?
S: Your knees.
T: (Records "knees.") All agree?
S: Your lips.
T: (Records "lips.") OK?
Here's your third question.
Which is nearer to my hair, the box or that chair?

STRUCTURING: A teacher sets a structure so students will know what they are to do as they work.

MAINTAINING A NONJUDGMENTAL ATTITUDE: Whatever the answer, the teacher provides no cues as to what he feels is correct.

Note that questions posed in this lesson cover comparison so close that measurement will be necessary to decide what is correct.

And so the lesson continues. About five or six such questions are posed, depending on how many the teacher feels the children can answer and still remember their first responses. At that point, if students don't raise the questions, "We had two answers for the second one. Which is right?" the teacher shifts the emphasis from having the children "theorize" to having them figure out how to test their answers.

T: Let's review what we've done so far. This was our first question: Which is farther from my lips, my toes or my hips? Everyone felt that "toes" was correct.

The second one was: Which is farther from my hips, my knees or my lips? We had some different ideas about that one.

(Teacher pauses. If no one suggests testing the two possibilities, he makes remark to guide them.)

Does anyone have any ideas about how you might work to find out which is correct?

STUDENTS DECIDE HOW THEY WILL WORK

If the students don't make any suggestions, the teacher has four alternatives. He can go on to the next question in an attempt to communicate the notion that if they want the problem resolved they will have to initiate an action. "Perhaps you want to think more about that one. Should we go on?"

A second alternative is to help by asking, "How might you find out which is farther for yourselves?"

A third is to suggest an operation the students can use. "Is there any way you can compare the distance from my hips to my lips (pointing) with the distance from my hips to my knees, to find out which is farther?"

A fourth way is to make a more specific suggestion, as: "Is there any way you can use a piece of string to compare the distance from my hips. . . ." Notice that each alternative provides increasingly more detailed help for the students. Keep trying to stop at an earlier step. The goal is to have children learn to test their ideas without any such support.

As students suggest ways to test their ideas, they are invited to carry out the proposed tests. Thus, they not only find out for themselves which theory or guess is best; they also gain experience in the intellectual task of moving from idea to test to idea substantiated or discarded.

At the end of the lesson, the teacher spends a few minutes inviting children to recount the ways they went about testing their ideas. They can also consider other ways they could have proceeded. To stimulate such thinking and discussion, the teacher can ask questions like these—not all at the end of any one lesson, but over the course of several [lessons]:

- What are some of the ways you've tried to find out for sure which thing was nearer or farther?
- Are there any other ways of testing that you thought of that we didn't try this time?
- How do you decide what to do to test your ideas?
- With this kind of problem, how do you decide which ideas are correct?
- Will you do anything differently when we do this kind of lesson again?
- How do you feel about what you did in the lesson?

- Encourage children's awareness and sensitivity regarding environmental stimuli.
- Reward creative achievement and imaginative excellence.
- Teach idea testing.
- Allow students to engage in scientific exploration and experimentation.
- Dispel the sense of awe associated with masterpieces and established authorities.
- Create "thorns in the flesh," confronting students with problems, contradictions, ambiguities, and uncertainties.
- Afford students opportunities to make something and then do something with it.
- Give children an opportunity to communicate what they have learned.
- Employ provocative and thought-producing questions.
- Encourage students to take the next step on their own beyond what they currently know.
- Encourage children's sense of self-esteem, self-worth, and self-respect.

Many factors interact to foster creativity. Cognitive, motivational, and personality characteristics all play a part. However, it is easy to overlook the role of situational and social factors such as those that come to bear within the classroom (Mansfield et al., 1978). Much of creativity has to do with people interacting with and stimulating one another (Suler, 1980; Gruber, 1981). As such creativity is also a social process. The classroom as a social environment does much to encourage or discourage the creativity process.

CHAPTER SUMMARY

1. Robert M. Gagné has formulated an integrated framework for dealing with various levels of learning. In Gagné's view, learning is cumulative. Individuals are portrayed as developing higher level skills or acquiring more knowledge as they learn capabilities that build successively on one another.

2. Gagné identifies eight types of learning, arranged as follows in the order of their complexity: signal learning, stimulus-response learning, chaining, verbal association, multiple discrimination, concept learning, rule learning, and problem solving.

3. According to Gagné, the learning of a skill or concept is a hierarchical process in which lower-order elements are gradually integrated to form higher-order ones. Achievement in each type of learning depends on acquiring the preceding skill. As a consequence, the teacher needs to consider the relevance of subordinate types of learning when preparing instruction for a higher type. This requires task analysis.

4. Problem solving is not so much a "happening" as a process. It involves five principal steps: sensing a problem, sharpening the dimensions of a problem, generating alternative solutions to a problem, evaluating the alternative solutions, and putting a solution into practice and appraising its effectiveness.

5. Three theoretical approaches have been employed by psychologists and educators to account for thinking and problem solving. Early behaviorist theorists emphasized stimulus-response associations. Cognitive theorists stress the importance of insight in problem solving. And a third group of theorists employ information-processing concepts for examining human thinking.

6. The more knowledge and skills we acquire, the more likely it is that our new learning will be influenced and shaped by our past learning. Prior knowledge functions as a point of departure for tackling new tasks. Hence, transfer of learning is a critical aspect of life and a central component in human adaptive capabilities. Transfer of learning is the objective of the vast majority of educational endeavors.

7. Transfer effects may be positive, negative, or absent. In positive transfer, the practice of one skill facilitates a second; it results in a strengthening of relevant responses. In negative transfer, the practice of one skill impedes another; it results in a weakening of correct responses or a strengthening of incorrect responses.

8. For the most part, psychologists and educators no longer ask if transfer of learning occurs. Instead, they have come to see their task as one of identifying the conditions that influence transfer between tasks. Moreover, most conclude that transfer may take place by identical elements or by general principles.

9. An above-average, although not exceptional, level of intelligence appears to be necessary for creative achievement. While high intelligence does not guarantee creative activity, low intelligence militates against it.

10. Highly creative persons tend to stress their inventiveness, independence, individuality, insightfulness, versatility, determination, enthusiasm, and industry. In contrast, the less creative tend to describe themselves in terms of their good character, concern for others, reliability, dependability, and conventional behavior.

11. Psychologists and educators have examined the family backgrounds of creative individuals. One recurrent finding is that creative people do not spend their childhood years basking in parental love and warmth. Instead, rather cool and even detached relationships often prevail between parents and their creative sons and daughters.

12. By virtue of their culture transmission function, schools are primarily conservative institutions. As a consequence, they can have the effect of stifling children's creativity and originality.

13. Creativity-oriented educators believe that creativity must not be left to chance. Carl Rogers outlines two environmental conditions that are conducive to maximizing creative abilities: psychological safety and psychological freedom.

CHAPTER GLOSSARY

brainstorming   A process by which a great many solutions to a problem are encouraged by deferring judgment and evaluation.

creativity   The occurrence of responses that are both new and useful.

problem   A stimulus situation for which an organism lacks a ready response.

synectics   The joining together of different and apparently unrelated or irrelevant ideas; the approach is based upon metaphorical thinking.

transfer of learning   The influence that prior learning has on performance in a subsequent situation.

EXERCISES

Review Questions

1. Here are some types of learning chosen from Gagné's hierarchy. Select the choice in which the learnings are ordered in proper sequence from simple to more complex.

   a. chaining, signal learning, verbal association
   b. stimulus-response learning, multiple discrimination, verbal association
   c. multiple discrimination, problem solving, rule learning
   d. verbal associations, concept learning, rule learning

2. Signal learning is to classical conditioning as stimulus-response is to

   a. cognitive theory
   b. observational learning
   c. operant conditioning
   d. assimilation

3. General assumption(s) concerning problem solving include

   a. the definition of a problem is a individual matter
   b. problem-solving abilities are generally related to the knowledge base of the individual
   c. problem-solving abilities have been used as indicators of intelligence

d. a, b, and c are true

e. a and c are true

4. Insight is a critical term in which theory?

    a. trial-and-error

    b. cognitive

    c. information-processing

    d. Piagetian

5. In the synectic approach to problem solving, which type of analogy is an individual using when he or she invents a zipper by imagining little insects manipulating hatches?

    a. direct

    b. personal

    c. fantasy

    d. innovative

6. The effectiveness of computers in simulating human problem solving lies primarily in the

    a. size of the computer memory bank

    b. sophistication of the computer language

    c. determination of the processes humans use

    d. selection of appropriate problem

7. The limitations of computers in simulating human problem solving reflect the fact that

    a. no provisions are made for emotion

    b. no programs now exist for problem identification

    c. the knowledge base of humans cannot be predetermined with certainty

    d. a, b, and c are true

    e. a and c are true

8. In which set of conditions listed below are you likely to have at least some positive transfer?

    a. different stimuli, same responses

    b. different stimuli, different responses

    c. same stimuli, different responses

    d. same stimuli, same responses

    e. a and d are true

9. According to Guilford, creativity is associated with what kind of thinking?

    a. productive

    b. divergent

    c. convergent

    d. analytical

10. The teacher who is interested in encouraging creativity in the classroom would find scholarly support in which of the following?

    a. The University of Chicago study revealed that the influence of teachers was generally minimal.

    b. Rogers believes that creative tendency resides in all of us.

    c. Unconventionality is generally more tolerated in the lower grades than in the upper grades.

    d. Teachers prefer brighter, more independent students.

Answers

1. d (See pp. 220–222)
2. c (See pp. 220–221)
3. d (See pp. 222, 224)
4. b (See pp. 229–230)
5. c (See pp. 227–228)
6. c (See pp. 230–231)
7. d (See pp. 230–231)
8. e (See p. 233) (The key element is the similarity of responses.)
9. b (See pp. 236–237)
10. b (See p. 240)

Applying Principles and Concepts

1. A number of behaviors that can be classified in Gagné's system as signal learning (SL), stimulus-response learning (SRL), chaining (C), verbal association (VA), multiple discrimination (MD), concept learning (CL), rule learning (RL), and

problem solving (PS) are listed here. Indicate in the space provided before each behavior the kind of learning demonstrated.

_____ a. Bill inserts his key in the lock, turns it, kicks the door, and twists the knob.

_____ b. Elaine says, "I'm so hungry my stomach is growling."

_____ c. Mary and Jim have been going over house plans similar to their own in order to get some ideas on how to increase the space in the bedroom.

_____ d. Jeannie surveys the sulfuric acid and the water and says to herself, "Add the heavier acid *to* the water."

_____ e. Mike opens up the circuit box and views the mass of colored wires. Without hesitation he reaches in and pulls out the ground wire.

2. A teacher is having a problem with a student in her chemistry class. The text suggests five steps in problem solving: (1) sensing a problem, (2) sharpening the dimensions, (3) generating alternative solutions, (4) evaluating alternative solutions, and (5) putting a solution into practice. Before each of the teacher's remarks, indicate by number which step the remark reflects.

_____ a. "I could simply have her memorize lists or try to explain how each symbol is derived. I'll split the elements and try both."

_____ b. "In her case each time I introduce a new element I'll try and explain how the symbol was derived."

_____ c. "Alice is not doing well in chemistry."

_____ d. "I'll test her on both lists and see which produces better results."

_____ e. "She can't seem to remember the symbols used for the elements."

3. A high-school teacher is interested in the brainstorming technique. Indicate which of the following

teachers' comments would *not* be helpful during the session.

_____ a. "Great idea, Jed."

_____ b. "C'mon, Gail, you can do better."

_____ c. "Hey, hold it, we've got too many ideas right now."

_____ d. "Bill, how does your idea tie in with Lisa's?"

_____ e. "That's far out."

4. A five-year-old is trying to catch a bird in her backyard. She is quite unsuccessful. What can she do? She notices some bread crumbs and throws them out one at a time to the bird. The bird eats them. Now, each succeeding time she drops the crumbs a little closer, and finally she makes a snatch at the bird. Fortunately for the little girl (and the bird) she misses. Here are three approaches to the problem solving. Rank in order the probability that the theory described can explain the child's behavior.

_____ a. Trial-and-error

_____ b. Cognitive

_____ c. Information-processing

5. Following are several instances in which the instructor is teaching for transfer. Indicate before each example whether the process is based on identical elements (E), general principles (P), or learning set (S).

_____ a. The teacher is instructing students in the use of a variety of saws. Emphasis is on the similarities of construction and usage.

_____ b. The instructor is showing student teachers the impact of grades on student performance. Emphasis is on analyzing grading practices with respect to principles of behaviorism.

_____ c. The teacher is instructing students how to solve polynomial equations. Emphasis is on showing them the procedures that can be used to analyze a variety of equations.

_____ d. The teacher is attempting to improve student critiques of art work. Procedures include presenting initially paintings that are quite primitive and moving toward more complex forms.

6. Here are some descriptions of children. Underline in each description those traits, behaviors, or aptitudes that are associated with creativity.

a. The student is average in intelligence and quite social. He is not particularly close to his parents, which may account for his rejection of authority.
b. The student is very intelligent, perhaps the brightest in the class. She comes from a very close family, which may account for her initiative and determination in taking on difficult assignments.
c. The student is above average in intelligence. He is asocial and quite nonconforming. In his own personal life, however, he insists on order and structure.

Answers

1. a, C; b, SL; c, PS; d, RL; e, MD (See pp. 220–221)
2. a, 3; b, 5; c, 1; d, 4; e, 2 (See pp. 224, 226, 228)
3. b, c (See p. 227)
4. a, 2; b, 1; c, 3 (See pp. 229–231)
5. a, E; b, P; c, P; d, S (See pp. 234–235)
6. a, Underline ''not particularly close to parents,'' ''rejection of authority''; b, Underline ''initiative and determination,'' ''taking on difficult assignments''; c, Underline ''above average in intelligence,'' ''asocial and quite nonconforming.'' (See pp. 237–240)

Project 1

OBJECTIVE: To determine ''the facts of life'' about creativity in the classroom.

PROCEDURES: You can visit any level of school for this subject. The content areas we suggest are art and English. At the elementary school level, the teacher will usually be the same for both areas.

Ask the teacher to name one student in the class who is creative in either English or art. Ask also for some samples of the student's work. Then use the following questions as guidelines:

1. How does the teacher define creativity?
2. In what ways does this student demonstrate creativity? (Refer to samples.)
3. How does the teacher try to provide an atmosphere conducive to creativity? (Check whether he or she sees creativity in terms of genetic inheritance or learning.)
4. What kinds of behaviors does the teacher look for in creative children?

ANALYSIS: Check the teacher's answers against the research findings in your textbook. Look especially for statements on intelligence, inheritability, and the like. In your estimation, does the teacher provide for creativity? What is the basis for your answer? You may want to talk to several teachers and determine areas of agreement or disagreement.

Project 2

OBJECTIVE: To see how people go about solving problems.

PROCEDURES: Ask someone (a peer or roommate will do fine) to solve the following problem: Three missionaries and two cannibals come to a river, which they must cross by boat. The problem is that, if at any point there are more cannibals than missionaries on the spot (in the boat or on the shore), the cannibals will eat the missionaries. Assume that all can row and that the cannibals do not run away (they love missionaries) and that the boat holds two people only.

ANALYSIS: Take note of how the individual attempts to solve the problem. Are his or her efforts systematic (that is, can you see the problem-solving steps suggested in the textbook)? Do they use paper and pencil or objects like coins? Do they attempt to work backward? Do they set up subgoals or steps that must be met? If they give up, why and how?

A typical solution follows:

1. Start 3M, 2C. A missionary and cannibal row over; the missionary returns.

End of step 1: Near shore, 3M, 1C; far shore, 1C.

2. Two missionaries row over; one returns.

End of step 2: Near shore, 2M, 1C; far shore, 1C, 1M.

3. Two missionaries row over; one returns.

End of step 3: Near shore, 1M, 1C; far shore, 1C, 2M.

4. One cannibal and one missionary row over.

End of step 4: Near shore, 0M, 0C; far shore, 2C, 3M.

CHAPTER OUTLINE

9

LANGUAGE SKILLS

CHAPTER PREVIEW

The previous chapters have dealt with processes involved in learning, such as remembering, thinking, and problem solving. The *medium* of most of school learning, though, is language. Without much effort, we can think of countless ways in which language is used in school, as well as in learning and thinking in general.

School is the place where written language assumes at least as much importance as spoken language. Thus, learning to read is one of the biggest tasks facing school-aged children. To provide a background for looking at language in the school, the nature of language itself and its connection to cognition, or thought, are first discussed. Various the-ories of language acquisition are also described, in order to explain how children come to learn and use language with such apparent ease. Because of the importance of reading to school and in school, characteristics of reading and reading instruction are reviewed here. The language students hear in school is not always the same as the one they speak and use outside of school. The difference may be one of dialect or of another language entirely. Problems encountered by students using Black English or speaking a language other than English are discussed, along with proposals for dealing with language differences in school.

Think about these questions as you read:

■ What is language, and of what three systems is it comprised?

■ What is the relationship between language and thought?
■ How do various theories of language acquisition differ in their explanations and emphases?
■ What do children have to learn in order to communicate effectively, and how do different contexts affect the way children use and comprehend language?
■ What do children have to do and know in order to learn to read English?
■ What factors seem to have the most effect on the success of reading programs?
■ Is the use of Black English a problem in school? If so, how? If not, why not?
■ How has the issue of bilingualism been addressed in schools?

When we encounter one another in everyday life, we communicate in terms of what we say and do. We know other people only through their behavior and the products of their behavior. This is not to deny the importance of mental states in shaping people's actions. Nor is it to deny that we have a powerful incentive to understand other people's attitudes and feelings; indeed, only by ascertaining others' attitudes and feelings can we hope to predict or influence their behavior. Nonetheless, the primary focus in the course of social interaction is on people's overt acts. The importance of what we say and do for the human enterprise leads us to a consideration of language.

THE NATURE OF LANGUAGE

Speech is civilization itself.

THOMAS MANN

Chapters 5–8 were primarily concerned with learning and cognitive processes, *internal* mental activities. This chapter examines an activity that allows people to transcend their individual beings so as to communicate with others. Although we often view internal and external behavior as sharply separated, in point of fact, complex links and feedback circuitry tie together the perceptual, cognitive, and motor processes making for an integrated, functioning organism. For instance, thought affects what we produce verbally through words, while language is the major medium through which we learn and with which we shape our conscious thoughts.

The Importance of Language

Language is by its very nature a communal thing; that is, it expresses never the exact thing but a compromise—that which is common to you, me and everybody.

THOMAS ERNEST HULME

The understanding and production of language is one of the most complex activities performed by human beings. Indeed, Leslie White, a cultural anthropologist, suggests that speech is the foundation of human societies and cultures:

> Without articulate speech we would have no *human* social organization. Families we might have, but this form of organization is not peculiar to man; it is not *per se, human*. But we would have no prohibitions of incest, no rules prescribing exogamy [outgroup marriage] and endogamy [ingroup marriage], polygamy or monogamy. . . . Without speech we would have no political, economic, ecclesiastic, or military organization; no codes of ethics; no laws; no science, theology, or literature. . . . Indeed, without articulate speech we would be all but toolless. . . . In short, without symbolic communication in some form, we would have no culture. "In the Word was the beginning" of culture—and its perpetuation also.[1949:33–34]

Many sociologists take a similar position (Mead, 1932, 1934; Blumer, 1969, 1977; Meltzer, Petras, and Reynolds, 1975). A fundamental premise of sociology is that humans are social beings. Of course, various "social insects" (ants, bees, and termites) likewise aggregate in organized groups. But in contrast to human beings, the behavior of these insects appears to be integrated chiefly on a physiological and instinctive basis. If human beings are largely lacking in such inborn mechanisms, then what is the basis for human groups and societies? Sociologists answer by pointing to the role of communication and symbols.

Through shared symbols (especially language) human beings impart "meaning" to their activities; they come to define situations and interpret behavior (for instance, what is good or bad, right or wrong, beautiful or ugly, and sacred or profane). And they act toward each other and modify their actions in terms of such socially derived meanings. Hence, sociologists say that the shared meanings afforded by common symbols provide the cement that links individual humans within the larger social fabric—society.

Over the past twenty years, *psycholinguists* (psychologists specializing in the study of language behaviors) have made startling advances in what

SHOW AND TELL
Many kindergarten and first-grade teachers hold show-and-tell sessions to assist children in the development of their communicative skills.

is known about children's speech and its development. Educators welcome these insights, since they provide information that can make the educational mission of the schools even more effective. Likewise, therapists and clinicians have benefited in their rehabilitative work from the practical applications afforded by these advances.

The Components of Language

When we study human language, we are approaching what some might call the "human essence," the distinctive qualities of mind that are, so far as we know, unique to man.

NOAM CHOMSKY
Language and Mind, 1972

Spoken **language** is a structured system of sound patterns (such as words and sentences) with socially standardized meanings. It provides a set of symbols that catalogs the objects, events, and relations that human beings experience in their environment (DeVito, 1970). Language finds expression in speech; writing systems use invented symbols to represent the ideas or sounds of spoken language. Sign languages utilize manual symbols to convey these aspects of language for hearing-impaired individuals. Three ingredients make up spoken language: **phonology**, the sound system of the language; **semantics**, a system of meanings associated with sounds; and **syntax**, rules for ordering the semantic units of language into meaningful patterns. Semantic elements of a language are represented in its *lexicon*, the body of words and word parts that are used in that language.

Language comprehension appears to be closely related to the general cognitive skills we employ in making sense of the world. Cognition, like language comprehension, involves organizing and ordering incoming perceptions, assigning meaning to units of perceptual information, and integrating new information with the stored knowledge we have of the world. Perhaps not surprisingly, some psycholinguists, such as Noam Chomsky (1972), view the study of language as a "branch of cognitive psychology" and claim that a theory of language is necessarily a theory of mind.

Language and Cognition

Over the years, two aspects of language have particularly fascinated writers, philosophers, and, more recently, psychologists. One is the relationship between language and thought (or cognition) and the other is language development—or how children learn to speak their native language. Although these two issues are related, especially in contemporary theories, each one will be considered in turn.

Similarities among related languages, such as French and Spanish, are readily apparent. However, in different languages, similar ideas seem to be conveyed very differently. This observation and the impression many people have that thinking is dependent on language have led to a great deal of speculation about the relationship between language and thought. In one form or another, the question has been raised as to whether people who speak different languages think differently. This issue is not only of theoretical interest. How we answer this question can influence, for example, the way we view children who come to school speaking a nonstandard dialect or a language other than English. This question is not an easy one to answer; it involves many linguistic and psychological factors. Most recent psycholinguistic theory and research, however, stress language universals, or commonalities in language and thought patterns among speakers of different languages.

The idea that the particular language someone speaks shapes the way that person thinks is known as the **linguistic relativity hypothesis**. In this century, this idea is most frequently associated with the linguist Benjamin Lee Whorf (1956) and thus is referred to as the ''Whorfian hypothesis.'' Whorf studied many American Indian languages and was impressed with the fact that these languages tend to express ideas very differently from Indo-European languages. For example, whereas we talk about a concept such as *heat* with a noun in English, *heat* is a verb in the Hopi language (Slobin, 1979). Whorf believed that these differences in describing experiences fundamentally influence how people understand the world.

What evidence exists that speakers of one language think differently from speakers of another? To answer this question, the psycholinguist Dan Slobin (1979) suggests that several aspects of language and language use need to be examined. One way in which languages may differ, for example, is in the ease with which they can express a particular idea. One language may have a word for a concept for which there is no readily available one-word equivalent in another language. This is one reason foreign words are often borrowed by the speakers of another language, as the French seem to have done with such English words as

camping and *weekend*. Additionally, certain discriminations are marked in some languages but not in others. Whorf (1956), for instance, pointed out that Eskimos have a great many words for snow, each denoting a different variety. We can only make such distinctions in English through the use of modifying phrases, as when we describe snow as ''fine-powdered'' or ''good-packing.''

Do these examples mean that certain concepts or discriminations can be understood correctly only by speakers of languages that have distinctive terms for them? Slobin (1979) thinks not. He believes that ''any concept can somehow be encoded in any language'' (1979:178), though more easily in some languages than in others. Because of this difference in encodability, though, Slobin draws the distinction between *habitual* and *potential* behavior. In general, people tend to use ideas that can be expressed rather easily in their own language, and thus they may define their experiences in terms of the words most accessible to them. This does not mean, however, that they cannot express or understand ideas that their language does not encode readily.

Another difference among languages is in the kind of grammatical distinctions speakers are obliged to make. For example, in French or German there is a difference between polite and familiar personal pronouns of address and in masculine and feminine forms of some nouns, such as *teacher*. Such distinctions may predispose people to attend to certain aspects of their experience because they are required to do so by the language they speak.

In concluding his analysis of the Whorfian position, however, Slobin (1979) emphasizes that the similarities among languages far outweigh their apparent differences. All languages perform the same basic communicative functions, such as making and negating statements, asking questions, and so forth. Further, certain aspects of the form of languages appear to be universal and to reflect fundamental human ways of perceiving and organizing experience (Clark and Clark, 1977). Ideas that are cognitively complex, as judged by reaction-time experiments, tend to be expressed by more complex language forms. Negations, for example, require more processing time than assertions. (Thus, *untie* is more complex than *tie*. *Don't stop* or *Do not stop* is more complex than *Stop!*) In addition, Eleanor Rosch and her colleagues (Rosch et al., 1976; Rosch, 1977) argue that people from different cultures organize the world into similar "natural" categories and make similar choices of examples to best represent these categories. That is, people's choices of the best example of a *circle* or a *bird,* for example, tend to be highly similar across languages, suggesting that some underlying cognitive process, rather than language itself, is shaping these perceptions.

Despite many apparent differences in the surface features of languages, such as word order, all languages seem to be sensitive to the limitations imposed by human processing capacity. Effective and efficient communication requires that a listener be able to follow a speaker's message without keeping too many words in memory or searching for a verb to go with a subject. All languages appear to be organized to facilitate this process in that, for example, verbs agree with subjects in number, and pronouns can be used to connect ideas across sentence boundaries. In sum, although there is some evidence that the words and grammatical forms used by a language influence people's thoughts and perceptions, an overwhelming amount of evidence suggests that cognitive functions restrict the way all languages are formed. This fundamental relationship between cognition and language also underlies much of the effort to understand and explain language acquisition.

LANGUAGE ACQUISITION

One of the most continually fascinating aspects of human development is the phenomenon of language acquisition. All over the world and regardless of the speech community into which they are born, children without restrictive handicapping conditions learn to speak their native language—beginning at approximately the same age and apparently without direct instruction. How does this occur? This question has prompted many responses, and various theories have been offered to explain the process of language acquisition. No one proposal seems to be able to account for all features of language development, but a complex picture of the way children come to learn and use language is emerging and becoming widely accepted.

For many years, two competing and conflicting theories dominated the discussion of language acquisition. One of these was espoused by the behaviorist B. F. Skinner and stressed traditional principles of learning theory, such as association, practice, imitation, and reinforcement. The other position, often called the "nativist" hypothesis, is associated primarily with the linguistic theorist Noam Chomsky. Impressed with the apparent ease with which the young child acquires productive knowledge of language, proponents of this view claim that human infants come biologically endowed with innate mechanisms to process speech and acquire the structure of language. In the late 1960s and early 1970s, however, students of language development became increasingly dissatisfied with the extreme forms of both these positions and turned instead to examining the underlying meanings and relationships expressed in early child speech, the role of cognitive processes in the acquisition of language, and the way parental speech affects children's language development. More recently, attention has been focused on children's development of *communicative competence,* or the ability to use language appropriately and effectively in different social contexts and for different purposes. Each of these approaches will be examined in turn.

Learning Theory

In his book *Verbal Behavior* (1957), Skinner asserts that operant conditioning underlies a child's learning to speak. He maintains that children learn language through the principles of reinforcement. In one kind of situation, parents hear and interpret random, babbling sounds made by infants. For instance, if a child says "wa-wa" by chance, parents may conclude that the child is asking for water and respond by providing it. If such a sequence is repeated on several occasions, the probability is increased that "wa-wa" or something like it will be uttered when the child is thirsty and desires water. In another case, a child may utter a random sound while playing with something. For example, a child might also make a "wa-wa" sound while hitting the water in a wading pool with a shovel. Although the child may not be identifying water with this sound, a nearby parent may make such an association and reward the child for this "linguistic accomplishment." If this event is repeated, the child learns to make a "wa-wa" response on coming in contact with water.

Skinner also suggests that children may acquire speech by imitating the verbal behavior of others. For instance, they may hear their parents refer to a clear liquid as "water" and in turn may attempt to mimic the response, producing "wa-wa." The parents may then reinforce the behavior by providing the child with water and perhaps also with a smile and a hug.

The process by which children learn syntax, or grammatical constructions, is said to occur in much the same way that they learn words. For instance, children learn specific "sentence frames" and then substitute words by means of generalization. Hence, a child may learn the sentence "I want water" through reinforcement. The child then finds that it is possible to substitute words to produce other sentences, for example, "I want milk," "I want ball," and so on.

Skinner's *Verbal Behavior* did not receive the acclaim accorded many of his other works. Psychologists tended to ignore it, while linguists dismissed it as laden with errors and imprecision. And Chomsky (1959) subjected it to a devastating critique, in which he pointed out many of the limitations of Skinner's approach for explaining language acquisition.

LANGUAGE ACQUISITION AND READING
Reading is one way for children to develop their language skills. (© *Alan Carey*)

Critics observe, for example, that children's speech is not a mechanical playback of adult speech. In learning language, children produce utterances—such as "Where I put book?," "I comed," "Daddy hat," "No mommy sit," and so forth—that they do not hear adults saying (except when imitating children). In fact, children have difficulty imitating grammatical constructions that they are not yet ready to produce themselves, tending to rephrase model sentences into the forms they would use themselves (Brown, 1973). Further, imitation cannot account for the ability of children to produce novel utterances they have never heard before. Additionally, if children are to generalize syntactical forms from reinforced sentences, only their utterances that are grammatically correct should be reinforced. This does not seem to be what occurs, however (Slobin, 1979). Parents are primarily interested in communicating with their children and thus tend to reward them for communicating successfully, whether or not mature language constructions are used. If what a child says is accurate or true, parents are likely to be pleased, since they do not expect children to speak like adults.

In spite of these criticisms, there has recently occurred a renewed interest in the operant conditioning view, in part fueled by the appearance of Stephen Winokur's book *A Primer of Verbal Behavior: An Operant View* (1976).

Innateness, or "Nativist," Theory

As noted, some linguists and psycholinguists claim that the learning theory of language acquisition is inadequate to explain the rapid and apparently effortless way in which normal children universally acquire the forms and structure of their native language. These theorists point out that very young children perform the incredibly difficult task of acquiring most of the complex rules of language so fast that learning from environmental stimuli and reinforcement are insufficient to explain this accomplishment. Moreover, children all over the world, living in very different language communities, go through very similar stages of language development. These facts have prompted some theorists to conclude that children are born with innate mechanisms specifically designed to facilitate the acquisition of language. In other words, children are somehow biologically "prewired" to learn how to use language. According to this view, then, the only environmental factor necessary for children to begin speaking is exposure to some specific language.

This innateness, or "nativist," position has been formulated principally by Noam Chomsky (1957, 1965, 1968, 1975, 1980), whose ideas have had

a major impact on subsequent studies of language and language acquisition. Both his supporters and critics acknowledge that his work has stimulated a great deal of investigation and theoretical development within the fields of linguistics and psycholinguistics. To account for the child's naturally endowed capacity to learn language, Chomsky proposed the existence of innate knowledge and language-specific processes or strategies, which together he called the *language acquisition device* (*LAD*). This is not conceived of as an actual physical structure but as a genetically set organizing mechanism specifically designed to process and code language into a rule-abiding system. The extent to which these processes are, in fact, either innate or distinct from general cognitive functions has been the subject of continuing debate and investigation.

Perhaps Chomsky's most significant contribution has been to linguistic theory, specifically with his formulation of *transformational*, or *generative*, grammar (1957, 1965, 1968, 1975). Chomsky was concerned with developing a grammar or rulelike system that could formally account for any and all possible well-formed sentences in a language and exclude any that a native speaker would judge to be "ungrammatical." He was impressed with the fact that sentences with different word orders, phrase structures, or functions could be related because of identical underlying elements, even though this relationship would not be apparent in the actual spoken or written sentences. On the other hand, two sentences could appear identical, in that they used the same words, but they could express very different ideas.

To explain these relationships and apparent ambiguities, Chomsky devised a grammatical theory with two levels and a series of transformational rules. The *deep structure* of a sentence consists of the kernel, or basic elements, of the sentence, such as noun phrases and verb phrases. The *surface structure* of the sentence is the actual sentence as spoken or written. Sentences with identical deep structures can have different surface structures because the latter have resulted from sequences of different transformations. Transformation rules convert deep structures into such forms as passive sentences, questions, and negative assertions (for example, "The dog is *not* hungry").

Consider the following two sentences:

1. Jack pushed the car.

2. The car was pushed by Jack.

These sentences have identical deep structures: the noun phrase *Jack* and the verb phrase *push car,* which is composed of the verb *push* and the noun phrase *car.* (Transformations add definite articles and tense markers.) The second sentence was transformed to the passive form in its surface structure through the application of a series of required rules, which, among other things, transposed phrases and added the preposition *by.*

Now consider the sentence "They are eating apples." This sentence is inherently ambiguous in its surface structure. It can mean two very different things depending on the arrangement of the phrases in its deep structure.

Either:

- They (meaning "some people") are engaged in the act of eating apples.

Or:

- They (meaning "some apples") are of the variety that are good to eat.

In this case, the ambiguity results when dissimilar deep structures can be converted via different transformations into sentences with identical surface structures. For the most part, transformational theory does not claim to describe what people actually *do* when they use language. Rather, its primary emphasis is on providing a formal and logical system to represent the knowledge that speakers of any language would have to have to produce well-formed sentences. This is also the kind of inherent knowledge that, according to Chomsky, is innate and enables children to begin to use language productively.

Transformational grammar primarily deals with *syntax,* or the permissible organization of words and phrases within a sentence. Therefore, researchers who were influenced by this theory were long concerned with identifying consistent patterns in child speech that might suggest beginning rule use and the gradual emergence of mature syntactic forms from two-word combinations (MacNeill, 1970; Brown, 1973). For a number of reasons, developmental psycholinguists and others concerned with language development began to question the direction this approach had taken, as well as many of the assumptions of the nativist position. Without adopting the exclusive emphasis on the environment characteristic of learning theory, they nevertheless recognized the role of several environmental factors in language learning. They were particularly interested, however, in the child's attempts to communicate meaning in different situations and in the relationship between cognitive development and the acquisition of language.

Cognitive and Semantic Aspects of Language Acquisition

In recent years, researchers have increasingly argued that language acquisition itself may be a function of overall cognitive development. In other words, the processes by which a child acquires language may not be specific to language but may be those by which the child comes to make sense of any category of experience. Further, the child's ability to use and comprehend language may rest on a previously acquired understanding of the concepts and relationships being communicated. This view reduces the emphasis on innate language acquisition mechanisms. Most theorists who accept this position, however, acknowledge that children need to acquire some specific knowledge about language, and the ability to do so may not depend entirely on cognitive processes. Melissa Bowerman summarizes initial language learning in this way:

The child comes to the language acquisition task already well equipped with a stock of basic concepts that he has built up through his nonlinguistic interactions with the world. The child's problem is to discover the linguistic forms or devices by which these concepts are expressed in his native language. [1978:102]

According to this view, children must have reached a certain level of cognitive development and have acquired prerequisite cognitive skills in order to begin to use language to communicate effectively (Harding, 1983). Many of these accomplishments are those that Piaget attributed to the sensorimotor stage of development (see Chapter 6). They include a sense of object permanence, the ability to recognize persons and objects in the environment and to note basic similarities and differences among them, an elementary understanding of the effect of actors' actions on objects ("John hit the ball"), the beginnings of representational thought along with the ability to remember symbolic information (such as words), and the ability to differentiate self from others so that genuine social interaction is possible (Bates, 1976; Cromer, 1976; Slobin, 1979).

The emphasis of this position is on the meaning that is encoded in children's utterances. Not surprisingly, then, researchers taking this perspective are concerned at least as much with *semantic* as with *syntactic* aspects of language development. Consequently, many of these investigators have been influenced by the development of *case grammars* (Fillmore, 1968; Schlesinger, 1971), which deal much more directly than transformational grammar with the semantic relationships expressed in sentences. Proponents of case grammars maintain that certain fundamental semantic roles or "cases" are expressed by the elements of sentences and that these should be represented in the deep structure of a grammar in a way that cannot be accomplished by a strictly syntactic analysis.

For example, contrast the meanings of the following sentences:

1. Carol opened the door.

2. A key opened the door.

3. Carol opened the door with a key.

Transformational grammar would treat *Carol* in Sentence 1 and *key* in Sentence 2 similarly. They would be subject noun phrases in both surface and deep structure. It is clear from Sentence 3, however, that *Carol* and *key* perform different functions, or *roles*, in these sentences. *Carol* is the person who does the action ("open"); *key* is the tool with which the action is performed. Case grammars could assign *Carol* the role of *agent* and *key* the role of *instrument*, thus marking the semantic distinctions between these functions. Charles Fillmore (1968) has suggested that such semantic roles, or cases, correspond to a set of universal concepts with which people organize and understand the world about them. Note that the basis for these roles is cognitive rather than linguistic.

Many studies of language development subsequently have used the kind of semantic relations proposed by case grammars to describe the functions expressed in children's early utterances (Bloom, 1970; Brown, 1973). Further, some investigators have attempted to show how even a child's first words encode a prelinguistic understanding of basic relationships, such as *agent-object*, which is revealed through the child's actions in specific situations (Greenfield and Smith, 1976). Advocates of this position claim that the child uses a word, and later two or more words, to encode that aspect of the situation that is most salient or novel at the time (Bates, 1976; Slobin, 1979). A basic premise of this view is that children first starting to speak know more than they are able to say. They have not yet acquired the cognitive skills and a sufficient grasp of grammatical rules to express all aspects of the situation (Antinucci and Parisi, 1973).

For example, two-year-old Robby may be sitting in a chair playing with a stuffed dog. His mother is standing nearby with her back turned to him. Robby accidently drops the stuffed animal and wants to get it back. He cannot yet say, "Look, Mommy, I dropped my doggie. Please give it back to me.'' So he may first say, ''Fall,'' to indicate the action that has occurred. If his mother turns around, he may then point to the floor and say, ''Doggie,'' to indicate what has fallen. If no immediate response is forthcoming, Robby may then say, ''Give!'' to express his request to have it back, or, perhaps, ''Mommy give,'' to show, as well, who he expects to take action. Adults usually have no trouble understanding what a child means in such a case.

Other evidence for the effect of cognitive development on language use comes from the observation that children fail to use some relatively simple language forms until they are able to understand the concepts that are expressed by them. Richard Cromer (1976) cites the example of the perfect tense in English, as in the sentence ''I *have gone* there.'' He found that two-year-old children used the component parts of this form (*have, gone*) in their speech but did not employ the perfect tense itself until about two years later. He attributes this delay to the conceptual difficulty of the perfect tense, concluding that ''the ability to use the perfect tense rests on a late-developing ability to consider the relevance of one timed sequence to another'' (1976:301).

However, even though most developmental psycholinguists now acknowledge the role of cognitive factors in language learning, they stress that cognitive development alone cannot account for language acquisition in its entirety (Cromer, 1976; Bowerman, 1978). To become mature language users, children must master many formal aspects of language that are not dependent on meaning and learn to express their intentions according to the grammatical rules of their native language. This is what Slobin (1979) refers to as ''the mapping problem.'' Children's efforts to accomplish this task are seen in their spontaneous self-corrections and in their explorations with syntactic forms, as if they were trying out different ways of saying the same things. For example, Slobin provides this excerpt from the speech of a three-year-old girl: ''She had Silly Putty like me had . . . like I . . . like I did'' (1979:99). Also, through

the preschool years, children use increasingly more complex linguistic forms to express ideas, such as negation and self-reference, that they have previously conveyed with simpler constructions. With self-reference, children gradually come to use *I* and *me* correctly, even though earlier utterances may have been well understood. In effect, their language becomes more and more ''adultlike.'' Whether children rely on general cognitive processes to learn these formal rules of language or whether, in addition, they need specific linguistic strategies is still not clear. As Bowerman notes, acquisition of grammatical knowledge may result from ''all-purpose inductive strategies that enable the child to recognize and abstract out regularities in linguistic and nonlinguistic input alike'' (1978:106), or some specialized language abilities may be required.

Language Used with Young Children

One important source of information for children about the content and structure of their native language is the speech addressed to them by parents and other caretakers. Although Chomsky (1965) claimed that the quality of adult speech to children was too imperfect to allow them to learn linguistic rules from it, later research has demonstrated that this is not the case. Many regularities have been described in such speech, and it is marked by several distinctive features (Newport, 1976; Ferguson, 1977; Bowerman, 1978). Since the speech of mothers to children has been studied most frequently, this simplified form of language has been called **motherese,** although fathers and other adults—and even older preschoolers (Shatz and Gelman, 1973; Sachs and Devin, 1976)—have been found to adjust their speech similarly when talking with toddlers.

Compared to that addressed to adults, the speech of parents to children consists of shorter, less complex sentences; is slower, higher in pitch, and marked by an exaggerated intonation pattern and more pauses; contains a more concrete and restricted vocabulary; and includes more questions and imperatives. In short, such "baby talk" seems to be particularly well suited to be understood by young children, to capture their attention, and to highlight important features of language. It could well serve, therefore, to instruct children in the use of their language and may help accomplish that purpose.

Is this why parents and others use baby talk? Roger Brown (1977) thinks not. He claims that the primary purpose of adults' using baby talk is communication. They want to be understood. And if they sense that a child has failed to understand, they will repeat or simplify what they have said to help ensure comprehension. The feedback adults receive from children, therefore, is a significant part of this process. Catherine Snow (1977) also stresses the *interactive* nature of such adult-child communication in showing how the adjustments parents make in talking with a child are guided by the child's own speech.

Thus, contemporary child language researchers emphasize both the role of cognitive development in language acquisition and the influence of the speech addressed to children. The complex picture of language development that they present shows that it is a finely tuned and very human pattern of interaction.

Pragmatics and Language Development

In recent years, increasing attention has been devoted to the study of *pragmatic* aspects of language development, or to the child's growing ability to communicate effectively in different situations. This ability involves knowing how to use language in socially appropriate ways and to achieve desired purposes. Elizabeth Bates defines **pragmatics** as "rules governing the use of language in context" (1976:420). "Context" refers to the setting and social situation in which language is used. Older people, for example, are usually addressed differently from young children. Conversational patterns used on the playground may or may not be suitable for the classroom.

To use language effectively and appropriately, a speaker must be able to take the point of view of the listener and observe implicit rules of conversation (Grice, 1973) that guide the interchange of remarks among participants. Children have to learn these contextually sensitive aspects of language in addition to the meanings of words and how to combine them into grammatically correct sentences. These are among the skills that mark the transition from egocentric to socialized speech according to Piagetian theory.

Interest in the pragmatic aspects of language development derives, in part, from *speeech act theory* (Austin, 1962; Searle, 1969), which analyzes how language is used to achieve different communicative effects. Studies of how young children express various intentions show that their use of language for these purposes evolves from earlier prelinguistic attempts to accomplish their aims, as through pointing or showing (Bates, 1976). Thus, using language to direct or obtain an adult's attention is among the earliest linguistic accomplishments of the child. "Daddy cup" may at first accompany and then replace a child's pointing under a nearby couch to get her father to retrieve a cup which has fallen there. Children seem to be able to understand some kinds of speech conventions such as indirect requests ("Can you close the door?" as an implied imperative instead of "Close the door!") as early as two years of age, but their own use of such forms does not occur consistently until several years later (Bates, 1976).

One of the more difficult language tasks facing children may be acquiring sensitivity to the communicative requirements of different situations, such as schools. Various environments often have special "rules of the game," which the participants have to recognize and learn if they are to function effectively in those settings. Studies of children's use and understanding of language (for example, Ervin-Tripp and Mitchell-Kernan, 1977) show that the real meaning of a verbal expression in a particular context may be very different from its literal meaning. For example, a kindergarten teacher who asks, "Who's ready to go?" at the end of the day is not just trying to determine which children are prepared to leave but also reminding them that they have to do certain things (such as pick up papers) before they *can* leave. Children interpret such expressions correctly if they share certain assumptions or presuppositions about the function of the expressions in that context. Without such shared background, comprehension does not occur. One of the problems facing many children in school is that they have not learned to speak "school language" and thus cannot participate fully in the "official" interactions that occur there. Children have to learn how language is used to achieve different purposes in school so they will know what is really expected of them.

LANGUAGE IN THE SCHOOL

Language pervades schooling. It is one of the most salient features of classroom life at all levels from kindergarten through graduate school. This is true whether that language is oral, written, communicated manually (as in signing), or communicated tactilely (as with Braille). Language, obviously, is an essential component of most instruction. Teachers talk and lecture; teachers and students engage in class discussions; and students are expected to learn the material contained in textbooks such as this one. Informal conversations among students are also a significant part of the school day. Needless to say, learning to use language effectively in all its forms and for a variety of purposes is a very important part of schooling and a basic requirement for academic success. Students who fail to accomplish this task are likely to face continued frustration and to

THE SCHOOL ENVIRONMENT
Students hear, see, and use many different aspects of language in school. (© *Elizabeth Crews*)

experience a range of academic and social problems. Several issues related to language use in school are presented in this section.

Use of Language in the School

By the time children enter school at age five or six, they are proficient language users, with an extensive vocabulary and a command of most of the syntactic structures of their native language. There are still some complex linguistic forms that they have not yet mastered, so that the acquisition of some aspects of syntax continues into the early school years and is closely related to cognitive development (C. Chomsky, 1969; Karmiloff-Smith, 1979). Children also have a great deal to learn about pragmatic aspects of language in school (Mehan, 1979). Before children come to school, their language is intimately connected to their own activity or embedded in a rich, interactive setting. These contexts support children's use of language. In school, many of these supports are missing. Language, both oral and written, becomes less personal and more formal (D. R. Olson, 1977). It becomes the object of attention itself, something to study and manipulate.

Speech conveys more information than the messages contained in spoken words. Intonation and pitch, for example, signal intended meanings that must be interpreted correctly if successful communication is to occur. A problem with these aspects of language use is that they tend to be dependent on the context and specific to various subcultures within the general community (Gumperz, 1981). Children in one ethnic group, therefore, may have experienced different speech conventions from children in another. Consequently, difficulties of interpretation are likely to arise in ethnically mixed classrooms, on the part of both teachers and students. These differences are more subtle than the variations in phonology and syntax apparent among dialects and thus may be more likely to lead to problems in communication.

John Gumperz (1981) provides an example of how such misinterpretation can occur. Observations at the beginning of the year in a first-grade classroom in an ethnically mixed school showed that a number of the black children did not follow the teacher's instructions to perform certain tasks, such as drawing with crayons or cutting out figures from paper. When asked why they were not carrying out these activities, many of the children replied with comments such as, ''I can't do this'' or ''I don't know how to do this.'' However, other evidence suggested that they did have the ability to accomplish these tasks. For example, all the children had done similar work in kindergarten. The observers became aware that the children's responses had distinctive intonation contours, and they tape recorded several of them. These taped samples of the children's remarks were played to both black and white judges who were asked whether they thought the children really did not know how to comply with the teacher's instructions. The black judges interpreted the taped responses to be children's requests for company so they would not have to work alone. The white judges tended to accept the statements as accurate admissions of inability to perform. Gumperz comments: ''Once we became aware of the special communicative import of the children's intonation contour, we began to see more and more evidence that the children really were asking for company rather than signaling lack of ability'' (1981:19). Appreciating these differences in language use requires some knowledge of sociolinguistics and great sensitivity to the environment in which speech occurs.

Reading

Reading is seeing by proxy.

HERBERT SPENCER

Perhaps the language activities most often associated with school are reading and writing. Instruction in the use of written language has been viewed historically as one of the fundamental purposes of formal schooling. Certainly, the ability to read is the basis for success in school and for functional participation in an adult world. However, census data reveal that approximately 1.4 million adult Americans are illiterate. They cannot read street signs, maps, restaurant menus, instructions for assembling simple appliances, telephone directories, labels on grocery items, letters and other correspondence, telephone and utility bills, and bank statements. In addition, an estimated one out of five persons is functionally illiterate. These people cannot read well enough to interpret a simple notice such as a store's check-cashing policy. Consequently, schools, particularly public schools, have remained under continuous scrutiny regarding the success with which they have met the challenge to produce a literate citizenry.

PRODUCING A LITERATE CITIZENRY
Because the basis for success both in school and in the adult world is the ability to read,
a fundamental purpose of formal schooling is to teach the use of written language.

The Nature of Reading

As we have seen, children come to school with a good command of both the production and comprehension of oral language. Although some children arrive at school knowing how to read, the majority of them face the task of acquiring a similar facility with written language. The ease with which they are able to accomplish this depends on a number of factors. These include, but are not limited to, the child's previous experience with written language; the quality of the instruction he or she receives in school; his or her own cognitive, linguistic, and perceptual capabilities; and the nature of the language itself.

Written English, of course, uses an alphabetic system. The primary characteristic of alphabetic systems (Gelb, 1952) is that they employ a limited set of conventional symbols to represent the *sounds* of the spoken language rather than ideas or concepts directly, as in Mandarin Chinese. Although alphabetic systems may be a step farther removed from a one-to-one encoding of meaning, they are also more flexible in that they potentially can represent any idea that is expressed in spoken language without the necessity of inventing new symbols for new concepts. Thus they require far fewer symbols than other writing systems. A basic task, then, for children beginning to read an alphabetic written language is to learn the conventional correspondences between letters or letter combinations and the sounds of their language. This process is often referred to as *decoding*.

Alphabetic systems differ in the extent to which they employ a consistent and distinct correspondence between individual letters and individual sounds. Thus Spanish **orthography** (spelling system), for example, is often considered to be highly "regular," whereas English orthography is described as "irregular," since in English the same letter or combination of letters may represent more than one sound, and the same sound may be expressed by different letters. For instance, consider the following sentence.

- Did h*e* bel*ie*ve that C*ae*sar could s*ee* the p*eo*ple s*ei*ze the s*ea*s?

In the above sentence, *e, ie, ae, ee, eo, ei,* and *ea* all represent the same sound, what basal reading series refer to as the "long *e*" sound (Fromkin and Rodman, 1974). Over the years, therefore, many people have advocated "reforming" English orthography to make it more "regular" or consistent (Downing, 1973). The argument offered is that children learn to read more easily with orthographically regular systems. However, the evidence for this position is largely inconclusive.

Although orthographic regularity seems to be a help in the initial stages of learning to read, it may offer no particular advantage for the acquisition of more advanced reading skills (Gibson and Levin, 1975). Simply knowing how to pronounce a word does not guarantee that successful reading will occur. Further, the reading theorist Richard Venezky (1970b, 1970c, 1978) has forcefully argued that a careful and systematic analysis of English orthography reveals consistent regularities, but at a *morphophonemic* rather than a *graphemic* (letter) level. That is, *morphemes,* or meaning units of the language, are regularly represented by clusters of *phonemes,* or sound units, though in a way that is sensitive to both word origin and spelling context. For example, the addition of the suffix *al* to the word *nation* changes the sound of the *a* in the first syllable. If different symbols were used to represent

the different sounds of *a* in *nation* and *national,* the common origin of the words would not be apparent. Venezky believes that spelling patterns that preserve resemblances in meaning assist the task of reading despite differences in pronunciation.

Is reading limited, though, to the pronunciation of words on a page? As mature readers, we would probably say no. We are aware that we read for a variety of purposes and that decoding is merely the means to a number of different ends. Since reading has become largely automatic for us (LaBerge and Samuels, 1974), we are probably seldom aware of making any effort to "sound out" a word except when we come across one that is strange or unfamiliar. What, then, is reading? Different people have offered widely different views. Definitions of reading vary from those that restrict the term "reading" to decoding to those that encompass such processes as comprehension and interpretation. Rudolph Flesch (1955), for example, defined reading as pronouncing sounds with or without understanding of those sounds. Most authors who equate reading with decoding, though, do so because they believe that correct identification of written symbols is the only unique aspect of reading (Fries, 1962), since the spoken language is already available and understood.

Generally, however, reading is defined more broadly. While recognizing that, to some extent, reading involves the translation of written symbols to a known language, most theorists see reading as a complex process that results in meaning and that should be viewed in its totality. One definition states that "Reading is extracting information from text" (Gibson and Levin, 1975:5). "Text," in this case, can be diagrams or graphs, as well as printed pages. Comprehension is implied in this definition, since something must be understood to "inform." "Extraction" also suggests a variety of processes. More recently, authors have emphasized that the meaning derived from reading is influenced greatly by the reader's background of knowledge, attitudes, and beliefs.

Obviously, these definitions represent diverse views of reading and emphasize different processes. For this reason, however, definitions of reading are important. They influence opinions of reading instruction and how reading actually is taught. As Mary Anne Hall, Jerilyn Ribovich, and Christopher Ramig note, ''What one believes the reading process to be underlies one's choice of instructional materials, classroom procedures, and overall methodology'' (1979:5). If reading is defined as decoding, then an instructional program will probably emphasize sound-symbol relationships. If, on the other hand, meaning is seen as an important aspect of reading, then comprehension instruction should be a part of a total reading program.

Learning to Read

A lot of mystery surrounds learning to read (Venezky, 1978) and apparently without good reason. When statistics on illiteracy, such as those at the beginning of this section, are cited, the impression is often created that some magic key needs to be found to unlock the complexities of learning to read. Yet, while the extent of functional illiteracy remains a national problem and while schools undoubtedly could do a better job of ensuring that more students become fluent and active readers, most children do acquire basic reading skills without much difficulty. In fact, some children learn to read—at home or in school— rather effortlessly. Why, then, the mystery? Partly because of the obvious failures and partly, perhaps, because it is difficult to put together a clear picture of how children learn to read. We can describe what teachers do, but then teachers do a great many things, often very differently. Learning to read involves a number of component processes— cognitive, perceptual, experiential, and linguistic.

Experiential factors may be particularly important, however (Coltheart, 1979; Torrey, 1979). Learning *about* written language is an often overlooked, but possibly crucial, part of learning to read (Ehri, 1979). First of all, children should understand that print is speech written down. The squiggles on the page are the words that they speak and hear. This may seem obvious, but many children in the initial stages of reading instruction do not realize this (Torrey, 1979) and thus are more mystified than they need be. One way that children acquire this concept is by being read to frequently during the preschool years, a practice that also encourages an interest in reading and an appreciation of its purposes (Trelease, 1982). Children learning alphabetic systems also need to become aware that language is segmented into words (Mason, 1980) and that words are composed of separate sounds (*phonemes*) (Elkonin, 1973), although they may not achieve these realizations until they have received some reading instruction (Ehri, 1979). They must also learn print conventions, such as the fact that word boundaries are marked by spaces (Holden and MacGinitie, 1972) and that English is read from left to right.

Debate over appropriate methods for teaching reading has a long and often stormy history, though with rather inconclusive results (Bond and Dykstra, 1967; Dykstra, 1968; Venezky, 1978). No one approach to reading instruction consistently has been found to be superior to another despite the occasional vocal advocacy of some particular system (Flesch, 1955). Greater differences in pupils' reading performance have been found among classrooms in which the same system was used than, overall, among different programs (Bond and Dykstra, 1967; Dykstra, 1968). This result suggests the importance of instructional factors other than reading method.

Jeanne Chall (1967) has distinguished between reading programs with a phonics emphasis and those with a meaning emphasis. **Phonics** is the term used to describe instruction in letter-sound correspondences or decoding. On the basis of her review of comparative studies, Chall recommended a code emphasis for beginning reading instruction. Actually, almost all contemporary reading programs, especially those that use a basal reading series, place strong emphasis on decoding and other aspects of word recognition in initial reading instruction. They are eclectic in that they provide for some sequential instruction in both decoding skills and reading for meaning (Gibson and Levin, 1975). (See the boxed insert on page 269.) Differences among them are largely in terms of

BASAL TEXTBOOK PROGRAMS

Most school systems within the United States have adopted the basal textbook approach for teaching reading. There are literally hundreds of commercially published programs that provide materials for sequential use from kindergarten through the sixth grade (some series are non-graded, focusing instead upon the readiness level of the students). Most basal programs follow a somewhat similar format:

- *Kindergarten:* Various readiness workbooks.
- *First grade:*
  Preprimer level—Three or more soft-covered texts with accompanying workbooks.
  Primer level—Hard-covered text with accompanying workbook.
  First level—Hard-covered text with accompanying workbook.
- *Second grade and above:* Generally two hard-covered texts and accompanying workbooks for each grade level.

Some publishers also provide readers for junior-high-school students. Each reader in a series has a teacher's guidebook or manual to explain how the material is to be used. Frequently, book companies also offer accompanying charts, tests, and various classroom aids. The series is usually marketed as the product of a team of specialists, the head of the team being a person of recognized authority and stature in the field of education. However, much of the material is prepared by an "in-house" staff within a publishing firm, individuals who may or may not have training in education.

Most commonly, a basal text lesson follows a number of steps:

1. *Orientation:* Students are provided with background material designed to arouse interest in the story they are about to read.
2. *New word presentation:* Pupils are presented with new words they will encounter in the story; these words are defined and explained.

BASAL READING SERIES

Most school systems in the United States use a basal reading reading series as their principal means for teaching reading. A basal series is characterized by a sequential set of graded materials, use of a controlled vocabulary, and detailed teachers' manuals.

3. *Guided reading:* Students are directed to read silently a certain amount of material and to find the answers to specific questions.
4. *Guided discussion:* The guidebook provides teachers with questions they are to ask students and with points they are to emphasize during the discussion session to help pupils interpret the story.
5. *Guided reading:* Students are asked to reread the story; usually a definite purpose for rereading is set forth, and the pupils are given a number of questions to facilitate their further interpretation of the material.
6. *Follow-up activities:* Pupils are provided with a series of exercises and activities correlated with the workbook.

Basal programs differ in what they teach. Some stress comprehension, others emphasize phonics, and still others attempt to fuel students' love of reading through the inherent appeal of a story. Over the past decade, however, most series have attempted to strike a balance between comprehension and phonic skills.

The authors of basal reading systems generally view their products as only part of a "total reading program." The material is designed to teach basic reading skills that are then to be supplemented throughout the year as pupils read library books. Too often, however, the basal books become *the* reading program, especially in inner-city schools.

emphasis and in how various components of the program are sequenced through the series (Venezky, 1978). For example, some programs place more emphasis on decoding than others. Regardless of the system used, explicit instruction in comprehension seems to be infrequent (Durkin, 1978–1979).

A more appropriate distinction may be between *analytic* and *synthetic* methods of teaching phonics. *Synthetic methods* teach the sounds represented by different letters or letter clusters in isolation; children then blend these sounds into words. Critics of this approach (for example, Hall, Ribovich, and Ramig, 1979) argue that such a system is artificial, in that consonants cannot be pronounced in isolation. (If you try to say the sound represented by *t*, for example, you will actually produce something like *tuh*.) Further, they claim that this method encourages a laborious "sounding out" habit and can lead to the production of many nonwords. *Analytic programs* begin with the teaching of whole words, including many that have regular letter-sound correspondences. Children are then led to detect these correspondences in words that have a common element (the *b* in *big, bat,* and *bed,* for example, or *-at* in *sat, bat,* and *cat*). A rather extreme example of this approach is the so-called *linguistic method* (Bloomfield and Barnhart, 1961; Fries, 1962), in which all initial reading instruction is based on the use of words with regular spelling patterns ("Dan can fan Nan"). Eleanor Gibson and Harry Levin (1975) emphasize that while it is important for children to learn to detect sound-symbol patterns within words, instruction should not focus on words or word parts in isolation. Words should be placed in the context of mean-

READING ACHIEVEMENT AND CLASSROOM PROCEDURES

The Stanford Research Institute undertook a comprehensive observation study of classroom processes and instructional practices (Stallings, 1976). The researchers secured data based on observations in 105 first grades and 58 third grades. Over 340 correlations between reading achievement and classroom processes were investigated. Of these, higher reading scores were most strongly related to the average time children spent in reading activity and the length of the school day (school systems varied by as much as two hours in the time students spent in classes). Hence, opportunity and exposure to reading were closely related to good performance on reading tests.

The researchers also found that positive reinforcement was related to test scores:

Higher reading scores were obtained in classrooms using systematic instructional patterns where the teacher provides information and asks a question about the information. The child responds and the teacher immediately lets the child know whether the response is right or wrong. If wrong, the child is guided to the correct answer. If correct, he/she receives praise, a token, or some form of acknowledgement. [Stallings, 1976:44]

Apparently, small groups were most effective for teaching first-grade reading. In contrast, groups of nine or more were productive in third grade. Likewise, reading scores were higher in classrooms where textbooks and programmed workbooks were used most often.

ingful connected discourse so that children can learn to use the many cues or natural redundancies that occur in language.

Venezky (1978; Venezky and Winfield, 1979) argues that continued emphasis on reading instructional methods may be misguided if schools are to be more successful in teaching reading. He urges, instead, that efforts be directed to managing and implementing reading programs within schools and school systems and to providing the kind of instructional leadership by principals and other administrators that has been shown to be effective. Support for this position comes from Gita Wilder (1977), who found that exemplary reading programs were marked by effective administrative leadership of educational programs and focused attention on the teaching of basic reading skills. After a review of successful reading programs, including those studied by Wilder, S. Jay Samuels (1981) concluded that such programs were marked by the following characteristics: a belief that schools can make a difference in the academic achievement of their students, strong administrative support, ongoing inservice training and supervision of teachers, clear objectives and an orientation emphasizing basic skills, the allocation of sufficient time for instruction, effective management of teacher time, and continuous monitoring of student progress.

Reading to Learn

For many years, much of the research concerning reading processes focused on cognitive and perceptual aspects of word recognition, and it related primarily to the early stages of reading acquisition. More recently, however, there has been increasing interest in the study of text comprehension. A number of theoretical trends are probably responsible for this development. One of these has been an effort to describe the way written discourse or text is organized or structured and to explore how various features of prose structure influence the way people remember and understand text (Meyer, 1975; Kintsch and van Dijk, 1978). Another has been the attempt to characterize the kinds of

complex knowledge that people acquire about the world and that they use to comprehend what they read (Rumelhart and Ortony, 1977; Schank and Abelson, 1977). In addition, developmental psychologists have been studying the processes schoolchildren use to comprehend prose material (Stein and Glenn, 1979; Brown, 1980). Since more and more of students' learning becomes text-based as they go on through school, these research directions can contribute to our understanding of instructional practices at all grade levels.

Research on text structure has shown how the organization of prose passages affects what people learn from them. Authors typically construct texts so that certain ideas are emphasized. Not surprisingly, adult readers judge such ideas to be more important and remember them better than other facts in the passage (Meyer, 1975; Brown and Smiley, 1977). College students can detect several levels of importance in a text, but elementary school pupils can only distinguish main ideas (Brown and Smiley, 1977). Also, children come to school with some understanding of the structure of simple stories, but their awareness of the components of story structure increases through the elementary grades (Stein and Glenn, 1979). Thus, sensitivity to the structure of texts and to the relations among ideas expressed in them is an important task to be accomplished by upper-elementary and secondary students if they are to learn successfully from written material.

While it may seem obvious that the comprehension of text depends to a great extent on the store of general knowledge a person has about the world, exploration of the relationship between such world knowledge and reading comprehension is a relatively recent phenomenon. It owes much to the elaboration of what has come to be called *schema theory* (Anderson, 1977), which suggests that people develop *schemata*, or generalized concepts, for the events, objects, or actions they experience repeatedly (Rumelhart and Ortony, 1977). For example, your "fire engine schema" may contain the information that a fire engine is usually red (though not always), is long, goes very quickly,

LEARNING TO READ AND READING TO LEARN
Reading to children and wide reading by children are among the best ways to ensure that children will learn to read well and will want to read to learn.

and may have a Dalmatian perched on it somewhere. Few of these features would be found in a dictionary definition of ''fire engine'' (try this one yourself), but they may be essential for the comprehension of a story about fire engines, since authors usually omit information that they assume readers already know. Studies with adults by Richard Anderson and his colleagues (Anderson et al., 1977; Anderson, Spiro, and Anderson, 1978) have demonstrated that readers do seem to make use of such organized frameworks in comprehending text. Readers with different backgrounds (for example, physical education or music majors)

interpret ambiguous passages according to their own orientations; and readers show better comprehension when passage content is consistent with their prior knowledge.

A *script* (Schank and Abelson, 1977) can be considered to be one type of schema. Scripts are described as stereotypical action sequences for common, everyday events, such as eating in a restaurant or shopping in a supermarket. Although one instance of such an event may differ in certain ways from another, there are certain characteristics that tend to be common to each of them. Such regularity in frequently repeated activities helps provide us with general expectations about them, and these expectations can be utilized in various ways. They tend to make daily living more predictable, and they can be used in comprehending texts that refer to such activities. Even preschoolers seem to develop script-like knowledge for events in which they participate frequently (Nelson, 1981). Such script knowledge may be a prerequisite for the successful accomplishment of a number of school tasks. Many stories in basal readers, for example, require that children have some knowledge of activities such as going to a library or visiting a zoo. Young children, even those of kindergarten age, apparently are able to use script knowledge to comprehend stories about common events, when information about those events is assumed, rather than stated, in the stories (Pace and Feagans, 1983). Teachers must be alert, however, to the fact that many children may not always have the background knowledge to understand either basal stories or classroom lessons.

Many school tasks require that students understand and remember *new* information presented in texts such as this one. To learn new information, they cannot rely on existing knowledge alone. Many techniques have been proposed over the years to help students read and study from texts. Study skills are taught in separate courses or as part of reading or English programs. Although many different procedures may be useful, research has not demonstrated that any one technique is consistently better than any other (Anderson, 1980).

What may be required is for students to develop internalized procedures for monitoring and controlling their own comprehension, strategies that they can use appropriately and flexibly in different situations and for different purposes (Brown, 1980). These skills include knowing when to reread texts to clarify understanding, being able to modify reading time and attention according to the purpose for reading, noticing inconsistencies in text and attempting to make sense of them, and using self-generated questions to guide reading. Existing studies indicate some positive results from students' use of such strategies. Secondary students can be trained to formulate broader and more comprehensive questions while reading, and middle and lower ability students, especially, may benefit from doing so (André and Anderson, 1978–1979). Better eighth-graders are able to notice comprehension difficulties while reading and spontaneously review preceding portions of text to resolve their confusion; younger students and those with poorer comprehension skills are less likely to do so (Garner and Reis, 1981). Elementary school children, particularly, may be deficient in comprehension monitoring skills (Brown, 1980; Markman, 1979), and the ineffective or infrequent use of such skills may characterize students with comprehension problems in the upper grades.

One challenge facing reading theorists and educators is to find ways to help students develop such comprehension monitoring strategies so that they can more effectively learn how to learn. By focusing on school-related tasks and materials that are similar to those used in actual instruction, these areas of research have the potential of providing useful recommendations for instructional practice by indicating how students might be taught to become independent and self-directed learners.

Black English

Educators have been concerned with the possibility that learning to read may be more difficult for children who speak ''nonstandard'' dialects of English. It is known, for instance, that individuals who speak one language encounter various difficulties when they try to master another language later in life. Accordingly, any number of educators have speculated that the dialect spoken by some blacks may contribute to the poor school performance of many inner-city black children. If Black English, as it is commonly termed, does represent a separate system of communication, then black children may confront problems in a school environment that operates in terms of Standard English.

Black and Standard English often differ in the affixes for tenses and possessives (Labov, 1970, 1972). For instance, *He is going home* in Standard English becomes *He going home* in Black English; *She said* becomes *She say*. The possessive affix *s* may be deleted in Black English yielding forms like *What's that guy name?* There are also phonological differences in the two dialects. For example, *r* is dropped before consonants and at the ends of words, so that words like *sore* and *saw* are homophones (words pronounced alike); likewise, *l* may be omitted so *bowl* and *bow* are homophones. Black English is rooted in a historical past that spans Africa, the Caribbean, the Creole heritage, the rural South, and now the northern cities.

According to the *linguistic difference hypothesis*, black children find school baffling when they are confronted with confusing and arbitrary relationships between unfamiliar sounds and symbols:

> All children acquire language but . . . many children, especially lower class black children, acquire a dialect of English so different in structural (grammatical) features that communication in school, both oral and written, is seriously impaired by that fact alone. [Cazden, 1970:35–36]

Those who accept this hypothesis call for a number of changes in those schools that serve children who speak Black English. These include (1) instructing teachers of black children on the differences between the two dialects so that they can communicate more effectively with black children, or hiring teachers who speak Black English; and (2) teaching black children Standard English as a second language (Hall and Turner, 1974; Harber and Bryen, 1976).

In a 1979 Ann Arbor court case brought by eleven black children, a federal judge held that bringing blacks into the mainstream of society requires more than integrated housing and the busing of students. In the ''Black English'' case, Judge Charles W. Joiner said that ''the evidence does clearly establish that unless those instructing in reading recognize (1) the existence of a home language used by the children in their home community for much of their nonschool communications, and (2) that this home language may be a cause of the superficial difficulties in speaking standard English, great harm will be done.'' The judge required the Ann Arbor school district to conduct classes for thirty-two teachers to help them to understand Black English and to distinguish between students' use of Black English and errors by students in understanding and interpreting materials that are unrelated to such English.

However, not all educators agree that a special approach dictated by Black English is necessary or desirable (Venezky, 1970a; Weber, 1970; Harber and Bryen, 1976; Hart et al., 1980). These educators suggest that, from a linguistic point of view, the differences between Black and Standard English are superficial and are far outweighed by the similarities between them. They claim that no acceptable, replicated research has found that the dialect spoken by black children presents them with unique problems in comprehending Standard English. Speakers of Black English seem to translate the Standard English into their dialect automatically (Hall and Turner, 1974). Further, not all blacks speak Black English. Nor is there any reason to believe that the use of Black English has any effect on cognitive development or the capacity to learn (Slobin, 1979).

Probably the safest conclusion we can draw at the present time is that research findings on the linguistic different hypothesis are contradictory

LINGUISTIC-DIFFERENCE HYPOTHESIS
According to the linguistic-difference hypothesis, some children who speak Black English in the nonschool environment find the classroom setting baffling when they are confronted with Standard English in reading and other assignments.

and inconclusive (Harber and Bryen, 1976). Large gaps remain in our knowledge. However, it seems unlikely that the hypothesis can explain observed differences in the reading levels of black and white students. Indeed, teachers' attitudes toward black students and Black English appear to be a more important determinant of school achievement than the dialect that is employed (Venezky, 1970a; Granger et al., 1977). Hence, teachers of all racial and ethnic groups must become more accepting of and sensitive to the dialects used by their pupils both inside and outside the classroom. In particular, they must avoid labeling dialectical differences ''errors'' and refrain from equating students' use of Standard English with their ability.

Bilingualism

The United States is a culturally diverse nation, a fact reflected in Table 9.1. As a consequence there are at present some 3.6 million pupils in the public schools with limited knowledge of English. For instance, in Fairfax County, Virginia (outside Washington, D.C.), more than fifty languages are represented among the students. About half the foreign language students speak Spanish, Vietnamese, or Korean. Other languages include Urdu, Farsi, and Swahili. In some cases only a handful of students speak a particular language. At some schools fifteen foreign languages are spoken by students. Situations such as those in Fairfax County pose special difficulties for students, teachers, and others concerned with education.

For the serious purposes of life within the United States literacy is confined almost exclusively to English. The identification of literacy with English is assured by the publication of textbooks in English and the representation of "appropriate" values in terms of the dominant Anglo-American culture. The notion that the United States is a melting pot of languages and cultures in which all become "American" and speak only English is as old as the Republic (Glazer and Moynihan, 1963; Christian, 1976). A non-English mother tongue has typically been viewed as a "disease of the poor" (Fishman, 1975). Individuals with a different cultural heritage have been expected to give up their language and distinctive traits and fuse with the dominant American group. This approach contrasts with the concept of "cultural pluralism," which aims to achieve uniformity within a society through conformity in those areas deemed necessary for the national well-being. Simultaneously, however, it permits individuals to maintain their own cultural traits in other areas that are not felt to be as essential.

Of the 3.6 million pupils in the United States who can speak little or no English, 70 percent are Hispanic. In Los Angeles, Hispanics are the largest

TABLE 9.1
Major Ethnic Categories, 1980

Caucasian (excluding Hispanic)	188,341,000
Black	26,488,000
Hispanic	14,600,000
American Indian	1,362,000
Chinese	806,000
Filipino	775,000
Japanese	701,000
Asian Indian	362,000
Korean	355,000
Vietnamese	262,000

Source: U.S. Census Bureau.

ethnic group in the school system. Yet in Los Angeles, of the 25,710 teachers in the system, only an estimated 2,000 can speak Spanish. New York City, Chicago, Dade County (Florida), and the Rio Grande Valley (Texas) are other centers of Spanish-speaking populations. The three largest Hispanic minorities in the United States are Mexicans, Puerto Ricans, and Cubans. Considerable variation exists among and within these Spanish-speaking groups. For instance, the vast majority of Puerto Rican families in New York City and Cuban-American families in Miami use Spanish as the most frequent means of verbal communication; among central Texas Mexican-American families, about one-fourth speak Spanish, another one-fourth English, and one-half a Spanish-English "mixture" (Laosa, 1975, 1977).

The schooling of Spanish-speaking youth is a national scandal. Even as late as a decade ago, little more than 1 percent of Puerto Rican high-school graduates in New York City received academic diplomas, whereas 8 percent received vocational certificates, and another 90 percent general diplomas (in effect, simply attesting to a student's class attendance). Until relatively recently, Mexican-American children in the Southwest were usually segregated for purposes of instruction either in separate buildings or in segregated classes within the same building. In many schools the speaking of Spanish was forbidden both in the classrooms and on the playground, and students were punished for lapsing into their native tongue. In school systems with few Spanish-speaking pupils, the children were at times placed in classes with the mentally retarded. It is little wonder that 40 percent of Mexican-American children who entered first grade never completed high school.

Over the past decade a political and pedagogical awakening has resulted in a rebirth of bilingual and bicultural programs that were prevalent in certain areas of the United States until World War I (for instance, there were German-English public bilingual schools in several states and French-English programs in Louisiana). These programs are designed to use the native language and culture of students as assets rather than a disadvantage (Zirkel, 1976, 1977). However, the typical definition of bilingual education as instruction employing two languages obscures a wide range of philosophical and programmatic differences. William F. Mackey (1970) identifies more than 400 types of bilingual education, depending on such factors as goals (assimilation or cultural pluralism), extent of subject matter taught through each language (for instance, a "fifty-fifty" program, offering a half-day in each language), and groups being served (for example, are only Spanish-speaking children involved, or are English-speaking children also taught Spanish?).

At present the focus on bilingualism has centered primarily upon two opposing approaches. The bilingual approach undertakes to teach non-English-speaking children the regular academic subjects such as reading, mathematics, and science in their own language by teachers who have mastered both English and the child's native language. As children learn to cope with English, they are shifted to regular classes.

A second approach views English as a second language (ESL). All non-English-speaking students are grouped together and are provided intensive language instruction by specially trained teachers. From the outset, the students take music and physical education with their English-speaking peers. Early in the ESL program, the students move into regular classes in subjects such as mathematics and science which are thought to require less extensive language skills. A somewhat similar approach is embodied in the commercial Berlitz method and the Army Language School in Monterey, California. The method—termed "immersion"—teaches a new language totally divorced from the native one. The goal is one of inducing students to think in the nonnative language without the aid of the first language (Hechinger, 1981b).

The Supreme Court has given impetus to bilingual education programs through its 1974 ruling in *Lau* v. *Nichols,* a case brought by 1,790 Chinese public school students in San Francisco. The nation's highest court held:

> There is no equality of treatment merely by providing students with the same facilities, textbooks, teachers, and curriculum; for students who do not understand English are effectively foreclosed from any meaningful education.

However, the Supreme Court did not mandate a specific approach to teaching national-origin students with English-language problems:

> No specific remedy is urged upon us. Teaching English to the students of Chinese ancestry who do not speak the language is one choice. Giving instructions to this group in Chinese is another. There may be others.

In a recent national poll of Hispanics conducted by the New York-based Hispanic Opinion and Preference Research, Spanish-speaking respondents were divided on the issue of bilingual education. Most support went for teaching mainly English, with supplementary Spanish. Others favored transitional teaching in Spanish while students learn English. And about the same proportion of respondents said that they favored an English-only school (19 percent) as preferred an all-Spanish program (18 percent). Underlying much of the disagreement about bilingual education is a basic dilemma: If Spanish-speaking children are taught in English, they do not learn, and the disadvantage they suffer in the early grades becomes permanent. If they are taught in Spanish, they do not become fluent in English in a nation in which the command of English is essential for full incorporation within American life and economic activity.

There is strong opposition to bilingual education among segments of the Anglo population. Critics contend that programs incorporating the use of Spanish pose obstacles to the long-term goal of having Hispanics enter the social and economic mainstream. They fear that unless Hispanic children learn English, the United States may drift toward a separate Spanish-speaking minority and one day confront the sort of problem posed for Canadian unity by the French-speaking minority in the province of Quebec.

Clearly, considerable controversy surrounds the nature and adequacy of contemporary bilingual programs. Research is spotty and not definitive (Engle, 1975; McLaughlin, 1977). All of this suggests that bilingual and bicultural education requires the urgent attention of educators and psychologists.

CHAPTER SUMMARY

1. The understanding and production of language is one of the most complex activities performed by human beings. Language provides a set of symbols that catalogs the objects, events, and relations that people experience in their environment. Three ingredients make up language: phonology, semantics, and syntax.

2. The relationship between language and cognition is complex. Although the linguistic relativity hypothesis proposed that a language shapes the way a person speaks, most evidence suggests that the syntax and vocabulary of a particular language merely predispose a person to think a certain way. Further, the formal similarities among all languages are greater than their differences, and all languages seem to reflect basic human ways of perceiving and organizing experience.

3. Different theories have been offered to explain children's acquisition of language. The learning theory of language acquisition, advocated by B. F. Skinner, emphasizes the principles of reinforcement, association, and imitation. One criticism of this approach is that even adults would be overwhelmed by the tasks children face in learning to speak and communicate in their native language.

4. The "nativist" theory of language acquisition, associated primarily with Noam Chomsky, proposes that children possess an innate organizing mechanism, termed the "language acquisition device" (LAD), genetically designed to process and code language into a rule-using system. Chomsky is also principally responsible for the formulation of transformational grammar, which focuses on syntactic features of language.

5. Other theories emphasize semantic aspects of language acquisition, as well as the relationship between language development and more general cognitive processes. From this perspective, children's use of language is seen as depending on their level of understanding and certain prerequisite cognitive skills. This view has also been influenced by the development of case grammars, which stress the underlying semantic relations expressed in language.

6. Children may learn a great deal about their native language from the speech addressed to them by parents, other adults, and even older children. This simplified form of speech, called "motherese" or "baby talk," is slower, less complex, and more concrete than speech to adults.

7. In addition to learning the syntax and semantics of their language, children also have to learn the pragmatic aspects of language, or how to communicate their intentions appropriately in different situations. This ability may depend on cognitive development and social experiences in a variety of situations.

8. One of the most important tasks facing children in school is learning to use written language

effectively. Learning to read successfully, of course, affects all later academic achievements. Reading an alphabetic system such as English requires learning the correspondences between sounds and the written symbols that represent them, which may be letters or letter clusters. Decoding is the process of recognizing the sounds represented by these symbols.

9. Recent studies of exemplary reading programs emphasize the importance of managerial and administrative aspects of programs, rather than particular instructional methods. Successful programs made academic achievement of students a clear goal, experienced strong administrative support, provided training and direction to school staffs, monitored student progress, and revealed careful organization and planning.

10. In addition to learning to read, students have to read to learn in most areas of the school curriculum. To do so, students must be able to comprehend different kinds of texts dealing with different subject area content. Research on reading comprehension and text structure shows that older students are more aware than younger children of the complexities of text structure and that they have a larger repertoire of successful strategies to use for comprehension.

11. Educators have been concerned with the possibility that learning to read may be more difficult for children who speak "nonstandard" dialects of English. Any number of educators have speculated that the dialect spoken by some blacks may contribute to the poor school performance of many inner-city children. Teachers' attitudes toward Black English may affect students more adversely than the rather superficial grammatical and phonological differences between Black English and Standard English.

12. Several million pupils in the public schools speak a language other than English. A great many of these students are of Hispanic origin. Schools are faced with the challenge of providing academic instruction to these students, while also helping them acquire a functional knowledge of English.

CHAPTER GLOSSARY

language   A structured system of sound patterns (words and sentences) with socially standardized meanings.

linguistic relativity hypothesis   The idea that the language spoken by a community affects the way the people in that community think about the world. Also referred to as the "Whorfian hypothesis," after the linguist Benjamin Lee Whorf.

motherese   A simplified form of speech used by mothers, other adults, and even other children in talking to babies.

orthography   The spelling system of a language.

phonics   A component of reading instruction concerned with teaching letter-sound correspondences or decoding.

phonology   The sound system of a language.

pragmatics   Sociolinguistic principles dealing with the relationships between the form or meaning of spoken expressions and their use for different communicative purposes.

semantics   That aspect of a language concerned with the meaning of words and sentences.

syntax   The rules of a grammar for ordering the semantic units of a language (words and sentences) into meaningful patterns.

EXERCISES

Review Questions

1. According to sociologists, the complexity of human society and culture is due primarily to

   a. social instinct
   b. language

c. intelligence

d. opposite thumb

2. The language system dealing with the meanings associated with sounds is

   a. phonology

   b. syntax

   c. semantics

   d. categorization

3. Among the arguments given against the Whorfian hypothesis is that

   a. surface features, such as word order, are highly consistent across all languages

   b. all languages seem to have terms for concepts that easily translate into other languages and few, if any, terms that cannot be so translated

   c. American Indian languages are not really fully developed languages

   d. many aspects of the form and processing of languages appear to be universal

4. Skinner's account of language acquisition has been criticized for which of the following reasons?

   a. Children must learn a tremendous amount of information about language in order to speak.

   b. Children use forms in speaking that are not exact replications of adult speech.

   c. Children produce novel utterances that they could not have heard in their environment.

   d. a, and c are true

   e. a, b, and c are true

5. In Chomsky's theory, deep structures are converted into surface representations by

   a. LAD

   b. phrase structures

   c. transformation rules

   d. semantics

6. According to theorists who stress cognitive contributions to language acquisition, which of the following skills are prerequisite to a child's effective use of language?

   a. an elementary understanding of causality

   b. a sense of object permanence

   c. the ability to distinguish self from others

   d. a, b, and c are true

   e. a and c are true

7. A characteristic of all alphabetic writing systems is

   a. the direct encoding of the ideas expressed in a language

   b. the use of a limited set of conventional symbols to stand for the sounds of the spoken language

   c. a one-to-one and distinct correspondence between a particular written symbol and a particular sound in the language

   d. a highly regular orthography

8. Successful reading programs appear to be distinguished by

   a. effective instructional leadership by principals or other administrators

   b. the use of synthetic phonics methods

   c. the adaption of the ''linguistic'' approach to reading instruction

   d. emphasis on reading for meaning rather than on developing decoding skills

9. The issue in Black English that produces most agreement is

   a. the differences between Black and Standard English are significant

   b. research indicates that the use of Black English is almost universal among blacks

   c. teacher attitudes may be a more critical deterrent in reading than dialect

   d. a, b, and c are true

   e. a and c are true

10. The largest non-English speaking group in the American public schools is

    a. blacks
    b. Hispanics
    c. American Indians
    d. Chinese

Answers

1. b (See p. 254)
2. c (See p. 255)
3. d (See pp. 256–257)
4. e (See pp. 258–259)
5. c (See pp. 259–260)
6. d (See pp. 260–262)
7. b (See pp. 266–267)
8. a (See p. 271)
9. c (See p. 274)
10. b (See p. 275)

Applying Principles and Concepts

1. Indicate whether the following examples would most likely be used in Skinner's theory of language acquisition (Sk), Chomsky's linguistic theory (Ch), or in cognitive approaches to language acquisition (cog).

_____ a. Teddy is sitting on his mother's bed looking at a picture book. He suddenly drops the book, and it falls from the bed. Teddy crawls to the edge of the bed, looks down at the book, and says, "Mommy get."

_____ b. A child is playing with stuffed animals and babbling. At one point, she says "duh-duh." A nearby parent, thinking the child has said "duck," hands her that animal and gives the child a hug.

_____ c. The sentence "They are visiting relatives" can mean your neighbors, the Joneses, are out of town visiting some of their cousins, or that the strange people you see on the Joneses' front porch are an aunt and uncle who have come to visit them from Toronto.

_____ d. A toddler is trying to tell her father that she broke one of her toys. She starts out by saying, "I break it." Then she shakes her head and says, "I breaked it." She realized this still isn't right, looks puzzled, and finally comes out with, "I broked it."

2. Underline in the following passage statements that are actually part of Chomsky's theory.

Chomsky is a behaviorist in terms of language acquisition. However, he argues that while there is an innate language-generating device, environmental factors preclude much commonalities among languages. He also suggests there is basically a *one to one* relationship between surface and deep structures.

3. In the following sentence, underline all the different letter combinations that represent the sound of "long *a*."

"Did he say that he paid eight dollars for the table Joe made?"

4. Before each of the following examples of different concepts or practices related to reading, indicate whether it represents the linguistic method (LM), a script (S), synthetic phonics (SP), or analytic phonics (AP).

_____ a. A teacher is pointing to the letter *p* on a chart and asking the children sitting in front of her to "say its sound." Then she points to *t* and makes the same request.

_____ b. First you take the cap off the tube of toothpaste. Then you hold your toothbrush in one hand and the toothpaste in the other and squeeze some of the paste onto the brush. Then you put the toothbrush in your mouth . . . and so on.

_____ c. The children already know the words *book, look,* and *cat.* The teacher writes them on the board, asks the group to read them, and then she erases the *b* and replaces it with a *c.* She then calls on a child to read the new word.

_____ d. The page in the reading book contains this sentence: "The fat cat sat on the hat."

5. A teacher at an elementary school with large numbers of blacks and Spanish-speaking children has made a number of comments about these children. Indicate by a checkmark those that appear to be substantiated by research.

_____ a. "Everyone agrees that black children must give up Black English in order to succeed in school."

_____ b. "Spanish kids have always been able to use their language in school to help each other."

_____ c. "Spanish kids seem to have a rougher time in school than black kids."

_____ d. "At least we can all agree on what a good bilingual program should be."

Answers

1. a, cog; b, Sk; c, Ch; d, cog (See pp. 257–262)
2. Underline "he argues that while there is an innate language-generating device." (See pp. 259–260)
3. *say, paid, ei(gh)t, ta-*ble, mad(*e*) (See p. 264)
4. a, SP; b, S; c, AP; d, LM (See pp. 270, 272)
5. c (See pp. 275–276)

Project

OBJECTIVE: To compare differing perceptions of some of the problems encountered by black and Spanish-speaking adolescents.

SCHOOL PROCEDURE: This project can be done either at a school or with campus peers. Visit a local junior or senior high school with either black or Spanish-speaking students. Visit a white Anglo teacher and a minority teacher and ask the same questions:

1. Does the adolescent black or Spanish-speaking student have problems similar to or different from those of white Anglo youth?
2. Are there sex differences with respect to these problems?
3. Does the school provide for remediation of these difficulties?
4. In the teacher's opinion is the plight of these students diminishing, increasing, or remaining the same?

ANALYSIS: The purpose of this project is to reveal the perception of problems and sensitivity in dealing with them.

1. Compare the answers of the Anglo and minority teachers. In what areas is there agreement? Disagreement?
2. What are the educational implications of these agreements and disagreements?
3. Which opinions seem more valid to you? Why?
4. What are the implications for your teaching?

CAMPUS PROCEDURE: Talk to Hispanic and/or black students about their high-school experiences.

1. What kinds of academic problems did they or their friends have?
2. What kinds of teachers were most helpful? Least helpful?
3. Were there differences in teacher expectations regarding their performances as compared to others?
4. Do they see any changes in college?

ANALYSIS: The student answers may be analyzed following the suggestions given in the school procedure analysis.

CHAPTER OUTLINE

10

PSYCHOMOTOR SKILLS

CHAPTER PREVIEW

When people think of school, they usually do so in terms of the teaching and learning of verbal, computational, or other intellectual skills. Thus, the major emphasis in this section so far has been on the acquisition of these aspects of schooling. However, motor behavior, as well as mental, is a vital component of a whole complex of school activities, as it is in everyday living. This is obviously the case on the playground and in the gymnasium, but it is also true for the classroom. This chapter, then, focuses on factors related to motor behavior and performance, such as motor development and the characteristics and learning of psychomotor skills.

Keep these questions in mind as you read:

- What are psychomotor skills and what factors are involved in skilled performance?
- How is motor development related to the acquisition of psychomotor skills?
- How is motor development related to students' school performance or behavior at different grade levels?
- What theories have been proposed to explain motor learning?
- What roles do practice and feedback play in perfecting motor skills?

Motor behavior is basic to the human condition. In an earlier age survival and maintenance often depended upon one's ability to extract a livelihood from nature, construct shelter, and fashion clothing. Today a complex division of labor no longer requires a high degree of self-sufficiency in making provision for ourselves and the members of our immediate family. But modern technology requires a host of new skills, including operating complicated machinery, computer programming equipment, automobiles, and jet aircraft. Further, many of our leisure activities, including playing musical instruments and participation in sports like skiing, golf, surfing, and baseball, demand a vast array of motor behaviors.

Within schools, motor skills are interwoven throughout the curriculum at all levels. Using a pencil, writing with chalk, making handwritten letters, drawing pictures, painting objects, employing measuring instruments, and walking from one place to another are all fundamental school activities. Similarly, playground activities and games in physical education involve complex and coordinated movements.

THE NATURE OF PSYCHOMOTOR SKILLS

Psychologists and educators commonly employ the term **psychomotor skills** to refer to motor skills that require neuromuscular coordination (Harrow, 1972). Motor skills are learned capabilities that find expression in processes producing expert, rapid, accurate, forceful, or smooth bodily movement (Posner and Keele, 1973; Gagné and Briggs, 1974). Separated into its two component parts, psycho and motor, the concept implies mind movement or voluntary movement. Thus, it is to be distinguished from involuntary, or reflex, movement.

Driving a car provides a good illustration of psychomotor skills. It requires that we adjust our behavior in accordance with continually changing perceptual input. Depending on environmental stimuli, we must slow down, apply the brakes, accelerate, and turn. Hence, our motor responses are linked within a complex network employing a variety of perceptual and mental operations.

Motor behavior pervades every school subject and extracurricular activity. Many activities involve manipulating an object or taking an object into account, like shooting a basketball, measuring a table top, or building a model airplane. Other activities entail fashioning symbols through bodily movements as reflected in speaking and handwriting. Still other activities have to do with the communication of attitudes, feelings, and emotions through the medium of movement as in the case of dance, the fine arts, and music (Ragsdale, 1950).

Characteristics of Psychomotor Skills

Motor skill performance has a number of characteristics (Sage, 1971). First, it requires an organized sequence of movements. Thus, a single muscle twitch is not classed as a motor skill. Rather, movement must occur with precision in speed and direction, and each muscle group must function at the proper time. For instance, in the jump shot in basketball, the ball must be released in the proper direction and propelled the right distance; knee-bending precedes elbow extension, elbow flexion precedes elbow extension, and wrist flexion takes place with the release of the ball.

A second characteristic of motor skill performance entails spatial and temporal organization. The activity requires the execution of a motor task in spatial continuity; for instance, in a tennis serve the movements of the legs, shoulders, arms, and wrists must be brought into play in a prescribed sequence if an awkward pattern is to be avoided. The motor activity simultaneously necessitates temporal organization so that a "dovetailing" or smoothness occurs from one subroutine (move-

MOTOR SKILL PERFORMANCE

Motor skill performance requires an organized sequence of movements, spatial and temporal organization, and accurate and deliberate execution.

SCORE A CURRICULUM VICTORY WITH SPORTS

ARTHUR E. SALZ

Have you used sports in your curriculum and taken advantage of the enormous fascination kids have with such activities? The opportunities are endless. Actually, this is not a new idea; it just hasn't been done to any extent in this country. The Greeks believed that athletics was a focal point of education, devoted long hours to it, and developed a balance between the physical, the aesthetic, the intellectual, and the spiritual that we have never quite attained in our education.

We're not going to talk about participation here, even though

Source: Arthur E. Salz, "Score a Curriculum Victory with Sports," Instructor, 89 (March 1980):62–64.

that is vitally important. Rather, we're going to explore ways to relate sports to the worlds of art, economics, psychology, mathematics, the social sciences, the physical and biological sciences, literature, and history. Here are some of the classroom activities appropriate for children ages ten to fourteen.

ARCHITECTURE

Kids can build scale models of such places as the Rose Bowl in Pasadena, the tennis complex at Flushing Meadow Park, a baseball stadium, or any other sports sites that come to mind. The use of graph paper, the concepts of ratio and proportion, mathematics, design, and artistic decisions

as to media, color scheme, construction materials, and so on, would all be involved in these projects.

PHYSICS AND SPORTS

What factors determine how far a baseball or golf ball curves in the air? What keeps a Frisbee flying? Why and how do quarterbacks throw spiral passes? Also, how does a bicycle work, what pushes the wheels forward, and how do its gears make pedaling easier? These kinds of problems will involve kids in the concepts of leverage, momentum, gear ratios, air pressure, aerodynamics, and other physical principles that can be appropriately examined by this age group.

ment) to the next, like in pacing the backswing in golf.

Third, motor skill performance involves accurate and deliberate execution to achieve some end. Thus, the activity is goal-directed. On occasion, the movements may be performed to conceal the ultimate objective. For example, fullbacks are taught to fold their hands close to their stomachs and to charge into the line after receiving a fake

handoff from the quarterback in order to mislead opponents.

Components of Psychomotor Skills

Paul M. Fitts (1965) surveyed forty coaches and physical education instructors at Ohio State Uni-

THE ANATOMY AND PHYSIOLOGY OF MOVEMENT

What do we mean by warming up? How does the nervous system control our every movement? Why must football linemen have quick reaction time? What role do our muscles play in moving our bones? What leverage factors are involved in running, throwing, kicking, punching, and swinging? What effect does exercise have on our cardiovascular system? What happens to pulse rate? Blood pressure? Breathing rate? Why do these changes take place? Why do we sweat? Why do we become fatigued? How long does it take to become tired? How can we postpone fatigue? How do athletes condition themselves?

GEOGRAPHY

On a map of Canada and the United States locate cities that have major league teams in baseball, football, hockey, and basketball. What is the distance between these cities in miles and kilometers? When the New York Yankees travel on a western road trip, how many miles do they cover? How many miles will the Los Angeles Dodges travel in one baseball season? On a map of the world, locate the places where the major golf, tennis, and soccer championships are held. Why does a basketball game in Portland begin at 10 P.M. in New York? Why, for that matter, are there different time zones? Why is it that if a baseball game is rained out in Cleveland on one day it usually rains in New York the next? What are the weather patterns across the United States?

THE SOCIOLOGY OF SPORTS

What are some of the basic rules in any given sport? Why were they made? How are they enforced? Who enforces them? What happens if someone violates a rule? Are all punishments the same? Do the rules apply to all players equally? What rules might you add or delete from a game to improve it? What has been the changing role of women in sports in the United States? How is it different from ten years ago? How has sexism affected women in sports? How does this compare to other fields of endeavor? Should women compete against men? In all sports?

STATISTICS

For openers, check out a baseball playing card any one of your kids might have. It's loaded with possibilities. The obvious one, of course, is figuring batting averages in class (we really mean batting percentages, or more precisely, parts of a thousand, for example, .378) but there are so many other statistics in sports. With or without the use of a calculator (its use is a natural here, however) children can figure out not only batting percentages but won-lost percentages, percentage of completed passes by a quarterback, scoring averages, average yards gained by a running back, average yards kicked by a punter, and earned-run average of a pitcher (this is not so easy to figure out). The four arith-

(continued)

versity regarding their experiences in teaching various skills. Despite the wide range of sports activities covered (football, basketball, baseball, tennis, swimming, diving, fencing, and soccer), considerable consensus existed among the instructors in the identification of four skill components.

First, many instructors stressed the cognitive aspects associated with an intellectual understanding of the task (commonly more advanced levels require judgment, decision making, strategy, and planning). Second, most instructors referred to the importance of perceptual factors in skill learning; students must learn what they are to look for, how to identify important cues, and how to make critical discriminations. Third, practically all instructors believed that coordination was vital (the ability to sequentially time successive movements with precision). And fourth, the instructors made comments

SCORE A CURRICULUM VICTORY WITH SPORTS
(continued)

metic operations with whole numbers and decimal fractions are involved here as well as concepts of ratio, average, and percentage.

ART, MOVEMENT, AND DANCE
From the Greeks to modern times, athletic endeavor has been the subject of myriad painters and sculptors. Through art books, visits to museums, filmstrips, and slides, students can be exposed to this heritage. And to really get a feel for it, have kids try their own hand at some artistic expression with sport as the subject. Photography is a good medium and marvelous photographic essays can be made of school-yard athletes in action. Setting up a darkroom would be a logical outgrowth of this type of activity. Sketching and simple modeling with clay should also be encouraged. The obvious relationship between the grace and ease of athletic movement and that of dance has been pointed out by many including the great dancer Jacques d'Ambois. His work in movement with boys, which has been publicized on television, dis-

pels the notion that dancing is a "sissy" activity. It is precisely this approach that should be emphasized in this exploration of art and sport.

LEARNING THEORY
How *does* someone learn a new motor skill such as shooting a basketball with the opposite hand, hitting a backhand in tennis, or driving a golf ball? (If our sixth-graders can figure this out, they'll make a million dollars.) Through the actual attempt to acquire a new motor skill, the students will be able to analyze the relative importance of goal setting, imitation, analysis of principles, insight, feedback, and practice, as they all relate to learning. Questions raised might deal with whether learning progress is linear, with gradual increments each session; or is there regression at certain points? Are there plateaus where learning appears to stop, and if so, when do these occur? How is the task affected by motivation, boredom, and so on? Is it possible to say that one day the skill did not exist and the next day

it did? Is learning sudden or gradual? As students go through the actual process of acquiring a new motor skill they will at the same time be investigating in the area of learning theory.

CREATING A SPORTS NEWS DESK
Students could publish a daily or weekly sports newspaper dealing not only with school events but major national items as well. As with any other paper it should contain factual reporting, analysis, editorials, features, humor, pictures, and puzzles. In addition, a radio broadcast can be developed which would announce sports news five minutes every day. This might be a natural lead-in to a full-scale current events broadcast touching on all other topics normally dealt with by the media.

SPORTS AS BIG BUSINESS
How much money are the superstars paid? How can the owners pay them so much? How much money is being made by a major baseball team? How does it make

about various personality and temperamental characteristics, such as the ability to maintain a cool, relaxed performance under tense circumstances.

Motor Development

Children's motor development is associated with their overall physical growth. For infants to crawl, walk, climb, and grasp objects with precision, they

must first reach certain levels of skeletal and muscular development. As their heads become smaller relative to their bodies, they improve their balance. Whereas the head is about one-fourth of the infant's body, it is only one-eighth of the adult's. Likewise, the trunk is a much larger portion of the infant's body than of the adult's, while the leg of the adult is proportionately twice as long as the infant's.

As children's legs become longer and stronger,

its money (ticket sales, television rights, stadium concessions, to name a few)? What is the role of media in sports? What's in it for the TV networks? The advertisers? The announcers? What is hype? How much hype is there in professional sports? How does this affect you as a spectator? How do you feel about this?

SPORTS AS UNIVERSAL PHENOMENA

Where did sports come from? What are the first records we have of sports? What sports familiar to Americans are played throughout the world? What sports are popular in other countries and less popular here? Any reasons? What sport did the American Indians invent? Where did tennis, soccer, basketball, and golf originate? Have there been many changes in a particular game since its inception? Why? A major project flowing out of this inquiry would be the actual participation in as many games and sports as possible from around the world and the compilation of a book describing each game in detail.

THE PSYCHOLOGY OF SPORT

Why are so many people interested in sports, both as participants and observers? What role does competition play? Cooperation? Is there a growing amount of violence in professional sports, especially football and hockey? Set up several "what would *you* do" role-playing situations involving cheating in a game, the importance of winning, the desire to be a star versus the team effort, the possible use of unfair physical tactics that could lead to injury, the show-off in front of others, and so on. Use these to explore some very basic feelings your kids have about sports and, whether we like it or not, about life. Avoid a "goody-goody, holier-than-thou" position. It will be death to any honest reaction by your kids.

INVENT A GAME

Challenge your kids to create a new sport. It must be one that is readily learned, can be played within the school yard, involves a significant number of participants, and can hold the interest of the

entire class. All rules must be written down, and it is the responsibility of the creator to teach the game to his classmates. Who knows, you might have another Abner Doubleday or James Naismith in your midst.

What appears above is certainly not the definitive and final word on the exciting possibility of bringing sports into your curriculum. It is, rather, a beginning look at some of the dimensions involved. No mention was made of the rich literature of sports, the biographies and autobiographies of the immortals, the histories and other accounting of dramatic moments in sports, or of the fiction of John Tunis, Ring Lardner, and others. The ore is a rich one just waiting to be mined. For the teacher who does so it might become a major step in the direction of bridging the school world with the real world in which that child resides after 3 o'clock. If placing the study of sports in the school accomplishes this, it will have served a vital role in curriculum development.

they are able to undertake new locomotive activities. As their shoulders widen and their arms lengthen, they increase their manual and mechanical capabilities. Motor development occurs in accordance with maturational processes. Certain behaviors appear when the structures and neural processes that make them possible have matured. The potential for these behaviors is built into the human organism and finds expression through interaction with the environment.

Development follows two patterns, the cephalocaudal principle and the proximodistal principle. The **cephalocaudal principle** involves development that proceeds from the head to the feet. Improvements in structure and function come first in the infant's head region, then in the trunk, and finally in the leg region. From birth to adulthood the head doubles in size, the trunk trebles in volume, the arms and hands quadruple in length, and the legs and feet grow fivefold (Bayley, 1935, 1956).

Motor development also follows this principle. Infants first learn to control the muscles of the head and neck, next their arms and abdomen, and finally their legs. When babies first begin crawling, they propel themselves with the upper part of their bodies while dragging their legs passively behind them. Likewise, infants learn to hold their heads up before they sit, and they learn to sit before they walk.

The **proximodistal principle** entails development that proceeds from near to far, outward from the central axis of the body toward the extremities. Initially, infants have to move their heads and trunks if they are to orient their hands when grasping an object. Only later do they become capable of employing their arms and legs independently, and it takes them still longer to make refined movements with their wrists and fingers. On the whole, large-muscle control precedes fine-muscle control. Kindergarten and first-grade teachers commonly find that children are somewhat more adept at activities such as jumping, climbing, and running, which involve the use of large muscles, than at activities like drawing and writing, which involve smaller muscles.

During the early teens children experience the adolescent growth spurt, a rapid increase in height and weight. Typically this spurt occurs in girls two years earlier than in boys. James M. Tanner (1972:5), an authority on adolescent growth, finds

PSYCHOMOTOR SKILLS IN PLAYGROUND ACTIVITIES
Many school activities require complex and coordinated movements.

that practically all skeletal and muscular dimensions of the body take part in the spurt, although not to an equal degree:

> Most of the spurt in height is due to acceleration of trunk length rather than length of legs. There is a fairly regular order in which the dimensions accelerate; leg length as a rule reaches its peak first, followed by the body breadths, with shoulder width last. Thus a boy stops growing out of his trousers (at least in length) a year before he stops growing out of his jackets. The earliest structures to reach their adult status are the head, hands, and feet. At adolescence, children, particularly girls, sometimes complain of having large hands and feet. They can be reassured that by the time they are fully grown their hands and feet will be a little smaller in proportion to their arms and legs, and considerably smaller in proportion to their trunk.

Asynchrony is the term developmentalists employ to describe this dissimilarity in the growth rates of different parts of the body. It has consequences for adolescent motor coordination. Many teenagers have a long-legged or coltish appearance that is commonly associated with clumsiness and misjudgments of distance. Middle-school and junior-high-school teachers in physical education encounter numerous incidents of asychrony each day. Asynchrony may lead to various minor accidents, such as tripping on or knocking over athletic equipment, benches, and tables. And it can contribute to an exaggerated sense of self-consciousness and awkwardness in adolescents.

The acceleration of muscular development during adolescence is accompanied by increases in strength, as measured by such indices as the pulling and pushing capabilities of the arms. Typically the greatest overall increment in strength takes place about one year after peak height and weight growth. The increases are greater for males than for females. Prepubescent boys and girls are roughly similar in strength, but after puberty boys become stronger. The greater strength of males is primarily a function of greater muscular development. However, other factors also play a part. Relative to their size, boys

develop larger hearts and lungs, higher systolic blood pressure, a greater ability for carrying oxygen in the blood, a lower resting heart rate, and a greater capacity to neutralize the chemical products of muscular exercise, which are experienced as fatigue (Conger, 1977).

ACQUIRING MOTOR SKILLS

Relatively little research is available on *how* children learn motor skills (Newell and Kennedy, 1978; Barclay and Newell, 1980). The field of motor development has been primarily concerned with charting the milestones of *when* children can perform different skills. Nonetheless, there are a number of theories dealing with motor learning and models for teaching motor skills.

Theories of Motor Learning

As with other areas of human behavior, psychologists have advanced a number of differing explanations of motor learning (Adams, 1977). One of the oldest of these is the *habit theory*. This view is rooted in behaviorist concepts of reinforcement, the notion that behavior is strengthened by its consequences. Certain motor activities are said to produce some sort of payoff for the organism, and hence they become entrenched within the organism's repertoire of behaviors. Such motor acts acquire habit strength and occur reliably in the presence of the appropriate environmental stimuli.

Jack A. Adams (1971, 1977), an educational psychologist, sees merit in habit theory but finds it an inadequate tool for understanding feedback mechanisms for error regulation. Habit theory depicts motor behavior as a simplistic black box operation in which input enters at one end of the box and comes out the other end as output. Adams

ACQUIRING MOTOR SKILLS
Properly chosen, playground games can provide children with the opportunity to develop
and practice many different motor skills. (© *Rick Friedman/The Picture Cube*)

contends that the approach fails to account for human compensatory capabilities. He points out that human beings do not function in the fashion of a traffic light locked into one pattern by a fixed timing device, snarling traffic when the load is heavy and impeding flow when traffic is light.

Instead, Adams advances a cybernetics, or *closed-loop, theory* of motor learning. Learning operations are seen as producing a reference mechanism, a mental specification of the correct response. As individuals engage in motor behavior, they check their movements against this internal standard. If a match occurs, the movements are maintained; if a mismatch occurs, an error is perceived and individuals make corrective adjustments. Hence, feedback and knowledge of results allow human beings to compensate for deviations from the standard. This process resembles the automatic home furnace. The thermostat setting is the reference, and the heat output of the furnace is compared against this desired value. If there is a

discrepancy, the furnace shuts on or off until the error is zero.

A third approach, the *motor program theory,* holds that motor behavior is channeled by commands originating in the brain with little moment-to-moment feedback guidance (Lashley and Ball, 1929). The nervous system is seen as activating responses based on *prior* programming. However, feedback stimuli may provide information from time to time that leads to an updating of the internal motor program.

A fourth view, the *recall schema theory,* says that motor behavior does not derive from habits or programmed mental traces but from a plan or mental model for behaving (Bartlett, 1932). Responses are "manufactured" by individuals on the basis of a small number of cognitive schemes. Versatility is viewed as a function of *applying* concepts or rules to specific situations—fitting bodily movements to the dictates of environmental conditions.

Although we would all prefer certainty regarding the nature of motor behavior, very little could be written about psychology or education if we had to wait for certainty. These contrasting theories, however, highlight the nature of the problem that various theorists are attempting to resolve.

Phases in Learning Motor Skills

The basic model for motor training in the schools remains essentially the same everywhere: explanation, demonstration, drill in basic skills, practice in integrating activities, and actual task performance. Paul M. Fitts and Michael I. Posner (1967) distinguish three main phases in learning motor skills:

1. *Early, or cognitive, phase:* Beginners initially attempt to "understand" the task and its demands. It is helpful if the instructor assists learners in identifying the component subparts of a skill, demonstrates each, and allows learners to practice each in turn. For example, swimmers may first be taught the kick, arm and hand movements, head positioning, and breathing techniques as part-skills. Learners are

---

AS THEY MOVE THEY LEARN

LEONA M. FOERSTER
Texas Technical University, Lubbock

Physical education activities can teach, reinforce, and enrich the communication skills of children. At first this may seem to be a rather unlikely combination, but as I tried to correlate language instruction with other subject areas, there seemed to be many possibilities for oral language development and listening through motor activities, games, and unstructured play.

When the school setting is

Source: Leona M. Foerster, "As They Move They Learn," *Instructor*, 81 (March 1972):59.

strange and perhaps even frightening for children, it may be very difficult to get them to talk enough to show their facility in oral English. So, at the beginning of the year I found it helpful to observe carefully the children on the playground during their "free play" period to see how readily and how well they communicated in English. While teaching games at the beginning of the school year, I saw how well children could listen and follow directions. I also noted their facility in oral language. Observations made in play situations would seem to be a little more realistic and effective than classroom observations, since they show how pupils function in life experiences outside of school. Once aware of pupils' facilities in these areas, teachers can develop them further.

LISTENING SKILLS
Attentive listening skills are best taught in meaningful situations. Listening is crucial if children are to learn how to line up, make a circle, count off, and so on, in order to play a game. Attentive listening requires that the listener

(continued)

AS THEY MOVE THEY LEARN
(continued)

avoid distractions and concentrate on one form of communication with a great deal of involvement. This does not come easily for children who have learned to "tune out" even before they come to school. But they can readily see the importance of concentrated listening in order to participate in some exciting activities on the playground. This becomes even more apparent if they fail to listen and consequently miss out on participating because they are unable to follow the directions.

Getting the children's attention is prerequisite to giving directions. Prearranged voice and hand signals work well with students, although at times a bell, whistle, drum, or other instrument will vary the procedure and be just as effective. Introducing the children to many different games during the year provides opportunities for meaningful attentive listening and for following different sets of directions. Initially I had to be cautious, making directions brief and simple, and increasing complexity and length only gradually. By the end of the year, much growth was noted. There was transfer into the classroom setting, with children becoming more attentive and better equipped to follow directions vital to classroom learning.

CONCEPTS AND VOCABULARY
Concept building and vocabulary building go hand in hand. They involve discrimination activities, classification, and verbal labeling.

How I struggled in the classroom to develop concepts and vocabulary on spatial relations! Then I decided to work on them during the physical education period. As we used balls, beanbags, and Indian clubs on the playground, as well as hands, feet, and other body parts, we considered such spatial relationships as *in, out, up, down, over, under, on top of, beneath, beside, between, here, there, to the right, to the left,* and so on. Children were actively involved with their whole bodies as they mastered these relationships. Further, play situations gave many opportunities for reinforcing labels for parts of the body.

Vocabulary related to such motor activities as *walk, step, jump, run, skip, hop, throw, catch, push, pull,* and the like was also developed as children actively participated in activities. This provided great kinesthetic reinforcement and helped make some of the words in our books come alive as children associated these words with their own recent pleasurable play experiences.

Not to be overlooked is the concept and vocabulary development related to the play equipment used. *Slide, ladder, rope, swing, ball, beanbag, jacks, marbles,* and so on, plus words related to the directions given in some of our activities which re-

ferred to *partners, twos, lines, circles, start, finish, sit, stand,* can be clarified and expanded for children out on the playground.

ORAL EXPRESSION
Children who are reluctant to participate actively in oral class activities often relax out on the playground and actively join in. I found it profitable to "draw out" my shyer students on the playground before trying to elicit responses within the classroom. During unstructured play activities, it was more rewarding to listen and talk with small groups of children engaged in activities of their choice than to stand at the side and attempt to "supervise" all the groups at once. The latter may be an assignment for an aide, freeing the teacher to proceed from one group of children to another, listening and talking with them, encouraging them and drawing them out with questions.

Structured physical education activities may also be used to encourage oral fluency by having children repeat directions, talk about what they are doing while they are doing it, learn games with verbal responses, and the like.

Play experiences provide a great medium for strengthening communication skills in a meaningful and purposeful way!

typically aware of a good many cues that later will go unnoticed; for instance, the inexperienced automobile driver looks for the pedals, and beginning typists may watch their fingers. Indeed, beginners commonly rely on visual feedback and only later develop sensitivity to cues associated with touch and pressure. Movements tend to be gross and effortful. During this stage, the task remains a collection of individual operations that bear only a superficial resemblance to the integrated performance of experienced individuals.

2. *Intermediate, or associative, phase:* As learning progresses, learners become increasingly sophisticated in performing the new patterns, and inappropriate responses are gradually eliminated. Feedback from other senses comes to supplement or minimize visual cues. The part-skills become progressively integrated in sequential order so that each part of the movement becomes the signal for the next.

3. *Final, or autonomous, phase:* In the final phase of motor skill learning, individuals no longer need to ''think about what to do next.'' The skill is said to be *autonomous* in that it can be executed while individuals are engaged in some other activity like conversing while driving an automobile. Hence, the movement pattern requires little conscious attention or cognitive regulation. At this point, conscious introspection may impair smooth performance. Now the eyes and ears, freed from their control functions, can concentrate on fine-tuning or the monitoring of relevant environmental stimuli.

Practice

Practice makes perfect.

EARLY ENGLISH PROVERB

One of the more obvious facts of learning a motor skill is that improvement occurs with practice. Skills like writing, shooting a basketball, typing, driving a car, and hitting a tennis ball must be practiced a good many times if they are to be performed effectively and efficiently. **Practice** involves repetition of a procedure with the intention of improving performance and securing appropriate feedback (Gagné, 1977). Practice allows individuals to increase the speed, the precision, and the accuracy of their performance (Sage, 1971).

Psychologists and educators are interested in identifying the optimum conditions of practice. One question is whether practice trials should be *massed* or *spaced*. The answer in part depends on the nature of the task. An operation requiring a substantial memory component may suffer if the lapses between sessions are too long. On the other hand, excessive repetition of a task without intervals of rest produces fatigue and boredom (Sage, 1971). It is generally recognized that a massing of trials depresses performance. However, a number of studies suggest that performance recovers after an interval of rest, reaching the same level over the long term as that of learners given distributed practice (McGeoch and Irion, 1952; Whitely, 1970). Thus, some authorities believe that the amount of practice is more important than its distribution.

Another question is whether learners should practice the entire task or should break the task up into its parts and practice them. The answer again depends on the nature of the skill. Some tasks involve the concurrent performance of several independent actions. Driving a car provides a good illustration of this kind of task, one in which it is advantageous to master the parts first (starting the engine, shifting, braking, turning, accelerating, parking, and so on). Other tasks depend on the synchronization of the subskills. Here timing becomes a critical feature as in driving a golf ball. Accordingly, the sooner the skill can be performed in its entirety, the better the results tend to be. Individual differences among learners also have a bearing on whether whole or part practice is more beneficial.

FEEDBACK IN MOTOR SKILLS
Among other functions, feedback enables us to adjust our motor behavior to reach a desired goal. Thus feedback permits the boy shown here to maneuver successfully from peg to peg. (© *Andrew Brilliant/The Picture Cube*)

Feedback

Much motor learning occurs through feedback. **Feedback** refers to information we receive about some performance or the consequences of the performance (Stallings, 1973). Feedback has a number of functions. First, it provides information that allows us to make adjustments in our responses in order to reach some desired objective. Second, feedback has reinforcing properties that derive from the rewarding effect of correct performance and the punishing effect of incorrect performance. And third, it provides motivation by ensuring an increase in interest level (Ammons, 1956; Sage, 1971). The corrective, reinforcing, and motivating influences of feedback make it one of the strongest and most important factors controlling motor performance (Bilodeau and Bilodeau, 1961; Nixon and Locke, 1973).

Feedback may be intrinsic or extrinsic. *Intrinsic feedback* refers to cues that we obtain from our own responses. For instance, professional baseball players develop a "feel" from the swing of their bats that allows them to distinguish between good and poor execution; violinists gain information from the tones they hear and from the feelings produced by their fingers pressing against the strings to inform them about the adequacy of each component in the movement pattern.

Extrinsic feedback involves information we receive from others about our performance. Beginners often overlook important cues regarding their performances. Instructors can provide advice and inform students what they are doing wrong. Recent technological innovations in photography, recording, and videotaping provide helpful aids for critically assessing performance.

The immediacy of feedback plays an important part in its effectiveness. In some cases, the adequacy of the response is readily apparent. For instance, the basketball either goes through the hoop or it misses; a tennis ball either goes out of bounds or lands in bounds. If the training has been limited, withdrawal of feedback results in a deterioration of performance (the effects are less noticeable after extended training) (Ellis, 1972). For instance, when we are learning to play golf, hitting a number of golf balls with no knowledge regarding the results typically produces no gains.

Children's ability to evaluate knowledge of results and to use this knowledge to improve motor performance improves with age (Newell and Kennedy, 1978; Barclay and Newell, 1980). This finding is consistent with other developmental research that reveals that as children grow older and gain experience, they become more capable in problem-solving situations. Presumably this adaptive ability is associated with knowledge derived from a response outcome that children use to adjust their behavior. Children in the early elementary grades do not perform as well as older children in processing information associated with knowledge of results and in using this information to meet better various task requirements.

CHAPTER SUMMARY

1. Motor skill performance has a number of characteristics. First, it requires an organized sequence of movements. Second, it entails spatial and temporal organization. And third, it involves accurate and deliberate execution to achieve some end.

2. Considerable consensus exists among coaches and physical education instructors in the identification of four motor skill components. First, many instructors stress the cognitive aspects associated with an intellectual understanding of the task (commonly more advanced levels require judgment, decision making, strategy, and planning). Second, most instructors referred to the importance of perceptual factors in skill learning; students must learn what they are to look for, how to identify important cues, and how to make critical discriminations. Third, practically all instructors believe that coordination is vital. And fourth, instructors mention various personality and temperamental characteristics, such as the ability to maintain a cool, relaxed performance under tense circumstances.

3. Children's motor development is associated with their overall physical growth. Development follows two patterns, the cephalocaudal principle and the proximodistal principle. The cephalocaudal principle involves development that proceeds from the head to the feet. The proximodistal principle entails development that proceeds from near to far, outward from the central axis of the body toward the extremities. During the early teens children experience the adolescent growth spurt, a rapid increase in height and weight. Asynchrony is the term developmentalists employ to describe the dissimilarity in the growth rates of different parts of the body during adolescence. It has consequences for adolescent motor coordination. The acceleration of muscular development during adolescence is accompanied by increases in strength.

4. As with other areas of human behavior, psychologists have advanced a number of different explanations of motor learning. One of the oldest of these is habit theory. This view is rooted in behaviorist concepts of reinforcement, the notion that behavior is strengthened by its consequences. A second approach is a cybernetics, or closed-loop, theory of motor learning. Learning operations are seen as producing a reference mechanism, a mental specification of the correct response. A third approach, the motor program theory, holds that motor behavior is channeled by commands originating in the brain with little moment-to-moment feedback guidance. A fourth view, the

recall schema theory, says that motor behavior does not derive from habits or programmed mental traces but from a plan or mental model for behaving.

5. There are three main phases in learning motor skills: the early, or cognitive, phase, in which beginners initially attempt to ''understand'' the task and its demands; the intermediate, or associative, phase, in which the part-skills become progressively integrated in sequential order so that each part of the movement becomes the signal for the next; and the final, or autonomous, phase, in which the skill requires little conscious attention or cognitive regulation.

6. One of the most obvious facts of learning a motor skill is that improvement occurs with practice. Psychologists and educators are interested in the distribution of practice (whether trials should be massed or spaced) and with whole-part learning (whether learners should practice the entire task or should break the task up into its parts and practice these).

7. The corrective, reinforcing, and motivating influences of feedback make it one of the strongest and most important factors controlling motor performance. Feedback may be intrinsic or extrinsic. Intrinsic feedback refers to cues we obtain from our own responses. Extrinsic feedback involves information we receive from others about our performance.

CHAPTER GLOSSARY

asynchrony Dissimilarity in the growth rates of different parts of the body; a process prevalent during adolescence

cephalocaudal principle A developmental pattern that proceeds from the head to the feet.

feedback The information we receive about some performance or the consequences of the performance.

practice Repetition of a procedure with the intention of improving performance and securing appropriate feedback.

proximodistal principle A developmental pattern that proceeds from near to far, outward from the central axis of the body toward the extremities.

psychomotor skills Motor skills that require neuromuscular coordination. Motor skills are learned capabilities and find expression in those processes producing expert, rapid, accurate, forceful, or smooth bodily movement.

EXERCISES

Review Questions

1. The example that would *not* be considered a psychomotor skill is
   a. kicking a soccer ball
   b. breathing deeply and slowly
   c. serving a tennis ball
   d. jogging
   e. a, b, c, and d are all psychomotor skills

2. One characteristic of a motor skill is that
   a. movements must be organized sequentially
   b. some end must be achieved
   c. organization may either be spatial or temporal, but not both
   d. a, b, and c
   e. a and b

3. An example of cephalocaudal development is that an infant
   a. can deliberately move its head before turning the body
   b. learns to sit before walking
   c. begins crawling by using the upper part of the body
   d. a, b, and c are true
   e. b and c are true

4. Which of the following illustrates the proximodistal principle of development?

    a. An infant orients a grasping response by moving the head and trunk.
    b. Fine-muscle control precedes large-muscle control.
    c. Generally kindergarten children are as adept at drawing as they are in climbing.
    d. Wrist control precedes independence of arms and legs.

5. According to Tanner, a characteristic of the adolescent growth spurt is that

    a. girls generally start their growth spurt about two years ahead of boys
    b. the growth patterns for both boys and girls can be generally characterized as symmetrical
    c. the greatest overall increment in strength occurs simultaneously with the peak in height and weight growth
    d. a and b are true

6. The increased strength of pubescent boys as compared to girls appears to be due to

    a. greater muscular development
    b. differences in cardiovascular size and functioning
    c. fewer chemical products resulting from muscular exercise
    d. a and b are true

7. The capacity of the individual to adjust a motor skill to a new situation is best explained by the which motor learning theory?

    a. habit
    b. cybernetic
    c. motor program
    d. recall schema

8. The motor learning theory that minimizes the impact of feedback is

    a. habit
    b. cybernetics
    c. motor program
    d. recall schema

9. The Fitts-Posner model of motor learning is based on three phases. The order of development is

    a. associative, cognitive, autonomous
    b. cognitive, associative, autonomous
    c. associative, autonomous, cognitive
    d. There is no sequential development implied.

10. Feedback serves a number of functions, including

    a. motivational
    b. corrective
    c. reinforcing
    d. a, b, and c are true

Answers

1. e (See p. 284)
2. e (See pp. 284, 286)
3. d (See pp. 289–290)
4. a (See p. 290)
5. a (See pp. 290–291)
6. d (See p. 291)
7. d (See pp. 290–292)
8. c (See p. 292)
9. b (See pp. 293, 295)
10. d (See pp. 296–297)

Applying Principles and Concepts

1. Following are a number of comments made by coaches about instructions they have given their athletes. Check those that could be supported by the Fitts (1965) study at Ohio State.

_____ a. "I'll tell my quarterback that unless he can read the defenses he will never do well."

_____ b. "Whatever else you can say, fencing is such a uniquely different sport that the general rules of coaching don't apply.''

_____ c. ''Temperamentally, girls are not suited for contact sports.''

_____ d. ''My best pitchers stay loose no matter what the game situation is like.''

2. An eighth-grade teacher is likely to hear which of the following statements by the students?

a. Pubescent girl: ''My hands and feet are just too big.''

b. Prepubescent boy: ''A lot of the girls are bigger and taller than I am.''

c. Prepubescent girl: ''Boys are always stronger than girls.''

d. Pubescent boy: ''My mother complains that I am always falling over or knocking over things in the house.''

3. The text suggests a number of theories of motor learning, including the habit (H) and closed-loop (L) theories. Indicate by an H or an L the theory represented by each of these behavior descriptions.

_____ a. Linda is cooking her favorite spaghetti sauce. As she adds spices, she adjusts the amounts to achieve ''just the right taste.''

_____ b. Sam has just hit the baseball well over the fence and immediately cocks his bat as he did before the swing.

_____ c. As Mike connects some wires in a high-voltage circuit, he keeps visualizing to himself the appropriate pattern. Suddenly he stops; something is out of place.

_____ d. Elizabeth taps her racquet twice before serving. All she knows is that if she fails to do it, her serve suffers.

4. A well-known football coach has written extensively about his technique for teaching blocking. Underline in the following passage those statements that appear to have been substantiated by research.

At the beginning I break down blocking, for example, into parts. In the end the player executes the block without worrying about how he's blocking. I try to spread practice over a period of time, and I don't give them too much to do at any one time. I also insist they practice each part of the block separately. And I watch my kids carefully; I tell them what they're doing. They seem to do better and like it when I explain their mistakes.

5. The following are examples of feedback. Indicate whether the example is indicative of intrinsic (I) or extrinsic (E) feedback.

_____ a. The player notices he has ''broken a sweat.''

_____ b. The coach tells his player, ''Let me know if the helmet is too snug.''

_____ c. A driver advises the shop mechanic that ''the steering doesn't feel right.''

_____ d. The wife hears her husband say, ''I think you put in too much salt in the stew.''

Answers

1. a, d (See pp. 286–287)
2. a, b, d (See p. 291)
3. a, L; b, H; c, L; d, H (See pp. 291–292)
4. Underline ''break down . . . into parts,'' ''executes the block without worrying about how he's blocking,'' ''spread practice,'' ''don't give them too much to do at any one time,'' ''watch my kids . . . tell them what they're doing,'' ''they seem to do better and like it.'' (See pp. 295–297)
5. a, I; b, both (player uses intrinsic feedback to advise coach); c, I; d, E (See pp. 296–297)

Project 1

OBJECTIVE: To determine what kinds of psychomotor skills are taught to kindergarten and first-grade children.

PROCEDURE: Visit the kindergarten or first-grade classroom. Ask the teacher the following questions:

1. What kinds of motor skills do you assume the child will have on entering?

2. What percentage of your children do not have these skills?

3. To what do you attribute these differences?

4. What kinds of motor skills do you teach as part of class?

5. Can you give me an example of how you would teach one such skill? What provisions are made for practice and feedback?

6. Do you have any alternative methods?

ANALYSIS: Compare your findings with those presented on pp. 291–297. Does the teacher seem to have any implicit or explicit theory of the acquisition of motor skills? What assumptions are made about the use of practice and feedback? In your opinion are the practices likely to be effective?

Project 2

OBJECTIVE: To determine the kinds of problems associated with junior- and senior-high-school sports.

PROCEDURE: Ask the physical education majors in the class to explain their approach to coaching and sports. Sample questions might include:

1. What are some of the advantages and disadvantages of participating in junior- and senior-high-school varsity sports? Do these differ from sport to sport? (Include in the discussion academic, social, emotional, and physical considerations.)

2. Would you consider more coed participation in sports that do not depend primarily on size and strength, for example, soccer? What would be the advantages and disadvantages?

ANALYSIS: The answers should give you some insight into the kinds of problems and decisions you will have to make eventually as a member of a school faculty, and how much uniformity and variance there are with respect to problems in junior- and senior-high-school and/or among sports.

CHAPTER OUTLINE

11

THE AFFECTIVE DOMAIN

CHAPTER PREVIEW

Just as the picture of schooling is incomplete without consideration of the role of motor skills in learning tasks and other school activities, so is it clearly inadequate without close attention to the pervasive influence of *affective factors* in school life. As this chapter will illustrate, students' attitudes toward school and about themselves affect their academic performance and behavior, and conversely, success—or failure—in school profoundly influences their conceptions of themselves. Likewise, students bring different values and differing conceptions of "right" and "wrong" to school. In turn, both explicit and implicit sets of values underlie the school curriculum. While educators may agree, in general, about the role of such factors in school, there is less agreement about whether schools should attempt to teach values directly or even to make students more aware of various moral choices. These issues are considered in depth in this chapter.

As you read, think carefully about the implications of the following questions:

■ How do children develop either positive or negative attitudes toward school or some aspect of it?
■ What is a person's self-concept, and how do children develop their self-concepts?
■ Why have there been different conclusions concerning the attitude of black children toward themselves?
■ What can or should schools do to help promote sound psychological growth in children?
■ What factors influence children's moral behavior?
■ How do three approaches to moral education differ as to intent, basic premises, and programs?

We must shift the emphasis from the three R's to the fourth R, human relations, and place it first, foremost, and always in the order of importance as a principle reason for the existence of the school. . . . We must train for humanity, and training in reading, writing and arithmetic must be given in a manner calculated to serve the ends of that humanity. For all the knowledge in the world is worse than useless if it is not humanely understood and humanely used. An intelligence that is not humane is the worst thing in the world.

ASHLEY MONTAGU
On Being Human, 1966

Too often we think of children as receptacles into which teachers pour knowledge that can then be inspected on test days. Such a view strips education of much of its vitality. It portrays children as isolated objects operating in a social vacuum. Yet, human elements pervade every aspect of the learning situation. The **affective domain**—all those aspects of human behavior involving feelings, emotions, tastes, preferences, values, attitudes, morals, character, philosophies of life, and guiding principles—plays a critical part in enhancing or blocking learning (Ringness, 1975).

Over the past two decades humanistic psychologists and educators such as Carl R. Rogers (1970), Abraham H. Maslow (1955, 1967, 1968, 1970), and Arthur W. Combs (Combs, Avila, and Purkey, 1971) have championed the view that education should take into account the whole human being— the total person. Seen from this perspective, education that imparts information while neglecting personal growth is inadequate and distorted. Indeed, the humanists say that such an education is potentially dangerous and destructive. They fear that its insensitivity to the human condition—its lack of "heart" and "soul"—all too often ends up fashioning individuals in its own sterile, frigid, callous image.

There are at least four reasons that affective goals are appropriate for the schools (Payne, 1974). First, affective factors influence learning. How students feel about themselves, others, their teachers, and the subject matter influences the progress they make toward the attainment of classroom goals (Ripple, 1965; Domino, 1971; Bodoin and Pikunas, 1977).

Second, affective factors influence people's ability to participate effectively within a democratic society. Individuals must be able to interact with others whether these others be young or old, men or women, black or white, liberal or conservative. The ability of people to live in modern societies— to maintain themselves and meet their needs— requires that they become sensitive to and respectful of other people's life-styles.

Third, affective factors play a large part in occupational and vocational satisfaction (Payne, 1974). This means that individuals must relate effectively to others, enjoy their work, feel that they can put their abilities to good use, and believe that they are making a contribution to society.

And fourth, it is important that individuals develop those abilities and skills to lay the foundation for a healthy and effective life. They must be able to adapt to new life circumstances and cope with stress and anxiety when these conditions present themselves. In sum, they must be able to meet the changes that occur in their lives and modify and adjust their behavior accordingly.

ATTITUDES AND SCHOOLING

Learning results in establishing attitudes that influence people's choices of action. An **attitude** is a learned and relatively enduring tendency to evaluate a person, event, or situation in a certain way and to act in accordance with that evaluation (Vander Zanden, 1984). It constitutes an *inclination* to respond in a given way, not the actual response itself. Thus, an attitude is a *state of mind* that makes certain classes of responses more or less probable (Warner and De Fleur, 1969; Wicker, 1969; Ajzen and Fishbein, 1973).

Prejudice provides a good illustration of an attitude. Prejudiced individuals may be disposed

relationship does not necessarily exist between the two factors.

Developing Attitudes Toward School

Schools are hardly neutral settings. Events take place continuously and have consequences for each person's sense of worth, adequacy, and security, aspects that touch the very core of one's sense of well-being. As such, these events mold the attitudes children develop toward school.

Students are commonly provided with some quantitative index (a mark or a grade) by the teacher based upon their performance on some learning task. In turn, children often appraise their success by inferring whether the teacher approves or disapproves of them and their work. Where students secure evidence that they performed a task superbly, they are likely to approach the next task in the series with enthusiasm and confidence. But it is the opposite for children who receive negative feedback.

Over a long series of learning tasks, students come to rate their capability with regard to given types of tasks as low, moderate, or high. For instance, by the end of third grade, students in the top fifth and bottom fifth of their math classes (as determined by achievement tests) feel quite differently toward mathematics. On a five-point scale measuring positive or negative attitudes toward mathematics, the top students are nearly two points higher than the lower students by the end of the third year; these differences persist in the eleventh grade (Bloom, 1977).

As the school year continues and as one year follows the next, the various indices accumulate; students begin to generalize about their adequacy or inadequacy in *school* learning tasks. Many studies have investigated the relationship between school achievement and the feelings that students have regarding school. Although no simple one-to-one relationship emerges, it does appear that

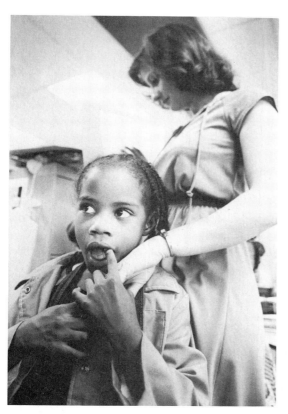

SHAPING SCHOOL ATTITUDES
Affective factors play a major role in influencing students' attitudes toward school and their academic performance.

to discriminate against members of another group. But this predisposition is no guarantee that they will, in fact, translate their state of mind into overt behavior. For example, when department stores in New York City first hired black sales personnel in the 1940s, some whites were displeased. Many of these whites nonetheless purchased merchandise from black clerks. They did so because they could not complete their shopping quickly and expediently if they engaged in discriminatory actions (Saenger and Gilbert, 1950). Thus, while attitudes influence actions and prejudiced individuals are more likely to discriminate against given groups of people than the less prejudiced, a one-to-one

ATTITUDES TOWARD MATHEMATICS

Over the past decade educators and psychologists have displayed a growing interest in student attitudes toward various subject areas, particularly mathematics (Aiken, 1970, 1976). A variety of measuring instruments has been developed for assessing *mathophobia,* anxiety in the presence of mathematics. When attitude scores derived from these measures are used as predictors of students' achievement in mathematics, a low but significant positive correlation is usually found between attitudes and performance. This finding holds across all levels of education from elementary to postgraduate schooling. And it holds true for students in other countries as well. An occasional study reports that attitude is the most important predictor of performance in mathematics, but most researchers find it secondary to ability as a forecaster of achievement.

Attitudes toward mathematics involve a complex interaction among student and teacher characteristics, course content, method of instruction, instructional materials, and parental and peer support (Aiken, 1976). Certainly, one of the most critical factors is the effect that teachers' attitudes have on students' attitudes (Phillips, 1973). One authority, Walcott H. Beatty, observes:

Arithmetic is not inherently unpleasant for any child. It becomes unpleasant when it doesn't make sense, when wrong answers lead to embarrassment, or when the child is judged inadequate because he does not perform as rapidly or accurately as someone else. [1976:279]

Another educator, John H. Banks, points out:

An unhealthy attitude toward arithmetic may result from a number of causes. Parental attitude may be responsible. . . . Repeated failure is almost certain to produce a bad emotional reaction to the study of arithmetic. Attitudes of his peers will have their effects upon the child's attitude. But by far the most significant contributing factor is the attitude of the teacher. The teacher who feels insecure, who dreads and dislikes the subject, for whom arithmetic is largely rote manipulation, devoid of understanding, cannot avoid transmitting her feelings to the children. . . . On the other hand, the teacher who has confidence, understanding, interest, and enthusiasm for arithmetic has gone a long way toward insuring success. [1964:16–17]

In recent years a number of behavior therapy techniques have been employed to decrease anx-

ATTITUDES TOWARDS MATHEMATICS
A student's achievement in mathematics tends to be related to his other attitudes toward mathematics.

iety toward mathematics. Most of these procedures expose the student to progressively more stressful mathematical activities while building upon techniques to promote relaxation. The results of these desensitization procedures are encouraging. However, although decreasing anxiety toward mathematics, desensitization does not always improve attitudes toward the subject or performance in it (Aiken, 1976).

academic success promotes satisfaction with school, which, in turn, increases the probability of future successes (Khan and Weiss, 1973; Good, Biddle, and Brophy, 1975; Marjoribanks, 1976). On the other hand, where students encounter repeated evidence of their inadequacy, they come to view the school as the source of their discomfort. They may then respond by retreating, attacking, or minimizing the school's effect upon them (Bloom, 1977).

Self-Attitudes

Treat people as if they were what they ought to be and you help them to become what they are capable of being.
JOHANN W. VON GOETHE

We acquire our attitudes in the course of interaction with others in a social environment. The same principle holds true of our self-attitudes. Indeed, no attitudes may be more important to us than the attitudes we have regarding ourselves. Not only do our self-attitudes influence our psychological sense of well-being, but what we think of ourselves and how we feel about ourselves affect our behavior. Many authorities believe that children and adults alike can have no stronger ally in life than a strong and positive self-concept.

Psychologists employ the term **self-concept** to refer to how individuals perceive themselves—the sum total of all the characteristics they attribute to themselves based on the roles they play and the personal attributes that they believe they possess (Beane, Lipka, and Ludewig, 1980). A related concept is self-esteem. **Self-esteem** refers to the positive or negative judgments individuals attach to these characteristics. Within many disciplines the notion of self-concept is coming to be recognized as one of the most useful integrative terms yet developed for understanding behavior. Self-concept involves both cognitive and affective components—mental "scripts" or frames by which we select and process information about ourselves and the feelings or emotions that we develop regarding these images. No aspect of school life is left untouched by the self-concepts that its members

SELF-ATTITUDES
Children's self-appraisals tend to reflect the appraisals they secure from others and the feedback they receive regarding their power and competence in the world about them.

hold of themselves, be it in the realm of social relationships, school discipline, academic achievement, or decisions for remaining in or dropping out of school. Likewise researchers have found that self-concept is associated with participation in class discussions, self-seating in a classroom, self-rewarding behaviors, self-direction in learning, and prosocial behavior (Ames and Felker, 1979; Dykman and Reis, 1979; Wylie, 1979; Beane Lipka, and Ludewig, 1980).

In the course of their daily lives, children receive continual cues regarding their desirability, worth, and status from parents, teachers, and peers. From the accepting and rejecting behaviors of others,

BUILDING POSITIVE SELF-CONCEPTS

ANN SURVANT
Hunter College

No students of human development will deny the importance of helping a child build a positive self-concept. Its relation to personality development, academic success, and mental well-being has been demonstrated time and time again. And as teachers we know that helping children see themselves in a positive light is one of our most important jobs.

What, specifically, are characteristic behaviors that help to tell us what kind of self-image a child has? And what can we do to promote development of a positive self-image?

Though all children are different, the behavior of a "typical"

Source: Ann Survant, "Building Positive Self-Concepts," *Instructor,* 81 (February 1972):94–95.

kindergarten child with a positive self-concept might be described like this: He

- Is unafraid in a new situation because he has a history of past successes when confronting new experiences.
- Makes friends with other children easily.
- Experiments eagerly with all kinds of new materials. Shows enthusiasm for new activities.
- Trusts his teacher although he or she is an adult and likely to be a stranger to him.
- Is cooperative and can usually follow reasonable rules.
- Is largely responsible for controlling his own behavior and can, to some extent, predict future outcomes of his behavior.

- Is creative, imaginative, and has ideas of his own.
- Talks freely and may have difficulty listening to others because of his eagerness to share his own experiences.
- Is independent, wanting, perhaps needing, only a minimum amount of help or direction from his teacher.
- Seems for the most part to be a happy individual.

Some of the characteristics of a child who has a poor self-image may reflect the opposite of characteristics listed above. A behavior profile of such a child might contain some of the following descriptions:

- He may be reluctant to enter into any new situation or to try

children are told the answers to the questions, "Who am I?" "What kind of person am I?" and "How valued am I?" Central to the writings of psychologists such as Carl R. Rogers (1970) and Benjamin S. Bloom (1977), social psychologists such as Charles Horton Cooley (1902, 1909) and George Herbert Mead (1934), and neo-Freudian psychiatrists such as Harry Stack Sullivan (1947, 1953) is the notion that people discover themselves in the behavior of others toward them.

Viewed from this perspective, individuals' self-appraisals tend to be *reflected appraisals*. If children are accepted, approved, respected, and liked for what they are, they acquire attitudes of self-acceptance and self-respect (Coopersmith, 1967; Sears, 1970; Gecas, 1971, 1972). But this is not true for those children who are belittled, blamed, and rejected by the significant people in their lives.

any new activity.

- He may have difficulty leaving one activity to go on to another, or may choose the same activity day after day until he acquires confidence to try something else.
- He may be particularly reluctant to enter into activity that involves close physical contact.
- He may be an isolate or cling only to one friend, or may force himself on other children.
- He is likely to talk only to his teacher or talk very little.
- He may be possessive of objects and make excessive demands on teacher's time.
- He may withdraw or be overly aggressive in his behavior toward the teacher and other children.
- He may react often with signs of frustration, characterized by tears or anger.
- His behavior in general does not suggest he is a happy child.

Sometimes a child shows few signs of being aware of his identity as a separate individual. He behaves as if he were an extension of his mother, his father, or an undefined member of his family.

Such a child might behave in the following manner:

- Seldom shows any initiative.
- Relies heavily on other children or the teacher for direction.
- Hesitates to do anything without first asking permission to do so, even where rules have been defined that grant permission.
- Almost always does precisely as he is told, sometimes in what might be called robot fashion.
- Seldom shows enthusiasm or spontaneity.

What can you do to encourage the development of healthy self-concepts?

- Give the child tasks which are interesting and challenging but within his range of ability so he can succeed and enjoy the feeling of accomplishment.
- Give him a lot of verbal reinforcement and encouragement.
- Accept the things he does. Comment honestly and positively about them. If you feel you can't comment honestly about something specific, re-

ward with a general comment such as "You've worked very hard today. I appreciate it."

- Help him feel he is an important member of the group.
- Solicit his suggestions and use them. Make him feel that his ideas are worthy and important.
- Listen to the child attentively. When he asks you something, stop what you are doing, get down on his eye level, and give him your undivided attention.
- After talking with him about it, bring some of his work before the group. Do it in such a way that it does not embarrass him.
- Show him your respect and consideration, and make him know that you value him as a unique human being.
- Be patient with his actions and slow to judge him.
- Give him opportunities to make choices and decisions (but not so many that he becomes confused or overwhelmed).

Remember that as a teacher you act as a model of behavior and the children's behavior is influenced by your example.

For the most part, an accumulating body of research has supported the postulate that we hold the keys to one another's self-concepts (Goffman, 1959; Gergen, 1965, 1971, 1972; Quarantelli and Cooper, 1966; Bloom, 1977).

Our self-concepts also derive from the feedback we receive regarding our power and competence in the world about us (Franks and Marolla, 1976). As we interact with others and our material envi-

ronment, we gain a sense of our energy, skill, and industry. Thus, we are not simply passive beings who mirror others' attitudes toward us; we *actively* shape our self-concepts as we encounter and cope with the realities of life (Wrong, 1961; Turner, 1962; Vander Zanden, 1984).

Psychologists and educators have been interested in the relationship between pupils' self-concepts and their academic performance (Shavelson and

Bolus, 1982). Students find that tests are as indigenous to the school environment as are textbooks and chalkboards. Bloom (1977) notes that the evaluations students receive of themselves in school-related tasks are consistent. Consequently, students commonly develop a deep sense of either adequacy or inadequacy in connection with school activities. When this feedback is generalized over a number of years. Bloom says that the object of appraisal becomes progressively shifted from the subject matter to the self. Hence, in Bloom's view the consistency of the appraisals students receive over the course of several years has a major effect on their academic self-concepts.

In support of his position. Bloom cites a study undertaken in three schools of a middle-class Chicago suburb (Kifer, 1973). The research revealed that first- and second-grade students are similar in their self-evaluations of ability despite differences in actual scholastic performance. But in each grade thereafter through junior high school, the achievement groups become increasingly differentiated in their academic self-concepts, with poor performers showing a steady drop in their self-appraisals.

Minority-Group Self-Attitudes

I have a dream that my four little children will one day live in a nation where they will not be judged by the color of their skin but by the content of their character.

MARTIN LUTHER KING, JR.
Speech, June 15, 1963

The notion that blacks suffer debilitating effects from the psychological stresses associated with racism found wide support in both the popular and the scholarly literature prior to the late 1960s (McCarthy and Yancey, 1971; Zirkel, 1971; Adam, 1978). Indeed, the Supreme Court assigned major importance to the argument that psychological damage results from segregation in reaching its 1954 school desegregation ruling (*Brown* v. *Board of Education of Topeka:* 347 U.S. 483, 1954). This view grew out of the work of Kenneth and

MINORITY-GROUP SELF-ATTITUDES
Some research shows self-esteem among black children to be higher than among white youth, though other studies suggest little difference.

Mamie Clark (1939, 1947, 1950). They found that black preschool children preferred white dolls to black dolls and concluded that the white-doll choice was a reflection of black self-hatred. There followed a proliferation of child studies that confirmed the existence of low self-esteem in black children (Goff, 1949; Stevenson and Steward, 1958; Morland, 1962; Porter, 1971).

Over the past decade, this early research has come under careful scrutiny. The doll studies have been criticized for the procedures that the researchers used in testing children's racial self-attitudes (Katz and Zalk, 1974; Banks, 1976). Recent investigators have found that black children's preference for whites or blacks is a function of a great many factors including the social situation (Banks and Rompf, 1973), the tester's race (Katz and Zalk, 1974), and the cleanliness of the dolls (Epstein, Krupat, and Obudho, 1976). Moreover, other studies have revealed that the levels of self-esteem among black children and adolescents are higher than among white youth, or at least there are no differences between the two groups (Rosenberg and Simmons, 1972; Yancey, Rigsby, and McCarthy, 1972; Paton, Walberg, and Yeh, 1973; Cummings, 1975; Simmons et al., 1978). Other research points to similar conclusions regarding native American (Indian) and Chicano (Mexican-American) children (Carter, 1968; DeBlaissie and Healy, 1970; Cockerham and Blevins, 1976; Stephan and Rosenfield, 1979).

Sociologists now recognize that a variety of factors may intervene to blunt the impact of the negative racist feedback minority groups receive (McCarthy and Yancey, 1971; Heiss and Owens, 1972). First, blacks do not necessarily judge themselves by white standards; assessment by blacks is much more relevant. Second, the situation that blacks confront within the United States allows them to blame the system rather than themselves should they be unable to realize American goals of success. And third, an increase in black militancy has contributed to enhanced feelings of black pride and unity.

PERSONAL ADJUSTMENT AND GROWTH

For many years it was assumed that the schools were only to deal with academic and cognitive material and were not to attend to the affective lives of students. This notion fostered the idea that affective and cognitive aspects are isolated and that it is possible to attend to one and ignore the other. Although many school administrators continue to operate on this premise, life in the classrooms dictates otherwise. All instances of interaction entail an affective component whether the participants recognize this fact or not.

The School and Mental Health

Ken is an obese, awkward fifth-grader; Sarah's parents are undergoing a conflict-ridden divorce and child-custody battle; Julia is the first black student to attend all-white Barrington elementary school; Andy is a small, fragile sixth-grader who is mercilessly tormented and bullied by the other boys; Debbie is a withdrawn child who often seems submerged in a world of fantasy. Can modern societies afford to ignore the affective lives of these schoolchildren? Do the schools have an obligation to promote the adaptive capabilities of their students and foster personal growth? These issues remain unresolved in many school systems.

It is estimated that from 10 to 30 percent of the children in schools within the United States have emotional disorders (Schulman et al., 1973). Popular stereotype has it that disturbed children are "troublesome" and disruptive. The problem is then defined by the public largely in disciplinary terms. Yet, investigations reveal that 80 percent of the children clinically adjudged as disturbed are anxious, withdrawn, apathetic, or depressed (Stringer, 1973).

The schools obviously cannot be responsible for remedying the troubles of all young people. Many of these emotional problems began in troubled families years before the children entered school. Even mental health professionals have difficulty helping some individuals. While many schools provide professional counseling services for those students who need special assistance, community health experts point out that these approaches have a pathology-oriented and treatment focus. Instead of merely following the traditional crisis-centered framework, these authorities emphasize the importance of programs keyed to early psychological intervention—the building of personal strengths and competencies rather than solely the amelioration of weaknesses (Allen et al., 1976). Eli M. Bower, a pioneer in popularizing early detection and prevention techniques, notes:

> For the most part, attempts have been made to promote mental health in our society by trying to

SCHOOL PHOBIA

GEETA RANIE LALL AND BERNARD M. LALL

Just before going to school each morning, third-grader Jody sits at the breakfast table and cries softly, complaining of a severe stomachache. She doesn't want to eat, and she doesn't want to go to school, either. Jody repeats this behavior every weekday morning, but on the weekends her symptoms somehow disappear.

Dick breaks out in a cold sweat whenever his second-grade teacher mentions the word *math*. He opens his workbook and stares blankly at the problems while his left hand twists a clump of hair in the middle of his head. He twists so hard that each day a little bit of hair comes out and a bare spot appears in its place. Dick is only eight years old, but already he's going bald.

Jennifer is six years old with a generally quiet and sweet disposition. Yet, when it's time to get ready for school, she screams and throws herself on the floor, hanging on to the nearest piece of furniture. But on Sundays, she goes to Bible school happily.

All three of these children are displaying the symptoms of a behavioral disorder known as "school phobia." Over the past eight years, its incidence has risen from three

Source: Geeta Ranie Lall and Bernard M. Lall, "School Phobia," *Instructor*, 89 (September 1979):96–98.

to seventeen cases per one thousand children. This rapid growth is cause for concern among teachers, parents, and administrators, all of whom need to know more about the problem if it's to be detected early enough for successful treatment to take place.

Defined simply as "an irrational fear of going to school," school phobia is characterized by an acute panic state; however, most children with this disorder are unable to tell exactly what they fear. The incidence of school phobia peaks between the third and fifth grades and it appears more frequently in girls than in boys. It also tends to be more common among children from higher socioeconomic levels, with parents who hold professional or managerial jobs.

The symptoms of school phobia are varied, but usually involve complaints of a physical nature, such as aches or pains in the stomach, nausea, vomiting, paleness, trembling, inability to move, dizziness, enuresis, diarrhea, and sleep disturbances. School-phobic children may be especially picky over food and often refuse to eat breakfast. They lose weight and, in the most dramatic cases, may even lose the use of their extremities.

Unfortunately, these symptoms are often mistaken for disciplinary problems and improper measures

are taken in futile attempts to correct them.

The causes of school phobia are complex and can be related to situations such as illness at home, divorce, separation, a sudden move, the birth of a sibling, harsh teachers, harassment from bullies, and school failure. But they may involve many other factors as well.

In some cases, for instance, the child and his mother may have a hostile-dependent relationship in which they fear separation and repress hostile feelings toward each other at the same time. When there is violent conflict between parents, the child may think that he should stay at home to protect his mother. She, in turn, feels guilty about causing his anxiety and may react with overindulgence or overcare. This only serves to intensify the child's dependence on her and often leads to a deep-rooted fear of abandonment which doesn't come to the surface until he is forced to attend school. Or the child's father may be passive, withdrawn, lacking in responsibility, competing with the child, or unable to define a paternal role. In other cases, there may be an interdependence between the child, his parents, and his grandparents. The mother and father may be neurotically involved with their own parents and have little or no interest in people or things outside of the family.

Parental indifference can also cause school phobia in children, who may then feel driven to gain attention. Conversely, overreactive or overprotective parents may cause their children to panic in situations in which they are away from parents.

Sometimes, an aspect of school itself may cause the phobia. Examples are peer pressure, a harsh and restrictive teacher, or having to undress for gym. This was the case with John, who mysteriously refused to go to school. Visits to the Child Guidance Clinic revealed that John, who was very tall and gangling, was self-conscious about undressing in front of the other boys. He was also apprehensive about riding the bus in the morning because of the smoking and general horseplay that went on. After both these causes were removed, the boy overcame his phobic reaction.

Finally, some researchers feel that children with this problem have an inbred tendency toward emotional disturbance and that school phobia is itself a symptom of some preexisting anxiety state.

Treatment for school phobia is most effective if begun immediately after the symptoms appear. Many different procedures can be used such as behavior modification, removing the child from school for a short time, and medication.

Behavior modification involves therapy right in the school situation. A therapist accompanies the child to school and they stay for only a short period of time. With each successive day, the child's stay increases until finally he remains in school for the entire day. This kind of therapy, known as "systematic desensitization," helps the child to cope with his anxiety by slowly increasing the time spent in school.

Phobic children above the fourth and fifth grade may have severe character disorders and are the most difficult group to treat successfully. They may be unable to cope with pressures that interfere with their normal ego development and cause regression. Treatment for these children frequently involves removing them from school for a period of time so they can discover their separate identities through individual psychotherapy. However, this kind of treatment should not be prolonged and the child should be returned to school as soon as possible. Withdrawal from the anxiety-producing situation does not allow the child an opportunity to confront his fears and "work through" them, and may be more damaging than helpful in the long run. In general, the longer a child stays out of school, the harder it is for him to go back.

Because of the danger of adverse side effects, medication should be used only as a final alternative, and then only under a doctor's supervision. In most cases, it is used in combination with family therapy, as school phobia and family problems are related.

Whatever treatment is used, keep the following points in mind. The child should receive immediate attention, beginning with a thorough examination by the family physician. Parents should be involved in treatment from the start and should have the final say in determining what type is used. The child must also be listened to and made to take part in finding a solution to his problem. After the child is returned to school, the parents or the entire family should receive therapy. If a family problem has caused the disorder to emerge, it may arise again and again if the situation is not improved. Also, a school-phobic child needs lots of reassurance and support from the school, such as praise for real success and recognition for efforts, no matter what the outcome. Instead of punishing the child, educators must view his problem as a disorder and try to understand all its factors. Finally, authoritarian methods, including the use of physical force to bring the child to school, may do more long-term harm than good. It's possible that the child's phobia began as a reaction to authority or a specific authority figure, and punitive methods may only serve to make the reaction stronger.

School phobia is *not* an imaginary disorder. It is a very real problem and it exists in all kinds of children and in all types of schools. This year, one of your students may have it—but will you be able to recognize the symptoms before it's too late? This is a challenge you face today.

deal with the consequences of mental illness and its allied manifestations. This, it has been suggested, is about as effective as trying to turn back the Mississippi at New Orleans. [1969:113]

Professionals in the field of mental health emphasize that prevention deserves a larger share of time and resources than has been allocated to it in the past. They have looked increasingly to the schools as one logical setting for preventive activities, since only in the school does society have an opportunity to reach all children. There is precedent for such programs in other preventive health measures instituted by many school districts, including mandatory immunization programs, physical check-ups, and dental reports (Schulman et al., 1973).

Over the past twenty years Ralph H. Ojemann (1959, 1961, 1967) has contended that one way to develop more satisfying human relationships is to introduce a "fourth R" into the schools, a program for human relations. He has formulated an approach that aims to educate children in causal thinking regarding their behavior. His program in preventive mental health has two underlying hypotheses. First, children can acquire an understanding of human behavior and learn to apply these insights to their interpersonal relationships. Second, the application of this knowledge will result in more satisfying human relationships and personal enrichment. The effectiveness of the approach has been demonstrated in a number of school settings (Levitt, 1955a, 1955b; Ojemann et al., 1955; Muuss, 1960). More recently, several authors have designed relatively well-defined, commercially available, packaged programs with an affective emphasis for use by classroom teachers, guidance counselors, and school psychologists (Medway and Smith, 1978).

Criteria of Optimal Adjustment

Education at its best will develop the individual's inner resources to the point where he can learn (and will *want* to learn) on his own. It will equip him to survive as a versatile individual in an unpredictable world. Individuals so educated will keep the society itself flexible, adaptive and innovative.

JOHN W. GARDNER
Self-Renewal: The Individual and the Innovative Society, 1963

Life compels us to find means for coping with the demands of our environment, a never-ending process termed **adjustment.** Coping mechanisms are judged in terms of their adequacy in promoting human well-being. According to the psychoanalyst Erich Fromm, the mentally healthy individual:

. . . is the productive and unalienated person; the person who relates himself to the world lovingly, and who uses his reason to grasp reality objectively; who experiences himself as a unique individual entity, and at the same time feels one with his fellow man; who is not subject to irrational authority, and accepts willingly the rational authority of conscience and reason; who is in the process of being born as long as he is alive, and considers the gift of life the most precious chance he has. [1955:275]

Among the best-known criteria for optimal adjustment are those set forth by Abraham H. Maslow (1970). According to Maslow, the human organism is self-directing and has not only the potential, but also the drive, for healthy growth and self-actualization. Maslow studied the lives of eminent figures from history whom he considered to be *self-actualizers,* such individuals as Abraham Lincoln, Albert Einstein, Walt Whitman, Jane Adams, and Eleanor Roosevelt. From the facts about their lives, he constructed the following portrayal of self-actualized persons:

- They have a firm perception of reality.
- They accept themselves and others for what they are.
- They show considerable spontaneity in thought and behavior.
- They are problem-centered rather than self-centered.
- They have an air of detachment and a need for privacy.

"YOU KNOW, I LIKE YOU"

ROBERT GEISER

Chief Psychologist at Nazareth Child Care Center, Jamaica Plain, Massachusetts

One day a class of first-graders and their teacher were watching their pet baby rabbit eat.

"Is the baby rabbit sad 'cause he left his mommy?" a child asked.

"Of course not," the teacher replied. "Rabbits don't have feelings."

Many teachers of young children would shudder at that answer, recognizing that the child was not asking an intellectual question about emotional states in rabbits but seeking permission to talk about his own feelings of sadness and loss at having left his mother to start school.

Teachers in the early grades usually accept children's need to talk about their feelings and encourage them with remarks like, "I think he is sad. What do you think?" Some teachers above third grade, however, still assume there is a mysterious process inside a child which enables him, by the time he has reached third grade, to separate his rational function from his emotions and believe it is possible to educate children by addressing themselves only to the intellect. They further believe that

children cooperate by asking only intellectual questions and being completely satisfied with factual answers.

Rationality exists and intellectual efficiency is promoted, however, only when the child's emotional needs have been satisfied to the extent that they no longer interfere with extended periods of intellectual activity. Children must, therefore, learn to accept their feelings and to find healthy and socially constructive ways of expressing their emotions. Children sense this and sometimes try to tell us if we fail to satisfy emotional curiosity. We must listen for their implied questions—their silent questions—as Miss Baker, a second-grade teacher, has learned to do.

One day, while she was working with a child in her individualized classroom, Phillip came up, put a paper in front of her, and asked, "Is this right?" She was annoyed at the interruption, but glanced at the arithmetic problem and said, "Yes, that's fine, Phillip." Phillip returned to his seat.

Five minutes later he was back at her desk with the same question. Her annoyance turned to anger at the persistence of his attention-seeking behavior. "I've

already told you it's right," she snapped. "I'm busy with Sally now. Stop interrupting me."

Shortly Phillip was back a third time. Miss Baker refused even to look at his paper. "Sit down and wait your turn," she ordered. "I don't want to see you up here again." Phillip went back to his desk, crumpled his paper into a ball, and threw it on the floor. He put his head down on his desk, through with learning for the day. Miss Baker kept him after school to make up the work he had failed to do.

The next afternoon during a staff meeting the school's mental health consultant suggested that Phillip might really have been asking whether the teacher approved of him.

"Why not put your arm around Phillip," he asked, "and say, 'Yes, I like you and what you are doing.'"

Two days later, Phillip and Miss Baker clashed again on the same issue. She was just about to explode following the third interruption when she remembered the group discussion. She smiled at Phillip, gave him a little hug, and said, "You know, I like you."

Phillip blinked, grabbed his pa-

Source: Robert Geiser, "You Know, I Like You," *Instructor*, 83 (April 1974): 72–73.

(continued)

"YOU KNOW, I LIKE YOU"
(continued)

per, and bolted back to his seat. He sat with a dazed expression on his face for a while, then went to work on his math. He did not interrupt Miss Baker again, but waited for his turn alone with her. As he was leaving the classroom at the end of the day, he dropped a note on her desk. It read: "I like you, too. Phillip."

Many teachers feel that devia-tions from the usual style of teach-ing (individualization, one-to-one relationships, concern with emo-tional development, freedom of expression) are necessary in spe-cial education. They fail to see that these departures, which give special education a humaneness often lacking in regular classes, are equally necessary and bene-ficial for normal children.

Because schools educate the total child, teachers of normal chil-dren need not only to hear the silent question, but to respond in ways that will encourage emo-tional growth. Only when chil-dren's emotional needs have been satisfied are they intellectually ready to learn.

- They are autonomous and independent.
- They resist enculturation and stereotyped be-havior, although they are not deliberately un-conventional simply for its own sake.
- They are sympathetic to the human condition and promote its welfare.
- They establish deep, profound relationships with a few people rather than superficial bonds with many people.
- They have a democratic world outlook.
- They have a considerable fund of creativeness.
- They transcend their environment rather than merely coping with it.
- They have a high frequency of "peak experi-ences" marked by rapturous feelings of excite-ment, insight, and happiness.

The Association for Supervision and Curriculum Development of the National Education Associa-tion has provided a definition of a mentally healthy child. According to ASCD, a mentally healthy child is one who is able to adapt to a changing environment, perceive reality accurately, manage stress in a healthy fashion, stand on his or her own feet, want to learn, and possess feelings of ade-quacy and well-being.

As psychologist Marie Jahoda (1958) points out, adjustment does not imply conformity to restricted social norms nor passive adaptation to stresses in order to be comfortable and free of symptoms. She considers "positive striving" to be the mark of a psychologically sound and healthy individual. Richard S. Lazarus (1976) similarly notes that adjustment consists of two processes: fitting oneself into given circumstances *and* changing the circum-stances to fit one's needs.

Some educators and parents attempt to limit and even eliminate stress from the lives of children. They view stress as a dangerous and destructive state. Yet, stress is an inevitable accompaniment of life. While it is true that excessive and prolonged stress can overwhelm an organism, a more common danger is that individuals will find it difficult to cope with even moderate amounts of stress. Hence, rather than sheltering children from everyday stress, wise educators and parents attempt to impart to children those skills for successfully dealing with it.

MORAL BEHAVIOR

If we are to live with one another in communities and societies, there must be a system of morality, shared conceptions of what is right and wrong.

Underlying families, schools, social clubs, armies, political groups, football teams, and other human endeavors are rules that guide social or interpersonal behavior. If people are to involve themselves in the collective enterprise—if they are to play their parts and make their contribution to ongoing activity—they must have confidence that others will follow the rules. Where some people get rewards, even disproportionate rewards, without playing by the rules—for instance, "idlers," "fakers," "chiselers," "sneaks," and "deadbeats"—others develop bitterness and resentment. Organized activity demands that people commit some resources, forgo some alternatives, and make some investment in the future. Hence, human life requires that there be rules, and people must be able to assume that, by and large, these rules will be observed (Cohen, 1966).

Moral behavior involves the adoption of principles that lead people to evaluate given actions as "right" and others as "wrong" and to govern their own actions in terms of these principles. We commonly feel a strong emotional commitment to certain ethical values. Such principles impart meaning to life. As we experience the world about us—people, objects, ideas, acts, and events—strong affective components touch us at every turn. We "feel" about things. We do not encounter the world in cold, aseptic terms.

Generality of Moral Behavior Across Situations

There is no well-defined boundary line between honesty and dishonesty. The frontiers of one blend with the outside limits of the other, and he who attempts to tread this dangerous ground may be sometimes in the one domain and sometimes in the other.

O. HENRY
"Bexar Script No. 2692," *Rolling Stones,* 1912

In a monumental and classic study carried out over a half century ago, Hugh Hartshorne and Mark A. May (Hartshorne and May, 1928; Hartshorne, May, and Maller, 1929; Hartshorne, May,

and Shuttleworth, 1930) were dismayed that they were unable to locate a stable personality trait such as honesty in schoolchildren. Nearly all the children cheated at one time or another depending on the situation. Further, attempts at character education had no influence on producing a general moral character trait that consistently resisted opportunities to cheat.

In their research, Hartshorne and May studied the moral behavior of some eleven thousand children in various circumstances including classroom work, home duties, party games, and athletic contests. The children were given opportunities to lie, cheat, or steal under conditions that, unknown to them, were being observed. Considerable inconsistency existed in the children's behavior. For instance, it was not possible for the researchers to predict whether a child who cheated on an arithmetic test would also cheat on a spelling test. Honesty, self-control, service, good temper, truthfulness, justice, and bravery were not a "bag of virtues" that the children either did or did not have. Rather, they were a function of the specific situations in which children found themselves.

Children's attitudes were also not simple and straightforward but diverse, complex, and often contradictory. Their scores on tests of moral knowledge and opinion differed widely depending on whether the test was taken at a children's club, at home, in the classroom, or in Sunday school. Thus, the situation in which the children found themselves did much to determine which of their varied attitudes and feelings would be brought into play. The researchers concluded: "A child does not have a uniform generalized code of morals but varies his opinions to suit the situation in which he finds himself" (Hartshorne, May, and Shuttleworth, 1930:107–108).

More recent findings have confirmed the Hartshorne and May conclusion that morality is not the product of a unitary "conscience" or a "character" trait but derives from the social context in which individuals find themselves (Mussen et al., 1970; Kohlberg, 1976; Rosenhan et al., 1976; Blasi, 1980).

GAMES AND MORAL CONDUCT
In games children learn the importance of rules for ordering human affairs.

Correlates of Moral Conduct

The finding that moral behavior is influenced by personal situational factors has led psychologists to undertake more concrete studies to identify those factors specifically associated with moral conduct.

Intelligence

A consistent finding has been the existence of an inverse relationship between cheating and IQ (Hartshorne and May, 1928; Parr, 1936; Hetherington and Feldman, 1964; Leveque and Walker, 1970). However, the relationship tends to be limited to academic-type tests and disappears or declines when the context is nonacademic (Burton, 1976). Apparently, the experience which low-IQ and low-achieving children have with failure in the schools leads them to try to improve their academic status by cheating. But being smart and being moral are not the same. The gift of intelligence simply makes a thief's capers better devised and a con artist's tongue more beguiling.

Age

It is sometimes asserted that younger children are more "innocent" than older children and hence more honest. Yet, research provides little evidence that children become less honest (or more honest) as they grow older. A small relationship may exist between age and honesty, but it seems to be the product of other factors that also correlate with increasing age, such as an awareness of risk and an ability to perform the task without the need to cheat (Burton, 1976).

Gender Differences

"Sugar and spice and everything nice . . ." is part of our cultural stereotype of girls being "good" and boys "bad." Indeed, research confirms that teachers do see girls as more moral than boys (Krebs, 1977). Yet, research also reveals that girls are not any more honest than boys (Bushway and Nash, 1977). Indeed, Hartshorne and May (1928) found that girls tended to cheat more often than boys on tests of the take-home variety. Overall, however, most of the studies undertaken over the past half century show no reliable gender differences in honesty (Burton, 1976).

Group Norms

Sociologists point out that much of our behavior is group-anchored. All of us are members of a surprising number of functioning groups, many of which have differing and even conflicting rules. Accordingly, in appraising people's attitudes or actions, it is necessary to know which group is operating in a situation to furnish individuals with their standards for behavior. The group supplying such standards is termed a *reference group*.

Reference groups play a critical part in providing the guidelines by which people map and channel their actions. Hence, it is hardly surprising that Hartshorne and May (1928) should have found that one of the major determinants of honest and dishonest behavior is the group code. When classroom groups were studied over time, the cheating scores of the individual members tended to become increasingly similar. This suggests that rules were evolved that then functioned to regulate each student's behavior. Other research demonstrates that the greater the disapproval of deviance by one's peers, the less likely the individual is to engage in deviant conduct (Bowers, 1964).

Motivational Variables

Fear of failure is an important factor contributing to dishonesty. When an individual's relatively poor performance stands a good chance of becoming public, the person is placed under considerable pressure to realize success even if it involves the use of dishonest means (Taylor and Lewit, 1966; Hill and Kochendorfer, 1969). Deception is especially likely when a high achievement motivation is coupled with high fear of failure (Gilligan, 1963). A low-risk and low-supervision situation similarly increases the chances for dishonest conduct (Tittle and Rowe, 1973; Leming, 1978).

Prosocial Behavior

Moral behavior does not merely consist of observing prohibitions against misbehavior. It also entails **prosocial behavior,** ways of responding to other people through sympathetic, cooperative, trusting, helpful, rescuing, comforting, and giving acts. Prosocial behavior is an umbrella concept that, as Lauren G. Wispé notes, takes various forms:

> "Altruism" refers to a regard for the interest of others without concern for one's self-interest. "Sympathy" refers to a concern with, or a sharing of the pain or sadness of another person. . . . "Cooperation" is the willingness and ability to work with others, usually but not always for a common benefit. "Helping" refers to the giving of assistance or aid toward a definite object or end. "Aid" usually refers to providing what is needed to accomplish a definite end. And "donating" refers to the action of making a gift or giving a contribution, usually to a charity. [1972:4]

Much of the research dealing with prosocial behavior has been guided by Albert Bandura's (1969, 1977) observational learning theory (see Chapter 5). In most studies, a child observes an adult model who provides assistance of some sort to others. The researchers then attempt to assess the extent to which the child subsequently imitates the helping, altruistic, or donating behavior. In most cases, when the model behaves generously, the children respond in a similar manner (Bryan, 1972, 1977; Rushton, 1976). For instance, Mary B. Harris (1970) found that fourth- and fifth-grade children would share with an adult model if the model had shared with them, would donate their winnings from a game to a charity if they had observed the model doing so, or would retain their winnings if that was the example they had witnessed.

Research reveals that verbal exhortations, such as "You should give," "It is good to give," and "Giving will make other children happy," have little impact on the overt prosocial behavior of children. Thus, teachers should be aware that their actions speak louder than a lip-service morality.

Further, one of the most recurrent findings is that when the model preaches charity but practices greed, the children are influenced by what the adult does, not by what the adult says. Indeed, one outcropping of adult hypocrisy is the production of hypocritical children (Bryan, 1972, 1977; Rosenhan, 1972).

There is little evidence that altruism is a character trait. At best, only low correlations exist between altruistic behavior in one context and altruistic behavior in others (Staub and Sherk, 1970; Bryan, 1972; Rushton, 1976). Psychologists find that much the same state of affairs prevails with respect to prosocial behavior as it does with regard to honesty. Some individuals may be more or less "other-centered" than others, but on the whole altruism is influenced by a variety of factors. Among these are expectations of approval, learned prohibitions, norms of responsibility, level of cognitive and social skills, susceptibility to feelings of anxiety, the cost or inconvenience of helping, and numerous situational variables (Yarrow and Waxler, 1976; Vander Zanden, 1984).

Erwin Staub (1973, 1978) has recently suggested a number of ways other than modeling by which prosocial behavior can be fostered. Children assigned responsibility for other children, especially for training them in prosocial activities, are themselves markedly affected by such teaching. Further, young children seem particularly eager to help the classroom teacher, affording opportunities for students to be plugged into helping activities. In contrast, circumstances that reward children's competitiveness (where achievement is accomplished at the expense of others) interfere with children's helping and cooperative behaviors (Bryan, 1977).

APPROACHES TO MORAL EDUCATION

Values education is now taking hold in educational institutions throughout America. It seems to be an idea whose time has come. But values education means different things to different people. Trying to define it

CURRICULUM FOR CARING

DOROTHY KOBAK

Let's just state it flat out: *Children . . . can . . . be . . . taught . . . to . . . care!* Just as math, reading, biology are taught, caring can be taught. Despite the fact that education has long ignored development of caring in individuals, there is ample evidence that it is a learnable, teachable subject that can be programmed into the curriculum, with teacher training and administrative support, on a structured daily basis. Moreover, if done properly, students *will* study and develop their "CQ" (Caring Quality) along with their academic growth.

Here are three ways to provide your kids with opportunities to experience and grow into caring!

1. A daily class dialogue period.
2. The use of creativity tools.
3. The use of action projects.

THE DIALOGUE PERIOD

This period should be consistent throughout the year, programmed into the day and always at the same hour. During this session, discuss either prepared topics or spontaneous subjects introduced by the kids—something that has just happened and touched off an emotional response. In our case, these included the drowning of a fellow student, the death of a parent, a national catastrophe, a misfortune to a staff member, and a playground fight.

Prepared topics should relate to reality. Your first sessions should include definitions and descriptions. Later, you can get into reasons behind, and understanding of, such things as truancy, stealing, fighting, drugs, underachieving, fears of rejection and inadequacy, peer pressure, and family relationships. Then you can move into more esoteric discussions, of topics involving empathy, sympathy, and sacrifice.

The following are examples of specific classroom topics that relate to caring. Discussion is geared to statement or question. This is followed by intensive dialogue directed to caring as a mandate in self-assessment and behavioral change.

Wonder Questions

"What's the hardest part of being a friend?" "Do you wonder why Frankie never smiles?"

Empathy Questions

"What are some of your parents' concerns about you?"

Answers: "I make them worry. I don't study very much. I'd rather watch TV."
Dialogue: "How can Judy be more caring, so her parents will not worry?"

Philosophical Questions

"Who is your enemy?"
Answers: "My sister is my enemy!" "My brother!"
Dialogue: "Why do persons become enemies?" "Can caring change enemies to friends?"

Identification Questions

"Who is the saddest person you know?"
Answers: "Old people, sick people, lonely people are sad."
Dialogue: "Why are they sad?" "Did you ever care for such people?" "Did it make a difference?"
Answers: "Yes, my grandmother, or the lady upstairs, or the old blind man. I helped them across the street, read them a book."

Alternative Questions

"Did you ever try to avoid a fight?"
Answers: "I wish I could. I can't stop beating other kids up. I'm scared. I'm afraid I'll get in real trouble."

(continued)

Source: Condensed from Dorothy Kobak, "Curriculum for Caring," *Instructor,* 89 (December 1979):53–55.

CURRICULUM FOR CARING
(continued)

Dialogue: "How can we help John? We care about his worry and fear. Let's see if we can think of other ways for him to act, so he can stop fighting and being afraid."

Solution: Make a list of cruel names to be eliminated. Probe and isolate sensitive feelings. Come up with ways to resolve disputes before they become fights.

Result: The entire class learns there are caring alternatives to fighting as the resolution of problems.

Problem Questions

"The principal, Mr. Jones, loaned Tom his personal book as a favor and Tom has not returned it. What can we do?"

Answers: "I'll beat him up for Mr. Jones!" "Make him pay!" "Flunk him!"

Reorientation: "But, class, we want to help Tom remember. What can we do to help Tom care that Mr. Jones feels bad?"

Dialogue: "I'll phone Tom and remind him." "I'll walk to school with him and talk about the book."

Result: Tom gets phone calls and companions who remind him about the book. He begins to care about his problem of forgetting. Then he starts to care about Mr. Jones feeling bad.

Truancy

Statement: "Sally does not come to school at all. How can we help her?"

Answers: "We don't care!" "If she doesn't want to learn, it's her tough luck!"

Reorientation: "Class, we are learning caring experiences. We want to show Sally that somebody cares when she is out of school." Then, "Why do you think she is skipping school?" "What can we do to help her?"

Dialogue: "Maybe she can't do the work. Maybe she has to help her mother. Maybe she has bad friends. We will send a letter. We will tell her she will not get a good job and make money if she does not go to school."

"But, class, how does such a letter show her you care about her and her problems and worries?"

Solution: The final letter to Sally: "We miss you. Your seat is empty in the back of the room. If you come back to school, we will be glad to see you."

Result: Sally returns to school and remains the rest of the term. She realizes: "I am missed in that seat back there. Somebody really wants me to come back. I'll take a risk and come back."

Dialogues in caring do not necessarily emphasize that it is "wrong" to be truant, borrow and not return, steal, and so on. Nor is punishment or getting caught the prime focus of dialogue, although these are significant realities. Rather, emphasis is placed on: "How do you think Wilma *feels* when you steal her ballpoint pen, or when you make fun of her or call her a name? Did anybody ever steal your pen? How did you *feel?*" Also, wherever possible, insults or degradation are handled immediately and discussed at once. Always, an apology and handshake are required. Then the incident is dropped and dialogue is resumed.

CREATIVITY TOOLS

The second large area of education for caring stresses creativity techniques such as poetry, drama, clay, murals, school newspapers, music, videotape, role playing, and psychodrama. All tools are focused on caring. Poems, for example, are a superb way to reach out for feelings and should be selected specifically for that reason. In reading a poem about "loneliness" in one of our classes, for example, we asked who felt lonely. One boy raised his hand and a caring dialogue was begun. The key was the boy's loneliness, which he described. The class was given an opportunity to respond with solutions.

Students evolved a plan to call him every afternoon and visit him on weekends. The poem was the springboard for this action.

Such response builds ego in the giver. It verifies feelings of effectiveness, self-satisfaction, and self-esteem. It helps boost a good self-image.

ACTION PROJECTS

The third method we have used to raise student CQ involves action projects, of which there are endless opportunities. Some examples of what we did include:

1. Pennies for People

Concern: "For whom would you like to collect pennies?" "Poor people who are hungry in Africa." "Why?" (A discussion follows on hunger, poverty, compassion, responsibility, and sharing.)

Commitment: "How should we do it?" "Let's have a jar and watch the pennies grow." "We'll put a label on the jar: 'Pennies for People'."

Post dialogue: To evaluate feelings, attitudes, disappointments, satisfactions, risks, and so on. This is a mandatory part of action projects, as it affords pupils the opportunity to observe and evaluate their own process safely and constructively.

Culmination: Five hundred pennies were collected and sent to CARE. Kids received a wonderful letter of thanks, information as to what village in Africa would use the money and for what purpose. The principal announced the results and congratulated the students. The process and feedback included learning and pleasure, yielding positive recall for future caring involvements.

2. Community Action Project

A class of fifth-graders "adopted" a nursing home. They made monthly visits and gave programs, discussions, gifts, and charts. Dialogue after visits got into feelings, attitudes, and results, all focusing on caring.

3. "Children Caring for Children"

Here an eighth-grade class was involved in a game, gym, and tutorial program with a fifth-grade class. Pairing took place at the beginning and remained the same throughout the year. Older students acted as caring role models to younger students, befriended them, helped them, and related to them in warm and supportive ways. The caring dialogues, prior to each encounter, related to *concern, commitment,* and *culmination.*

4. "Citizens of the Week"

This is a teacher-pupil project in which students are chosen by the teacher to become "Citizens of the Week." There is no limit to how many can be chosen in each class. The basis is doing or saying something caring which is then acknowledged and recognized, giving pleasurable recall to the recipient and, thereby, reducing fears of caring in the future. Recognition comes by the naming of those honored over the loudspeaker—by the principal—and by the placement of their pictures on a special "Caring Bulletin Board" outside the principal's office. A letter is sent to the parents telling them that their child was selected as "Citizen of the Week."

The effectiveness of a program for teaching children to care is contingent largely upon administrative acceptance of the concept. And this means giving ample time, support, and encouragement to staff for developing expertise in the area. Where school principals have given support and included caring in the curriculum formally, consistently, and effectively, there have been gains in academic achievement, classroom management, and school harmony. The implications for family and community are far-reaching, in addition to personal mental health and happiness.

is somewhat like attempting to peel an onion: You keep taking off layer after layer and you wind up with nothing but tears.

EWALD B. NYQUIST
Commissioner of Education, State
of New York, Speech, March 27, 1976

Educators face the constant problem of moral issues and values in the classroom. Over the past two decades the United States has been struggling with what some have termed a "crisis of conscience." Political assassinations during the 1960s, the violent eruptions of the black civil rights struggle, the Vietnam War, the issue of women's rights, the agony of Watergate, widespread drug use, sexual experimentation, and scandals revolving around corruption in business and government have kept moral concerns center stage for a generation of Americans. All of this has had an impact on the schools. Considerable controversy exists regarding the responsibility of the schools for educating a moral citizenry—indeed, whether the schools should even have a part in moral education, leaving the matter to the home and the church.

The Values-Transmission Approach

What are our schools for if not indoctrination against Communism?

RICHARD M. NIXON

All education indoctrinates.

ROBERT M. MAC IVER
Politics and Society, 1969

The belief that the schools should teach moral values is at least as old as the nation itself. Thomas Jefferson, in his *Bill for the More General Diffusion of Knowledge,* argued for an educational system that would fortify citizens with moral fiber sufficient to resist the schemes of the enemies of liberty. The assertion of the nineteenth-century English philosopher Herbert Spencer that "education has for its object the formation of character" was a truism on both sides of the Atlantic, finding

embodiment in *McGuffey's Readers* (see the boxed insert on page 325). And John Dewey, the dominant figure in American education during the first half of this century, saw moral education as central to the mission of the schools:

> The child's moral character must develop in a natural, just, and social atmosphere. The school should provide this environment for its part in the child's moral development. [1934:85]

Recent Gallup polls show that four out of every five Americans favor instruction in the schools that would deal with morals and moral behavior. Indeed, there are those like political scientist Reo M. Christenson (1977) who believe that moral training may be the most important subject in the curriculum. He argues that certain basic values and attitudes inherent in the American system should be cultivated by the schools: "What is needed, to put it bluntly, is a revival of the *McGuffey Reader* concept—using a modernized version appropriate in style and content to our times, one that sets forth some of the timeless principles of responsible moral behavior every young person should know" (1977:739).

To be sure, there is the opposite view that the schools should stick to imparting basic knowledge and skills and should not teach morality. Many Americans fear that arbitrary values may be imposed on unsuspecting children.

One version of the values-transmission approach takes the position that certain ethical standards are "right," namely those of one's own group or society. The task of the schools is defined as one of imparting these values to the youth (Oldenquist, 1981). Thus, Nikolai Lenin, the Bolshevik leader, wrote, "The overall aim of bringing up young people today should be the teaching of Communist morality" (quoted by Connell, 1975:702).

Many sociologists and anthropologists advance a somewhat different version of the values-transmission approach. Rather than asking whether or not the schools should transmit particular sets of values, these social scientists say that the schools inevitably promote the values of the groups that

THE McGUFFEY READERS

William Holmes McGuffey (1800–1873) gave his name to one of the most remarkable educational ventures in this nation's history, the *McGuffey's Readers* (Westerhoff, 1978). Some 120 million copies of the books were sold between 1836 and 1920, placing their sales in a class with the Bible and *Webster's Dictionary*. Indeed, today the cry "Back to *McGuffey's Readers*" is heard in some quarters almost as frequently as "Back to the Bible." The distinguished historian Henry Steele Commager has written: "They [the readers] played an important role in American education . . . and helped to shape that elusive thing we call the American character" (quoted by Westerhoff, 1978:16).

McGuffey was responsible for the compilation of the first four readers but not the fifth or sixth (which were prepared by his brother, Alexander). Further, he was not responsible for any of the editions after 1857. The earlier editions compiled by McGuffey reflected McGuffey's theologically conservative, Presbyterian Calvinist philosophy. They stressed such values as salvation, righteousness, and piety. The publishers of the later editions replaced his Calvinistic emphasis with one that affirmed the morality and lifestyles of the emerging middle class. Although the specific moral content of the readers changed with time, an underlying theme pervading all editions was a strong commitment to the moral education of the nation's youth. The following are illustrative excerpts from a number of the readers.

It is well for us all to have work to do. It is bad for us not to work. John was a good boy, and he did not love to play so much that he could not work. No—he knew it to be right to work, and when his work was done he would play.
Eclectic First Reader, 1836

You cannot receive affection unless you also give it. You cannot find others to love you, unless you also love them.

If you are not loved, it is good evidence that you do not deserve to be loved.
Eclectic Third Reader, 1837

Ralph Wick was five years old. In most things, he was a fine boy. But he was too apt to cry.

When he could not have his own way, he would cry about it. This was wrong. All good boys and girls know better.

They should take what their kind friends see fit to give them. They should be glad to get this.
New Second Eclectic Reader, 1865

No little boy or girl should ever drink rum or whiskey, unless they want to become drunkards. . . .

Whiskey makes the happy miserable, and it causes the rich to become poor.
Eclectic First Reader, 1836

Do all in your power to make others happy. Be willing to make sacrifices of your own convenience that you may promote the happiness of others . . . .

When you are playing with your brothers and sisters at home, be always ready to give them more than their store of privileges. Manifest an obliging disposition, and they cannot but regard you with affection.
Eclectic Third Reader, 1837

The little boy took care of his faithful dog as long as he lived and never forgot that we must do good to others, if we wish them to do the same to us.
New Fourth Eclectic Reader, 1857

control the schools. According to this view, schooling is inescapably a moral enterprise; no institution is neutral, since certain behavioral preferences pervade every aspect of its operation. All social or interpersonal behavior is regulated by rules; institutional functioning takes place in terms of rules, many of which are taken for granted—the background understandings or "stuff" out of which we fashion our lives (Garfinkel, 1964, 1967; Zimmerman and Wieder, 1970; Mehan and Wood, 1975, 1976). Within the schools a "hidden curriculum" lurks beneath the surface and implies many underlying moral assumptions and values; for example, an emphasis on obedience to authority— "Stay in your seat," "No talking unless called on," "Get a hall pass," and so on (Jackson, 1968). (See the boxed insert on page 327.) To carry on one's daily activities within an institutional context is to take on the ways of that institution. Viewed from this perspective, all education, no matter how benign, indoctrinates.

The Cognitive-Developmental Approach

The aim of education is growth or development, both intellectual and moral. Ethical and psychological principles can aid the school in the greatest of all constructions—the building of a free and powerful character. Only knowledge of the order and connection of the stages in psychological development can insure this. Education is the work of supplying the conditions which will enable the psychological functions to mature in the freest and fullest manner.

JOHN DEWEY
*What Psychology Can Do
for the Teacher*

The cognitive-developmental approach to moral education denies the premise of the values-transmission approach that it is possible to drill principles of morality or citizenship into the minds of children. This orientation was launched by Jean Piaget's (1932) early investigations of moral development. According to Piaget, there is an orderly and logical pattern in the development of children's moral judgments. This development is rooted in the stages that characterize the emergence of logical thought (see Chapter 6). Piaget says that it is no more possible to teach children moral codes than it is to teach them to conserve quantities. Children evolve new and higher standards of morality as they become intellectually ready through interaction with their environment. They generate their conceptions of right and wrong out of their own active efforts to understand the world about them and organize their social experiences (Turiel, 1973).

Lawrence Kohlberg (1963, 1968, 1975, 1980, 1981), a Harvard psychologist, has further elaborated Piaget's stage theory of moral development. Like Piaget, Kohlberg describes how individuals reason about moral issues at different life stages. He contends that moral development is a culturally universal, invariant sequence of six stages. Children move step-by-step through each of the stages, and reaching any stage requires passing through the preceding series. Additionally, each successive stage is morally superior to those preceding it (Kohlberg and Kramer, 1969; Rest, Turiel, and Kohlberg, 1969).

The advance from a lower moral stage to the next higher one does not represent an increasing knowledge of cultural values; instead, it entails a restructuring and transformation of earlier modes of moral judgment. Hence, moral development "emerges through a process of development that is neither direct biological maturation nor direct learning, but rather a reorganization of psychological structures resulting from organism-environment interactions" (Kohlberg and Mayer, 1972:457). Although individuals may stop at any stage in the invariant sequence, they can be stimulated to ascend the scale, Hence, Kohlberg asserts that the primary aim of education is to facilitate development through these stages.

Like Piaget, Kohlberg focuses on the development of moral *judgments* in children rather than on their actions. He gathers his data by asking individuals questions about hypothetical stories. One of these stories has become famous as a classic ethical dilemma:

THE HIDDEN CURRICULUM

Perhaps the greatest of all pedagogical fallacies is that a person learns only the particular thing he is studying at the time. Collateral learning in the way of formation of enduring attitudes, of likes and dislikes, may be and often is more important. . . . For these attitudes are fundamentally what count in the future.

John Dewey
Experience and Education,
1938

Schools teach much more than the skills and information specified in the academic curriculum. Intentionally or unwittingly, they impart a whole complex of unarticulated values, attitudes, and behaviors, what is termed the hidden curriculum (Dreeben, 1968; Jackson, 1968; Cartledge and Milburn, 1978). Although not *stated,* the hidden curriculum contains instructional objectives vigorously pursued by the educational system. Students learn not only from the official courses of study but from the physical environment of the school, the attitudes teachers and pupils exhibit toward one another, the social climate, and the bureaucratic organization of the school.

Those behaviors constituting the hidden curriculum are modeled by teachers and reinforced by them in their dealings with students. The characteristics preferred by teachers are those that embody middle-class values and morality—industry, responsibility,

conscientiousness, reliability, thoroughness, self-control, efficiency, and emotional stability. These behaviors resemble those of the marketplace and the world of work, where the emphasis falls on economically ambitious, materialistic, competitive, adaptable, and conforming behavior (as opposed to behavior that is humanistic, open-minded, curious, and creative). In this sense, schools provide a bridge between the values of intimacy, acceptance, and authority pervading the family and the more demanding, impersonal rules of the larger society (Eisenstadt, 1956). As Alton Harrison, Jr., and John E. Westerman observe:

It is pointless to ask whether or not schools should reflect major societal values. A more germane question is, Could schools do otherwise? [1974:636]

Surveys reveal that teachers rate those social skills concerned with order, rules, and obedience as most important. They attach less overall value to skills that involve taking the initiative and being assertive and outgoing in interpersonal relationships (Cartledge and Milburn, 1978).

Within school settings pupils must become accustomed to being judged and having their work evaluated and compared in quality with that of others. All of this compels students to cope with varying degrees of success and

failure. In few if any areas of school life can they escape from an atmosphere of competitive achievement, be it in "hard-core" subjects, music, art, or physical education (Dreeben, 1968).

William Kessen, a Yale University developmental psychologist, studies the hidden curriculum operating in one first-grade classroom in a New Haven school that drew its students from a predominantly upper-income neighborhood (Radloff, 1975). The hidden curriculum centered on the "importance of getting ahead." The children undertook each task only partly for its own sake; they saw its main function as allowing them to get on to the next task. For instance, in working with a reading series, the six-year-old children were eager to finish the blue unit so they could get to the more advanced orange one, then to the purple one, and so on.

The first-grade children were adept "social diagnosticians." They threw out answers and guesses on the basis of the teacher's cues, smiles, nods, and body language rather than focusing on the problem at hand. The students continually ranked themselves and others in terms of each accomplishment and evolved complex sets of hierarchies. Some pupils found it easier to feign stupidity than to fight the system. They would respond by saying, "I can't do it," although in working personally with the teacher they were able to relax and do the work.

TEACHING MORAL VALUES
Church-related schools are established with the express purpose of transmitting a particular set of values to students.

In Europe, a woman was near death from a special kind of cancer. There was one drug that the doctors thought might save her. It was a form of radium that a druggist in the same town had recently discovered. The drug was expensive to make, but the druggist was charging ten times what the drug cost him to make. He paid $200 for the radium and charged $2,000 for a small dose of the drug. The sick woman's husband, Heinz, went to everyone he knew to borrow the money, but he could only get together about $1,000, which is half of what it cost. He told the druggist that his wife was dying, and asked him to sell it cheaper or let him pay later. But the druggist said, "No, I discovered the drug and I'm going to make money from it." Heinz got desperate and broke into the man's store to steal the drug for his wife. Should the husband have done that? [Kohlberg, 1963:18–19]

Based on children's and adults' responses to this type of dilemma, Kohlberg identifies six stages in the development of moral judgment. He groups these stages into three major levels: the *preconventional level* (stages 1 and 2); the *conventional level* (stages 3 and 4); and the *postconventional level* (stages 5 and 6). Table 11.1 summarizes these levels and stages, together with typical responses to the story of Heinz. Study the table carefully for a thorough understanding of Kohlberg's theory. Note that the stages are not based

TABLE 11.1
Kohlberg's Stages in the Development of Moral Judgment

Level One	Preconventional	Child's Responses to Theft of Drug
Stage 1	*The obedience-and-punishment orientation:* The child obeys rules to avoid punishment. The physical consequences of an action determine its goodness or rightness irrespective of the broader human meaning of these consequences. As yet, moral standards remain external to the child.	Pro: Theft is justified because the drug did not cost much to produce. Con: Theft is condemned because Heinz will be caught and go to jail.
Stage 2	*The naive hedonistic and instrumental orientation:* Right consists of that which satisfies the child's needs, allowing the child to obtain benefits and rewards. Although reciprocity occurs, it is self-serving, manipulative, and based upon a marketplace outlook: "You scratch my back and I'll scratch yours."	Pro: Theft is justified because his wife needs the drug and Heinz needs his wife's companionship and help in life. Con: Theft is condemned because his wife will probably die before Heinz gets out of jail, so it will not do him much good.

Level Two	Conventional	Child's Responses to Theft of Drug
Stage 3	*The "good boy"—"nice girl" morality:* Good behavior is that which pleases others. The child is concerned with winning the approval of others and avoiding their disapproval. Behavior is often judged by intention. The child has a conception of a morally good person as one who possesses a set of virtues; hence the child places much emphasis upon being "nice."	Pro: Theft is justified because Heinz is unselfish in looking after the needs of his wife. Con: Theft is condemned because Heinz will feel bad thinking of how he brought dishonor on his family; his family will be ashamed of him.
Stage 4	*The "law-and-order" orientation:* The individual blindly accepts social conventions and rules. Emphasis is placed on "doing one's duty," showing respect for authority, and maintaining a given social order for its own sake.	Pro: Theft is justified because Heinz would otherwise have been responsible for his wife's death. Con: Theft is condemned because Heinz is a lawbreaker.

Level Three	Postconventional	Child's Responses to Theft of Drug
Stage 5	*The social-contract orientation:* The individual believes that the purpose of the law is to preserve human rights. Moral behavior rests on an agreement among individuals to conform to laws that are necessary for the community welfare. But since law is a social contract, it can be modified so long as basic rights like life and liberty are not impaired.	Pro: Theft is justified because the law was not fashioned for situations in which an individual would forfeit life by obeying the rules. Con: Theft is condemned because others may also have great need.

(continued)

TABLE 11.1 *(continued)*
Kohlberg's Stages in the Development of Moral
Judgment

Level One	Preconventional	Child's Responses to Theft of Drug
Stage 6	*The universal ethical principle orientation:* Morality is viewed as a decision of conscience, an internalized set of ideas which, if violated, results in self-condemnation and guilt. The individual follows self-chosen ethical principles based on abstract concepts (for example, the equality of human rights, the Golden Rule, and respect for the dignity of each human being) rather than concrete rules (for example, the Ten Commandments). Unjust laws may be broken because they conflict with broad moral principles.	Pro: Theft is justified because Heinz would not have lived up to the standards of his conscious if he had allowed his wife to die. Con: Theft is condemned because Heinz did not live up to the standards of his conscience when he engaged in stealing.

Sources: Adapted from Lawrence Kohlberg, "The Development of Children's Orientation Toward a Moral Order," *Vita Humana,* Vol. 6 (1963), pp. 11–33; and "The Cognitive-Developmental Approach to Moral Education," *Phi Delta Kappan,* Vol. 56 (1975), pp. 670–677.

on whether the moral decison about Heinz is pro or con, but on the reasoning that the individual employs in reaching the decision.

Kohlberg and his associates have tested individuals in the United States, Great Britain, Israel, Mexico, Turkey, Taiwan, and Malaysia. He interprets this data as supporting his claim that all individuals, regardless of culture, go through the same stages of moral development. Although societies may differ in the specific details of their culture, Kohlberg says that they all share a common principle of justice—regard for the value and equality of all human beings and for reciprocity in human relations. Like Socrates, he believes that virtue is ultimately one, not many, and it is always the same ideal regardless of culture. Thus, Kohlberg and his associates (Turiel, 1973) deny that moral values are acquired through processes of socialization in which individuals internalize cultural content (a position held by many sociologists and psychologists of the behaviorist and observational learning schools).

All of this has implications for moral education:

Because the experiences necessary for structural development are believed to be *universal,* it is possible for the child to develop the behavior naturally, without planned instruction. But the fact that only about half of the adult American population fully reaches Piaget's stage of formal operational reasoning and only 5% reach the highest moral stage demonstrates that natural or universal forms of development are not inevitable but depend on experience. [Kohlberg and Mayer, 1972:486–487]

Until recently Kohlberg insisted that it is useless for teachers to instruct children directly in moral values. Instead, he argued that teachers should provide the conditions where children can "stretch" their existing moral thinking and evolve more effective cognitive structures for dealing with the realities that they encounter as they interact with their environment. As such he objected to the teaching of specific values. He thought that as children passed from one stage to the next in moral reasoning, they would simultaneously acquire more mature and positive moral values and perspectives.

However, over the past several years Kohlberg (1978) has revised a number of his formulations. He has appeared to drop his sixth stage, which some have criticized as Ivy League elitist and culturally biased. In the sixth stage, Kohlberg had

PRECONVENTIONAL MORALITY
Children at the first-grade level tend to follow rules from a desire to obtain rewards and benefits. Rules, including rules about appropriate classroom behavior like sharpening pencils, are external to the self.

attempted to capture the ideal of brotherhood, equality, and community embodied in the philosophies of individuals such as Martin Luther King, Jr. But at a symposium in the late 1970s, Kohlberg lamented his increasing difficulty in finding stage-six persons: ''Perhaps all the sixth-stage persons of the 1960s had been wiped out, perhaps they had regressed, or maybe it was all in my imagination in the first place'' (quoted by Muson, 1979:57).

As noted, Kohlberg had held that children can be stimulated to climb the stage ladder by discussion of moral dilemmas in the classroom. However, he now advocates an approach that even he acknowledges to be ''indoctrinative'':

Although the moral stage concept is valuable for research purposes, . . . it is not a sufficient guide to the moral educator, who deals with concrete morality in a school world [stealing, cheating, aggression, and drug use]. . . . In this context the educator must be a socializer, teaching value content and behavior, not merely a Socratic facilitator of development. . . . I no longer hold . . . negative views of indoctrinative moral education, and I now believe that the concept guiding moral education must be partly ''indoctrinative.'' [Kohlberg, 1978:84]

Kohlberg and his colleagues have been directly involved in the design and conduct of a number of programs for moral education, including the

Cluster School in Cambridge, Massachusetts, and a Connecticut prison (Blatt and Kohlberg, 1975; Mosher, 1980; Reimer, 1981). Much of this work has focused on the establishment of "just communities" (based on the democratic ethos) in the high schools and prisons. Kohlberg and his associates have also developed classroom curricula for promoting growth in moral reasoning. One technique that Kohlberg recommends involves stimulating dialogues in which students are confronted with contradictions in their moral thinking:

> In terms of moral discussion, the important conditions appear to be:
> 1. Exposure to the next higher stage of reasoning.
> 2. Exposure to situations posing problems and contradictions for the child's current moral structure, leading to dissatisfaction with his current level.
> 3. An atmosphere of interchange and dialogue combining the first two conditions, in which conflicting moral views are compared in an open manner. [Kohlberg, 1975:675]

A book of dilemmas, *Hypothetical Dilemmas for Use in Moral Discussions,* has been prepared and distributed by the Moral Education and Research Foundation at Harvard University.

Kohlberg (1969, 1975) also suggests that moral development is facilitated by providing pupils with opportunities to take different roles, allowing them to view circumstances from contrasting perspectives. The impact of these techniques apparently lies in the instigation of disequilibrium and its resolution through the transformation of the child's cognitive structure.

Critics of the cognitive-developmental approach point out that the theory deals with moral judgments—an attitude or state of mind—and not with moral behavior. This is a serious limitation, since moral judgment is not a sufficient condition for moral action. Moreover, Kohlberg, like Piaget, is particularly weak on the development of the affective side of morality, such matters as emotion, guilt, concern for others and remorse (Peters, 1975).

The Values-Clarification Approach

There's no place to hide from your values. Everything you do reflects them. Even denying that your values show in your every act is a value indicator.

SIDNEY B. SIMON AND POLLY DE SHERBININ
Values Clarification, 1975

Over the past decade, the values-clarification approach has experienced a rapid rise in popularity throughout the United States and Canada, becoming the most widely used method of moral education. The foundation stones of the approach are two books: *Values and Teaching* (Raths, Harmin, and Simon, 1966) and *Values Clarification: A Handbook of Practical Strategies for Teachers and Students* (Simon, Howe, and Kirschenbaum, 1972). The program does not go further than eliciting awareness of values; it assumes that becoming more self-aware about one's values is an end in itself:

> When discussing value-laden areas and controversial issues, the value-clarifying teacher or parent accepts all viewpoints and does not try to impose his or her own views (although they may be shared). In that sense, the approach is indeed "value free." . . . Responses are not judged as better or worse; each student's views are treated with equal respect. [Kirschenbaum et al., 1977:744]

Although Kohlberg also termed his original approach "non-indoctrinating," he nonetheless saw his method as leading students to the highest stage of morality, one which places a premium on human life, equality, and dignity. Sidney B. Simon and other sponsors of the values-clarification approach disavow even this goal. Further, Simon and his associates question Kohlberg's claim that certain values are culturally universal and conclude that "a person in the Antarctic would not be expected to have the same values as a person in Chicago" (Raths, Simon, and Harmin, 1966). Despite these differences, both approaches stress the open discussion of value dilemmas.

VALUES: TOOLS FOR DISCUSSION

A fifth-grade student discovers a friend stealing from the closet. He doesn't want to mention it to the teacher, but he's afraid not to. The teacher has been making a big deal about thefts in the classroom recently. What does the student do?

He may turn the friend in and feel like a traitor. Or perhaps he will ignore the incident and feel guilty. What he does depends largely on his values.

His dilemma is real, taken from Mimi Comerchero's concerns class at Anna C. Scott School in Leonia, New Jersey. Her concerns class examines worries of students, providing a forum where they can study their feelings and reactions. This is one way of studying values.

Another way is to use everyday life experiences, as did Arnold B. Cheyney of the University of Miami, Coral Gables, Florida, and Rosemarie Roth, an educational consultant for the *Miami Herald.*

THE CONCERNS CLASS
When you look at the notes students pass back and forth to each other, you see their hurt feelings

Source: "Values: Three Tools for Discussion," *Instructor*, 86 (August/September 1976):120–123.

and obvious failures in dealing with group pressures, Ms. Comerchero told *Instructor.* They need a forum for discussing their problems. She developed a concerns class to talk about peer pressures, role problems, and family troubles. How does it work?

Several students act out a scene about a person with a particular problem. The class serves as a "third ear," allowing students to hear themselves as others do. Ms. Comerchero establishes the scenarios, using everyday situations. Students clarify the issues and provide good reasons for acting one way or another. The scenes are emotional but not threatening. Following are some instances the class examined, but you can find other situations just by observing the problems that trouble your own students:

- Susan wants to be friendly with two groups of girls who oppose each other. Friendship with one group means being left out of the other. Which does she choose? How does she choose? Is any choice the "right" one? Why? What might be the consequences of a good or a bad choice?
- Robert has always been critical of his father's smoking. Now, on three separate oc-

casions, friends suggest he join them for a smoke. Robert finally gives in, and is seen by a neighbor who tells his parents. What does he say? Is he wrong for smoking?
- Linda's mother specifically forbids her to use her favorite perfume. Disobeying, Linda uses it and accidentally drops it, breaking the bottle. What does she do? How could she have avoided the problem?

Students eagerly participate. All want to air their opinions and see how others react. Even if little analyzing goes on, playing a different role leads to thoughtful reconsideration of their values. Students learn to recognize that morality has a social dimension, that other persons have feelings and rights, as well as responsibilities. No moral decision can be made unless they study the alternatives.

"I do very little talking once I present the situation. I reserve my comments to probing, restating, and clarifying," Ms. Comerchero noted. "Above all, I try to help youngsters hear between the lines. I surprise myself by feeling little need to pass judgment on what I hear. The kids' solutions are rich, multifaceted, and revealing."

(continued)

VALUES: TOOLS FOR DISCUSSION
(continued)

Examining values is a constant task, and establishing a concerns class raises interesting questions. Do you have a responsibility to yourself or to the group? Do your values match those in your community? Does ignorance excuse you? Can you live with complicity? How do you stand up against group pressures?

Not knowing all the answers is no crime. There are no pat answers or solutions, and discussing values is always enlightening.

INVESTIGATIVE REPORTERS
Have you ever thought of using your local newspaper as a tool for teaching values? Arnold Cheyney and Rosemarie Roth suggest that the paper cannot only clarify values for students, but also make them aware of the values of others.

How can a newspaper do all this? Below are twenty activities tailor-made for using the paper as a tool for teaching values. Begin the project by making sure students understand the meaning of a *value*. Suggest each child bring in a daily newspaper or a week's supply, if needed. Copy each activity on 5″ × 8″ index cards.

Students may read the cards to the entire class, individually at an interest center or as part of a panel discussion. They may also work with their families at home.

1. On one side of the card, make a list of as many values as you can. How does it compare with the list on the backside of the card: beauty, loyalty, brotherhood, obedience, courage, patience, democracy, patriotism, dependability, perseverance, freedom, peace, promptness, friendship, responsibility, honesty, reverence, industry, kindness, liberty, and truthfulness. Select an article that illustrates a particular value. How does the article describe the value you selected?
2. Find an example of honesty (or the lack of it) in government, advertising, business, or individuals. In what ways are the parties honest or dishonest? Would everyone agree with your choice?
3. Is there an article about someone with a particularly frustrating problem? How should they solve it? What alternatives do they have? What are the consequences if they don't solve the problem at all?
4. Cut out a picture of people working together. Why is cooperation valuable? Is their job easier because they are working together? How?
5. Read an article about an angry person. Why is the person angry? Does he have good reason? What can he do to lessen his anger? Have you ever felt angry? How do you react when you are angry? What are the consequences of anger for the individual? For others?
6. Select a picture or article about one person. (The sports page is a natural place to look.) On a sheet of paper, make two columns listing qualities you do and don't admire about this person. Put an X next to the qualities you possess yourself.
7. Is there a picture of someone who looks lonely? Ask others in your class: "Why does the person feel this way?" "What would you do to help the lonely person overcome his problem?" "What can you do when you're lonely?" "Is loneliness always undesirable?"
8. Turn to the television programming section. What programs will you watch after school or at night? While you watch the programs, fill in the following survey. Report your findings to the class.

Values-clarification proponents claim that contemporary youth are confronted by many more choices than in previous generations. Areas of confusion abound: politics, religion, love, premarital sex, family, friends, drugs, race, work, leisure time, school, health, aging, and death:

Values clarification begins with the observation that both individuals and societies are suffering from many ailments, not the least of which are *value problems*. In individual lives the symptoms are apathy, flightiness, overconformity, overdissention, and other behaviors indicative of lack of

Program: _____

Channel: _____

Date and time: _____

Number of children: _____

Number of men: _____

Number of women: _____

Number of violent actions: _____

_____

Number of people of a race different from yours: _____

9. Choose someone who would make a good friend. What qualities do you like about this person? What would you do together? What is friendship, and why do you value it?

10. Would you like to be involved in an event described in the newspaper? Why would you like to participate? In what ways would this activity improve you as a person? Is self-improvement important? Why?

11. Look through food advertisements. Are there foods mentioned that you have never eaten? Look in reference books to discover where the food is grown. Draw a picture of how it looks. What do you think it tastes like? What is its texture? Would you want to try eating this food? (Why or why not?) Is it good to widen our tastes? How is an aesthetic value, such as taste, different from a moral or a social value?

12. Are there people described in the news who are from a different country or who have customs different from your family's? Do the articles tell how the people live or raise their children? What are their religious beliefs? How are they similar to you and your family? How are they different?

13. Cut out pictures of fashions and hair styles you like. Paste them on construction paper. Would the styles be appropriate for recreation? School? Or church? Label each picture accordingly. See if your classmates agree.

14. Use a crayon to circle the things you like to do. Cut them out and paste on a piece of paper. Next to each, mark whether you like to do it alone, with friends, or with parents. What do you like to do that is not listed in the paper?

15. Read through the comic section of the daily or Sunday paper. What character would you like to be? Why?

16. List values found in feature stories, letters to the editor, question-and-answer columns, Ann Landers, or Dear Abby. Choose two of these values that are important to you, and write a paragraph stating why. Write your own Dear Abby column for classroom problems.

17. Cut out a single cartoon that points out a specific value. Show the cartoon to a friend. What does he think the cartoon means? Draw your own cartoon illustrating that value.

18. Play charades. Pick an article about a value you found in the paper and act out the story in front of the class. See who in your class can find the article you're describing. Then ask the winner to act out the next scene.

19. Is there an article or a picture about elderly people? Describe the people in one paragraph. What are they like? Are they interested in any of the same things you are? Make a list of the values you think they have. Are those values the same as yours? How are they different?

20. If you had all the time and money in the world, what situation described in the paper would you change? Tell how you would accomplish that change.

values or of value confusion. . . . Values clarification is *an intervention* that attempts to change this state of affairs. [Kirschenbaum et al., 1977:743]

The process of values clarification is taught in classroom simulations in which students are taken through a set of activities or "strategies." These strategies offer students various choices and encourage them to make a conscious effort to discover their own values. They are designed to help students learn an approach for formulating their values and to apply this process to value-laden areas and moral dilemmas in their own lives.

Strategy No. 49 is the "Cave-In Simulation." Students are brought together in a darkened room with a candle in their midst. The teacher tells the students to imagine that they are all trapped in a cave-in. They are to dig out single file. The nearer a person is to the front of the line, the better his or her chance of survival:

> Each member of the class will give his reasons for why he should be at the head of the line. After hearing each other's reasons, they will determine the order by which they will file out.
>
> The teacher concludes his scene-setting and instructions by saying, "So now we will go around our circle, one at a time, and each person will give his reasons for why he would like to be near the head of the line. Your reasons can be of two kinds. You can tell us what you want to live for; or what you have yet to get out of life that is important to you. Or you can talk about what you have to contribute to others . . . that would justify your . . . survival. Both types of reasons will be considered equally. . . ."
>
> Each student gets a chance to offer his reasons. Students may pass; although in this situation, a pass means the student is deciding to allow himself to be placed near the end of the line. [Simon, Howe, and Kirschenbaum, 1972:287–288]

In Strategy No. 56, called "Obituary," the child writes and then publicly shares his or her obituary with the class. The teacher hands out a sample format, "James Clark, age ten, died yesterday from . . ." (Simon, Howe, and Kirschenbaum, 1972:311).

The values-clarification approach has sparked its own controversy. Some criticize the program for failing to affirm the existence of certain "absolute" values, a charge made most often by patriotic and religious groups. Others take the opposite tack. They contend that, although the approach's sponsors claim it to be "value-free," in point of fact the authors have built their own values into the system (Stewart, 1975; Eger, 1981). William J. Bennett and Edward L. DeLattre analyze the various strategies and conclude that many have a basic underlying theme: "People are bundles of wants; the world is a battlefield of conflicting wants; and no one has room for goodness, decency,

or the capacity for a positive exercise of will" (1978:86).

In conclusion, there are many approaches for dealing with the moral education of a nation's youth. But whatever approach is followed, most schools cannot proceed very far in promoting values not shared by the community at large. Education of any sort, whether via the hidden curriculum or the conventional one, mirrors the society in which it occurs. Hence, morality is ultimately the product of the world in which children and the educational enterprise are immersed (Etzioni, 1977).

CHAPTER SUMMARY

1. Affective elements pervade every aspect of the learning situation. There are at least four reasons why affective outcomes need to be assessed in considering education. First, affective factors influence learning. Second, they influence people's ability to participate effectively within a democratic society. Third, affective factors play a large part in occupational and vocational satisfaction. And fourth, it is important that individuals develop those abilities and skills that form the foundation for a healthy and effective life.

2. Learning results in the establishment of attitudes that influence people's choices of action. Schools are hardly neutral settings. Events continuously take place that have consequences for each person's sense of worth, adequacy, and security, aspects that touch the very core of a person's sense of well-being. These events mold the attitudes that children develop toward school.

3. Individuals' self-appraisals tend to be reflected appraisals. If children are accepted, approved, respected, and liked for what they are, they acquire attitudes of self-acceptance and self-respect. Our self-concepts also derive from the feedback we receive regarding our power and competence in the world about us. Thus, we are not simply passive beings who mirror others' attitudes toward us; we actively shape our self-concepts as we encounter and cope with the realities of life.

4. The notion that blacks suffer debilitating effects from the psychological stresses associated with racism found wide support in both the popular and the scholarly literature prior to the late 1960s. Over the past decade, however, this early research has come under careful scrutiny. More recent studies reveal that the levels of self-esteem among black children and adolescents are higher than among white youth, or at least that there are no differences between the two groups.

5. While many schools provide professional counseling services for those students who need special assistance, community health experts point out that these approaches have a pathology-oriented and treatment focus. Instead of merely following the traditional crisis-centered framework, these authorities emphasize the importance of programs keyed to early psychological intervention—the building of personal strengths and competencies rather than solely ameliorating weaknesses.

6. Adjustment consists of two processes: fitting oneself into given circumstances and changing the circumstances to fit one's needs. Wise educators and parents attempt to impart to children skills for successfully dealing with stress.

7. If we are to live with one another in communities and societies, there must be a system of morality, shared conceptions of what is right and wrong. However, simply because there are rules does not guarantee that people will conform to them. In a monumental and classic study carried out over a half century ago, Hugh Hartshorne and Mark A. May were unable to locate a stable personality trait such as honesty in children. Nearly all the children cheated at one time or another depending on the situation. Further, attempts at character education had no influence on producing a general moral character trait that consistently resisted opportunities to cheat.

8. Intelligence, age, and sex differences play a small part in moral conduct. Group codes and motivational factors have a much larger role.

9. Moral development represents more than simply learning prohibitions against misbehavior. Like honesty, prosocial behavior has a strong situational component, although some individuals may be more or less "other-centered" than others. Among the factors influencing prosocial behavior are expectations of approval, learned prohibitions, norms of responsibility, level of cognitive and social skills, susceptibility to feelings of anxiety, the cost or inconvenience of helping, and numerous situational variables.

10. One version of the values-transmission approach to moral education takes the position that certain ethical standards are "right," namely those of one's own group or society. The task of the schools is defined as one of imparting these values to the youth. A somewhat different version of the values-transmission approach asserts that schooling is inescapably a moral enterprise. To carry on one's daily activities within an institutional context is to take on the ways of that institution.

11. The cognitive-developmental approach to moral education asserts that the primary aim of education is to facilitate children's moral development by confronting them with moral dilemmas. Such techniques instigate disequilibrium. The resolution of moral dilemmas leads to the transformation of the child's cognitive structure and advancement to a higher moral level.

12. The values-clarification approach to moral education does not go further than eliciting awareness of values. It assumes that becoming more self-aware about one's values is an end in itself. When discussing value-laden matters, the teacher accepts all viewpoints and does not try to impose his or her own values.

CHAPTER GLOSSARY

adjustment The process of finding means for coping with the demands of our environment.

affective domain All those aspects of human behavior involving feelings, emotions, tastes, preferences, values, attitudes, morals, character, philosophies of life, and guiding principles.

attitude A learned and relatively enduring tendency to evaluate a person, event, or situation in a certain way and to act in accordance with that evaluation.

moral behavior The adoption of principles that lead people to evaluate given actions as "right" and others as "wrong" and to govern their own actions in terms of these principles.

prosocial behavior Ways of responding to people through sympathetic, cooperative, trusting, helpful, rescuing, comforting, and giving acts.

self-concept How people perceive themselves; the sum total of all the characteristics they attribute to themselves, based on the roles they play and the personal attributes that they believe they possess.

self-esteem The positive or negative judgments individuals attach to the characteristics which they attribute to themselves.

EXERCISES

Review Questions

1. Student attitudes toward school
   a. are strongly influenced by academic performance
   b. tend to vary considerably between grades
   c. are subject-specific, rather than generalized
   d. are based on unrealistic estimation of capability

2. Psychologists feel that self-concept is
   a. based on both affective as well as cognitive components
   b. not related to academic performance
   c. basically self-generated rather than influenced by the reactions of others
   d. equivalent to self-esteem

3. Within the last decade, research on minority self-attitudes revealed that
   a. the levels of self-esteem among blacks have been replicated in other minority groups
   b. black preference for white or black dolls is a function of the testing situation as well as the tester's race
   c. more recent studies show a lower self-esteem for black adolescents as compared to whites
   d. a and b are true

4. Which of the factors listed below has been found in school phobias?
   a. Phobias peak between the first and second grade.
   b. The incidence is greater among girls than boys.
   c. They are more common in lower socio-economic groups.
   d. The symptoms are universal among students.
   e. a and c are true

5. In treating school phobias, school authorities should remember that
   a. therapy can be done within the school setting
   b. prolonged withdrawal from school may be harmful
   c. the entire family generally should be involved in therapy
   d. a, b, and c are true

6. In their classic study of cheating, Hartshorne and May determined that
   a. honesty is a relatively stable virtue
   b. situational factors were critical in determining children's attitudes and behavior
   c. boys cheated more than girls
   d. character education was successful in changing attitudes

7. Research findings on prosocial behavior show that

    a. altruism, unlike the other prosocial behaviors, appears to be a character trait

    b. children will invariably model prosocial but not antisocial adult behaviors

    c. when the verbal behaviors and actual practices of an adult conflict, actual practices are more influential

    d. children are little affected by the attitudes of adults

8. Proponents of the values-transmission approach argue that

    a. polls show the majority of Americans favor instruction in moral behavior

    b. up to the last decade or so moral instruction was ignored in the school curriculum

    c. children do not learn moral behavior within the school unless it is explicitly taught

    d. good must be defined as a universal

9. In Kohlberg's stage theory of moral development

    a. higher stages can only be reached sequentially

    b. higher stages differ from lower stages in terms of the knowledge base

    c. the focus is on behavior rather than judgment

    d. the order of stages is culture-specific

    e. b and c are true

10. The values-clarification approach stresses that

    a. becoming aware of one's values is the critical educational goal of moral growth

    b. there are no universals among human values

    c. clarification of personal values is done through simulations of moral dilemmas

    d. a, b, and c are true

    e. b and c are true

Answers

1. a (See pp. 305, 307)
2. a (See p. 307)
3. d (See pp. 310–311)
4. b (See pp. 312–313)
5. d (See pp. 312–313)
6. b (See p. 317)
7. c (See p. 320)
8. a (See pp. 324, 326)
9. a (See p. 326)
10. d (See pp. 332–336)

Applying Principles and Concepts

1. Ms. Carr, a black, is the first minority teacher hired in a previously all-white lower-class school. Place a check before each of the following statements that is *not* likely to be true of students in her class.

_____ a. Louise, who has previously been doing badly in school, will welcome Ms. Carr as a change for the better.

_____ b. Eric's parents' dislike of blacks will cause them to remove him from that class at all costs.

_____ c. Paul has been doing well in school. He has no special feelings for or against blacks and therefore is most likely to regard Ms. Carr as just another teacher.

2. In the following passage underline those words or phrases that refer to events or situations likely to contribute to or indicate poor self-esteem.

Shauna is quite a good student academically. She is above average in appearance. Students do tease her a lot because athletically she does quite poorly. She does not make friends easily and faces new situations quite anxiously. Although Shauna trusts her teacher, she shows little affection and rarely speaks to her.

3. In the textbook, criteria defining optimal adjustment are listed from various sources. Which of the following behavior characteristics are *not*

generally agreed to be measures of good adjustment?

_____ a. Reactive rather than passive
_____ b. Highly gregarious
_____ c. Quite independent
_____ d. Very intelligent
_____ e. Reality-oriented

4. Mr. Owens, a math teacher, is making some observations to a student teacher about proctoring a test. Place a check before each of the following statements that is supported by research.

_____ a. "I watch the boys like a hawk; they cheat more than girls."
_____ b. "There's just more cheating in some classes than in others."
_____ c. "There's a lot more cheating today than when I was in school."
_____ d. "The smart ones seem to cheat less."
_____ e. "I look for kids who are pretty worried; they're more likely to cheat."

5. Which of the following statements reflect a values-transmission approach to education?

_____ a. The teacher has a sign on his or her desk that says "Think Positive."
_____ b. The math textbook uses examples of selling at a profit or loss.
_____ c. The teacher conducts a discussion on the moral implications of a specific problem situation.
_____ d. The teacher rewards the student for finishing first.

6. Kohlberg has identified six stages of moral development: obedience-and-punishment orientation (1), naive hedonistic and instrumental orientation (2), the "good boy"–"nice girl" morality (3), the "law-and-order" orientation (4), social-contract orientation (5), and the universal ethical principle orientation (6). Following is a description of an experiment conducted by a psychologist some years ago. After the description we have included a number of statements by subjects. Indicate by number the stage of reasoning exhibited by the subject.

In the experiment the subject was led into a room where he was told he would be administering electric shocks to another "subject" in a separate room. To administer the shocks, he would turn a rheostat. At one point on the rheostat, the subject was told, the shock could be lethal. As the subject was ordered to turn the rheostat higher, the person in the other room began to moan and cry out. (In reality there was no connection; the other "subject" was a paid participant who had been told what to do.) At a certain point this other "subject" cried out and then fell silent. The experimenter ordered the real subject to continue.

_____ a. "You're the boss; I guess it's all right if you say so."
_____ b. "I know we both volunteered, but he may be hurt. I can't go on."
_____ c. "I guess if I stop now, I'll ruin the experiment. You wouldn't like that."
_____ d. "No, and I don't care what you think."
_____ e. "All right; I'm just as interested as you are in what happens next."

Answers

1. b (See pp. 304–305)
2. Underline "students do tease her," "does not make friends easily," "faces new situations quite anxiously," "shows little affection and rarely speaks to her." (See pp. 307, 309–310)
3. b (See pp. 314, 316)
4. b, d, e (See p. 319)
5. a, b, d (See pp. 324, 326)
6. a, 4; b, 5; c, 3; d, 6; e, 2 (See pp. 328–332)

Project

OBJECTIVE: To obtain a measure of social responsibility among high-school students.

PROCEDURE: Visit a secondary school, and ask permission to tell the following story to at least ten students. Choose boys and girls. There are two versions of the story. Tell Version 1 to half the students and Version 2 to the other half. At the end of the story ask for the students' reactions and reasoning. This project can also be carried out using peers.

Version 1:

Tom is a very good student and a great athlete. Bill, his friend, is surprised to find that Tom is peddling cocaine in school. Tom insists he isn't forcing anyone, and he doesn't use it himself. But he says, "Some guys are hooked, and if I don't sell, some one else will." Tom's parents ask Bill if Tom is pushing drugs. What should Bill do?

Version 2:

Tom is a very good student and a great athlete. Bill, his friend, is surprised to find that Tom is using drugs and helping others find a supplier. Tom insists he isn't forcing anyone, and he isn't making money himself. But, as he says, "I'm on coke and I know how others feel." Tom's parents visit and ask Bill if Tom is on drugs. What should Bill do?

ANALYSIS: The stories differ in that in one instance Tom is a user and in the other a seller. Determine the effects this difference has on people's empathy for Tom and on their choice of Bill's decision. Try to relate the reasons to Kohlberg's levels.

CHAPTER OUTLINE

12

MOTIVATION

CHAPTER PREVIEW

As Chapter 11 indicated, an important relationship exists between students' attitudes toward themselves and school and their experiences of success or failure. This relationship is explored further in this chapter, which seeks to explain why some students are motivated to do well while others seem to have given up hope of achievement. Differences between intrinsic and extrinsic motivations are explored, along with the explanations or attributions people make for task outcomes. The effect of anxiety on perfor-

mance, as well as differences among individuals in their desire to set and realize goals, are also examined. In addition, classroom reward structures, or the arrangements by which students' interdependence—or lack of it—determines rewards, are discussed. Understanding the many motivational factors that influence students' achievement is important both for planning instruction and in dealing with individual students.

After reviewing the chapter outline, think about the following questions while reading this chapter:

▪ What are some appropriate uses of extrinsic motivators in the classroom, and how can students' use of intrinsic motivation be encouraged?

▪ How do people come to make different attributions regarding their task performance, and how do these attributions, in turn, affect later achievement?
▪ How does the phenomenon of learned helplessness develop?
▪ How does anxiety influence achievement?
▪ What different classroom reward structures have been described, and how might each be used appropriately?
▪ In what ways do people differ in their desire to seek and attain competitive success?

Among the most frequently asked questions about human behavior are "why" questions. Why does Mark, despite his high intelligence, do so poorly in school? Why is Jennie so perseverant in her studies? Why did Cathy watch television last evening rather than complete her homework assignment? These questions concern motivation. By understanding motivation, teachers can encourage their students to invest more of themselves in the educational enterprise and achieve a variety of educational objectives. Indeed, good teachers concern themselves with motivation. Philip Jackson (1968) asked a group of outstanding elementary school teachers how they determined when they were teaching effectively. Unlike most educational researchers who would resort to measures of student learning, the teachers indicated that they used evidence of motivation. They scrutinized their students for signs of interest during class time and for indications that this interest continued beyond formal lessons.

Motivation influences the rate of learning, the retention of information, and performance. Accordingly, psychologists have attempted to identify the factors that affect motivation. They broadly group motives in two general categories. The first group consists of *biological motives,* since they derive from various physiological needs such as hunger, thirst, sleep, sex, pain avoidance, elimination, oxygen, and temperature control. The second category involves *social motives,* since they arise in the course of human interaction, for instance, the need for social status, achievement, affiliation, security, and self-esteem.

Considerable controversy exists among psychologists regarding the nature of motivation. Despite the claims of this or that theorist, no current theory provides a full picture of motivation in education (Ball, 1977). Motivation is a complex topic, one that is not completely understood. Here only a small portion of the topic will be considered—motivation that is most immediately relevant to educators.

EDUCATIONAL MOTIVATION

The important thing is not so much that every child should be taught, as that every child should be given the wish to learn.

LORD AVEBURY
The Pleasures of Life, 1887

Most of us assume that behavior is functional, that people do certain things because the consequences somehow meet their needs (Levine, 1975). This premise underlies the concept of motivation. **Motivation** involves those inner states and processes that prompt, direct, and sustain activity. It is a central concept in educational psychology. Yet, motivation is something we never directly observe. Instead, we observe people's behavior and the environment in which that behavior occurs. From these observations, we make inferences regarding their motivation (Ball, 1977).

Intrinsic and Extrinsic Motivation

We destroy the . . . love of learning . . . in children by encouraging and compelling them to work for petty and contemptible rewards—gold stars, or papers marked 100 and tacked to the wall, or A's on report cards, or honor rolls, or dean's lists, or Phi Beta Kappa keys. . . .

JOHN HOLT
How Children Fail, 1964

Mark Twain once observed that work consists of whatever we are obligated to do, whereas play consists of whatever we are not obligated to do. Work is a means to an end; play, an end in itself (Greene and Lepper, 1974). Many psychologists make a similar distinction between extrinsic motivation and intrinsic motivation. **Extrinsic motivation** involves activity that is undertaken for some purpose other than its own sake. Rewards such as school grades, honor rolls, wages, and promotions are extrinsic, because they are independent of the

TERMINOLOGY

In reading psychological literature dealing with motivation, one encounters a complex terminology, which is itself a problem. But perhaps even more disconcerting is the fact that not all psychologists use the same definitions for the concepts or make similar use of them. Among these terms are the following, each of which is provided with its most widely accepted definition:

Needs Those things that the organism requires to survive or function in a reasonably healthy manner.

Drive A mechanism that incites activity when conditions depart from some physiological or psychological optimum, and that sustains activity until the physiological or psychological balance again returns to normal.

Motive Any condition that affects an organism's readiness to initiate or continue a sequence of activity.

Goal The end state or condition toward which an organism is directing its activity.

Incentive External stimuli employed to arouse and direct the activity of an organism toward some goal (usually by threat or promise of reward).

actual activity itself and because they are controlled by someone else. **Intrinsic motivation** entails activity that is undertaken for its own sake. Intrinsic rewards are those inherent to the activity itself and over which we have a high degree of self-control (Notz, 1975; Deci, 1980).

Undermining Intrinsic Motivation

Many progressive educators point out that the schooling process all too often fails to capitalize on children's spontaneous curiosity and desire to learn. A hallmark of childhood is the enormous amount of energy children expend in exploring, learning about, and mastering their environment. Indeed, few characterizations of childhood are more apparent than youngsters' relentless pursuit of competence (White and Watts, 1973). Children want to feel effective and self-determining in dealing with their environment (White, 1959; Deci, 1975, 1980). Unhappily, formal education often undermines these positive tendencies. For instance, one survey reveals that 41 percent of fourth-grade students still retain excellent or outstanding motivation for learning; this percentage declines in

EXTRINSIC MOTIVATION
The use of extrinsic rewards like gold stars may decrease children's intrinsic motivation.

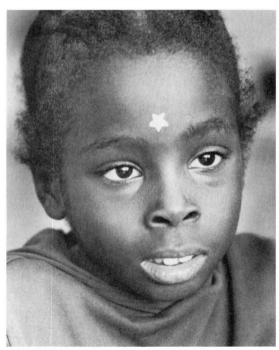

INTRINSIC MOTIVATION
Children engage in many activities because they find them satisfying in their own right, and thus the children do not require external rewards as motivating agents.

subsequent years, until it reaches 12 percent for twelfth-grade students (Flanagan, 1973).

Most psychologists agree that punishment and pain are detrimental to learning. But over the past decade they have also become aware that even rewards, under some circumstances, are the enemies of curiosity and exploration (Condry, 1977). An accumulating body of research suggests that extrinsic rewards decrease intrinsic motivation (Swann and Pittman, 1977; Deci and Ryan, 1980; Deci et al., 1981). Based on his review of the

literature and his own research, Edward L. Deci concludes:

> Children are intrinsically motivated to learn; the activities of learning and discovery are rewarding in their own right because they allow a child to feel competent in relation to his environment. The use of rewards or punishments to encourage this learning will only interfere with the learning because it will make the child's learning dependent on the reward and cause him to do things that will lead him to the reward in the easiest way. This, in turn, will undoubtedly leave him having "learned" less. [1975:212]

The research by Mark R. Lepper and David Greene has demonstrated that parents and educators can unwittingly undermine children's intrinsic motivations by providing them with extrinsic rewards (Lepper, Greene, and Nisbett, 1973; Greene and Lepper, 1974; Lepper and Greene, 1975). The researchers observed children in a nursery school setting and recorded which ones enjoyed drawing with felt-tipped pens of various bright colors. They then had the teachers remove the pens from the classroom for two weeks. After this interval, the researchers brought those children who had earlier shown interest in drawing with the felt pens one by one to another room in the school. The children were asked to make drawings using the felt pens.

Before beginning their drawings, one-third of the children were shown a "good player" award with a gold star and a red ribbon and told that they would receive it upon completing their drawing. Another third did not suspect that they were to receive an award until they were presented with it upon finishing the project. The final third neither expected nor received an award.

A week later, the teachers once again set the felt pens on several tables in the playroom. Lepper and Greene found that the children who had been experimentally induced to expect a reward for their drawings now spent only half as much time with the pens as they had at the time of the first observations. However, the children who had received no award or had unexpectedly received an award at the end of the session displayed the same amount of interest in the felt pens as they had previously. The researchers took this as evidence that the expectation of extrinsic rewards impairs children's intrinsic interest in many activities.

Using Motivators

Many psychologists and educators find that both extrinsic and intrinsic motivators have their uses (Bates, 1979; Brophy, 1981). For instance, extrinsic rewards work effectively to induce individuals to do something they would not otherwise do. A chemistry major may never have considered taking a course in English literature had it not been a college requirement (an extrinsic motivation). Yet, once in the course, the student may become fascinated with the subject. Thus, as involvement and skills increase, intrinsic motives often also develop.

One solution to the problem of rewards is a gradual movement from tangible to intrinsic incentives as children increasingly begin to learn solely for the sake of being competent. Parents and educators can use rewards as necessary to draw children into activities that do not at first attract their interest. But then the extrinsic rewards should be phased out as soon as possible. In the years ahead, it is hoped that research will further clarify the circumstances in which intrinsic or extrinsic rewards are to be preferred. It may also be found that each motivates different types of behavior (Benowitz and Busse, 1976; Deci, 1980).

Attributions of Causality

Closely linked to the matter of intrinsic and extrinsic incentives is another matter—people's perceptions of the factors that produce given outcomes. Consider the following experience. You have been watching a game involving your favorite football team. With five seconds left in the game and the score tied, a player on your team intercepts a pass and races for the goal line. As the player stumbles into the end zone, the gun sounds ending the game. Your team has won. Your friend, who

has a low regard for your team, says, "Your guys sure were *lucky!*" You indignantly respond, "Luck my eye! That was true *ability.*" "Naw," exclaims another friend. "Your guys were more psyched up. They put out more *effort.*" To which a fourth observer interjects, "Heck, it was an *easy* interception. No one was between him and the goal line. Anyone could've done it!" Four differing explanations were set forth for the same event: luck, ability, effort, and the difficulty of the task.

The psychologist Bernard Weiner (1972, 1979) has formulated an approach to the attributions (explanations) people make regarding outcomes that he bases on these four concepts. He notes that psychologists have typically assumed that when people make an internal attribution of causality, they are doing so in terms of inferences about personal *ability* (one's own or another person's intelligence, skill, talent, or resourcefulness). In contrast, when people make an external attribution regarding some success or failure, they are assigning causality to *chance* factors. Weiner says that such assumptions are inadequate and even misleading. They confuse an internal-external dimension with a stability-instability dimension (whether an occurrence is stable or unstable across various events). Consequently, Weiner proposes that attributions regarding outcomes be considered in terms of a *stability* (stable-unstable) dimension and a *control* (internal-external) dimension. This scheme provides four attributional factors: *effort* (internal and unstable), *ability* (internal and stable), *luck* (external and unstable), and *task difficulty* (external and stable). In sum, in life we tend to attribute an outcome to our own or another person's ability or effort, to sheer luck, or to the difficulty of the task.

Educational psychologists find that when students attribute their successes to high ability, they are more likely to view future success as highly probable than if they attribute their success to other factors. By the same token, the attribution of an outcome to low ability makes future failure seem highly probable (Nicholls, 1979). The perception that one has failed because one has low ability is considerably more devastating than the perception that one has failed because of bad luck, lack of effort, or task difficulty.

Some educational psychologists say that both success and failure feed on themselves. Students with histories of performing better than their peers typically attribute their superior performances to high ability, and thus they anticipate future success. Should they encounter periodic episodes of failure, they attribute them to bad luck or lack of effort. However, those with histories of low attainment commonly attribute their successes to good luck or high effort and their failures to poor ability. Consequently, high attainment leads to attributions that maintain a high self-concept of ability, high academic motivation, and continued high attainment. It is otherwise for those students with low attainment (Covington and Omelich, 1979; Nicholls, 1979; Forsyth and McMillan, 1981). Moreover, students who usually attribute their achievement to ability are likely to prefer tasks in which competence is required for the outcome. Conversely, students who attribute success to luck tend to avoid ability tasks and to prefer games of chance (Fyans and Maehr, 1979).

Attainments are relative when they derive from social comparison. Without comparison, individuals are unable to distinguish between the contributions that such factors as ability and difficulty make to outcomes. In this context, the more positive motivation of the higher-achieving students is a product of the presence of the poorer performers. In sum, the academic achievement of some students is enhanced at the expense of their peers. This outcome has led some educators and psychologists to search for noncompetitive reward structures, a topic that will be deferred until later in the chapter.

Locus of Control

The research on attributions of causality has been influenced by the concept of locus of control (Lefcourt, 1976; Phares, 1976; Fanelli, 1977). **Locus of control** refers to people's perception of who or what is responsible for the outcome of events and behaviors in their lives. As noted, people differ in the extent to which they believe that they influence the happenings in their lives. When people perceive the outcome of an action as the result of luck, chance, fate, or powerful others, they believe in *external control*. When individuals interpret an outcome as the consequence of their own abilities or efforts, they believe in *internal control* (Rotter, 1966; Chan, 1978).

A number of questionnaires have been developed for measuring an individual's perception of locus of control (Lefcourt, 1976; Phares, 1976). The best known of these was devised by Julian B. Rotter (1966) and is termed the Rotter Internal-External Control Scale. The questionnaire consists of twenty-nine pairs of statements that require the respondent to select one statement of each pair with which he or she most strongly agrees. The following are items 5 and 13 from the Rotter questionnaire:

5. a. The idea that teachers are unfair to students is nonsense.
   b. Most students don't realize the extent to which their grades are influenced by accidental happenings.
13. a. When I make plans, I am almost certain that I can make them work.
    b. It is not always wise to plan too far ahead because many things turn out to be a matter of good or bad fortune anyway.

In these illustrations, the "a" responses are scored as internal control; the "b" responses, external control.

A good many studies have shown a relationship between locus of control and academic achievement. It appears that locus of control plays a mediating role in determining whether pupils become involved in the pursuit of achievement. Externally controlled children tend to follow the theory that no matter how hard they work, the outcome will be determined by luck or chance; they have little incentive to invest personal effort in their studies, to persist in attempts to find a solution to a problem, or to change their behavior to ensure success. In contrast, internally controlled children believe that their behavior accounts for their academic successes or failures and that they can direct their efforts to succeed in academic tasks. This may account for the finding that those students who have an internal sense of control generally show superior academic performance (Massari and Rosenblum, 1972; Bar-Tal and Bar-Zohar, 1977).

Individuals are not irreversibly locked into a fixed pattern of interpreting events. For instance, internal control typically increases with the age of the child (Penk, 1969). Scores on the Rotter Internal-External Control Scale tend to be relatively external at the third grade, with internality increasing in the eighth and tenth grades (Crandall, Katkovsky, and Crandall, 1965). Further, there is some evidence that perception of locus of control can be modified by restructuring the environment (Bar-Tal and Bar-Zohar, 1977). For example, one group of black, disadvantaged children showed a clear and significant change toward a more internal-control orientation as a consequence of their involvement in an educational enrichment program (Follow Through) (Shore, Milgram, and Malasky, 1971). Likewise, pupils in classrooms that use individualized programs of instruction apparently have more internal perceptions of control than do students in classrooms employing traditional methods of teaching (Bar-Tal, Bar-Tal, and Leinhardt, 1975).

Learned Helplessness

Life requires that organisms continually attune their behavior to the realities they encounter in the world about them. Adjustment consists of coping mechanisms that organisms use both to fit themselves to environmental circumstances and to change those circumstances to fit their needs. Yet, research over the past ten years by psychologist Martin E. P. Seligman and his colleagues (Seligman, 1975, 1978; Abramson, Seligman, and Teasdale, 1978) has shown that some organisms exposed to uncon-

trollable events acquire a learned helplessness that then impairs their adjustment to later events that are controllable. **Learned helplessness** refers to a generalized expectancy that events are independent of one's responses. Individuals characterized by learned helplessness view their own actions and consequent events as causally unrelated. Hence, they believe that active coping efforts are futile.

Seligman and his associates stumbled on the phenomenon of learned helplessness while experimenting with dogs whom they had traumatically shocked to test a learning theory (Seligman and Maier, 1967; Overmier and Seligman, 1967). The dogs had been strapped in a harness and given electric shocks. Later, the researchers placed the dogs in a two-compartment shuttlebox where they were supposed to learn that they could escape shock by jumping across the barrier separating the compartments. (For obvious reasons animal lovers have been highly critical of the research.)

Dogs who had not previously been exposed to shock quickly learned the exercise, but this was not true for the dogs who had experienced shock under inescapable conditions. These latter dogs typically did not cross the barrier and escape. Although at first they would run about the compartment and howl, they soon settled down and passively took the shock, whining quietly. The researchers concluded that the experience in the harness had taught the dogs that their responses did not matter and thus they simply gave up.

Donald Hiroto (1974) undertook a learned helplessness experiment with a sample of college students. The students were assigned to one of three groups. The first group heard loud noise that they could terminate by pushing a button four times. The second group heard the noise but could not escape from it. The third group did not receive any noise. In the second phase of the experiment, all groups were tested with a "noise box" in which the subjects could turn off the sound simply by moving a lever from one side of the box to the other.

The results were strikingly similar to the dog experiment. The first and third groups—those

SEX DIFFERENCES IN LEARNED HELPLESSNESS

A growing body of research suggests that girls are more likely to show evidence of learned helplessness than boys. For example, girls are more apt than boys to attribute failure to uncontrollable factors like lack of ability and to decrease their efforts following failure (Dweck and Repucci, 1973; Dweck and Gilliard, 1975; Nicholls, 1975). This occurs despite the fact that on school-related tasks girls are at least as proficient as boys. Indeed, girls receive consistently higher grades than boys and are more favorably rated by teachers and other adults on most attributes (Coopersmith, 1967; Achenbach, 1970; Brophy and Good, 1970; McCandless, Roberts, and Starnes, 1972).

At first sight it would seem that the feedback girls receive from their academic and social achievements would tell them that they are highly regarded. But, then, why do girls so readily indict their abilities when confronted with failure? Why do boys display greater confidence and persistence, despite the fact that they receive more negative evaluations? Carol S. Dweck and her associates (Dweck and Bush, 1976; Dweck et al., 1978) sought answers to these questions in classroom observations and experimental settings. Their research suggests that the pattern of evaluative feedback teachers provide boys and girls with differs.

Teachers tend to be much more critical of boys than girls. This, says Dweck, allows boys to attribute negative feedback to a characteristic of the teacher and not to themselves. Moreover, much of the negative evaluation (45 percent) boys receive for their work is unrelated to its intellectual quality and is based instead upon neatness or instruction following. Accordingly, boys can view negative feedback as irrelevant to the intellectual adequacy of their work. Finally, teachers attribute boys' failures to lack of motivation (laziness, not trying, not studying, and so on) more often than they do the failures of girls. Hence boys can more often blame their academic inadequacies upon a lack of effort rather than a lack of ability.

In contrast, teachers use negative feedback in a highly specific manner for girls' intellectual failures (less than one-third of the boys' negative evaluation is contingent on the intellectual aspects of their work; for girls, more than two-thirds). Further, since they tend to view girls as highly motivated and diligent, teachers do not emphasize motivation as a determinant of girls' failures. Dweck says that as a result boys come to attribute their failures to

SEX DIFFERENCES IN LEARNED HELPLESSNESS
Despite the fact that girls are at least as proficient as boys on school-related tasks, girls are more likely to show evidence of learned helplessness than boys.

inadequate effort and girls to inadequate ability. And since effort can be altered but ability cannot, girls come to see their academic lot as uncontrollable—in brief, they learn helplessness. This effect has consequences for the differences in the long-term academic achievement of men and women (Dweck, Goetz, and Strauss, 1980).

receiving prior controllable noise and those receiving no noise—quickly learned to shut the noise off. But the second group—those receiving prior uncontrollable noise—typically listened passively to the aversive sound. They had learned that they were helpless.

Seligman notes considerable parallels between the behaviors that characterize learned helplessness and the symptoms of depressive disorders. Perhaps the most prominent of these is passivity, a seeming paralysis of will. Similarly, depressed patients interpret their responses as either failing or doomed to failure. It is as if the depressed person is locked within a mental set that repeatedly registers, "I am a born loser." However, critics have pointed out that there are a great many different types of depressive disorders, each evidencing somewhat different symptoms (Depue and Monroe, 1978). In recognition of this fact, Seligman (1978) has recently narrowed his interpretation to encompass a more limited subclass of depressions.

Educational psychologists find that children who give up when they confront failure in achievement situations are also victims of learned helplessness (Dweck, 1975; Diener and Dweck, 1978; Weisz, 1981). Their motivational deficit in learning situations arises from the expectation that outcomes are uncontrollable. This perceived inability to surmount failure leads to apathy. Likewise, learned helplessness may find expression in social situations when children believe they cannot surmount rejection. Children who emphasize their personal incompetence as the source of their rejection are less likely than other children to pursue approval from their peers (Goetz and Dweck, 1980).

In a study undertaken in a school setting, Carol S. Dweck and N. Dickon Reppucci (1973) had one teacher give solvable problems and another unsolvable to fifth-graders. When the "unsolvable" teacher later presented solvable problems, some children did not solve them despite the fact that the problems were of the same sort as the ones they had solved for the other teacher. The researchers were able to compare those children who gave up in the face of failure with those who persevered.

They found that the less persevering students took less personal responsibility for their successes and failures; further, to the extent to which they took responsibility, they attributed success and failure to ability rather than to effort.

In another study involving learned helplessness, Carol I. Diener and Dweck (1978) found a striking difference between "helpless" and "mastery-oriented" children in their approach toward failure. Helpless children tend to ruminate about the cause of their lack of success. However, since they attribute failure to uncontrollable factors, they spend little time searching for ways to overcome failure. In contrast, mastery-oriented pupils appear to be less concerned with explaining past errors and more concerned with finding a solution for the problem that confronts them. Other research reveals that helpless children underestimate their number of successes and overestimate their number of failures. Nor do helpless children, in contrast with mastery-oriented children, expect their successes to continue (Diener and Dweck, 1980).

Dweck (1975) has successfully trained children characterized by learned helplessness to attribute their failure to a lack of effort rather than to a lack of ability. The children who were taught to make attributions that stressed motivation rather than ability as determinants of failure showed striking improvement in their coping responses to failure. However, another group of helpless children who were only provided with success experiences (such as contained in programmed instruction) continued to display difficulty when confronted with failure situations.

Significance of Anxiety

Anxiety—apprehension, dread, or uneasiness—is a key motivational element in classroom behavior and achievement. Depending on the individual and the circumstances, it can facilitate or impair learning. Some psychologists use the terms "anxiety" and "fear" interchangeably. Others define anxiety as a diffuse, unfocused emotional state, and fear as a response to tangible stimuli (for example, tests, high places, snakes, or flying in airplanes). In practice, however, it is usually difficult to distinguish between anxiety and fear.

Charles D. Spielberger (1966, 1972) differentiates between **state anxiety,** a transitory condition of apprehension resulting from the perception of threat in a situation, and **trait anxiety,** apprehension associated with a relatively stable personality attribute. Research reveals that trait anxiety influences state anxiety. In general, anxiety-prone persons are more likely than other individuals to respond with high levels of state anxiety to situations that pose threats to their self-esteem (O'Neil, 1972).

Although most studies find that anxiety impairs school achievement, some research shows that anxious students may on occasion perform better than nonanxious students (Hansen, 1977). Apparently, much depends on the nature of the task. Under some circumstances, anxiety impairs performance (Sarason, 1960; Hill, 1972; Weiner and Samuel, 1975); under others it aids performance (Alpert and Haber, 1960; Wittmaier, 1974); and under still others, there is a curvilinear relationship (up to a certain point, anxiety serves to arouse the individual, leading to improved performance, but if the level of anxiety increases beyond that point, performance is hindered) (Sarason, 1961; Doob and Kirschenbaum, 1973). On tasks of low complexity or on tasks in which the individual is already skilled, anxiety seems to facilitate performance; on tasks of high complexity or on tasks where the individual is not well practiced, anxiety appears to lower the level of performance (Hansen, 1977).

On the whole, anxiety-prone children do less well than unanxious children on such indices of school learning as achievement tests, report-card grades, and grade repetition (Hill and Sarason, 1966; Munz and Smouse, 1968; Spielberger, 1972). Nonetheless, highly test-anxious individuals perform as well or better than the less anxious when evaluative stress is low (Gaudry and Bradshaw, 1970; Sarason, 1972, 1973). For these individuals, high levels of anxiety interfere with their performance.

Recent theory suggests that anxiety may impair people's performance by contributing to selective attention (Wine, 1971; Sarason, 1972; Deffenbacher, 1978). According to this interpretation, anxiety-prone individuals become more alert to evaluative cues when they are under stress. They become increasingly preoccupied with self-worth and other self-oriented responses that direct their attention away from the task. Consequently, their performance suffers.

More specifically, three types of distractions interfere with the performance of highly anxious individuals (Morris and Liebert, 1969, 1970, 1973; Morris and Fulmer, 1976; Deffenbacher, 1977, 1978). First, they worry a good deal about their performance, the consequences of failure, and how well they are doing relative to others (Nottelmann and Hill, 1977). Second, they experience emotional interference in the form of physiological arousal that produces such symptoms as a "racing" heart and an upset stomach. And third, highly anxious people often attempt to compensate for their apprehension by taking a "safe" approach to problem solving that leads to rigid and unimaginative responses.

All of this has implications for education. Psychologists have developed various techniques by which people can restructure worrisome thoughts, promote self-managed relaxation, and ignore irrelevant responses (Meichenbaum, 1972; Holroyd, 1976). For example, Jerome B. Dusek, Nancy L. Mergler, and Marguerite D. Kermis (1976) have recently demonstrated that highly anxious children can improve their performance on learning tasks by consciously sorting out and labeling the relevant stimuli. Consequently, these children should be explicitly taught to identify and then direct their attention to the critical aspects of a task.

R. Jon Leffingwell, an educational psychologist, provides the following advice:

> A teacher can do much to reduce anxiety within his own classroom. Modeling nonthreatening behavior is a primary step in the reduction of

maladaptive behavior. It is difficult for a student to learn new material if he perceives his environment as hostile. Demonstrating a sincere concern for students and verbalizing interests in them, and the material to be learned is necessary. Defining objectives of the course so that the requirements are clearly understood will increase the probability that adaptive learning behaviors will occur. Providing study guides which further clarify what information is important to be learned, and dividing the amount of knowledge into digestable quantities is advisable. [1977:362]

Some researchers find that programmed and computer-aided instruction offers benefits to anxiety-prone children (Spielberger, O'Neil, and Hansen, 1972). (See Chapter 14.) First, these instructional programs provide task-inherent direction and task-relevant feedback (Nottelmann and Hill, 1977). Second, they minimize fear and failure (Papay et al., 1975). And third, students can proceed at their own pace, unencumbered by the traditional lock-step method of instruction.

Classroom Reward Structures

Certainly, aggressiveness exists in nature, but there is also a healthy nonruthless competition, and there exist very strong drives toward social and cooperative behavior. These forces do not operate independently but together, as a whole, and the evidence strongly indicates that, in the social and biological development of all living creatures, of all these drives, the drive to cooperation is the most dominant, and biologically the most important. . . . It is probable that man owes more to the operation of this principle than to any other in his own biological and social evolution.

ASHLEY MONTAGU
On Being Human, 1966

Teachers differ in the reward structures they employ in their classrooms. **Reward structures** refer to the rules under which students receive some sort of payoff for academic performance. Teachers can evaluate students within a competitive, cooperative, or individualistic context (Deutsch,

1962; Johnson et al., 1981). A *competitive* condition implies that a reward can be had by one person if, and only if, others do not receive rewards; the goals of individual students become so closely linked that their goal attainments are negatively related. A *cooperative* condition is one in which a reward can be had by an individual if, and only if, others in the group also receive rewards; the goals of individual students become so closely linked that their goal attainments are positively related. In an *individualistic* condition, the individual receives a reward independent of whether other individuals secure rewards; whether or not one student accomplishes a goal has no bearing on whether other students accomplish their goals.

Competitive Reward Structures

Much classroom work is structured so that students compete with one another for grades and other rewards. Teachers compare students to determine whose performance is superior or inferior. It is little wonder that most students within the United States see school as competitive, become increasingly competitive the longer they remain in school, and are more competitive than children in most other cultures (Johnson and Johnson, 1974; Thomas, 1975; Johnson and Ahlgren, 1976).

Educational reformers have been especially critical of the competitiveness that pervades the schools of Western nations. They level the following criticisms against competition:

- Since there can be only one winner in a competitive situation, the vast majority of students experience failure. Moreover, fairly stable patterns of achievement operate so that the majority of students always "lose" and a few always "win." Consequently, some students are placed in situations in which they spend twelve years as "losers" (Ames et al., 1977; Johnson et al., 1981). Indeed, if the level of effort required to achieve high performance varies inversely with ability, then those who need to try the hardest are given the least incentive to do so; judged

MOTIVATING STUDENTS

RICHARD M. GORMAN

What are the best motivational techniques for a teacher to use in his classroom? Here are some suggested applications from what we have seen. Perhaps you can think of others.

GENERAL

Use a variety of motivating techniques: personal goals, practical value of a subject, individual

Source: Richard M. Gorman, *The Psychology of Classroom Learning: An Inductive Approach* (Columbus, Ohio: Charles E. Merrill Publishing Company, 1974), pp. 140–142. By permission.

interests, felt needs, and praise. Motivating students is often difficult; having a repertoire of techniques will prove valuable. Emphasize intrinsic motives such as curiosity, involvement, and discovery as much as possible. When necessary use extrinsic incentives to a lesser extent.

CURIOSITY

Provoke curiosity in students before starting a topic by pointing up a problem or conflict, or giving a pre-test to make them realize what they don't know about the topic. Arouse surprise and a feeling of contradiction in students by presenting a phenomenon that violates their expectations or runs counter to their experience and former training, for example, plants that live without sunlight or chlorophyll (fungi). Arouse doubt, uncertainty, bafflement by giving students a problem with no indications for its solution, for example, how to find one's position (latitude and longitude) in the middle of the desert.

ATTENTION

Arouse attention in students by starting a class with something novel, different, unusual, for example, a brainstorming demon-

against the achievements of others, they constantly fall short (Michaels, 1977).

- John Holt (1964) argues that the most interesting aspect of school for students is the other students. Yet, in competitive situations, children must set themselves apart from others. They cannot interact with them, visit with them, or on occasion even look at them. Some schools go so far as to bar conversations in the halls between classes and during lunchtime in the cafeteria. Holt says this is splendid training for a world in which people relate to others either by doing them in or paying them no heed.

Further, evidence suggests that competitive environments encourage students to enhance themselves at the expense of others (Bryant, 1977). Indeed, if they are to realize academic success, students must often alienate themselves from their peers.

- Some educators say that competition subverts intrinsic motivation in learning. Students learn to "win" extrinsic rewards (grades, gold stars, listing on honor rolls, and so on). This discourages intellectual pursuit for its own sake and leads to the view that knowledge that does not help a person win is "wasted effort"

stration or a copy of an old newspaper in history. Maintain attention and interest through variety and change: Never start a class the same way three times in a row.

LEVEL OF ASPIRATION
Provide for different levels of aspiration among students by encouraging them to strive for levels of performance in keeping with their abilities and by having differentiated materials, activities, and projects available for students of different ability and aspiration levels. This is as important for the student's involvement as it is difficult for a teacher. The contract system and the task-oriented nongraded programs can be of help here.

With individual ability levels in mind, set standards and provide tasks of intermediate difficulty that are within the reach of students but still offer some challenge. Provide easier tasks for students who are discouraged because of low or failing grades. Mastering easier tasks will help them set realistic—and gradually higher—levels of aspiration for their work.

ACHIEVEMENT MOTIVATION
On occasion, try to increase the basic achievement motivation of some students through talking with them, having them read about highly motivated persons, putting them in with a group of highly motivated students, etc. Chances of an increase in achievement motivation are greater with above-average socioeconomic class students. Make students aware of their successes and the satisfaction they bring through comments such as: "You really did well in that," "Didn't it feel good to get so many right?" etc. Try to divert students' attention away from their failures by not threatening or punishing them or dwelling on their errors.

REINFORCEMENT
Use praise and encouragement often, particularly for average and slower students and those who are more introverted and lack self-assurance. Give personal, encouraging comments on tests and other work rather than just a grade. Inform students regularly on how they are doing in a course, the sooner after a test or assignment the better. Use positive comments as much as possible.

COMPETITION
Use group cooperation and team competition as incentives rather than have individuals compete against each other through such methods as group murals and "spelling baseball" (with correct words getting "on base" and misspelled words as "outs").

(Johnson and Johnson, 1974; Johnson et al., 1981). Moreover, critics of competition claim that marks and grades discourage students from studying "hard" subjects and from selecting "tough" teachers.

Other educators and psychologists argue that competition has its place in education. While admitting that competition can be both overused and misused, they point out that individual competition can be an effective means for developing and strengthening the ability of students to work independently. Indeed, some researchers find competition a more potent educational mechanism than other arrangements (Michaels, 1977).

Cooperative Reward Structures
Among the strongest proponents of the use of cooperative reward structures are David W. and Roger T. Johnson (brothers and educational psychologists):

> Beyond all doubt, cooperation should be the most frequently used goal structure. The conditions under which it is effective and desirable are almost

COMPETITIVE REWARD STRUCTURES
Competition pervades a great many aspects of contemporary schooling.

too many to list. Whenever problem solving is desired, whenever divergent thinking or creativity is desired, whenever quality of performance is expected, whenever the task is complex, when the learning goals are highly important, and when the social development of students is one of the major instructional goals, cooperation should be used. Students will expect the group to achieve the learning goal, and they will also expect to have positive interaction with other students, and to share ideas and materials, to get group support for taking risks in thinking and trying out skills, to have every member contribute in some way to goal achievement, and to divide the task between each other in a division of labor when desirable. [1975:66]

Little disagreement exists among educational psychologists that cooperative reward structures are superior to competitive and individualistic structures in strengthening group-related factors such as trust, coordination of activities, interpersonal skills, social collaboration, interpersonal attraction, effective communication, and empathic role-taking (Michaels, 1977; Johnson et al., 1981; Skon et al., 1981). Whereas competitive environments teach enhancement of self at the expense of others, cooperative environments teach both the enhancement of self *and* others (Bryant, 1977; Ames, 1981). On the whole, research suggests that students involved in cooperative environments are more likely than those working in competitive environments to like the subject matter, share information, work together, and talk with one another.

Individualistic Reward Structures

Little research exists that compares individualistic to cooperative and competitive reward struc-

IMPORTANCE OF COOPERATIVE ACTIVITIES
Cooperative arrangements are important for cultivating interpersonal skills associated with social collaboration, the coordination of activities, effective communication, and empathetic role-taking.

tures (Johnson et al., 1981). One area in which individualistic environments find expression is in mastery and programmed learning (see Chapter 14). Individualistic structures appear preferable for teaching specific skills, such as how to use a microscope or a calculator, or for learning a specific series of facts, such as important dates in American history (Johnson and Johnson, 1975). But since learning occurs in isolation, individualistic structures do not foster interpersonal skills or promote social connectedness (Johnson et al., 1976, 1981).

Conclusion

Discussions regarding the benefits of various reward structures easily jump to highly judgmental conclusions about the relative virtues of one and the evils of the others. Yet, most educators and psychologists are increasingly coming to recognize that competitive, cooperative, and individualistic reward structures are not mutually exclusive alternatives (Ebel, 1975; Johnson and Ahlgren, 1976; Michaels, 1977; Slavin, 1977). All three structures are appropriate and effective under different conditions. Further, their complementary strengths and weaknesses suggest that mixtures of differing structures often offer the most positive benefits. Indeed, students need to be taught to function in all three types of environments (Johnson and Johnson, 1974). Mature individuals should be able to compete, cooperate, and work alone under appropriate conditions.

ACHIEVEMENT MOTIVATION

Climb high
Climb far
Your goal the sky
Your aim the star.

INSCRIPTION ON STEPS OF HOPKINS MEMORIAL,
WILLIAMS COLLEGE, WILLIAMSTOWN, MASS.

Individuals differ greatly in their desire to set future-oriented goals for themselves and then to strive to realize these goals. Over the past thirty years the matter of achievement motivation has been the focus of a number of research programs. The initial investigations derived from Henry A. Murray's (1938) formulations regarding human motivation. Among the "universal needs" identified by Murray was the need to achieve, which he defined as the striving to "overcome obstacles, to exercise power, to strive to do something difficult as well and as quickly as possible" (1938:80–81). Murray's notion was taken up by David C. McClelland, John W. Atkinson, and their associates in the late 1940s and early 1950s (all of whom were at the time at Wesleyan University). They viewed the need to achieve—commonly referred to as **need for achievement,** or *n-Ach*—as involving "success in competition with some standard of excellence" (1953:110–111).

MOTIVATING STUDENTS
One of the many tasks confronting teachers is the motivation of their students.

Need for Achievement

Ah, but a man's reach should exceed his grasp. Or what's a heaven for?

ROBERT BROWNING
Andrea del Sarto, 1855

Achievement motivation is an attitude—a state of mind. As such it is not identical with observable accomplishments such as high test scores, high rank, or high salary. Individuals may have a high need for achievement but for one reason or another never attain success. Since it is an attitude, achievement motivation may be found among individuals from all walks of life.

Measuring Achievement Motivation

One of the first tasks that confronted McClelland and his associates was to devise some way to measure achievement motivation. In the 1930s, Murray (1938) had developed the Thematic Apperception Test (TAT) as a means of studying personality and needs. The test consisted of a number of pictures. Subjects are asked to make up a story about the individuals or things portrayed. The assumption behind the test is that motivation influences fantasy and that a person's underlying motives are therefore revealed in the content of his or her story.

In their research McClelland and his colleagues devised a number of TAT-type pictures designed to assess achievement motives. For example, one picture depicts a boy in the foreground with a vague scene of a surgical operation in the background. Individuals are generally given about five minutes in which to write a story about the picture. They are instructed that their stories are to provide answers to the following questions: (1) What led up to the scene being depicted? (2) What is now happening? (3) How do the characters feel? and (4) What will be the outcome?

Individuals with high achievement motivation may write that the boy is daydreaming about becoming a surgeon, saving lives, and making a substantial income. Those with low motivation

may say that the boy is thinking about his mother undergoing surgery, that he is worried about the operation's outcome, and that he will miss his mother if she were to die.

Achievement-Oriented Persons

Over the past twenty-five years, a large number of studies have explored the personality characteristics of people with high achievement motivation. McClelland finds a strong relationship between high need for achievement and entrepreneurial behavior. He reports that individuals with high need for achievement (high n-Ach scores) generally behave like successful, rationalizing business entrepreneurs. Perhaps not surprisingly, many go into business activities (McClelland, 1965). They attune themselves to various barometers that provide concrete feedback on how well they are doing. These individuals with high achievement needs like to assume personal responsibility for problems. In this manner they gain a sense of achievement satisfaction from completing a task. In contrast, they derive little satisfaction when success depends on luck or the problems are set for them by others. They generally are self-initiating people who scrutinize the world about them for challenges they can successfully meet and master (McClelland and Winter, 1969).

Atkinson's Formulation

John W. Atkinson (1964, 1966; Atkinson and Raynor, 1974) has refined many aspects of achievement theory. One of his contributions has been the distinction he makes between two different motivational orientations. One involves a need to strive for success; the other, a need to avoid failure. People vary in the relative strength of these traits; they may be basically success oriented or failure threatened.

Life confronts people with tasks of varying difficulty and for which they must evaluate their probability of success. People whose need for success is stronger than their need to avoid failure will be achievement oriented and will seek out achievement tasks. This is most likely in situations in which they calculate their likelihood of success as being in the 50 percent range; such circumstances afford the greatest amount of realistic challenge. Their level of motivation will be less when they believe that success is either highly improbable or virtually certain.

In contrast, individuals who have a stronger need to avoid failure than to strive for success will shun achievement tasks when they calculate their chances of success as approximately 50 percent. However, their resistance will diminish when they believe that the likelihood of their success is either very high or nearly impossible. If success is highly likely, they need not confront the prospect of failure. If success is improbable, they can write off their resulting failure as the product of impossible odds.

Gender and Achievement Motivation

Apparently all societies have seized on the anatomical differences between men and women for the assignment of *gender roles*. These roles define the behavioral expectations regarding what constitutes appropriate male and female conduct. Within the United States men traditionally have been assigned the economic-provider role and women the homemaking and childbearing role. This has contributed to a dichotomy between the public and domestic spheres. Public labor has been rewarded with wealth, prestige, and power, whereas domestic labor has remained isolated and undervalued.

When women have entered the wage economy, they have been largely relegated to lower-paying "women's jobs," primarily clerks and secretaries. Physicians, lawyers, judges, engineers, accountants, college educators, and architects are more likely to be men than women. In contrast, noncollege teachers, nurses, librarians, dietitians, and health technologists are usually women. Even in "female fields"—nursing, social work, librarian-

GENDER AND ACHIEVEMENT MOTIVATION
The sexual structuring of the job market has influenced women's perception of the occupational avenues available to them.

ship, and elementary school teaching—women are disproportionately underrepresented in the administrative phases of the profession (Vander Zanden, 1984).

The prevalence of sexism within American life has led psychologists like Matina S. Horner (1968, 1970, 1972) to speculate that women may develop somewhat different achievement orientations than men. It is known that numerous research findings concerning achievement motivation in men do not apply for some reason to women (Veroff, Wilcox, and Atkinson, 1953; Atkinson, 1958; French and Lesser, 1964). Horner hypothesized that an underlying cause of these sex differences is that women are hampered by "fear of success."

Horner says that the motive to avoid success is "a stable, enduring personality characteristic" (1970:47). When women anticipate a high probability of achieving academic or vocational goals considered prestigious in our society, they become anxious because the "motive to avoid success" is activated. By virtue of their socialization, women learn that success in competitive situations is inconsistent with standards of femininity: "Whereas men are unsexed by failure . . . women seem to be unsexed by success" (1970:55).

Horner based her conclusions on research she carried out with a sample of undergraduate students at the University of Michigan in the 1960s. In the study she asked ninety women to tell a story based on the following beginning: "After first-term finals, Anne finds herself at the top of her medical school class." Sixty-five percent of the women were disconcerted, troubled, or confused by the cue. Their responses were filled with negative consequences for women who excelled, such as a loss in their femininity and social rejection.

Eighty-eight University of Michigan men also participated in the study, responding to the following cue: "After first-term finals, John finds himself at the top of his medical school class." Only 9 percent of the men wrote fear of success stories. In another phase of the study, Horner gave male and female students a variety of tasks to perform under competitive and noncompetitive conditions. She found that women who expressed a fear of success performed more poorly in competitive than in noncompetitive situations. On the other hand, most of the men and those women who had not shown fear of success performed better under competitive conditions.

It is now widely recognized that serious technical flaws characterized Horner's research (Levine and Crumrine, 1975; Zuckerman and Wheeler, 1975; Sassen, 1980). For instance, she never asked the "John" cue to women or the "Anne" cue to men. A number of researchers have since found that males provide a high incidence of "fear of success" stories to the "Anne" cue. This finding raises the question as to whether "fear of success" is a "personality trait" in women or a gender-role stereotype shared by both men and women (Feather and Raphelson, 1974; Hoffman, 1974; Sassen, 1980). Many psychologists also fault Horner for

not adequately defining "success," and little consensus exists on scoring students' essays as to what precisely constitutes fear-of-success imagery.

Many scientists reject the view that characteristics like competitiveness, assertiveness, and competence are sex-linked on the basis of either genetic predispositions or socialization factors (Darley, 1976). Strong social pressures compel people to conform to their society's gender-role expectations. What Horner terms "fear of success" frequently reflects realistic appraisals by women of the negative consequences that will likely follow should they deviate from gender-related norms and of the occupational opportunities available to them in a sexist world (Condry and Dyer, 1976; Meeker and Weitzel-O'Neill, 1977).

Rather than assuming that women have a general disposition to avoid success, some psychologists hold that both sexes will shun success when such success conflicts with norms relating to one's gender role, and both will seek success when the norms allow for success (Darley, 1976). Indeed, in the early 1970s, substantial numbers of youth took a negative view of success. A relatively high proportion of *both* college-age men and women believed that it was not "cool" to be too successful, criticized "grinds" and "cutthroats" (students who study hard and value high grades), and ridiculed materialism and suburban life (Langman, 1971; Prescott, 1971; Krussell, 1973).

All of this in no way detracts from Horner's contribution. If nothing else, her speculations regarding fear of success in women spawned a large body of significant research and continues to do so.

CHAPTER SUMMARY

1. Most of us assume that behavior is functional, that people do certain things because the consequences somehow meet their needs. This premise underlies the concept of motivation. Psychologists broadly group motives in two general categories.

The first category consists of biological motives, since they derive from various physiological needs. The second category involves social motives, since they arise in the course of social interaction.

2. An accumulating body of research suggests that extrinsic rewards decrease intrinsic motivation. It seems that the expectation of extrinsic rewards impairs children's intrinsic interest in many activities. However, extrinsic motivators do have their use within education. For instance, extrinsic rewards work effectively to induce individuals to do something they would not otherwise do.

3. The psychologist Bernard Weiner has formulated an approach to the attributions that people make regarding task outcomes. He suggests that attributions regarding outcomes be considered in terms of a stability (stable-unstable) dimension and a control (internal-external) dimension. This scheme provides four attributional factors: effort (internal and unstable); ability (internal and stable); luck (external and unstable); and task difficulty (external and stable).

4. People differ in the extent to which they believe that they influence the happenings in their lives. When people perceive the outcome following their action as the result of luck, chance, fate, or powerful others, they have belief in external control. When individuals interpret an outcome of behavior as the consequence of their own abilities or efforts, they have a belief in internal control. A good many studies show that students who have an internal sense of control show superior academic performance.

5. Individuals characterized by learned helplessness view their own actions and consequent events as causally unrelated. Hence, they believe that active coping efforts are futile. Some psychologists find that children who give up when they confront failure in achievement situations are victims of learned helplessness.

6. Depending on the individual and the circumstances, anxiety can facilitate or impair learning. On tasks of low complexity or on tasks in which the individual is already skilled, anxiety seems to facilitate performance; on tasks of high complexity or on tasks where the individual is not well practiced, anxiety appears to lower the level of performance. Recent theory interprets performance deterioration in the presence of anxiety as deriving from selective attention.

7. Quite different reward structures prevail in classroom settings. Students can be evaluated within a competitive, cooperative, or individualistic context. These structures are not mutually exclusive alternatives. All three structures are appropriate and effective under different conditions. Students need to be taught to function in all three types of environments.

8. Individuals differ greatly in their desire to set future-oriented goals for themselves and then to strive to realize these goals. Achievement motivation is an attitude—a state of mind. As such it is not identical with observable accomplishments like high test scores, high rank, or high salary.

9. The Thematic Apperception Test (TAT) is one means to study personality and needs. David C. McClelland and his associates find a strong relationship between high need for achievement and entrepreneurial behavior.

10. John W. Atkinson has refined many aspects of achievement theory. He distinguishes between two different motivational orientations. One involves a need to strive for success; the other, a need to avoid failure. People vary in the relative strength of these traits.

11. Matina S. Horner speculates that women are hampered by ''fear of success.'' By virtue of their socialization, women learn that success in competitive situations is inconsistent with standards of femininity. Critics point to serious technical flaws that characterize Horner's research. Many scientists reject the view that characteristics like competitiveness, assertiveness, and competence are sex-linked on the basis of either genetic predispositions or socialization factors. What Horner terms ''fear of success'' frequently reflects realistic appraisals by women of the negative consequences that are likely to follow should they deviate from gender-related norms and the lack of occupational opportunities available to them in a sexist society.

CHAPTER GLOSSARY

anxiety   Apprehension, dread, or uneasiness.

drive   A mechanism that incites activity when conditions depart from some physiological or psychological optimum and that sustains activity until the physiological or psychological balance again returns to normal.

extrinsic motivation   Activity undertaken for some purpose other than its own sake.

goal   The end state or condition toward which an organism is directing its activity.

incentive   External stimuli employed to arouse and direct the activity of an organism toward some goal (usually through treat or promise of future reward).

intrinsic motivation   Activity undertaken for its own sake.

learned helplessness   A generalized expectancy that events are independent of one's responses.

locus of control   People's perception of who or what is responsible for the outcome of events and behaviors in their lives.

motivation   Those inner states and processes that prompt, direct, and sustain activity.

motive   Any condition that affects an organism's readiness to initiate or continue a sequence of activity.

need for achievement   Success in competition with some standard of excellence.

needs   Those things that the organism requires to survive or function in a reasonably healthy manner.

reward structure   The rules under which students receive some sort of payoff for academic performance.

state anxiety   A transitory condition of apprehension resulting from the perception of threat.

trait anxiety   Apprehension associated with a relatively stable personality attribute.

EXERCISES

Review Questions

1. Of the motives listed below, which would be considered social in origin?
   a. hunger
   b. self-esteem
   c. pain avoidance
   d. affiliation
   e. b and d are true

2. In motivation terminology, a teacher's encouragement of a student to obtain a reward is best defined as a(n):
   a. need
   b. incentive
   c. goal
   d. motive

3. The research by Lepper and Greene suggests that
   a. no useful distinction can be made between intrinsic and extrinsic motivation
   b. intrinsic rewards are more powerful than extrinsic
   c. extrinsic rewards can undermine intrinsic motivation
   d. motivation has little impact on learning

4. Which of the following is *not* a dimension in Wiener's theory of attribution?
   a. effort
   b. control
   c. abilities
   d. luck

5. The explanation of failure most likely to be devastating to a student is
    a. "I just studied the wrong materials."
    b. "I was too tired to read the book."
    c. "The material is beyond me."
    d. "There is just too much work."

6. The locus of control issue suggests that
    a. locus of control bears little relationship to academic performance
    b. most children start with a sense of internal control and move to an external orientation
    c. locus of control can be modified by environmental restructuring
    d. b and c are true

7. Research on learned helplessness leads to the conclusion that it
    a. appears to be a generalized response
    b. tends to resemble certain types of depression
    c. is displayed more by boys than by girls
    d. has not been observed in other than humans
    e. a and b are true

8. Which of the following situations best describes state anxiety?
    a. worry about the future
    b. concern over one's appearance
    c. fear of not having a date for the dance
    d. apprehension of not doing as well as one's peers

9. Among the arguments given concerning competitive reward structures is
    a. too many students experience failure
    b. intrinsic motivation can be subverted
    c. there has been little research done in the area
    d. competitive reward situations are not typical of real life
    e. a and b are true

10. Individuals characterized as high achievers
    a. prefer professional rather than entrepreneurial roles
    b. tend to assume personal responsibility for their actions
    c. depend less frequently on feedback from others
    d. tend to let others initiate the problem

Answers

1. e (See p. 344)
2. b (See p. 345)
3. c (See pp. 346–347)
4. b (See p. 347)
5. c (See pp. 347–348)
6. c (See pp. 348–349)
7. e (See pp. 349, 351)
8. c (See p. 352)
9. e (See pp. 353–355)
10. b (See p. 359)

Applying Principles and Concepts

1. Suppose you observe the following events in a classroom. Indicate whether the activity reflects intrinsic (I) or extrinsic (E) motivation.

_____ a. During recess Marilyn goes back to class and reads.
_____ b. Mr. Betts puts a "smiley face" on Tim's spelling test.
_____ c. At an all-school meeting, the principal reads the names of the students on the honor roll.
_____ d. Louise watches television alone several hours a day.
_____ e. Albert wears his college letterman's jacket whenever he can.

2. Just before an exam, a teacher overheard the following comments. Which of these indicate an external locus of control (E), an internal locus of control (I), or learned helplessness (L)?

_____ a. "Those trick questions of hers will get you every time."

_____ b. "I used Cynthia's notes; I just can't take notes in class."

_____ c. "I never can figure out how she'll grade."

_____ d. "I got the exam figured out; boy, am I ready."

_____ e. "I've looked over some other exams, and I think I know what questions she'll ask."

3. A school counselor is describing an individual whom he considers to be highly anxious. Underline those parts of the description that can be substantiated by research.

> His anxiety really comes out during test time. He shakes so hard before an exam I think he'll never be able to write. During the test he keeps telling me how hard he's trying. His essays are at best average. He'll guess at objective test answers even when there is a penalty for mistakes.

4. The same counselor is trying to help the student in Question 4. Underline those parts of the following passage that research findings suggest are appropriate.

> Before the exam I warn him that the exam will be hard, so he will be prepared. However, I go over the kinds of questions I will ask, and give him some examples of the kinds of test items I will ask. During the test I walk around encouraging him.

5. Which of the following grading practices are examples of competitive (C), cooperative (CP), and individualistic (I) goal structures?

_____ a. Grading on the curve

_____ b. Mastery testing

_____ c. Setting 90 percent for A, 80 percent for B, and so on

_____ d. Giving all students involved on a project a common grade

_____ e. Setting the highest grade equal to 100, then ranking all others

6. Following are statements by several individuals. Place a checkmark before those indicating high need for achievement or striving for success.

_____ a. "I know it's risky, but I think it's worth a try."

_____ b. "If I can have a reasonable chance of success, I'll do it."

_____ c. "That's so simple it isn't worth the effort."

_____ d. "Bet everything we have; the race is fixed."

_____ e. "John invests in Treasury notes; he says he hasn't got enough capital for the futures market."

7. Professor Clements is teaching his doctoral seminar in theoretical physics. He is concerned that his students do the best they can. To be accepted in this class students have to be exceptional. According to Darley (1976), which of the following students are *not* likely to do their best?

_____ a. Donna, a very attractive and feminine girl, who comes from a middle-class family

_____ b. James, a black, whose family is lower class

_____ c. Louise, who is married to a car salesman and has no children

_____ d. Bill, who is unmarried and comes from a family of professional people

Answers

1. a, I; b, E; c, E; d, I; e, either I or E (See pp. 344–347)
2. a, E; b, L; c, E; d, I; e, I (See pp. 348–349, 351)
3. Underline "comes out during test time," "shakes so hard," "keeps telling me how hard he's trying," "essays are at best average." (See pp. 351–352)
4. Underline "go over the kinds of questions," "some examples of the kinds of test items," "I walk around encouraging him." (See pp. 352–353)
5. a, C; b, I; c, I; d, CP; e, C (See pp. 353–357)
6. b, e (See pp. 359–360)

7. According to Darley's research, there is no reason to suspect any of them will not try to do his or her best. Remember, this is a *doctoral* seminar, and all are exceptional students who have already proved themselves. (See p. 361)

Project

OBJECTIVE: To conduct a study similar to Horner's experiment (see pp. 360–361) on sexual stereotyping of achievement. It is to be a cross-sex study in that men will react to a woman in the story and vice versa.

PROCEDURE: Use peers or secondary school students. After each story, ask the subject to rank the choices in terms of desirability for Anne or John. Try to show each version to at least ten students.

Version 1 (show to females):

After the first-term finals, John finds himself at the top of his class. Following are a number of choices open to John. Rank from 1 (most) through 5 (least) the desirability of these choices. There are five choices, and *each* should be ranked:

_____ a. Explain to everyone how lucky he was

_____ b. Stay near the top but avoid being number one

_____ c. Deliberately try to move more toward the middle

_____ d. Strive to maintain number-one status

_____ e. Become active socially so people will not think of him as just a "brain"

Version 2 (show to males):

After the first-term finals, Anne finds herself at the top of her class. Following are a number of choices open to Anne. Rank from 1 (most) through 5 (least) the desirability of these choices. There are five choices, and *each* should be ranked:

_____ a. Explain to everyone how lucky she was

_____ b. Stay near the top but avoid being number one

_____ c. Deliberately try to move more toward the middle

_____ d. Strive to maintain number-one status

_____ e. Become active socially so people won't think of her as just a "brain"

ANALYSIS: To determine evidences of sexual stereotyping carry out the following data analyses:

1. For *each* version determine the mean rankings for each choice. To do that, add all the ranks assigned to that choice, and divide by the number of subjects. For choice a, if the rankings for ten subjects were 3, 2, 4, 4, 5, 1, 1, 2, 4, 3, the mean ranking would be 2.9. After you have the mean rankings for each choice, arrange them in value from low (most desirable) to high (least desirable). If the mean rankings were a, 2.7; b, 3.1; c, 2.1; d, 4.2; and e, 1.6, the order would be e, c, a, b, d.

2. Compare the rank order of choices between the two groups. Look especially at the high-low choices. If they agree, there is less evidence of cross-sex sexual stereotyping than if they disagree. If they disagree, examine the differences. Choice d is considered a stereotyping of male behavior, whereas choice c would be a stereotype for female behavior. Choices a, b, and e according to recent research (see pp. 360–361) may not be stereotyped.

3. On the basis of your findings do you see evidence of cross-sex stereotyping? Is it true for one or both sexes? What are the implications?

PART
THREE

TEACHING

CHAPTER OUTLINE

13

INSTRUCTIONAL PLANNING AND OBJECTIVES

CHAPTER PREVIEW

The focus now shifts from learning to teaching, to the activities of the teacher in planning and carrying out instruction. The first chapter in this section presents different views of instructional planning and the setting of objectives. Bloom's taxonomy of educational objectives in the cognitive domain is discussed, along with recommendations for its use in planning. A description of behavioral objectives is followed by critiques of such objectives from cognitive and humanist perspectives.

To achieve your objectives for learning this material, keep these questions in mind:

- What are the major components of the taxonomy of educational objectives in the cognitive domain, and how can the taxonomy be used in planning instruction?
- What are the components and functions of behavioral objectives?
- What objections have been raised to the use of behavioral objectives by cognitively oriented educators?
- How do humanist approaches define the goal and purposes of education?
- What criticisms have been aimed at the humanist movement in education?

"Would you tell me, please, which way I ought to go from here?"

"That depends a good deal on where you want to get to," said the Cat.

"I don't much care where—" said Alice.

"Then it doesn't matter which way you go," said the Cat.

"—so long as I get *somewhere*," Alice added as an explanation.

"Oh, you're sure to do that," said the Cat, "if you only walk long enough."

LEWIS CARROLL
Alice's Adventures in Wonderland

The previous eight chapters dealt primarily with learning and with what the learner does. Learning involves a relatively permanent change in behavior that results from experience. It is what occurs when individuals can now do something that they could not do earlier (Goldsmid and Wilson, 1980). In this and the chapters that follow the emphasis falls on teaching. **Teaching** is purposeful activity designed to induce learning or to change behavior. As such, teaching is a more limited process than learning. It implies formal, conscious, and systematic training. There is usually a degree of consciousness regarding the process on the part of the teacher, or the learner, or both (Mercer and Carr, 1957).

Educators and psychologists are concerned with explaining, predicting, and controlling the ways in which teacher behavior affects the learning of students. Teacher behavior involves a great many elements. As a starting point for considering teacher behavior, let us first examine instructional planning. Before setting out on some venture—be it teaching or any other undertaking—we should know what we intend to accomplish and how we plan to accomplish it. In some respects, the first task confronting teachers resembles that of a captain whose ship is about to leave port. An error in taking one's bearings at the beginning may result in entirely missing one's mark at the end. This holds true despite the sturdiness of one's craft or the excellence of one's seamanship.

INSTRUCTIONAL PLANNING

Schools organize their programs of instruction in a variety of ways (Gagné, 1977). The most comprehensive category of the instructional program is the **curriculum.** For instance, most schools have a curriculum in mathematics that extends from kindergarten through high school. In turn, a curriculum is made up of *courses* that usually extend over a half or full school year. The segment of a course that has a single purpose or a set of interrelated concepts is termed a *topic* or *unit*. A topic or unit generally requires several *lessons,* each of which occupies a standard interval of time, such as forty-five minutes.

Components of a Psychology of Instruction

The three R's of our school system must be supported by the T's—teachers who are superior, techniques of instruction that are modern, and thinking about education which places it first in all our plans and hopes.

LYNDON B. JOHNSON
Message to Congress, January 12, 1965

Structuring a body of knowledge so that it can be readily grasped by the learner is a critical problem in curriculum development and the formulation of instruction. The search for a set of procedures to guide the preparation of effective instruction has long occupied the attention of educators. Jerome S. Bruner (1966) points out that theories of learning such as B. F. Skinner's theory of operant conditioning and Albert Bandura's observational learning theory are *descriptive* (see Chapter 5). They tell us how learning occurs, focusing on the conditions under which some competence was acquired *after* instruction had taken place. But Bruner says that a theory of instruction is *prescriptive* in that it proposes in advance rules for the most effective achievement of some body of knowledge or of a skill and

THEORIES OF LEARNING AND INSTRUCTION
Theories of learning deal with how learning occurs, while theories of instruction propose rules in advance for effective teaching. Nonetheless, the focus of each type of theory is the student.

provides techniques for measuring and evaluating outcomes. It is also *normative* in that it sets up criteria for judging performance.

The educational psychologist Robert Glaser (1973, 1976) suggests a prescriptive theory for the design of instruction that consists of four components:

■ First, it is necessary to analyze the content of the subject matter to determine what it is that the student is expected to learn. Educators must ask themselves what distinguishes the competent performer from the novice (for instance, a skilled reader from an unskilled one). This involves **task analysis,** or identification of the subordinate skills and knowledge learners must

acquire before they can achieve the educational goal (the terminal objective). (See Figure 13.1.)

■ Second, instructional planning requires a description of the students' initial or entering characteristics. This calls for careful assessments of the strengths, weaknesses, styles, background interests, and abilities of individual learners. Educators must establish what readiness skills the students already possess—the perceptual, cognitive, and motor concepts and processes that are fundamental to subsequent effective learning and performance.

■ Third, educators need to establish the conditions under which students will work, from their initial or entering status to the successful com-

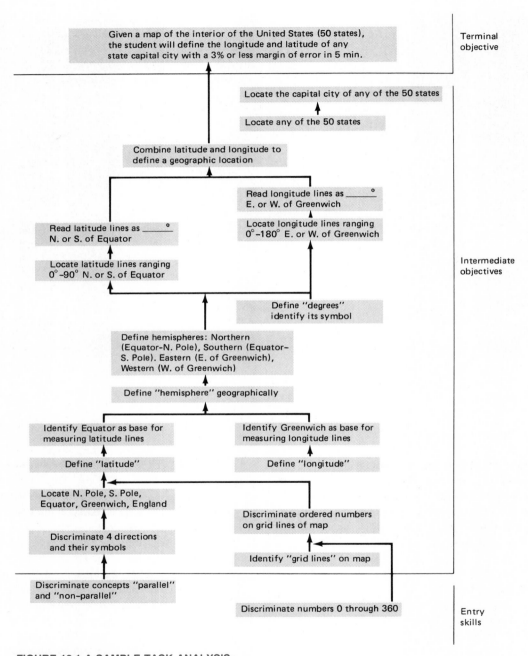

FIGURE 13.1 A SAMPLE TASK ANALYSIS
Task analysis enables the teacher to identify the subordinate skills and knowledge that students must acquire if they are to realize the terminal goal. *(Source: R. Packard,* Psychology of Learning and Instruction *[Columbus, Ohio: Charles E. Merrill, 1975], p. 233. By permission.)*

PLANNING
Good teaching requires good planning.

pletion of the educational objectives. This involves determining the instructional procedures that the teacher is to follow as well as specifying the required materials and resources.

- Fourth, plans for instruction must have provisions for monitoring a student's progress. Such assessment takes place at regular intervals and determines to what extent the educational program is producing the desired outcomes. This allows for appropriate adjustments in the instructional program.

The Taxonomy of Educational Objectives

One attempt to provide a framework for the design of instruction is the taxonomy of educational objectives, begun in the 1950s by Benjamin S. Bloom and his colleagues. A **taxonomy** is a device for identifying, naming, and classifying things in terms of their characteristics. Chemists find a periodic table a helpful taxonomic tool for organizing information about elements; similarly, biologists classify plants and animals in terms of a nomenclature based on a hierarchical scheme of species, genus, family, order, class, phylum, and kingdom. A taxonomy of educational objectives allows teachers to identify the different types of learning embodied in an instructional context (Furst, 1981).

Bloom and his associates (1956) classify educational objectives in three domains: the cognitive, the affective, and the psychomotor. The cognitive domain includes those educational objectives related to the recall of knowledge and the development of intellectual abilities and skills (Bloom, 1956). The affective domain is concerned with changes in pupils' interests, attitudes, values, and emotional states (Krathwohl, Bloom, and Masia, 1964). The psychomotor domain contains objectives that involve muscular or motor skills, the manipulation of materials and objects, and neuromuscular coordination (Harrow, 1972).

Bloom's taxonomy for the cognitive domain has generated the greatest interest. It contains six major classes (see also Table 13.1):

- *1.00 Knowledge:* Knowledge involves the recall of specific facts, universal principles, methods, processes, structures, or settings. Little more is asked of the student than to bring to mind the appropriate material.

- *2.00 Comprehension:* Comprehension entails ''the lowest level of understanding.'' The student is required to paraphrase knowledge accurately or to summarize it without necessarily being able to relate it to the other material or see its fullest implications.

- *3.00 Application:* Application is the use of abstractions in particular and concrete situations. The student is asked to select an idea, rule of procedure, or generalized method that is appropriate to a situation and then to apply it correctly.

- *4.00 Analysis:* Analysis involves breaking down a communication into its parts to illustrate the relative hierarchy or internal organization of the ideas. The student is required to clarify the communication, indicate how the communication is organized, and specify the way in which the communication manages to convey its message.

- *5.00 Synthesis:* Synthesis entails putting together elements and parts to form a larger whole. The student is asked to work with pieces, parts, or elements and to arrange them in such a way that a pattern or structure is devised that was not clearly there before.

- *6.00 Evaluation:* Evaluation involves rendering judgments about the value of material and methods for particular purposes. The student is asked to provide qualitative and quantitative judgments about the extent to which material and methods satisfy certain criteria.

Bloom points out that it is possible to conceive of these six classes in several different arrangements. He prefers to view them as consisting of a hierarchical order (the objectives of one class commonly make use of and build on the behaviors found in the preceding class in the list, thus giving the hierarchy cumulative properties). The educational behaviors are arranged from simple to complex. This arrangement is based on the idea that one behavior may become integrated with other similar level behaviors to form a more complex behavior. Evidence supports the ordering of the first four levels better than the ordering of the last two (Seddon, 1978; Kunen, Cohen, and Solman, 1981).

Bloom believes that the taxonomy helps teachers to (1) communicate the properties of the educational enterprise in concrete and explicit terms, (2) determine goals that they may wish to incorporate within their own curriculum, (3) identify new directions for extending their instructional activities, (4) plan learning experiences, and (5) prepare measuring devices.

Table 13.1 contains an outline of Bloom's cognitive domain taxonomy of educational objectives. The table also provides a series of verbal guidelines that are useful in operationalizing specific levels of the taxonomy. The use of infinitives and direct objects should facilitate writing instructional objectives (see the boxed insert on pages 379–380). Further, the taxonomy calls teachers' attention to the higher level cognitive objectives and the need to achieve an appropriate balance of objectives (teachers tend to spend an inordinate amount of time focusing upon the lower level objectives of knowledge and comprehension while giving little time to the higher level objectives).

TABLE 13.1
Instrumentation of the Taxonomy of Educational
Objectives: Cognitive Domain

Taxonomy Classification	Key Words	
	Examples of Infinitives	*Examples of Direct Objects*
1.00 Knowledge		
1.10 Knowledge of Specifics		
1.11 Knowledge of Terminology	to define, to distinguish, to acquire, to identify, to recall, to recognize	vocabulary, terms, terminology, meaning(s), definitions, referents, elements
1.12 Knowledge of Specific Facts	to recall, to recognize, to acquire, to identify	facts, factual information, (sources), (names), (dates), (events), (persons), (places), (time periods), properties, examples, phenomena
1.20 Knowledge of Ways and Means of Dealing with Specifics		
1.21 Knowledge of Conventions	to recall, to identify, to recognize, to acquire	form(s), conventions, uses, usage, rules, ways, devices, symbols, representations, style(s), format(s)
1.22 Knowledge of Trends, Sequences	to recall, to recognize, to acquire, to identify	action(s), processes, movement(s), continuity, development(s), trend(s), sequence(s), causes, relationship(s), forces, influences
1.23 Knowledge of Classifications and Categories	to recall, to recognize, to acquire, to identify	area(s), type(s), feature(s), class(es), set(s), division(s), arrangement(s), classification(s), category/categories
1.24 Knowledge of Criteria	to recall, to recognize, to acquire, to identify	criteria, basics, elements
1.25 Knowledge of Methodology	to recall, to recognize, to acquire, to identify	methods, techniques, approaches, uses, procedures, treatments
1.30 Knowledge of the Universals and Abstractions in a Field		
1.31 Knowledge of Principles, Generalizations	to recall, to recognize, to acquire, to identify	principle(s), generalization(s), proposition(s), fundamentals, laws, principal elements, implication(s)
1.32 Knowledge of Theories and Structures	to recall, to recognize, to acquire, to identify	theories, bases, interrelations, structure(s), organization(s), formulation(s)

(continued)

TABLE 13.1 (*continued*)

Taxonomy Classification	Key Words	
	Examples of Infinitives	*Examples of Direct Objects*
2.00 Comprehension		
2.10 Translation	to translate, to transform, to give in own words, to illustrate, to prepare, to read, to represent, to change, to rephrase, to restate	meaning(s), sample(s), definitions, abstractions, representations, words, phrases
2.20 Interpretation	to interpret, to reorder, to rearrange, to differentiate, to distinguish, to make, to draw, to explain, to demonstrate	relevancies, relationships, essentials, aspects, new view(s), qualifications, conclusions, methods, theories, abstractions
2.30 Extrapolation	to estimate, to infer, to conclude, to predict, to differentiate, to determine, to extend, to interpolate, to extrapolate, to fill in, to draw	consequences, implications, conclusions, factors, ramifications, meanings, corollaries, effects, probabilities
3.00 Application	to apply, to generalize, to relate, to choose, to develop, to organize, to use, to employ, to transfer, to restructure, to classify	principles, laws, conclusions, effects, methods, theories, abstractions, situations, generalizations, processes, phenomena, procedures
4.00 Analysis		
4.10 Analysis of Elements	to distinguish, to detect, to identify, to classify, to discriminate, to recognize, to categorize, to deduce	elements, hypothesis/hypotheses, conclusions, assumptions, statements (of fact), statements (of intent), arguments, particulars
4.20 Analysis of Relationships	to analyze, to contrast, to compare, to distinguish, to deduce	relationships, interrelations, relevance, relevancies, themes, evidence, fallacies, arguments, cause-effect(s), consistency/consistencies, parts, ideas, assumptions
4.30 Analysis of Organizational Principles	to analyze, to distinguish, to detect, to deduce	form(s), pattern(s), purpose(s), point(s) of view, techniques, bias(es), structure(s), theme(s), arrangement(s), organization(s)
5.00 Synthesis		
5.10 Production of a Unique Communication	to write, to tell, to relate, to produce, to constitute, to transmit, to originate, to modify, to document	structure(s), pattern(s), product(s), performance(s), design(s), work(s), communication(s), effort(s), specifics, composition(s)

TABLE 13.1 (*continued*)

Taxonomy Classification	Key Words	
	Examples of Infinitives	*Examples of Direct Objects*
5.20 Production of a Plan, or Proposed Set of Operations	to propose, to plan, to produce, to design, to modify, to specify	plan(s), objectives, specification(s), schematic(s), operations, way(s), solution(s), means
5.30 Derivation of a Set of Abstract Relations	to produce, to derive, to develop, to combine, to organize, to synthesize, to classify, to deduce, to develop, to formulate, to modify	phenomena, taxonomies, concept(s), scheme(s), theories, relationships, abstractions, generalizations, hypothesis/hypotheses, perceptions, ways, discoveries
6.00 Evaluation		
6.10 Judgments in Terms of Internal Evidence	to judge, to argue, to validate, to assess, to decide	accuracy/accuracies, consistency/consistencies, fallacies, reliability, flaws, errors, precision, exactness
6.20 Judgments in Terms of External Criteria	to judge, to argue, to consider, to compare, to contrast, to standardize, to appraise	ends, means, efficiency, economy/economies, utility, alternatives, courses of action, standards, theories, generalizations

Source: W. S. Metfessel, W. B. Michael, and D. A. Kirsner, "Instrumentation of Bloom's and Krathwohl's Taxonomies for the Writing of Educational Objectives," *Psychology in the Schools,* 6 (1969):227–231. By permission.

USE OF THE TAXONOMY OF EDUCATIONAL OBJECTIVES

The taxonomy of educational objectives contained in Table 13.1 provides a valuable tool for the classroom teacher. It assists the teacher in breaking down the decisions that need to be made regarding levels of complexity. More specifically, will the learner (1) simply possess knowledge, (2) comprehend it, (3) apply it, (4) analyze it, (5) synthesize it, or (6) evaluate it?

Consider the teacher who is interested in familiarizing his or her students with the nature and operation of the human body. By referring to Table 13.1 and looking under the first level, the teacher can find a set of infinitives (action verbs) that are useful for formulating "knowledge" objectives. For instance, at this level the teacher would be concerned with writing objectives in which students are asked to define, distinguish, identify, recognize, or recall the major organs of the human body. The table also provides examples of

(continued)

USE OF THE TAXONOMY
(*continued*)

direct objects. In this case, the students may be asked the "names" of the major organs.

Having dealt with the task of providing students with the basic information, the teacher can move to the second level, "comprehension." The teacher may select from category 2.20 (interpretation) the verb "prepare" and ask the students to prepare a sketch of the body showing the placement of the major organs. The teacher may believe that comprehension is insufficient and wish to go on to "application." He or she may want the students to "relate" the structure of the lungs to the process the body uses to utilize oxygen.

The teacher may then wish to proceed to "analysis," for instance, to have the students "categorize" the functions of the major organs of the body. Next the teacher may move to "synthesis" and ask the students to "derive" or "develop" a scheme showing the transformations occurring in ingested material as the material passes through the various organ systems. And finally, the teacher may have the students engage in "evaluation," for example, "appraising" the efficiency of the specific organs.

Norris M. Sanders provides an illustration of the taxonomy in teaching social studies students the concept of gerrymandering. He has modified the levels slightly by substituting the term *memory* for "knowledge" and *interpretation* for "comprehension":

Memory: What is meant by "gerrymandering"? (The student is asked to recall the definition presented to him earlier.) Restate this definition in your own words.

Interpretation: Each country in the diagram of the mythical state has about the same population and is dominated by the designated political party "A" or "B." The state must be divided into five voting districts of about equal population. Each district must contain three countries.

What is the greatest number of districts that Party A could control if it is in charge of the redistricting and chooses to gerrymander? What is the greatest number of districts that Party B could control if it is in charge of the redistricting and chooses to gerrymander? (The students have previously been given a definition of gerrymandering).

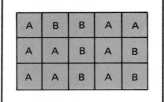

Application: The mayor recently appointed a committee to study the fairness of the boundaries of the election districts in our community. Gather information about the present districts and the population in each. Determine whether the present city election districts are adequate. (The student is expected to apply principles of democracy studied in class to this new problem.)

Analysis: Analyze the reasoning in this quotation: "Human beings lack the ability to be fair when their own interests are involved. Party X controls the legislature and now it has taken upon itself the responsibility of redrawing the boundaries of the legislative election districts. We know in advance that our party will suffer."

Synthesis: (This question must follow the application question given above.) If current election districts in our community are inadequate, suggest how they might be redrawn.

Evaluation: Would you favor having your political party engage in gerrymandering if it had the opportunity? [1966: 3–5]*

EXERCISE
Select a topic in which you have interest and formulate appropriate educational objectives for teaching the topic at each level in the taxonomy (use Table 13.1).

EDUCATIONAL OBJECTIVES

Of necessity teachers must plan. Indeed, their survival depends on it, since an absence of planning would quickly plunge the classroom into chaos. Since teaching is goal-directed activity, it requires that teachers determine their objectives *before* they proceed to learning activities (Colbert, 1979; Yinger, 1979). As such, objectives provide direction for teaching and curriculum development. Having defined their instructional objectives, the teacher can then design the means or learning activities that will achieve those objectives. Finally, instructional objectives provide the teacher with guidance in later evaluating the students' learning.

Behaviorist, cognitive, and humanist educators differ to some extent in their educational goals and programs. Some psychologists believe that these approaches have incompatible underlying assumptions and cannot be assimilated to each other (Reese and Overton, 1970). In practice, however, many teachers find that each model has insights and suggests certain applications to their particular classroom situations. Behavioral orientations, with their focus on actions, provide techniques for teaching specific skills. Cognitive perspectives, stressing thought processes, make a contribution to the understanding of problem solving and the higher levels of information processing. And humanist approaches, with their emphasis on feelings and emotions, have much to offer teachers in the affective domain of classroom life. Let us examine each of these approaches in turn.

Behavioral Objectives

For decades educators and psychologists have stressed the need for precise educational statements. However, it was not until 1962 when Robert F. Mager published his classic book, *Preparing Instructional Objectives*, that the educational community began to take instructional objectives seriously. Since then there has been growing interest in many educational circles in stating behavioral objectives at high levels of specificity. Such high-level specification is compatible with current developments in educational technology such as programmed and computer-aided instruction. And it has received additional impetus from the requirements being written into accountability legislation.

Definitions

Educational goals are statements regarding the outcomes of instruction (Gagné and Briggs, 1974). When goals are formulated in terms of teacher activity, they are usually referred to as *aims* or *directions;* when expressed in terms of student outcome, they are called *objectives* (Mehrens and Lehmann, 1978). **Behavioral objectives** are statements regarding the specific changes educators intend to produce in pupil behavior. The emphasis of behavioral objectives falls upon the *products* of learning rather than the *process* of learning (Gronlund, 1976). Accordingly, behavioral objectives are formulated in such a manner that their attainment (or lack of it) can be observed and measured.

Educational goals are usually stated in general terms, for instance, ''To be familiar with human respiration.'' In contrast, behavioral objectives are stated in specific terms that express the performance expected of the learner after instruction, for example, ''Given a list containing the names of ten parts of the respiratory system, a diagram of the respiratory system, ten minutes to complete the task, and no references or aids, the student will correctly identify eight of the ten parts in the appropriate places on the diagram.''

Functions

The advocates of behavioral objectives claim the objectives have a good many advantages. First, behavioral objectives act as a guide to instruction. Because the goals of instruction are specific and observable, they provide criteria for sequencing material, they direct learning activities, and they offer an overall instructional design. The objectives provide clear and precise targets at which teachers can take aim.

BEHAVIORAL OBJECTIVES AS GUIDES TO INSTRUCTION
Behavioral objectives provide criteria for the sequencing of material, the direction of learning activities, and the overall design of instruction.

Second, since the objectives state the terminal behavior that is expected, they can be easily translated into a test of student achievement. From this, the quality of the instruction can be inferred (Davis, Alexander, and Yelon, 1974). On the basis of such information, educators can make appropriate adjustments in their programs and gain insights into curriculum development.

Third, behavioral objectives communicate to relevant parties what is to be learned:

> Basically, a meaningfully stated objective is one that succeeds in communicating to the reader the writer's instructional intent. It is meaningful to the extent it conveys to others a picture (of what a successful learner will be like) identical to the picture the writer has in mind. [Mager, 1962:6]

Behavioral objectives tell pupils exactly what learning outcomes are expected of them, giving them cues for guiding their educational activities. They provide parents with standards by which they can appraise their children's academic achievement. They supply other teachers with vital information for coordinating the curricula between grades to minimize redundancy and to maximize coverage. And they inform principals and other school administrators about what students have mastered and what they still must master.

Components

A behavioral objective consists of three parts (Mager, 1962; Davis, Alexander, and Yelon, 1974;

Gronlund, 1976). First, it must state the *behavior* a student will be able to perform as the intended outcome of instruction. The behavior must be able to be observed or recorded. As such, the statement will contain an *action* verb (for example, *identify, write, name, describe, solve, classify, draw, select, state*, and so on) and a *reference to the product* of the student's behavior (for instance, a diagram, an essay, a procedure, a speech, and the like). The following are illustrations:

- Draw a diagram showing the chamber of the heart.
- Conduct a medical history interview with a patient.
- Present an impromptu speech on the effects of the Norman invasion upon Anglo-Saxon culture.
- Identify by underlining statements that are examples of positive conservation management.
- Arrange the objects in the tray from highest to lowest in the order of their weights.
- Demonstrate a procedure for calculating the temperature of a gas.

Second, a behavioral objective describes the *conditions* under which the expected behavior is to be performed. Three general types of conditions are relevant (Davis, Alexander, and Yelon, 1974):

- The aids or tools pupils will be permitted to use (for instance, source books, a calculator, reference tables, and the like).
- The restrictions under which the student will operate (for example, the amount of time to be allowed).
- The manner in which the information is to be provided (for instance, videotape recording, checklist test, written essay, and so on).

Third, a behavioral objective describes the *criteria* by which the behavior is to be judged as acceptable or unacceptable. The following are illustrations:

- Correctly identifies five out of eight (a statement

of the minimum acceptable proportion of correct responses).
- Solves the problem correctly.
- Is accurate within plus or minus 0.10 meters (a statement of the acceptable deviation from some standard).
- Must include four of the six reasons.

The three components are brought together, usually with the condition stated first, the behavior next, and the criteria of performance last. Consider the following two illustrations:

> 1. When given a list of twelve states, the pupil should be able to supply the capital cities for at least ten of them.

In this statement, the *condition* is "when given a list of twelve states"; the *behavior* is "to supply the capital cities"; and the *standard of performance* is "for at least ten of them."

> 2. Given seven cultures of fungi, thirty minutes to complete the assignment, and using no references or aids, the student will identify five of the seven cultures by their scientific names.

In the statement, the *conditions* are "given seven cultures of fungi, thirty minutes to complete the assignment, and using no references or aids"; the *behavior* is "the student will identify by their scientific names"; and the *standard of performance* is "five of the seven cultures."

Levels

In preparing written educational objectives, it is often helpful to proceed from general to more specific statements. David A. Payne (1974) distinguishes four levels of objectives based on their degree of specificity. The first, the most abstract level, consists of the long-term global goals of education, such as mastery of basic reading and writing skills, vocational efficiency, self-realization, and informed citizenship practices.

At the second and more concrete level, the general objectives are translated into specific behaviors that represent the expected outcomes of

PRACTICE IN PREPARING BEHAVIORAL OBJECTIVES

In order to gain practice in preparing behavioral objectives, examine college textbooks in the following four areas: (1) a biological or physical science, (2) a social science, (3) English literature, and (4) mathematics. Select from each textbook a manageable unit of instruction and formulate a behavioral objective for it. First, separately write the behavior, the condition, and the standard of performance and then bring the components together, stating the condition first, the behavior next, and the criteria of performance last. Illustrations are provided below.

BEHAVIOR

1. A biological or physical science: The student will list one harmful effect for each chemical.
2. A social science: The student will be able to write a check, balance a checkbook, and reconcile a bank statement.
3. English literature: The student will describe in writing one instance of psychological conflict for each of three different characters.
4. Mathematics: The student will write a proof of the Pythagorean theorem.

CONDITION

1. A biological or physical science: Given the names of six common household chemicals

---

education. By way of illustration, basic reading and writing skills can be broken down into more concrete components:

- The pupil can distinguish among and name the letters of the alphabet.
- The pupil can read and complete a job application form written at the sixth-grade level.
- The pupil can write a simple letter of inquiry to a business firm that contains no more than X errors of spelling and punctuation.

The third level provides even greater specificity and detail. It consists of behavioral objectives describing the expected behavior, the conditions under which it will be performed, and the criteria by which it will be evaluated. For example, "Given a simple newspaper clipping consisting of five paragraphs and ten minutes to complete the assignment, the student will correctly answer six out of eight multiple-choice questions on the content of the article."

The fourth level consists of the instructional materials and the test items. It provides the most specific level. Each level is seen as linked in an interactive relationship to the others and has implications for the other levels. By working back and forth among the various levels, the major developmental lines can be clarified and refined, leading to more sophisticated instruction.

Experimental Evidence

A good many studies have attempted to assess the effectiveness of using behavioral objectives for improving student learning. When this research is reviewed, the data for and against benefits appear to be evenly matched (Jenkins and Deno, 1971; Duchastel and Merrill, 1974; McKeachie, 1974; Good, Biddle, and Brophy, 1975). These mixed results suggest that in their own right behavioral objectives are not a particular critical factor. Rather, much depends on other associated factors that as yet have not been clearly identified, such as teacher

such as bleaches, detergents, and insecticides.

2. A social science: Given a simulated problem situation.

3. English literature: After reading Shakespeare's *Hamlet* and having access to the book.

4. Mathematics: Given a right △ABC in which ∠ACB is a right ∠, the sides are a, b, and c, and the formula is $c^2 = a^2 + b^2$.

CRITERIA OF PERFORMANCE

1. A biological or physical science: With no more than two errors.

2. A social science: Each of which must be 90 percent correct.

3. English literature: Which must

have been cited in the student workbook and must be completed within thirty minutes.

4. Mathematics: Employing all six steps stated in the textbook.

INTEGRATED BEHAVIORAL OBJECTIVE

1. A biological or physical science: Given the names of six common household chemicals such as bleaches, detergents, and insecticides, the student will list one harmful effect for each chemical with no more than two errors.

2. A social science: Given a simulated problem situation, the student will be able to write a check, balance a checkbook, and rec-

oncile a bank statement, each of which must be 90 percent correct.

3. English literature: After reading Shakespeare's *Hamlet* and having access to the book, the student will describe in writing one instance of psychological conflict for each of three different characters who must have been cited in the student workbook, and the task must be completed within thirty minutes.

4. Mathematics: Given a right △ABC in which ∠ACB is a right ∠, the sides are a, b, and c, and the formula is $c^2 = a^2 + b^2$, the student will write a proof of the Pythagorean theorem employing all six steps stated in the textbook.

skill, learner characteristics, and type of content (Merrill, 1974; Tennyson and Part, 1980). Furthermore, several studies have indicated that teachers typically do not make use of behavioral objectives in planning (Zahorik, 1970; Peterson, Marx, and Clark, 1978; Yinger, 1980). Instead they tend to focus on lesson content and instructional activities, though they may be implicitly aware of objectives (Morine-Dershimer, 1978–1979; Shavelson and Stern, 1981.)

Cognitive Approaches

Behavioral objectives have their roots in the behaviorist tradition of learning that was discussed in Chapter 5. In keeping with a behaviorist orientation, their primary concern is with behavior (what students do and say). Accordingly, they focus on the products of learning, what can be observed, recorded, and measured.

In contrast with behaviorist approaches, cogni-

tive educators and psychologists stress the *inner* dynamics of learning and thinking. They are interested in the structural organization in thinking—the internal frameworks that individuals employ for transforming, elaborating, storing, recovering, and using information. Their primary concern is with assisting students to refine their information-processing procedures and to evolve new and more effective structures for thinking about the environment (see Chapter 6).

Criticisms of Behavioral Objectives

Cognitive educators and psychologists are critical of highly specific behavioral objectives. They, together with those taking a humanist approach (to be considered later in the chapter), advance a number of arguments against the use of behavioral statements. First, they claim that behavioral objectives tend to focus educational attention on the trivial (Wright, 1976). Important and broad objectives are often discarded because of the difficulty of specifying them in measurable terms. The problem is compounded, they claim, by the tendency to strip learning of its "guts" by deemphasizing the human ingredients in the teacher-student relationship (Scandura, 1977).

A second argument against behavioral objectives is advanced by Albert R. Wright (1976). He points out that most behavioral objectives are statements of measurements that are to be taken at the completion of a program, under stipulated conditions, and with specified performance criteria:

> Most so-called behavioral objectives are not really objectives. . . . They are only indicators (samples of behavior or tests that serve as evidence) that the true objectives have been achieved. Calling them objectives can mislead the teacher and the student into believing that the sample of behavior (the indicator) . . . is the desired end result of the learning activity. . . . With the focus on the indicators, it is easy to lose sight of the true objectives. Providing the student with a comprehensive set of behavioral objectives amounts to explaining in some detail the kinds of examinations he will be given. The indicators help him understand what he must do to satisfy the teacher . . . [but] performing the prescribed act or demonstrating the behavior may have little meaning for the student. [Wright, 1976:82–83]

Hence, according to Wright, the behavior itself often becomes the goal and not an indication of the attainment of the goal. When objectives are written in measurement terms, teachers tend to teach and learners tend to learn for the test, not for the true objective.

Third, critics say that behaviorist approaches are undemocratic since they result in teachers "programming passive students" for given behaviors. The educational goals call for changing behavior rather than imparting knowledge (Simons, 1973). As a consequence, knowledge becomes fragmented—just so many isolated bits and pieces—rather than larger integrated wholes. Robert L. Ebel observes:

> Educational development . . . is concerned with the student's understanding, his resources of useful and available knowledge, his intellectual self-sufficiency. It sees him not as a puppet on strings controlled by his teachers, but as one who needs and wants the help of his teachers and others as he tackles the difficult problems of designing and building a life of his own.[1970:172]

Fourth, critics charge that the use of behavioral objectives is impractical by virtue of the time required for their preparation. James B. Macdonald and Bernice J. Wolfson note:

> Let us assume that the teacher cares nothing about individualization. (Should he wish to individualize, he must multiply our descriptions by 30.) He plans to teach all children the same thing at the same time. This means that every day he must have time to plan behavioral objectives for six to nine curriculum areas. Further, he must think through and plan alternative activities, organization, and evaluation procedures for each objective. Such a task is impossible unless the teacher is handed a daily schedule preplanned by experts, or unless he puts much of his program on a teaching machine or uses programmed materials.[1970:123]

And even if teachers could find the time for their preparation, teachers would find themselves with encyclopedic lists of detailed objectives that would be unmanageable.

And fifth, cognitive educators and psychologists say that behavioral objectives are inappropriate for some content areas that cannot readily be broken down and stated in behavioral terms. For example, in literature, teachers point out that they aim to foster certain kinds of perception, awareness, and emotional growth (internal experiences) rather than to teach specific skills that can be readily measured in overt behavior (Gurth, 1974).

Nonbehavioral Objectives

Although there are problems associated with communicating via behavioral objectives, many teachers find them useful tools for some classroom purposes. This is most apparent when the focus is primarily on teaching particular skills rather than

MENTALISTIC AIMS
Teachers are not only concerned with teaching students specific skills. They also want their students to appreciate and enjoy various types of activities.

promoting more effective thought processes. The major merit of behavioral objectives is that they compel teachers to think clearly, and in some detail, about what they wish to accomplish. Further, they provide teachers with a vehicle for evaluating whether or not they are achieving their educational goals.

However, as cognitive educators point out, teachers do not limit themselves to teaching specific skills. They also have "mentalistic" aims; they want their students to appreciate, understand, enjoy, or comprehend something and to think in a creative and imaginative fashion (Waks, 1969). These processes do not readily lend themselves to behavioral statements. Thinking and feeling are events that go on inside people; they are not directly observable by the unaided senses.

The principal way we have of finding out what students are thinking or feeling is by what they say or do. For instance, we may have as our goal teaching students to appreciate classical music. How are we to explain what we mean by "appreciate"? One way we might approach the matter is

to describe how a person who "appreciates" classical music behaves differently from one who does not. We can specify certain kinds of behavior, for example, the time they spend listening to classical music, the proportion of their incomes they use to purchase classical recordings or attend concerts, and the attentiveness they exhibit in listening to classical music (Mehrens and Lehmann, 1978).

In many cases, then, it may not be possible to state objectives in strictly behavioral terms. Rather than specifying the behavior a student will perform as the outcome of instruction, it may be necessary to indicate the kinds, frequency, or levels of performance we will accept as evidence that an objective has been achieved or has a reasonable hope of being achieved over time. Under these circumstances, the behaviors stated in the objectives are not ends or products themselves but simply indicators of inner cognitive interests, feelings, and capabilities (Gideonse, 1969). Hence, nonbehavioral objectives involve the separation of the goal and measurement components; unlike behavioral objectives, the two elements are not combined within one statement (Wright, 1976). Indeed, in some circumstances, the statements may lack a measurement component, being formulated only in broad and general terms to provide a focus or direction for teaching activities (Zahorik, 1976a, 1976b).

Humanist Approaches

If we value independence, if we are disturbed by the growing conformity of knowledge, of values, of attitudes, which our present system induces, then we may wish to set up conditions of learning which make for uniqueness, for self-direction, and for self-initiated learning.

CARL R. ROGERS
On Becoming a Person, 1970

During the first half of the twentieth century, behaviorist and Freudian psychoanalytic theories dominated psychological thought. In the 1940s

humanistic psychology (also called *humanism*) began to emerge, in part as a reaction against what some psychologists considered to be the inadequacies of the two established traditions. For this reason it is sometimes referred to as a *third-force psychology*. Humanists (as they are termed) criticize behaviorists for depicting people as ''robots'' who are mechanically programmed by the conditioning force of environmental stimuli. And they find unacceptable psychoanalytic approaches, which they believe portray people as locked by unconscious instincts and irrational forces into a lifetime programmed by childhood events.

As viewed by humanists, the major goal of education is the development of the total person. They stress the uniqueness of the human condition in that human beings can actively intervene in the course of events to control their destinies and shape the world around them. Accordingly, humanism aims to help people to understand themselves and to develop their full capacities and potentialities. It assigns particular emphasis to the affective domain—the ability to experience empathy for others and to come to terms with one's own and others' emotional feelings. Hence, humanistic psychology centers on the experiencing person.

Among those who have made significant contributions to humanism are Abraham H. Maslow, Carl R. Rogers, Rollo May, Kurt Goldstein, Gordon W. Allport, Charlotte Buhler, Arthur W. Combs, and James F. T. Bugental. However, there is no single position that can be readily identified as the humanistic psychology. Rather, there are certain common themes in the writings of most humanists.

Focus on the Inner Person

In contrast to their behaviorist counterparts, humanists are more concerned with people's ''inner behaviors'' than with behaviors that are externally observable and measurable. The humanist Arthur W. Combs points out:

> It [humanism] regards behavior only as symptom, the external manifestation of what is going on inside a human being. The humanist believes that effective understanding of persons requires understanding, not only of behavior, but also the nature of an individual's internal life. It holds that the primary causes of behavior lie in people's feelings, attitudes, beliefs, values, hopes, perceptions, and aspirations. These are the things that make us human and these, say the humanists, are the fundamental dynamics of behavior. [1978:301–302]

Behaviorists focus on the external world as it impinges on individuals via stimuli and not, as humanists do, on the person who experiences the stimuli. This results in differing educational goals and techniques. As the behaviorist B. F. Skinner notes, the humanist ''wants to change things inside people, and I want to change the world in which people live'' (quoted by Holden, 1977:31). Accordingly, behaviorists pay less attention to individual differences among children than humanists do. And whereas behaviorist programs stress external reinforcement, humanists seek to cultivate the learner's intrinsic motivation, to assist the child to become a self-motivated and enthusiastic scholar.

Human Growth and Fulfillment

Underlying the humanist perspective is the notion that people are basically good (Primack and Aspy, 1980). Like plants, their natural tendency is to grow and realize their potential. But if compelled to grow in a poor environment, like a plant trying to develop under a brick, growth becomes distorted and the plant or organism is stunted. Humanists assist students to grow and develop in their own unique ways by providing a warm and accepting environment. They do not seek to impose their own ideas on the direction students should take, any more than a gardener would attempt to make a lily a rose. Rather, they would have students come to think for themselves, weigh decisions, consider evidence, and relate their learning to their own values.

Three terms continually reappear as educational aims in humanist literature—''self-actualization,'' ''self-fulfillment,'' and ''self-realization.'' The humanist Abraham H. Maslow states what he believes to be the "ultimate goal" of education in the following terms:

> According to the new third psychology, . . . the far goal of education—as of psychotherapy—is to aid the person to grow to fullest humanness, to the greatest fulfillment and actualization of his highest potentials, to his greatest possible stature. In a word, it should help him to become the best he is capable of becoming, to become *actually* what he deeply is *potentially*. What we call healthy growth is growth toward this final goal. [1964:49–50]

A person's self-concept (what an individual thinks and feels he or she is) assumes critical importance in humanist formulations. Indeed, Combs (1978) says that a positive self-concept is a person's "most precious possession" and that what happens to the self in the course of schooling may be more important than any other aspect of education.

Relevance in Education

A basic humanist principle of learning is that information will be acquired and used by a person only to the degree to which the learner has discovered the personal meaning of the information (Combs, 1978, 1981). Students must find the information significant and relevant. Combs (1978:302) asserts, "Education must be affective [have a feeling component] or there is none at all!" Humanists point out that things have no inherent, absolute meanings in their own right. Rather they derive their meanings from the qualities people attribute to them.

Humanistic educators say that if teachers are to maximize their effectiveness, they must start where their pupils are and not where they themselves happen to be. Don E. Hamachek points out:

> Humanistic approaches to teaching and learning keep in mind that students bring their total selves to class. They bring heads that think and feel. They bring values that help them to selectively filter what they see and hear, and they bring attitudinal sets and learning styles that render each student unique and different from all the rest. Humanistic teachers do not only *start out* with the idea that students are different, but they recognize that students may still be different at the *end* of an academic experience. [1977:156]

Humanists believe that many educational practices derived from behaviorist theories violate this premise and as a result bring about only surface and superficial learning.

Student-Centered Education

Humanists highly value personal autonomy and self-determination (Moses and Dickens, 1980; Combs, 1981). They believe that the freedom to choose—to make decisions regarding one's own activities and to set goals for one's own life—is essential if people are to fully realize self-actualization. By virtue of their self-awareness, people are capable of intervening in the course of human affairs to effect given outcomes; their ability to choose means that they are not bystanders but active participants in experience.

The concern with human freedom leads humanists to favor student-centered education, an approach that finds expression in the open classroom movement (to be considered in Chapter 15). Since schools presumably exist for the benefit of students, humanists argue that the instructional process should be based on and geared to student needs, interests, and problems. They insist that students should play an active role in making decisions about what is to be learned and when it is to be studied—that learners should select their own directions, formulate their own problems, discover their own learning resources, decide upon their own courses of action, and live with the consequences of their choices. Further, they believe that students should take the primary responsibility for evaluating their activities and work. In this manner, self-criticism and self-evaluation become of primary importance and that of others of only secondary significance (Rogers, 1967). Hence, humanists believe that, when given the opportunity, people can figure out what is best for them.

HUMANISTIC APPROACHES
Humanist educators value self-awareness and freedom to choose one's own activities. They say that people learn only to the degree to which they personally relate to information.

The Teacher as Facilitator

Humanists conceive of teachers primarily as facilitators. Humanistic psychologists such as Carl R. Rogers question whether anyone can "teach" anyone else anything worthwhile; they believe that real learning is self-initiated. Thus, teachers have the task of providing a climate in which students can feel free to take responsibility for their own education.

Rather than functioning as behavioral engineers, teachers as humanistic facilitators are seen as helpers who free students to achieve their higher human needs. Teachers permit students choice, a share in responsibility, power, and control, and enter into activities as participant learners (Rogers, 1977). They regard themselves as flexible resources to be used by students and as providers of the widest possible range of resources for learning (books, materials, equipment, trips, audiovisual aids, other people, and the like).

Criticisms

All major educational theories have their own particular view of human beings and the world— a unique philosophical outlook or model. If one accepts the underlying tenets of humanism, then its educational formulations and programs make a good deal of sense. Of course, if one rejects these tenets, the programs seem less perfect. And various educators and psychologists, especially those associated with behaviorist schools of thought, do indeed find much in humanism to which they object.

Many behaviorists view humanism as moralistic, pious, and value-laden, as a kind of "secular religion." They deny the humanist notion that people are basically good, saying instead that people are neutral and acquire given behaviors only as responses to environmental stimuli. Moreover, Norman A. Sprinthall charges that qualities like open-mindedness, spontaneity, sensitivity, empathy, and self-awareness are "a bag of virtues"—they are vague, arbitrary, and culture-bound concepts:

The virtues are topical and current but are still an arbitrary list of static traits, time-limited and situational. In this sense it is no different to talk about openness, spontaneity, etc., than it would have been to talk about being brave, clean, and reverent in a previous era. The traits are more up to date, but we are still dealing with a bag of virtues as educational objectives. [1972:352]

It is said that the qualities emphasized by humanists resemble those studied over a half-century ago by Hugh Hartshorne and Mark A. May (1928). They found that such behaviors as honesty, good temper, truthfulness, and bravery are not stable character traits but a function of the specific situations in which children find themselves (see Chapter 11).

Critics also ask how one might use scientific methods to measure self-awareness, freedom, healthy relationships, and human potential. They find it difficult to come up with firm evidence that reveals whether or not humanistic teachers are achieving their educational goals. And the critics are distressed by what they view as the absence among humanists of a "tough-minded" and "hard-headed" orientation for rigorously testing hypotheses.

There are also those who reject as without merit humanist programs that allow students to make up their own courses of study and then to provide the definitive appraisal of the adequacy of the work. Psychologist Albert Ellis says: "Unless you have very good directive teaching, education is a waste of time. People almost always do the wrong thing" (quoted by Holden, 1977:33).

CHAPTER SUMMARY

1. A prescriptive theory for the design of instruction consists of four components. First, it is necessary to analyze the subject matter content to determine what it is that the student is expected to learn. Second, instructional planning requires a description of the initial or entering characteristics

of the students themselves. Third, educators need to establish the conditions under which students will work, from their initial or entering status to the successful completion of the educational objectives. Fourth, planning must provide for monitoring a student's progress.

2. One attempt to provide a framework for instructional planning is the taxonomy of educational objectives begun in the 1950s by Benjamin S. Bloom and his colleagues. Educational objectives are classified in three domains: cognitive, affective, and psychomotor.

3. Bloom's taxonomy for the cognitive domain has generated great interest. It contains six major classes: knowledge, comprehension, application, analysis, synthesis, and evaluation. Bloom views the six classes as consisting of a hierarchical order. The hierarchy has cumulative properties. It is based on the idea that one behavior may become integrated with other similar-level behaviors to form a more complex behavior.

4. Since teaching is a goal-directed activity, teachers should determine their objectives before they proceed with learning activities. Objectives provide direction for teaching and curriculum development. Having defined their instructional objectives, teachers can then design the means or learning activities to achieve them. Finally, instructional objectives provide teachers with guidance in later evaluating the students' learning.

5. Over the past two decades, there has been considerable interest in educational circles in stating behavioral objectives at high levels of specificity. Behavioral objectives serve a variety of functions. First, they act as guides to instruction. Second, since objectives state the expected terminal behavior, they can be easily translated into a test of student achievement. Third, behavioral objectives communicate to relevant parties what is to be learned.

6. A behavioral objective consists of three parts. First, it must state the *behavior* a student will be able to perform as the intended outcome of instruction. Second, a behavioral objective describes the *conditions* under which the expected behavior is to be performed. Third, a behavioral objective describes the *criteria* by which the behavior is to be judged as acceptable or unacceptable.

7. A good many studies have attempted to assess the effectiveness of behavioral objectives for improving student learning. When the research is reviewed, the data for and against benefits appear to be evenly matched. In actual practice, moreover, teachers may make little use of written behavioral objectives.

8. Behavioral objectives have their roots in the behaviorist tradition of learning. In contrast with behaviorist approaches, cognitive educators and psychologists stress the inner dynamics of learning and thinking. Their primary concern is in assisting students to refine their information-processing procedures and to evolve new and more effective structures for thinking about the environment.

9. Cognitive and humanist educators and psychologists are critical of highly specific behavioral objectives. First, they claim that behavioral objectives tend to focus educational attention on the trivial. Second, most behavioral objectives are statements of measurements that are to be taken at the completion of the program, leading teachers to teach and learners to learn for the test (and not the true objectives). Third, critics say that behaviorist approaches are undemocratic, since they result in teachers "programming passive students" for given behaviors. Fourth, critics charge that the use of behavioral objectives is impractical by virtue of the time required for their preparation. And fifth, behavioral objectives are inappropriate for some content areas (like literature).

10. Although not stated in behavioral terms, many educators nonetheless find it useful to state instructional objectives. Nonbehavioral objectives involve the separation of the goal and measurement components; unlike behavioral objectives, the two elements are not combined within one statement. Often, rather than specifying the behavior a student will perform as the outcome of instruction, it may be necessary to indicate the kinds, frequency, or

levels of performance that will be accepted as evidence that an objective has been achieved.

11. Humanistic psychologists view the major goal of education as the development of the total person. They stress the uniqueness of the human condition in that human beings can actively intervene in the course of events to control their destinies and shape the world about them. A number of themes are common to the writings of most humanists: a focus on the inner person, an emphasis upon human growth and fulfillment, concern with relevance in education, student-centered education, and the definition of the teacher as a facilitator.

CHAPTER GLOSSARY

behavioral objectives   Statements regarding the specific changes that educators intend to produce in pupil behavior.

curriculum   The most comprehensive category of the instructional program.

educational goals   Statements regarding the outcomes of instruction.

humanistic psychology   A psychological school of thought that stresses the uniqueness of the human condition. It maintains that human beings, unlike other organisms, actively intervene in the course of events to control their destinies and shape the world around them.

task analysis   The identification of the subordinate skills and knowledge learners must acquire before they can achieve the educational goal (the terminal objective).

taxonomy   A device for identifying, naming, and classifying things in terms of their characteristics.

teaching   A purposeful activity designed to induce learning or to change behavior.

EXERCISES

Review Questions

1. Bruner argues that a theory of instruction should be
   a. descriptive
   b. normative
   c. prescriptive
   d. a, b, and c are true
   e. b and c are true

2. In Bloom's taxonomy, the simplest and most complex categories are
   a. knowledge and analysis
   b. comprehension and synthesis
   c. application and comprehension
   d. knowledge and evaluation

3. A teacher who uses the key words *translate, interpret,* and *estimate* in her questions is emphasizing which category in Bloom's taxonomy?
   a. comprehension
   b. application
   c. knowledge
   d. analysis

4. A teacher who uses the key words *write, propose,* and *produce* in her questions is emphasizing which category in Bloom's taxonomy?
   a. comprehension
   b. application
   c. knowledge
   d. synthesis

5. Which of the following is *not* considered a contribution of Bloom's taxonomy?
   a. It avoids need for writing instructional objectives.

b. It calls teachers' attention to need for higher order questions.

c. It helps prepare evaluation instruments.

d. It assumes learning proceeds from simple to complex.

6. Among the advantages claimed for behavioral objectives is that they

a. assist in overall planning of instruction
b. form the basis for test items
c. emphasize process rather than product
d. a and b are true

7. Which of these statements would *not* be considered true in David Payne's levels of specificity?

a. Behavioral objectives are considered to be at the least level of specificity.
b. Global objectives are the most abstract.
c. The third level is represented by test questions.
d. Specific behaviors hold a position of specificity between global objectives and behavioral objectives.
e. a and d are true

8. Among the arguments advanced against behavioral objectives is that they

a. tend to be equated with true goals
b. encourage passivity in students
c. often reduce teacher planning time
d. a and b are true

9. Unlike behaviorists, humanists

a. emphasize empirical positions regarding human growth and development
b. assume that learners must take an active role in choosing learning experiences
c. argue that significant learning experiences have universal meaning
d. a and c are true

10. Criticisms leveled against humanist education include

a. it is too pragmatic
b. definitions of key concepts are too narrowly specified
c. outcomes are often not amenable to scientific analyses
d. a and c are true

Answers

1. e (See p. 372)
2. d (See p. 376)
3. a (See p. 378)
4. d (See pp. 378–379)
5. a (See p. 376)
6. d (See pp. 381–382)
7. e (See pp. 383–384)
8. d (See pp. 385–386)
9. b (See p. 389)
10. c (See p. 391)

Applying Principles and Concepts

1. A high-school history teacher is preparing to teach a class unit on the battle of Gettysburg. Glaser has listed four steps in instruction: task analysis, initial or entry-level skills, determination of institutional procedures, and monitoring students' progress. Here are listed some steps in the teacher's planning. Which, if any, of Glaser's components are missing?

a. Students will report daily on their projects.
b. Students should be able to list the sequence of events leading up to the battle itself.
c. The teacher will have each student construct a map of the terrain.
d. Students will prepare papers summing up the major outcomes of the battle.
e. The teacher will need additional books on the subject.

2. An educator is conducting a seminar on Bloom's taxonomy. Classify each of the following questions he intends to ask as an example of Bloom's knowledge (K), comprehension (C), application (AP), analysis (AN), synthesis (S), or evaluation (E) question type.

_____ a. Can anyone give me some examples of a synthesis-type question?

_____ b. What assumptions about learning appear to underlie Bloom's taxonomy?

_____ c. What are the categories in Bloom's taxonomy?

_____ d. How useful do you think his taxonomy is to the average classroom teacher?

_____ e. What do you see as common elements to these taxonomy approaches?

3. Here is a list of behavioral objectives. Indicate whether the objective is complete or lacking a statement of conditions (C), an action verb (V), and/or a standard of performance (S).

_____ a. The students will identify all examples of adverbs.

_____ b. Given a diagram of the eye, the students will identify all the numbered structures.

_____ c. After listening to a lecture on geothermal energy, the students will recall at least five advantages of this source.

_____ d. The students will understand the concept of democracy.

4. A behaviorist has written the following criticism of humanism. Underline those passages that the author of the textbook would consider an *unfair* statement of position or that cannot be substantiated by research (not including criticisms by others mentioned in the textbook).

> Humanists see absolutely no place for the teacher. They believe in intrinsic motivation and automatically assume that all students can immediately assess their own needs. Frankly, they don't seem to care if anyone learns anything.

5. A humanist has written the following criticism of the behaviorist position. Underline those passages that the author of the textbook would consider an *unfair* statement of position or that cannot be substantiated by research (not including criticisms by others mentioned in the textbook).

> The behaviorists don't like to accept anything they can't hear or see. They have no concern for the individual child. Their so-called behavioral objectives have never been shown to help improve achievement; all they are is an excuse for imposing the teacher's ideas on the student.

Answers

1. The teacher did not assess initial or entry-level skills. (See pp. 373, 375)
2. a, C; b, AN; c, K; d, E; e, S (See pp. 376–379)
3. a, C; b, complete; c, complete; d, C, V, and S (See p. 383)
4. Underline "Humanists see absolutely no place for the teacher," "automatically assume that all students can immediately assess their own needs," "they don't seem to care if anyone learns anything." (See pp. 387–389, 391)
5. Underline "no concern for the individual child," "behavioral objectives have never been shown to help improve achievement," "all they are is an excuse for imposing the teacher's ideas on the student." (See pp. 381–384)

Project

OBJECTIVE: To analyze the kinds of questions used in a discussion.

PROCEDURE: You can do this project in one of your classes or in a public school classroom if you have access. Look over Table 13.1 of the textbook. You may want to copy some of the key words used. Use a class meeting that is not a straight lecture. During the class categorize the teacher's questions using the following chart, and rank their order.

Type	Rank Order
Knowledge-comprehension	
Application	
Analysis	
Synthesis	
Evaluation	

Note that, instead of merely indicating frequency, we are asking you to rank the *order* in which the questions appear. Hence, if the first four questions are typed as knowledge-comprehension, analysis, application, and analysis, the following numbers will appear in the "Order" column: knowledge-comprehension, 1; analysis, 2, 4; application, 3.

ANALYSIS: The analysis should yield two types of information:

1. First, the types of information sought can be obtained by simply counting all the numbers listed in a given category (regardless of rank order). Heavy concentrations in knowledge-comprehension would indicate the teacher's emphasis on factual information. Conversely, concentration in the other areas would indicate emphasis on higher order thinking.

2. Second, the rank orders should yield information on whether the teacher is following some hierarchical structure or skipping about. That is, if the lower ranks (earlier questions) are concentrated in knowledge-comprehension, then it would appear that the teacher is trying to secure an information base. A quick way of estimating this point is to count the rank orders obtained in each category and to divide by the number of items, which will yield the mean rank order. If the rank orders obtained for knowledge-comprehension are 8, 14, 19, 20, 39, the mean rank order will be:

$$\frac{8 + 14 + 19 + 20 + 39}{5} = 20.0$$

The lower the mean rank order, the earlier in the discussions such questions were used. Discuss the implications of your findings with the teacher.

CHAPTER OUTLINE

398

14

INSTRUCTIONAL STRATEGIES AND TECHNIQUES

CHAPTER PREVIEW

Planning is only an initial step in instruction. The lesson or unit designed must then be presented to the student. Many techniques have evolved or been developed for the delivery of instruction, and several of these are discussed in this chapter. They are classified into those that are primarily teacher centered, such as the familiar lecture format; those that involve group activity, such as discussions and simulations; and those that focus on the student, in that they are designed to be adapted to the needs and interests of individuals. Included in the latter category are the concept of mastery learning, programmed instruction, and computer-assisted instruction. The advantages and disadvantages of these various approaches are weighed.

Consider these questions part of your self-instructional strategy while reading:

- What are the advantages and disadvantages of the use of the lecture in instruction?
- What are the characteristics of classroom recitation as typically used?
- In what ways can discussion groups, games, and simulations be used most effectively?

- What three general approaches have been taken to designing programs for aptitude-treatment interactions?
- What are the basic premises of mastery learning? How would this concept alter classroom instruction as usually practiced?
- How might computers (especially microcomputers) be used most effectively in schools and classrooms?

Teachers organize and structure classroom instruction in quite different ways. They may talk a great deal or very little. They may expect students to sit quietly or allow them to move about. And they may treat pupils en masse or individually. Likewise, the instructional focus varies. Attention may be centered on the teacher, the class, or the individual student. Each emphasis entails a somewhat different set of techniques and strategies.

TEACHER-CENTERED TECHNIQUES

It is not the system or method in itself that is important, but whether the teacher is happy with it and capable of using it effectively.

JAMES COLLINGE
Teachers and Teaching Methods, 1976

When most of us imagine a classroom setting, the teacher emerges as the central figure. This stereotype derives from our own schooling experience in which lectures and discussion have been the typical approaches. The activities and attention of the students revolve about the teacher. Although the chapter will consider a variety of strategies, let us begin our discussion with this familiar and traditional pattern—teacher-centered techniques.

LECTURE
The major advantage of the lecture method is that it allows the teacher to communicate with a large number of students at one time. Its chief disadvantage is that students tend to become passive participants in the learning process and hence are not necessarily attentive to the lecturer.

Lecture

Teacher talk comprises at least half of all the time spent in normal classroom interaction. Lecturing is a special kind of teacher talk characterized by formal communication. It takes up between a sixth and a fourth of all classroom interaction time. Teachers in the higher grades generally make more use of lecturing than do those in the lower grades (Dunkin and Biddle, 1974).

The major virtue of the lecture is that teachers can communicate with large audiences economically. They can personally present the chief elements of their subject, directly inspire an audience with their own enthusiasm, and key their presentation to audience responses. The popularity of the lecture method derives from its effectiveness in summarizing content in a form understandable by a group of students. Moreover, especially on the college level, instructors typically believe it "the easiest thing" to do, "the accepted thing" to do, and "the safest" thing to do. The chief disadvantage of the lecture is that the lecturer often fails to engage the attention or active participation of the students. Critics say that all too often lecturing results in dreary classes and the "spoon-feeding" of students (McLeish, 1976).

Student "intake" patterns during lectures tend to resemble those found in the work patterns of the industrial labor force (McLeish, 1976). Most commonly an initial spurt takes place at the beginning of the period. This is followed by a middle sag that results from boredom and fatigue. Finally, an end-spurt is found with a return to a level approximating the initial stage.

Surveys of college students reveal that they consider "systematic organization" and the "ability to explain clearly" as the most important qualities for a successful lecturer in the sciences. They cite "ability to encourage thought," "enthusiastic attitude to the subject," and "expert knowledge" as the most important qualities of arts and social science lecturers. Deemed to be of lesser importance are the lecturer's personality, fairness, tolerance, sympathetic attitude, and speaking ability. Overall, then, college students believe that effective teaching is the result of knowledge of the subject, good organization of the material, and commitment to the area of specialization (Riley, Ryan, and Lifshitz, 1950; Musella and Rusch, 1968; Smithers, 1970).

Recitation

Classroom recitation is another highly used teaching method. It consists of repeated episodes of *structuring, soliciting, responding,* and *reacting* (Gage, 1976; Clark et al., 1979). Structuring entails telling students what they will be doing and talking about and how the teacher plans to deal with the material. Soliciting is similar to question-asking, except that the teacher need not state the question in a complete sentence and may employ body language. Responding involves student answering. Reacting is what the teacher does once a student has provided an answer.

Teacher questions play a prominent role in recitation sessions. Classroom surveys reveal that from 40 to 75 percent of teacher talk is in the form of questions. Lee Banton (1977) finds from the analysis of videotape teaching sessions that some

teachers ask as many as thirty-five questions in five minutes—an unbelievable rate of about seven questions per minute. Teachers at the lower grade levels make greater use of questions than do those at the higher grade levels. Further, teachers address more questions to boys than to girls (Dunkin and Biddle, 1974). The vast majority of teacher questions call for a recall of facts, whereas only 17 to 29 percent require thought responses (Gall, 1970).

The questions teachers ask take a number of forms. For convenience, James J. Gallagher (1965) distinguishes among four types of teacher questions: cognitive-memory, convergent-thinking, divergent-thinking, and evaluative-thinking.

Cognitive-memory questions require the pupil to engage in perception, comprehension, or retention of content. They generally do not call on the student to go beyond the retention and recall of information. Such questions generally involve:

- Reading or spelling ("How do you spell marine?")
- Recapitulation or review ("What did you observe on our trip to the museum today?")
- Giving facts, labels, or definitions ("What is the definition of biology?")
- Detailing or describing ("What are the parts of the respiratory system?")

Convergent-thinking questions call for thinking, analyzing, reasoning, or integrating information to arrive at the right, conventionally accepted answer:

- Make relationships ("How are a robin and a blue jay alike?")
- Give explanations ("Why can't fish live on land?")
- Reason ("There are four dogs in the kennel. Two dogs run away. The owner then buys three new dogs and puts them in the kennel. How many dogs are now in the kennel?")
- Arrive at conclusions, principles, or inferences ("If people cut all the trees down on a mountainside for firewood, what will happen in a heavy rainfall?")

MEDIA OF INSTRUCTION

One consideration in instructional design is choosing media to serve as an extension of the teacher. Print is, of course, the oldest and most important medium. It has provided the foundation for a literate population and universal public education. Textbooks and reference books are so fully accepted as part of education that most of us now take them for granted. As a result, when we talk about "instructional media," we usually think in terms of the photographic and electronic media: photographs, slides, slide-tapes, transparencies, films, recordings, videotapes, radio, television, and computers. Like print these are information-carrying technologies that are not specifically designed for instruction, although they can be used for educational purposes (Schramm, 1977).

Beginning in the 1920s, instructional radio was widely used in the United States. By virtue of adverse regulatory decisions and the advent of television, the use of the radio has dwindled. However, developing countries like Thailand, Upper Volta, and Mexico are making increasing use of radio. Its principal attraction has been its cost, which is low in comparison with many other media. Research shows that when appropriately supplemented by visual material, radio is an effective media for instruction (Jamison, Suppes, and Wells, 1974).

There have been well over two hundred studies comparing instructional television with tradi-tional classroom instruction (Chu and Schramm, 1967; Dubin and Hedley, 1969). Overall, the research suggests that instructional television can teach all grade levels and subject matters about as effectively as live teachers. Although a significant number of teachers and students initially have negative attitudes toward instructional television, these attitudes tend to lessen with time. Generally, teachers and pupils are more favorable toward the use of instructional television in elementary school than in secondary school and college. The introduction of "Sesame Street" (a television series for preschool children) in the late 1960s did much to build a favorable climate for educational television.

On the basis of a survey of the research on teaching with television and film, Aimee D. Leifer reaches the following conclusion:

Television and film can (a) capture the uncommon or hard to duplicate and make it available to everyone; (b) present static and moving visual information easily; (c) alter visual, auditory, and temporal characteristics of material and phenomena; (d) resort to animation; (e) reach a very large audience; and (f) be repeated endlessly. On the other hand, television and film cannot as easily (a) respond to students as they are learning the lesson; (b) foster practice of reading, writing, and speaking skills; (c) oversee students learning through their own activity; and (d) take the idiosyncrasies of each student into account. [1976:326]

Most authorities agree that the various teaching media are interchangeable for most educational tasks. Further, no one medium has properties that make it best for all purposes. Thus Wilbur Schramm concludes:

Can the media teach? has been asked over and over again, and over and over again the answer has come back: Of course, students can learn effectively from the media, from any medium. Can they teach as well as a teacher? The answer: what they can do, they can do as well as a classroom teacher, sometimes better. It depends on the performance of the teacher, the content of the media, what is being taught, and to whom. Is one medium any more effective than others? For some purposes, probably yes, but overall there is no superlative medium of instruction. [1977:14]

Consequently, an evaluation of the utility of any given medium as a teaching device must be based on criteria such as the expertise with which it presents a particular topic, ease of delivery, cost per pupil, and size of class. Moreover, a teacher need not worry about whether or not to use various instructional media; rather, the educator must decide when to use them and how best to integrate them into the larger educational program (Leifer, 1976).

Divergent-thinking questions involve thinking that leads to a variety of acceptable responses. In contrast to convergent thinking, there is no one right answer:

- Create new ideas ("What would be another title for *Treasure Island*?")
- Generate a number of differing responses ("What are the functions of the respiratory system?")
- Arrive at novel responses through reasoning or inference ("What would happen if the sun would disintegrate?")

Evaluative-thinking questions require the pupil to judge or rate information on the basis of certain criteria:

- Judgments based on certain specified criteria ("What is the best way to reach an object hanging from the ceiling if you have three wooden blocks of large, medium, and small size?")
- Judgments based on unspecified criteria ("Which one doesn't belong—a dog, a rabbit, a robin, and a donkey?")
- Express an opinion ("Do you like Mozart's music?")

Experimental data on the relative value of the differing types of teacher questions are as yet inconclusive (Clark et al., 1979; Winne, 1979; Dillon, 1981).

CLASS-CENTERED TECHNIQUES

Some instructional techniques have the class as their focus. Rather than revolving about either the individual student or the teacher, the activities center on the whole or the group. In these arrangements the parties engage in a variety of actions in which they mutually and reciprocally influence one another's attitudes and behavior. The principal class-centered techniques involve discussion groups, games, and simulations.

Discussion Groups

The discussion method provides both the teacher and the pupil with control over the treatment of the subject. It allows a good deal of give-and-take to occur among people. Usually the teacher serves as the moderator-leader and channels the communicative interaction in keeping with the instructional objectives. Discussions permit students to express themselves and to interact with each other. It is particularly effective in instructional settings where students spend considerable time working in isolation from one another. The satisfaction inherent in discussion sessions serves to enhance learning outcomes, contributes to class morale, and compels students to identify what they do and do not know (Gall and Gall, 1976). Further, the participants can learn from one another.

Although discussions are usually designed to promote student involvement and thinking about problems and issues, researchers find that most discussions at the elementary school level are characterized by a preponderance of teacher talk and fact questions (Gall and Gall, 1976; Gall and Gillett, 1980). The result is that students tend to talk to the teacher, often playing the game of "guess what is on the teacher's mind" rather than talking to one another in an open matter (Stanton, 1977). The teacher then functions like a telephone switchboard routing communications from one pupil to another.

Another limitation of the method is that all too often classroom discussions are boring, aimless, and even threatening to various students (Applegate, 1969). Some pupils are afraid to engage in group discussion even when they receive considerable encouragement. Others participate but show little self-confidence. Frequently, only a few children are self-assured enough to take part, and these students become the dominant participants in the

DISCUSSION GROUPS
Although discussion sessions are designed to provide student involvement, all too often
teachers do most of the talking.

discussion (Trosky and Wood, 1976). Hence, a discussion typically involves three or four assertive students, with the remainder of the group playing the part of passive onlookers (Stanton, 1977). Indeed, a relatively large discussion group can only work if a considerable proportion of the members participate infrequently or say nothing at all. Still another limitation is that a discussion simply for the sake of discussion quickly tends to degenerate into a ''pooling of ignorance.''

The educational psychologist Wilbert J. Mc-Keachie reaches the following conclusion regarding the discussion method:

> Since discussion offers the opportunity for a good deal of student activity and feedback, it could be (according to theory) and is (according to research results) more effective than typical lectures in developing concepts and problem-solving skills. However, because the rate of transmission of information is slow in discussion classes, we would expect lecture classes to be superior in attaining the objective of teaching knowledge. Research results tend to support this generalization. [1965:216]

Meredith D. Gall and Joyce P. Gall (1976) have surveyed the literature on the discussion method to identify those features that can make it a more reliable and effective tool in the hands of teachers. They make a number of recommendations. First, the best group size appears to be about five members. This is because (1) a strict deadlock is not possible with an odd number of members; (2) the group tends to split into a majority of three and a minority of two, so that being in a minority does not isolate the individual (as in a three-person group), but allows each person sources of gratification; and (3) the group appears to be large enough for the members to shift roles easily and for any individual to withdraw from an awkward position without necessarily having to resolve the issue at hand (Hare, 1976).

Second, Gall and Gall recommend that teachers form discussion groups in which students are heterogeneous rather than homogeneous in their abilities and attitudes. This ensures a variety of perspectives and a more lively encounter.

Third, they suggest that teachers foster moderate rather than strong group cohesiveness. Highly cohesive groups are more likely to resist attitude changes and to reject deviant members who do not share the majority members' standards. On the other hand, groups with very low cohesiveness tend to be so fragmented and polarized that meaningful interchange is virtually impossible.

Fourth, Gall and Gall find that a discussion promotes effective communication if the teacher establishes seating arrangements that place students in easy eye contact and hearing range of each other. Fifth, they recommend that teachers exercise a democratic rather than an authoritarian leadership style.

A final recommendation comes from Odarka S. Trosky and Clifford C. Wood (1973). They point out that many students lack the necessary skills for effective participation in discussions. Teachers can sensitize students to the components of a discussion by examining with their students such features as listening to someone else, asking questions, giving answers, taking turns, talking about something, and planning ahead what one will say. Students then can participate in a series of small-group discussions that provide practice in the various "jobs" that have to be done.

Games and Simulations

A half century ago, John Dewey (1928) noted the link between play and social life and advocated the use of games as an integral part of the instructional program. A distinguishing characteristic of a game is that it involves a free, make-believe activity in which the participants agree on certain objectives and a set of rules whereby these objectives may be attained (Suits, 1967). Many teachers recognize that any drill can be turned into a game. The old-fashioned "spelling bee" is a good example. Indeed, the number of ways games can be used in schools is virtually limitless (Seidner, 1976; Borman, 1979).

Simulation games involve students in a mode of learning that differs from the usual information-dispensing model. In a simulation game, students act and observe concrete events that result from their actions in an artificially produced environment (Coleman, 1970; Seidner, 1978; Cohen and Bradley, 1978). They become players rather than spectators in the process of learning. In this manner, students encounter cues and consequences very much like those in real environments. The pupils act as they would in a real environment and receive feedback through natural channels (Davis, Alexander, and Yelon, 1974). An illustration is a social studies course in which students are asked to assume the role of diplomats representing various nations. The students must arrive at decisions and treaties as part of the game. Another illustration of a different sort is equipment for simulating actual driving conditions that allows student drivers to encounter real situations without jeopardizing their own lives or those of other people.

In a simulated environment students can discover various concepts and principles for themselves. The games provide a self-motivating activity that is gratifying in its own right. They offer an enjoyable change of pace from traditional methods of instruction. The students learn not so much from interacting with the teacher but from the medium and the other students (Cruickshank and Telfer, 1980).

A major problem with simulations is that they are not always effective in helping students to generalize from the particular experience provided in the game to the more general principles appli-

SELECTING CLASSROOM GAMES

MATTIE EDWARDS
Springfield College

The great proliferation of educational games demands increased expertise in the decision-making process. With little effort, "gadgets" and "gimmicks" may be acquired for almost any aspect of classroom learning. Many such aids are designed for reinforcement purposes, others to help children make discoveries on their

Source: Condensed from Mattie Edwards, "Selecting Classroom Games," *Instructor*, 83 (September 1973):170.

own. Some may be recommended for both. For whatever purposes, teachers and students are putting games to greater use in a variety of ways.

But we must now view this necessarily as an indication of increased academic achievement. Educational games, though admittedly helpful, have their shortcomings. Many, for example, tend to eliminate early in play those students whose needs could be served best by remaining in the game. Under the best circumstances, students are not always

given the feedback needed for answering the crucial questions: Where did I go wrong? Why is this answer not correct? What must I do to improve?

In spite of claims made, reasonable caution and sound judgment must be exercised in the use of classroom games. The following suggestions may be helpful in your selection.

- Consider the special needs of the children who will be using the games. Select games which will meet these needs.

cable in real-life situations (Coleman et al., 1973; Baker et al., 1981). Accordingly educators need to take care to provide an appropriate mix of lesson formats so that each may complement and supplement the others.

STUDENT-CENTERED TECHNIQUES

Although human beings share much in common, each is nonetheless unique. No matter how much society—parents, teachers, religious leaders, and others—encourage conformity, each person exhibits strikingly individual characteristics. By capitalizing on the uniqueness of each child, teachers can aid their students to attain their maximum

potentialities. Over the past two decades educators have shown considerable interest in individualizing education. Indeed, individualized instruction is one of the most promising recent emphases in education. Yet, adapting education to the student is not new. Socrates' famous dialogue with Meno and a Greek slave boy is an early attempt to suit instruction to the student.

Assumptions of Individualized Instruction

Individualized instruction takes a good many forms. There are, however, three assumptions underlying most programs (Hunter, 1977). First, every student has the potential for learning the next thing beyond that which he or she already

- Avoid using the same games with the same children over and over again. To provide variety for those whose needs persist, make available several games with the same purpose.
- Minimize the use of "win-lose" games. Competition should be with others whose chances are nearly equal.
- "Self-teaching" games do not exonerate the teacher of any responsibility. Individualization of instruction should be reflected in the use of games as in other teaching materials.

- Games cannot prove to be equally successful for every child. A lack of progress may indicate that other activities would better serve a particular learning style.
- To avoid undue anxiety and unnecessary interruptions by the child who constantly seeks reassurance, withhold games to be played alone until an increased degree of independence is established.
- Intersperse games with other activities.
- Select games of durable qual-

ity, especially those used excessively.
- Look for ways to make games on hand serve more than one purpose.
- Although most games are in some way educational, evaluation should be based on established purposes.

These suggestions are not intended to take the fun out of games. Rather, let these tips help you introduce effective and instructional games into classroom learning.

knows. Accordingly, the "next thing" is ideally the area in which the teacher should focus attention. The teacher should assess tasks to arrive at the correct level of learning difficulty for each student.

A second assumption of the individualization movement is that students use different modes and strategies in learning. This implies that teachers should identify the strategies a student successfully employs and the strategies that require development or strengthening.

A third assumption of an individualized program is that students require different types of assistance from and stimulation by teachers. Students need instruction that gears *what* they are taught and *how* they are taught to the interests and abilities they bring to the teaching-learning process (Anderson and Block, 1977). This notion implies that there is a certain optimal level of difficulty for each student.

Numerous misconceptions exist regarding individualized instruction. It does not imply, for example, that teachers must teach each student separately or that they must see to it that each student is doing something entirely different from the other students. As Henry Pluckrose, a British educator, states, "The teacher then becomes rather like a master juggler at a circus, whose aim is to keep thirty plates spinning on thirty poles. This he does by moving to where he is most needed when he is most needed, increasing the momentum of individual poles to prevent the plates from falling to the ground" (quoted by Kepler and Randall, 1977:339). Under these circumstances, children are often waiting, off-task, confused, and frustrated.

Even teachers who use programmed or packaged multimedia materials must carefully introduce opportunities for group projects, group discussions,

INDIVIDUALIZED SPELLING

JENEVIE SHARKNAS

Fourth-Grade Teacher,
Grand Blanc, Michigan

There was no doubt about it—spelling books were not the answer to my fourth-graders' spelling problems. Those neat, usually perfect spelling papers on Friday gave no indication of the errors to appear on next week's compositions, letters, and other written work. In an attempt to achieve some carry-over, I decided to individualize spelling instruction.

In a folder I placed a sheet of paper for each student. Whenever I found a spelling error in a student's work, I noted the word on his sheet. I kept this cumulative list for two or three weeks. Then I made up a file folder for each student, putting in his word list and a piece of graph paper.

I also proceeded to pair students. Some research, reading, and review of students' standardized tests indicated a relationship between reading and spelling ability. So in pairing I kept reading abilities in mind. I also considered personalities.

After explaining the program, I discussed with students how to study spelling words. Then we were ready to start.

Monday: Each student chose from his cumulative list the words he wanted to learn that week, and wrote them on a dated 3″ × 5″ card. Which words and how many were his own choice, though I gave guidance when needed. Since many words were misspelled because of mispronunciation, the dictionary pronunciation was written after each word on the card. Students kept this card in the front of their file box.

Tuesday: Students wrote a sentence for each spelling word, which they underlined. I checked the sentences, making a list of any misspelled words at the bottom. I also checked sentences with the word wrongly used.

Wednesday: Tuesday's papers handed back, students added any new misspelled words to their cumulative lists. They also rewrote any sentences in which they used the word incorrectly. On Wednesdays and Thursdays, I did some teaching of generalized spelling rules to the whole group. Then the children spent a few minutes studying their lists.

Thursday: Partners worked together, reading sentences and words to each other. They spent a few minutes drilling and giving each other quick tests.

Friday: Partners gave each other their weekly test. Using sentence sheets, they pronounced the spelling word, used it in a sentence, pronounced it again. Test papers were handed in.

The following Monday I returned test papers. Students recorded their score on their graph, then X'd the correctly spelled words on their cumulative word list. Wrongly spelled words were put on this week's list to be learned. Last week's file card was also checked, misspelled words transferred to the new list, and the card filed at the back of the box.

With this spelling program, preview tests were not necessary; neither were review tests. Instead, I encouraged students to refer to their cards when doing creative writing and other work.

After indivdualizing, I found the children actually enjoyed spelling! I noticed a great improvement in word awareness—of pronunciation and meaning as well as spelling. There was a definite carry-over to other written work; sentence structure greatly improved, as did the appearance of the papers. Individualized spelling was better meeting my students' needs.

Source: Jenevie Sharknas, "I Individualized Spelling," *Instructor,* 79 (March 1970):64.

INDIVIDUALIZED INSTRUCTION
Individualized instruction is not something new but is as old as education itself.

and peer teaching to offset the negative effects of always working alone or following the built-in orders of the "learning package" (Hyman, 1973). Not all learning or development is best accomplished in isolation through solitary scholarship. Children's learning and development also result from attending to other children's thoughts and ideas. Indeed, as noted in Chapter 6, Piaget and other cognitive psychologists stress the important relationship between social interaction and cognitive development. Accordingly, teachers should optimize the range and depth of experiences available to their students.

All of this is to suggest that teachers need to use a mixed bag of teaching methods and schedules since students have multiple learning needs. Further, even the same student differs from time to time and from task to task in learning efficiency.

Aptitude-Treatment Interactions

As noted, it is widely assumed that some children learn best from one method, while others profit from a different type of instruction. Thus a strategy that works well in general may not be the best strategy for everyone. Some psychologists attribute the differing effectiveness of various methods to

CHILDREN AS TUTORS

Qui docet discit. (He who teaches, learns.)

An ancient dictum

By teaching the younger children, the more advanced are constantly reviewing their studies. . . . The monitorial plan, as I used it, is the true democratic one. . . . No child . . . was so low that she could not teach something, and that something *I always required her to teach.*

William Bentley Fowle
The Teacher's Institute, 1866

Tutoring represents one approach to individualized instruction because it provides a one-to-one teaching situation. The approach has a long history. In the one-room schoolhouses of early America, pupils often helped less capable or younger peers with their lessons. Today tutoring programs are increasing in both number and variety (Allen, 1976; Devin-Sheehan, Feldman, and Allen, 1976). For instance, some programs have matched tutors and tutees in terms of age, sex, background characteristics, or academic difficulties, while others have not; some programs require tutors to follow prescribed lessons, while others allow tutors considerable leeway; some programs have specifically selected only youngsters judged to be dependable and responsible, while others have relied on volunteers; and some programs have paid tutors for their time, while others have depended on student good will and interest (Medway and Baron, 1977).

One of the most interesting findings emerging from research on tutoring is the benefits it provides the child who teaches another child. Indeed, the impressiveness of the results have led some to conclude that "every child must be given the opportunity to play the teaching role, because it is through this role that he may really learn how to learn . . ." (Gartner, Kohler, and Riessman, 1971:1). The following are some benefits the tutor can derive from teaching:

- *Improved achievement:* Tutors frequently show substantially greater gains in their areas of tutoring than do control groups composed of students exposed only to traditional forms of teaching (Allen and Feldman, 1976; Dineen, Clark, and Risley, 1977). Of particular significance, many low achievers in reading make significant gains in reading achievement following their tutoring of younger children (Devin-Sheehan, Feldman, and Allen, 1976).
- *Empathy for the teacher:* Children who enact the role of teacher come to see the student-teacher relationship from another vantage point. By "exchanging" roles, the child can better grasp the requirements for social interaction—what kinds of behaviors a teacher can expect of students and students from teachers (Lippitt, 1976).
- *Improved classroom behavior:* Writing in 1803 in his book for teachers, Joseph Lancaster noted:

I have ever found, the surest way to cure a mischievous boy was to make him a *monitor* [tutor]. I never knew anything to succeed much better, if as well. . . . Lively, active tempered boys are the most frequent transgressors of good order, and the most difficult to reduce to reason; the best way to reform them is by making monitors of them. It diverts the activity of their minds from mischief, by useful employment, which at the same time adds greatly to their improvement. [1803:31, 73]

Contemporary research confirms Lancaster's observation that tutoring contributes to a decrease of classroom behavior problems among tutors (Paolitto, 1976; Strodtbeck, Ronchi, and Hansell, 1976).

- *Improved self-esteem:* Tutoring can give a student an enhanced sense of self-esteem. Tutors gain responsibility, status in the eyes of other students, attention and reward from adults, feelings of competence, and respect from

CHILDREN AS TUTORS
Teachers are increasingly having students help one another with various learning activities.

younger children (Allen and Feldman, 1976; Lippitt, 1976; Ehly and Larsen, 1976).

■ *Improved interpersonal skills:* Being a tutor is thought to enhance a child's skills in relating to another person, especially in a nurturant role. Students learn to take responsibility for another person and to sensitize themselves to another's needs (Allen, 1976; Argyle, 1976).

While research suggests that a very broad range of students may benefit from acting as a tutor, the evidence is mixed on whether or not the tutee also shows improvement. Some studies find that the tutee gains (Cloward, 1976; Dineen, Clark, and Risley, 1977); others show no significant benefit (Erickson and Cromack, 1972; Allen and Feldman, 1974).

This variation in outcomes may be partially accounted for by the preparation tutors receive for their role. One difficulty confronting tutoring programs is that tutoring skills are not intuitive (Horan et al., 1974; Lippitt, 1976; Melaragno, 1977). For instance, Grant V. Harrison (1976) finds that when left to their own devices, many students use ineffective tutoring techniques. He concludes that low-achieving students will not be helped simply by bringing them together with tutors:

> After extensive observations, we discovered that effective tutors needed to perform the following specific tasks in order to help their students: establish and maintain rapport with the child; orient the child to the task; let the child know precisely how he is expected to respond; deal appropriately with different types of responses from the child; properly praise the child; avoid punishing the child; teach new information; make decisions about learning rates; properly reinforce the child; focus the child's attention on the instructional materials; and avoid the use of subtle cues to prompt the child. [1976:170–171]

Accordingly, Harrison advocates a structured tutoring approach and has developed a training package (for instance, trainer's guide, practice booklets, and tapes) that can be used to teach tutors.

In conclusion, peer tutoring offers much promise as an individualized method of instruction. As Steward W. Ehly and Stephen C. Larsen point out: "Every pupil has something to contribute and to gain from experience as a tutor, if proper training, supervision, and follow-up are part of the tutoring program" (1976:477). Further, a tutorial system can be established with relative ease (Melaragno, 1977).

differences in pupil aptitudes (Cronbach and Snow, 1977; Greene, 1980; Corno and Mitman, 1981). Programs concerned with adapting instructional treatments to differing student aptitudes are termed **aptitude-treatment interactions** (abbreviated ATI). *Aptitude* is defined as any characteristic of an individual that increases (or impairs) his or her probability of success in a given treatment, and *treatment* is defined as variations in the pace or style of instruction (Cronbach and Snow, 1977). Many educators prefer the idea of aptitude-treatment interactions to the search for one "best" method of instruction.

Gavriel Salomon (1971) distinguishes between three models of aptitude-treatment interactions. The first he labels the *remedial* approach. Here teachers seek to overcome the learning deficiencies of slow or disadvantaged learners. It is assumed that some critical ingredient of knowledge is missing and that progress can occur only when this deficiency is overcome. Accordingly, teachers design instruction to close the gap. This view is consistent with that of psychologists such as Robert M. Gagné who view knowledge as organized into increasingly more complex hierarchies of capabilities (see Chapter 8).

The second model entails a *compensatory* approach. For instance, highly anxious students often do poorly on problem-solving tasks. Many of these students have difficulty recalling the intermediate steps and hence repeat their errors. By assisting anxious pupils to employ visual memory supports, their problem-solving capabilities frequently improve. This approach differs from the remedial model where one tries to fill in knowledge or performance gaps. In the compensatory model, the deficiencies are left untouched but their debilitating effects are circumvented.

A third approach, the *preferential* model, seeks to capitalize on what the student is already capable of doing. It exploits various strong points, calling on the kinds of style or aptitude with which the learner is best equipped. For instance, some students perform better when achievement feedback is provided; others, under circumstances of affili-

ation feedback (see Chapter 12). Here the problem confronting teachers is to find the best "match" between the student's aptitudes and the task. Unfortunately, aptitude-treatment interactions are not always easily identified (Hunt, 1975; Ysseldyke, 1977; Miller, 1981).

Mastery Learning

What any person in the world can learn, almost all persons can learn *if* provided with appropriate prior and current conditions of learning.

> BENJAMIN S. BLOOM
> *Human Characteristics and School Learning*, 1976

The concept of **mastery learning** provides a totally different view of instruction and its assessment from that found in conventional education. Mastery learning refers to a student's successful attainment of a prespecified instructional goal. Its basic premise is that virtually all students, rather than just a small number, can acquire most of what is now being taught in schools. Students master one unit before proceeding to the next unit in an educational sequence. It eliminates two stalwarts of traditional schooling, grades and semesters. The vast majority of the students earn A grades and take whatever time is required to achieve a high level of competency in each unit of instruction (Block, 1980; Guskey, 1980).

Bloom's Thesis

Mastery learning is closely identified with the work of Benjamin S. Bloom, a University of Chicago educational psychologist. In 1976 Bloom summarized his approach in *Human Characteristics and School Learning,* a book that some educators have heralded as a "revolutionary" approach to education (Havighurst, 1976; Chall, 1977; Harvey and Horton, 1977). Bloom's basic thesis is that "most students can learn what the schools have to teach—if the problem is approached sensitively and systematically" (1976:1).

Bloom (1976, 1980) says that if the proper conditions are provided, 95 percent of the students can master most instructional objectives to the degree now only reached by the "best students." This leaves 1 to 3 percent at the bottom who cannot master the curriculum and another 1 to 2 percent at the top who have superior abilities and do not fit the pattern. The trick, Bloom argues, is one of defining what constitutes mastery of a subject and then providing students with the quality of instruction and the time they need to demonstrate mastery.

Bloom credits John B. Carroll's (1963) model of school learning with influencing him in the development of his concept of mastery learning. Carroll argued that if students are normally dis-tributed (the traditional bell curve) with respect to aptitude for some subject, and if all students are given exactly the same instruction (in quality and amount of instruction and learning time), then achievement measured at the completion of the subject will be normally distributed. Under these conditions the correlation between aptitude measured at the beginning of the instruction and achievement measured at the end of the instruction will be relatively high. Conversely, if students are normally distributed with respect to aptitude, but the kind and quality of instruction and learning time allowed are made appropriate to the characteristics of each learner, the majority of students will achieve mastery of a given subject.

MASTERY LEARNING
Students master one unit of instruction before moving on to the next unit. Each unit builds on the knowledge and skills acquired in the previous units.

Bloom denies that some students are "good learners" while others are "poor learners." Instead, he says that most students become very similar with regard to learning ability, rate of learning, and motivation for further learning when they are provided with favorable conditions. He asserts that if students are systematically and appropriately taught, individual differences in what they learn approach the vanishing point. Underlying this concept is the belief that individuals do not differ in their capacity for learning but only in their capacity to benefit from a particular instructional mode or form (Anderson and Block, 1977; Block, 1980). In contrast, when provided with unfavorable conditions, Bloom says that students become more dissimilar, so that the gap between high and low achievers widens at each successive grade level. In effect, Bloom sets aside the concept of "intelligence," claiming that the quality measured by IQ tests need not control how much or little a student learns in school.

Elements in School Learning

It is Bloom's view that school learning is a function of three factors:

Student cognitive entry behaviors. Bloom places great emphasis on what the learner brings to the learning situation. To the extent to which knowledge is cumulative and sequential, new learning builds step-by-step on previous learning. Certain competencies and skills are essential if one is to learn a new task or set of tasks. For instance, in order to learn elementary algebra effectively, a student must be familiar with at least fifth-grade arithmetic. Since students differ in their previous learning, they exhibit considerable variation in their learning outcomes.

According to Bloom, as schools currently operate, students are graded and evaluated not on what they have learned from a particular unit of instruction but on the cognitive entry skills they possessed prior to beginning the course. Hence, under the ordinary school treatment, the entering variation among students is increased from year to year. Students with inadequate entry behaviors are incapable of mastering fundamental new tasks and consequently become increasingly incapable of learning subsequent tasks. The net result is that these students fall farther and farther behind in a snowballing fashion.

Given student differences in entry competencies, Bloom says that teachers have the task of accurately diagnosing where the student stands with respect to prerequisite skills. Based on such an appraisal, the teacher needs to "plug" the student into the proper level of material to maximize development and success. Bloom emphasizes that remedial instruction should be given at the earliest time possible. This is particularly true of reading, which he believes is the key to most school learning.

Student affective entry characteristics. A second factor in school learning stressed by Bloom is the motivation students bring to learning tasks. Students differ in their effective entry characteristics—their interest in achieving a desired outcome and the confidence they have that they possess the ability to achieve it. As pointed out in Chapter 12, if students secure evidence that they have done a task superbly, they are likely to approach the next task in the series with more enthusiasm and confidence. But they feel the opposite if they find that they did poorly.

After completing a large number of tasks, a student gradually evolves a pattern of performance. This has consequences for the pupil's interest, attitude, and self-image as a learner. Depending on their academic adequacy or inadequacy, students become progressively locked within motivational mind-sets that breed patterns of success or failure. Accordingly, Bloom believes that teachers should structure learning activities so that they develop positive feelings for each subject area and the schooling experience.

Quality of instruction. The third factor Bloom considers important is the quality of instruction. He acknowledges that numerous studies show that "the characteristics of teachers rarely account for more than 5 percent of the achievement variation of their students—and usually much less. Similarly, many studies have been done on the characteristics of the classroom or school . . . here again the relation between student achievement and selected variables rarely yields correlations that account for more than 5 percent of the achievement variation" (1976:110–111). However, Bloom believes that what does make a difference is the *teaching* and not the *teacher*. He says that in contemporary schools teachers are likely to spend most of their time "managing students" rather than "managing learning."

Bloom's ideal model of teaching is one in which the teacher (1) provides each student with *cues* regarding what is to be learned, (2) ensures that the pupil is actively involved through *participation* in the learning process, (3) supplies the learner with *reinforcement*, and (4) provides a *feedback* and *corrective system*.

Instructional Design

Central to mastery learning strategies is the formulation of a set of instructional objectives that all students will be expected to achieve by the end of a course. The course is then divided into a sequence of smaller learning units. The material in one unit builds directly on the material in previous units. Each unit contains a small set of lessons that typically require between one to ten hours of student time. Next the teacher constructs brief, diagnostic progress tests. These instruments provide detailed information (feedback) about each student's grasp of a unit's objectives. Finally, the teacher prepares a set of alternative learning materials (instructional correctives) that students use as necessary to complete mastery of the instructional unit (Block, 1974a, 1980; Anderson and Block, 1977).

No student is allowed to progress until he or she has mastered the preceding unit. Bloom (1976) recognizes that some students require a somewhat longer period of study than others.

Evaluation

Bloom and other proponents of mastery learning claim that it offers a means for an overwhelming majority of students from all backgrounds to acquire the knowledge and competencies necessary to function in and contribute to a highly technological society. Bloom says that an investment of only 10 to 20 percent over present instructional effort would be required. Such promises are mindboggling given the high price we now pay in loss of human potential. Yet, Bloom's formulations are still tentative. Karen Harvey and Lowell Horton point out:

> His theory raises many questions; it seems imperative, therefore, to pursue further research and to develop a great deal more empirical data before we jump onto the mastery learning bandwagon. These questions remain: Will it work? What is needed to make it work? Should we try? [1977:191]

A number of studies lend support to the validity of Bloom's arguments but are not substantial enough to support them with unequivocal certainty (Block, 1974b; Grabe and Latta, 1981; Stinard and Dolphin, 1981). Norman D. Kurland provides this summary statement regarding many educators' thinking about Bloom's work:

> Bloom has made a persuasive case in logic, but it still lacks the evidence necessary to win the confidence of any large numbers of educators or the public. However, if Bloom is right, the schools can be far more effective than they have been, and it is the responsibility of educators to see to it that schools do achieve what they are capable of achieving. If Bloom is taken seriously, there could be a revolution in our thinking about schools if not in our educational practice. [1977:159]

Self-Instructional Programs

A human being should not be wasted in doing what forty sheets of paper or two phonographs can do. Just because personal teaching is precious and can do what books and apparatus cannot, it should be saved for its peculiar work. The best teacher uses books and appliances as well as his own insight, sympathy, and magnetism.

EDWARD L. THORNDIKE
Education, A First Book, 1912

Over the past twenty-five years educators have shown a growing interest in various types of self-instruction, particularly varieties of programmed and computer-based instruction. The educational psychologist Sidney L. Pressey in the 1920s and B. F. Skinner in the 1950s provided the earliest attempts to "automate" teaching. Pressey developed a rather primitive type of teaching machine, while Skinner contributed to the introduction of programmed instruction. Self-instruction offers the promise of meeting a student's individual needs, presenting basic factual material without the aid of teachers, and saving student learning time.

Programmed Instruction

The programmed instruction movement hit American education like a whirlwind in the early 1960s (Bunderson and Faust, 1976). It was promoted as a quick-fix solution for education's ills. However, flooding the market with literally thousands of poorly prepared and ill-conceived "programs" quickly led to considerable disillusionment with the approach. Nonetheless, it has enjoyed a comeback in recent years in the military and industrial communities where a number of carefully designed programs have been successfully employed. For instance, the army reports significant improvement among its personnel in the use of equipment ranging from the hand grenade to the Chaparral antiaircraft missile by employing programmed-instruction-type materials (Middleton, 1976).

Programmed instruction commonly consists of (1) a definition of the objectives of the learning experience, (2) sequential activities that enable users to accomplish these prescribed objectives, and (3) feedback devices that allow learners to evaluate their progress in such a way that each learning and evaluation builds on the previous activity. Typically, a series of "frames" are carefully arranged to successively "shape" the desired outcome. In this fashion a point must be understood before the pupil moves on, material is presented only when the student is ready, and the learner derives immediate confirmation of every correct response (the student uncovers the correct answer by moving a marker or turning the page). The prompt feedback of a positive sort is viewed as reinforcing and provides the student with motivation to continue the task.

Programmed texts employ either a linear or branching format (Holcomb, 1972). *Linear programming* involves a step-by-step order in which every student follows the identical sequence. Generally the learner is given a small amount of information and then is asked a question about it. In the next step, the student is provided with the correct answer. After the learner receives the correct answer, regardless of the accuracy of his or her answer, he or she proceeds to the next step without additional information.

Branching programming provides a number of alternative sequences leading the learner along an individualized path that will depend on his or her responses to key questions. For instance, after completing a unit the student may be asked to answer a number of multiple-choice questions. If the correct responses are selected, the pupil is directed to proceed to the next frame. If an incorrect response is made, the student is referred to one or more frames that supply appropriate "remedial" instruction. More sophisticated programs contain questions interspersed throughout the exercise and designed to detect an advanced learner. These students are directed to skip the frames that would be superfluous for them. In this fashion the program is designed to be "individually responsive" to each student.

DESIGNING PROGRAMMED LEARNING SEQUENCES

A programmed learning sequence (PLS) is a set of instructions which helps a student learn a complex task by breaking it into a series of simple, one-at-a-time steps. A student can use a PLS to learn to tie a shoe, to recognize silent *e*, or even to conserve energy and pursue new sources.

Programmed learning sequences are based on several basic principles:

- *One item is presented at a time on a 5" × 7" index card:* A single concept or skill is introduced through a simple, written statement. After reading the statement, the learner is required to answer a question or two to demonstrate that

Source: Condensed from Instructor Workshop, "How to Design Programmed Learning Sequences," *Instructor,* 87 (February 1978):124–125.

he understands what has been introduced on that card, then go on to the next card.

- *The student is required to be an active, rather than a passive, learner:* Unlike large group instruction where a student can merely sit and appear to be listening, a PLS requires that a response be made for each card.
- *The student is informed of the correctness of each response immediately:* As soon as a youngster has read the card and answered the question based on the material he has just read, he turns to the back of the card where the correct answer is stated. The student, therefore, is immediately made aware of the accuracy of his response. This immediate reinforcement is an extremely effective teaching strategy with most learners.

- *The student does not continue onto the next index card until the material on each previous card has been understood:* When the student's response to the question covering the material on a given frame is correct, he is directed to the next card. When the response is not correct, he is directed to restudy the previously read card, to ask for help from an adult, or to turn to another card in the program that will explain the material in a different way.
- *The student is exposed to material that gradually becomes more difficult:* The index cards are written so that the first few in the series are very simple. Gradually, as the student's correct answers demonstrate his increased understanding of what is being taught, more difficult aspects of the topic are introduced.

Programmed texts offer a number of advantages. First, they permit students to control and work at their own rate of learning. Second, students can use the material at their own convenience and, if they choose, carry it home or to the library for use as they have time. Third, programmed materials make it possible to learn by doing. Fourth, they afford prompt feedback to students. And fifth, programmed texts allow teachers to spend their time with students developing concepts, attitudes, and appreciations (Joiner, Miller, and Silverstein, 1980; Papert, 1981).

Programmed texts also have limitations. First, the development of effective and rigorously tested materials involves considerable time, effort, and expense. Second, some learners experience boredom with programmed frames once the initial novelty has worn off (Jamison, Suppes, and Wells,

1974). And third, critics charge that programmed instruction fosters student passivity and stifles creativity and initiative.

Research reveals that no significant differences exist between the results realized by traditional classroom and programmed instruction (Zoll, 1969; Jamison, Suppes, and Wells, 1974). However, programmed texts may decrease the amount of time required for students to achieve specific educational goals. As a teaching tool, programmed instruction appears to be best adapted to the transmission of facts and skills. All of this suggests that programmed materials should be viewed as supplements and not as replacements for other forms of instruction (Cross, 1976).

Computer-Assisted Instruction

Computer-assisted instruction (CAI) has had a history paralleling that of programmed instruction. The year 1965 marked the beginning of a boom in computerized education. During the Johnson Administration, federal aid for research and development in new educational technology flowed freely, and many projects were initiated in schools and universities. During this same period, various computer companies were merging with publishing companies in anticipation of a vast new market. By the early 1970s, however, the initial flush of enthusiasm for computer-based instruction had subsided—the educational magic promised by early proponents failed to materialize, federal funding began to dry up, and the hope for a large new educational market did not live up to early projections. Many of the computer firms either retrenched or went out of business (Bunderson and Faust, 1976).

It was unfortunate that computer-assisted instruction was oversold and the complexities of mastering its technology greatly underestimated. Many computer systems were developed, but as Frank B. Baker points out, "most demonstrated only the feasibility of CAI, not its practicality" (1971:51). Computer enthusiasts warn that we should not confuse the present reality of computer-assisted instruction with its potential. They note that the use of computers for teaching purposes has taken place only over the past fifteen years. As Lawrence Stolurow observes, "Projections based upon today's systems would have the same degree of fidelity as projections based upon the Wright brothers' first plane would have had for predicting the design of the supersonic transport" (quoted by Cross, 1976:62).

Computer-assisted instruction refers to a variety of educational programs in which the student interacts with an electromechanical device that has as its purpose the dissemination of certain information or the transmission of specific skills. In some respects computer-assisted instruction resembles programmed texts. However, in contrast with programmed texts, computer-assisted instruction can be readily synchronized with audiovisual materials. Further, the computer provides vast opportunities for test scoring, diagnosing, prescribing, and reporting (Baker, 1971). For example, at the beginning of a unit of instruction, a student may take a computer pretest to determine his or her status relative to the instructional objectives. The computer scores the student's performance, and on the basis of the pretest assigns specific learning tasks to the student. In some cases, the computer may then implement the decisions, leading the student through a sequence of learning activities. Not only can the computer supply achievement feedback to the student, it can also provide the teacher with the student's test results and with information regarding the trend of the student's performance. In turn, the computer can store and indefinitely update data on the student's academic achievement.

Computer systems developed in the 1960s used either an electric typewriter or a teletype terminal as the intermediary device through which students received information from the computer and transmitted their responses to the computer. Ordinarily, the computer typed instructions, information, diagnostic questions, and feedback messages, while the student responded by means of the keyboard. Some systems provided supplementary material that the student received via an audio headset. More recently, newer systems have employed a

COMPUTER-ASSISTED INSTRUCTION
The use of computers in classrooms is becoming more and more widespread. Computer-assisted instruction has many advantages, including the possibility of more easily providing alternative lessons for individual student needs. (© *Tyrone Hall/Stock, Boston*)

small television screen as the primary display device. The television equipment has a typewriter keyboard and a light-pen (an electronic stylus) through which students can feed responses to the program (with the light-pen the student can point to positions on a chart, graph, or map).

Computer-assisted instruction has many of the same advantages and disadvantages of programmed instruction. However, there are a number of differences. The computer can offer and manage more alternative lessons and more opportunities for individual learning paths (branching programming) than programmed instruction can. Further, it affords a more effective tool for testing, evaluating, and storing information. But unlike programmed instruction, computer-assisted instruction usually must be used in a prescribed place. Computer-

assisted instruction is also usually more expensive, requires special programming training, and consists of complicated equipment that can be repaired only by electronic technicians.

The computer has enormous potential for individualizing instruction. K. Patricia Cross points out:

> Its patience, its memory, and its endless capacity for detail are assets that defy competition from ordinary human teachers. Although such characteristics undoubtedly cannot replace the charm of a Mr. Chips, there are times and situations and subjects where such "inhuman" virtues are undeniably important. [1976:61]

Before the advent of the computer, there was only limited flexibility in manipulating the flow of instruction in a classroom. Now, with the computer, a new dimension for teaching has emerged (Atkinson, 1974).

Students receiving information from a computer may respond anywhere from once every four seconds to once every thirty seconds. This means that each student who is receiving computer-based instruction is responding and deriving feedback from 20 to 150 times during a ten-minute session. In contrast, in a typical classroom of thirty students, only the bright and assertive students will be able to respond and receive feedback from a teacher in a regular class period. Slower and more reticent students may receive feedback only a few times during the entire week.

Computer-assisted instruction appears to be a particularly useful teaching tool where it is employed to augment traditional instruction, particularly for slower students (Fletcher and Atkinson, 1972; Jamison, Suppes, and Wells, 1974). It can provide students opportunities for drill and practice that otherwise might be unavailable to them. And for some subject matter, such as mathematics, it may offer an efficient and effective form of remedial instruction (Smith, 1973). Further, computer-assisted instruction does not appear to have the dehumanizing consequences some critics attribute to it (Hess and Tenezakis, 1971; Smith, 1973).

SPECIFIC SELF-INSTRUCTIONAL PROGRAMS

Over the past twenty years a number of specific self-instructional programs have been developed. Four of the better-known programs are detailed here.

INDIVIDUALIZED PRESCRIBED INSTRUCTION (IPI)

Individualized Prescribed Instruction was developed jointly during the 1960s by the Learning Research and Development Center at the University of Pittsburgh and by Research for Better Schools, an educational laboratory. Major contributors have included Robert Glaser, John O. Bolvin, C. M. Lindvall, and Richard Cox. The learning materials consist of units arranged so that a student goes through a sequence of worksheet exercises that build on one another in a cumulative and sequential manner. Tests are given before, during, and after the learning sequence for diagnostic purposes, and the results are almost immediately made available to the student. Pupils work at their own rate and do not move ahead until they have mastered a particular skill. The teacher's role is primarily one of evaluation, diagnosis, and facilitation.

INDIVIDUALLY GUIDED EDUCATION (IGE)

Individually Guided Education was first introduced by the Research and Development Center for Cognitive Learning at the University of Wisconsin during the 1960s (Nussel, Inglis, and Wiersma, 1976; Klausmeier, Rossmiller, and Saily, 1977). Contributors have included Herbert Klausmeier, William J. Goodwin, Richard A. Rossmiller, and James M. Lipham. It involves cooperative team teaching and grouping students without regard to age. IGE seeks to replace the age-graded, self-contained classroom at the elementary level and the subject-centered department at the junior- and senior-high levels. The approach places considerable emphasis on each student's beginning level of performance, rate of progress, style of learning, and level of motivation. IGE teachers formulate instructional objectives for each student. Instructional materials (including printed matter, filmstrips, and cassettes) are placed in a sequential fashion, and diagnostic testing occurs be-

With the advent of the new computer technology, some teachers have expressed fear that some day they might be replaced by a mechanical gadget. This is extremely unlikely. As noted, computers render their greatest benefits when employed in conjunction with more traditional forms of instruction. Further, someone must prepare the programs for the computers. And finally, there are some functions human teachers perform uniquely well. Ernest R. Hilgard (1971) cites a number of these— assisting the pupil to initiate inquiry, helping the student to acquire a positive self-image, and aiding the student in developing effective interpersonal skills. As J. David Holcomb (1972) points out, one wonders how teachers must have felt when Johannes Gutenberg invented the printing press, since the printed word could also be considered a substitute for the teacher.

CHAPTER SUMMARY

1. Teachers conduct classroom instruction in quite different ways. Attention may be focused on the teacher, the class, or the individual student. Each emphasis entails a somewhat different set of techniques and strategies.

fore, during, and after each instructional unit. Students may work independently, with a teacher or another student, or in groups.

PERSONALIZED SYSTEM OF INSTRUCTION (PSI)

The Personalized System of Instruction was initiated during the 1960s by Fred Keller, Gil Sherman, Rodolpho Azzi, and Carolina Martuscelli Bori, four psychologists well versed in behavioral reinforcement theory (Spencer and Semb, 1977). It is designed for use in higher education. A college course is broken down into learning modules. Students are required to master one module before proceeding to the next. A module typically consists of a set of instructional objectives and a number of reading assignments. Student proctors (teaching assistants) are available to answer questions, clarify ambiguities, and administer quizzes. Students pace themselves over the school term and decide when they are ready

to be tested on each unit. Mastery is defined as scoring above 80 percent on a quiz. Pupils are allowed to redo an assignment without penalty and to take alternative forms of the quiz until the specified level of mastery is achieved. Lectures and demonstrations are provided at periodic intervals for those students wishing to attend. They provide an opportunity for enrichment and serve a motivational function.

PROGRAM FOR LEARNING IN ACCORDANCE WITH NEEDS (PLAN)

Project PLAN is a major ungraded, computer-supported individualized program developed in the 1960s by the Westinghouse Learning Corporation, the American Institute for Research, and twelve school districts. The project was initiated by John C. Flanagan, an educational psychologist. In 1972 the Westinghouse Learning Corporation took over the program. It is responsible for

marketing and monitoring PLAN materials and operating the computer installation necesary for the proper functioning of the program in a school.

At the beginning of the school year, a program of study is prepared for each student on the basis of the pupil's responses to a variety of questionnaires and testing instruments. The basic unit is an instructional package or module that normally takes a student two weeks to complete. For each module there are different instructional approaches or "teacher-learning units" (TLUs) that differ in reading difficulty, degree of group involvement, and variety of activities. A particular TLU is assigned a student based upon his or her aptitude scores, interests, and learning style. Students are tested on each module. On the basis of the test results, the students either are moved on to the next module, review a number of items before moving on, or restudy the module (Hambleton, 1974).

2. In lecturing, the teacher is in control of the subject matter and lectures without much interruption. The major advantage of the lecture is that it makes it possible for a teacher to communicate with a large audience in an economical fashion. The chief disadvantage of the lecture is that there is no guarantee that the lecturer will succeed in engaging the attention or active participation of the students.

3. The recitation strategy consists of repeated episodes of structuring, soliciting, responding, and reacting. Teacher questions play a prominent role in recitation sessions, consisting of from 40 to 75 percent of teacher talk.

4. The discussion method allows both the teacher and the pupil some control over the treatment of the subject. It provides a vehicle for a good deal of give-and-take among participants.

5. A distinguishing characteristic of a game is that it involves a free, make-believe activity in which the participants agree on certain objectives and a set of rules whereby these objectives may be attained. In a simulation game, students act and observe concrete events that result from their actions in an artificially produced environment. They become players rather than spectators in the process of learning.

6. There are three assumptions that underlie most

programs of individualized instruction. First, every student has the potential for learning the next thing beyond which he or she already knows. Second, students use different modes and strategies in learning. And third, students require different types of assistance from and stimulation by teachers.

7. It is widely assumed that some children learn best from one instructional strategy while others profit from a different type of instruction. Some psychologists attribute the differing effectiveness of various methods to differences in pupil aptitudes. Programs concerned with adapting instructional treatments to individual differences are termed aptitude-treatment interactions.

8. The basic premise of mastery learning is that virtually all students, rather than just a small number, can acquire most of what is now being taught in schools. Students master one unit before proceeding to the next unit in an educational sequence. It eliminates two stalwarts of traditional schooling—grades and semesters. The vast majority of the students earn A grades and take whatever time is required to achieve a high level of competency in each unit of instruction.

9. The programmed instruction movement hit American education like a whirlwind in the early 1960s. It was promoted as a quick-fix solution for education's ills but was soon found incapable of living up to the glowing promises of its proponents. Currently available research suggests that no significant differences are apparent between the results achieved by traditional classroom and programmed instruction.

10. Computer-assisted instruction (CAI) has had a history paralleling that of programmed instruction. It was unfortunate that computer-assisted instruction was oversold and the complexities of mastering its technology greatly underestimated. Computer-assisted instruction offers enormous potential for individualizing instruction. It appears to be a particularly useful teaching tool when it is employed to augment traditional instruction, particularly for slower students.

CHAPTER GLOSSARY

aptitude-treatment interactions (ATI)   Programs concerned with adapting individual treatments to individual differences among student aptitudes.

computer-assisted instruction (CAI)   A variety of educational programs in which the student interacts with an electromechanical device that has as its purpose the dissemination of certain information or the transmission of specific skills.

mastery learning   A student's successful attainment of a prespecified instructional goal. The basic premise of mastery learning is that virtually all students, rather than just a small number, can acquire most of what is now being taught in schools.

EXERCISES

Review Questions

1. In using the lecture method, one should consider that
   a. the major points should be reserved for the middle of the lecture
   b. students generally rate the lecturer's clarity ahead of personality
   c. one disadvantage is it fails to involve the student
   d. a, b, and c are true
   e. b and c are true

2. Teacher questioning in the recitation episode is included under
   a. structuring
   b. soliciting
   c. responding
   d. reacting

3. Studies of teacher questioning indicate that
   a. less than one-fourth of teacher talk involves questions
   b. as grade level goes up, teachers make greater use of questions
   c. teachers address more questions to boys than to girls
   d. the majority of teacher questions require thought responses

4. Research on small group discussions suggests that
   a. as the size of the group increases so does the number of participants
   b. classroom discussions usually result in increased student motivation
   c. discussions can be characterized as involving high rates of information transmission
   d. none of the above are true

5. A teacher who matches student strengths with the nature of the task is employing which model of aptitude-treatment interaction?
   a. compensatory
   b. remedial
   c. preferential
   d. a and b are ture

6. Carroll argued that the key instruction variable in determining whether children will master a given task is (are):
   a. student aptitudes
   b. validity of assessment instruments
   c. time
   d. kind and quality of instructional materials
   e. c and d are ture

7. Bloom's ideal model of teaching includes
   a. cues
   b. learner participation
   c. reinforcement and feedback
   d. a and b are true
   e. a, b, and c are ture

8. Research on programmed instuction has found that
   a. achievement levels are almost invariably higher with programmed instruction
   b. time required for instruction may decrease
   c. all levels of cognitive activity can be handled equally well
   d. programmed instruction can, in many situations, replace other forms of instruction
   e. a and b are ture

9. Which of these self-instructional programs is *least* likely to use computers?
   a. IPI
   b. IGE
   c. PSI
   d. PLAN

10. The major advantage cited for computer-assisted instruction over traditional instruction includes
   a. greater opportunity for integrating instructional media usage
   b. more direct instructional time for the individual student
   c. endless patience and capacity for detail
   d. a, b, and c are true
   e. a and b are true

Answers

1. e (See pp. 400–401)   6. e (See pp. 414–415)
2. b (See pp. 401, 403)   7. e (See p. 415)
3. c (See p. 401)   8. b (See p. 418)
4. d (See pp. 403–405)   9. b (See pp. 420–421)
5. c (See p. 412)   10. d (See pp. 418–419)

Applying Principles and Concepts

1. Classify each of the following questions as an example of either cognitive memory (CM), convergent thinking (CT), divergent thinking (D), or evaluative thinking (E).

_____ a. Which of the following is not a renewable energy source?

_____ b. What dangers are present in all nuclear reactors, regardless of design?

_____ c. What are the major elements of a nuclear reactor?

_____ d. What could we do with those nuclear reactors we have now if they were all shut down?

2. Mr. Jones and his student teacher, Mr. Perkins, have arranged for a series of group discussions on the role of high-school athletics. They have arranged for two sessions a day, with Mr. Jones and Mr. Perkins each taking charge of one session. They have decided on the following arrangements for Day 1. Indicate by a checkmark which of these Gall and Gall would approve.

_____ a. The students will conduct the discussions in a circle.

_____ b. The group size will average five students.

_____ c. The students can choose the members of their discussion groups.

_____ d. Mr. Jones tells Mr. Perkins to "be in control at all times."

3. The textbook proposes a number of assumptions about individualized instruction. Here are a number of statements make by teachers about such instruction in their classroom. Check those that do not contradict the text.

_____ a. "I try to allow students as often as possible to make decisions regarding their work."

_____ b. "Frankly, I don't have the same ultimate objectives for each student."

_____ c. "My goal is to have each child doing something different at the same time."

_____ d. "Some kids you can praise; a couple need a kick in the pants to get them moving."

4. The local elementary school has instituted a tutorial program. After the first semester the principal interviews the tutors. Check the one statement made by a tutor that is *least* substantiated by research.

_____ a. "You know, I've been in less trouble myself this year."

_____ b. "My guys have really done much better in class."

_____ c. "It's weird—but my grades have gone up."

_____ d. "Those kids in the class where I tutor look up to me like a teacher."

5. Which of the following are considered typical elements of a mastery-learning program?

_____ a. Students are expected to finish assignments at about the same time.

_____ b. Student's cognitive behaviors are assessed at the beginning of the semester; this is not true for affective behaviors.

_____ c. It is assumed that every student can eventually learn what is being taught.

_____ d. Students have primary responsibility for determining instructional sequences.

_____ e. Evaluation is frequent and at the unit level.

6. Here are some elements of instruction. Indicate by a checkmark in Column A (programmed instruction) or Column B (computer-assisted instruction) whether or not the element is likely to be used for that method.

	Column A: Programmed Instruction	Column B: Computer-Assisted Instruction
a. Use of objectives	_____	_____
b. Data storage	_____	_____
c. Linear programming	_____	_____
d. Immediate feedback	_____	_____
e. Diagnosis of student answers	_____	_____
f. Prescribing new tasks	_____	_____

Answers

1. a, E; b, CT; c, CM; d, D (See pp. 401, 403)
2. a, b (See pp. 404–405)
3. a, b, d (See pp. 406–407, 409)
4. b (See pp. 410–411)
5. c, e (See pp. 412–415)
6. a, A and B; b, B; c, A and B; d, A and B; e, B; f, B (See pp. 416–420)

Project

OBJECTIVE: To help you prepare a self-instructional program on computing the square root.

PROCEDURE: Following is a detailed breakdown of a method for computing by hand the square root of a four-digit whole number. Your task will be to transfer the steps and illustrations to a set of index cards, which when complete, will allow anyone to solve a new problem. (Hint: The steps given will have to be expanded in certain areas. For example, you may want to include some test examples within the program.) For the purposes of simplicity we will use a four-digit number, 1379:

1. Divide the number into two groups, 13 and 79.
2. Place the groups under a division symbol:

$$\overline{)13\ 79}$$

3. Determine the largest number that when multiplied by itself is less than or equal to the first group, that is, 13. For example, $4 \times 4 = 16$ is more than 13; but $3 \times 3 = 9$ is less than 13.
4. Place the number 3 above 13:

$$\frac{3}{)13\ 79}$$

5. Multiply the number by itself and enter the results as follows:

$$\frac{3}{)13\ 79}$$
$$\longrightarrow 9$$

6. Subtract 9 from 13 as follows:

$$\frac{3}{)13\ 79}$$
$$\longrightarrow \frac{9}{4}$$

7. Double 3, and enter 6 as follows:

$$\frac{3}{)13\ 79}$$
$$\frac{9}{6\ )\ 4}$$

8. Drop the 79 as follows:

$$\frac{3}{)13\ 79}$$
$$\frac{9}{6\ )\ 4\ 79} \longleftarrow$$

9. Now select the largest two-digit number that begins with 6 and, when multiplied by its second digit, is equal to or less than 479. For example, $68 \times 8 = 524$ (more than 479), whereas $67 \times 7 = 469$.

10. Enter 7 in two places as follows:

$$\frac{3\ 7}{)13\ 79} \longleftarrow$$
$$\frac{9}{67\ )\ 4\ 79}$$

11. Multiply 7×67:

$$\frac{3\ 7}{)13\ 79}$$
$$\frac{9}{67\ )\ 4\ 79}$$
$$\frac{4\ 69}{10}$$

We will not go into decimals, but, if you are interested, the next step is:

$$\frac{3\ 7.1}{)13\ 79.\ 00}$$
$$\frac{9}{67\ )\ 4\ 79}$$
$$\frac{4\ 69}{741\ )10\ 00}$$
$$\frac{7\ 41}{2\ 59}$$

Construct your cards, and give them to a subject

who does not know how to find the square root. Do not prompt, but sit quietly, and respond only to direct questions.

ANALYSIS:

1. After the subject has finished, you should know what gaps (concepts, illustration, and the like) are missing.

2. Revise your cards, and give them to a second student.

3. If the set appears complete, give it to a third student, ask him or her to do the square root of 1851. The answer is:

$$
\begin{array}{r}
4\ 3 \\
\overline{)18\ 51} \\
16 \\
83\ \overline{)\ 2\ 51} \\
2\ 49 \\
\overline{2}
\end{array}
$$

CHAPTER OUTLINE

15

CLASSROOM DYNAMICS

CHAPTER PREVIEW

The previous two chapters focused on reasoned *prescriptions* for the planning and organizing of instruction. Such proposals, however, are not always sensitive to the complexities of the classroom environment. Classroom teaching does not occur in a vacuum, but in a multifaceted social setting in which school climate, teachers, and students all interact. This chapter, therefore, describes how several aspects of classroom organization and interaction affect the teach-

ing-learning situation. The effects of class size and ability grouping are considered, as are the principles and practices of open education. Recent research that has examined effective schools and effective teaching is also reviewed. The possible role of teachers' perceptions and expectations of students in teacher-student interaction is discussed. Finally, attention is paid to the important influence of students on each other.

Attend to these questions as you interact with the content of this chapter:

- What are some of the advantages and disadvantages of ability grouping?
- In what ways does open education differ from traditional education?
- According to recent studies,

what features characterize academically effective schools and what distinguishes effective teachers?
- How are teachers' judgments of students influenced by personality characteristics, physical appearance, or race?
- According to the original description, by what process does the teacher-expectation effect occur? Does it really work this way? Why or why not?
- How do peer groups influence student learning and behavior?

School is a place where tests are failed and passed, where amusing things happen, where new insights are stumbled upon, and skills acquired. But it is also a place in which people sit, and listen, and wait, and raise their hands, and pass out paper, and stand in line, and sharpen pencils. School is where we encounter both friends and foes, where imagination is unleashed and misunderstanding brought to ground. But it is also a place in which yawns are stifled and initials scratched on desktops, where milk money is collected and recess lines are formed.

PHILIP W. JACKSON
Life in Classrooms, 1968

In their own right classrooms are self-contained "little worlds" teeming with behavior. Indeed, each classroom possesses its own unique characteristics, so much so that teachers frequently talk about how "the personality" of this year's class differs from that of the year before. The "fit" among individual students, the teacher, and the students as a group jells to produce what sociologists term a **social system**—a configuration in which individuals are bound together within a relatively enduring network of relationships. As a consequence, classroom activities have a considerable element of organization to them. Each person more or less knows what various other individuals are likely to do.

STRUCTURAL INFLUENCES

Social life does not consist of large numbers of individuals haphazardly interacting with one another. Rather, individuals relate to one another in organized, recurrent, and stable patterns. Thus, much of life presents a picture of order and regularity. This is also true of the interaction that transpires in the classroom. Among the factors influencing classroom interaction are class size, social composition, communication patterns, and degree of "openness."

Class Size

It would be wrong to conclude, based solely on the lack of evidence to the contrary, that class size has no effect whatever on student performance. But on the basis of what has been presented to us, we must caution against the use of pupil-teacher ratios as instant measures of anything remotely approaching the quality of education.

The President's Commission on School Finance, 1972

One of the basic beliefs of our educational system is that reduced class size provides a more desirable learning environment for students and increases the teacher's effectiveness. Common sense indicates that in smaller classes teachers have more time to spend on each pupil and students have more opportunities to participate in class discussions and ask questions. Class size is an issue that has been raised with increasing frequency in recent years in teachers' contract negotiations. And polls show it to be an important factor in teacher morale (Fiske, 1978).

School administrators have generally opposed cutting class size since doing so is very costly. Salaries constitute about 80 percent of a school district's expenditures, and the added costs can be sizable. Assume, for instance, that a medium-sized school system enrolls fifteen thousand students, the average class size is thirty pupils, and the average teacher's salary is $17,000. A reduction in average class size from thirty to twenty-nine pupils would require seventeen additional teachers and a budget increase of $289,000 per year. If classes were reduced from thirty to twenty-five students per class, the system would require one hundred additional teachers. This would add $1.7 million to the annual budget requirements of the system.

Research dealing with the influence of the student-to-teacher ratio on pupil learning is somewhat contradictory (Jamison, Suppes, and Wells, 1974; Marsh, Overall, and Kesler, 1979; Shapson et al., 1980). Indeed, some studies, defying all the conventional wisdom, show students achieving more

about twenty-five to thirty-four pupils, class size seems to have little if any decisive impact on the academic achievement of most students. It does point out, however, that smaller classes increase achievement of certain groups of students under some circumstances. Students with learning problems, economically or socially disadvantaged pupils, and early primary-level students in reading and mathematics may benefit more from smaller classes than other students.

Research suggests that even these positive effects occur only when teachers adapt their methods to take advantage of the opportunities afforded by fewer students. Small classes do not always lead to individual instruction, even if they create the opportunity. According to the National Association of Elementary School Principals, only half of the teachers with classes of twenty or fewer students actually take advantage of individualized instruction methods (Fiske, 1975). The teachers simply continued to handle instruction in the traditional manner. The principals' association concludes that class size *could* be one of the factors that influence pupil achievement, but research has not proved that it *is* one of them.

It is also conceivable that if classes got down to ten or fewer students, then class size might make a difference. This is one of the findings reported by Gene V. Glass of the University of Colorado Laboratory of Educational Research after he and his associates made an exhaustive study of data on nearly 900,000 students (Glass and Smith, 1978; Smith and Glass, 1980). Glass finds that the achievement curve starts to rise rapidly only when class size gets down to about fifteen students. Accordingly, he suggests that instead of having two classes of twenty-five students each, it might be better to have one of forty students and one of ten—where the teacher could work closely with students—at least part of every week.

Further, the literature has dealt primarily with academic achievement. Martin N. Olson (1971) found that smaller classes were advantageous in terms of individualism, interpersonal regard, and

CLASS SIZE
In order to secure optimal results, class size must be appropriate for the needs of the students, the subject matter, and the skills of the teacher.

in large classes than in small ones. A recent review of studies on class size undertaken by the Educational Research Service, a nonprofit educational organization, says that decades of research have failed to justify small overall reductions in class size as a matter of general policy (Fiske, 1978). The report suggests that within the mid-range of

creativity in a survey of 18,528 elementary and secondary school classrooms in 112 school systems over a seven-year period. All of this suggests that in order to produce optimal results, the size of the class must be appropriate for the learning tasks, the needs of the students, the nature of the subject matter, and the skills of the teacher.

Ability Grouping

One of the issues that has been hotly debated in recent decades is ability grouping. **Ability grouping** is the practice of placing together children of a given age and grade who have similar standings on measures of learning achievement or capability. Large school systems tend to employ this pattern of organization more frequently and in higher proportion than small school systems. Further, the practice becomes increasingly prevalent as students proceed through the educational system. In the primary grades, ability grouping generally occurs in reading; students within a classroom are divided into groups with names like ''Robins,'' ''Bluejays,'' and ''Chickadees.'' By seventh grade, many school systems group students by achievement for instruction in mathematics. In junior and senior high schools, ability grouping is often accomplished by ''self-selection'' in which individual students ''choose'' whether to follow a college preparatory or vocational curriculum.

The debate between proponents and opponents of ability grouping centers on whether or not homogeneous grouping results in better conditions for teaching and learning. The rationale for homogeneous ability grouping usually includes the following arguments (Martin and Pavan, 1976):

■ Grade placement by age tends to ignore individual differences among students by presenting the same basic grade-level curriculum to all students. In contrast, ability grouping allows pupils to advance at their own rate with others of similar capabilities (for instance, brighter students are not held back by the slower ones).

■ Ability grouping specifically allows teachers to adapt methods and materials to their students, since the pupils have more characteristics in common (drill with slower students, projects with abler students, and so on).

■ Students are challenged to do their best within the group by a realistic range of competition (less able students will not have to make invidious comparisons with their more able peers).

■ Ability grouping reduces the range of learning rate differences within a group, and this makes teaching easier and more manageable.

Alternatively, the following are arguments advanced in favor of heterogeneity (and against ability grouping):

■ The self-concept of children is adversely affected by ability grouping. It places a stigma on those in lower ability groups, contributing to their losing interest in learning. Simultaneously, homogeneous grouping gives high-ability children an inflated sense of their own worth.

■ Most life experiences do not occur in homogeneous settings and pupils must learn to work with a wide range of people (Leinhardt, 1980).

■ Students learn from one another. Pupils of lesser ability may profit from learning with those of greater ability (in the absence of superior students, slow learners have fewer opportunities to learn vicariously through paying attention during class discussions and receiving stimulation from other children as models and helpers). Fast students learn something from slow students, even if it is nothing more than a feeling of compassion and understanding for those who experience difficulty in learning (Urevick, 1974; Beckerman and Good, 1981).

■ It is impossible to achieve a truly homogeneous grouping. Scores on intelligence and achievement tests are usually not reliable or valid enough for this type of distinction. Further, a student's ease and rate of learning vary greatly from one subject area to another. Indeed, more than one psychologist has observed, ''The only way it is possible to have a homogeneous group is to have one pupil—and the pupil continues to change.''

- Ability grouping goes against the grain of American ideals and democratic principles. Our society cannot afford to let its youth be stratified in the schools. Everyone deserves the same opportunity (Urevick, 1974). Homogeneous grouping particularly penalizes the ''late bloomer.''
- Homogeneous grouping tends to segregate children along ethnic, racial, and socioeconomic class lines. As such, it deepens and perpetuates the cleavages of the larger society from one generation to the next (Rosenbaum, 1976). Tracking becomes the instrument the school uses to reproduce and reinforce the inequalities of the larger society (selection takes place as early as the seventh grade and tends to be permanent, except for those who lose a match or two in the college track and are dropped from the competition).
- Ability grouping results in an inferior education for slower learners. ''Low groups'' become dumping grounds for students who, because of low motivation, emotional difficulties, poor health, or environmental handicaps, perform poorly in their academic work. Teachers expend their energy on maintaining order, fostering among these students a ''culture of defeat'' (Ravitz, 1963; Trow, 1968).

Unfortunately, the arguments of both those favoring and opposing ability grouping appear to be based more on rhetoric than on any solid research evidence (Kier, Styfco, and Zigler, 1977). Some findings favor homogeneous grouping, while others favor heterogeneous grouping. The exact results of grouping as such are difficult to sort out from other factors, especially variables associated with socioeconomic differences. Moreover, the strong personal preferences of educators suggest the likelihood of experimenter bias in many of the studies (Boocock, 1972).

After reviewing the evidence, such as it was,

from 1910 to the late 1960s, Warren G. Findley and Miriam M. Bryan concluded:

> Ability grouping, as practiced, produces conflicting evidence of usefulness in promoting improved scholastic achievement in superior groups, and almost uniformly unfavorable evidence for promoting scholastic achievement in average or low-achieving groups. Put another way, some studies offer positive evidence of effectiveness of ability grouping in promoting scholastic achievement in high-achieving groups; students seldom show improved achievement in average or low-achieving groups.
>
> The effect of ability grouping on the affective development of children is to reinforce (inflate?) favorable self-concepts of those assigned to high achievement groups, but also to reinforce unfavorable self-concepts in those assigned to low achievement groups. [1971:3]

Recent research has done little to alter this basic appraisal (Kelly, 1975; Marting and Pavan, 1976). However, one study by Michael W. Kibby (1977) provides additional light on ability groupings. At a midwestern elementary school, Kibby compared the less able readers from a class of second-grade high achievers with the best readers in a low-achieving class. The attitudes and behaviors of both groups of students were more indicative of their classroom social ranking than their actual abilities. Although all the children in the high-achieving group were reading at sixth- to eighth-grade levels, those at the ''bottom'' of their class had lower self-concepts and more negative attitudes toward reading than did those at the ''top'' of the low-achieving group. Apparently, a student's position within a group has more influence over the individual's attitude than the status of the group itself.

Communication Patterns

Even when the teacher acts like a broadcasting station, it is doubtful that all the pupils are tuned in. A more plausible model is that the teacher is communicating with different individuals for brief sporadic periods and that these pupils are responding to other stimuli the rest of the time.

HARRY F. SILBERMAN
Journal of Teacher Education, 1963

A major goal of education is to impart information and skills to students. This necessitates effective communication. Indeed, communication is the heart of classroom life. Philip W. Jackson (1968) estimated from his observations in several elementary classrooms that teachers average over two hundred interpersonal exchanges every hour of the school day.

The only consistently active communicator in most classrooms is the teacher. Much of the communication is one-way (Boocock, 1972; Wiemann and Backlund, 1980). Usually the teacher is *telling* and the students are *listening*. One difficulty with this arrangement is that it tends to produce individuals who are programmed for input but not communication output. Donald W. Olson observes:

Covertly, if not overtly, the teacher often short-circuits the students' response channel early in

their school career. . . . If one operates from the premise that human beings learn communication proficiency by communicating, and if stifled communication channels have existed since early in the students' scholastic career, the students simply have not had the necessary communication training by the time they reach the secondary level. Their use of the tool of oral communication is comparable to the ape who used the flute to scratch his back. [1977:161]

Further, since the teacher functions as the communication "gatekeeper" in the classroom, student initiative in communication interaction is frequently blocked (see the boxed insert on pages 435–436).

The physical arrangement of the classroom does much to structure communication patterns. In the traditional classroom twenty to thirty-five students are seated in rows facing the teacher. The teacher has a larger desk and chair and often stands at the front of the room. Generally the teacher is bigger, older, and more knowledgeable in the subject matter. Under these circumstances, almost all the communication flows through the teacher:

COMMUNICATION PATTERNS
Communication patterns reflect networks of social relationships among students and the physical arrangement of the classroom.

HEY, DID YOU REALLY HEAR THAT KID?

CHARLES M. GALLOWAY AND TRUMAN WHITFIELD

Effective communication is the most essential ingredient in the learning process. Mrs. Wilson, a sixth-grade teacher, communicates with her students daily, but the message she sends out is not always what she intends. One day, after assigning a creative writing lesson to her class, she moved around the room helping children work on their stories. Billy finished and asked to read his story to her. He began reading with gusto and excitement. At first, Mrs. Wilson listened attentively and seemed interested, but as he read on, her attention strayed. She began to look around, nodding at other students.

Billy was still reading as Sharon approached Mrs. Wilson with her story and stood there. Mrs. Wilson glanced from Billy to Sharon as though she didn't know which one to listen to. She finally turned all her attention to Sharon and Billy was left reading to himself. As he realized that she was no longer listening, his voice dwindled and soon he returned to his seat although he hadn't finished his story.

After listening to Sharon, Mrs. Wilson again began to move around the room. Coming to Billy's desk, she remembered they had been interrupted.

"Now, let's see, Billy, where were we?"

Billy responded, "Oh, that's OK. It didn't matter anyway."

It didn't matter? Of course it *did!* Billy thought he had a great story, but Mrs. Wilson's inattentive behavior signaled him that it apparently didn't matter to her. Her message was unintentional. There was no deliberate attempt to favor one child over another, but it did seem that way. Other teachers are all too likely to make similar mistakes. They fail to recognize the impact of their inadvertent behavior as it functions in the classroom.

Communication is a total process. When the communication system is not functioning well, the chances for optimal learning become pretty slim. The first step toward becoming an effective communicator is to understand the communication process.

A simplified communication model consists of five basic components (see Figure 15.A). Because of the feedback relation-ship, receiver and sender constantly alternate roles and their nonverbal behaviors become as crucial to effective communication as their verbal ones.

Mrs. Wilson, as a receiver and sender, was doing a pretty ineffective job. After all, being a good listener is not an easy task. Listening is difficult because the listener must move out of his natural concern for self and relate empathically to the other person's message.

Breakdown occurs when the listener sends inappropriate feedback cues to the sender. When these cues indicate inattentiveness, they are a signal that the listener isn't interested in what is being expressed. They are not planned or intentional messages, but carry the same weight as if

Source: Condensed from Charles M. Galloway and Truman Whitfield, "Hey, Did You Really Hear That Kid?" *Instructor,* 86 (October 1976):84–85.

FIGURE 15.A SIMPLIFIED COMMUNICATION MODEL

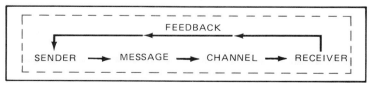

(continued)

HEY, DID YOU REALLY HEAR
THAT KID? (*continued*)

they were carefully planned. Children are quite perceptive at interpreting cues which imply inattentiveness. When they think they are being ignored, the mutual bond necessary for effective communication is lost.

The second important step for becoming a more effective communicator is to know what constitutes an appropriate cue of attentiveness. Through a study we have done on how students perceive teacher listening behaviors, it seems clear that kids are keen at interpreting cues of inattentiveness.

A simple fact jumps out of our study. Get control of your eyes!

Look the kids straight in the eye. Your mind may wander, but your eyes mustn't, unless you want to tell the children that their messages are of little significance.

What can you do to improve your own listening skills? Probably the first thing is to admit that improvement is necessary. In making such an admission, it is important to recognize that things are not always what they seem. The behaviors associated with listening may not be perceived the same by all people.

Your best source of information is the students themselves. Engage their assistance to find out how well you communicate. To

obtain honest student responses, an open and nonjudgmental classroom climate is necessary. It is also important that students feel you will take their responses seriously and use them to modify your behavior. Start with the general questions, "What do I do that tells you that I am listening to you?" "What do I do that tells you that I am not listening to you?" Keep the climate safe, and students will respond with a wealth of information—invaluable to you in your effort to become a better communicator.

And that kid will say to himself, "Hey! She really heard what I said!"

The teacher plans—the students obey without question except for clarification; the teacher lectures—the students take notes; the teacher tests—the students take exams; the teacher evaluates—the students wait to find out whether or not they learned anything. [Gorman, 1974:38]

Some researchers have reported that verbal communications are highly concentrated in the center-front and middle of the classroom, a zone of increased activity labeled the "action zone" (Adams and Biddle, 1970). Teachers typically spend up to 70 percent of their time in the center-front of the room, 15 percent along the sides and back, and the remainder of the time in the aisles. However, Peter Delefes and Barry Jackson (1972) report a greater diffusion of teacher-pupil interactions throughout the classroom than reflected in these figures.

Robert Sommer, a psychologist specializing in the significance of physical space, observes:

One can learn to "read" the physical arrangement of chairs and desks, the use of decorations and real and symbolic barriers to gauge the present and desired levels of interaction. Such an analysis reveals immediately the tremendous imbalance of power that exists in the classroom. The instructor has freedom of space, the students do not. The teacher can direct students to move their desks and chairs, and to use them in specified ways. The teacher has control over the use of blackboards, walls, and other display areas. [1977:174]

Sommer goes on to point out:

There is no ideal classroom layout for all activities. The straight row arrangement with all chairs facing ahead was designed for sit-and-listen teaching. If that is the teacher's style and objective, then straight rows are logical. If the teacher wants to have work groups sharing tasks and working cooperatively, then cluster tables are best. [1977:175]

Good teaching involves more than the clear articulation of facts and the proper timing of their

DO YOU "HEAR" THEIR BODIES "TALKING"?

SUE BLAKE AND W. D. RICHARDSON

The importance of body language came to one kindergarten teacher in a moment when she "saw herself as others see her." The children were playing school. There stood the pint-sized teacher, hands on hips, feet planted firmly apart, head and shoulders bent slightly forward. In front of her cowered the offender, too intimidated to defend himself.

By using simple basics in nonverbal communication any teacher can improve interpersonal relations and help avoid many potentially unpleasant situations:

■ *See, and try to understand, your children's body language:* We all know that when a child asks to go to the bathroom and is doing an unrhythmic dance, the urgency of the situation warrants a quick

positive reply. Much body language is more subtle, of course. There is no pat formula for understanding it. Close, sympathetic observation can sharpen your ability to sense a child's needs, however.

Does Billy walk with slouched shoulders? Does Jennifer make nervous hand movements? Does Dan move his head in a negative swing when he stumbles over words? These questions suggest ways you can tell when children have problems. Only sensitive reflection and probing will disclose what the problems are and raise ideas for dealing with them. Is Billy's mother pushing him too hard in reading? Should he be given new tasks, ones in which he can succeed and thus rebuild his shaken self-confidence?

■ *Be alert to your own body language and check to see if it carries the same message*

you express in words: A smile or a grin, a friendly hug, even a casual swat on the seat can express a friendly mood and encourage a pleasant classroom climate. Conversely, a frown, foot-tapping, or cold stare expresses impatience and disapproval. Example:

Sharon had a cold and remained inside at play period. "I watered the plants for you," she announced, beaming, as the class came in. Mrs. Shepherd looked at the milk cartons sitting on the window sills, each neatly labeled with a child's name and the type of seed. Now, from each carton a muddy trickle of water oozed down the side. In the terrarium, one green leaf bravely floated on water standing two inches deep.

Mrs. Shepherd kept outwardly calm and repaired the damage while explaining to Sharon the proper method of
(continued)

Source: Condensed from Sue Blake and W. D. Richardson, "Do You 'Hear' Their Bodies 'Talking'?" *Instructor*, 85 (March 1976):100–101.

delivery. *Nonverbal communication*—the sending and receiving of nonlanguage cues indicating attitude and feeling—also play an important part in classroom interactions (Hall et al., 1977; Woolfolk, 1978; Smith, 1979). We communicate by using a vast array of wordless expressions portrayed by the face, hand, and body. Words miss their mark when compared to the furrowing of a brow, to the smile of greeting, to the nod of the head, to the droop of the hand or body, or to the wink of the confidante (Galloway, 1977). Through nonverbal cues, teachers forcefully communicate to students their attitudes and feelings toward them and toward the subject matter (see the boxed insert above).

DO YOU "HEAR" THEIR BODIES "TALKING"?
(continued)

watering plants. Later in the day, as she surveyed the collection of desk litter, she found a note in Sharon's second-grade scrawl: "I luv you and you luv me, but not as much as I luv you." Puzzled, Mrs. Shepherd recalled Sharon's questioning face across her desk. Normally she would have invited the child around her desk and under her arm simply by holding out her hand. Today, without deliberate meaning, she hadn't, and Sharon had been too unsure to press herself. Mrs. Shepherd's anger, though not verbalized, had come through in nonverbal behavior and the child had picked up the vibrations.

Of course you can't carefully measure, calculate, or plan each physical movement you make each day. But, awareness of the body language you use and the effect it has on children will result in both conscious and subconscious changes in attitudes and actions.

- *Establish body contact with your children in the early school years:* Every primary teacher knows that young children need to be reassured by physical contact with a compassionate teacher. In fact, a person who doesn't enjoy being punched, pinched, pulled, and patted by fifty little hands doesn't belong in a primary room. Through an awareness of body language

and a positive use of the medium, you can avoid unintentionally destroying a child's desire to communicate and be understood.

- *See eye to eye with children in private conversations:* Don't tower over your children, even to reprimand. Not many teachers consider themselves giants, but everything depends on point of view. Remember when as a third-grader your thirty-one-year-old teacher was aged? And the principal was a different colored version of the Jolly Green Giant—sometimes without the *jolly*? Consider the angle from which your children see you as they approach. How accessible are you? A timid child may easily be intimidated by the sheer distance from your eye to his. Primary teachers must have very flexible knees. Often, a child should be met at his physical level, especially during personal, one-to-one situations. When you stoop to communicate with a child you are telling him, "I want to hear what you have to say. Your ideas are important to me."

It is especially desirable to greet children on their level during the first days of school. Get a small chair and sit when you meet for the first time. It is important that they feel comfortable with you, and sense warmth and sincerity in your presence.

- *Recognize barriers between you and the children:* Your desk is a formidable obstacle to a child whose shoulders barely show above the top. Ideally, of course, a primary teacher spends little time behind her desk, but when fatigue threatens to overcome even the most energetic director of learning, the desk offers a refuge. There are moments, then, when a barrier is desirable, and you should not feel duty bound to be completely accessible at all times—unless a child is compelled by some need to approach the refuge. In that case he should be welcomed to come within the invisible limits. An outstretched arm, an open palm, a movement to face the child directly will let him know he may move nearer if he so desires.

A warm and friendly atmosphere, good communication, and a happy teacher are vital elements of the classroom. If children are to grow and learn, a good environment must be maintained. Each child must be comfortable, realize that he is accepted regardless of his limitations, and know that he is loved and is free to give love. Words alone cannot convey all this. Body language, too, conveys important messages. When employed properly our unspoken language can do much to promote a desirable teaching-learning situation.

Open Education

I hold that the aim of life is to find happiness, which means to find interest. Education should be a preparation for life.

A. S. NEILL
Summerhill, 1960

Major upheavals occurred throughout the field of education during the late 1960s and early 1970s. In response to growing dissatisfaction among both the public and professionals with prevailing educational practices, new programs were developed to offer alternatives to the traditional methods of instruction. Probably the most conspicuous of these new ideas was **open education,** an umbrella concept referring to approaches that stress individual differences in learning and the informal structuring of the schooling process.

Open education (also termed *informal education*) has generated considerable controversy. Critics of open education complain that its permissive atmosphere encourages a dangerous lack of discipline and results in ill-prepared college students. Enthusiasts like to believe that informal structure promotes creativity and instruction geared to the child's individual needs.

The movement derived its early impetus from the practices of some British elementary schools (Silberman, 1970; Weber, 1971). For the most part, open education has grown out of practical experience rather than out of a specific philosophical or scientific position. It is not so much a theory of education as a set of ideas and methods (Walberg and Thomas, 1972). To some extent open education derives its rationale from the writings of cognitive developmental psychologists like Jean Piaget and Jerome S. Bruner (see Chapter 6), while its educational orientation is much in tune with the ideas of self-actualization and freedom found within humanistic psychology (see Chapter 13).

Open education is based on the assumption that children want to learn, learn only what has meaning to them, and learn best in the absence of fear and threat (Campbell, 1976). Above all, it values individual differences and builds on them. Children are seen as differing in the ways they learn and the times at which various aspects of development take place. Further, pupils are viewed as possessing the competence and the right to make significant decisions concerning their own learning. Children are permitted to make errors and to learn from their mistakes so that their direct experiences and actions become vehicles for learning.

Characteristics

Despite several attempts to define open education in precise terms, there is a notable lack of agreement on exactly what the concept means. The best way to describe open education is to specify the characteristics commonly used to distinguish it from traditional approaches.

An environment rich in learning resources. Manipulative materials are supplied in great diversity and range. Among other things, there may be sand and water tables, two or three boxes of odd-shaped macaroni for counting, bottle caps, popsicle sticks, common household utensils, typewriters, books and other media, measuring instruments, printing and drawing materials, and perhaps live animals. Each is there because the teacher has concluded that certain learning possibilities are inherent in the materials (Rogers, 1976). Children learn directly through manipulating materials, taking things apart, and creating items rather than by listening to lectures in which they are simply told certain facts and principles.

Environmental design of space. The physical environment is characterized by the flexible use of space, including open doors, work areas in corridors, and tables and chairs instead of desks. It provides a total environment aimed to break down distinctions between work and play, between subject matters, and between the inside and outside of the classroom. The key to open-space usage is that the instructional area is divided into a number of smaller learning centers such as a reading corner, writing nook, science lab, math section, and art center.

Children's interaction with their physical environment is held to be an essential part of the learning process. They move freely about the area without permission, selecting the activity of interest to them at the time. Indeed, the openness of the physical setting is designed to encourage movement, thereby enhancing the possibilities for the use of materials and the sharing of ideas among children. Although open education can take place within self-contained classrooms, many schools have been designed as open-space buildings, walls are movable or removable, creating spaces of varying sizes and dimensions that allow interaction among pupils of various ages and grade levels.

Individualized instruction. Teachers base their instruction on each individual child and the child's interaction with the materials and equipment. They

OPEN EDUCATION
Open education emphasizes individual differences in learning and the informal organization of classroom activities.

work "alongside the child," continually prodding, challenging, and stimulating (guiding more than directing and listening more than telling). Human variability and differences are seen as desirable attributes that require nurturing and encouragement. As such teachers work with individual children or with two or three, only infrequently presenting the same material to the class as a whole.

Individualized instruction demands constant planning. It is based on an ongoing diagnosis of each child's strengths and weaknesses and an assessment of his or her intellectual, social, emotional, and physical growth. This evaluation involves keeping careful records and individual histories in order to evaluate the child's development and to guide teaching activities. And it necessitates a continual appraisal of the alternatives available in the environment to maximize each child's potential.

A humane, accepting environment. Within the open classroom teachers behave in a warm, responsive manner toward the students. They foster interpersonal communication skills and patterns of cooperative interaction. The climate is one where humanness, respect, and consideration prevail among teachers and pupils.

Open schooling emphasizes spontaneity, creativity, and independence. Children are not compared with one another nor judged as "good" or "bad." Rather they find teachers accepting partners and catalysts in the learning process. Hence, the concept of failure is removed from open education.

Evaluation

There are many variations in open classroom practices. Indeed, "openness" is best viewed as a set of continuous variables or dimensions. Hence, classrooms may be open on some characteristics but closed on others (Marshall, 1981). Further, observers in classrooms these days are finding an expanding array of hybrid instructional practices, methods, and beliefs (Barth, 1977; Horwitz, 1979).

Aside from anecdotal and descriptive accounts by journalists or testimonials by exponents, research on and evaluation of open education is limited (Day and Brice, 1977; Marshall, 1981). Much of what has been written about the open-classroom movement is more suited to rhetoric than to experimental consideration. Overall, there is little research to show whether what supporters assert is going on in open classrooms is actually what is going on.

It is often claimed that an open classroom is superior to a traditional classroom in promoting academic achievement, creativity, positive self-esteem, and healthy school attitudes. However, the most relevant research suggests that, when judged by results on standard indices of academic achievement, there are either no differences between the two types of classrooms or that traditional classrooms are superior to open classrooms (Ward and Barcher, 1975; Wright, 1975; Solomon and Kendall, 1976; Groobman, Forward, and Peterson, 1976; Forman and McKinney, 1978). Some, but not all, studies reveal that students in open classrooms are more creative (Haddon and Lytton, 1971; Solomon and Kendall, 1976; Elias and Elias, 1976; Hyman, 1978) and have more positive attitudes toward school than do students in more conventional settings (Arlin, 1976; Groobman, Forward, and Peterson, 1976; Seidner et al., 1978). In terms of positive self-esteem, neither approach appears to provide a significant advantage over the other (Ruedi and West, 1973; Wright, 1975; Klaff and Docherty, 1975; Day and Brice, 1977; Seidner et al., 1978; Horwitz, 1979).

These mixed findings suggest that the type of classroom setting is only one among a large number of determinants of educational outcomes. Research indicates that there are some children who perform about as well or as poorly in one setting as the other, while others do better in open, and still others in traditional classrooms (Friedlander, 1975; Solomon and Kendall, 1976; Marshall, 1981). Although open education is not a panacea for all the problems facing educators, it is a promising new approach for benefiting some types of students. Hence, a more profitable question than "Is open

TEAM TEACHING

Over the past thirty years one of the better known educational innovations has been team teaching. **Team teaching** is a type of instructional organization in which two or more persons cooperatively plan and implement a learning program for a group of students. Among the purported advantages offered by team teaching are that (1) a group of teachers is better able than a single teacher to identify the problems of the individual child; (2) children are exposed to the strengths of different teachers; (3) team teaching results in better sequencing and pacing of units of instruction, since the perceptions of one teacher must be verified by other team members; and (4) multiple teachers permit a more flexible approach to teaching (Martin and Pavan, 1976; Armstrong, 1977; Marusek, 1979).

Studies of team teaching have failed to confirm that it affords benefits substantially superior to those achieved by the solitary teacher. After reviewing the research dealing with team teaching, David G. Armstrong observes:

> Realizing the limitations of the studies reported here, one still is struck by the relatively large number of investigations reporting no observed differences in the achievement of team-taught and solitary-teacher-taught pupils. . . . In those studies where significant differences between the two conditions were reported, those differences favored team-taught groups slightly more frequently than solitary-teacher-taught groups. [1977:68]

Further, results of a study by Carol J. McCallum and Albert E. Roark (1974) do not support the claim that teachers in teams can identify children's problems in some superior way.

At least two factors may contribute to the failure of researchers to find significant differences in achievement between groups of students taught by solitary teachers and teachers in teams (Armstrong, 1977). First, teachers appear to view team teaching primarily as an administrative management scheme having little connection with the nature of the instructional process (Rutherford, 1975). Accordingly, the patterns of interaction between teachers and students may show little difference between the practices labeled "solitary teacher teaching" and "team teaching." Second, studies comparing the two approaches are usually based on instances of team-teaching behavior after only a single school year. This may be too short a time period for team teaching to "take hold" among both teachers and students (Kennamer and Hall, 1975). All of this suggests that team teaching is an innovation that merits more careful consideration and evaluation.

TEAM TEACHING
In team teaching two or more teachers cooperate in planning and implementing an instructional program.

education better than traditional?'' might be ''For whom is open better and for whom is traditional better?'' (Arlin, 1976).

EDUCATIONAL EFFECTIVENESS

In large measure educators and the general public believe that schools affect their students' intellectual and social development and that ''good'' schools produce more favorable outcomes than ''poor'' schools. Thus the Coleman Report of 1966 startled the nation by its conclusion that schools contribute relatively little to the academic and social development of their pupils. The study—named after its principal author, James S. Coleman, a leading sociologist—was funded by Congress and involved tests and surveys of 645,000 pupils and 60,000 teachers in 4,000 public schools. The report concluded that:

> Schools bring little influence to bear on a child's achievement that is independent of his background and general social context [the family and community from which the child comes]; and that this very lack of an independent effect means that the inequalities imposed on children by their home, neighborhood, and peer environment are carried along to become the inequalities with which they confront adult life at the end of school. [1966:325]

The Coleman findings contributed to public skepticism toward schools and to the erosion of educational funding. Not surprisingly, educators and psychologists subjected the Coleman Report to careful scrutiny. They pointed out that Coleman collected the data at the school level rather than at the classroom level. Consequently, Coleman's large-scale sociological study provided us with data about the mythical ''statistical average'' school. But the process of collecting and averaging the data masked the differences among teachers and students.

More recent research reveals that good schools and good teachers *do* make a difference. For instance, Eigil Pedersen, Thérèse A. Faucher, and William W. Eaton (1978), employing a complicated and innovative methodology, were able to demonstrate a positive relationship between one first-grade teacher and the adult success of children from a disadvantaged urban neighborhood. Two-thirds of ''Miss A's'' pupils achieved the highest adult status, compared to less than half of the former pupils of other first-grade teachers. None of her pupils were in the lowest category, although more than a third of other teachers' students were.

''Miss A'' enjoyed the reputation as an excellent teacher, and it was said of her that ''there was no way that the pupil was not going to read by the end of grade one.'' ''Miss A'' gave extra time to slow learners and invariably stayed after hours to assist children. The researchers concluded that ''Miss A,'' by helping to shape the academic self-concept and achievement of a pupil, laid an initial foundation that yielded cumulative benefits in later stages of life.

Effective Schools

An accumulating body of research is providing an answer to the question of what it is about an effective school that makes it effective. Michael Rutter (1979), a professor of child psychiatry, led a University of London team in a three-year study of students entering twelve London intercity secondary schools. The research found that schools only a scant distance apart and with students of similar social backgrounds and intellectual abilities engendered widely different educational results.

Perhaps the most critical element emerging from the Rutter research is the ''ethos''—the overall tone—of the school. The successful schools fostered expectations that order would prevail and did not leave matters of student discipline to be worked out by individual teachers for themselves. Consequently, it was much easier to be a good teacher in some schools than in others. Likewise, the effective schools emphasized academic concerns—care by teachers in lesson planning, group instruction, high achievement expectations for student performance, a high proportion of time spent on instruction and learning activities, assignment and checking of homework, and use of the library. Rutter also found that respect for students as responsible people and high expectations for appropriate behavior contributed to academic success. In the better schools, many students held responsibilities as group captains or as participants in school assemblies. Factors that were unrelated to student achievement or discipline included the size and age of the building.

Other reserach similarly points to a strong association between a school's climate and student achievement and discipline (Brookover et al., 1979; Clark, Lotto, and McCarthy, 1980; Wynne, 1981). A sense of social order and community and high academic expectations pervade successful schools. Much depends on a school's leader, usually the principal. Effective schools are typically led by principals who provide (1) assertive, achievement-oriented leadership; (2) an orderly, purposeful, and peaceful school climate; (3) high expectations for teachers and students; and (4) well-designed instructional objectives and evaluation systems (Shoemaker and Fraser, 1981). Consequently, such schools are run for well-formulated purposes rather than running from force of habit (Austin, 1979). They possess "coherence" in that things stick together and bear predictable relationships with one another.

Effective Teachers

The successes of such individuals [outstanding teachers] tend to be born and to die with them; beneficial consequences extend only to those pupils who have personal contact with such gifted teachers. . . . The only way by which we can prevent such waste in the future is by methods which enable us to make an analysis of what the gifted teacher does intuitively, so that something accruing from his work can be communicated to others.

JOHN DEWEY
The Sources of a Science of Education, 1929

Over the past decade a number of educators and psychologists have studied what makes for an effective teacher. The generalizations that have emerged from this research provide guidelines for understanding various teacher behaviors and for assisting teachers in formulating their courses of action. But such generalizations do not provide a set of prescriptive rules or recipes by which teachers can conduct their classes. Researchers find few, if any, specific teaching behaviors that work in all contexts. Educational generalizations are necessarily indeterminate, since they cannot predict precisely what will occur in a particular case. At best they allow teachers to assess the likely consequences of alternative strategies within highly complex situations (Good, 1979; Brophy, 1979, 1982).

When research data are integrated at a high level of generality, several clusters or patterns of teacher

EFFECTIVE TEACHERS
Good teachers make a difference in shaping children's self-images and academic achievement.

behaviors are consistently related to student gains. One cluster has to do with teacher expectations. Effective teachers view the instruction of students in the curriculum as central to their role. They expect to conduct serious instruction, and they define the classroom situation for their students in these terms. Moreover, they translate these definitions into classroom realities (Brophy, 1979, 1982). Successful teachers allocate more of their time to instruction than unsuccessful teachers do. Indeed, research reveals that the amount of time students are engaged in reading and math is positively associated with learning gains (Fisher et al., 1978; Gage, 1978). Effective teachers begin lessons on time, do not end classes early, and do not waste time when they prepare and distribute materials (Rutter, 1979).

Another cluster revolves about direct instruction (Rosenshine, 1979; Good, 1979). Elements in direct instruction include (1) the formulation of clear learning goals, (2) the promotion of extensive content coverage and high levels of student involvement in classroom tasks, (3) the active monitoring of student progress, (4) the structuring of learning activities and the provision of immediate feedback to students, and (5) the creation of a task-oriented but relaxed environment. Direct instruction entails active teaching. The teacher presents the process or concept under study, supervises student work, and holds students accountable for their work. Research shows that higher achievement gains are associated with orderly classrooms, persistent application of students to academic tasks, and well-defined and structured learning contexts (Gage, 1978; Stallings and Hentzell, 1978; Good, 1979).

Still another cluster of teacher behaviors has to do with teacher managerial skills, the subject of the next chapter. Whereas instruction focuses on the achievement of various learning goals, management is centered on the creation of conditions under which learning can proceed. If teachers are to instruct students effectively, they must limit interruptions and intrusions into class activities and control negative behavior. Well-managed classrooms allow students to use efficient routines for

carrying out their tasks and to work without distraction in calm, pleasant environments.

Linda M. Anderson, Carolyn M. Evertson, and Jere E. Brophy (1979) investigated the effectiveness of instructional techniques in teaching first-graders to read. The study involved twenty-seven first-grade teachers and their students. Elements that were associated with learning gains included the following:

- The more effective teachers spent more time with their reading groups and hence covered more content than did ineffective teachers (thirty minutes as opposed to twenty minutes). They also carefully assigned seatwork to follow the group lesson.
- Teachers fostered student achievement by providing students with opportunities for practicing their skills. Practice sessions allowed teachers to monitor student understanding, provide feedback, and adjust the lesson.
- The most effective teachers were those who had good managerial skills. They started the lesson immediately and did not waste time organizing materials or assembling students.
- Ordered turns in reading afforded the most effective technique for working individually with students within a group setting. This procedure was preferable to random selection or volunteering to respond.
- Teaching effectiveness was associated with the asking of questions that provided a high rate of correct answers. The first-graders profited from lessons that resulted in a low rate of errors since correct practice permitted the students to internalize the skills.
- Successful teachers transmitted to their pupils a good deal of appropriate information about the structure of the skills rather than focusing only on the memorization of rules and labels. They used overviews to set the stage for a lesson, feedback following errors, ongoing explanations of the steps involved, questioning procedures, and explicit specification of correct and incorrect behaviors.
- When call-outs occurred, effective teachers re-

minded the child that each pupil got a turn and that he or she must await his or her turn to answer. When a child was unable to respond within a reasonable time, the teachers assisted the student by appropriate probing.

- Successful teachers employed praise in moderation. Both praise and criticism were as specified as possible, identifying the desirable or correct alternatives.

Thomas L. Good and Douglas A. Grouws (1979) studied a sample of over one hundred fourth-grade teachers so as to determine the practices that optimize mathematics instruction. Among the key teacher behaviors identified by this research were the following:

- The more effective teachers taught the class basically as a whole within one instructional group.
- Successful teachers opened each session with a review (lasting about eight minutes) of the concepts and skills stressed in the homework assignment.
- The more effective teachers presented information more actively and clearly than did the less effective teachers. They focused on meaning and promoted student understanding with lively explanations, demonstrations, and illustrations.
- Successful teachers were task-focused and spent most of the period on mathematics as opposed to socializing.
- Effective teachers assigned both seatwork and homework. They let students know that their work would be checked and followed through by correcting the assignments. In this fashion students were held accountable for assigned work.
- The more effective teachers were basically nonevaluative and created a relatively relaxed learning environment. They provided relatively little praise or criticism.

This description of good mathematics teachers is very similar to that of Carolyn M. Evertson and her associates, who undertook a study of junior-high-school teachers.:

> In *mathematics classes,* the results form a consistent picture of the practices of ''good'' teachers (using both achievement and student attitudes as criteria). The more effective teachers were active, well-organized, and strongly academically oriented. They tended to emphasize whole-class instruction, but with some time also devoted to seatwork. They managed their classes efficiently, and tended to ''nip trouble in the bud,'' stopping a disturbance before it could seriously disrupt the class. They asked many questions during class discussions. Most were ''lower order'' product questions, but ''higher order'' process questions were also fairly common.
>
> The best mathematics teachers were not martinets, however. They were also rated as more enthusiastic, nurturant, and affectionate than their less successful colleagues. [1980:58]

In sum, research linking teacher behavior to student learning is making solid progress.

TEACHER-STUDENT INTERACTION

Central to classroom settings is the interaction between the teacher and the student. When American teenagers grade their teachers and their schools, they are considerably more generous to the teachers than to the schools. The Gallup Youth Survey (1980d) finds that whereas two out of three teens award an A or B to their teachers, fewer than 50 percent are willing to give top grades to their schools. Fully 26 percent give A's to their teachers but only 9 percent to schools in their community. Nationally, only 9 percent of all teens think their teachers deserve a D or an F; 15 percent give their schools these grades. Teens of above-average academic standing view their teachers and schools more favorably than do average or below-average students.

Teacher Perceptions and Ratings of Students

The secret of education is respecting the pupil.

RALPH WALDO EMERSON

Human life does not consist of a neutral world, one devoid of evaluations and judgments relative to an individual's desirability, worth, merit, or beauty. Schools are no exception. Both teachers and students continually judge and rank one another and their peers. The difference, however, is that teachers enjoy greater power resources for translating their value preferences into the operating realities of classroom life.

Attitudes Toward Various Children

A variety of studies reveal that teachers feel differently about different children in their classrooms (Willis and Brophy, 1974; Helton and Oakland, 1977). Further, these differing attitudes have consequences for a teacher's behavior. One procedure for studying these matters is to ask a teacher to nominate students to each of four attitude groups and then to observe the teacher's interactions with these students over a period of time. The attitude categories commonly used are the following (Silberman, 1969):

1. *Attachment:* If you could keep one student another year for the joy of it, whom would you pick?

2. *Concern:* If you could devote all your attention to a child who concerns you a great deal, whom would you pick?

3. *Indifference:* If a parent were to drop in unannounced for a conference, whose child would you be least prepared to talk about?

4. *Rejection:* If your class was to be reduced by one child, whom would you be relieved to have removed?

Sherry Willis and Jere Brophy (1974) find that three factors tend to influence teachers in placing students in one of these four categories: the students' general level of academic success, the degree to which students reward teachers in their personal contacts with them, and the degree to which students conform to classroom rules. More specifically:

1. *Attachment students:* Attachment students are usually successful academically, obey school rules, and reward teachers in their interactions with them.

2. *Concern students:* These students have academic difficulty but are obedient and personally rewarding to teachers, so that teachers are concerned about them and spend considerable time providing them with remedial help.

3. *Indifferent students:* Indifferent students respond negatively to teachers, failing to provide them with interpersonal rewards.

4. *Rejection students:* These students not only fail to provide teachers with rewarding experiences but also constitute discipline problems.

Overall, Willis and Brophy conclude that the personal qualities of the student-teacher relationship tend to take precedence over student achievement in influencing the attitudes of teachers toward students.

Physical Attractiveness

Social psychologists have shown that people who are judged good-looking enjoy advantages in life solely because of their external attributes (Dion, Berscheid, and Walster, 1972; Dermer and Thiel, 1975; Bennetts, 1978). It is not particularly surprising, therefore, that researchers should find that teachers rate children thought to be attractive by prevailing cultural standards more favorably than they do unattractive children (Algonzzine, 1977; Lerner and Lerner, 1977; Adams and Crane, 1980). For instance, one pair of investigators (Ross and Salvia, 1975) attached photographs of attractive and unattractive children to identical, fictitious case studies of mildly handicapped children. Experienced teachers who appraised the material indicated that the unattractive children would have more difficulty academically and socially. Moreover, these teachers favored special class placement more for the unattractive than for the attractive pupils.

In another study. Margaret M. Clifford and Elaine Walster (1973) sent twelve report cards filled out for above-average students to a sample of fifth-grade teachers in Missouri. Each card had a photograph of an attractive or unattractive boy or girl attached to it. Accompanying each report card and photograph was an opinion sheet the teachers were asked to complete. It was found that the children's attractiveness was significantly associated with the teachers' appraisals of how intelligent the children were, how interested in

education their parents were, how far they were likely to progress in school, and how popular they would be with their peers.

Race and Social Class

Although the Declaration of Independence states that "all men are created equal," research shows that educational equality for students from different racial and social-class backgrounds is a myth (DeMeis and Turner, 1977, 1978; Beady and Hansell, 1981). Teachers' assessments of students are affected by their stereotypes of different racial and social-class groups. In general, white teachers rate whites higher than either black or Chicano students, and middle-class white and black pupils fare better than lower-class whites and blacks (Jensen and Rosenfeld, 1974).

RACIAL MEMBERSHIP
Studies show that teachers' assessments of students are influenced by the racial stereotypes the teachers hold regarding the members of given racial groups.

Thomas K. Crowl and Walter H. MacGinitie (1974) investigated the concept of vocal stereotyping within an educational context. Tape recordings were made of six white students of an upper-middle-class socioeconomic background and six black students of a lower socioeconomic background. The boys, all ninth-graders, read identically worded answers to typical school questions in Standard English. To ensure that each student's ethnic membership could be accurately identified from his speech, twelve judges drawn from the same population of teachers who participated in the study listened to the tapes and were able to identify each student's ethnic group with an average accuracy of 88 percent. Subsequently, sixty-two experienced white teachers appraised the answers spoken by black students as inferior to the answers spoken by white students (despite the fact that the verbal content was the same). Crowl and MacGinitie note, "Even though teachers may not be recording marks in a grade book every time a student speaks, it may be that the teacher makes some kind of judgment about what kind of person the student is, and these subtle judgments may ultimately affect the teacher's behavior toward a student" (1974:308). The findings of the Crowl and MacGinitie study are consistent with other research that shows that students judged to have "more nonstandard speech" are expected to perform academically less well than students whose speech is judged "more standard" (Williams, Whitehead, and Miller, 1972).

Teacher-Expectation Effects

Children who are treated as if they are uneducable almost invariably become uneducable.

KENNETH B. CLARK
Dark Ghetto, 1965

As noted, teachers perceive the competencies and potentialities of children quite differently. Some educators and psychologists say that teachers reflect these expectancies in their interactions with children and thus produce differential achievement among them. The term **teacher-expectation effects** has been coined to refer to this tendency (also referred to as a *self-fulfilling prophecy*). According to this view, our beliefs or expectancies about other people affect the way we behave toward them, and the way we behave often causes the other people to respond just as we expected they would. For instance, a teacher who expects a child to be friendly may treat the child in a warm responsive manner causing the child to respond in a friendly way. In contrast, a teacher who expects a child to be difficult and troublesome may treat that student with overt gingerliness or coldness and cause the child to feel rejected and to respond negatively and with hostility (Brophy and Evertson, 1976).

Considerable controversy was aroused in 1968 with the publication of *Pygmalion in the Classroom,* by Robert Rosenthal and Lenore Jacobson, a study that concluded that a teacher's expectations can appreciably affect a pupil's academic achievement. Rosenthal and Jacobson arranged at the beginning of the school year to have an intelligence test administered to all the children in grades one to six of a south San Francisco elementary school. Teachers were told that the test was an instrument to identify intellectually late-blooming students. Within each of the classes, approximately 20 percent of the pupils were *randomly* chosen to form an experimental group. The names of these students were given to their teachers. The teachers were falsely told that the test scores of these children predicted that they would show dramatic gains in intellectual achievement over the course of the year.

At the end of the school year, the intelligence test was again administered to the children. Across all classrooms there were average IQ gains of 12.22 points among the children for whom a learning "spurt" was predicted; this compared with 8.42 points for the rest of the student body. Of even greater significance, at the first-grade level, the pupils in the experimental group showed gains of 15 points more than the other children (and at the second-grade level, 9 points).

FACILITATING PROACTIVE TEACHING

As pointed out in the text, teachers respond differently to group and individual differences in students. At times, these differences in teacher behavior have implications for their pupils' learning. Yet, teachers are typically unaware of many of these differences in their behavior, even when they appear obvious and systematic to the classroom observer. For instance, Roy Martin and Albert Keller (1976), on the basis of observations carried out in thirty classrooms within eight schools, found that teachers inaccurately recalled the extent to which they call on boys or girls, the frequency with which students approach them, the number of times they initiate private contacts with students, and the amount of class time spent on procedural matters.

Jere E. Brophy and Thomas L. Good (1974) have suggested a number of reasons for this. First, there is so much activity usually going on in the classroom that it is difficult for a teacher to be conscious of it all. Second, many teacher-training programs fail to provide prospective teachers with the conceptual framework required to ascertain, process, and interpret this kind of information. Third, teachers seldom have feedback from an objective source regarding what is happening in the classroom.

Teacher awareness is a key to facilitating better and more responsive teaching. Generally, when teachers are made aware of inappropriate teaching on their part, they are willing and eager to change. Of course, a good deal depends on the source and nature of the feedback. Teachers often reject feedback because they do not agree with the standards their supervisors employ (McNeil, 1971). Too often supervisors' comments boil down to "your way is wrong, do it my way"; such implications lead teachers to become defensive (Good and Brophy, 1974).

Good and Brophy (1974) undertook to determine if feedback based on observational data would be more acceptable to teachers than the feedback usually provided by supervisors. In the study observers separately tabulated a teacher's interactions with each student. This allowed Good and Brophy later to interview each teacher on the basis of the observers' data and to show the teacher that some students were being taught appropriately and others inappropriately. In making suggestions for improvement, Good and Brophy were in effect saying to a teacher, "You are doing a fine job with Mary, now try to do the same kinds of things with Stella."

On the basis of earlier research, Good and Brophy were convinced that few teachers consciously give up on certain students or treat them with rejection or discouragement. Rather, they gradually drift into a pattern in which they continue to react in an inappropriate way toward certain students without necessarily realizing it. By providing teachers with information to make them aware of what they are doing, Good and Brophy believe, teachers can and will be able to make appropriate changes in their teaching. The study largely confirmed this assumption.

Two types of students were called to the teachers' attention. The first involved students with strikingly low rates of interaction with the teacher, both because they avoided the teacher and because the teacher avoided them. The second group consisted of students whom teachers ignored if the students did not succeed on their first recitation opportunity. By virtue of a single interview with Good and Brophy, the teachers significantly increased their rates of interaction with the first group of students and their rates of staying time with the second group. In addition, student behavior was positively influenced by the change in teacher behavior.

Initially the Rosenthal-Jacobson findings had a considerable impact on the thinking of educators. The following statement is illustrative:

> What we "see" is a product of what we believe to be "out there." We see things not as "they" are, but as we are. . . . The teachers "perceived" these children as intelligent because they were expected to see "intelligent behavior." The teachers . . . "made" the reality that was "there." But we can assume that once the teachers "made" that reality, the children began to "make" one of their own. The children modified their behavior in accordance with the positive expectations of their teachers. In other words, the children changed their perceptions of themselves, and they did so because their environment had a positive effect on their purposes and assumptions. [Postman and Weingartner, 1969:95]

It was not long, however, before critics charged that the data-gathering methods, the techniques of analysis, and the data presentation of the Rosenthal-Jacobson study were not sufficiently precise to warrant the generalizations the report contained (Thorndike, 1968; Snow, 1969; Jensen, 1969; Elashoff and Snow, 1971; Cooper, 1979). In the intervening years since 1968, a good many studies have been undertaken to test the teacher-expectation effect further. The great majority have offered little or no support to the notion that teachers bias

TEACHER-EXPECTATION EFFECTS
Research suggests that how a teacher feels about a student influences how that child performs in an academic setting.

the performance of their pupils as a result of having correct or incorrect knowledge about the children's IQ or achievement scores (Finn, 1972; Dusek, 1975; Braun, 1976; Wittrock and Lumsdaine, 1977).

Critics of the Rosenthal-Jacobson thesis do not deny that teachers' interactions with students vary with their expectations. For instance, studies reveal that teachers spend more time and interact verbally in more positive and supportive ways with high-achieving children than with low-achieving pupils (Rubovits and Maehr, 1971, 1973; Good, Cooper, and Blakey, 1980; Good, 1981). Moreover, these expectancies (and presumably their behavioral expressions) have been shown to relate to students' academic achievement (O'Connell, Dusek, and Wheeler, 1974; Sutherland and Goldschmid, 1974). However, the critics say that simply because teachers treat "bright" and "dull" students differently does not bias students' performance. Rather, they claim that teachers are merely good predictors of students' achievement potential; if they treat their students differently, it is because teachers adjust their teaching style to the differing abilities and needs of their pupils (Dusek, 1975).

All of this highlights two competing explanations of the relationship between teacher expectations and students' academic performance. Rosenthal and Jacobson set forth one position, the view that teachers are the causal agents whose varying expectations influence the differential development of pupils' skills and abilities. The other interpretation holds that student achievement shapes teacher expectations. According to this viewpoint, teachers make valid assessments of children's abilities and reflect their expectations in adapting their instruction to each student's unique needs.

Recent research by William D. Crano and Phyllis M. Mellon (1978) sheds additional light on these contrasting interpretations. The study involved the assessment of 4,300 British elementary school children at various points over a four-year period. Using complex statistical procedures, Crano and Mellon concluded that teachers and students influence one another so that both interpretations contain

an element of truth. However, teachers' expectancies were found to have more influence on children's achievement than children's performance had upon teachers' attitudes.

Crano and Mellon were able to assess two different types of teacher expectancies. One set concerned a child's social skills and conduct; the other, a child's academic status. They found that teachers' expectations of students' social development exerted a greater effect on children's later academic performance than did those expectancies specifically associated with academic potential. The study shows that how a teacher feels about a child has a strong impact on the child's academic performance.

Crano and Mellon argue that the experimental procedures used to test teacher-expectancy effects serve to bias research against confirming the Rosenthal-Jacobson thesis. Telling teachers that certain children are "late bloomers" or feeding them phony IQ data is not sufficient to overcome naturally occurring expectations. Often the fictitious information provided by the experimenters is too obviously and sharply discrepant from the students' observable characteristics (Good and Brophy, 1973). Indeed, say Crano and Mellon, it would be a very poor teacher who, on the basis of past training and experience, could not differentiate children in terms of their actual academic potential.

Significance of the Teacher's Gender

Boys and girls differ in their classroom behavior and performance. For one thing, boys have more academic problems in elementary school than girls (Schaeffer, 1969). Some reports indicate that school-related problems are three to four times higher for boys than for girls (Bentzen, 1963; Ringness, 1967). For instance, surveys of remedial reading programs generally find that about 70 percent of all referrals are boys (Blom, 1971). Moreover, boys generally do more poorly than girls in areas requiring verbal and reading skills (Maccoby and Jacklin, 1974; Vroegh, 1976). On the other hand, beginning at about age twelve or thirteen, boys' mathematical skills typically increase faster than those of girls (Maccoby and Jacklin, 1974).

Various explanations have been advanced to account for these sex differences. Some stress the role of heredity, pointing to what they believe are genetic and maturational differences. Most educational psychologists, however, appear to favor an environmental explanation (Stein, 1971; Good, Sikes, and Brophy, 1973; Vroegh, 1976). This latter interpretation is supported by a number of cross-cultural studies. Although in the United States girls at the elementary level outscore boys on achievement tests, in Germany the reverse is true, and this reversal also holds in the incidence of reading retardation (Preston, 1962). Other surveys show that although girls outscore boys in several aspects of reading achievement in the United States and Canada, boys outscore girls in England and Nigeria (Johnson, 1972).

Some educators and psychologists suggest that the reason for greater academic problems for boys in the United States derives from women staffing the schools. Of interest, boys outscore girls in Germany, where the majority of teachers are male. The same holds true of England and Nigeria, where there are more male elementary teachers than in the United States and Canada.

Patricia C. Sexton (1969) has been an especially vehement critic of what she views as "feminizing" influences in inducing passive, conforming, and uncertain types of behavior among students. This, says Sexton, works a particular hardship on boys:

Women teachers know almost nothing about boys games, and most couldn't care less. Typically, the woman teacher is about as involved in the World Series as boys are in the score of *La Traviata*. This is not a trivial matter. Sports and games . . . are central to the boy personality. Much of a boy's life is spent playing sports, watching them, or talking about them. Thus this intense inner life of boys is given little chance for exposure in the academic classroom. [1969:121]

A number of advantages are alleged to flow from having more male teachers in the classroom (Vroegh, 1976). First, men offer male models who can help children to clarify the male role. Second, male teachers can bring to the schools many diversified interests and activities that can benefit both girls and boys. And third, men can provide a different kind of nurture than female teachers.

Proponents of the feminizing thesis make two assumptions: First, female teachers treat boys and girls differently, and second, the differences in treatment lead to differences in learning performance by boys and girls. There are not, however, any firm data that clearly show that female teachers discriminate against boys or that male teachers treat boys differently than female teachers do (Good, Sikes, and Brophy, 1973; Travis, 1977; Good, Cooper, and Blakey, 1980; Prawat and Jarvis, 1980). While it does appear that teachers give boys more frequent and harsher criticism, some research suggests that boys may also receive more positive feedback than girls do. Further, findings that boys receive relatively more negative treatment may result from the failure of researchers to divide male and female students into finer categories; much teacher criticism usually centers on a small group of misbehaving boys rather than on boys in general (Martin, 1972).

The great majority of studies also reveals that male and female teachers on the whole treat their male and female students similarly. Not untypical is the conclusion reached by Thomas L. Good, J. Neville Sikes, and Jere E. Brophy:

Male and female students are not treated the same way, since important student sex differences appear regularly. However, the present data show that the same kind of sex differences that have been repeatedly demonstrated to exist in classes taught by female teachers also exist in classes taught by male teachers. The presence of male teachers does not eliminate or reverse these sex differences. . . . Previous writers describing the "plight" of male students have overemphasized that the teachers were female and placed too little stress on the fact that they were teachers. [1973:83]

Since teachers are trained for similar roles, and the expectations placed on them by parents and school authorities are identical, teachers of both sexes may behave similarly in the same situations.

All of this suggests that the characteristics of good teachers are not sex-linked. Both men and women teachers are needed in schools. Children should see and experience a world that is not constrained by narrow stereotyped sex roles. In this manner children can feel free to approach resources on the basis of individual needs rather than on the basis of outmoded traditions of what is appropriate for males and females (Vroegh, 1976). Further, innovations are needed that are capable of changing the tendency for both male and female teachers to behave negatively toward low-achieving boys and to help modify the largely passive role played by many low-achieving girls (Good, Sikes, and Brophy, 1973).

Reciprocal Influence

Students influence teacher behavior at the same time that their own behavior is being influenced by the teacher.

JERE E. BROPHY AND THOMAS L. GOOD
Teacher-Student Relationships, 1974

Teachers do not play their roles in a social vacuum. Students have clear, well-defined expectations regarding how teachers should administer discipline, handle subject matter, and communicate explanations and fairness. Roy Nash observes:

A new class is not a clean slate passively waiting for the teacher to inscribe his will on it. It is an ongoing social system with very definite expectations about appropriate teacher behavior. If these are not confirmed, the pupils will protest and the renegotiated patterns of behavior may not prove to be just what the teacher intended. [1976:286]

It is often overlooked that many classroom problems arise out of the reciprocal nature of the teacher-student relationship. For instance, when we say that a teacher "lost control" of the class, it is actually a case of some student or students gaining control (Schlechty and Atwood, 1977).

Further, student discipline problems are attributable at least in part to mutual antagonism between certain pupils and their teachers. For any number of reasons, one party displeases the other party. A cycle of mutual disapproval is unleashed and locks the teacher and the student into a hostile, destructive relationship (Polirstok and Greer, 1977).

A number of studies have shown how students alter teacher behavior (Feldman and Prohaska, 1979). Susan S. Klein (1971) demonstrated that college education classes could change the verbal behavior of guest lecturers from approving to critical statements by shifting from positive, attentive behavior to negative, inattentive behavior on cue. In another study, Carol G. Noble and John D. Nolan (1976) observed the number of students volunteering and the amount of directed teacher questioning that occurred in high-school classes at the beginning of the school year and again three months later. The initial observations revealed no relationship between the amount of volunteering and the amount of directed teacher questioning. Three months later this situation had changed, with teachers directing more questions to those students who had exhibited a high rate of volunteering. It appeared that the students had shaped the frequency with which teachers called on them by the amount of volunteering they did.

Power relationships within the classroom are often portrayed as involving all-powerful teachers and vulnerable, powerless students. Although the dimensions of classroom power are uneven and unequal, power is hardly a one-way street. As Phillip C. Schlechty and Helen E. Atwood (1977) point out, teachers know that students are the principal source of their reputations among school officials, colleagues, parents, and other students. The ability of students to report to others as to what *really* goes on in a classroom gives them an element of leverage. Nor are teachers unaware of the fact that some students have contact with powerful community members, for instance, the student whose parent is a member of the school board.

Schlechty and Atwood also note that some students typically perform "director" roles:

There are some students from whom the teacher will take cues about the quality of his own performance, or when it is time to move on to the next "act." For example, when teachers ask questions like "Now, does everyone understand?" they usually look to the same one or two students for signals of understanding. If the signals are positive, the teacher will move ahead with the lesson; if they are negative, the teacher is likely to go back over the material that is proving difficult. But of more interest, perhaps, is that when these student-directors give cues that are at odds with other cues given off in the class, the teacher tends to move with the directors rather than with [the] majority of the class. Furthermore, teachers are seldom conscious of this behavior. [1977:288]

Thus, students play an important part in shaping patterns of classroom interaction.

STUDENT-STUDENT INTERACTION

Man is a knot, a web, a mesh into which relationships are tied.

ANTOINE DE SAINT-EXUPÉRY

At birth children enter a world of people, a social network that, although changing in form, intensity, and function, stretches across the life span. Among the most important social relationships human beings form are their bonds with **peers**—individuals of roughly the same age. Peer relationships assume a vital part in children's development and provide a critical ingredient within the educational enterprise.

PEER INFLUENCE
Students exert a powerful influence on one another's learning.

SCHOOL DESEGREGATION AND INTERGROUP RELATIONS

The goals of integration and quality education must be sought together; they are interdependent. One is not possible without the other.

Kenneth B. Clark
Dark Ghetto, 1965

How to reduce racist attitudes and behaviors is a problem that has plagued our society since the United States became the Great Melting Pot. Among the goals of school desegration programs, the reduction of dominant group prejudice is cited almost as frequently as the promotion of minority group academic achievement. Many of the social scientists who testified in the 1954 Supreme Court case of *Brown* v. *Board of Education* (in which the nation's highest court held mandatory school segregation unconstitutional) believed that school desegregation would lead to more positive racial attitudes (Stephan, 1978). However, experience has demonstrated that merely creating desegregated classrooms is not sufficient for improving race relations among students.

Although some studies suggest that school desegregation can have a positive impact on intergroup attitudes and behavior, a good many others reveal no effect or even a negative effect (Carithers, 1970; St. John, 1975; Cohen, 1975; Gerard and Miller, 1975; Pearce, 1980). All of this suggests that there is more to successful integration than simply mixing children from different racial backgrounds. Rather than asking whether or not desegregation improves intergroup relations, social scientists are increasingly studying the *conditions* that make desegregation effective. This has drawn attention to the distinction between desegregation and integration. **Desegregation** refers to the removal of formal barriers within a society, both legal and social, that are premised on racial or ethnic membership. It involves the elimination of segregation in institutional functioning and the achievement of what is often termed "civil rights." **Integration,** however, embraces the idea of eliminating prejudice as well as discrimination. As such, integration refers to much more than desegregation. It involves attitudinal changes and the removal of fears, hatreds, and suspicions—in brief, the acceptance of individuals without regard to their race within informal, personal, intimate, and voluntary relationships.

Children bring to school the prejudices and fears of their parents and the larger community (St. John and Lewis, 1975). Research involving large samples of black and white students in the public high schools of Indianapolis shows that racial attitudes that are important predictors of negative interracial behavior are students' own prior unfavorable attitudes and those of their families and peers (Patchen, Hofmann, and Davidson, 1976; Patchen et al., 1977). In contrast, interracial friendliness in high school is fostered by policies that encourage friendly interracial contact at early ages in grade schools and neighborhoods (Singleton and Asher, 1977). Further, positive family and peer racial attitudes contribute substantially to friendly interaction. These findings suggest that when desegregation is opposed by parents and significant segments of the community, powerful social norms operate to discourage informal interracial contact. It is illogical and unreasonable to expect the schools to undo the racist patterns that the larger society continually recreates in the course of its daily functioning.

Efforts to reduce intergroup friction and prejudice have often proceeded from the maxim "Bring differing groups into contact and their ill feelings will wither away." Indeed, an almost mystical faith resides among Americans in "get-

POSITIVE INTERGROUP RELATIONSHIPS
Positive relations among individuals of different racial groups are fostered by circumstances in which the individuals work together toward common goals.

ting to know one another" as a solvent of racial tensions. Yet, much research reveals that things do not always work out this way, since the social contacts may simply serve as occasions for intensifying conflict (Allport, 1954; Sherif et al., 1961; Amir, 1969).

It is true, however, that under favorable conditions intergroup contact may be beneficial. One of these conditions involves equal status contacts (Schofield and Sagar, 1977). Individuals who are similar in social class and home background, share like values, and possess mutually admired skills and traits tend to be attracted to one another. Thus, the mutual popularity of blacks and whites is affected by many of the same factors that other researchers have identified as contributing to peer group popularity generally (Lott and Lott, 19174; St. John and Lewis, 1975; Clore et al., 1978).

Another condition favorable to the development of positive intergroup relationships is the creation of multiracial interdependencies.

The possibilities for achieving harmony are greatly enhanced when groups are brought together to work toward common goals. Hostility gives way when groups pull together to achieve overriding goals that are real and compelling (Allport, 1954; Sherif et al., 1961). One way to structure interdependencies is the creation of biracial work groups or teams in which similar rewards are administered to all teammates. Research suggest that the use of biracial student teams is a way to create greater interracial cooperation and acceptance (DeVries and Edwards, 1974; DeVries, Edwards, and Slavin, 1978).

Most studies using sociometric measures find that as the proportion of students from the other race increases in a student's class, interracial friendship choices also increase (St. John, 1975). Even though students tend to prefer classmates of their own race, the polarization tends to be somewhat less extreme in balanced than in unbalanced classes (Koslin et al., 1972).

Teachers also play a critical part in shaping the social climate of the classroom (Gerard and Miller, 1975; Miller and Gerard, 1976). Their likes and dislikes are examples for most of the children. Thus, a teacher's bias may influence a minority child's popularity among his or her classmates. As Norman Miller and Harold B. Gerard note in their study of desegregation in Riverside, California:

Acceptance by classmates and teachers may be most important of all. Schools have to create classroom settings in which minority children will be accepted and not threatened, thereby raising the odds on making desegregation a benefit. The classroom setting is also easier to change than personality, which has its origins far back in the family. [1976:100]

All of this suggests that, as in most other aspects of life, desegregation works where people are dedicated to making it work; it fails where people are indifferent or determined to see it fail.

Peer Groups

Students exert a strong influence on one another's cognitions, attitudes, and behaviors, all of which affect academic performance (Schmuck, 1977; Moore, 1981). This derives from the important functions performed by peer groups (Vander Zanden, 1984). First, they give children experience with relationships in which they are on equal footing with others; these relationships contrast with children's subordinate position in their relations with adults. Second, peer groups allow children to acquire status and realize an identity in which their own activities and concerns are central and supreme. Third, they are agencies for the transmission of informal knowledge, superstitions, folklore, fads, jokes, games, secret modes of gratification, and sexual information. And fourth, by virtue of the support they receive from their peer group, children can gain the courage and confidence necessary to exercise a measure of independence from adult controls.

The social maturity of children develops rapidly in the early school years. A. Jackson Stenner and William G. Katzenmeyer (1976) found that in one school system 50 percent of the first-graders said they would rather play with younger children, a figure that dropped to one-third among third-graders. Further, whereas one out of three first-graders would rather play alone, less than one in five third-graders reported such a preference. And while being with other children bothered one out of three first-graders, this was true of only one out of five third-graders.

Although as children move through the early school years they typically exhibit a higher level of social maturity, they also are more likely to report that other children do not like them and are "mean" and try "to take advantage" of them (Stenner and Katzenmeyer, 1976). Indeed, it appears that some children go through school with few or no friends. For instance, Norman E. Gronlund (1959) found that about 6 percent of third- through sixth-grade children in one school system were not selected by any classmate on a sociometric questionnaire (see the boxed insert on pages 459–460); an additional 12 percent were selected by only one classmate.

Aggression

One of the complicating and often disconcerting aspects of classroom life to teachers and students alike is the recurrent and inappropriately aggressive behavior of one or more students. **Aggression** is behavior that is socially defined as injurious or destructive. One particularly disheartening and prevalent school problem has to do with those students who are classroom outcasts and the steady targets of cruelty.

Students who are the victims of aggression (they are ridiculed, teased, hit, and pushed about) usually differ from their classmates in appearance or interests. Typically, "whipping boys" are found to be anxious, insecure, and isolated among their peers, with less self-esteem and a more negative attitude toward themselves than boys in general. They also tend to be physically weaker and athletically inept (Olweus, 1977). Research reveals that frequently attacked boys are for the most part unprovocative; rather than attempting to "attract" aggression, they find themselves in situations where they are simply the victims of other children's aggression (Denham and Keese, 1977; Olweus, 1977, 1978). Girls who are victimized tend to be poor students and to be viewed by their classmates as "strange."

School authorities and teachers generally find it difficult to reduce aggressive and antisocial behavior in preadolescent and adolescent boys (Burchard and Harig, 1976). Dan Olweus (1977, 1978) found in his sample of Swedish boys that there was no relationship between the boys' aggressiveness and their popularity (the bullies enjoyed average popularity among their peers). The bullies tended to be average or slightly below average in school ability. This led Olweus to conclude that the boys' bullying behavior did not derive from unusual frustration or failure in the school setting. On the

SOCIOMETRIC TECHNIQUES

Sociometry is a method for assessing patterns of attraction, rejection, or indifference among members of a group. It is a relatively simple technique in which the investigator asks individuals to indicate those individuals with whom they prefer to associate. A typical sociometric questionnaire is shown in Figure 15.B. The data secured from a sociometric questionnaire can, in turn, be represented in a **sociogram,** which graphically shows the patterns of choice existing among members of a group at some point in time (see Figure 15.C).

Sociometric data has a number of uses (Gronlund, 1976; Morrison, 1981): First, they provide a basis for forming congenial committees and work groups. Second, the data assist teachers in identifying students who are encountering difficulty in social adjustment. Third, they provide information teachers can use to evaluate the influence of given practices on students' social relations. And fourth, the data provide insights for using peer ties to channel and build classroom cohesiveness. Teachers who employ sociometric techniques report that they have at times misjudged the network of relationships prevailing among their pupils. Classroom interaction is so complex that even the keenest observer is likely to overlook some elements.

Name _____

DIRECTIONS: Read the sentences below. Write the names of the students in our class whom you would like to be with you for each activity. Include students who are absent. Your choices will <u>not</u> be seen by anyone but you and your teacher.

1. SCIENCE PROJECT: I would like to work with these students on a science project:

First Choice: _____

Second Choice: _____

Third Choice: _____

2. FIELD TRIP: I would like these children to be in my group when we go on our next field trip:

First Choice: _____

Second Choice: _____

Third Choice: _____

3. PARTY COMMITTEE: I would like to plan a party with these students:

First Choice: _____

Second Choice: _____

Third Choice: _____

FIGURE 15.B SOCIOMETRIC QUESTIONNAIRE
This sociometric test identifies three activities and asks for first, second, and third choices. The choices should reflect real ongoing classroom activities. Each student's choices should be kept confidential. The choices should be used by the teacher in organizing some classroom activities. *(continued)*

SOCIOMETRIC TECHNIQUES
(continued)

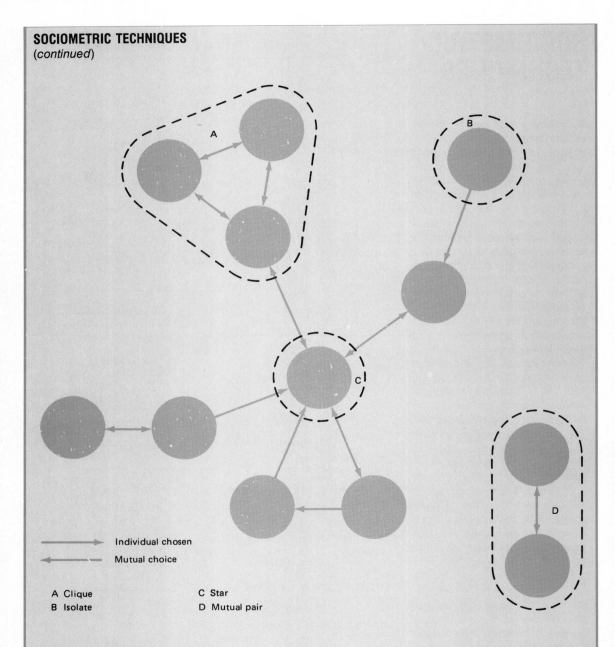

FIGURE 15.C SIMPLIFIED SOCIOGRAM
Sociometry is a simple technique that is inexpensive and easy to administer. The data gathered by a sociometric questionnaire can be graphically depicted to portray the network of relationships and to identify popular individuals (stars), cliques, friendship pairs, and social isolates.

whole the aggressive boys were nonanxious, confident, masculine, and self-assured. Olweus concluded that the aggressive behavior of the bullies did not have its primary origin in the school environment. Rather, the boys appeared to bring relatively established tendencies toward aggression with them to the school.

Other researchers point out that not all children internalize the social norm that aggression is reprehensible (Bandura, 1973b; Perry and Perry, 1974). For some youths delinquent behavior is often a source of self-satisfaction and heightened feelings of self-worth and pride. These youths are socialized in contexts where direct reinforcement for aggression and exposure to aggressive models are common (Lefkowitz et al., 1977). Aggressive interactions become an important part of their lives (Perry and Bussey, 1977).

CHAPTER SUMMARY

1. One of the basic beliefs of our educational system is that reduced class size provides a more desirable learning environment for students and increases the teacher's effectiveness. However, research dealing with the influence of the student-to-teacher ratio on pupil learning is contradictory and inconclusive. It is conceivable that if classes were reduced to ten or fewer students, then class size might make a difference.

2. One of the issues hotly debated in recent decades is ability grouping. Proponents of ability grouping argue that it allows pupils to advance at their own rate with others of similar capabilities and permits teachers to adapt methods and materials to their students. Critics believe that children's self-concepts are adversely affected by ability grouping and that ability grouping goes against the grain of American ideals and democratic principles.

3. The only consistently active communicator in most classroom interaction is the teacher. Much of the communication is one-way. Since the teacher

functions as the communication "gatekeeper" in the classroom, student initiative in communication interaction is frequently blocked. The physical arrangement of the classroom also does much to structure communication patterns.

4. The best way to describe open education is to specify the characteristics commonly used to distinguish it from traditional approaches: (1) Manipulative materials are supplied in great diversity and range; (2) the physical environment is characterized by the flexible use of space, including open doors, work areas in corridors, and tables and chairs instead of desks; (3) teachers base their instruction on each individual child and the child's interaction with materials and equipment; (4) teachers behave in a warm, responsive manner toward the students.

5. An accumulating body of research is providing an answer to the question of what it is about an effective school that makes it effective. Perhaps the most critical element is the "ethos" of the school—the overall tone. A sense of social order and community and high academic expectations pervade successful schools. Much depends on a school's leader, usually the principal. Effective schools are typically led by principals who provide assertive, achievement-oriented leadership; an orderly, purposeful, and peaceful school climate; high expectations for teachers and students; and well-designed instructional objectives and evaluation systems.

6. Several clusters or patterns of teacher behaviors are consistently related to student gains. One cluster has to do with teacher expectations. Effective teachers view the instruction of students in the curriculum as central to their role. Another cluster revolves about direct instruction. Direct instruction entails active or intentional teaching. The teacher presents the process or concept under study, supervises student work, and holds students accountable for their work. Still another cluster of teacher behaviors has to do with teacher managerial skills. If teachers are to instruct students effectively, they must be well prepared, proceed quickly from one activity to another, limit interruptions and intrusions, and control negative behavior.

7. A variety of studies reveal that teachers feel differently about different children in their classrooms. These various attitudes have consequences for a teacher's behavior toward particular children. For instance, researchers find that teachers rate children thought to be attractive by prevailing cultural standards more favorably than they do unattractive children. Teachers' assessment of students are also affected by their stereotypes of different racial and social class groups. And finally, evidence exists for gender bias within schools.

8. Some educators and psychologists say that teachers reflect their differing expectancies in their interactions with children and thus produce differential achievement among them. The term "teacher-expectation effects" has been coined to refer to this tendency. There are, however, two competing causal explanations of the relationship between teacher expectations and students' academic performance. Robert Rosenthal and Lenore Jacobson set forth the view that teachers are the causal agents whose varying expectations influence the differential development of pupils' skills and abilities. The other interpretation holds that student achievement shapes teacher expectations. According to this viewpoint, teachers make valid assessments of children's abilities and reflect these expectations in adapting their instruction to each student's unique needs.

9. Boys and girls differ in their classroom behavior and performance. For instance, school-related problems are three to four times higher for boys than for girls. Some educators suggest that the reason for the greater academic problems among boys derives from having large female staffs. However, there are not any firm data that female teachers treat boys and girls differently. Further, the great majority of studies reveals that male and female teachers on the whole treat their male and female students similarly.

10. Researchers have typically proceeded from the assumption that the flow of classroom interaction is from teachers to students. Viewed from this perspective, teachers act and students respond. Such formulations overlook the fact that teachers do not play their roles in a social vacuum. A two-way or reciprocal relationship exists among teachers and students.

11. Peer relationships assume a vital part in children's development and provide a critical ingredient within the educational enterprise. Students exert a strong influence on one another's cognitions, attitudes, and behaviors, all of which affect academic performance.

12. One particularly disheartening and prevalent school problem has to do with those students who are classroom outcasts and the steady targets of cruelty. Typically, "whipping boys" are found to be anxious, insecure, and isolated among their peers, with less self-esteem and a more negative attitude toward themselves than boys in general. They also tend to be physically weaker and athletically inept.

CHAPTER GLOSSARY

ability grouping The practice of placing together children of a given age and grade who have nearly the same standing on measures of learning achievement or capability.

aggression Behavior that is socially defined as injurious or destructive.

desegregation The removal of formal barriers within a society, both legal and social, that are premised upon racial or ethnic membership.

integration The acceptance of individuals without regard to their racial or ethnic membership within informal, personal, intimate, and voluntary relationships.

open education An umbrella concept referring to approaches that stress individual differences in learning and the informal structuring of the schooling process.

peers Individuals of roughly the same age.

social system A configuration in which individuals are bound together within a relatively enduring network of relationships.

sociogram   A diagram showing the patterns of choice existing among members of a group at some point in time.

sociometry   A method for assessing patterns of attraction, rejection, or indifference among members of a group.

teacher-expectation effects   Beliefs about other people affect the way we behave toward them, and the way we behave often causes the other people to respond just as we expected they would.

team teaching   A type of instructional organization in which two or more persons cooperatively plan and implement a learning program for a group of students.

EXERCISES

Review Questions

1. The research in class size has found that
   a. a reduction of average class size by one or two pupils results in a minor decrease in the typical school budget
   b. most teachers do not significantly modify their strategies when class size is reduced to twenty
   c. academic achievement seems to be the only classroom variable significantly affected by classroom size
   d. the achievement curve only begins to show a rapid increase when class size is about fifteen students
   e. b and d are true

2. The proponents and opponents of ability grouping seem to agree that ability grouping
   a. provides a realistic basis for pupils to compare themselves to others
   b. reflects the fact that in real life people group themselves homogeneously
   c. tends to break down segregation barriers
   d. increases student self-esteem
   e. none of the above are true

3. Research comparisons between open and traditional classrooms have shown
   a. achievement in the traditional classroom to be equal or superior to that in open classrooms
   b. open classrooms to be possibly superior in creativity and attitudes toward school
   c. that there is more positive self-esteem in the open classroom
   d. that teachers invariably prefer the open classroom
   e. a and b are true

4. Studies on team teaching indicate that
   a. team teaching is favored over solitary teacher-taught groups in terms of achievement
   b. teachers tend to view the arrangement primarily as an administrative one
   c. team teaching may require time to "take hold"
   d. teachers can identify student problems more easily
   e. b and c are true

5. The least significant aspect of a school in terms of its educational effectiveness is the
   a. school climate
   b. physical plant
   c. academic expectations
   d. sense of order

6. Among the clusters of teacher behaviors associated with effectiveness is
   a. teacher expectation regarding academics
   b. direct instruction
   c. classroom management
   d. a, b, and c are true
   e. b and c are true

7. Summarizing the research on the instructional techniques of good teachers, one would *not* find

 a. strong academic orientation
 b. good managerial skills
 c. lavish use of praise and criticism
 d. careful explanations of content

8. One of the findings of the Brophy and Good study on proactive teaching was that teachers

 a. still preferred supervisory feedback to observational data
 b. could not significantly alter their attitudes toward disabled pupils
 c. increased time spent helping students who did not answer correctly the first time
 d. made changes only after numerous interviews with the researcher

9. Reseach concerning gender differences in classroom teacher behavior and pupil performance has demonstrated that

 a. in all Western societies girls do better than boys in reading
 b. male and female teachers discriminate against pupils of the other sex more frequently
 c. boys tend to receive harsher criticism and more praise than girls
 d. some characteristics of good teachers are sex-linked
 e. c and d are true

10. Which of the following is *not* true about student outcasts?

 a. They have lower self-esteem.
 b. They cannot make friends.
 c. They provoke attacks by others.
 d. They are often distinguishable from peers in appearance and interests.

Answers

1. e (See pp. 430–432)
2. e (See pp. 432–433)
3. e (See p. 441)
4. e (See p. 442)
5. b (See pp. 443–444)
6. d (See pp. 444–446)
7. c (See p. 446)
8. c (See p. 450)
9. c (See pp. 452–453)
10. c (See pp. 458, 461)

Applying Principles and Concepts

1. A consultant to the local school district has made a number of recommendations. Check those that agree with the findings presented in the chapter.

_____ a. Even if class size is cut from thirty-five to thirty at the elementary school level, student achievement will not increase significantly.

_____ b. Ability grouping cannot be recommended on the basis of gains in achievement, for research has not clearly demonstrated that brighter students necessarily do better.

_____ c. One danger in ability grouping is the impact on self-concept; regardless of initial self-concept, however, students in the high group all eventually have more positive self-images.

_____ d. Desks should be clustered, rather than all facing front. Research has shown that students are then more likely to communicate with one another than with the teacher.

2. A professor has sent her students out to observe open-education classrooms and file reports. Following is a section taken from one report. Underline the passages that are *not* considered typical of such classrooms.

Instruction is based on diagnosis of each child's strengths and weaknesses. There are learning centers in each class with lots of materials. The child often helps to decide what she or he wants to do. The teacher stresses competition between them, in order, as she says "to get them to do their best in this kind of environment."

3. Teacher attitudes toward children can be characterized as attachment (A), concern (C), indiffer-

ence (I), or rejection (R). In the space provided before each description of a child, indicate which category is likely to apply.

_____ a. The student is quite a problem in class, a constant source of irritation.

_____ b. The student is one of those kids who will learn ''in spite of the teacher.''

_____ c. The student tries hard but is always in academic difficulty.

_____ d. The student is a ''closed book.''

4. Mr. Snow, a white Anglo, is looking over photographs and all academic records of the students coming into his sixth-grade class. He is new to the school and has never met or seen the students. On the basis of the research described in the textbook, rank each of the following student descriptions from 1 (highest) to 4 (lowest) as determining probable expectations Mr. Snow may have concerning academic achievement.

_____ a. Paul is a rather unattractive boy, white, with below-average grades.

_____ b. Lisa is a very attractive girl, white, with very high grades.

_____ c. Jennifer is an average looking girl, black, with slightly above-average grades.

_____ d. Leonard is an above-average looking boy, Spanish-American, with above-average grades.

5. Assume that Mr. Snow in Question 4 has acquired additional information on the social development of each child. According to Crano and Mellon's research (1979), which of the children would be likely to produce the most conflict in Mr. Snow's expectations?

_____ a. Paul is very poor socially.

_____ b. Lisa is above average in terms of social development.

_____ c. Jennifer is quite a bit behind socially.

_____ d. Leonard is quite adept socially.

6. Following are a number of high-school situations involving attempts at desegregation. Place a checkmark before those situations in which positive intergroup relationships are more likely to occur. The minority group in this instance is black.

_____ a. SCHOOL A: Students have been drawn from racially segregated neighborhoods; school population comes from markedly different socioeconomic levels.

_____ b. SCHOOL B: Students have been drawn from racially segregated neighborhoods; the school minority population is less than 10 percent.

_____ c. SCHOOL C: Students have been drawn from racially segregated neighborhoods; school population from all groups is primarily upper-middle class.

_____ d. SCHOOL D: Students have been drawn from racially segregated neighborhoods; school athletic teams are not segregated and are very successful.

7. Below are a number of sociograms. Indicate which represents a clique (C), isolate (I), star (S), and mutual pair (MP).

_____ a.

_____ b.

_____ c.

_____ d.

Answers

1. a, b (See pp. 430–437)
2. Underline ''teacher stresses competition.'' (See pp. 439–441)
3. a, R; b, A; c, C; d, I (See p. 447)
4. a, 4; b, 1; c, 3; d, 2 (See pp. 447–448)

5. c (See p. 452)
6. c, d (See pp. 456–457)
7. a, I; b, MP; c, S; d, C (See pp. 459–460)

Project 1

OBJECTIVE: To assess the accuracy of teachers' perceptions of student-student relationships.

PROCEDURE: Visit a classroom, and ask permission to conduct a sociometric analysis. An elementary school classroom may be preferable. Tell the teacher you will share the results:

1. Ask the teacher to select one student who would be a popular choice—a star—and one who would be an isolate if the class members were asked the following question: ''Name three children with whom you would like to plan a party.''

2. Prepare a sociogram by asking each child to submit the names of three classmates with whom he or she would like to plan a party (see pp. 459–460).

ANALYSIS: Sociograms can be quite complex, but we shall try to simplify this one:

1. Distribute the names of all the children on a large sheet of paper, and circle each name. Do not put the names all in a row.
2. Take each sheet on which a child has listed three names, and draw an arrow from the child's name to those chosen. That is, if Mary chose Beth, Paul, and John, you draw:

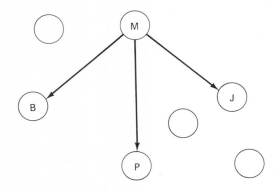

3. As you go through the lists, you will find evidence of mutual attraction. For example, Beth also chose Mary. As you already have an arrow from Mary to Beth, make it a double arrow:

4. When the sociogram is complete, look for the children whom the teacher initially selected. The star should have been chosen by at least five or six children, the isolate by one or no one.
5. Show the data to the teacher. Do they coincide with her expectations? What other findings surprise her? Discuss the implications.

Project 2

OBJECTIVE: To compare teacher perceptions and student performance.

PROCEDURE: You can use a classroom at any level. Your task will be to locate a student who has done very well with one teacher but not with another. At the elementary school level, this difference will involve teachers in different grades, whereas at the secondary school level, it will involve teachers in different courses. Interview the teacher in whose class the student has done well and also the one in whose class the student has done poorly. Use the following questions as a guide:

1. How well do you remember _____?
2. How would you describe _____?
3. Why, do you think, _____did well (or poorly) in your class?
4. Were you surprised that she (he) did well (or poorly) in _____'s class? Why?

ANALYSIS: There are two levels of analysis you can use. Do not use data from a teacher whose answer to Question 1 indicates poor recollection:

1. Look at the answers from Question 2, and determine whether the relation between traits used to describe the student and teacher expectations fits the research described in this chapter of the textbook. Can you locate any unusual findings?

2. Look at the data from Questions 3 and 4. Can you determine differences between teachers in the categories used (physical, social, intellectual, and so on)? Does your data lead you to believe that teacher gender is involved? Why?

CHAPTER OUTLINE

16

CLASSROOM MANAGEMENT

CHAPTER PREVIEW

As Chapter 15 indicated, effective classroom management is an essential ingredient in effective instruction. Further, beginning teachers, especially, identify control of a class as one of their major concerns, if not the most important one. This chapter will show that successful classroom management and discipline are very different from a system of harsh, punitive measures. In fact, they derive primarily from careful planning, good organization, consistency, and smooth pacing of instruction. Various approaches to classroom management are described, with particular attention given to research illustrating how good classroom managers begin the school year and to behavior modification strategies. How peer groups can be used to help achieve control, as well as how self-control (by students) might be fostered, are also considered.

As you read this material, consider the following questions:

■ What are some of the characteristics, identified by Kounin, of teachers with good management skills?
■ What can teachers do at the beginning of the year to help ensure a smoothly functioning classroom thereafter?
■ How else can teachers help prevent discipline problems?
■ How can behavior modification strategies be used in the classroom? When might they be most useful?
■ How can students be encouraged to employ self-control?

Teaching involves both instruction and management. Instructional activities are aimed at attaining specific educational outcomes. Management activities attempt to establish and maintain conditions under which instruction can occur effectively and efficiently (Buckley and Cooper, 1978). Teachers spend about two-thirds of class time on these two activities (Flanders, 1963; Gump, 1967).

Adequate control of a class is a prerequisite to achieving instructional goals. A classroom that is "out of control" is hardly a pleasant experience for either teachers or students. Accordingly, a successful teacher must function as a manager of group behavior—a kind of ringmaster who channels and orchestrates an incredible number and variety of interpersonal interchanges (Jackson, 1968).

CLASSROOM DISCIPLINE

To many, the terms "classroom management" and "classroom discipline" have an unpleasant connotation. "Managing" often conveys the notion of manipulating in some devious or secretive manner. And "discipline" is equated by some with repression, coercion, czarism, tyranny, and authoritarianism (McDaniel, 1977). Yet effective classroom management and discipline are at the opposite ends of the spectrum from these concepts. When classroom management is inept and discipline is weak, students are frustrated and learning is placed in jeopardy (McCarthy, 1977).

Nature of Discipline Problems

The American public has identified discipline as the number-one problem facing the schools in twelve of the last thirteen annual Gallup polls (Gallup, 1981). Order in the classroom is also a primary concern for teachers. It is particularly worrisome for beginning teachers. How will they manage a room full of energetic and at times unruly youngsters? How will they "stay on top" of the classroom action and "turn on" so many different and contrasting types of students? Will they be able to "survive" for an entire academic year? Indeed, the inability to manage their classrooms is the single most important factor in why many novice teachers fail (Vittetoe, 1977).

Surveys of the incidence of problem behavior in school-aged children reveal that teachers view 20 to 30 percent of the general school population as having problems at any one time. Only a small number of this group, perhaps 2 to 3 percent, show recurrent or persistent problems in adjusting to school situations (Wood and Zabel, 1978). In the course of their schooling experience, approximately one-half of all students experience a learning or adjustment problem serious enough to be recorded on their cumulative records (Kindsvatter, 1978).

Daniel L. Duke, (1978) surveyed school administrators in New York state and California high schools to identify their most pressing problems. Truancy (absence from school without permission), skipping class (absence from class without permission), and lateness to class were singled out respectively as their number-one, two, and three problems. They identified their least pressing problems as profanity, fighting, and drug use.

Sources of Classroom Authority

The basis of classroom management lies in the authority inherent in the position of teacher as supervisor. John R. P. French and Bertram Raven identify five sources of supervisory power (French and Raven, 1959; Collins and Raven, 1969; Raven, 1974):

- *Reward and coercive power:* Reward and coercive power derives from the ability of one party to determine the rewards or punishments received by another party.
- *Legitimate power:* One party is recognized as having a right to make decisions involving another party.
- *Expert power:* Expert power derives from the

knowledge, experience, skills, or special competence that one party possesses or is believed to possess.

- *Informational power:* Power frequently depends less on the social relationship than on the specific content of the communication or new facts that are transmitted.
- *Referent power:* Referent power operates when one party looks up to another party as a model and a "frame of reference" for self-evaluation.

Research reveals that supervisors who manage primarily with expert, informational, and referent power are most successful as group leaders (Vander Zanden, 1984). This is hardly surprising, since individuals come to take on the behaviors preferred by their supervisors; they undergo an authentic change in their behavior. In contrast, reward-coercive and legitimate power do not necessarily entail an underlying change in people's motivation for engaging in given activities. They may conform simply because they find it expedient to do so. The primary duty of teachers is to mobilize students around the various tasks that are to be done. This is most effectively achieved when teachers gain the willing compliance of their pupils. When teachers focus on power without consideration of whether or not the students believe their instructions are legitimate, they invite student opposition (Larkin, 1975).

Regardless of the provisions of state law or school board regulations, the actual exercise of teacher authority is an uncertain and precarious enterprise (Wegmann, 1976). As sociologist Chester Barnard observes, "Authority lies always with him to whom it applies" (1964:183). Much of the responsibility for classroom order falls on the students themselves. There are a great many ways that students can challenge a teacher's authority, including coming late to class, doing the exact opposite of what one was told, loudly slamming a book, and making insulting remarks. When a student fails to follow a teacher's request, how other students react is often critical. If they respond negatively, the student then faces peer disapproval and is not likely to continue. Hence, teachers must

engage in many-sided management, negotiating their way through a surprisingly complex and highly problematic series of interaction sequences (Wegmann, 1976).

Classroom Climate and Leadership Styles

Effective teachers are those who are, shall we say, "human" in the fullest sense of the word. They have a sense of humor, are fair, empathetic, more democratic than autocratic, and apparently are more able to relate easily and naturally to students on either a one-to-one or group basis.

DON HAMACHEK
"Characteristics of Good Teachers," 1971

We hear a good deal nowadays that "the schools should enforce stricter discipline and force the students to shape up." Yet experienced classroom teachers know that becoming more stringent and repressive often serves to worsen an already difficult situation. A more thoughtful solution lies in finding ways to improve the classroom climate.

The climate of a classroom has been likened to an "organizational personality." Just as each individual has a unique personality, so each classroom has its unique characteristics—a blend of the various individuals and the classroom environment (Halpin and Croft, 1963; Hamachek, 1977). Classes may be quiet and withdrawn, outgoing and assertive, cold and detached, or warm and receptive. Even subject matter influences classroom climate. For instance, French classes are regularly "closer" in climate to English and history than to mathematics classes (Moos, 1978; Hearn and Moos, 1978).

Fashioning a positive classroom climate cannot be reduced to a formula. It is a tenuous and fluctuating response to a variety of factors (Kindsvatter, 1978). One key ingredient, however, is the teacher's **leadership style**—the instructor's characteristic ways of handling information and of applying sanctions. The manner in which teachers handle their classes can have important conse-

GAMES TEACHERS PLAY

LESLIE J. CHAMBERLAIN AND MORRIS WEINBERGER

Although there are differences of opinion concerning classroom control and methods for achieving it, all teachers will agree that a pleasant, well-disciplined classroom atmosphere results in more effective learning for all. Good teachers realize that to a very large extent they themselves create the climate in their classrooms. But even a good teacher may play classroom "games" that lead to pupil boredom and disinterest, and result in behavior problems.

The game of ambiguous rules, for example, is a common cause of classroom disturbance. Teacher and pupils learn the rules and then spend hours playing the game with repeated student testing to make the rules specific. In "How

Source: Leslie J. Chamberlain and Morris Weinberger, "Games Teachers Play," *Instructor*, 80 (February 1971):69.

wide is an aisle?" for example, the students' team "scores" whenever there is a foot in the aisle without reprimand and the teacher "scores" when he catches someone. Repeated trials by students, with a scolding each time ("Get your foot out of the aisle"), result in both sides' eventually agreeing on an imaginary line that is the boundary. A foot inside or on the line is acceptable but one-quarter inch over is not. This game may take an hour to play on a day early in the fall but is played more quickly when students reopen the game out of boredom in the spring. Similar games are "But you've been to the bathroom" (a game more often won by students) and "When is a pencil dull?" (a game the teacher usually wins).

Uncritical enforcement of traditional rules is another cause of classroom misbehavior. Too often teachers perpetuate rules without

knowing why they do so, what purpose the rules serve, or what the total effect of the rule is on either the class as a whole or an individual student.

Among the most common classroom "games" are the teacher's attitudes and behavior. Children behave much like the adults around them. While it is flattering to have a student imitate him, the teacher must realize that anything he does before children, for good or ill, remains with them longer than most adults realize. Though a teacher may recognize the pupil imitations of his virtues, it is much more difficult to recognize faults secondhand, and he may be using a teaching technique which has become a disciplinary pitfall and the cause of problem after problem. Flippant remarks, sarcasm, and unfriendly looks are often unconsciously used in teaching. A person who is truly objective will notice antagonistic

quences for their students' learning, satisfaction, and development (Baird, 1973).

Through the years the classic experiments in leadership by Kurt Lewin and his associates (Lewin, Lippitt, and White, 1939; Lippitt, 1939; White and Lippitt, 1960) have generated considerable enthusiasm among researchers in education and

group dynamics. In these pioneering investigations, adult leaders working with groups of eleven-year-old boys were trained to follow three leadership styles: (1) an *authoritarian* style, in which the leader formulated group goals, dictated activities, set forth work procedures, assigned members to tasks, used personal praise and criticism, and

or belligerent pupil feedback, but many teachers fail to recognize it. When one *knows* one is right, it is hard to hear or see contradictory evidence.

The art of listening is not to be taken lightly, for this is how the teacher interprets what people, especially his students, are trying to tell him. Unfortunately, most teachers feel they are listening when they are only hearing the words. Listening involves understanding from the speaker's viewpoint, a detail often missed by even good teachers. Teaching involves the interactions of human beings and a good teacher learns from what he hears as well as from what he sees.

Teachers should also realize that the life goals of children and of adults are usually different, and that children of different ages have different goals. A student's actions should be evaluated in terms of the individual or group goal being sought at the time. A student will select from his different behavioral patterns the actions he believes will help him to achieve his personal goal and then behave accordingly. Teachers who learn to adjust their thinking to what is appropriate student behavior in terms of the child's age and his goals will seldom need to

apply external controls. Failure to see this viewpoint means that the teacher will be out of step with his class most of the time, and have many disciplinary situations.

Using the lecture method is a pitfall for many beginning teachers. It often fails to meet the interest, needs, and abilities of the students. Yet a lecture can be an efficient technique occasionally, if the content is at the children's level of understanding, is adapted to student needs and goals, and is brief. A teacher who comes to class poorly prepared, with a bare minimum of correct information, and no thought of its interest level, should hardly be surprised when the students fail to pay the rapt attention he would like.

Too many people believe that a knowledge of subject matter is nearly all of the professional preparation required to teach. This point of view defines learning as the mere acquisition of actual knowledge. But learning affects not only factual knowledge but habits, understandings, attitudes, emotional control techniques, and social values as well. In fact, learning to like to learn may be the most important thing a teacher can help a student acquire.

Some problems develop from

the way a teacher implements his teaching. Classwork that is too advanced, too verbal, or in a poorly planned sequence will create difficult situations for both the teacher and the students. Behavior standards that are too high or too low, or a classroom that has too much or too little organization, may result in boredom or fatigue.

An important factor affecting the environment of every classroom today is the increased emphasis on education. Students are expected to read more, study more, write more, and learn more. The problems posed by this pressure are creating anxiety and additional indirect disciplinary pressures within the classroom. It takes conscious effort and constant readjustment for even experienced teachers to match their teaching to student needs, abilities, interest, and time.

Many problems of discipline are actually responses to inadvertent teacher behavior. Difficult as self-assessment always is, a conscientious teacher will examine his day-to-day habits with care, to make certain that what he calls student misbehavior isn't really his, and to understand the behavior games that he and his students play.

remained aloof from participation; (2) a *democratic* style, in which the leader submitted policies, activities, and work procedures for group decision, outlined goals and suggested alternative procedures, let the group arrive at its own division of labor, was objective in praise and criticism, and exhibited group spirit; and (3) a *laissez-faire* style,

in which the leader supplied materials but adopted a passive, uninvolved stance and refused to provide structure, make suggestions, or render help in answering questions.

In general the researchers found that authoritarian leadership was accompanied by high levels of frustration and some degree of aggression toward

LEADERSHIP STYLES
Teachers show considerable variation in their leadership styles—their characteristic
ways of handling information or applying sanctions.

the leader. When the leader was present, productivity was high; when the leader was absent, productivity sagged severely. Under democratic leadership the boys were happier, felt more group-minded and friendly, exhibited more independence (especially when the leader was absent), and displayed lower levels of aggressive behavior than the other groups. Laissez-faire leadership was least conducive to productivity. In fact, productivity actually went up in the leader's absence. Considerable in-group aggression characterized the laissez-faire groups.

The work of Lewin and his associates prompted any number of educational researchers to explore the relative effects of "authoritarian" and "democratic" leadership styles on learning. Other labels that have often been employed to designate a somewhat similar kind of dichotomy have included "teacher-centered" versus "student-centered," "directive" versus "nondirective," and "leader-centered" versus "group-centered instruction. On the whole, this research has shown that neither the authoritarian nor democratic procedures are consistently related to greater learning. A major difficulty encountered by this research is that the terms are so global that they fail to discriminate among the particulars of leadership behavior.

Classroom Behaviors of Teachers

Teachers differ in their classroom management skills. Jacob S. Kounin (1970) undertook a number of studies in which he compared videotapes of successful and unsuccessful classroom managers. The classrooms of successful teachers ran smoothly and more or less "automatically," while those of unsuccessful teachers were chaotic and strife-rid-

COLLECTIVE BEHAVIOR
Social contagion operates to communicate patterns of collective behavior among students. Here a child looks down a sewer. Other children, intrigued by his behavior, join the activity.

den. Kounin had initially expected that the two groups of teachers would differ in the manner in which they handled misbehavior. Accordingly, he carefully scrutinized the tapes to determine the degree of clarity, firmness, and intensity with which the teachers handled discipline problems. Yet, he could not identify any differences between successful and unsuccessful teachers in their techniques for coping with classroom misbehavior.

In analyzing the videotapes, however, Kounin

gradually came to identify a variety of classroom management practices that set the two groups of teachers apart. The first of these Kounin termed *withitness*. Teachers who were "with it" communicated to their students that they knew "what was going on." They were teachers with the proverbial "eyes in the back of the head." Withit teachers were sensitive to early clues of misbehavior and promptly intervened.

Good timing and being on target (accurately

THE EYE-CONTACT METHOD

FREDERIC H. JONES

Let's say you want to shape up your classroom. There are many disruptions and you're trying to get on top of them. First, review classroom rules. Keep only those you really want to enforce. These should be the few that even people who differ philosophically wouldn't quibble with. Very simple things like sharing, not bothering each other. Beyond that, any rule you make is simply to suit your format. For example, if a student is working independently with certain math materials, getting up and going to the math center is not breaking a rule at all. However, getting up and kicking his

Source: Frederic H. Jones, "The Eye-Contact Method," *Instructor,* 88 (November 1978):64.

buddy's desk on the way is. So the rules should reflect whatever is sensible. Explain the difference between disruption and nondisruption. "You can work with your neighbor as long as you don't get too loud." If kids know from experience what you mean by "too loud," then it's a perfectly enforceable rule. If they don't know, and you don't know, then your enforcement will be inefficient.

Second, arrange your classroom in a U-shape, semicircle, or other configuration that is compact and open so that you can move in a small area and be close to any child.

Third, move among the kids, during group discussions, while giving individual help, or just walking as you talk with the kids.

Fourth, catch disruptions early. As soon as something starts, deal with it. Now we'll talk about how.

Being assertive is the key. Assertiveness is 95 percent body language. Sometimes it's difficult to be assertive without feedback because most people aren't aware of what they're doing with their bodies. You can come across as *tentative* even though you're trying to be *assertive.* What, then, is assertive body language? First, turn and face the child. If you're not willing to commit your body in that direction, don't expect the child to respond. If you look over your shoulder and say, "Timmy, stop," he won't stop because you haven't said to him with your body that you're going to deal with his

---

identifying the "wrongdoers") were key ingredients in withitness. This allowed successful teachers to employ the *ripple effect* (when the impact of behavior directed toward one or two students influences other students who view the incident) to their advantage. By quickly stopping misbehavior—"nipping it in the bud"—witit teachers prevented the disorder from spreading. Yet they did not overreact or "blow up." As a result they did not contribute to new classroom tension and anxiety that subsequently erupted in additional disciplinary problems.

Another practice Kounin found that successful

teachers employed was *overlapping*—attending to two matters simultaneously. Consider the following illustration. The teacher is working with a reading group. Debbie is reading aloud. Elsewhere in the room Bill and Mark are supposedly doing seatwork but begin intermittent scuffling. The teacher quickly identifies the developing problem and says, "Debbie, continue reading. I'm listening" and then more loudly, "Bill, Mark, back to your seats. Complete your math problems."

Now consider another classroom illustration. The teacher is also working with a reading group. Observing a problem developing between Jeff and

disruptions before you do anything else.

Next, work on facial expressions. Don't yell—that shows a child he's getting your goat and that reinforces his behavior. But don't be sweet because that indicates you're not serious. Just put an edge on your voice and say the student's name in a straight, flat tone.

Next, make eye contact. Drill your eyes right through him. If they dart around, it's like having a conversation with somebody who won't look you in the eye. (You assume from his body language that he's afraid, and it's a correct assumption. The kids will assume the same thing.) So fix your eyes on his. Lean toward him. Don't fold your arms because that's self-protective. Instead extend your hand toward him as you say his name and look him in the eye.

You want the child to quit messing around and get back to work. Maybe he'd rather mess around. At some point you're going to have to raise the ante as in poker until he folds. Watch the child's body. Let's say he is turned toward his neighbor, has his elbow on the desk, and having a conversation. He looks at you but his body is still turned toward his neighbor. What he's saying is "Big deal." Or in poker terms, "I'll raise you." At that point you have a choice. You either play or fold. If you give him a little shake of the finger and say, "Now you get back to work"; and you turn your back on him, you fold. What do you do to raise him? Very slowly walk right up to his desk so your leg is touching it, stand and look at the child. Don't say anything, don't hurry. By that time most kids will fold. They'll turn around, they'll pick up their pencil. At that point you can terminate the interaction by simply reinforcing it and saying, "Good." Stay for three seconds looking right at the child.

Let's say the kid doesn't fold. He's still turned sideways with his elbow on his buddy's desk. What now? It's one thing to say "I mean business" and another thing to enforce it. At this point, put your palms flat down on his desk and face him at his level. Stay there until he caves in. Now, suppose he's turned away from you toward his buddy. Then face him at his level, right between him and his buddy. At this point, he'll probably decide that it's a lot easier to turn around and settle down to work.

Over a period of time, teacher control follows a predictable sequence. Early in the school year, you might go through this entire routine. But when children learn you follow through consistently, that you can't be undone, or faked out, they will quit testing you. A couple of weeks later you will say a kid's name and he'll stop what he was doing, not because of what you said, but because . . . there's a 100 percent probability that if he doesn't stop, he'll get the eyeball treatment!

Several weeks later you may then go from verbal to nonverbal. You might just make the gesture, and get the same response from the child because you have been consistent about the few simple meaningful rules your class knows must be followed.

Mike, the teacher gets up and walks over to the two boys and angrily declares, ''Get back in your seats. That's enough of that nonsense. You haven't finished your math problems. Hurry up. Get to it.'' In the interval, Debbie has stopped reading aloud. The teacher returns to the reading group and says, ''Okay, let's continue where we left off.''

In the first example, the teacher remained seated with the reading group and issued a statement to Debbie almost simultaneously with her instruction to Bill and Mark. The teacher attended to both the reading group and the developing discipline problem by overlapping. In this manner the teacher remained ''on top'' of both situations. In contrast, the teacher in the second illustration temporarily ''shut down'' one activity to attend to another, Kounin found that the ability to overlap actions contributed to managerial success in the classroom.

Successful teachers were also adept at handling lesson flow. They *smoothly* initiated, maintained, and terminated activities. In contrast, unsuccessful teachers engaged in behaviors that frequently interrupted the ongoing flow of classroom events. These included *stimulus-boundedness* (the teacher became easily distracted and would pay attention to irrelevant details); *thrusts* (the teacher would "burst in" on the children's activity with an order, statement, or question); *dangles* (the teacher would introduce an idea and then leave it "hanging in mid-air" only to pick it up at some later time); and *flip-flops* (the teacher would terminate one activity, start another, and then initiate a return to the activity that had been terminated).

In addition, successful teachers had a feeling for maintaining class *momentum*. They did not overdwell on how the children were behaving and they did not continually "nag" or "preach" to children about their misbehavior. Nor did they preoccupy themselves with instructional details and physical props (pencils, crayons, paper). They minimized boredom by dealing with the substance of a matter and by getting on with learning tasks. Further, successful teachers avoided excessive fragmentation. In contrast, unsuccessful teachers would have members of the class do things singly and separately that a whole group could do better as a unit and at one time (this would result in significant "waits"). Likewise, unsuccessful teachers would break a meaningful unit of instruction into subparts when the behavior could be better performed as a single, uninterrupted sequence.

Finally, successful teachers held their students *accountable* for work. The teachers monitored and maintained student performance during recitations. Other accountability behaviors include requiring students to show their work or recite as a group, calling for a show of hands to indicate readiness to perform, and circulating about the classroom to check pupils' work.

APROACHES TO CLASSROOM CONTROL

All teachers are faced at one time or another with the problem of a noisy, disruptive classroom. Disorder impairs pupils' academic progress. Yet disciplinary problems occur at all grade levels from kindergarten through high school. Although class-room management cannot be reduced to a formula, a good deal of contemporary research has provided teachers with a repertoire of strategies to maximize desirable student behavior and minimize undesirable behavior.

Prevention

Good academics compete with disruptive behavior and good academics are the main way to avert poor behavior.

HOWARD N. SLOANE
Classroom Management, 1976

Many educators are convinced that the key to successful classroom management is the *prevention* of disciplinary problems. And the heart of prevention is keeping students actively engaged in productive activities. Indeed, researchers find that teachers can control disruptive behavior by strengthening academic behavior (Ayllon and Roberts, 1974). As Kounin's research revealed, successful teachers are not notably better than other teachers in dealing with problems once they have arisen. But by carefully planning and pacing instruction, successful teachers keep students engaged in learning endeavors, thus preventing problems from getting started in the first place.

Below are presented in summary form a list of "teacher-should" statements that have been extracted from various research reports:

1. Teachers should provide students with a set of rules that allows them to attend to their personal and procedural needs without constantly checking with the teacher (Jackson, 1968; Brophy and Evertson, 1976; Gage, 1978). These rules should be:
   a. Relatively few in number so as to be manageable;
   b. Fairly general and flexible so that the teacher can interpret them strictly or loosely depending on the immediate situation; and
   c. Well-explained at the beginning of the year so that the students understand each rule and the reason behind it.

HEADS ON DESKS
In order to break the self-perpetuating quality of widespread classroom disorder or to mark the end of a free period, some teachers have the students cease all interaction for a brief time and place their heads on their desks.

2. Teachers should set forth rules covering five broad categories of behavior (Jackson, 1968). These deal with the questions of:
   a. Who may enter and leave the room and under what circumstances;
   b. How much noise is acceptable;
   c. How to respect an individual's privacy and rights in a crowded setting;
   d. What to do when work assignments are prematurely completed; and
   e. What general standards of social etiquette will prevail.

3. Teachers should keep their daily directions to the class to a minimum. One mechanism is to write the daily schedule on the board (Gage, 1978).

4. Teachers should move about the classroom frequently, monitoring students' work and communicating to their students an awareness of their behavior (Brophy and Evertson, 1976; Gage, 1978; Emmer et al., 1980, 1981).

5. Teachers should develop ''automatic''mechanisms so that students can get help if they need it. Often one or more students can be designated as the person or persons to whom a fellow student can turn for help with an assignment (Brophy and Evertson, 1976; Emmer et al., 1980, 1981).

6. Teachers should hold each student accountable for the appropriate completion of an assignment, and the student should know that his or her

NO RESPONSE? ASK YOURSELF THESE QUESTIONS

GLORIA GILBERT

Each year you are undoubtedly faced by at least one child with a behavior problem. If his behavior is disruptive enough, you will seek help from the principal, the guidance counselor, or the school psychologist. Eventually you may even refer him to a medical or psychiatric clinic for evaluation and treatment. But there are courses of action you can take while a child awaits agency help, or, as is the case in many areas, there is no agency nearby to see the child.

Even after work with health specialists and agency officials major changes in a child's behavior will come about mainly by making environmental changes— at home and at school. Since the classroom is your province, you may, with minor adjustments, be able to effect a noticeable change in your problem child. If you're getting no response in dealing with behavior problems, ask yourself these questions.

- *Does the child understand what he is expected to do?* Some children do not readily understand oral-verbal instructions. Your child may have

Source: Condensed from Gloria Gilbert, "No Response? Ask Yourself These Questions," *Instructor*, 84 (November 1974): 96, 98, 100.

a memory problem and may need you to break down a complex task into a series of smaller operations.

- *Does your child resist doing written assignments?* Does he neglect to complete them, or, worse, does he not even begin? Notice how he holds his pencil. Is his writing slow and laborious? There are exercises available to improve fine motor coordination and to develop efficient writing habits. Put them to use. Also, consider making such accommodations as providing paper with wider spaces, a sample alphabet taped to the child's desk, and, most important, a reduced assignment.
- *Do you find yourself scolding a problem child frequently?* Shift gears and concentrate on what he does right, even if you have to strain to discover what it is. The child will try harder if he feels that you will notice his efforts and that you will praise him appropriately. Instead of paying attention to behaviors you want to get rid of, call attention to those you want to encourage.
- *Do you expect the child to perform at the wrong level?* Wrong, that is, for him? Usu-

ally, "wrong" means *too difficult*. If achievement tests and school records indicate that the child functions at a third-grade reading level, you may expect problems if his assignments are geared to a fifth-grade book. If you think you are too busy to plan other work at a more appropriate level, stop and think. Fifteen minutes of extra planning each day may save the child and will also save considerable wear-and-tear on you. The bright child who may be getting into trouble because he is bored may need a more advanced and challenging program, or, at least, an enriched one.

- *Are you overcorrecting verbal responses or written assignments?* If the pupil is making many errors, reevaluate your expectations. If, however, it is necessary for him to work at the regular class assignment, concentrate on only one or two kinds of errors and help him correct those. Covering a pupil's paper with red pencil corrections will discourage him if he is generally trying. His productivity may "dry up" and soon you will be saying, "He won't work for me! Why?"
- *Does the child refuse to read*

aloud or recite before the class? A child's embarrassment, for whatever reason it is caused, should be respected. If you find that the child has some sort of articulation problem or other speech handicap, share your concern with the parents, and refer the child for a speech and hearing evaluation.

- *Does trouble seem to erupt at the same time every day?* Be your own detective. Is there a disturbance just before lunch when children are hungry and tempers short? Mid-morning milk or juice may be the solution. Are some children overstimulated by recess? Try more structured playground activities. If children fail to settle down after play period, schedule an enjoyable activity requiring quiet attention when the group returns to the classroom.

- *Can you train the explosive child to operate his own defusing device? Can you teach him to recognize the build-up of tension?* Consider allowing him, with a prearranged signal from you, to walk out of the classroom for a tension-releasing drink of water or a trip to the bathroom. Then, when he is calm, permit him to re-enter without paying a penalty. If the child cannot be allowed out of the classroom alone, a sheltered place for quiet withdrawal within the classroom may be provided. Teaching an impulsive child to remove himself from overstimulating situations may be one of the most important lessons of his life.

- *Are you patient with the difficult child? Do you stop to consider the situation from his point of view? Do you listen to his explanation? Or does your tone of voice suggest to the other children in the room that they may "scapegoat" the difficult child and earn subtle approval from you?* Structure the task so that the child can do it acceptably and watch his resistance melt. Clinical studies of poor achieving children have made it clear that such descriptions as "He's lazy," or "He could do it if he would," would be more accurately stated as "He would do it if only he could."

Here, then, is a summary of ways to manage problem children in the classroom:

1. Provide an optional work place for the child which is relatively free of visual and auditory distractions.

2. Reduce assignments in length and divide them into separately assigned parts.

3. Use color for underlining and bordering work sheets so that the child can distinguish important features of the lesson.

4. Make corrections on written work promptly. If possible, give immediate feedback.

5. Don't overcorrect. If there are many errors on the paper, mark only one or two for the child's attention and ignore the others. If the child is making many errors, the work is too difficult. Reteach at a lower level.

6. Select a few basic skills and basic rules of behavior to work on. Let the rest go. Don't overload the child.

7. Give simple, explicit directions for seatwork. Don't just tell the child: *show* him what you expect him to do.

8. Don't talk too much. Use short sentences and brief directions.

9. Try to follow a consistent work schedule in the classroom.

10. Teach a few rules of behavior for the class; then follow them firmly and consistently.

11. Pay more attention to what's right than to what's wrong. Reward effort, no matter how small. Shape behavior by encouraging what is positive, even though it may be only part of the picture. Praise such things as beginning work promptly, paying attention, expressing original ideas, completing work, waiting patiently—in short, any behavior which you value and wish to be continued or increased.

12. Try to convey to the child by your manner that you are not being punitive or impatient. Be honest about recognizing that he has problems which you want to help him with.

13. Use your sense of humor. A lighthearted approach will get and hold the attention of distractible children. Just remember not to ridicule.

work will be checked (Brophy and Evertson, 1976).

7. In recitation sessions, teachers should call on a child by name before asking a question (this ensures the participation of all students) (Gage, 1978).

8. Teachers should minimize "I don't know" responses by rephrasing a question, giving cues, or asking supplementary questions to evoke a response (Gage, 1978).

9. Teachers should cultivate the respect of their students (McDaniel, 1977). Students will respect teachers who:
   a. Know their subject;
   b. Approach their classes with a serious (but not humorless!) purpose;
   c. Conduct the class in an efficient and businesslike way;
   d. Plan lessons thoroughly;
   e. Set reasonable, clearly understood, and fairly administered standards of performance and behavior for the class; and
   f. Respect themselves and their role.

Beginning the School Year

Good classroom management begins immediately with the first day of school. Effective teachers are aware that classroom order and discipline are essential for teaching and learning. Consequently, they assign classroom behavior a top priority as they inaugurate the new school year. They provide the students with clear definitions and expectations for appropriate behavior. Moreover, they promptly undertake to structure and pattern classroom behaviors that are conducive to serious work. These teachers recognize that once a high level of disruptive and disorderly behavior is established, it is exceedingly difficult to reverse (Doyle, 1979).

Researchers like Edmund T. Emmer, Carolyn M. Evertson, and Linda M. Anderson (1980, 1981) find that beginning-of-year activities are critical in determining student cooperation during the re-

mainder of the year. They studied twenty-eight third-grade teachers and their pupils. Successful managers spent a good deal of time during the first three weeks explaining rules to the students and then reminding the students of them. They carefully formulated procedures by which students secured assistance, contacted the teacher, lined up, turned in their work, conducted group work, and undertook seatwork. The effective managers typically reviewed these procedures as "survival" skills and the foundation for a workable learning environment. Some teachers had the students rehearse some of the procedures. And most taught their pupils to respond promptly to specific signals such as the ringing of a bell or the clapping of the hands.

Very often the effective classroom managers launched the initial period of the first school day with a simple, enjoyable task such as drawing and coloring. The teachers remained with the entire class, provided clear, specific instructions, and monitored the pupils closely. Over the ensuing days the teachers gradually introduced new procedures and content. If they had to work with an individual student or carry out some clerical task, they provided the class with a specific assignment and continuously monitored the activities. When misbehavior occurred, it was stopped quickly. Eye contact was employed more frequently by effective than by ineffective managers.

Poorer managers, like the better managers, had rules for their pupils. But the rules were often vague and not clarified, for instance, "Be in the right place at the right time." Moreover, in many instances the ineffective managers introduced rules casually and failed to discuss or elaborate upon them. Nor were the poorer managers as likely as the better managers to review the rules periodically. Perhaps of even greater significance, the ineffective managers frequently failed to monitor classroom behavior and did not follow through on warnings. In effect, they lessened their role as classroom leaders and, by default, allowed students considerable freedom to do as they pleased. In fact, one particularly ineffective teacher left the room three times during the first hour of the first day. In sum, the poorer managers were less likely to work on rules during the first three weeks and to socialize their students within the classroom system than were the better managers.

Behavior Modification Strategies

Over the last two decades a large body of research and many new educational programs have appeared employing a behavioristic approach, especially the principles of operant conditioning (see Chapter 5). Termed **behavior modification,** the approach applies the results of learning theory and experimental psychology to the problem of altering maladaptive behavior (Ullmann and Krasner, 1965). It focuses on the control of actual behavior, what an individual says or does such as talking out of turn or hitting another person. Behavior modification procedures provide classroom teachers with a direct tool for dealing with specific problems without having to delve into deep-rooted psychological mechanisms as do many clinical psychologists and psychiatrists. The aim of behavior modification is not to alter a child's personality but to change only certain problem behaviors. The strategy rests on the assumption that learning depends on the connections between what you do and what subsequently happens to you.

Steps in Behavior Modification

Finding that traditional methods for handling classroom problems are often ineffective, many teachers have sought to implement behavior modification procedures. There are four steps in the use of behavior modification principles (Clarizio, 1976). First, the teacher must define the *specific* behavior that will be the focus of attention. The target behavior should be one that is likely to

TIME-OUT PROCEDURES
Some teachers employ the time-out procedure in which inappropriate behavior is followed by a brief period of social isolation.

contribute significantly to the student's academic and social adjustment. Most frequently a teacher will err by stating an objective in excessively global terms, for instance, ''Getting Mike to behave in class.'' Rather, it is necessary to pinpoint exactly what behavior is to be modified, for example, to stop bothering other children during seatwork, to refrain from talking out of turn, or to desist in playground fighting. The objective should be stated in such a way that it refers to an *observable* behavior, one that lends itself to counting. The teacher should then keep a record over a week's time of the frequency and duration of the behavior (termed a *baseline measure*).

In the second step, the teacher attempts to identify the ABCs of the behavior (Clarizio, 1976). ''A'' refers to the antecedents of the behavior, the environmental event that typically precedes the misbehavior (for instance, an unstructured setting, boredom, or the absence of the skills necessary to complete an assignment). ''B'' is the behavior itself, the target of the modification procedures. ''C'' makes reference to the consequences associated with the behavior, clues as to its reinforcing properties (for example, the misbehavior may result in a reprimand from the teacher that brings the reward of classroom recognition and attention). By examining what happens immediately *before* and *after* the target behavior, the teacher can pinpoint the kind of events that encourage and perpetuate the misbehavior.

Having identified the ABCs, the teacher is ready to begin the third step—the selection of techniques. Charles H. Madsen, Jr., Wesley C. Becker, and D. R. Thomas (1968) have employed a threefold strategy of *rules, praise,* and *ignoring* for dealing with talking or seat-sitting problems. The teacher formulates four or five explicit rules for behavior with the child's help (''Sit quietly while working,'' ''Walk,'' ''Raise hand,'' and so forth). A number of times each day the teacher reviews the rules with the child. Praise and approval are employed to reinforce appropriate behavior, based on the tenet, ''Catch the child being good'' (''I like the way you are staying in your seat and getting your work done, Mike''). Disruptive behavior is ig-

nored, unless it involves hurting another child, so as not to reward the behavior inadvertently.

The fourth step involves an evaluation of the results of the behavior change program. The teacher continues recording the frequency of the misbehavior. Based on this feedback, the teacher can determine the effectiveness of given strategies.

Contingency Management

Contingency management refers to the rearrangement of environmental rewards and punishments to strengthen or weaken specified behaviors (Tharp and Wetzel, 1969: Lovaas and Bucher, 1974). Chapter 5 considered at some length the principle of reinforcement and the principle of punishment. It also examined various schedules of reinforcement and shaping and extinction procedures. The reader may wish to review the material in Chapter 5 dealing with these matters since it is these mechanisms that provide the foundations for contingency management.

Token Economies

Over the past decade token reinforcement systems have become one of the most prominent techniques for modifying children's classroom behavior (Kazdin, 1977). The approach commonly operates as a miniature economy similar in many ways to that of the larger society. Within everyday life money functions as a token or medium of exchange. Although money in its own right does not satisfy any basic needs, it can be exchanged for services and objects that do. Accordingly, money is a generalized conditioned reinforcer (MacMillan, 1973).

In much the same way, some teachers who are confronted with twenty or more children who differ in terms of what is reinforcing to them have turned to a token economy on a slightly different scale. But instead of money, the token is some stimulus like a poker chip, a checkmark, a star, a stamp, or a numerical rating that can be exchanged by a student for some desired object or activity. The objects and activities for which the tokens are

THE INADVERTENT REINFORCEMENT OF MISBEHAVIOR

Just as teachers train students, students also train teachers. In this case, they [students] train us to shout and to become upset over them. Such attention, although unpleasant, is nonetheless better than none.

Harvey F. Clarizio
Toward Positive Classroom Discipline, 1976

Some teachers disapprove of the use of behavior modification principles. Or they may not consciously apply the procedures since the procedures strike them as complicated and time-consuming. Nonetheless, they may be unwittingly modifying behavior by these very techniques. Since behavior is largely determined by its consequences, behavior that produces positive consequences is likely to be repeated. This principle often conjures visions of a teacher with a large bag of candy "bribing" students. Yet, the most prevalent reinforcers employed by teachers are their own behaviors—their use of praise, attention, and proximity (Broughton, 1974).

Many teachers rely primarily on negative responses to control their classrooms. In fact, classroom observational studies show that in every grade after second, the rate of teachers' verbal disapproval tends to exceed the rate of teachers' verbal approval (White, 1975). This can have major consequences, since research reveals that teachers who employ primarily negative methods for handling disruptive behavior actually serve to maintain and even increase the incidence of this very behavior. Charles H. Madsen, Jr., and his associates (1968) found that the more teachers tell children to sit down when they get out of their seats, the more they get out of their seats. The less teachers respond to out-of-seat behavior and the more they respond with praise to in-seat behavior, the less out-of-seat behavior they get. Hence, responses that teachers often mean to be punishing boomerang, serving to reinforce the behavior they hoped to eliminate. The more efficient approach is to reinforce the appropriate behavior from the outset.

In another study, researchers systematically varied teachers' approving and disapproving behaviors at different phases of a study and observed the effects on pupils' classroom behavior (Thomas, Becker, and Armstrong, 1968). Here also disapproving responses served to increase disruptive behavior, while approving behavior resulted in its decrease. Apparently, disapproval reinforced disruptive behavior just as sit-down commands had reinforced out-of-seat behavior. Further, the failure of teachers to reinforce appropriate behavior led to an increase in those disruptive behaviors that were most likely to be reinforced by peers (presumably the students were searching for social approval and got it from either one party or the other).

In still another study, researchers found that an eleven-year-old boy was unable to learn to spell the words he had studied (Zimmerman and Zimmerman, 1962). The boy would repeat letters that had no relation to the word he was to spell. The teacher would respond by patiently having him sound out the word, giving him a good many cues, and encouraging his efforts. The researchers suggested to the teacher that her responses were actually serving to reinforce the boy's spelling difficulties and recommended that she rearrange the reinforcement contingencies. The boy was not sent to the board to do his spelling exercises. The teacher would sit at her desk occupied with other tasks and would ignore the boy's statements, "I can't spell it" or "I can't remember how." However, invariably the boy would in due course spell the word correctly, at which point the teacher would smile, praise him, and give him another word. At the conclusion of the study, the boy was working efficiently and his spelling had greatly improved. This research suggests that under some circumstances a teacher's attention can contribute to learning problems. In sum, even teachers unconscious of the consequences of their behavior may be unwittingly reinforcing disruptive and problem behavior.

exchanged are termed *backup reinforcers*. The success of the system depends on the provision of a wide enough variety of backup reinforcers so that each child will presumably find something that is appealing (MacMillan, 1973).

A token should have several properties (O'Leary and Drabman, 1971): (1) Its value should be readily understandable to children; (2) it should be easy to dispense; (3) it should be readily portable; (4) it should require minimum bookkeeping duties for the teacher; and (5) it should be identifiable as the property of a particular child. A checkmark usually entails fewer administrative problems but generally lack the appeal of a physical token. Further, physical tokens can be used to teach mathematics. But tangible reinforcers also present problems since they can be thrown, chewed on, played with, lent, stolen, or used to buy favors (Craighead, Kazdin, and Mahoney, 1976).

In selecting reinforcers for token economies, teachers should be aware of the **Premack principle**—high-frequency behaviors may be used to reinforce low-frequency behaviors (Premack, 1959). Translated into classroom reality, this means that those tasks children voluntarily engage in most often (reading comic books or playing games) can be used to get them to engage in tasks they do not willingly perform often (such as mathematics assignments). The principle has also been termed "Grandma's Law": "First you clean your plate, and then you get dessert" (Homme, 1970). Hence, a child gets to engage in the activity that he or she prefers (the high-probability behavior) only when the child completes the task assigned by the teacher (the low-probability behavior).

Three ingredients characterize a token reinforcement program (O'Leary and Drabman, 1971): (1) a set of instructions to the class specifying the behaviors that will be reinforced; (2) an arrangement where the receipt of a token is made contingent on behavior; and (3) rules governing the exchange of tokens for backup reinforcers. Most educators recommend that token reinforcement programs be employed to "prime the pump," allowing natural reinforcers to take over after the desired behaviors are well established. Since tokens

function as extrinsic rewards, the danger always exists that students will become "hooked" on mechanisms of extrinsic motivation, decreasing their intrinsic motivation (see Chapter 12). Thus, it is important that a token arrangement be phased out as soon as possible. Further, as noted in Chapter 5, behavior maintained by continuous schedules of reinforcement tends to extinguish very rapidly once reinforcement is discontinued. For this reason intermittent schedules of reinforcement should be instituted as quickly as feasible, followed by progressive "weaning" from extrinsic reinforcers altogether.

Should a teacher institute a token reinforcement program with only one student, the teacher can share with the class what is being done. For instance, one teacher told her class, "Jimmy needs some help to remind him to stay in his seat until his work is done." From this point on the other classmates could be heard to say "Good for you" whenever the teacher gave Jimmy his token reinforcement, thus adding peer reinforcement.

Contingency Contracting

A **contingency contract** is a negotiated agreement, usually in writing, that specifies the behaviors required of a party and the reinforcements the party is to receive on completing these requirements. The rationale underlying the contingency contract is, "You can achieve a pleasant outcome (realize some desired object or engage in some valued activity) if you perform this task." Hence, like the token reinforcement program, the contingency contract is based on "Grandma's Law."

To be effective, the contract must confer a reward that is highly attractive and not obtainable outside the conditions of the contract (Homme, 1970). It is important that the contract spell out clearly and explicitly what task the student is expected to perform and what reinforcer the student will secure on successful completion of the task. Generally, the contract should focus on the *positive,* what the student is to do and what benefit the student is to receive. A poor contract provision might read, "Mike is not to speak in class unless first called upon by the teacher, and, if he speaks without permission, Mike will not go out on the playground during the next recess period." The contract might more appropriately read, "Mike will raise his hand if he wishes to speak in class and he will receive one stamp for each time that he follows this procedure and the teacher judges that he makes a useful contribution to the class discussion."

Usually students who fail to fulfill their contracts go unrewarded. They are not directly punished, but they are deprived of the rewards that they could have enjoyed had they fulfilled the conditions of the contract. However, if a student does not fulfill his or her contract, the contract should be adjusted so that the student can succeed. One side benefit of the contingency contract is that it can place the student and the teacher in direct communication with one another, therefore facilitating mutual understanding.

Ethical Considerations

Any number of educators and psychologists have raised ethical questions regarding the use of behavior modification. For instance, Richard A. Winett and Robin C. Winkler (1972) surveyed the papers in a leading professional journal (*Journal of Applied Behavior Analysis*) dealing with the use of behavior modification procedures for educational purposes. They found that inappropriate behavior was consistently defined as behavior that interferes with order, quiet, and stillness. This led Winett and Winkler to observe critically, ". . . if a quiet classroom is needed for every type of lesson, be it reading, spelling, social studies, or any of the other many types of lessons where behavior modification has been used, then the children are being forced to spend almost their whole day not being children but being quiet, docile, and obedient 'young adults' " (1972:500).

Virtually all the early proponents of behavior modification believe there is a very close linkage between their research and various social and ethical applications and implications. This has been most marked in the writings of B. F. Skinner,

considered by many to be one of the founders of the behavior modification movement. Over thirty years ago Skinner wrote *Walden Two* (1948), a novel that has sold over a million copies. In it Skinner portrays a utopian society in which life is governed by the principles of positive reinforcement. More recently, in *Beyond Freedom and Dignity* (1971), Skinner calls for the restructuring of our contemporary society using behavioral technology as a guiding framework.

As viewed by Skinner, the technology of behavior modification "is ethically neutral." It can be used by villain or saint. And Skinner believes that it is inevitable that some group will manage humanity. He argues, therefore, that it had better be the "good guys." Albert Bandura takes a somewhat similar position: "The basic moral question is not whether man's behavior will be controlled, but rather by whom, by what means, and for what ends" (1969:85). Thus Skinner and the behaviorists are not upset by the idea of control since they maintain that humans are always controlled by other humans in any system of interaction (Tharp and Wetzel, 1969; Cooke and Cooke, 1975). Indeed, the behaviorists point out that education itself involves the control of people, an organized effort to influence students' attitudes and change their behavior (MacMillan, 1973).

Accordingly, some psychologists suggest that the ethical problem is not whether behavior influence is proper or improper. We all influence one another in the course of our daily lives. Instead, they call for a specification of the circumstances under which behavior influence is appropriate. More particularly, they suggest that, to the extent it is practical, the person who is the focus of a behavior modification program should have an active voice in the formulation of its goals and procedures.

Peer Group Contingencies

The peer group provides powerful reinforcing effects which if properly employed can bring about changes in students' behavior (McGee, Kauffman,

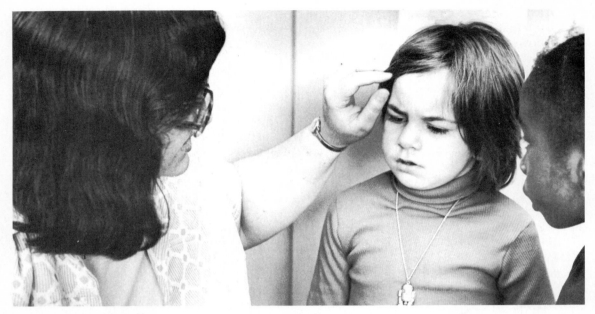

CLASSROOM PROBLEM
These two students were engaged in a hostile encounter over which child would
have the use of a particular desk. The teacher had the children come up to her
desk to discuss the matter and evolve appropriate ways to deal with the dilemma.

and Nussen, 1977). Indeed, the peer group may well represent the greatest untapped reservoir of aid for intervention programs available to teachers and school officials. The potential effectiveness of *peer group contingencies*—rewards and punishments delivered by associates of roughly equal status—is dramatically illustrated by Soviet methods of education. Urie Bronfenbrenner (1970) reports that teachers in the Soviet Union emphasize the training of the peer group to promote appropriate behavior and to punish misbehavior. Group members are enlisted in classroom control, disciplining each other and exerting pressure to conform to adult expectations. This arrangement is in marked contrast to situations in the United States where the adolescent peer group frequently functions to enforce peer as opposed to adult standards. However, many Americans find the Soviet approach abhorrent, arguing that it fosters a "big brother mentality" and undermines individual rights and achievement.

Peer group contingencies are usually of two types. The first type involves group consequences for group behavior. The same rewards and punishments are simultaneously in effect for all group members and are applied to a level of group performance. It has frequently been employed when many students are involved in disruptive behavior. It has also been found effective when peers reinforce classroom misbehavior. The technique has been successfully used in cases of misbehavior among mentally retarded children (Sulzbacher and Houser, 1970). The target behavior was the "naughty finger" (raised fist with middle finger extended). The teacher imposed a one-minute reduction in a special ten-minute recess at the end of the day for each episode of the behavior. The success of the procedure derived from the fact that the naughty finger behavior had previously been maintained by the reinforcement afforded by approving peer reactions.

The second type of peer group contingencies

THE GOOD BEHAVIOR GAME

One of the simplest yet most powerful procedures involving group contingencies employed to date is The Good Behavior Game (Barrish, Saunders, and Wolf, 1969). In this procedure, the teacher lists on the blackboard several rules that specify those occasions when the children are not to be out of their seats or to talk with their classmates without permission. The class is divided into two teams, each roughly paired in terms of students with behavior problems. The teacher explains that whenever a pupil on either team is seen breaking a class rule, that team receives a mark. The winning team (or both teams if neither team has more than five or some other number of marks) receives privileges and free time at the end of the period or at the end of the day.

In a modified version of the game, V. William Harris and James A. Sherman (1973) formed a third team composed of three students in a fifth-grade classroom who announced they would no longer play the game and were responsible for the largest proportion of their team's marks. For each mark scored over a given number, team members were required to remain after school for five minutes. The "third" team lost the game the first day this procedure was in effect and "stayed after school" for fifteen minutes. Over the next four days, none of the teams lost the game and after the fifth day of this condition, the members of the third team asked to be re-turned to their original teams. The teacher permitted them to do so.

A number of students have shown the game to have a powerful effect in reducing disruptive behavior (Medland and Stachnik, 1972; Harris and Sherman, 1973; Warner, Miller, and Cohen, 1977). The game is relatively easy to implement and can be used for a variety of behaviors. However, some educators believe that the game poses ethical questions (Warner, Miller, and Cohen, 1977). One issue has to do with excesses in peer pressure. Another matter is that some teachers become carried away by the ease of the game's implementation, and behavior control becomes the primary feature of their classrooms.

involves group consequences for the behavior of a particular student. In this procedure, a single child, usually with a problem behavior not common to other classmates, determines the consequences for the whole group. For instance, the technique can be used to bring a child's classroom tantrum behavior under control. The class is informed that they are to ignore (face forward in class) the target child whenever the child throws a tantrum. At the end of each school day in which the child does not throw a tantrum, everyone in the class receives a treat or the opportunity to participate in a special activity.

Peer group contingencies have a number of advantages. The procedures harness the motivation inherent in peer group approval toward the achievement of socially desirable goals. Researchers have found that group contingencies contain considerable potential for accelerating academic behavior and controlling disruptive behavior (Hayes, 1976). In addition, group consequences based on the academic scores of low performers have had the side effect of increasing cooperative classroom interactions and student tutoring behavior (Hayes, 1976; McGee, Kauffman, and Nussen, 1977). And many teachers find that group contingencies entail easier record keeping and administration than token-economy systems.

There are also occasional problems associated with peer group contingencies (O'Leary and Drab-

LUNCHROOM ORDER
One problem confronting principals and teachers is the containment of lunchroom noise and activity within manageable and acceptable levels.

man, 1971). First, there is always the possibility that some child cannot perform the required behavior. Second, peer pressure on a particular child can become excessive and even threatening and abusive. Third, from time to time one or two children find it gratifying (reinforcing) to subvert the program or "beat the system." And fourth, many teachers are concerned with the unfairness of group consequences for well-behaved children.

Punishment

Probably the most common yet most controversial technique for weakening behavior is punishment. For many years psychologists had warned parents and teachers to avoid punishment and, as a consequence, it has tended to acquire a stigma among "rational, thinking" people (Walters and Grusec, 1977). Nonetheless, almost all parents and teachers make daily use of some form of punishment, be it a well-practiced scowl or a verbal reprimand. Both common observation and research evidence clearly show that punishment is a commonly used behavioral device (Musemeche and Sauls, 1976). Apparently, many people believe punishment is an effective means for suppressing and eliminating behavior but are reluctant to admit it. Indeed, one repeatedly hears the cry for more severe penalties for lawbreakers.

As discussed in Chapter 5, punishment is any consequence of behavior that has the effect of decreasing the probability of that response. It is not what we do that indicates whether we are employing punishment; it is the *effect* that an act has upon the person that determines if it is punishment. Thus, as employed by psychologists, the definition of punishment differs from its everyday use in which punishment refers merely to a penalty imposed upon misbehavior (Craighead, Kazdin, and Mahoney, 1976).

Types of Punishment

By virtue of the negative connotations often associated with punishment, it is important to dispel certain notions that do not apply to the psycholog-

ical use of the term. Punishment need not entail pain or physical coercion, nor is it necessarily a means of retribution or retaliation (Craighead, Kazdin, and Mahoney, 1976). As noted in Chapter 5, punishment is of two types: first, *punishment by application* involves bringing an aversive stimulus (negative reinforcer) to bear following a response (a spanking, frown, criticism, or loud "No"); second, *punishment by removal* entails bringing about a loss in a pleasant stimulus (losing a privilege like watching television, being deprived of a smile, or no longer receiving a commendation).

Corporal punishment is the most controversial form of punishment. It refers to pain inflicted on the body of a person by an agent of authority using some instrument such as a whip or paddle (Maurer, 1974). Only Maine, Massachusetts, Maryland, New Jersey, and Hawaii forbid the use of corporal punishment in the schools. In a survey of school districts within the United States, 90 percent of larger districts and 69 percent of smaller ones reported that corporal punishment was administered in their schools (Musemeche and Sauls, 1976).

Corporal punishment for schoolchildren has been banned in Poland since 1783, in the Netherlands since 1850, in France since 1887, in Finland since 1890, and in Sweden since 1958. Most Communist nations, including the Soviet Union, bar corporal punishment in public schools (McDaniel, 1980). However, corporal punishment continues in nations with an "Anglo-Saxon" heritage like the United States, Great Britain, and Australia. In 1977 the United States Supreme Court (*Ingraham* v. *Wright*) held that the cruel and unusual punishment clause of the Eighth Amendment does not apply to disciplinary corporal punishment in public schools and that the due process clause of the Fourteenth Amendment does not require notice and a hearing prior to the imposition of corporal punishment. In sum, the nation's highest court said that the Eighth Amendment was intended to protect criminals, not schoolchildren (Cryan and Smith, 1981). However, the American Psychological Association opposes the use of corporal punishment in the schools, in part because it views corporal punishment as relatively ineffective.

Undesirable By-Products

At times punishment produces a number of undesirable side effects. Accordingly, psychologists and educators are concerned that it be employed with great care. First, punishment often teaches individuals what *not* to do but fails to teach them what *to* do. Many times students do not know exactly what their teacher expects of them. Rather, they hear a powerful authority figure declaring, "Ed, quit fooling around," "Mary, stop that, you hear," or "Jack, cut it out." It is essential that teachers also explicitly inform students what they are to do.

A second problem with punishment is that children may attempt to avoid the punishing agent, be it a parent or teacher. This can prove a serious hindrance to learning, since it deprives the student of the opportunity to acquire the socially desired attitudes and behaviors. Where escape is not possible, the individual may "tune out" the aversive stimulus through daydreaming or other mental wanderings. Further, individuals who are excessively and unreasonably punished often find alternative avenues to achieve the desired but forbidden end, for instance, cheating, lying, secretly carrying on the activity, blaming others, finding excuses, and so on.

A third problem with punishment is that a teacher or parent who yells at and slaps a child is unwittingly supplying a model for aggression. Punishing children for aggression often results in more, not less, aggressive behavior. Albert Bandura observes:

> Indeed, parental modeling may often counteract the effects of their direct training. When a parent punishes his child physically for having aggressed toward peers, for example, the intended outcome of this training is that the child should refrain from hitting others. The child, however, is also learning from parental demonstration how to aggress physically and this imitative learning may provide the direction of the child's behavior when he is similarly frustrated in subsequent interactions. [1967:43]

The command, "Do as I say, not as I do," boomerangs. We are more influenced by the model's behavior—the "as I do" part of the command—than by the punishment associated with the "as I say" part.

Self-Control

Thus far the chapter has stressed the operation of external mechanisms of control. However, the most effective form of control is clearly *self-control*—the management and regulation of one's own behavior. The use of self-control procedures in classroom settings has recently increased in popularity, although the idea that students should manage their own classroom behavior is hardly new.

Frederick H. Kanfer (1975, 1976) has suggested a three-stage sequence that occurs in the self-regulatory process:

- *Step 1: Self-monitoring.* Individuals observe their own performance and the context in which it occurs. For instance, a student may systematically record at regular intervals over the course of an hour the amount of time she attends to a reading assignment and the amount of time she devotes to daydreaming.
- *Step 2: Self-evaluation.* Individuals compare their performance with some standard to appraise its adequacy.
- *Step 3: Self-reinforcement.* Individuals administer to themselves positively reinforcing or punishing stimuli (self-produced consequences) on the basis of either good or poor performance. Self-reinforcement may be a simple self-verbalization such as "I really did well" or "I sure did blow it." Or self-reinforcement may entail a self-reward, such as getting to watch a favorite television program, or a self-penalty, such as not viewing the program.

One procedure for inducing self-control in schoolchildren has involved the use of "countoons" (Kunzelmann, 1970). A countoon has three components: (1) pictures that tell the child what he or she does; (2) a column of numbers the child circles each time he or she emits the behavior; and (3) a "what happens" column that shows the child the consequences of the behavior. For instance, one teacher recorded the frequency of whining behavior shown by a boy for thirty school days (revealing an average of 2.5 times per hour). The child was given a countoon, and he recorded his own whining behavior. Within ten days, the whining behavior had been eliminated.

An accumulating body of research suggests that behavior can be modified and maintained as effectively with self-control procedures as with externally derived reinforcement (McLaughlin, 1976; Jones and Evans, 1980). However, the maintenance of self-control over time appears to be enhanced by a student's prior exposure to external reinforcement programs (McLaughlin, 1976; Jones and Evans, 1980). The advantages of self-control are that it is an economical way to change behavior and is not dependent on the presence of external control agents. A major difficulty with the technique is that some students reinforce themselves without earning rewards, especially when self-recording is related to immediate payoffs as in a token reinforcement program (O'Leary and O'Leary, 1976). Further, some students fail to record their disruptive behavior (Santogrossi et al., 1973). It is reasonable to assume that refinements will be made in self-control procedures in the years ahead and that they will come to play an increasingly prominent part in classroom behavior modification programs.

CHAPTER SUMMARY

1. Teaching involves both instruction and management. Instructional activities are aimed at attaining specific educational outcomes. Management activities attempt to establish and maintain conditions in which instruction can occur effectively and efficiently.
2. Surveys of the incidence of problem behavior in school-aged children reveal that teachers view 20 to 30 percent of the general school population as having problems at any one time. Only a small number of this group, perhaps 2 to 3 percent, show recurrent or persistent problems in adjusting to school situations.
3. There are five sources of power available to teachers: reward and coercive power; legitimate power; expert power; informational power; and referent power. Research reveals that supervisors who manage primarily with expert, informational, and referent power are most successful as group leaders. When teachers focus on power relationships without consideration of whether or not the students believe the instructions are legitimate, they invite student opposition.
4. Fashioning a positive classroom climate cannot be reduced to a formula. It is a tenuous and fluctuating response to a variety of factors. One key ingredient is the teacher's leadership style. The manner in which teachers handle their classes can have important consequences for their students' learning, satisfaction, and development.
5. Teachers differ in their classroom management skills. Successful teachers are characterized by withitness. Teachers who are "with it" communicate to their students that they know "what is going on." Good timing and being on target are key ingredients in withitness. This allows successful teachers to employ the ripple effect (when the impact of behavior directed toward one or two students influences other students who view the incident) to their advantage. Another practice characterizing the successful teacher is overlapping (the ability to attend to two matters simultaneously).
6. Many educators are convinced that the key to successful classroom management is the prevention of discipline problems. And the heart of prevention is keeping students actively engaged in productive activities. Successful teachers pace their lessons smoothly with few interruptions. Further, underlying classroom order is a carefully designed set of rules.
7. Good classroom management begins immediately with the first day of school. Effective teachers are aware that classroom order and discipline are essential for teaching and learning. Consequently,

they assign classroom behavior a top priority as they inaugurate the new school year. They provide students with clear definitions and expectations for appropriate behavior. Moreover, they promptly undertake to structure and pattern classroom behaviors that are conducive to serious work. And when misbehavior occurs, they stop it quickly.

8. Finding that traditional methods for handling classroom problems are often ineffective, many teachers have sought to implement behavior modification procedures. There are four steps in the use of behavior modification principles. First, the teacher must define the specific behavior that will be the focus of attention. In the second step, the teacher attempts to identify the ABCs of the behavior. The third step involves the selection of techniques. And the fourth step entails an evaluation of the results of the behavior change program.

9. Over the past decade, token reinforcement systems have become one of the most prominent techniques for modifying children's classroom behavior. The approach commonly operates as a miniature economy similar in many ways to that of the larger society. But instead of money, the token is some stimulus like a poker chip, a checkmark, a star, a stamp, or a numerical rating that can be exchanged by a student for some desired object or activity.

10. The peer group provides powerful reinforcing effects which if properly employed can bring about changes in students' behavior. The peer group may well represent the greatest untapped reservoir of aid for intervention programs available to teachers. Peer group contingencies are usually of two types. The first type involves group consequences for group behavior. The second type entails group consequences for the behavior of a single student.

11. Probably the most common yet most controversial technique for weakening behavior is punishment. At times, punishment produces a number of undesirable side effects that have contributed to the concern among many psychologists and educators that it be employed with great care.

12. The most effective form of control is self-control. One proposed self-regulatory process in-

cludes three steps: self-monitoring, self-evaluation, and self-reinforcement.

CHAPTER GLOSSARY

behavior modification   An approach that applies the results of learning theory and experimental psychology to the problem of altering maladaptive behavior.

contingency contract   A negotiated agreement, usually in writing, that specifies the behaviors required of a party and the reinforcements the party is to receive upon completing these requirements.

contingency management   The rearrangement of environmental rewards and punishments to strengthen or weaken specified behaviors.

leadership style   The instructor's characteristic ways of handling information and applying sanctions.

Premack principle   High-frequency behaviors may be used to reinforce low-frequency behaviors.

EXERCISES

Review Questions

1. Studies of discipline problems reveal that
   a. teachers perceive the majority of pupils in their class as having problems at any one time
   b. about 10 percent of the pupils in any given school are likely to have recurrent or persistent problems
   c. a survey of school administrators found truancy to be a more pressing problem than drugs

d. less than 5 percent of all pupils actually ever have a problem serious enough to be put on their cumulative record

e. a and d are true

2. According to Kounin the teacher who stops the misbehavior of a few children to prevent the problem from spreading is exhibiting

a. withitness
b. ripple effect
c. accountability
d. overlapping

3. The teacher who is preoccupied with mundane details and constantly reminding students of their shortcomings is, according to Kounin, failing to exhibit

a. withitness
b. momentum
c. accountability
d. smoothness

4. Among the solutions *not* proposed by Gloria Gilbert's article on the problem child is

a. giving immediate feedback and relatively short assignments
b. overloading the work required so the child has less opportunities for mischief
c. making few but carefully defined rules
d. making a special effort to reward good behavior

5. Research on effective management procedures for beginning the school year suggests that

a. rules should be given early, but explanations can wait until appropriate situations arise
b. rules need not be reviewed periodically, since students perceive this as nagging
c. classroom monitoring is critical
d. a and c are true

6. When using the behavior modification approach to classroom problems, the first step, according to Clarizio, is

a. identifying the ABCs of the behavior
b. planning the appropriate strategies to be used
c. identifying the target behavior
d. constructing appropriate assessment instruments

7. The text suggests that the property of a token that may present the greatest problems is

a. an easily perceived value
b. portability
c. minimum bookkeeping requirements
d. tangibility

8. Among the problems associated with peer group contingencies is that they

a. are useful only with handicapped children
b. may exact undue peer pressure on an individual
c. encourage children to subvert the system
d. are detrimental to academic behavior

9. Among the findings on punishment is that

a. punishment, like reinforcement, can teach the child what to do
b. after a brief initial phase children do not attempt to avoid the punishing agent
c. punishment often leads to more aggressive behavior
d. corporal punishment has been considered cruel and unusual by the Supreme Court
e. c and d are true

10. The "countoon" technique for self-control among children does not provide for

a. self-monitoring
b. self-evaluation
c. self-reinforcement

Answers

1. c (See p. 470)
2. b (See p. 476)
3. b (See p. 478)
4. b (See pp. 480–481)
5. c (See pp. 482–483)
6. c (See pp. 483–484)
7. d (See p. 486)
8. b (See pp. 489, 491)
9. c (See p. 492)
10. c (See pp. 492–493)

Applying Principles and Concepts

1. French and Raven have identified five sources of supervisory power: reward and coercive (R/C), legitimate (L), expert (E), informational (I), and referent (R). Five student statements made about teachers are listed here. In Column A note the type of power represented by each, and in Column B check those types the text considers likely to lead to success in the classroom.

	Column A	Column B
a. "He'll know the answer to the problem."	_____	_____
b. "I like her; she's so cool."	_____	_____
c. "It'll earn me brownie points."	_____	_____
d. "He's the teacher."	_____	_____
e. "She'll know how to fix the computer."	_____	_____

2. Kounin has identified a number of types of teacher behavior, including withitness (W), ripple effect (RE), overlapping (O), stimulus-boundedness (SB), thrusts (T), dangles (D), flip-flops (F), momentum (M), and accountability (A). On this basis, categorize the teacher behaviors listed here (not all are represented).

_____ a. The teacher is handing back an exam to Louise: "Mark, I think you had better leave Irene alone."

_____ b. "I know what you're thinking, Timothy, so cool it."

_____ c. The class is doing seatwork: "Hold it; has everyone got the right assignment?"

_____ d. "Let's go on to our social studies unit. I forgot—has any one any questions on the health assignment? Now, today's lesson is on the War of 1812."

_____ e. "In colonizing America, England managed to send over a great many different types of people. Has anyone seen my pen?"

3. Below is an extract of a report written by a principal describing the kind of teacher who is generally successful at preventing discipline problems. Underline those statements that can be supported by the research.

My composite of the successful teacher is one who makes as few rules as possible. However, these rules are tightly defined to avoid situational problems. The teacher may not be loved, but he or she is respected. Good teachers don't monitor the classroom too much, but students must be held accountable for what they do.

4. Following are a number of classroom problem situations that teachers have identified. Indicate whether or not the description completely represents the ABCs of the problem (A = antecedent, B = behavior, C = consequence). If the situation is incomplete, indicate which element or elements are missing.

_____ a. "Just before lunch Mandy gets fidgety in her seat. I ignore her because if I don't she starts to cry."

_____ b. "Dick gets to calling out during a questioning period. I reprimand him sharply. Usually he just slumps in his seat."

_____ c. "If Cynthia does not turn in a perfect spelling test, she starts to cry."

_____ d. "Bill gets very tense every so often during class. When that happens, I send him outside for a few minutes, and that seems to relax him."

5. Percy is a student in a third-grade class. He has been in a behavior modification program designed to improve his reading. Every time he reads a sentence without error he receives a poker chip. These chips can be turned in for backup reinforcers. He has been in the program for three months, and the teacher notices that he is not as eager to obtain tokens as he once was. What should she do next?

_____ a. Give Percy two tokens for each response.

_____ b. Stop issuing tokens immediately.

_____ c. Give Percy a token after every second or third correct sentence.

_____ d. Remind Percy about the value of tokens and give him several extra ones.

6. Check any of the following statements that are *not* good examples of contingency contracts.

_____ a. "After you eat your pie, mow the lawn."

_____ b. "If you don't stop calling out, I won't let you go to recess."

_____ c. "Clean your room; then you can watch TV."

_____ d. "For every five correct examples, you will get one token."

Answers

1. a, I/√; b, R/√; c, R/C; d, L; e, E/√ (See pp. 470–471)
2. a, O; b, W; c, T; d, F; e, SB (See pp. 475–478)
3. Underline "makes as few rules as possible," "the teacher may not be loved, but he or she is respected," "students must be held accountable for what they do." (See pp. 478–479, 482)
4. a, complete; b, A (note that the teacher does not say *when* during the questioning); c, C; d, A (See p. 484)
5. c (See pp. 484, 486)
6. a, b (See pp. 486–487)

Project 1

OBJECTIVE: To assess the effectiveness of a peer group contingency approach.

PROCEDURE: Visit an elementary school classroom, and explain to the teacher that you would like to try a group contingency program. Select a child who has a specific behavior the teacher would like to decrease or eliminate:

1. A good start is to select a student whose behavior involves some form of interaction (talking to others, trying to gain peer approval for disruption, or the like). Select a behavior that can be counted.
2. There are two phases to the experiment. Allow several days for the baseline and at least a week for treatment.

Baseline Phase

3. Sit in back of the room, and ask the teacher to conduct class as usual. Observe the child during this period, and count the frequency of the targeted behavior. Observe for at least forty minutes. At the end of the period summarize the data, that is, the total frequency.
4. Prepare a graph, indicating on the ordinate (vertical dimension) the total frequency above Day 1 on the abscissa (horizontal axis). If the child has displayed the inappropriate behavior five times, your graph will look like this:

5. For the next three or four days keep a daily record. On the same graph put the results for Days 2, 3, and 4. Connect the results with a line to indicate the baseline period. Your graph might look like this:

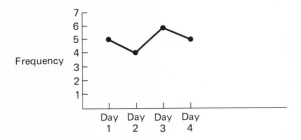

Treatment Phase

6. Determine with the teacher, in advance, an appropriate response to the problem from the class. Ignoring the problem student might be a good start. Choose the appropriate reinforcement (for example, an extra recess, a special story, or the like). During the treatment phase the problem student may not participate in the reinforcer.

7. Tell the class what you intend to do. Explain carefully that, if the class members ignore the student (be sure to define the inappropriate behavior carefully), they will receive a specified reward. Be sure to explain what ''ignore'' means—turning eyes to the front and *not* yelling, touching, smiling, laughing, looking, and so on.

8. Carry out the treatment observations as you did during the baseline phase. You will construct a graph for the next week. Draw a vertical line to separate the phases, and connect the data points. Note that sometimes during extinction behavior may show a temporary increase. Do not be discouraged.

ANALYSIS: If you have been successful, the graph might look like this:

Success in this case represents an overall decrease. If the inappropriate behavior has been extinguished, ask the teacher to reward the student for good behavior and to allow him or her to share in group rewards. If the experiment has failed, see whether or not you can determine the causes.

Project 2

OBJECTIVE: To establish a token economy

PROCEDURE: This project is very much like Project 1; for example, you will use the same type of graphs:

1. Visit a teacher who would like a student to display more of a given behavior.

2. Have a teacher define the behavior carefully. As you will carry out the experiment yourself, be sure the behavior is likely to occur often enough during the time you are there (at least forty minutes).

3. Observe and construct a baseline graph for at least three days. You may use either duration or frequency to record each instance of the desired behavior. If you use duration, break it up into small units (a minute or less).

4. Go over with the teacher your use of tokens (poker chips) and a backup reinforcer. The reinforcer, in this early stage of the economy, should be available daily. The teacher may know of something the child would like to do. You or the teacher should be in the position to give the reinforcer. If the experiment is to continue beyond

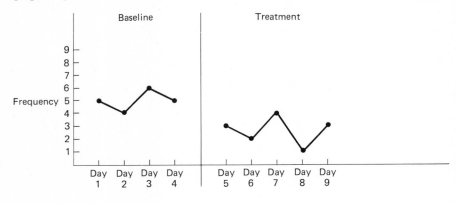

a week, you will raise the response requirements for the tokens. Use the baseline data to obtain some idea of how much you think you can increase the behavior of the first day of the treatment phase. The idea is to reward often. If you want the child to stay in his seat, hand out a chip every minute or two. In setting up the schedule with the child, use enough reinforcement so that he or she can see that there is a chance to obtain the reward each day.

5. Visit the child before the experiment begins, and explain *what* behavior will be rewarded, by how much, and how many tokens are needed to obtain the backup reinforcer. Check to make sure that the child knows what the backup reinforcer is. It may help to have the teacher explain to the class that you are working this week with _____

6. On Day 1 begin distributing chips for each instance of behavior on the schedule agreed upon. Be sure to praise the child each time you reward him or her. If the child does not earn enough on the first day, announce that he or she can carry chips over to the next day. Ignore inappropriate behavior, but do not take away chips. Graph your results during the treatment phase. That is, record each unit (of time or frequency) of the behavior observed. This behavior may not coincide exactly with your reinforcement schedule.

ANALYSIS: Study the graph, and discuss the results with the teacher. If the tokens have been successful, the treatment phase will show an increase. You may suggest continuing the project, with the teacher giving out the tokens and increasing requirements. Be sure to remember to praise the child; eventually praise alone can be used.

CHAPTER OUTLINE

17

STUDENTS WITH SPECIAL NEEDS

CHAPTER PREVIEW

Several ways in which children—or adults—may differ from one another have been discussed thus far, and many programs for adapting instruction to the requirements of individual students have been described. However, many students need or deserve arrangements or services that go beyond minor alterations in the usual classroom routine. These are students who are "exceptional" in some way—either those who have some kind of disability or those who may possess some unusual ability or talent. Programs for such students are the focus of this chapter, and particular attention is devoted to learning disabilities and to the educational needs of gifted and talented individuals. Problems in identification and categorization are discussed, and methods for providing recommended services are described. Since more and more students with various handicapping conditions are being mainstreamed into regular classrooms for at least part of the school day, it is becoming increasingly important for all teachers to understand the educational, physical, and emotional needs of these youngsters.

Think carefully about the following questions as you read:

■ Why has defining "learning disabilities" proved to be so difficult?

■ What are some of the advantages and disadvantages of using categories like "learning disabled"?

■ What factors have to be considered in order for mainstreaming to work successfully?

■ Why is parent counseling important in programs for students with learning and behavioral problems?

■ In what different ways have gifted and talented children been identified? What kinds of programs have been offered for them?

501

Most children and young people experience an occasional learning or behavioral problem in the course of growing up. But for the most part the problems are not so severe that they preclude the students from mastering the basic elements of a traditional educational program. This is not true, however, for an estimated one out of eight of this nation's schoolchildren who have a problem that requires special teaching techniques.

Over the past ten to fifteen years, efforts to solve the problems associated with various disabilities and handicaps have commanded growing attention. Today, education, psychology, and medicine are all devoting appreciable resources to the study and remedying of these problems. The public has also been made more aware of learning and behavioral problems through extensive press and television coverage. And the subject has become a fertile field of specialization for students seeking a marketable degree and for industries seeking new markets (Coles, 1978).

THE NATURE OF THE PROBLEM

During the past decade a new approach to children and young people with special needs has been moving to the forefront. This outlook is more positive and empathic in several respects. It derives

FEDERAL LEGISLATION FOR THE HANDICAPPED

During the 1970s, Congress passed legislation designed to provide free, appropriate educational opportunities for all handicapped individuals who require special educational services. In 1973 it enacted Section 504 of the Vocational Rehabilitation Act which reads:

No otherwise qualified handicapped individual in the United States shall, solely by reason of his handicap, be excluded from the participation in, be denied the benefits of, or be subjected to discrimination under any program or activity receiving Federal financial assistance.

Two years later in 1975, Congress passed PL 94–142, the Education for All Handicapped Children Act (the "PL" stands for Public Law; "94" indicates that the law was passed by the 94th Congress; and the "142" indicates that it was the 142nd law passed by that session of the Congress to be signed into law by the president). The following are among the major provisions of PL 94–142:

DEFINITION
Handicapped students are defined by the act as those who are:

mentally retarded, hard of hearing, deaf, orthopedically impaired, other health impaired, speech impaired, visually handicapped, seriously emotionally disturbed, or children with specific learning disabilities who by reason thereof require special education and related services.

FREE APPROPRIATE PUBLIC EDUCATION
The legislation operates under the "zero reject" principle and mandates a free appropriate public education for all handicapped children and young people. This

from the following assumptions (Milofsky, 1974; Willenberg, 1977):

■ Individuals with special needs function and behave as they do by virtue of forces largely beyond their ability to comprehend or control. This assumption removes the stigma of willful and deliberate intent on the part of the students for their problems and poor achievement.

■ The condition of students with special needs is most commonly caused by factors beyond the scope of traditional child-rearing practices. This assumption helps to relieve parents of feelings of guilt and shame.

■ Students with special needs, many of whom were once thought largely ineducable, are ca-pable of benefiting from instruction, although to varying degrees. The possibility of cognitive and emotional growth encourages educators, parents, and others to provide appropriate ed-ucational programs. This assumption proclaims that all children and young people possess the right to a full and adequate education.

■ The remediation of learning and behavioral problems is justifiable from both an economic and humanitarian standpoint. This assumption provides the basis for demanding public support to underwrite the additional expense of appro-priate educational programs. In 1975, a break-through was scored with congressional passage of the Education for All Handicapped Children Act (PL 94–142). (See the boxed insert below.)

requires that handicapped stu-dents must be provided special education and related services at public expense under public su-pervision and direction. Schools must plan to serve all handi-capped students, adopt policies that serve all handicapped stu-dents, and conduct searches to locate handicapped individuals of school age.

NONDISCRIMINATORY EVALUATION

The act mandates that evaluative procedures be adopted to ensure the appropriate classification of handicapped students and the ex-tension of relevant educational services to them. This provision is designed to remedy against evaluating students in ways that may prove racially or culturally biased.

LEAST RESTRICTIVE EDUCATIONAL ENVIRONMENT

A handicapped student may not be segregated inappropriately from his or her nonhandicapped schoolmates. Accordingly, hand-icapped students must be edu-cated in regular classrooms to the extent possible. However, the provision does not mandate main-streaming (placement of handi-capped students in regular class-rooms), since some students may have particular educational needs that cannot be met in this fashion.

INDIVIDUALIZED EDUCATION PROGRAMS

The principal method under the act for furnishing an appropriate education to a handicapped stu-dent is the Individualized Educa-tion Program (IEP). Such a pro-gram requires a written statement for each handicapped student that indicates the present levels of the student's educational perfor-mance, the short-term and long-term educational goals, and the special and regular educational services that will be provided for the student. The program is to be drawn up by the teacher or teach-ers of the student, a representa-tive of the local educational agency, the parents or guardians, and, whenever appropriate, the student.

PROCEDURAL SAFEGUARDS

The act guarantees full due proc-ess for parents and students in all matters of educational assess-ment and placement and provides strict guidelines and procedural safeguards in the administration of the act.

There are a vast number of terms and labels applied to children and young people afflicted with one or more difficulties— minimal brain damage, mentally retarded, information-processing disability, memory problems, emotionally disturbed, visual- and auditory-perceptual problems, learning disability, cognitive and language processing problems, and so on. (See the chapter appendix, which provides a glossary of terms.) The absence of a valid and reliable classification for learning and behavioral problems has posed a major and persistent problem to progress in this field.

Rather than becoming bogged down in a quagmire of confusing nomenclature, the chapter will focus primarily on one group of problems termed "learning disabilities." This category includes students with both academic and behavioral problems and thus provides a perspective on many types of handicaps confronted by regular classroom teachers. Indeed, educators are increasingly coming to realize that considerable overlap occurs among groups of students having very different diagnostic labels applied to them.

Definition

The term "learning disabilities" emerged from a need to identify and serve a group of individuals who experience school failure yet elude existing categories like mentally retarded and emotionally disturbed (Mercer, Forgnone, and Wolking, 1976; Rie and Rie, 1980). In the 1950s the term "brain injury" was employed to refer to these students, only to be displaced in the 1960s by the term "minimal brain dysfunction," and more recently by the term "learning disabilities." (Unlike the earlier terms, "learning disabilities" is purely descriptive and carries no implication regarding cause.) Indeed, more than forty English terms are used in educational and psychological literature to identify essentially the same group of students (Cruickshank, 1972; Forness, 1981). Many educators view **learning disabilities** as an umbrella concept referring to children and young people who encounter difficulty with school-related subject matter, despite the fact that they are of normal intelligence and have no demonstrable physical, emotional, or social handicap (Ross, 1976).

Probably the most widely accepted definition of learning disabilities is that proposed by the National Advisory Committee on Handicapped Children (1968:34) and since incorporated in slightly modified form in the 1975 federal law on the education of the handicapped (PL 94–142):

> Children with specific learning disabilities are those children who have a disorder in one or more of the basic psychological processes involved in understanding or in using language, spoken or written, which disorder may manifest itself in imperfect ability to listen, think, speak, read, write, spell, or do mathematical calculations. Such disorders include such conditions as perceptual handicaps, brain injury, minimal brain dysfunction, dyslexia, and developmental aphasia. Such term does not include children who have learning problems which are primarily the result of visual, hearing, or motor handicaps, of mental retardation, of emotional disturbance, or environmental, cultural, or economic disadvantage.

It is apparent that this definition is extraordinarily vague. Further, it is primarily a definition by exclusion. The definition says that learning disabilities are not primarily due to mental retardation or to underlying emotional disorder. It excludes students with visual, hearing, or motor handicaps (although students having these difficulties may be encompassed by the term if these handicaps are not judged to be the primary disabilities). Also excluded are students whose difficulties arise primarily from "environmental, cultural, or economic disadvantage," leading some critics to charge that the definition covers only students from middle- and upper-socioeconomic-class backgrounds.

The definition, however, does cover students with handicaps having a neurological foundation ("brain injury, minimal brain dysfunction, dyslexia, and developmental aphasia"). Although the government definition does not do so, many other definitions of learning disability include a *discrep-*

ancy component—an inconsistency between a student's estimated ability and his or her academic performance (Mercer, Forgnone, and Wolking, 1976). Some definitions also mention "uneven performance across a variety of tasks" or "scatter effect on test profiles" (the child may perform at very high levels in some skill areas and very low levels in others).

From this discussion, it is apparent that the field of learning disabilities has been plagued by the problem of defining and describing a group of students who exhibit quite different behaviors (Chalfant and King, 1976; Kass et al., 1982). Most commonly school learning problems are first identified by the classroom teacher, who, in turn, makes a referral to a school psychologist or counselor. Nearly all teacher referrals are made on the basis of one or both of two types of problems: (1) A student is experiencing difficulty learning skills of an academic nature, or (2) a student is having difficulty with social behavior (either acting out or not interacting sufficiently with the teacher and classmates). At this point, the school psychologist or counselor takes over and after consultation with others in the system (including parents), the student is usually placed in one of three categories: (1) educable mentally retarded, (2) emotionally disturbed, or (3) learning disabled (Forness, 1981).

One difficulty with existing disabilities programs is that they have too often become "dumping grounds" for all the academic or discipline-problem students regular teachers cannot handle. Indeed, at times students are classified as learning disabled solely because they are judged to be underachievers or referred to the school psychologist for sundry other reasons (Coles, 1978). Psychologist William M. Cruickshank (1972) notes that he has found students labeled "learning disabled" for such diverse problems as stuttering, teasing the family cat, having a hard time with tenth-grade geometry, having nightmares, not being able to swim, masturbating, being able to type but not to write legibly, and not liking to date girls. "Teachers have questioned me about disrespectful children, children who will not listen to the adult,

children who cry, children who hate, children who are sexually precocious, children who are aggressive—all in the belief that these are learning disability children" (1972:382).

Unlike diagnostic categories such as retardation, which are restricted by definition to a specified proportion of the population, the learning disabilities category is relatively unrestricted (Rie and Rie, 1980). In a very real sense learning disabled individuals present a paradox. They are "normal," yet they have serious difficulties that impair their academic performance. As a consequence, in trying to secure adequate funds for school budgets, school officials seem to have little difficulty in reclassifying pupils to fit any program that provides special financial assistance (Sartain, 1976; Phipps, 1982).

Identifying Learning Disabled Students and Their Problems

Among children and young people designated learning disabled, there are those whose eyes see correctly but whose brains do not properly receive or process the information. For instance, a student who gets letters mixed up (reads *saw* for *was* or *dog* for *god*) may have visual processing problems. Other learning disabled students have trouble selecting the specific stimulus that is relevant to the task at hand from among a mass of sensory information. Still others may hear but cannot remember what they have heard by virtue of an auditory-memory problem. (The student may turn to the wrong page in the book or attempt the wrong assignment when relying solely upon oral directions.) And some seem impulsive, hyperactive, underactive, distractible, or undermotivated. Before any remedial program can be initiated, it is crucial that the student's specific difficulties be determined.

The tests comprising a learning disabilities battery usually evaluate a student's perception, language, intelligence, and neurological function. Although each test is designated as dealing with a

RICK'S A PART OF THE TEAM

DWIGHT WOODWORTH, JR.

Worcester Public Schools, Massachusetts

Would they really be able to accommodate Rick Hoyt, to accept him and emotionally cope with his limitations? This question ran through the minds of teachers at South Middle School when they learned that a very severely physically disabled student would be attending their western Massachusetts school.

Structurally the school could accommodate those in wheelchairs by moving classes from the second to the first floor, but Rick would presumably need a lot more help than the other 1,100 students.

Born with cerebral palsy, fourteen-year-old Rick is virtually nonverbal and physically helpless. Since psychological testing and observations indicated he had a keen mind, the recommendation was that he be placed in the sixth grade. But wouldn't he be better off in specialized facilities?

Mr. and Mrs. Hoyt decided against special placement. They recognized Rick's many limita-

tions, but wanted him to live as "normal" a life as possible. Since Rick had attended regular kindergarten and an out-of-state public school part-time, Mrs. Hoyt felt he was ready to be mainstreamed as a regular public school student.

With federal funds the school hired aide Kathy Armstrong as Rick's full-time school helper. Although Ms. Armstrong had no background in education and, like other staff members, had never worked with a handicapped child, her sincere interest in helping soon overcame these obstacles.

At first science teacher Joe Wright felt uneasy. "When I first met Rick," he admitted, "I had to leave the room to compose myself." But after spending one school day with Rick, feelings of apprehension turned into concerted efforts to help Rick develop his full potential.

Rick expresses himself by using a Tufts Interactive Communicator (TIC), an electronic device developed by Tufts University's Bio-Medical Engineering Center. A light scans columns of letters and numbers. Through a single-input switch operated by his knee, Rick can select the desired char-

acter which then appears on a display and also on a ticker tape.

Since communication with TIC is too slow for regular classroom participation, Mr. Wright hopes to use the school's computer as a more effective communicative device. An eighth grader has already developed many computer programs for Rick. Hopefully, Rick will soon be developing his own programs. Said Wright: "I see a career for Rick in the computer programming field." This doesn't jibe with Rick's ambition to become a sportswriter, but time will tell.

Rick is presently weakest in reading and spelling, so Ms. Armstrong, under the direction of a language teacher, stresses these subjects with Rick. Rick has even opted to drop art and music classes—giving him more time to complete assignments. "He's just like any other kid. At times he gets stubborn," tattled Ms. Armstrong, "but we get along just fine." Rick's assignments, though not as lengthy, are equivalent in quality to those given other students. "Rick is marked on the work he *can* do, to the extent that he can make his ideas understood," she explained. He is given

Source: Dwight Woodworth, Jr., "Rick's a Part of the Team," *Instructor*, 87 (October 1977):202–203.

"modified" grades in subjects like social studies and science where he cannot physically do the work. Ms. Armstrong functions as Rick's hands, making or setting up things for him, and explaining the procedure as she goes along.

Rick's comprehension is excellent according to Rick's social studies teacher. "Rick stays on top of current events," he said. During class elections last fall, Rick was the only student who was aware of the simultaneous national, state, and local elections. Even with no communication device at hand, Rick was able to get his message across. Sometimes it may become "20 questions," but even this has benefits, for it rivets the attention of the class to the topic under discussion.

Rick usually answers questions with yes, no, or a number. In studying decimals, math teacher Barbara O'Connor writes 94.167 on the board and asks, "Rick, which number is in the tenths place?" Rick taps the underside of his tray once with his knee.

Lunchtime finds Rick leaving Ms. Armstrong and going to the cafeteria with his eighth-grade helper, Tom Romani. Teachers may warn Rick about dragging in the corridors or committing other "traffic violations" but he takes it as good-naturedly as it is given.

An attaché case holds Rick's lunch, towels for under his chin, and his drinking cup. Ten high-school students (two per day) help Rick with lunch and are finding it a rewarding experience. It takes patience because of Rick's involuntary muscular movements, but these students have developed an efficient system. One handles the sandwich, the other the drink, and both still manage to eat their own lunch in half an hour. Many mutually beneficial relationships have developed beween Rick and his helper friends. Some of these students are "class problems"— students who crave recognition. They find a constructive way of gaining it through helping Rick. Students take over in Ms. Armstrong's absence and Rick becomes a motivating force for these children: "If Rick can do it, so can I."

Gym class is an exciting experience for Rick. In gym trunks along with his classmates, Rick does exercises by having a student move his arms and legs to the instructor's commands.

"To a greater or lesser degree," explains the gym instructor, "Rick participates in everything we do." Rick was certainly a star player in a recent soccer game. A unique play was for Rick's teammates to corral the ball under the wheelchair, move as close to the goal as possible, and then kick the ball through the footrests to score.

Time permitting, gym [concludes] with a shower for all, including Rick.

Since a van transports Rick and other special-needs children to and from school, afterschool activities are limited. Rick does his fair share of socializing, however. His election to the student council shows his popularity.

Place Rick in special facilities? Why? Ms. Armstrong claims, "We don't think of Rick as 'different.'" And perhaps this is why he has integrated so well.

Rick is getting a lot more from this mainstream experience than would be possible in specialized settings. He will never have to make the difficult transition from a sheltered special setting to a community of able-bodied people. He will never question whether he can "measure up," for he is receiving feedback on this every day.

As Rick learns to deal with his limitations, he is also recognizing his developing abilities, and his schoolmates are recognizing them as well. Comments like "Rick's a good kid" indicate that these students are growing up with both a more understanding attitude toward those with disabilities, and with an awareness of Rick as a *person*.

The mainstream may be turbulent, but with continued support Rick will stay afloat.

distinct area, most tests overlap, since they are structured to fit the model of impairment specified in federal learning disabilities legislation (Coles, 1978). In part, the tests have been developed in an attempt to provide a rational means for understanding students whose inability to learn seems otherwise unexplainable.

To date no foolproof tests have been developed for diagnosing learning disability (Milofsky, 1974; Owen, Braggio, and Ellen, 1976; Kochanek, 1980). Most special educators agree that the state of the art in education, psychology, physiology, and medicine does not enable them to diagnose the causes of a student's difficulties with great specificity or to design a program of instruction that is tailored to each student's specific needs with great accuracy. But the growth in public awareness of the problems of learning disabilities and the commitment of public resources to identification and treatment have encouraged those in the field of special education to accelerate their search (Milofsky, 1974). In the interval the principal burden

for the early identification of learning disabled students continues to fall on the classroom teacher. Fortunately, a good many recent studies contain evidence that classroom teachers are quite accurate predictors of students' future school success and problems (Keogh, Tchir, and Windeguth-Behn, 1974; Schaer and Crump, 1976).

Although there is no totally satisfactory battery of tests for screening early school problems, most educators believe nonetheless that screening is a useful and helpful procedure. Most authorities agree that the earlier a child's diagnosis, the better the prognosis. The purpose of screening is to identify possibilities of trouble ahead. Screening assists the diagnostician in determining whether or not a learning problem exists, and if it exists, identifying its nature and how it affects the child's learning behavior. A battery of learning disability tests supplies one of a number of mechanisms for screening (and for individual diagnosis where this is necessary). Some educators compare the practice to preventive medicine (Arnold, Cranwell, and

LEARNING DISABILITIES AMONG THE EMINENT

It is all too easy to despair in the face of the learning disabilities that confront some of our students. At these times it is worth reminding ourselves of the eminent who have also experienced a variety of learning disabilities. Albert Einstein, for example, was a rare, imaginative, productive scientist whose unique contributions to theoretical physics may

have been based upon an equally unique visual method of conceiving and solving problems (Patten, 1973). The young Einstein did not speak before three years of age. Until he was seven, Einstein would laboriously search for words and silently repeat with his lips each spoken sentence. Indeed, in his verbally oriented elementary school in Munich, Einstein was

judged by some to be retarded. A number of Einstein's verbal disabilities persisted into adult life, including the difficulty he experienced in spelling. Evidence suggests that the creative thought process responsible for his theory of relativity was nonverbal and mediated through the constructive manipulation of mentally visualized images. Apparently, Ein-

SCREENING TO IDENTIFY POSSIBLE LEARNING DIFFICULTIES
Many educators believe it is desirable that all children be screened for learning problems at the kindergarten level in order to detect and begin correcting as early as possible any difficulties that may be present.

stein overcame his verbal handicap by circumventing it and compensating by an unusual way of visual thinking.

The young Thomas A. Edison also had his share of childhood difficulties (Thompson, 1971). Many relatives and neighbors believed the boy to be "abnormal." When enrolled in a one-room school at the age of eight, he overheard his teacher say that his mind was "addled" (muddled and confused). He refused to return to school, and his mother, unwilling to admit backwardness in her son, taught the boy at home. Edison wrote in his diary, "I remember I used never to be able to get along in school. I was always at the foot of the class," and "My father thought that I was stupid, and I almost decided that I was a dunce" (1948:20, 14). One biographer writes of Edison:

> [He] never learned how to spell; up to the time of his manhood his grammar and syntax were appalling. We see that he was hard to teach. Whatever he learned, he learned in his own way. In fact, though his mother inspired him, no one ever taught him anything: he taught himself. [Josephson, 1959:22]

Overall, it appears that Edison had a definite disability in learning to read, spell, and write.

Nelson A. Rockefeller (1908–1979), vice-president during the Ford Administration, achieved eminence, even though he had to struggle since childhood to spell correctly and to read—and to remember that he perceived numbers in the wrong order, so that what he saw as 92, for instance, was really 29. Similarly, King Karl XI (1655–1697) was judged one of Sweden's wisest kings but had difficulty reading and spelling all his life. Among other eminent individuals who are believed to have experienced early language problems are Woodrow Wilson, Auguste Rodin, and General George Patton (Thompson, 1971).

Spar, 1977), and thus they call for the screening of all kindergarten children (Cowgill, Friedland, and Shapiro, 1973; Eaves, Kendall, and Crichton, 1973; Forness, Hall, and Guthrie, 1977).

Screening children for learning disabilities offers a number of advantages (Johnson and Morasky, 1977; Beers and Beers, 1980; Bagnato, 1981). First, problems diagnosed early are often less firmly entrenched and hence are more easily treated. For instance, since many children with academic problems learn quite well but, unfortunately, learn the wrong things (like incorrect phonic strategies in reading), an early identification of misdirected learning leads to easier extinction of bad habits. Second, there are economic advantages because it is cheaper to treat problems in an early stage of development. For example, early problems may become complicated as frustrated students develop sporadic attendance records. Third, another profitable aspect of screening is that it provides baseline data that can be used for later comparative and diagnostic purposes.

Screening data can also provide insights that educators can use in designing an instructional program for a student. The rationale for this type of assessment is that an understanding of *how* a particular student learns becomes the basis of how to *teach* the student. The resulting remediation program should take into account both the student's assets and his or her liabilities. Any comprehensive educational plan ideally seeks to sustain and maximize a student's strengths, while attempting to overcome weaknesses that interfere with the learning process. This commonly involves diagnostic-prescriptive teaching, a matter that will be considered later in the chapter.

Categorization: Stigma or Benefit?

The placement of children in a category like "learning disabled" is a serious business. As Nicholas Hobbs points out:

Classification can profoundly affect what happens to a child. It can open doors to services and experiences the child needs to grow in competence, to become a person sure of his worth and appreciative of the worth of others, to live with zest and to know joy. On the other hand, the classification, or inappropriate classification, or failure to get needed classification—and the consequences that ensue—can blight the life of a child, reducing opportunity, diminishing his competence and self-esteem, alienating him from others, nurturing a meanness of spirit, and making him less a person than he could become. Nothing less than the futures of children is at stake. [1975:1]

Some educators and psychologists believe that the disadvantages of categorization outweigh the benefits. They advance a number of arguments:

- Once children are given a label such as "learning disabled," it is difficult for them to regain the status of being "normal" like everyone else. The label becomes a stigma, a harmful badge, that is psychologically damaging to a child and an instrument for isolating the child from many meaningful social experiences and relationships.
- Large numbers of lower-socioeconomic-class and minority-group children, victims of classist and racist institutions, have been inaccurately assigned to the learning disabled category, adversely shaping their development.
- Labeling children "learning disabled" prejudices the responses of teachers, parents, peers, and others, thereby creating a self-fulfilling prophecy. Negative labels influence the social feedback these children receive. This has consequences for their self-conceptions and, in turn, for their subsequent behavior.
- The deficit label enables teachers and parents to "explain" a lack of academic progress in terms of the label ("After all, Jack is a learning disabled child"). The label diminishes the sense of responsibility for all concerned and provides a nice, antiseptic rationale for failure. The student is seen simply as the victim of his or her own neurology or other biological malfunctioning.
- Labeling a student "learning disabled" results

in perceiving as deviant behaviors that otherwise would be considered of little consequence. Those of us not so labeled blame our own forgetfulness, impatience, or other undesirable behaviors on external causes. But behavior lapses that previously would have been overlooked in a "learning disabled child" now are more likely to be recorded and follow the student for years to come (Kronick, 1976, 1977).

Other educators and psychologists point to the benefits that can follow from the appropriate categorizing of students as learning disabled:

■ Classification makes it possible for society to identify specific learning problems and to marshal resources of money, facilities, and talent to attack these problems. Categorizing is necessary to get help for students, to write legislation, to appropriate funds, to design service programs, to evaluate outcomes, to conduct research, and to communicate about the problems of certain students (Hobbs, 1975).

■ A label provides a name so that parents can obtain information about the problem, learn of types and sources of help, and seek specific forms of assistance. It can afford parents the opportunity to affiliate with a volunteer organization, meet other parents with similar problems, share information, and gain a sense that they are not alone with their problem (Kronick, 1977). And it enables parents to reach out for community or professional assistance when they are not equipped to deal with their difficulties.

■ A label helps parents recognize that the child's problems have not resulted from their own failings and child-rearing practices. This knowledge relieves guilt and shame. Further, informed parents are less likely to "blame" the child for his or her academic shortcomings.

■ Students need to be grouped as a matter of convenience and economic necessity. Although one-to-one instruction may be an effective means of remedial teaching, it is not always feasible or practical. In many cases, students with the same difficulties can be served as a class or by the same resource teacher.

Research confirms that a label like "learning disabled" is not a neutral term. Diagnostic labels lead teachers to view specific behaviors as more incapacitating than when descriptions are used alone (Herson, 1974). Further, the label "learning disabilities" generates negative expectancies in teachers and affects their objective observations of children's behavior (Foster, Schmidt, and Sabatino, 1976; Algozzine and Sutherland, 1977). On the other hand, there is some evidence that children whose parents are aware of their neurological malfunctioning have a better self-image than children of unaware parents. Presumably, this is because aware parents are less likely to impute moral failure to the child and are better able to provide the child with emotional support (Rosenthal, 1973).

All of this highlights the dangers lurking in categories and labels. Categories and labels can be employed for obscure, covert, or hurtful purposes. Teachers should be aware of the possible harmful effects that labels may have on their expectations for student performance and on their behavior toward pupils. Classification procedures must not be used to undermine respect for children's individuality. By the same token, categories and labels can be turned to advantage if they open up opportunities for children, facilitate the passage of legislation in their interest, and provide rallying points for concerted action programs (Hobbs, 1975).

Hyperactive Children

Fidgety Phil
He won't sit still
He wiggles
He giggles. . . .

and when told off:

The nauthy restless child
Grows still more rude and wild.

HENRICH HOFFMAN
"Fidgety Phil," 1845

Hyperactivity in children has become a matter of intense popular concern and controversy since the late 1960s. Hyperactivity is not a disease but merely a label for a collection of rather vague and global symptoms. Children labeled ''hyperactive'' tend to be characterized by excessive restlessness, high distractibility, short attention spans, academic difficulties, and behavior problems (Ross and Ross, 1976; Rosenthal and Allen, 1978; Weiss and Hechtman, 1979). To describe such children the American Psychiatric Association has adopted the term ''attention deficit disorder'' (ADD). Some psychologists take the view that hyperactivity is a disorder of the total personality, while minimal brain dysfunction is a neurological condition, and learning disability is an educational classification (Rosenthal and Allen, 1978). However, the three categories overlap considerably so that in practice there is a tendency to view them as somewhat synonymous.

Medical experts disagree on the nature of the hyperactive syndrome (or even if it is a syndrome) and the means for diagnosing it. The diagnosis of a hyperactive condition is made on the basis of a child's observed behavior and not on the basis of hard, unequivocal medical or laboratory findings (Sandoval, Lambert, and Yandell, 1976; Sandoval, 1977; Weiss and Hechtman, 1979). Experts have advanced a number of theories to explain the cause of hyperactivity, including genetic defects, poor parenting, food additives, allergies, lead poisoning, fluorescent lights, insufficient oxygenation, inadequate school environment, and too much television (Johnson, 1981).

Hyperactivity is a descriptive term that implies a judgment about a child's behavior. It is not surprising, therefore, that estimates vary widely on its prevalence. Medical authorities indicate that symptoms of hyperactivity are present in from 4 to 10 percent of children, or 1.4 to 3.5 million children. If one surveys parents of children aged six to twelve and asks them if their children are restless, 35 to 50 percent of the parents of boys and 20 to 30 percent of the parents of girls respond affirmatively (Tuddenham, Brooks, and Milkovich, 1974; Safer and Allen, 1976). Teachers report

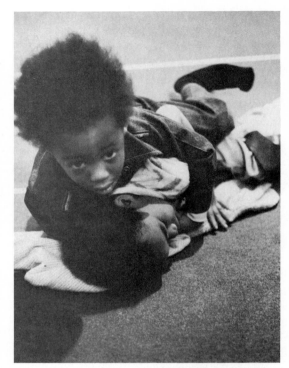

ACTIVITY NOT NECESSARILY HYPERACTIVITY
Hyperactivity is a descriptive term, and authorities do not always concur as to which children fit in the category.

that about 40 percent of their students are restless and that over a third are inattentive. But if teachers are asked, instead, to identify only those children who have a notable degree of hyperactivity and inattentiveness and have had it since they began school, then the figure drops to 5 to 10 percent of the elementary school population (Safer and Allen, 1976).

Parents often report that their hyperactive schoolchildren were ''difficult'' to rear during infancy and early childhood. The children were fussy and hard to feed, had a high incidence of colic, had difficulty sleeping, cried a good deal, and did not learn to speak or speak adequately until age three or later (Stewart et al., 1966; Ross and Ross, 1976; Safer and Allen, 1976). Some medical and psychological experts believe that hyperactivity is a developmental disorder that begins to fade during adolescence (Safer and Allen, 1976). Others say that hyperactive children continue to experience various difficulties during adolescence that find expression in school problems, unsatisfactory family and peer relations, and trouble with the law (Huessy, Metoyer, and Townsend, 1974; Ross and Ross, 1976; Weiss and Hechtman, 1979).

There is little information about what happens to hyperactive children in adulthood. Some research suggests that the hyperactive behavior pattern might be a childhood prologue to psychiatric disorders in adulthood (Anderson and Plymate, 1962; Ross and Ross, 1976). Other research indicates that while childhood hyperactivity may be associated with greater adult "nervousness" and restlessness, a faster pacing of one's life, and entry into the work force at a somewhat lower status level, it is not necessarily associated with a higher incidence of social or psychiatric problems (Borland and Heckman, 1976).

Considerable controversy surrounds the use of drugs, primarily amphetamines, in the management of hyperactive children. Although some psychologists report success employing behavior modification procedures (Walden and Thompson, 1981; Sandoval, Lambert, and Sassone, 1981), the major approach to managing hyperactive children has been the prescription of Ritalin (methylphenidate) or Dexedrine (dextroamphetamine). Precise figures on the use of these drugs are difficult to come by. Current estimates place the number of American schoolchildren who are receiving amphetamines for the control of hyperactive behavior at between 500,000 and 1.5 million. Medical experts disagree on the precise mechanisms by which amphetamines produce their paradoxical, calming effect on hyperactive children, since amphetamines have an opposite, stimulating effect on adults.

Proponents of drug therapy point to a number of well-designed and carefully executed studies that show that between 60 and 90 percent of hyperactive children benefit from Ritalin; the rate is somewhat lower for Dexedrine (Conners, 1972a; Millichap, 1973; Whalen and Henker, 1976). Of course, this still leaves about 10 to 40 percent who

do not show significant behavioral improvement. Further, amphetamine treatment does not cure the condition, and there is serious question whether those receiving drug treatment fare any better over the long run than those who do not.

Amphetamines appear to enhance children's ability to attend to critical aspects of the learning situation and to plan and control their responses (Conners, 1972b; Ellis et al., 1974; Swanson and Kinsbourne, 1976). However, most researchers find that reasoning, problem solving, and academic learning are not usually affected by amphetamine therapy (Whalen and Henker, 1976; Adelman and Compas, 1977; Cunningham and Barkley, 1978; Kolata, 1978). Some children's irritability, disruptiveness, and temper outbursts have proven responsive to Ritalin treatment. It is not entirely clear, however, whether it is the children's behvior or the adults' perception of the children's behavior that changes.

As with any medication, some individuals experience adverse side effects with Ritalin and Dexedrine therapy. These include insomnia, moodiness, stomachaches, and dizziness. The symptoms tend to be most prominent during the first week of treatment, although they may persist into the second week. Some children also experience retardation of growth. However, when taken off the drug, the children show a distinct growth rebound.

Advocates of amphetamine treatment say that hyperactive children should not be deprived of the possible benefits it can afford. They see parallels between amphetamine therapy and the eyeglasses provided to those with vision problems, the anticonvulsants given to epileptics, and the insulin administered to diabetics.

But there are also those who fear that the widespread enthusiasm for administering amphetamines to "hyperactive" children has led to abuses and to the acceptance of drug therapy for children who may not benefit from it. Indeed, one study has reported that 58 percent of the children referred for treatment as hyperactive may not have been (Kenny et al., 1971). It becomes frighteningly easy for parents and teachers to control behavioral "problems" under the guise of giving children ''medicine.'' The drugs may then function as ''conformity pills'' for rebellious youngsters. The suspicion exists that children, especially those in some inner-city communities, are ''being subdued pharmacologically because drugs are cheaper than providing an adequate learning environment'' (Wolff and Hurwitz, 1973:113). Psychologist Alan O. Ross observes:

> Learning disability is primarily a problem for the child; hyperactivity is primarily a problem for the adults around the child. Since adults are ''in charge,'' it is not surprising that the focus of intervention is more often on what is troubling the adult than on what the child really needs. That is, treatment is more often directed at the hyperactivity than at the learning problem. [1976:105]

All of this suggests that a recommendation that a child receive medical evaluation as a likely candidate for Ritalin treatment should be made carefully. There should be reasonable assurance that the child's problem does not stem from teaching inadequacies or other aspects of the school environment. Drug therapy is not appropriate when the difficulty resides in boredom or inappropriate teacher standards. A teacher should not assume the responsibility for such a recommendation. Should medical evaluation be undertaken, the teacher can play a significant part by supplying the physician with a characterization of the child's behavior. Further, the teacher and physician should collaborate in the development of a monitoring system for the child being treated with drugs (Bosco, 1975). Unhappily, one survey revealed that only 22 percent of elementary school teachers had ever been requested by a physician to evaluate the behavior of a child receiving Ritalin (Robin and Bosco, 1973).

SERVING STUDENTS WITH SPECIAL NEEDS

It is apparent from our consideration of learning disabilities that a good deal of controversy characterizes the field. As is often true of many new areas of scientific inquiry, researchers and practitioners continually turn up findings that do not necessarily fit existing interpretations. While fueling disagreement, these circumstances also stimulate additional investigations that seek to resolve the difficulties. Perhaps not surprisingly, some of the most intense controversy has to do with what constitutes the best strategy for assisting students with special needs.

Mainstreaming

In the past decade there has been a dramatic change in the policy and philosophy of educating mildly and moderately handicapped students. The current shift has been away from separate or

OPENING DOORS
Mainstreaming is designed to open regular classroom doors to a larger segment of the school-age population.

segregated classrooms toward **mainstreaming**—the integration of students with special needs within regular school programs. The movement has received added impetus from federal legislation that has mandated that handicapped students must be educated in the least restrictive environment to the maximum extent that is possible. Some have hailed this legislation as an achievement comparable to that of the Civil Rights Act.

Mainstreaming has been proposed as a means of ensuring equality of educational opportunity and equal protection under the law. Critics of separate classrooms charge that they are an inappropriate training ground for individuals who must live in the mainstream of society on completion of their formal education. Advocates of mainstreaming view it as a means for reducing isolation and

prejudice (Woodward, 1980; Leyser and Gottlieb, 1981). Integrated placement is assumed to lessen the stigma associated with segregated classes, promote peer acceptance of students with special needs, and increase the effectiveness of educational programming (Jones et al., 1978; Zigler and Muenchow, 1970).

Although much hope exists for mainstreaming, many educators and psychologists warn that the mere physical presence of a student with special needs in a regular classroom will not guarantee academic or social success (Burton and Hirshoren, 1978; Zigler and Muenchow, 1979; Glick and Schubert, 1981). Although the setting may change, the problems do not. Unless *basic* changes are made in school programs, the children are simply returned to the very failure situations that originally

PATIENCE
All students can benefit from patient and dedicated teachers.

led to their specialized placements. A host of factors must be taken into account if mainstreaming is to be a successful alternative and not just a passing fad. Mainstreaming is not a panacea (if indeed there is such a thing as a panacea in education). It works where school officials, teachers, parents, and students are committed to making it work through designing, implementing, and supporting appropriate reprogramming (Macy and Carter, 1978; Hoben, 1980; Leyser and Gottlieb, 1981).

Perhaps the biggest barrier to successful mainstreaming is the historic attitude among Americans: "The handicapped are different. They trouble us in deep, unexplainable, irrational ways. We would like them somewhere else, not cruelly treated, but out of sight and mind" (Martin, 1974). In general, studies reveal that many classroom teachers believe

HE'S BLIND, HE'S IN OUR CLASS, EVERYBODY'S LEARNING

MARY LOU ALSON

First-grade teacher, Oceanside, California

Teachers who visit my class ask, "What's it like to have a totally blind child in a sighted class?"

Generally it is not much different from having many of the other children the regular classroom teacher works with—the shy, the neglected, the sensitive, the dominating, the child of low ability. Besides the blind student in our class, we have one child who attends a learning disability class for one hour each day, two who attend speech, three who attend English as a second language, one who works with the teacher for Vietnamese, and one who is

Source: Condensed from Mary Lou Alson, "He's Blind, He's in Our Class, Everybody's Learning," *Instructor*, 87 (September 1977):222–224.

a mentally gifted minor. All these children require some extra planning on the part of the classroom teacher. But the regular classroom offers children with special limitations a more normal natural learning and social environment.

The regular classroom teacher should be prepared to spend extra time planning for the blind child just as she has to for any of the other exceptional children. Probably there are more demands on the first-grade teacher's time than on any other.

As he becomes a more effective reader, the blind child will be more self-reliant. The blind child needs, and will need for several years to come, activities that develop manual dexterity. Since no one knows at the beginning reader

level whether he will eventually earn his living by manual dexterity or intellectual skills, he needs training in both areas. For the regular classroom teacher it means that she must prepare for both types of activities and provide space for listening, for dictation tape materials, and for the braille-writer, besides the regular desk where the child can work with the manipulative materials. He needs a tray on his desk with a rim around it so the materials he uses to develop manual dexterity do not fall on the floor out of reach. And he needs many sets of materials for sorting, matching, stacking, and so on.

The blind child in our class goes to the resource room for the visually impaired, to work for one

that children with special needs would have a negative effect on their programs (Shotel, Iano, and McGettigan, 1972; Vacc and Kirst, 1977). Further, the vast majority of regular classroom teachers feel that they are ill-equipped to deal with handicapped children (Gickling and Theobold, 1975; Vacc and Kirst, 1977; Flynn, Gacka, and Sundean, 1978). Overall, a good many teachers believe that their instructional practices are not geared toward accommodating students whose ability levels and needs are widely discrepant from the majority of pupils in their classes. This clearly points to the need to provide teachers with knowledge about handicapped children and with more specialized skills to deal with specific academic and behavioral problems.

Instructional integration is assessed by the extent to which a child with special needs shares in the

hour a day. There he works on reading and writing braille. The remainder of the day he works in our classroom with the other "regular" students. The blind child as well as all the other exceptional children are accepted by the other children who work and learn in our class. None of the children is thought of as different or peculiar.

It takes careful planning by the classroom teacher so that the special children are not gone from the room when a learning activity they should take part in is scheduled. It is very easy for the speech teacher to say, "Send Larry and Cathy at 10:15." But if that time is right in the middle of a reading group, it's difficult for the classroom teacher to watch the time and keep an eye on the lesson. It is easier if the special children are scheduled right after a recess break or something else that they can associate their own special time with. If this is not possible, then the resource teacher should send a messenger for the children.

The sighted teacher, untrained in reading braille, will need a code sheet for reference although the resource teacher should have most materials needed for first grade penciled in with regular print. The resource teacher should also supply word cards, sentence strips, and books with the traditional printed symbols so the sighted children can share vocabulary game drills and read along with the blind child. In later school years this is not necessary, but on the first-grade level where extra vocabulary drill practice is needed, it is important.

The blind child can operate his own cassette player for dictated word or vocabulary drills for writing braille. The tapes should be made or supplied by the resource teacher, but it is the classroom teacher who will change the tapes and load the braillewriter with paper for use in the classroom.

Although all first-grade teachers should have a full-time aide, few do. Often the sighted children in the room can help by getting materials ready for the blind child. They can separate the manipulative pieces so that they are ready for the blind child to sort, match, and otherwise put together. An older student might help as a tutor. Fifth- and sixth-grade students generally make good tutors for listening and encouraging the blind child to read. A fifteen- or twenty-minute session is enough. Later in the day another tutor may help with math. The classroom teacher or the resource teacher can train or instruct the tutoring student in the correct procedure for working with the blind child.

The classroom teacher should be careful to plan time blocks that alternate guided review, independent work activities, taped braille writing, and manipulative activities for the blind child much as she would balance the type of activities for the sighted children. The blind child in a regular first-grade classroom does require more concern and care for the classroom teacher without an aide, as do all exceptional children. Smaller classes for the beginning reader stages is important. But even with the extra time needed for the exceptional child in the regular classroom, the advantages for those children make the extra time worthwhile.

educational environment of the regular classroom. Successful mainstreaming requires that at least three conditions be satisfied (Kaufman et al., 1975; Jones et al., 1978). First, the child's educational needs must be compatible with the instruction that is being provided his or her classmates. For instance, although all the students may be assigned reading seatwork, the content of the work is varied to meet the individualized needs of each student.

The second essential condition for instructional integration is a willingness on the part of the teacher to accommodate children with different learning styles and abilities. Mara Sapon-Shevin notes, "Mainstreaming must be conceived of, not as changing the special child so that he will fit back into the unchanged regular classroom, but rather as changing the nature of the regular classroom so that it is more accommodating to all children" (1978:120).

The third facet of instructional integration is the development of a cooperative relationship between the regular classroom teacher and the special educational teachers. Commonly, children with special needs spend portions of their time receiving specialized or intensive instruction from a resource, itinerant, or other special educator. Coordination is essential lest excessive scheduling or abrupt transitions be very difficult for the child to negotiate. Further, all too often the regular and special class teachers attempt to communicate on a catch-as-catch-can basis. It is difficult to evolve an effective, well-articulated program based on haphazard meetings.

Research suggests that segregated classrooms do not tangibly benefit mildly retarded or emotionally disturbed students. Equally handicapped pupils placed in regular classrooms perform at least as well (Dunn, 1968; Bradfield et al., 1973; Macy and Carter, 1978). As early as two decades ago, G. Orville Johnson noted:

> It is indeed paradoxical that mentally handicapped children having teachers especially trained, having more money (per capita) spent on their education, and being enrolled in classes with fewer children and a program designed to provide for their unique needs, should be accomplishing the objectives of their education at the same or at a lower level than similar mentally handicapped children who have not had these advantages and have been forced to remain in the regular grades. [1962:62]

Also of importance is the social acceptance of students with special needs. Research reveals that integrated retarded children adapt socially about as well as their nonretarded peers. Yet their popularity tends to be considerably below average (Guinagh, 1980; Leyser and Gottlieb, 1981).

Various factors contribute to the lesser popularity of children with special needs within peer group settings. First, in some cases the children suffer from a stigma resulting from being labeled or treated as a special educational problem. Second, deficits in attention, language, or perception may hinder the children in detecting critical cues and making inferences about people. Third, the regular classroom has traditionally been a place where recognition and high grades have been allocated on the basis of academic achievement; thus, less able children generally receive lower grades and recognition, making them less attractive as friends (Kavanagh, 1977; Gottlieb, Semmel, and Veldman, 1978). Finally, some children, especially the emotionally disturbed and learning disabled, exhibit behaviors their peers interpret negatively, for example, short attention spans, distractibility, hyperactivity, aggressiveness, frequent statements of rejection, and "ritual insults" (Bryan et al., 1976). Clearly, educational interventions are needed to improve the social acceptance of mainstreamed children (Ballard et al., 1977).

Contrasting Models

There are a number of different approaches to learning disabilities. The major frameworks within which academic and behavior problems are considered are the educational deficit, behavior modification, social environmental, medical, and psychotherapeutic models. Each suggests that the causes of students' problems reside in a somewhat different area of study. And each recommends different strategies for dealing with students' difficulties.

Educational deficit advocates contend that students have individual strengths and weaknesses that must be addressed by a program of instruction. Behavior modification proponents say that both appropriate and inappropriate behavior result from learning experiences. Social environmental advocates argue that children's school difficulties result from the failures of the educational institution and the larger society. Medical proponents look to structural (neurological) or metabolical malfunctioning to account for learning and behavior problems. And psychotherapeutic advocates focus on faulty personality development and functioning.

Educational Deficit Model

The educational deficit approach is primarily concerned with devising and implementing appropriate diagnostic and teaching procedures. It focuses only on those behaviors that pose difficulty for a student. The teacher makes no tacit assumption that the child is handicapped by virtue of some internal deficit. Rather if the teacher finds that the child is underachieving in one or more subject areas (mathematics, reading, spelling, or handwriting), instructional efforts are directed at diagnosing and reteaching the particular skills or subskills not yet mastered (Larsen, 1976). Most commonly this involves **diagnostic-prescriptive teaching**—identifying the most effective instructional strategy for each child. As noted in previous chapters, some children learn best under one instructional strategy, while others learn best under another.

A diagnostic-prescriptive teaching strategy can proceed on the basis of two different theoretical orientations: the ability-training orientation and the task-analysis orientation (Ysseldyke and Salvia, 1974). The first approach employs diagnosis to identify *ability* strengths and weaknesses in order to prescribe remediation for the abilities themselves. Here the primary concern is with establishing the perceptual, motor, information-processing, or other abilities presumed to cause inadequate skill development. In contrast, the task-analysis approach undertakes to assess a child's academic *skill* development and then to tailor instruction to move the student from where he or she is to where the teacher desires the student to be. The emphasis falls on teaching specific skills as opposed to cultivating more general abilities.

Those who use a diagnostic-prescriptive teaching orientation reason that there is little evidence to indicate that the exact cause of a learning problem can be precisely determined. Even if it were possible, this knowledge would not appreciably alter the academically oriented remediation. They also point out that any program must ultimately address itself to teaching those processes or skills that relate directly to scholastic proficiency and normal classroom functioning. And finally, they argue that that responsibility for teaching mainstreamed students falls upon regular classroom teachers who should direct their efforts to those areas in which they possess demonstrated competence (Larsen, 1976).

Behavior Modification Model

Like the educational deficit model, the behavior modification model is not concerned with underlying obscure forces or the inner causes of behavior. Rather, it concerns itself with the child's performance (what the child does and says). The behavioral model deals specifically with the observable symptoms of a problem. As such it tends to minimize and deemphasize traditional diagnostic labels (Forness, 1976).

Viewed from a behavioral perspective, all behavior, good or bad, is learned; maladaptive behavior is learned and unlearned in the same fashion as any other behavior. This means that all behavior is capable of being changed in accordance with the principles of learning (see Chapter 5). Accordingly, they use contingency management procedures—the rearrangement of environmental rewards and punishments to strengthen or weaken specified behaviors (see Chapter 16).

Full-fledged behaviorists take the student's organic structure as given. Consequently, they focus on the immediately available and changeable elements in the environment. John M. Throne articulates this view:

> A child who is brain-injured or emotionally disturbed usually learns academic and related skills less well than one who is neither. But the cause of this difference is not his injured brain or emotional disturbance. Being brain-injured or emotionally disturbed, in order to learn he needs a different environment than a child who is not. To the extent that the environment proves sufficient, his learning will improve. To the extent it is insufficient, it will not improve. . . . [Likewise] a visually handicapped or blind child may be enabled to learn academic and related skills by being fitted with glasses or taught to read Braille (through tactual sensory channels) regardless of neurological or ocular considerations. If the environment does not see to it that he is fitted or so trained, he will be unable to learn, but not because he cannot see or cannot read books. He will not learn because the environment fails . . . to rearrange itself to see that he learns despite his defect. [1973:543–544]

In sum, behavior modification proponents seek to change the environment to elicit or eliminate given behaviors.

Social Environmental Model

The social environmental model resembles the behaviorist model except that it stresses sociological rather than psychological factors. The environmental model seeks the roots of children's classroom problems in institutional and societal malfunctioning. The school and society are seen as contributing to and even creating children's difficulties in acquiring basic skills. According to this view, only by changing the broader social system can education be remedied. Gerald S. Coles says:

By positing biological bases for learning problems, the responsibility for failure is taken from the schools, communities, and other institutions and is put squarely on the back, or rather within the head, of the child. Thus, the classification [like minimum brain dysfunction, learning disabled, emotionally disturbed, and so on] plays its political role, moving the focus away from the general educational process, away from the need

SOCIAL ENVIRONMENTAL MODEL
Some educators believe that the schools are failing minority-group children. They call for fundamental changes in the schools and the broader society.

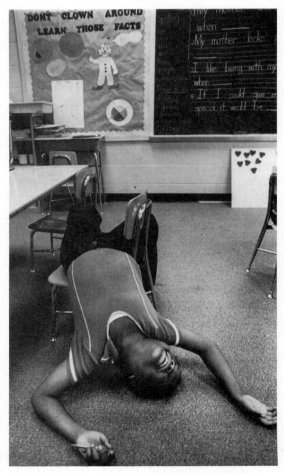

to change institutions, away from the need to rectify social conditions affecting the child, and away from the need to appropriate more resources for social use. [1978:333]

Seen from this perspective, society and the schools are failing children. But through a perverse logic, the child is defined as the failure, a classic case of "blaming the victim" (Ryan, 1972). For instance, one study found that 23 percent of the children in classes taught by adequate teachers (as rated by their principals) failed in reading. Of the children in classes taught by poor teachers, 49 percent failed (Jansky and de Hirsch, 1972). Similarly, a substantial proportion of students with reading problems come from inner-city schools.

Medical Model

In sharp contrast with the educational deficit, behavioral, and social environmental models, the medical model seeks the cause of learning difficulties *within* the child. Educational problems are seen as symptoms of an underlying "disease," "disturbance," or "disorder." Since learning involves the brain, advocates of the medical model reason that if learning fails to occur, there must be something wrong with the child's brain. Presumably a physical lesion, abnormality, or chemical imbalance results in the failure of the brain to function properly, a condition of "brain dysfunction." A by-product of this conception is the notion that it is relatively ineffective to treat a child's maladaptive behaviors, since the behaviors are merely external expressions of some more basic cause.

The medical model calls for a diagnosis of the neurologial malfunctioning, and, where possible, appropriate medical intervention. It recognizes that some children like the mentally retarded cannot be "cured," but they can receive some degree of help. In some instances the disorder is believed to respond to biochemical treatment, as in the case of Ritalin administered to hyperactive children and sodium valproate to children with epilepsy.

Psychotherapeutic Model

The psychotherapeutic model resembles the medical model in considering factors within students to be the source of their learning and behavioral problems. Although both models embrace the disease concept of behavior abnormalities, the proponents of the psychotherapeutic model see these problems as symptoms of an underlying personality disturbance rather than a neurological malfunctioning. Many of the notions associated with the psychotherapeutic model derive from the principles originated by Sigmund Freud. Freud stressed the part that unconscious motivation—stemming from impulses buried below the level of awareness—plays in a person's behavior.

Therapeutic intervention is directed toward "working through" these unconscious motivations with a psychiatrist, psychologist, or counselor and fashioning "healthier" modes of behavior. Unfortunately, the success record of traditional psychotherapeutic approaches for dealing with learning and behavior problems in children has not been good (Levitt, 1971; Hewett and Blake, 1973; Johnson and Morasky, 1977). Although psychotherapy may not be the treatment of choice for many academic and behavior problems, it may be beneficial as an adjunct to other forms of treatment if the initial problem has given birth to secondary emotional and coping difficulties.

Specialists and Allied Professionals

Regular classroom teachers need not feel that they stand alone in dealing with the learning and behavioral problems of their pupils. Nor should teachers expect that they will have all the skills demanded by their classroom circumstances. The complexity of some students' difficulties may require interprofessional assessment and treatment. A thorough knowledge of the more serious problems in learning and behavior transcends the knowledge available to any one individual or profession.

FOR THE LOVE OF PETE

CYNTHIA L. JARZEN
Fourth-grade teacher, Lorain, Ohio

I spoke to his back because he wouldn't turn to face me as we were introduced. Looking at him, a muscular, eleven-year-old, I remembered yesterday, the first day of school, when I had scanned my class roster for his name. Since spring, I had known he would be coming to me from an intensive instruction class. He had not been able to cope in a regular classroom before, but was now ready to again be "tried out." When his name wasn't on the list I felt somewhat relieved, but now, here he was, his back to my front.

Source: Cynthia L. Jarzen, "For the Love of Pete," *Instructor,* 85 (October 1975):159–161.

As I touched him and invited him to come in and sit at one of the desks, he shook my hand from his shoulder. Shuffling noisily into the room, he threw down supplies, then walked out the door with me in pursuit. The pursuit would occur many times during the coming weeks.

Each morning I went to school with a leaden lump in my stomach, expecting the worst from Peter and usually getting it. Each day the words from his record came to life: *aggressive, potentially dangerous, seriously disturbed.* Within a week, he was known to all the teachers and most of the children in our wing. He was loud, mean, and hurtful. His presence upset many of the children. When

I questioned his placement, the psychologist told me the other children would be better for it—eventually. Would I try to "bend"?

So I bent. But the day came when I could bend no longer. I called Leon to lead "Simon Says." Peter ran to the head of the class screaming, "I'm the leader. I'm the leader!" Boiling inside, I told the class to ignore him and follow Leon. "I am the teacher of this class," I told them, trying hard to believe it. For several minutes the game continued with the two leaders trying to outshout each other. Finally, Peter stood aside, stopped shouting, and watched. A point for my side!

Expecting any work from him was a task to be postponed. I

In practice what can be done to help a student depends on several factors, including (1) the severity of the child's problems, (2) the age of the child, (3) the availability of well-qualified professionals, (4) the financial resources of the school district and the child's parents, and (5) the location of the diagnostic and treatment facilities (Peters, 1977). Teachers need to exercise caution in controlling the common tendency of assuming that the more members there are on a team, the better the service will be.

The following is a list of some of the types of professionals involved in giving special services to students with learning and behavioral problems:

- *Audiologist:* A nonmedical specialist who evaluates hearing defects and rehabilitates persons with impaired hearing.
- *Endocrinologist:* A medical physician who specializes in the diagnosis and treatment of problems associated with the secretions of the endocrine system.
- *Neurologist:* A medical physician who specializes in the branch of medicine dealing with the structure, functions, and diseases of the nervous system.
- *Ophthalmologist:* A medical physician who specializes in the branch of medicine dealing with the structure, functions, and diseases of the eye.

considered myself fortunate if he stayed in his seat and looked at me as I taught. One day, as I was explaining a math problem at the board, he arose, walked in front of me, and went to the listening center. All eyes followed him. He proceeded to put a record on the turntable and hook up the earphones. Flames encircled my neck. He was being rude; he was not learning; he was interfering with the learning of others; he was hurting *my pride.*

"Peter, you're being RUDE! Put those things down and return to your seat. I am teaching YOU as well as the other children. I expect you to pay attention! If you're bored, then *be* bored, but don't prevent the others from learning. SIT DOWN!" He stared at me. Slowly—deliberately slowly—he rolled up the cord, placed the headset back in the container,

and sauntered back to his seat, not once removing his eyes from mine. The lesson went on.

At the next progress conference with his counselors I would *tell* them he was *not ready* to be in a regular classroom. That very day he had walked around the room with a black-handled, three-pronged *thing* that looked like a marshmallow fork, thrusting it toward a few classmates' faces before I got to him. "Peter, give it to me," I said, trying to steady my outstretched hand. "Where do you want it?" I pictured my hand—*gored,* but held it out anyway. "NOT where you're planning to give it to me!" I glared at him. He threw his head back in laughter and slapped the weapon into my palm.

I kept him after school one afternoon and talked to him about his behavior. Or rather I talked to

the back of his head again. I told him that I really liked him (a small white lie) but that I didn't like many of the things that he did; that he could be a good student and a very kind person. I went on and on, although I felt I was talking to deaf ears.

The next day he came to my desk and started to talk about football. Although my knowledge of the subject is meager, I did know a few names that seemed to impress him. "I'm gonna be a football player. I'm strong. See how strong I am?" And he lifted my desk on end causing me to throw myself down upon papers, pencils, and books that went sliding downhill. I laughed, "O.K., Peter, you're strong!"

Then he noticed that my desk drawer was broken. "I'll fix it," he

(continued)

- *Optometrist:* A licensed nonmedical specialist who tests the eyes for defective vision and prescribes corrective glasses or lenses where necessary.
- *Otolaryngologist:* A medical physician who specializes in the branch of medicine dealing with the structure, functions, diseases, and disorders of the ear, nose, and throat.
- *Pediatrician:* A medical physician who specializes in the medical care of infants and children.
- *Psychiatric social worker:* An individual trained in providing social and human services; many hold master's degrees.
- *Psychiatrist:* A medical physician who specializes in the diagnosis and treatment of mental and emotional disorders.
- *Remedial reading teacher:* An educator who specializes in the teaching of children who experience severe problems in learning to read at a level that is appropriate for their current grade placement.
- *School psychologist:* A nonmedical specialist who administers educational and psychological tests for diagnostic purposes and treats school adjustment problems.
- *Speech pathologist:* A nonmedical specialist who works with individuals who misarticulate

---

FOR THE LOVE OF PETE (continued)

said, and was down on his hands and knees beside the desk, fishing around inside the drawer for the missing parts. Within seconds he had some nuts, bolts, and metal pieces on the floor and soon had them reassembled and the handle in place. I was truly pleased and surprised.

"You're not only strong, you're a good mechanic, too. Thank you, Peter." I rested my hand on his back and this time he didn't shake it off. "Anytime you want your desk fixed, just call me."

Things seemed to go better from then on. He smiled more and was cooperating more. One morning he came into the classroom before the bell rang dressed in a brand-new outfit. "Hi handsome," I called to him. As he turned away embarrassed, I caught sight of a smile. A few seconds later he turned back grinning and said, "I ain't handsome—I'm *cool.*"

I really *was* beginning to like him. Later that week, I felt we had definitely reached some kind of understanding. We were on the playground and I had to scold a student for using a jump rope as a whip on another child. He did it again and Peter skated over to him, yanked the rope from him, and shouted, "Didn't you hear the teacher? She said STOP!" Then he skated back and asked, "Would you like me to skate for you?"

"I'd love you to skate for me." I watched him glide gracefully around the yard. The lump in my stomach had become definitely smaller.

As the weeks went by, I came to realize that the best way to treat this child was to acknowledge and somehow reward his positive behavior and try to ignore his negative behavior. Hopefully, the second personality would eventually fade out. I did it, though it was most difficult.

Near Christmas he began working more—not much—but it was a start. If I assigned ten math problems, he'd ask if he could do five. I'd say, "How about seven?" then he'd agree to six. He always did all that he said he would and sometimes surprised himself by doing the work easily and continuing to do more. He preferred to print his work, but with encouragement he grew gradually more skillful and would write in cursive about half the time. Whenever he completed a nice paper, I pasted

---

speech sounds, stutter, have voice disorders, or are delayed in language use.

Parent Counseling

The parents of handicapped and learning disabled children hold the key to any successful program for helping their children. Professionals are increasingly coming to recognize the critical role that parents play (McDowell, 1976; Abrams and Kaslow, 1977; Shapero and Forbes, 1981). Consequently, parent counseling is a necessary component of programs providing services for handicapped and learning disabled students. Unfortunately, little is currently being done along these lines. Many excuses are given: not enough money, inadequate staff, not enough time, and parents' problems with work schedules. Yet a commitment to children with special needs also clearly carries the responsibility of providing assistance to their parents (McDowell, 1976).

Parents of children with special needs often experience a host of associated difficulties, including depression, lowered self-esteem, and a lessened enjoyment in parenting (Voysey, 1975; Cummings, 1976; Prince-Bonham and Addison, 1978; Wikler, 1981). Not uncommonly the parents pass through several phases including disbelief, guilt ("What did I do to cause this to happen?"), rejection ("I don't want a handicapped child!"), shame ("What will everyone think?"), denial ("There's nothing wrong with the child!"), and a feeling of helplessness (McDowell, 1976; Wikler, 1981).

The addition of a child with special needs to a family unit affects all the members' lives, the parents' marriage, sibling relationships, and ties with friends, relatives, and the community (Princea small red dot on it. He took pride in these red-dot papers and counted them each day.

He was becoming more pleasant and cooperative with his classmates to such a degree that one of the girls, after witnessing some nicety performed by Peter, whispered to me, "Miss Jarzen, that *can't* be Peter!"

The child who seems the most unlovable is often the one who needs love the most. One afternoon during a values discussion, I arranged various objects on the chalk tray. We all agreed that they represented values that were important to us: a bottle of aspirin—good health; a dollar bill—money; a Valentine card—someone loves you; a *TV Guide*—entertainment, and so on. I then called on volunteers to arrange the objects in order of importance to them. Most of the children attached little importance to the Valentine, putting it in last place. Peter was the only child to place it first.

A year with Peter cannot adequately be contained in words. It was a year of agony and ecstasy; of victory and defeat; of laughter and tears. Did he really improve in as many ways as I thought he did, or, as one teacher put it, did I simply become immune to him? Did I help him at all, or didn't I? How does a teacher ever really know? What will happen to him next year? Ten years from now? I'll probably never know the answer to these questions. Or, perhaps the answer came in a note that he wrote to me on the last day of class.

I had asked the children to write me letters telling me what they liked about the year and what they disliked about it. Peter was finished with his letter in two minutes and brought it to my desk folded into a small square. I was almost afraid to open it, but I thanked him and read it as he returned to his seat. At the top of the page was his name (in cursive) and under that, printed neatly in green, inch-high letters were the words:

YOU DID NICE.

I looked up and said, "Thank you, Peter"—to the back of his head.

Bonham and Addison, 1978; Faerstein, 1981). The divorce rate among parents of mentally retarded children is three times that of parents with normal children (Love, 1973); the desertion rate of fathers is disproportionately high (Reed and Reed, 1965); and the suicide rate is twice the national average (Love, 1973). A family's social life suffers. Members commonly feel embarrassed at having a mentally retarded child. Further, the child usually requires extra time, care, and attention. Many parents withdraw, cutting down on the number of their acquaintances and their contacts with relatives (Prince-Bonham and Addison, 1978).

Through counseling and participation in groups with other parents experiencing similar difficulties, parents may develop more healthy and successful coping techniques. Most parent counseling strategies fall into three categories: (1) informational programs to provide parents with facts concerning their child's handicapped condition, (2) psychotherapeutic programs to help parents deal with their own problems and to understand the conflicts that bring about emotional difficulties in themselves and their children, and (3) parent-training programs to help parents develop effective child management and teaching skills (McDowell, 1976; Shapero and Forbes, 1981).

TEACHING GIFTED AND TALENTED CHILDREN

The world . . . is only beginning to see that the wealth of a nation consists more than in anything else in the number of superior [gifted] men [and women] it harbors.

WILLIAM JAMES
Speech at Stanford University, 1906

Concern for the identification and training of gifted individuals is hardly a recent development. Over 2,300 years ago Plato speculated on ways of telling which children were gifted so that they might be educated for leadership in the Greek state. The Romans later adopted some of Plato's ideas and gave special training to talented youths so that they might become military and governmental leaders. Today rapid scientific advances and widespread social change have expanded the need for competent and talented personnel at all levels of contemporary life.

Yet, as too often in the past, human societies remain extravagantly wasteful of talent (Gallagher, 1982). Within the United States there are an estimated 1 to 2 million gifted children who represent 2 to 4 percent of the nation's elementary and secondary school pupils. They are, says Sidney P. Marland, Jr., the former United States Commissioner of Education, among "our most neglected" students. In a 1970 report to Congress, Marland admitted that federal efforts to aid the gifted and talented were "all but nonexistent." Although the Office of the Gifted and Talented was established within the U.S. Office of Education in 1972 (ironically as part of the Bureau of Education for the Handicapped), little has happened over the past decade to change Marland's assessment. In the great majority of the nation's communities, programs for the gifted are at most piecemeal, sporadic, and sometimes totally absent.

Advocates of programs for the gifted are frequently accused of elitism, which in a democratic order is often viewed as a grievous sin. And some black parents view such programs as a new version of old tracking systems that relegated black children to the slow-track classes. Indeed, American society seems to have a strong love-hate relationship with the gifted (Gallagher, 1982). On the one hand, we revere the gifted individual, especially one who has risen from a humble background. On the other, we are suspicious of attempts to subvert our commitment to an egalitarian society.

Experts in education insist that gifted children have a tough row to hoe (Karnes, Shwedel, and Linnemeyer, 1982; Whitmore, 1982). An unusually able child is frequently made to feel like an oddball among his or her peers. Even teachers may respond with hostility. Bored with regular classwork and uncomfortable with their uniqueness, many gifted children turn into behavioral problems. Some of them become disruptive and uncooperative, while others adapt by excessive withdrawal.

Defining Gifted

Genius and precocity are not necessarily the same thing, nor, even, are giftedness and precocity. . . . Yet in this country giftedness of children has meant high IQ, and genius has meant an even higher IQ.

DAVID FELDMAN
A book review, 1977

The term *gifted* became the prevalent designation for individuals of superior ability during the early part of this century. Indeed, until relatively recently, it was almost impossible to bestow the title "gifted" on a child without having the label legitimized through an IQ test. Part of the appeal of using IQ in defining the gifted is that an IQ score seemingly provides a tangible and objective basis for the designation.

In the 1950s psychologists began to stress creativity rather than IQ in the study of intellectual giftedness. As noted in Chapter 8, this research has revealed that high IQ is a relatively poor predictor of truly outstanding achievement. Many researchers have found that once the IQ is higher than 120, other factors become increasingly important (Getzels and Dillon, 1973; Albert, 1975). Indeed, Robert S. Albert advances the argument that "genius" is a matter of social definition and recognition, a question of how people evaluate and react to an individual:

Genius is not a blessing, a danger, or a fortuitous occurrence; it is not a trait, an event, or a thing. Rather, it is, and always has been, a judgment overlaid with shifting values. What genius has often been based on is far more solid—behavior. [1975:150]

And there are those psychologists like David Feldman (1979) who hold that all children are gifted and that it is the burden of the educational system to find out what a child's gifts are and then to foster their expression.

In the 1920s, Lewis B. Terman, a Stanford University psychologist who developed the Stanford-Binet intelligence test, launched a study of children with IQs over 135 (Goleman, 1980). Over the intervening sixty years, teams of investigators have undertaken to follow up on how the original group of 1,528 young people have fared. On the whole the group did well by societal standards. They are happier, healthier, wealthier, and more productive than their peers. However, none made any truly noteworthy creative breakthroughs or achieved a Nobel Prize or similar honor.

The outcome of the Terman and related research has led educational psychologists to conclude that no single criterion like high IQ serves to identify giftedness. Instead psychologist Joseph S. Renzulli (1978) suggests that unique accomplishments and creative contributions are a product of three interlocking clusters of traits. These clusters consist of above-average general ability, task commitment, and creativity. Traditional indicators of academic success have at best only a very modest correlation with various indicators of success in the adult world. Also necessary are dedication to a task and originality and constructive ingenuity.

Over the past decade or so the focus of attention has shifted to a concern with *talent*. Although talent is no less ambiguous a concept than intelligence or creativity, it generally is taken to refer to superior abilities valued by society (Getzels and Dillon, 1973). Illustrative is the working definition of the gifted and talented employed by the U.S. Office of Education: "Children capable of high

TALENT
Talent is increasingly coming to be defined in social terms as those behaviors that are valued by society.

performance, including those with demonstrated achievement or ability in any one or more of these areas—(1) general intellectual ability, (2) specific academic aptitude, (3) creative or productive thinking, (4) leadership ability, and (5) visual and performing arts, or psychomotor ability.'' Applying this definition, it is generally believed that approximately 3 to 5 percent of the school-age population—some 2 to 5 million children—could be considered gifted and talented (Sisk, 1977).

Myths Regarding the Intellectually Gifted

There is no great genius without madness.

ARISTOTLE

The facts regarding the intellectually gifted are befogged by a great many myths that have little or no foundation in fact. Indeed, the essential picture regarding intellectually gifted children was drawn in the 1920s and has not been substantially altered in the intervening years. Numerous investigations continue to discover and rediscover and to state and restate what has been known for decades (Getzels and Dillon, 1973):

- *Myth:* Intellectually gifted children are puny and physically underdeveloped.
- *Fact:* Although individuals with high IQs are often stereotyped as frail and weak, research reveals that as a group they are likely to be healthy and robust (Terman, 1925; Monahan and Hollingworth, 1927; Witty, 1930; Hobson, 1948; Miles, 1954; Goleman, 1980). They have been found to have better than average bodily development (height and weight) and superior neuromuscular capacity. Overall, their general physical health tends to be better than average. Their physical development is usually accelerated, and they generally enter puberty earlier than do children in the general population.

- *Myth:* Intellectually gifted children are mentally unstable.

- *Fact:* Throughout much of history the gifted have been thought to be emotionally unstable. The ancient Greeks equated genius with madness, demigods, or both. Even today many people believe that ''whiz kids'' are ''peculiar.'' But research does not support the idea that intellectual superiority is related to emotional instability. If anything, intellectually gifted children tend to be more emotionally stable, less tense, and better able to handle personal problems than children in the general population (Terman, 1925; Gallagher, 1976). Unhappily, all too often we call anything that is different ''unhealthy.'' Hence, children who are interested in atomic physics rather than football are thought to be ''odd.''
- *Myth:* Intellectually gifted children are socially maladjusted.
- *Fact:* Gifted children are likely to be more socially popular and accepted than their peers (Terman, 1925; Miller, 1957; Bell, 1958; Grupe, 1961). There is some evidence, however, that the superior social adjustment of the gifted may be partially the product of their more favored socioeconomic class position and opportunities (Bonsall and Stefflre, 1955).

- *Myth:* Intellectually gifted children blossom and then fade to mediocrity.
- *Fact:* No research has confirmed the ''early ripe, early rot'' thesis. As Lewis M. Terman observes, ''So far no one has developed post-adolescent stupidity'' (1954:23).

Programs for Gifted and Talented Children

Gifted and talented children all too often confront the problem of adjusting their skills and interests to the curriculum being offered in the classroom. This frequently means that they must endure the systematic presentation of material that they have long since mastered. Advocates of special instructional programs for the gifted and talented say that this is an unhealthy situation. It breeds frustration, bitterness, anger, and eventually alienation. But even more important, proponents of programs for the gifted and talented say that every student has a *right* to an *appropriate* education. Robert L. Trezise argues:

> This principle applies to all students, from the most handicapped child to the most gifted. To provide for the gifted, therefore, is not undemocratic, as is so often implied; it is in keeping with the best traditions of American schools. [1976:243]

Yet, as pointed out earlier in the chapter, the gifted and talented are among "our most neglected" students. Many lay persons and also some school personnel contend that providing educational programs specially for the talented will contribute to the establishment of an intellectual elite. Of interest, many of those who express this concern accept unhesitatingly and uncritically the fact of first teams in sports, first violins in orchestras, and winners in races, art contests, and competitions in essay writing about American democracy (Newland, 1976).

Adding to the difficulty of winning support for the gifted and talented is the belief in many circles that children of extraordinary ability should be able to make it on their own. Bruno Bettelheim, a psychologist renowned for his work with emotionally disturbed children, takes this position: "I feel that the gifted child, despite the concern of many parents, is well able to take care of himself. If he isn't, then he isn't gifted" (quoted by Maeroff, 1977a:31). But advocates of aid for the gifted reject this view. They maintain that the failure to nurture talent causes it to wither. Marland, the former U.S. Commissioner of Education, says: "Intellectual and creative talent cannot survive educational neglect and apathy" (quoted by Maeroff, 1977a:31).

Programs for the gifted and talented are commonly categorized under the headings of enrichment, grouping, and acceleration. Although the categories overlap to some extent, this practice will be followed here.

Enrichment

One approach to the education of gifted and talented children is to "enrich the curriculum." This entails the introduction of activities designed to further develop the particular skills and talents of the gifted child within the context of an otherwise undifferentiated or heterogeneous classroom (Renzulli, Smith, and Reis, 1982). As such, enrichment programs are simply a variety of individualized instruction in which teaching is adjusted to the needs and abilities of a child. One approach involves an independent study program based on a written contract between the student and the teacher for the completion of specified work. Unfortunately, much of what commonly passes as enrichment is simply busywork. The assignments consist of more of the same, greater in quantity than is required of average students, but little different in level or challenge.

Grouping

Grouping involves placing students in special classes, "tracks," or "streams" according to ability or interest. It long has been the focus of sharp controversy revolving as much about democratic and egalitarian issues as about effectiveness in improving academic achievement (Getzels and Dillon, 1973). (See Chapter 15.) Grouping may be achieved in a number of ways. Probably the rarest arrangement is the special school devoted entirely to the education of the intellectually gifted, an arrangement New York City has employed at the high-school level. A more usual arrangement is to place children of a similar level of ability together in the same classroom. Another approach is to separate students in special groups by ability level for a part of the day. Still another arrangement, an itinerant teacher program, places gifted children with a teacher who specializes in the education of high-ability children for a few hours each week.

Acceleration

Acceleration refers to programs that allow students to complete their schooling in less time or at an earlier age than usual. Such programs take a variety of forms: early entry to kindergarten through college, combining two years' work into one, skipping a course or grade, taking extra courses or attending summer sessions to shorten total time in school, earning college credit for high-school work, and "proficiencing" (getting credit for certain courses by examination (Passow, 1958).

Acceleration enjoys a poor reputation among the lay public as well as many educators. This is tragic, since the preponderance of research reveals that those who have been accelerated, one way or another, generally do well both in school and in later life (Pressey, 1949; McCandless, 1955; Stanley, 1976). Not untypical are D. A. Worcester's findings regarding the early admission of gifted children to school in a number of communities in Nebraska:

> [The children] who were admitted to kindergarten on the basis of individual mental tests were, on the average, approximately eight months younger than those admitted regularly. There were no statistical differences in physical development. In academic work, the younger did as well or better than their older classmates. Judged by their peers or by teacher ratings, they are socially and emotionally as well or better adjusted. They have as good or better coordination. They are accepted by their peers. They like school. They do as well or better than those of the same age who were a year later in getting started in school. Indeed, no negative effects have been discerned. As compared with those who took the test but did not pass it, the younger ones had gained a year of school life without loss in social adjustment. [1956:28]

Study after study confirms that early admission is undeniably favorable (Hobson, 1948, 1956; Justman, 1953, 1954). Julian C. Stanley (1976) and his associates at Johns Hopkins University also claim favorable results based upon their program of radical acceleration for gifted math students (Fox, 1981). Despite such overwhelming evidence, considerable resistance still persists toward acceleration. As James J. Gallagher observes, "When

negative attitudes still persist in the face of strong evidence, some more persuasive emotional factor would seem to be present and needs to be identified if these procedures are to be put into operation in our public schools" (1966:100).

CHAPTER SUMMARY

1. During the past decade, a new approach to children with special needs has been moving to the forefront. This outlook is more positive and emphathic. It seeks to remove the stigma of willful and deliberate intent on the part of the children for their problems and poor school achievement. Further, it aims to relieve parents of feelings of guilt and shame.
2. The term "learning disabilities" emerged from a need to identify and serve a group of children who experience school failure yet elude existing categories like mentally retarded and emotionally disturbed. Most definitions of the term are extraordinarily vague.
3. The tests comprising a learning disabilities battery usually evaluate a child's perception, language, intelligence, and neurological function. To date, however, no foolproof tests have been developed for diagnosing learning disability. Most special educators agree that the state of the art in education, psychology, physiology, and medicine does not enable them to diagnose the causes of a child's difficulties with great specificity or to design a program of instruction that is tailored to each child's specific needs with great accuracy. Although there is no totally satisfactory battery of tests for screening early school problems, most educators nonetheless believe that screening is a useful and helpful procedure.
4. The placement of children in a category like "learning disabled" is a serious business. It can profoundly affect what happens to a child. The label generates negative expectancies in teachers that affect their objective observations of children's

behavior. On the other hand, classification makes it possible for society to identify specific learning problems and to marshal resources of money, facilities, and talent to attack these problems.

5. Hyperactivity is not a disease but merely a label for a collection of rather vague and global symptoms. Medical experts disagree on the nature of the hyperactive syndrome and the means for diagnosing it. Hyperactivity is a descriptive term that implies a judgment about a child's behavior. Considerable controversy surrounds the use of drugs, primarily amphetamines, in the management of hyperactive children.

6. In the past decade, there has been a dramatic change in the policy and philosophy of educating mildly and moderately handicapped children. The current shift has been away from separate or segregated classrooms toward mainstreaming. Mainstreaming has been proposed as a means of ensuring equality of educational opportunity and equal protection under the law. Successful mainstreaming requires that at least three conditions be satisfied. First, the child's educational needs must be compatible with the instruction that is being provided his or her classmates. Second, there must be willingness on the part of the teacher to accommodate children who have different learning styles and abilities. And third, a cooperative relationship must prevail between the regular classroom teacher and the special education teachers.

7. Several different models exist within the field of learning disabilities, and each accounts for children's academic and behavioral problems from a somewhat different perspective and recommends different strategies for dealing with these difficulties. Educational deficit advocates contend that children have individual strengths and weaknesses that must be addressed by a program of instruction. Behavior modification proponents say that both appropriate and inappropriate behavior result from learning experiences. Social environmental advocates argue that children's school difficulties result from the failures of the educational institution and the larger society. Medical proponents look to structural (neurological) or metabolical malfunc-

tioning to account for learning and behavior problems. And psychotherapeutic advocates focus upon faulty personality development and functioning.

8. The complexity of some students' difficulties may require interprofessional assessment and treatment. A thorough knowledge of the more serious problems in learning and behavior transcends the knowledge available to any one individual or profession.

9. The parents of handicapped and learning disabled children hold the key to any successful program for helping their children gain mastery of their disabilities. A commitment to children with special needs carries the responsibility to provide assistance to their parents. Most parent counseling strategies fall into three categories: (1) informational, (2) psychotherapeutic, and (3) parent training.

10. The term "gifted" became the prevalent designation for individuals of superior ability during the early part of this century. Indeed, until relatively recently, it was almost impossible to bestow the title "gifted" on a child without having the label legitimized through an IQ test. In the 1950s psychologists began to turn from the study of intellectual giftedness as defined by IQ to creativity. Over the past decade the focus of attention has again shifted, this time to a concern with talent.

11. The facts regarding the intellectually gifted are befogged by a great many myths that have little or no foundation in fact. Intellectually gifted children are not puny and physically underdeveloped, mentally unstable, or socially maladjusted.

12. Programs for the gifted and talented are commonly categorized under the headings of enrichment, grouping, and acceleration. Enrichment entails the introduction of activities designed to further develop the particular skills and talents of the gifted child within the context of an otherwise undifferentiated or heterogeneous classroom. Grouping involves placing students in special classes, "tracks," or "streams" according to ability or interest. Acceleration refers to programs that allow students to complete their schooling in less time or at an earlier age than usual.

CHAPTER GLOSSARY

diagnostic-prescriptive teaching   Identifying the most effective instructional strategy for each child.

hyperactivity   A collection of rather vague and global symptoms including excessive restlessness, high distractibility, a short attention span, academic difficulties, and behavior problems.

learning disabilities   An umbrella concept referring to children who encounter difficulty in school-related subject matter despite the fact that they are of normal intelligence and have no demonstrable physical, emotional, or social handicap.

mainstreaming   The integration of children with special needs into regular classroom programs.

APPENDIX OF SPECIAL EDUCATION TERMS

agnosia   The individual receives information from a sense organ but is unable to comprehend or interpret it.

agraphia   The inability to relate the mental images of words to the motor movements required for writing them.

alexia   Loss of the ability to read, usually as a result of a brain lesion.

aphasia   The loss of the ability to employ language symbols as in speech.

apraxia   (also termed **dyspraxia**) Loss of the ability to perform purposeful movement in the absence of paralysis or other motor impairment.

articulation   The production of speech sounds (words and sentences).

ataxia   A condition of the central nervous system resulting in marked inability to control and coordinate bodily movement.

auditory blending   The ability to put separate sounds together to form a word.

auditory discrimination   The ability to distinguish or differentiate among sounds that are nearly alike.

autism   A condition characterized by absorption in fantasy to the exclusion of reality.

brain damage   Any structural (tissue) injury to the cerebellum, cerebrum, or cerebral cortex resulting in some degree of malfunctioning.

central nervous system (CNS)   The brain and the spinal cord.

cerebral dominance   The notion that one hemisphere of the brain is dominant in controlling particular body functions.

closure   The ability to recognize or achieve a complete conception or idea, especially when some of the information is absent.

culturally disadvantaged   Children who find that the social norms, values, and beliefs of the school differ radically from those found in the environment in which they have been reared.

deaf   Lacking functional hearing, usually defined as hearing losses greater than sixty decibels.

decibel   A unit of volume; one decibel is roughly equal to the smallest difference in loudness that the human ear can detect.

dissociation   The inability to perceive things as a whole or unity; segments are seen without relation to the total configuration.

distractibility   The tendency to be easily drawn away from the task at hand and to become involved with extraneous stimuli.

dyslexia   A reading difficulty not attributable to ordinary learning causes.

echolalia A meaningless repetition of sounds or words.

educable mental retardate (EMR) An individual whose IQ score is in the 60 to 80 range and who can benefit from educational programs.

electroencephalography (EEG) A technique for recording the electrical activity of the brain for the purpose of detecting pathological conditions.

emotional lability A psychiatric term referring to instability in emotions or moods that is characterized by rapid shifts from one extreme to another extreme.

etiology A medical term referring to the origin or cause of a particular disease or abnormality.

glaucoma A disease of the eye involving increased pressure within the eyeball and leading to a progressive loss of vision.

grand mal seizure A form of epilepsy characterized by considerable neural discharge in which there is a sudden loss of consciousness accompanied by muscular spasms.

hyperkinesis A condition characterized by excessive restlessness, high distractibility, and short attention spans.

hypoglycemia An abnormally low level of glucose in the blood.

hypokinesis A condition characterized by diminished motor activity and function, often giving the appearance of listlessness.

impulsivity The tendency to act without forethought or concern for subsequent results.

kinesthesia The sense by which the organism perceives muscular movements and the position of the body.

laterality Awareness of the relative position of one side of the body to the other side.

lesion Any injury or other localized, abnormal structural change in the body.

malfunction A failure to operate in the proper or usual manner.

meningitis Inflammation of the membranes of the brain or spinal cord.

mental retardation A condition characterized by significantly subaverage general intellectual functioning and significant deficits in adaptive behavior apparent in the course of the individual's development.

minimum brain dysfunction An unspecified but not severe neurological impairment that results in learning and/or behavioral problems.

mixed cerebral dominance The theory that some learning disorders, especially language, are caused by the fact that neither hemisphere of the brain is dominant.

modality An avenue by which the organism acquires sensation; a sensory pathway such as the visual or auditory.

motility The range and speed of an organism's motion.

neonatal The newborn during the first two weeks following birth.

neurological Having to do with the nervous system.

neurosis A form of mental or emotional maladjustment that is not severe enough to produce a profound personality derangement, as in psychotic disorders.

nystagmus A continuous, involuntary, rapid, rolling movement of the eyeball.

ocular Pertaining to the eye.

olfactory Pertaining to the sense of smell.

ontogeny The developmental or life history of an organism.

orthopedic malfunction A defect in the skeletal system.

pathological   A diseased or abnormal condition.

perceptual disorder   An inadequate functioning of the sensory system resulting in difficulty in acquiring and processing relevant information.

perseveration   The tendency for a specific form of behavior to be maintained when it is no longer appropriate.

phobia   An excessive or inappropriate fear.

phylogeny   The evolutionary development of a species or class of organisms.

prenatal   The period elapsing between conception and birth.

prognosis   A prediction about the eventual course of an illness or response to treatment.

prophylaxis   Preventive treatment.

psychosis   A severe form of emotional or mental illness that constitutes a disease entity.

schizophrenia   A psychosis characterized by one or more symptoms such as hallucinations, disordered and illogical thinking, inappropriate emotional responses, personality deterioration, bizarre behavior, and gradual withdrawal from reality.

soft signs   Some behavior or test result suggestive of brain dysfunction.

stereopsis   Three-dimensional perception.

strabismus   A disorder of vision in which the optic axes of both eyes do not allow focusing at the same point; sometimes termed squinting or cross-eye.

Strauss-syndrome   A cluster of symptoms considered characteristic of the ''brain-injured'' child.

syndrome   A group of symptoms that together are characteristic of a disease, disability, or disorder.

visual discrimination   The ability to distinguish between and see similarities in shapes, colors, numbers, and related stimuli.

visual memory   The ability to recall what has been seen.

EXERCISES

Review Questions

1. The increasing emphasis on improving educational programs for students with special needs has been influenced by which of the following?
   a. These students can control much of their behavior, and hence education is relevant.
   b. Their problems are related to failures in traditional child rearing.
   c. The students have been shown to benefit in varying degrees from instruction.
   d. Assistance can be justified from an economic viewpoint.
   e. c and d are true

2. Under the definition included in PL 94–142, which of these types would be included in a learning disabled class?
   a. mildly mentally retarded
   b. minimal brain dysfunction
   c. emotionally disturbed
   d. blind

3. The identification of learning disabled children has been helped considerably by the fact that
   a. there are several universally satisfactory test batteries now available for screening
   b. classroom teachers are quite accurate predictors of future school success
   c. ''learning disabled'' is a relatively restricted diagnostic category
   d. a, b, and c are true

4. Proponents and opponents of categorizing children seems to agree that

a. a designation such as "learning disabled" is semantically neutral

b. teachers at least are not likely to "explain" a child's behavior because of a label

c. these children are more likely to receive sympathetic treatment from peers

d. there is no agreement on a, b, and c

5. Hyperactivity in children

a. is generally a description of the child's behavior

b. is attributed primarily to organic defects

c. occurs in less than 1 percent of all school-children

d. is generally assumed to lessen considerably during adolescence

6. Successful mainstreaming depends on

a. compatibility of the child's educational needs with the instruction being provided

b. willingness of the classroom teacher to adjust

c. a cooperative relationship with the special education teacher

d. a, b, and c are true

e. b and c are true

7. A factor that contributes to the loss of popularity among handicapped children being mainstreamed is their

a. stigmatization as special education students

b. determination to succeed academically, which is at variance with usual group norms

c. behavior, which may draw negative reactions from peers

d. a, b, and c are true

e. a and c are true

8. Families of children with special needs

a. find that having such a child usually draws them closer together

b. discover that their embarrassment disappears once school starts

c. tend to expand their social life to compensate

d. feel a personal guilt

9. Until recently, the most widely used criterion for defining the gifted was

a. age at which the child started talking

b. performance in school

c. IQ

d. talent

10. Among the teaching practices associated with the gifted is

a. grouping

b. enrichment

c. acceleration

d. a, b, and c are true

e. a and b are true

Answers

1. e (See p. 503)
2. b (See pp. 502–503, 504)
3. b (See pp. 505, 508)
4. d (See pp. 510–511)
5. a (See pp. 512–513)
6. d (See pp. 516–518)
7. e (See p. 518)
8. d (See pp. 524–525)
9. c (See pp. 526–527)
10. d (See pp. 529–530)

Applying Principles and Concepts

1. Choose those items that are included in PL 94–142, the Education for All Handicapped Children law.

_____ a. Handicapped is defined in terms of physical or neurological, but not psychological, impairment.

_____ b. Districts must locate and serve *all* handicapped children of school age in the district.

_____ c. All handicapped students must be mainstreamed.

_____ d. An individual educational program is to be drawn up for each student.

_____ e. Placement of a child in a program is left entirely to the district professional staff.

2. According to the texbook, which of the following students could validly be placed in a learning disabled class?

_____ a. The student is twelve years old, is in the sixth grade, has an IQ of 110, and reads at second-grade level.

_____ b. The student is six years old, is in the first grade, has an IQ of 130, cannot read, and is hard of hearing.

_____ c. The student is ten years old, has an IQ of 65, and cannot read or write.

_____ d. The student is thirteen years old, is in the seventh grade, has an IQ of 100, reads at seventh-grade level, and cries constantly.

3. A fourth-grade teacher is reporting on one of her students, who is supposedly hyperactive. Underline those passages that are _not_ typical of hyperactive children.

Marty [the child] is very restless, always squirming. However he can work for long periods of time once he gets started. He is quite irritable, but Ritalin seems to have a calming effect. Indeed, I am convinced his scholastic achievement has improved immeasurably since he started taking the drug.

4. A junior high school has recently decided to mainstream mildly retarded students. Which of the following statements made by a regular classroom teacher might be considered valid?

_____ a. "I don't have the skills to deal with these children."

_____ b. "Some of my students are going to give these kids a real hard time."

_____ c. "It will work if the special education teacher stays away."

_____ d. "These retarded kids just can't cope socially."

5. There are five models of learning disabilities: educational deficit (ED), behavioral modification (BM), social environmental (SE), medical (M), and psychotherapeutic (P). Identify each example below with the appropriate model.

_____ a. "Where he came from, poor neighborhoods have poor schools."

_____ b. "You can't change her genes, but you can change the classroom."

_____ c. "Let's first find out what the specific learning problems are, and then attack those."

_____ d. "That child seems hell-bent on self-destruction."

6. Which of the following descriptions of gifted children would be supported by research?

_____ a. John has had a history of mental instability, although his grades have been excellent when he was not having problems.

_____ b. Jane has always managed to deal effectively with older children in high school because she matured earlier.

_____ c. Poor Sam, he showed so much early promise that he never fully realized.

_____ d. A teacher: "I wonder why so many of my gifted kids come from families that are economically and socially well-off."

Answers

1. b, d (See pp. 502–503)
2. a (See pp. 504–505)
3. Underline "can work for long periods of time," "scholastic achievement has improved immeasurably since he started taking the drug." (See pp. 512–514)
4. a, b (See pp. 516–517)
5. a, SE; b, BM; c, ED; d, P (See pp. 518–521)
6. b, d (See p. 528)

Project 1

OBJECTIVE: To assess how mainstreaming is actually implemented.

PROCEDURE: Visit a school where mainstreaming is practiced, and use the following questions as guidelines. Interview one or more teachers who have actually had handicapped children in class:

1. How long has mainstreaming been in effect?
2. What kinds of students are mainstreamed?
3. Who determines which students are placed in a regular class?
4. What has been the attitude of your other students toward these children?
5. What kinds of instructional and classroom-management problems have you encountered?
6. What kinds of skills do you wish you had?
7. Have you received any special help with these children (for example, resource teacher, special education teacher, and the like)?
8. How optimistic are you about mainstreaming?

ANALYSIS: The data lend themselves to several types of analysis:

1. *Teachers' perceptions:* Questions 4, 5, 7, and 8 reflect current classroom practices. If the teachers' answers are quite divergent, then you may infer that the impact on such children in the regular classroom is unique to that situation. Common responses may, however, permit the development of certain general expectations among teachers.
2. *Diagnosis and management:* Questions 1, 2, and 3 reflect how much "give" there is in diagnosing and administering the program. As the text suggests, labeling children "handicapped" is often a way of dumping them. Do the answers reflect a precise, tight definition of handicapped?
3. *Teacher preparation:* Question 6 will give you some insight into what you may be personally lacking. Look especially for common perceptions of weaknesses.

Project 2

OBJECTIVE: To determine how a school handles the gifted.

PROCEDURE: Visit a school at any level, and ask the following questions:

1. How does the school define "gifted"?
2. How are gifted children selected?
3. What kinds of programs are available in the school? In the district?

ANALYSIS: Two dimensions of analysis are possible:

1. The answers to Questions 1 and 2 will yield information on whether giftedness is viewed simply as academic potential or in broader terms. You can almost bet that if IQ scores are critical, "gifted" means intellectual.
2. In the textbook, enrichment, grouping, and acceleration are described. Determine which are used in the school or district.

CHAPTER OUTLINE

18

MEASUREMENT

CHAPTER PREVIEW

As you saw in Chapter 13, one of the important steps in the design of instruction is evaluation, or some means of determining whether the instructional unit has been successful. Such assessment not only gives a teacher information about student achievement, but it also provides feedback about the preparation and presentation of the unit. While careful evaluation of each lesson taught may not occur regularly in school, assessment of many kinds is ever present. This chapter focuses on *measurement*—the

systematic collection and quantification of information about some area of interest. It may take the form of a standardized achievement test, a teacher-made test at the end of a social studies unit, or a rating scale about career preferences. Whatever form it takes, teachers must understand the qualities and characteristics of good tests, be sensitive to the uses and abuses of test information, and appreciate the range of factors to be considered in trying to evaluate student progress fairly.

To help accomplish these aims, keep these questions in mind as you read:

■ What are the major differences between norm-referenced and criterion-referenced tests, and when might each type of measurement be most appropriate?

■ Why are the concepts of test reliability and validity important?
■ What are the characteristics of good essay tests? Of good objective tests? What are some of the problems in the construction and scoring of each type of test?
■ What different systems have been employed for recording and reporting student progress? What advantages or problems are associated with each approach?
■ What factors should be considered in assigning grades?

Measuring, evaluating, and testing have been in the forefront of educational controversies over the past decade. Increasingly, legislators, taxpayers, and parents have raised the demand for accountability on the part of educators. Mounting criticism has been directed toward the quality of the educational product. There are those who charge that "Johnny can't read," "he can't write effectively," and "he can't perform simple mathematical computations." Critics point to the decline in college board scores since the early 1960s and to the drop in other standardized test scores to support their contention that public schools are ineffective. And there are also minority-group leaders who say that educational testing functions as a device to ensure the continued advantage of existing white elites.

Nonetheless, for the general public as well as most educators, schools without testing remain as inconceivable as schools without teachers, books, paper, and pencils. Further, decision making requires information, and wise decision making necessitates accurate and relevant information. This brings us to a consideration of evaluation, measurement, and testing.

THE NATURE OF MEASUREMENT

In common, everyday usage we employ the terms "evaluation," "measurement," and "test" interchangeably. Yet, as used in educational assessment, each term has a distinct meaning. **Evaluation** is the most inclusive of the concepts. It refers to the process of using qualitative or quantitative data to make judgments and decisions. Qualitative data include anecdotal and observational records of a person's behavior, generally a word description of a characteristic, property, or attribute ("Susan is a bright, resourceful youngster"). Quantitative data involve numerical values or scores, a measure of the magnitude, extent,

amount, or size of a characteristic, property, or attribute ("Susan has an IQ of 118 on the Wechsler Intelligence Scale for Children"). Whatever the form of the data, evaluation entails the use of information for judging alternative courses of action, determining the congruence between performance and objectives, or rendering an opinion about the desirability of a state of affairs.

Measurement is the systematic ascertaining of a characteristic, property, or attribute through a numerical device. The device may be an inventory, checklist, questionnaire, scale, or test. Measurement is limited to quantitative description of behavior and does not include qualitative descriptions or judgments of the desirability of the behavior being measured (Gronlund, 1976). In this respect, measurement differs from evaluation.

Test is a still more limited concept and refers to a type of measurement tool or instrument. It consists of a group of questions or tasks to which a student is asked to respond. The pupil may be requested to solve a mathematical problem, define a word, assemble an apparatus, or draw a figure.

Uses of Measurement Data

School administrators, guidance personnel, classroom teachers, and individual students require information that will allow them to make informed and appropriate decisions regarding their respective educational activities. Ideally, they should be aware of all the alternatives open to them, the possible outcomes of each alternative, and the advantages and disadvantages of the respective outcomes. Educational and psychological measurement can help individuals with these matters.

Data secured through testing procedures have many uses (Gronlund, 1976; Thorndike and Hagen, 1977; Salmon-Cox, 1981; Sproull and Zubrow, 1981). First, measurement data may be employed in the *placement* of students in one or another instructional program. Usually pupils take a *pretest* to measure whether they have mastered the skills that are prerequisite to admittance to a particular course or instructional sequence. For instance,

IMPORTANCE OF MEASUREMENT
Measurement provides students, teachers, administrators, and guidance personnel with
information for making informed educational decisions.

foreign language and mathematics programs are usually arranged in some hierarchical order so that achievement at each level of learning depends on mastery of the preceding level. The student is led from the entering position in the hierarchy to the terminating phase via intermediate steps. On the basis of the information provided by a pretest, a student can be placed (1) at the most appropriate point in the instructional sequence, (2) in a program with a particular instructional strategy, or (3) with an appropriate teacher.

Second, measurement data can be used in *formative* evaluation. Tests are administered to the students to monitor their success and to provide them with relevant feedback. The information is employed less to grade a student than to make instructions responsive to the student's strengths and weaknesses as identified by the measurement device. Mastery learning procedures emphasize the use of formative tests to provide detailed information about each student's grasp of a unit's objectives (see Chapter 14).

Third, measurement data have a place in *diagnostic* evaluation. Diagnostic testing takes over where formative testing leaves off. When a student fails to respond to the feedback-corrective activities associated with formative testing, a more detailed search for the source of the learning difficulty is indicated. Remediation is only possible when a teacher understands the basis of a student's problem and then designs instruction to address the need.

Fourth, measurement data may be used for

summation purposes. Such testing is employed to certify or grade students at the completion of a course or unit of instruction. Often the result is "final" and follows the student throughout his or her academic career (as in the case of college and university transcripts). It is this aspect of evaluation that some educators find particularly objectionable.

Fifth, measurement data are used by employers and educational institutions in making *selection* decisions. Many jobs and slots in educational programs are limited in number, and there are more applicants than positions. In order to identify the most promising candidates, standardized tests may be administered to the applicants. The information provided by the tests presumably increases the accuracy and objectivity of administrators' decision making. Results of college board examinations are used by many universities in admitting students to freshman classes, and graduate and professional schools likewise employ data from standardized testing programs to make their entrance decisions.

Sixth, measurement data are employed by school officials in making *curricular* decisions. In order to evaluate existing programs and to decide among instructional alternatives, school administrators need to assess their students' current levels of performance and the strengths and weaknesses the students evidence.

Seventh, measurement data find a place in *personal* decision making. Individuals confront a variety of choices at any number of points in their lives. Should they attend college or pursue some other type of post–high-school training? What kind of job seems most suited to their needs? What sort of training program should they enter? Measures of interest, temperament, and ability can give individuals insights that can prove helpful in the decision-making process.

Steps in Measurement

Robert L. Thorndike and Elizabeth P. Hagen (1977) point out that three steps are involved in developing a measurement device. First, we must identify and define the quality or attribute that is to be measured. We never measure a person, only a quality or attribute of the person like intelligence or emotional maturity. Similarly, we do not measure a table but the *length* of the table; not the fire but the *temperature* of the fire; not the automobile tire but the *durability* of the tire. Having identified the quality or attribute that interests us, we need to define it. For instance, if we are concerned with the durability of a tire, do we mean its resistance to puncture, its endurance against road wear, or its ability to hold up against deterioration?

Likewise, when educators and psychologists study intelligence, emotional maturity, achievement, and similar attributes, they find it necessary to specify the behaviors involved. If we are interested in measuring intelligence, do we define the term by the individual's ability to deal with ideas and abstract concepts, to exhibit innovative responses in novel situations, to show a particular speed and fluency in response, or to display some other property or properties?

The second step in developing a measurement device is to devise a set of operations to isolate the attribute and make it apparent to us. Take the durability of an automobile tire. Once we have identified and defined the attribute that interests us, we need to develop some standard to allow us to gauge or index it. If our concern is with the tire's resistance to roadway abrasion, we need to develop a procedure for ascertaining the rate at which the rubber wears away.

Similarly, various educators and psychologists have developed the Stanford-Binet and other tests that include operations for eliciting behavior that we take to be indicative of intelligence. But as Thorndike and Hagen note:

> The fact that there is no single universally accepted test, and that different tests vary somewhat in the tasks they include and in the order in which they rank people is evidence that we do not have complete consensus as to what intelligence is on the one hand, or what the appropriate procedures are for eliciting it on the other.[1977:13]

The third step in measurement is to express the results of the operations established in the second

MINIMUM COMPETENCY TESTING

Many states have established minimum standards that students must meet to graduate from high school and, in some cases, to progress from grade to grade. The minimum competency movement began in 1975. By 1981, three-fourths of the states had enacted some form of minimum competency legislation. The movement has been a response to widespread public dissatisfaction with the educational performance of the schools. Employers have complained that large numbers of high-school graduates do not have the basic reading, writing, and calculating skills required for many entry-level jobs. Colleges and universities have found it necessary to add remedial courses to their freshman programs. And parents whose seventeen-year-olds remain functionally illiterate after eleven or twelve years of schooling have voiced angry outrage.

Minimum competency programs vary widely. New York has made the passing of basic competency tests a requirement for high-school graduation. New Jersey has extended the principle to promotion from grade to grade, beginning with the third grade, but does not require a test for graduation. Some programs specify only that students must demonstrate general competency in reading or communications and arithmetic. Others, such as that of Vermont, spell out dozens of specific competencies students must demonstrate, ranging from arithmetic to "listening." Florida mentions life skills, and Rhode Island, survival skills. Many states have set up statewide norms and tests. Still others mandate that local districts set up their own systems for defining and measuring competency.

Oregon was the first state to adopt minimum competency requirements. Each of Oregon's 330 school districts was told to come up with its own program. The implementation of the directive confronted districts with a variety of problems. For instance, Portland began its program with 143 competencies, but the testing and recording were so time-consuming and expensive that local authorities subsequently reduced the number to 34. Further, lists of competencies differ from district to district (for instance, "life skills" thought necessary in Oregon's urban areas may receive low priority in rural districts).

As the movement has gained momentum, more state legislatures have been calling for testing at earlier grade levels in order to establish several checkpoints (for example, Maryland in grades 3, 7, 9, and 11; Kentucky, grades 3, 5, 8, and 11; and so on). Moreover, more emphasis is falling on remedial work, and on problems created by, or not directly handled in, the minimum competency legislation (Pipho, 1978).

Minimum competency programs have proven highly controversial. Proponents say that the programs (Popham, 1981; Lerner, 1981):

- Raise academic standards and encourage increased emphasis on core academic subjects.
- Produce greater accountability by educators and the schools in the use of public monies and resources by setting benchmarks of acceptable academic performance.
- Compel teachers and the schools to define more precisely what it is that students are expected to learn.
- Restore integrity to the high-school diploma by guaranteeing that the holder has certain skills.
- Allow schools to identify those students who need remedial work most and to provide help before it is too late.
- Provide a rational way to distribute federal, state, and local funds for remedial programs.
- Increase motivation to learn through the threat of holding students back or denying them a diploma.

(continued)

MINIMUM COMPETENCY TESTING *(continued)*

Critics say that minimum competency programs (Madaus, 1981; Pullin, 1981):

- Result in an unhealthy preoccupation with test scores and teachers "teaching to the test."
- Lead teachers to overemphasize isolated skills that can be easily measured at the expense of overall comprehension and to formulate trivial and narrow educational goals.
- Exceed the present measurement arts of the teaching profession.
- Make the minimum the maximum, since the emphasis falls on the performance of the academically weakest students.
- Hold teachers responsible for academic results rooted in conditions that extend well beyond their control within the classroom situation.
- Encourage students who do poorly on the tests to drop out of school when they reach age sixteen or the age when compulsory school attendance is no longer required.
- Discriminate against minority group youth (for instance, in the first year that minimum competency legislation was in effect in Florida, twice as many blacks as whites failed the test).
- Drain scarce school resources away from teaching and into devising, administering, and revising the tests.

One issue that has confronted the minimum competency movement has been that of defining competence. Some states are depending on definitions and standards of reading and calculating competence based on what is presumed to be within the "real-world" needs of contemporary adults. This requires a distinction between "school skills" and "life skills." Here is a question from a school skills test:

If John has 70 marbles and gives José 13 marbles and gets 26 marbles from Slim and gives 38 marbles to Alice, how many marbles does John have left?

Here is an item from a life skills test:

Balance this checkbook by adding these deposit slips and subtracting these cancelled checks.

Henry M. Brickell (1978) points out that there are seven elements to think about in planning a competency policy:

- What competencies will be required?
- How will the competencies be measured?
- When will the competencies be measured?
- How many minimums will be set?
- How high will the minimums be set?
- Will the results be used for students or for schools?
- What will be done about those students lacking the competencies?

If the American dream of education for all is to be achieved, the dialogue on these issues must be open and continuous.

step in numerical or quantitative terms. This involves an answer to the question, "How many or how much?" For example, we may employ millimeters as the units for indicating the thickness of the tread on the face of the tire and therefore express the amount of wear on the tire in terms of millimeters.

Similarly, educators and psychologists require numerical units for gauging anxiety, emotional maturity, intelligence, and other attributes. In the case of intelligence, they may have individuals perform a number of tasks and count the total number of successes that they then convert into IQ units.

Clearly each step in measurement rests on human-fashioned definitions. In the first step, we define the attribute that interests us. In the second step, we define the set of operations that will allow us to identify the attribute. And in the third step, we define the units in which we will state the results of our operations. Thus, what is measured is always a function of our definitions, and they have their own inherent limitations.

Norm- and Criterion-Referenced Testing

There are two principal ways in which we can interpret test scores. We can compare the level of a student's performance with that of others on the same test, termed a **norm-referenced measure.** Or we can compare the level of a student's performance against some established standard or criterion, termed a **criterion-referenced measure.** In the former case, we are interested in how the student compares with others in a group; in the latter, with what the student can do and with what he or she knows. A norm-referenced measure is used to differentiate among students and to rank them on the basis of their performance. For instance, on a given vocabulary test, we may find that Jerry can perform better than 85 percent of a national sample of fifth-graders. A criterion-ref-

INTERPRETING MEASURES OF PERFORMANCE
There are two chief ways for appraising a student's performance. We can administer a test to all the students and then compare one student's performance with that of the other students'—a norm-referenced measure. Or we can administer a test to one or more students and compare each student's performance against some standard— a criterion-referenced measure.

erenced measure is employed to ascertain a student's mastery of course content. For example, on a given vocabulary test, we may find that Jerry can correctly define 85 percent of the words.

The concern in criterion-referenced testing is not with the performance of others but with whether or not an individual is able to perform at an acceptable level (Nitko, 1980). It can tell us if a student has mastered the skills necessary to advance to the next level in a learning sequence. Or on a driver's license test, it can tell us if the student has attained what is commonly judged to represent a minimum proficiency in auto handling and safety. On a criterion-referenced test the standard is fixed and independent of the performance of others. The student knows that he or she will receive the desired grade or licensing certification if the required level of performance can be achieved.

In terms of appearance, both norm- and criterion-referenced tests are alike. They differ, however, in the content of the items. The items in a norm-referenced test are selected to produce a wide range of scores. This permits a teacher to differentiate the performance levels of the pupils and to rank the students in order of achievement from high to low. In contrast, the items in a criterion-referenced test are designed to reflect whether or not the pupil has attained specific knowledge and skills. The distributions of scores on criterion-referenced tests tend to "bunch" and are less useful for ordering individuals on measured ability.

Criterion-referenced testing has aroused particular interest over the past fifteen years, paralleling the movement toward mastery learning and individualized instruction (see Chapter 14). Common to these approaches is the notion that given enough time and suitable instructional materials, nearly every student can achieve proficiency with respect to the chosen instructional objectives. Criterion-referenced testing is employed to determine when a student's competence in an area is sufficient to allow him or her to progress to the next unit in an educational sequence. Accordingly, in constructing this type of test, it is essential to have a clear definition of the knowledge or skills the device is to assess.

One reason for the current popularity of criterion-referenced testing is that it diminishes the competitiveness often associated with norm-referenced testing. In theory, every child can perform at an acceptable level, since an absolute standard is used. In contrast, norm-referenced testing forces 50 percent of the pupils to perform "below average." Some educators also believe that the assessments based on criterion-referenced tests tend to be less judgmental and evaluative and more diagnostic and prescriptive. Criterion-referenced measures are best adapted to testing basic skills such as reading and mathematics at the elementary school level. These skills are specific and are prerequisite to the acquisition of higher-level skills.

There are, however, limitations and disadvantages to criterion-referenced testing. One potential danger, especially with nationally standardized tests, is that a school will "teach for the test" and downgrade other equally important and legitimate objectives. Further, students may be induced to learn material by rote instead of striving to understand. Robert L. Ebel observes, "One can teach badly by being too specific about the goals of learning, as well as by being not specific enough" (1975:85). Finally, criterion-referenced tests describe *what* students can do but not how well the students *should* be doing (Popham, 1976, 1978, 1980a, 1980b). Standards for performance derive from comparisons between the achievement level reflected by students in one classroom, school, or school district and that in other classrooms, schools, or school districts. This calls for norm-referenced scores or the use of criterion-referenced test scores for normative purposes.

In more advanced and less structured academic areas, less agreement exists regarding what constitutes achievement, and hence evaluation is less absolute and more open-ended. Here the focus falls on norm-referenced evaluation in assessing a person's degree of attainment. However, the distribution of assigned grades tells us nothing about the overall quality of performance in a classroom; it only affords a gross measure of a student's standing relative to that of the other students in the class. In order to determine the quality of instruction, a norm-referenced test would have to be administered for comparative purposes to a similarly situated citywide, statewide, or national sample of students.

THE QUALITY OF TESTS

A measurement device should possess several qualities. Among the most important are reliability, validity, and practicality. A good many statistical procedures are available to educators and psychologists for evaluating these properties of a test. Here we shall consider what each quality involves, although a statistical treatment is usually reserved for more advanced courses in education and psychology.

Reliability

In deciding on or fashioning a measuring device, we are concerned with how accurately it measures what we set out to measure and the precision of the resulting score. Thus, we need to know whether it will yield a similar result under similar conditions if we again measure the property in which we are interested. **Reliability** refers to the degree to which an instrument yields a consistent measurement of the same thing. For instance, if we take our temperature and the thermometer registers readings varying from 95 degrees to 103 degrees when we are known to have a normal temperature, we will have little confidence in the instrument. Nor will we feel easy with the measurements of a house taken by an elastic ruler.

We confront the problem of reliability when we administer an achievement test to our students. Would the students realize the same scores if they took the test last week, yesterday, tomorrow, or next week? Would their scores be the same had we provided another test with a differing sample of what we believe to be equivalent items? These matters deal with how generalizable test results are over different occasions or over different samples of the same type of behavior.

A good many factors affect the reliability of a measuring device. The individuals taking the test may themselves change from one time to the next. Such changes include state of health, motivation, fatigue, emotional strain, attention, forgetting, guessing, and training. The simple fact of having previously taken a similar test also introduces change. Further, the task itself may change, since the second test usually contains somewhat different items. And finally, the test administrator may not adhere to the time limits rigidly or the scorer may not grade the tests in the identical fashion (especially those with essay items). Such factors introduce some element of error to all test scores (Gronlund, 1976).

One way to establish the reliability of a test score is to administer an equivalent test to the same individuals and to correlate the scores (Green, 1981). A correlation of 1.0 indicates that the relative standing of the individuals is the same on the two tests. However, correlations of 1.0 are seldom achieved although reliabilities above .90 are frequent. In practice, a duplicate test is often not feasible because of the fatigue of the test-takers or because of the difficulty in constructing an equivalent test. Consequently, psychologists often use a *test-retest* procedure, in which the same test is administered twice at different times to the same individuals. The tester hopes that at the second testing the individuals will not remember either the items or their earlier responses. Another alternative for evaluating reliability is the *split-halves* procedure. In the split-halves procedure a test is divided into two halves that are matched as well as practical and then administered separately. Reliability of the total test is inferred from the correlation of the scores on the two halves.

Validity

Perhaps the most important question we have regarding a measuring device is whether it measures what we want it to describe, represents all the components of what we wish to describe, and describes nothing else but what we want it to describe. The matter is similar to the edict that the courtroom witness tell the truth, the whole truth, and nothing but the truth. The extent to which an instrument serves the purpose for which it is intended is termed **validity**.

If we are interested in the length of a desk, it is of little use to have a scale that determines its weight; instead, we require a ruler. Should we be interested in determining the mathematical achievement of a group of students, we would need to prepare a test that adequately samples a variety of mathematical skills. The score would represent a measure of each student's mathematical proficiency. However, the score itself is not the student's proficiency but merely a record of a sample of the pupil's behavior. Any appraisal regarding the student's proficiency is an inference from the number of problems the pupil solves correctly. The validity of the score is not self-evident but must be established on the basis of adequate evidence (Thorndike and Hagen, 1977; Messick, 1980; Green, 1981).

Three basic types of validity have been identified: content validity, criterion-related validity, and construct validity. *Content validity* refers to the extent to which a test measures a representative sample of the subject matter content or the behavioral changes in which we are interested. Finding the content validity of a test is equivalent to ascertaining how well it samples certain types of subject matter or behaviors. If we are concerned with the vocabulary comprehension of a group of students, we would need to measure each student's performance on a sample of questions intended to represent a phase of word achievement.

Criterion-related validity refers to the extent to which test performance is related to some other external measure. We are, in effect, asking with what confidence we can generalize or predict from these test results how well a student will do on a *different* task. For example, a test may be used to estimate a student's *present status*. Thus, a mathematics test may be interpreted as telling us about the accuracy with which a student can perform the

necessary arithmetic operations in metal shop. The validity of the test can then be assessed by how well the student actually solves mathematical problems in metal shop. Or a test may be employed to make a *prediction* about a student's future achievement. Colleges commonly use academic aptitude tests as part of their admission procedures. The tests are designed to forecast the probability of a student's college success. The validity of the test can be experimentally determined by administering the test to a group of high-school seniors and then later assessing how well the test predicted these same students' grades at the end of their freshman year in college.

Construct validity refers to the extent to which some hypothetical trait is reflected in the test performance. Various psychological and educational tests seek to measure general traits (constructs) like a person's verbal fluency, reasoning ability, spatial visibility, mechanical comprehension, anxiety, and introversion. Tests of these qualities are deemed valid insofar as they reveal the traits being expressed in the way that our existing body of knowledge says such traits should be expressed. For instance, from what we know regarding assertiveness we would expect that a group of sales personnel should score especially high on a measure of assertiveness and a group of librarians should score low.

Practicality

In selecting or devising a test, practical considerations need to be taken into account. A primary consideration is the ease with which the test can be administered. The directions should be complete, simple, and clear. They should be in written form. The more complicated the directions and the greater the number of subtests, the more likely errors will occur that distort the results.

The scoring of tests has traditionally been a particularly tedious, cumbersome, and troublesome operation. However, the trend toward objective standardized tests, the availability of separate answer sheets, and machine scoring have considerably eased many of the burdens. Test developers and publishers have produced tests that can be processed using sophisticated equipment. The costs are not prohibitive and represent a savings over hiring special clerical help or the false economy of imposing the burden upon already busy teachers.

The practicality of a test is also dependent on the ease with which the results can be interpreted and applied. Generally, publishers of a test provide a manual or guide to explain the uses of the test and how the results are to be evaluated. This material should contain tables and information about the test norms and their uses. And there should be comprehensive suggestions for applying the results to problems such as diagnosing student weaknesses, structuring remedial instruction, organizing class groupings, and the like.

TEACHER-MADE TESTS

Central to a school's evaluation process are teacher-made tests. Such instruments are designed to appraise the outcomes of local classroom instruction. Generally, commercial standardized tests are too general in scope and too inflexible to meet the special requirements of each classroom context.

Experienced educators know that good tests do not simply happen. Nevertheless, test construction all too often occurs at the last possible moment and in haste. This is unfortunate, since testing is an integral aspect of the total instructional program. Various uses of tests were identified earlier in the chapter. In preparing a test, the teacher needs to have a clear conception of how the test results are to be used. This requires prior specification of instructional objectives and decisions regarding the sequence and method of instruction (see Chapter 13). Therefore, evaluation is but one phase in an encompassing web of continual classroom planning.

Essay Tests

Teachers are often as concerned with measuring the ability of students to think about and use knowledge as they are with measuring the knowledge their students possess. In these instances, tests are needed that permit students some degree of latitude in their responses. Essay tests are adapted to this purpose. They provide items in which students supply, rather than select, the appropriate answer. Usually, the students compose a response in one or more sentences. Essay tests allow students to demonstrate their ability to recall, organize, synthesize, relate, analyze, and evaluate ideas.

Freedom of Response

Essay questions differ in the degree of freedom they permit students in fashioning responses. At one extreme, the students are limited both to the content and form of their answers, termed *restricted response questions*. The test statement defines the scope of the answer and the way the answer is to appear:

> List in statement form the major issues that divided the colonists and the British in 1775 on the eve of the American Revolutionary War.

At the other extreme, students are provided considerable leeway in selecting what they believe to be pertinent information, organizing the response as they deem appropriate, and evaluating the matters they judge to be significant. This is termed an *extended response question*. The test statement allows for a global attack on a problem and measures more general learning outcomes:

> Some historians claim that the issues dividing the colonists and the British in 1775 on the eve of the American Revolutionary War were so deep and irreconcilable that war between the two groups was inevitable. Evaluate the accuracy of this appraisal.

However, the latitude that is provided students makes the extended response question inefficient for measuring specific learning outcomes and poses difficulties to the grader in deriving a reliable score.

Advantages and Disadvantages

There are both advantages and disadvantages to essay questions. The major advantage is that they provide students with an opportunity to integrate and apply their thinking and problem-solving skills creatively. Rather than simply selecting a correct response, the pupils must *supply* an appropriate answer. As such, essay tests can provide an effective instrument for tapping higher levels of reasoning.

Some educators claim that essay questions have a desirable effect on students' study habits. The questions compel students to consider larger units of subject matter rather than preoccupying themselves with many isolated bits and pieces of knowledge. Thus, essay questions are thought to encourage students to learn how to organize and integrate their ideas and to express them effectively.

Essay questions have proven popular with teachers because they are viewed as quick and easy to prepare. However, this advantage can be misleading. Well-constructed essay questions that clearly define tasks in terms of instructional objectives require considerable time and effort.

There are important disadvantages to essay tests. The most severe difficulty is the unreliability of their scoring. An answer may be scored differently by different teachers and even by the same teacher at different times. Further, reading and scoring essays is laborious and time-consuming.

Another difficulty with essay questions is that they cover only a limited segment of a course's content. Since they take a good deal of time to answer, only a few questions can be completed during a class period. The teacher cannot sample a course's content as well with a few essay questions as with fifty multiple-choice questions.

Constructing Essay Test Questions

In preparing essay questions, teachers commonly find it helpful to keep the following suggestions in mind:

- Phrase the question with sufficient specificity so pupils know what they are asked to do. Avoid vague questions with ambiguous wording. For example:

  Poor: What causes climate?
  Better: Chicago and Rome are in the same general latitude yet their climates differ. Give reasons why the climates of Chicago and Rome differ.

- The question should be written in a way that will elicit the desired response in terms of objectivity and evidence. This is especially important in asking students a question dealing with a controversial issue. Asking students ''What is your opinion?'' or ''What do you think?'' provides no basis for arriving at a generally acceptable answer. Instead, students should be asked to marshal evidence and arguments in support of one or another position. For example:

  Poor: What is your opinion regarding a federal health insurance program?
  Better: Considerable disagreement prevails regarding the desirability of a federal health insurance program. Outline evidence and arguments either in support of or in opposition to the enactment of a federal health insurance program.

- When possible, phrase a question in a novel manner. For example:

  Poor: Explain the effect of a meander on the banks of a river.
  Better: You are planning to purchase land along a meandering river. Would it be better to purchase land on the inside or outside bank of a meander? Give the reasons for your choice.

- Begin essay questions with such words or phrases as *classify, compare, state the reasons for, illustrate, differentiate,* and *present an original example of.* Avoid essay questions that start with such words as *what, who, when,* and *list.* These latter words lead to the simple reproduction of information and defeat the organizing, synthesizing, and evaluating functions of essay items.

- Avoid the use of optional questions. It is a common practice among teachers to provide students with a number of essay questions and to allow them to select a certain number (for instance, answer four of the following seven questions). Providing alternatives undermines the common basis for evaluating students' achievement. Further, pupils can selectively study for the examination by omitting some material, since they know the test will contain an escape hatch.
- Allow enough time for students at all levels of competency to complete the examination.

Scoring Essay Tests

Professional educators recommend a number of guidelines to maximize the reliability of scores on essay items:

- Prepare a model answer or key at the time the essay question is formulated.
- Check the appropriateness of the model or key against a number of randomly selected papers before actually beginning the grading process.
- Grade only one essay question at a time for all students rather than all the questions on one student's paper (teachers are often influenced in scoring a question by how well the student did on the previous question).
- Identify the factors that are irrelevant to the learning outcomes that the test is seeking to measure (for instance, legibility of handwriting, spelling, punctuation, grammatical structure, and neatness).
- To the extent it is possible, grade the papers

anonymously so that prejudicial considerations do not bias the scoring process.

- Randomly reshuffle or rearrange the papers before grading the next question in a series (teachers are frequently influenced in scoring a paper by its position, particularly if the preceding paper was unusually good or poor).
- Score all the responses to a question at one sitting with only short breaks (teachers tend to vary from one time to another in scoring essay answers).
- When papers are to be returned, place appropriate written comments and answers on the paper for the benefit of the student.
- When important decisions rest on the outcome of the test results, obtain two or more independent ratings of a pupil's performance.

Objective-Item Tests

Objective-item tests are of two types. The *supply* type asks the student to provide a short answer or to complete a blank. The *select* type provides the student with alternative responses in the form of matching, true-false, or multiple-choice items. Proponents of objective-item tests contend that they assure good content sampling and easy and reliable scoring. Critics say that the tests foster rote learning, encourage guessing, and neglect the cultivation of integrating and organizing skills.

Short-Answer Items

Short-answer items are of two types: *simple-direct questions* (Who was the first president of the United States?) and *completion items* (The name of the first president of the United States is _____.). The items can be answered by a word, phrase, number, or symbol. Short-answer tests are a cross between essay and objective tests. The student must supply the answer as with an essay question but in a highly abbreviated form as with an objective question.

TEACHER-MADE TESTS
Evaluation is a continual and indispensable part of the teaching process.

Short-answer items have a number of advantages. First, they reduce the likelihood that a student will guess the correct answer. Second, they are relatively easy for a teacher to construct. Third, they are well adapted to mathematics, the sciences, and foreign languages, where specific types of knowledge are tested (The formula for ordinary table salt is _____.). Fourth, they are consistent with the Socratic question-and-answer format frequently employed in the elementary grades in teaching basic skills (8×4 is _____.).

There are also a number of disadvantages associated with short-answer items. First, they are limited to content areas in which a student's knowledge can be adequately portrayed by one or two words. Second, they are more difficult to score

than other types of objective-item tests, since students invariably come up with unanticipated answers that are totally or partially correct. Third, short-answer items usually provide little opportunity for students to synthesize, evaluate, and apply information.

Matching Exercises

The matching exercise consists of two parallel columns. The column on the left contains the questions to be answered, termed *premises;* the column on the right, the answers, termed *responses*. The student is asked to associate each premise with a response to form a matching pair. For example:

Capital City	Nation
_____ 1. Paris	a. Denmark
_____ 2. Copenhagen	b. Spain
_____ 3. Lisbon	c. Portugal
_____ 4. Madrid	d. France
_____ 5. The Hague	e. Netherlands
	f. Hungary
	g. West Germany

In some matching exercises the number of premises and responses are the same, termed a *balanced,* or *perfect, matching exercise*. In others the number of premises and responses may be different (as in the illustration above), termed an *unbalanced,* or *imperfect, matching exercise*.

The chief advantage of matching exercises is that a good deal of factual information can be tested in minimal time, making the tests compact and efficient. They are especially well suited to who, what, when, and where types of subject matter. Further, students frequently find the tests fun to take because they have puzzle qualities to them.

The principal difficulty with matching exercises is that teachers often find that the subject matter is insufficient in quantity or not well suited for matching items. An exercise should be confined to homogeneous items containing one type of subject matter (for instance, authors-novels; inventions-inventors; major events-dates; terms-definitions; foreign words-English equivalents; rules-examples; and the like). Where unlike clusters of questions are used, the adept but poorly informed student can often recognize the ill-fitting items by their irrelevant and extraneous nature (for instance, in a list of authors the inclusion of the names of capital cities).

True-False Items

The *true-false* (also termed *alternative-response) item* consists of a declarative statement that the pupil judges to be either correct or incorrect. Each question contains only two possible answers. Teachers find that the items are easy to construct and score, and that even students who are relatively poor readers can cope with them. However, true-false questions have decided limitations. In most fields only the most trivial statements can be reduced to absolute terms. Accordingly, the items found on true-false tests too often focus on unimportant pieces of information. The chief exceptions have to do with questions distinguishing between fact and opinion and in identifying cause-and-effect relationships. Further, since there are only two alternatives, a student has a fifty-fifty opportunity of guessing the correct answer on chance alone.

Multiple-Choice Items

The multiple-choice question is probably the most popular as well as the most widely applicable and effective type of objective test. It consists of two parts: (1) the *stem*, which states the problem, and (2) a list of three to five *alternatives*, one of which is the correct (or best) *answer* and the others distractors ("foils" or incorrect options that draw the less knowledgeable pupil away from the correct response).

The stem may be stated as a direct question or as an incomplete statement. For example:

Direct question:	What is the capital city of Denmark?
	a. Paris
	b. Lisbon
	c. Copenhagen
	d. Rome
Incomplete statement:	The capital city of Denmark is
	a. Paris
	b. Lisbon
	c. Copenhagen
	d. Rome

The chief advantage of the multiple-choice question is its versatility. For instance, it is capable of being applied to a wide range of subject areas. In contrast, short-answer items limit the writer to those content areas that are capable of being stated in one or two words. Nor is a multiple-choice item necessarily bound to homogeneous items containing one type of subject matter as are matching exercises. And a multiple-choice question greatly reduces the opportunity for a student to guess the correct answer from one chance in two with a true-false item to one in four or five, thereby increasing the reliability of the test. Further, since a multiple-choice item contains plausible incorrect or less correct alternatives, it permits the test constructor to "fine tune" the discriminations (the degree of homogeneity of the responses) and control the difficulty level of the test.

Multiple-choice items are difficult to construct. Suitable distractors are often hard to come by, and the teacher is tempted to fill the void with a "junk" response. This has the effect of narrowing the range of options available to the test-wise student. They are also exceedingly time-consuming to fashion, one hour per question being by no means the exception. Finally, they generally take students longer to complete (especially items containing fine discriminations) than do other types of objective questions.

Constructing Objective Test Questions

In preparing objective test questions, teachers commonly find it helpful to keep the following suggestions in mind:

- Test students for important information and avoid trivia. Many teachers find that constructing objective-item questions is taxing and tedious work. Since core material is often complex and many-sided, it may not immediately or easily lend itself to question formation. In contrast, trivial points frequently appear clearcut and readily available for precise test packaging. Teachers should resist the temptation to take the easy way out.

- Write the items clearly; avoid excessive verbiage, inappropriate choice of words, and awkward sentence arrangement. Too often tests measure the students' reading ability or the size of their vocabulary rather than their mastery of the course content. Teachers need to strike a balance between leaving out so much that the item is ambiguous and leaving out so little that the item is excessively easy. Consider the following examples (the answer is option *b*):

  Poor: The formulation of hypotheses
      a. is required to accomplish a descriptive study
      b. guides the direction of research
      c. states scientific fact
      d. is proven correct by research

  Better: A hypothesis is a statement that a researcher
      a. employs as a technique for collecting data
      b. uses as a guide in defining the nature of the study
      c. accepts as a proposition of scientific fact
      d. proves correct in the course of scientific investigation

- Do not give the answer away with irrelevant clues. Some test-wise students capitalize on the characteristics of the test to obtain a high score independent of their knowledge of the course content. Among common defects are stereotyped language, a systematic difference in the structuring of correct answers, grammatical clues, and word definitions. For example, in the following illustration the use of the indefinite article *an* gives the answer, "electron," away since it begins with a vowel:

  A subatomic particle that has a negligible mass and carries a unit negative electrical charge is an
      a. proton
      b. neutron
      c. molecule
      d. electron

- In some instances the student can use clues from one or more items to figure out the answers to other items. For instance, in the illustration below, the word *maestro* allows the pupil to identify the answers as *c* and *b* respectively:

  Maestro means
      a. employer
      b. letter
      c. teacher
      d. shirt

  El maestro es joven means
      a. the tie is old
      b. the teacher is young
      c. the tree is beautiful
      d. the clown is funny

- Make each item independent of other items. It should not be necessary for a student to get the correct answer to one item in order to answer another item correctly. Teachers should avoid writing items like the following that are interrelated (the answers to the questions are respectively *d* and *c*):

  A type of radiation that travels at the speed of light is
      a. a beta particle
      b. an alpha particle
      c. a cathode ray
      d. a gamma ray

  This type of radiation has the following charge
      a. positive
      b. negative
      c. no charge
      d. electric

- Avoid the use of negative questions. It takes students longer to answer a negatively phrased question than an equivalent positively phrased question. Further, more errors in interpretation are associated with a negative question. For example (the answer is option *a*):

Poor: The nucleus of the following element does not contain neutrons
a. hydrogen
b. sodium
c. helium
d. neon

Better: With the exception of the following element, the nuclei of all elements contain neutrons
a. hydrogen
b. sodium
c. helium
d. neon

■ **Avoid lifting a statement verbatim from a textbook or other source.** The practice favors pupils who can detect a textbook expression. Further, verbatim statements are frequently ambiguous since they are used out of context. For example:

Poor: (Shale) is clay that has become rock, mainly by pressure.

Better: Clay that has become rock through the action of the earth's pressure is termed (shale).

Mechanics of Objective Tests

The items comprising an objective test can be arranged in a manner to assist both the test-taker and the scorer. Measurement experts recommend that items be grouped together according to format (short-answer, matching exercises, true-false, and multiple-choice). Within each item type, those items dealing with the same subject matter can be placed together. This presents the pupil with an orderly, integrated arrangement rather than a disorganized mosaic of just so many bits and pieces of knowledge. Finally, educators advise that the items be arranged in order of their difficulty from easy to hard. Most commonly this entails beginning with true-false items, followed in order by matching

exercises, short-answer items, multiple-choice items, and finally essay questions.

The test should contain clear and concise directions. The student should be provided with a brief statement of the purpose of the test. This is frequently accomplished orally, usually at the time the test is announced and again immediately prior to its administration. The student should be informed as to the length of time available for completing the test, the procedure for recording the answers, and how the test is to be scored. This information should be provided in the form of written directions. With inexperienced test-takers, it is advisable to provide practice-test items to verify that the directions are understood by each student. Where appropriate the student should be instructed as to what to do about guessing (include information as to whether some correction formula or weighting scheme will be employed in scoring the test).

STANDARDIZED TESTS

The development of standardized tests in the United States has produced a situation unique in history. Never before has a society so conscientiously sought to evaluate the abilities and characteristics of its members.

MARJORIE C. KIRKLAND
"The Effects of Tests on Students and Schools," 1971

A **standardized test** is a measurement device that is commercially prepared by educational specialists for widespread use in a large number of schools. It is characterized by a fixed set of questions designed to measure a clearly defined sample of behavior. The test is administered under uniform conditions using the same set of directions for timing constraints and scoring. This permits educators to give the identical test to students in different locations and at different times.

Most commonly test designers establish performance norms for a standardized test based on representative groups of individuals (including various age and grade groups on a state, regional, or national level). This feature allows educators to interpret a pupil's performance in a norm-referenced manner. Accordingly, it is possible to compare the level of a student's performance with that of other groups of students. Further, a student's level of performance on one set of questions can be compared with his or her performance on other sets of questions (provided all the tests were normed using the same sample of students).

Standardized tests can be classified in any number of ways. The most popular classification is according to *what* is measured (Mehrens and Lehmann, 1978):

- Aptitude tests (general, multiple, and special).
- Achievement tests (diagnostic, single-subject matter, and survey batteries).
- Personality, attitude, interest, self-concept, and adjustment inventories.

The first two categories usually seek to measure maximum performance; the third, typical performance.

Aptitude tests are employed to make decisions about what an individual can do. They are a predictor of some *future* performance. *Achievement tests* tell us what an individual knows and has learned to do. They provide a measure of a person's *present* level of knowledge or skill. The distinction between an aptitude and an achievement test lies more in the purpose for which the results are to be used than in the nature of the test itself (Thorndike and Hagen, 1977). However, in some instances aptitude tests provide a broader coverage of behavior than do achievement tests.

Some educators and psychologists suggest that a student's performance on an achievement test is more likely to be influenced by environmental factors than performance on an aptitude test. Aptitude tests that assess the general cognitive functioning of individuals independent of any specific training or instruction they may have received are termed *intelligence tests*. But as discussed in Chapter 4, the matter of "intelligence" is exceed-

ingly controversial. Since "intelligence" has come to carry a good many highly charged meanings and associations, many psychologists prefer to speak of "general cognitive ability" or "scholastic aptitude." Perhaps the safest generalization that can be made regarding these matters is that the more content oriented the aptitude test, the more useful it will be in predicting future academic success in the *same* content area, but the less useful it will be in predicting general future learning (Mehrens and Lehmann, 1978).

Schools have been turning to standardized tests, especially since World War I. The trend has become particularly pronounced over the past twenty-five years. It is estimated that in 1952 more than 75 million standardized tests were taken by 25 million students in North American educational institutions. The figure rose to 100 million tests a year in 1961. Current estimates are that at least 200 million standardized tests are administered each year to North American students. No attempt will be made here to provide a survey of available tests (see the boxed insert on page 557 for sources of information regarding standardized tests). Indeed, the treatment would be outdated before publication by virtue of the rapidity with which tests are revised and new tests appear.

MARKING AND REPORTING

Most educators recognize the wisdom of ascertaining the academic progress of their students. By clearly defining instructional objectives and carefully implementing measuring procedures, they can greatly facilitate the task of reporting the results of their evaluative efforts. On the surface, the assignment of grades—giving and reporting marks—appears to be among the easier tasks teachers have. Yet a good many teachers find it a disconcerting process, one that, when undertaken responsibly and conscientiously, requires a good deal of serious thought and hard work (especially

INFORMATION ON STANDARDIZED TESTS

A number of sources are available for securing information regarding standardized tests. The American Psychological Association published a forty-page booklet in 1974 entitled *Standards for Educational and Psychological Tests*. The booklet contains recommendations for test publishers and test users prepared by a committee of selected psychologists and educators. It provides guidelines for evaluating test materials and manuals, and a checklist of factors to keep in mind when selecting, administering, scoring, and interpreting standardized tests.

Perhaps the most valuable and important single source of information about tests is *The Mental Measurements Yearbook* edited by Oscar K. Buros until his death in 1978. It has appeared at periodic intervals since 1938 and provides detailed information and critical reviews by experts of each new standardized test that is published. The reviewers attempt to point out the strengths and weaknesses of each test and the uses for which it is best suited. Other practical information provided by the *Yearbooks* are test author, test publisher, norms, costs, publication and revision dates, administration time, and references. After Buros's death, the University of Nebraska announced that the yearbook series would be taken over by the university and publication continued.

Other useful guides to be used in conjunction with the *Yearbooks* are *Tests in Print*. Most commonly a test is reviewed in the first *Yearbook* that appears following the test's development. *Tests in Print* updates the bibliographic and other information on each test. Accordingly, *Tests in Print* provides a ready reference guide where the user can obtain critical and detailed information about the vast majority of standardized tests.

where detailed progress letters need be prepared for the parents of each child at periodic intervals during the school year). The matter is further complicated by the controversies that have traditionally surrounded marking and reporting. These issues have included who should have access to reports on a child's academic performance, what types of grading procedures should be employed, and what criteria should be used in assigning grades.

Functions of Marks

Grading systems are the source of much dissatisfaction, anguish, and criticism. Indeed, some critics suggest that schools ought to dispense with grades altogether. These educators cite a number of points (Ebel, 1974; Yarborough and Johnson, 1980). First, they say that grades are basically meaningless (great diversity exists among institutions and teachers in grading practices, a single symbol cannot adequately report a person's performance, and grades are often used to enforce discipline rather than to report exclusively on achievement). Second, critics charge that grades are unimportant (grades do not correctly predict later achievement and marks have as their focus the adequacy of students rather than the adequacy of educational programs). Third, they argue that grades are unnecessary (when the emphasis falls on mastery learning, differential levels of achievement no longer remain to be graded). And fourth, critics claim that grades are harmful (they reward conformity and penalize creativity, foster competition rather than cooperation, and employ extrinsic rather than intrinsic mechanisms of motivation).

Although a wide variety of alternative systems for evaluation and reporting have been proposed, the traditional system of grading has demonstrated remarkable resilience and durability. There are a good many reasons for this, stemming in large measure from its historical functions:

- Marks provide an efficient and useful method for communicating with pupils and their parents.
- Symbols can be readily converted into numbers, permitting the computation of grade-point averages (GPAs).
- A mark serves as a convenient and standardized capsule summary of a student's performance and is easily and readily understood by a wide range of potential audiences.
- Marks provide a manageable format for portraying data useful in making decisions concerning promotion, certification, graduation, transfer, and future education.
- Grades are the "currency" of the academic realm and are convertible into desirable positions, ego satisfactions, and other rewards, all of which have motivating properties.
- Marks simplify the task of record keeping by giving a highly condensed evaluation of a student's achievement.
- Grading compels an instructor to evaluate a student and in the process implicitly assess the adequacy of his or her own teaching.
- Marks provide a composite report on a student's achievement that can be made available to employers in making hiring decisions or to colleges in reaching admission decisions.

Through the years considerable controversy has raged over who should have access to a student's school records. The Family Educational Rights and Privacy Act of 1974 (PL 93–380) sought to correct what many considered to be abuses in earlier procedures. The act provides that parents have the right to inspect and review all records, files, and data directly related to their children, including all material incorporated within each child's cumulative record folder. Prior to congres-

sional enactment of the measure, school authorities commonly withheld aptitude test scores, behavioral evaluation data, and other selected information from parents. The legislation also gives parents the right to a hearing for purposes of challenging the content of their child's school record. Further, the 1974 act provides safeguards over the release of personally identifiable records or files to individuals or organizations without the written consent of a child's parents.

Marking and Reporting Procedures

The most common procedures for marking and reporting are letter-number systems, pass-fail options, checklists, progress letters, and teacher-parent conferences.

Letter-Number System

The traditional method for reporting a student's performance continues to be the assignment of a letter grade (A, B, C, D, or F) or a number (100 to 0). The arrangement has the advantage of being widely understood and interpretable. The major disadvantage is the failure of a single symbol to communicate what it is that is being reported: a level of achievement (measurement) or a teacher's satisfaction with that level (evaluation). Nor does the symbol necessarily tell us whether it is a summary representation of the student's final achievement, growth, effort, ability, deportment, or a combination of these characteristics. At times school systems have attempted to "solve" these difficulties by employing some other system like G, S, and U (good, satisfactory, and unsatisfactory). More often than not this has simply compounded the problem since parents often claim that they do not know what the symbols "really mean." It seems that regardless of the innovation, a system tends to drift back over time toward some sort of five-category arrangement.

GRADING
Although often viewed as a tedious task, grading students' work is a vital aspect of the teacher's role.

Pass-Fail Options

In the late 1960s and early 1970s a high proportion of North American colleges and universities and a smaller proportion of high schools introduced a pass-fail option to students for a limited number of courses. Under the plan students are permitted to take some courses, usually electives, without having the grade included in the computation of their grade-point average (GPA). The justification for the arrangement is that it encourages students to take courses in new areas of study without fear of receiving a poor grade. Other stated reasons are that it emphasizes learning rather than "grade getting," reduces student anxiety, and allows pupils to arrange their study time more beneficially.

However, evidence reveals that most students who elect to take a course on a pass-fail option would have taken the course anyway (Mehrens and Lehmann, 1978). Further, many educators express dissatisfaction with the option, claiming that pass-fail students tend to be less highly motivated and to do less well than students enrolled under the regular program. And admissions officials in professional and graduate schools and prospective employers say that the system provides a less reliable and less informative means of communication. In contrast, a modified version of the plan, a pass-no grade marking system, appears well suited to mastery learning arrangements in which a student's record remains a blank until an acceptable level of competence is demonstrated.

Checklists

The letter-number system provides a global evaluation but little specific information regarding a pupil's strengths and weaknesses. One remedy has been to replace or supplement the traditional system with a list of behavior descriptions to be checked or rated. This approach has the advantage of permitting the teacher to appraise a student's strengths and weaknesses in relation to specific instructional objectives (see Figure 18.1). It is important that the list of items be kept to a workable number and that the statements be simple and concise.

Progress Letters

Another means for communicating with parents is a letter discussing various aspects of the pupil's school experiences, behavior, and growth. The chief advantage of a letter is the freedom it affords the teacher in adapting the report to each child's unique requirements. The primary difficulty is that it requires a considerable amount of time to prepare a carefully formulated letter. All too often progress letters are highly stereotyped, generalized, and platitudinous, revealing little in the way of substance. In part, this derives from a concern among

FIGURE 18.1 A CHECKLIST REPORT
This format permits the teacher to rate the pupil's academic performance and the student's effort. The report also provides space for a teacher's comments, incorporating in modified form a component of the progress letter.

PUPIL PROGRESS REPORT

STUDENT'S NAME _____ GRADE: 4 5 6   YEAR: 19 ____ 19 ____
(Circle One)

TEACHER'S NAME _____ SCHOOL _____

THIS REPORT OFFERS THE TEACHER'S BEST PROFESSIONAL JUDGMENT OF YOUR CHILD'S PERFORMANCE IN RELATION TO SCHOOL EXPECTATIONS AND THE CHILD'S EFFORT. ALL CHILDREN DO NOT ATTAIN THE SAME LEVELS OF ACHIEVEMENT AT THE SAME TIME OR AT THE SAME RATE OF DEVELOPMENT.

PERFORMANCE — G. S. U

G = GOOD
S = SATISFACTORY
U = UNSATISFACTORY
√ = INDICATES WEAK AREA

	DAYS ABSENT TO DATE			
	TIMES TARDY TO DATE			

EFFORT – 1, 2, 3, 4

1 - CONSISTENTLY TRIES HARD
2 - TRIES MOST OF THE TIME
3 - TRIES WHEN URGED
4 - PUTS FORTH LITTLE EFFORT

	FALL			MID-YEAR (OPTIONAL)			APRIL			TEACHER'S COMMENTS
	PERFORMANCE	EFFORT	WEAK AREA	PERFORMANCE	EFFORT	WEAK AREA	PERFORMANCE	EFFORT	WEAK AREA	
READING										
INTERPRETS WHAT IS READ										
IS BUILDING A LARGER VOCABULARY										
APPLIES WORD ATTACK SKILLS										
READS WELL ORALLY										
DOES INDEPENDENT READING										
LANGUAGE and SPELLING										
SHOWS ORIGINALITY AND EXPRESSES IDEAS WELL IN DISCUSSION AND ORAL REPORTING										
USES ACCEPTABLE ENGLISH										
WRITES EFFECTIVE SENTENCES AND ORGANIZED PARAGRAPHS										
USES LANGUAGE MECHANICS OF CAPITALIZATION AND PUNCTUATION CORRECTLY										
SHOWS CREATIVITY IN WRITTEN EXPRESSION										
WRITES LEGIBLY IN ALL WRITTEN WORK										
SPELLS ASSIGNED WORDS CORRECTLY										
SPELLS ACCURATELY IN DAILY WORK										
MATHEMATICS										
KNOWS & USES NUMBER FACTS & TERMS ACCURATELY										
USES NUMBER PROCESSES ACCURATELY										
SOLVES STORY PROBLEMS										
SOCIAL STUDIES and SCIENCE										
USES MAP AND GLOBE SKILLS										
GATHERS AND ORGANIZES INFORMATION FROM A VARIETY OF MEDIA										
UNDERSTANDS AND APPLIES CONCEPTS IN DIFFERENT SITUATIONS										
DISPLAYS INTEREST IN CURRENT EVENTS										
IS DEVELOPING AN UNDERSTANDING OF HIS RIGHTS AND RESPONSIBILITIES AS AN AMERICAN CITIZEN										
ARTS, MUSIC, and PHYSICAL EDUCATION										
EXPLORES POSSIBILITIES IN THE USE OF ART MATERIALS										
BECOMES INVOLVED IN SOLVING ART PROBLEMS										
PARTICIPATES IN SINGING ACTIVITIES										
PARTICIPATES IN RHYTHMIC ACTIVITIES										
EXHIBITS SPORTSMANSHIP IN PHYSICAL ACTIVITIES										
DISPLAYS STRENGTH FLEXIBILITY, ENDURANCE, AND BALANCE NECESSARY FOR THE DEVELOPMENT OF EXPECTED MOTOR SKILLS										
APPLIES SKILLS SUCCESSFULLY IN PHYSICAL ACTIVITIES										

PERSONAL HABITS and VALUES	Fall	Mid Year	Apr.	
WORKS INDEPENDENTLY				
COOPERATES IN GROUP ACTIVITIES				
COMPLETES ASSIGNMENTS ON TIME				
LISTENS AND FOLLOWS THROUGH				
PROOF-READS WRITTEN WORK				
IS NEAT ABOUT PERSONAL APPEARANCE				
COMPLIES WITH SCHOOL RULES				
USES TIME WISELY				
RESPECTS THE PROPERTY AND RIGHTS OF OTHERS				
EXERCISES SELF-CONTROL				
SHOWS SPIRIT OF INQUIRY				
REFLECTS GOOD SLEEP AND REST HABITS				

YOUR SIGNATURE BELOW INDICATES THAT YOU HAVE EXAMINED THIS REPORT.

Parent's signature for Fall Report _____

Parent's signature for Mid–Year Report _____
(Use of the checklist in mid-year is a parent–teacher option)

Parent's signature for April Report _____

some teachers that the letter be phrased as diplomatically as possible so as not to offend parents. Figure 18.2 provides an example of a reasonably good letter prepared by a fifth-grade teacher. Figure 18.3 is a letter dealing with the same student written by a sixth-grade teacher. Note the superior quality of the letter by the fifth-grade teacher in providing specific and detailed information about the child's school experiences. The two letters also highlight another problem with this procedure. They fail to provide over an extended period of time a systematic and cumulative record of a student's progress toward the objectives of the educational program.

FIGURE 18.2 PROGRESS REPORT OF A FIFTH-GRADE TEACHER
The letter contains much specific detail and provides concrete insight regarding the student's school experiences.

Dear Mr. and Mrs. [parent's surname],

    As the school year nears its close, it seems important that an overall summary of the student's strengths and weaknesses in work habits, attitudes, and achievements be made, so that, in the fall, he understands clearly where to exert his greatest effort in order to ever-improve his academic status. Anything not specifically mentioned would fall somewhere between the extremes— or has not changed since a recent report.

    There is little to mention in terms of Brad's attitude and approach to school, his work habits, or use of study techniques. They were excellent when he entered the class and are a part of his self-discipline. He is becoming meticulous about detail, and it might be worth mentioning here that he would do well to consider when to be particular with others and when not to be, if he is at all concerned about reactions of classmates. Some tend to resent his being critical on small points, even though he and I may like perfection!

    In the latest diagnostic test, he ranked near the top of the class with perfect scores in two sections of the test. But the achievement test shows a drop in vocabulary (not a loss, but greater challenge), and comprehension is stationary. In reading news items and more challenging classroom materials, it is very evident that Brad does not take time to approach new words by syllables or bother with a dictionary, for he miscalls them or glides over them awk-

(continued)

FIGURE 18.2 (*continued*)

wardly. This is something that needs careful attention for it affects proper understanding of an item or passage and the oral
interpretation of it to others.

Language skills, related in various ways
to the above, showed just a four-month gain
for the year. Work-study skills (map, graph,
table and reference material reading) indicate a gain of eight months.

In math, surprisingly, Brad dropped a bit
on the latest test. His daily work has been
as accurate as ever, so some other factor
may have caused this. He is still almost
two years above national norms and a year
above that of his class. I have lately kept
him working with the class most of the
time, but let him work ahead of the discussions or use his own methods much of the
time, though I make sure he understands
other approaches to the problem solving he
may run into later.

Brad's creative writing has improved tre-
mendously! Every project is more perfectly
done than the one before; there is more detail, organization is fine, etc. He understands and appreciates your desires for him
and takes them seriously. You can be thankful for that—it is the exception rather
than the rule in most families, for children to try to please parents.

I have truly enjoyed Brad's sojourn in
my class! I hope we have managed to contribute something to his well-being and
self-image. He should not be lacking in
this area! I shall continue to be interested in his future progress. I know I have
not heard the last of him as a student.

Sincerely,

[teacher's name]

Dear Mr. and Mrs. [parent's surname],

Brad has completed his sixth-grade work with fine achievement in all areas. He has outstanding qualities as a student. His genuine interest in learning, his steady, thorough work habits, and excellent ability to express himself in written and oral form, account for a most successful year. He has a fine sense of fairness and a genuine regard for people. He is regarded as a leader and is highly respected by his teacher and his classmates.

In all academic areas Brad was top in our class. It is my fondest hope that he was challenged and stimulated by his teacher this year. It seemed that Brad enjoyed all of our units of study and long-range assignments and here especially is where he could extend himself and produce extraordinary work.

Brad is a fine young man who did much to set high standards in our classroom. It was truly my privilege to share this year with Brad. I will watch for his future accomplishments in the years to come.

Sincerely,

[teacher's name]

FIGURE 18.3 PROGRESS REPORT OF A SIXTH-GRADE TEACHER
The letter is a progress report concerning the same child discussed in Figure 18.2 by a fifth-grade teacher. The letter is platitudinous. While making the child and parents "happy," it contains little specific or helpful information.

Parent-Teacher Conferences

Parent-teacher conferences offer opportunities for establishing two-way communication between the home and the school. In addition to receiving a report from the teacher, the parties can clarify information, overcome misunderstandings, discuss their common concerns, and plan a joint program to assist the child. Enough time, minimally thirty minutes, should be allowed for a conference. Experienced teachers also know that good conferences do not simply happen but are the result of careful thought and preparation. Probably the teacher's main task is to "open parents up" so they can raise the matters that most trouble them.

Parent-teacher conferences also have limitations. Perhaps the most basic difficulty is that both teachers and parents often feel defensive and "on guard" (Kleiman, 1981). Further, conferences are commonly too short and too few in number (one or two per year tend to be typical). Finally, teachers find that some parents are unwilling or unable to attend a conference.

PARENT-TEACHER CONFERENCES

For the student, the parent/teacher conference has the potential of being the single most education-ally valuable event of the entire school year.

James A. Rabbitt
"The Parent/Teacher
Conference," 1978

Very frequently, both parents and teachers dread the parent-teacher conference (Rabbitt, 1978; Klei-man, 1981). Both parties fear that the other will blame, criticize, or otherwise hurt them. Yet the conference can afford a unique opportunity for forging cooperative ties between the parties. Teachers can do much to make for a positive conference outcome by anticipating parental concerns. Generally the most frequently asked questions are: How does my child behave? How is my child doing in school work? How does my child get along with the other children in the class?

When teachers feel threatened by a conference, they often respond by assuming a pedagogical style in which they simply *give* parents information. Unfortunately, their apprehensive response too often blocks a two-way interchange. As a consequence, teachers may fail to *get* helpful information. Moreover, they are unable to *draw* the parents into the search for and implementation of solutions to academic or behavioral problems. The net result can be disaster for all the parties—teachers, students, and parents. Where parents develop negative attitudes toward the teacher and the school, teachers lose an indispensable ally. Perhaps even more important, the parents' negative attitudes are communicated to their children, dramatically compounding the difficulties of any educator.

In parent-teacher conferences teachers often find it useful to go over with parents examples of the child's work. At times it is appropriate to listen to tape recordings of the child during an actual lesson. It helps considerably if teachers point out several positive things about the child and his or her work. Sensitive teachers quickly involve the parents in the conference. Ice-breaking questions include: Could you tell me a little about how your child feels about school? What is a typical day like for your child? What would you like to see changed in our program?

Often teachers attempt to accomplish too much in a conference. It is best to single out no more than one problem—at most two—for attention. Working on one's problem at a time keeps all parties from being overwhelmed and increases the chances for success. In the course of the discussion, the teacher and parent can work out a joint program

Criteria for Assigning Grades

Most commonly teachers are expected to allocate letter or number marks to students on the basis of their demonstrated competence as measured by achievement tests. Yet in practice the task is hardly a simple one. An issue that continually confronts teachers is whether or not to take effort into account in assigning grades. Sooner or later most teachers encounter a student who puts forth considerable effort but performs poorly on tests. If the teacher grades the student on his or her demonstrated competence, will the student then become discouraged and no longer work diligently? Or should the teacher reward the student's effort? If the teacher takes into account a student's attitude, is the teacher misleading the student, the student's parents, and others, since marks are usually interpreted as indicating degree of competence rather than degree of effort? Further, is the teacher who rewards effort "fudging" the mark and thus failing to communicate to the student the real situation, precluding more realistic adjustment processes by the student? In response to these dilemmas, many

and their specific contributions to its implementation. And both should plan a specific date and method for a follow-up conference to review their efforts (Rabbitt, 1978). Telephone miniconferences may prove helpful in the interval.

At times parents are afraid to come to school and feel uncomfortable if they do. Under some circumstances it may be advisable for the teacher to make a home visit. Indeed, the site of the conference may assume more importance than educators commonly assign to it. The territorial factor is known to have major consequences for human interaction (Vander Zanden, 1984). For example, it finds expression in athletic contests in which the home team generally enjoys the advantage. And police interrogation is based on the same principle: never question suspects on their home ground but on the detective's home ground—the police station (Inbau and Reid, 1962).

The school is the teacher's home territory. When teachers see parents in the school setting, parents often feel themselves to be intruders in a foreign land. Teachers should consider making adjustments in the parent-teacher conference should this element constitute a severe obstacle to mutual trust, comfort, and spontaneity.

The parent-teacher conference should be viewed as but one aspect of an encompassing program to establish links between the home and the school. A decade or so ago a parent asking a teacher "How can I help my child do better in school?" was likely to be told: "Don't. We teach the new math now and you'll just confuse the child." Or "Our reading program builds on itself and unless you know what you are doing, you'll cause more harm than good." This attitude is now on the way out. Teachers realize that parents play, and indeed they should play, a vital part in their children's education.

It is desirable that teachers send evaluated papers and other work home at regular intervals. Periodic personal letters and newsletters provide additional channels for communication. Teachers can assist parents to help their children at home with flash cards and multiplication-fact and other learning-oriented games. During the early school years, time can be set aside each evening for the child to read to the parent. Since most schools fail to provide sufficient writing situations, parents can help by having their children write themes, keep journals and diaries, and write thank-you notes. By involving parents, teachers can reap untold benefits in better attitudes and performance on the part of students.

educators recommend that letter and number systems be reserved for reporting on academic achievement (using explicit standards) while checklists and progress letters be employed for detailing other aspects of a child's behavior.

The teacher confronts a somewhat similar dilemma in deciding whether to grade on a student's level of achievement (current status) or level of improvement (growth). Consider the following cases. John entered the course at an unusually high level of competence as ascertained by the pretest administered during the first week of the course. At the end of the course, he scored among the top two students on the final examination, yet he showed little evidence of growth. In contrast, Mike scored the lowest of any of the students on the pretest. Nonetheless, on the final examination he ranked fourteenth from the top in a class of thirty-two students. Appraised by levels of achievement, John should receive a high mark and Mike an average mark. Yet judged by improvement, John demonstrated little and Mike considerable growth. Here again many educators believe that letter and number marks should be reserved for reporting

FEEDBACK TO STUDENTS
In the course of interaction with a student, a teacher provides significant, although often subtle, clues as to the teacher's assessment of the student's work. Marking and grading are simply more formal mechanisms for communicating to a student and others how well the student is doing.

upon academic achievement. (They would also point out that ideally John should have been placed in a more advanced course on the basis of his pretest score.) These educators maintain that grading on growth advantages those students with low initial scores and that pupils soon learn to fake ignorance on pretests (Mehrens and Lehmann, 1978).

CHAPTER SUMMARY

1. Educational and psychological measurement can help individuals at all levels of education make better decisions. Measurement data may be em-

ployed by placing students, formative evaluation, diagnostic evaluation, making selection decisions, arriving at curricular decisions, personal decision making, and for summation purposes.

2. Three steps are involved in developing a measurement device. First, we must identify and define the quality or attribute that is to be measured. Second, we need to determine a set of operations that will isolate the attribute in question and make it apparent to us. Third, we have to express in numerical or quantitative terms the results of the operations established in step two.

3. With a norm-referenced measure we are interested in how a student compares with others in a group; with a criterion-referenced measure, with what the student can do with what he or she knows. The concern in criterion-referenced testing is not

with the performance of others but with whether or not an individual is able to perform at an acceptable level.

4. A measurement device should possess several qualities. Among the most important of these are reliability, validity, and practicality. Reliability has to do with how accurately a measuring device measures what we set out to measure and the precision of the resulting score. Validity concerns whether a device measures what we want it to describe, represents all the components of what we want to describe, and describes nothing else but what we want it to describe. Practicality entails the ease with which a test can be administered and scored.

5. Teachers are often as concerned about measuring the ability of students to think about and use knowledge as they are with measuring the knowledge their students possess. In these instances, tests are needed to permit students some degree of latitude in their responses. Essay tests are well adapted to this purpose.

6. Objective-item tests are of two types. The supply type asks the student to provide a short answer or to complete a blank. The select type provides the student with alternative responses in the form of matching, true-false, or multiple-choice items. Proponents of objective-item tests contend that they assure good content sampling and easy and reliable scoring. Critics say that the tests foster rote learning, encourage guessing, and neglect integrating and organizing skills.

7. Standardized tests are administered under uniform conditions using the same set of questions and the same set of directions for timing constraints and scoring. This permits educators to give the identical test to students in different locations and at different times.

8. Critics of grading systems say that marks are meaningless, unimportant, unnecessary, and even harmful. Yet the traditional system of grading has demonstrated remarkable resilience and durability. There are a good many reasons for this, stemming in large measure from its historical functions. Of these, the primary reason appears to be that marks

provide an efficient and useful method for communicating with pupils and their parents.

9. The most common procedures for marking and reporting are letter-number systems, pass-fail options, checklists, progress letters, and teacher-parent conferences. Of these, the letter-number system is the most prevalent.

10. Most commonly teachers are expected to allocate letter or number marks to students based upon their demonstrated competence as measured by achievement tests. Yet, in practice the task is hardly a simple one. Two issues that continually confront teachers are whether to take (1) effort and (2) growth into account in assigning grades.

CHAPTER GLOSSARY

criterion-referenced measure An evaluation instrument by which a student's performance is compared against some established standard.

evaluation The process by which qualitative or quantitative data are used to make judgments and decisions.

measurement The systematic ascertaining of a characteristic, property, or attribute by a numerical device.

norm-referenced measure An evaluation instrument by which a student's performance is compared with that of others on the same test.

reliability The degree to which an instrument yields a consistent measurement of the same thing.

standardized test A measurement device that is commercially prepared by educational specialists for widespread use in a large number of schools.

test A type of measurement tool or instrument consisting of a group of questions or tasks to which a student is asked to respond.

validity The extent to which an instrument serves the purpose for which it is intended.

EXERCISES

Review Questions

1. The term used to describe judgments made on the basis of data is

   a. measurement
   b. evaluation
   c. tests
   d. normative selection

2. Among the claims *not* made for minimum competency programs is that they

   a. identify students needing help
   b. provide data for educational accountability
   c. raise academic standards by encouraging weaker students to leave school
   d. increase emphasis on core academic skills

3. Criterion-referenced tests have been criticized because

   a. all students can do well
   b. they may encourage rote learning
   c. "teaching for the test" can become an important instructional objective
   d. a, b, and c are true
   e. b and c are true

4. Procedures for determining test reliability may include

   a. correlation with equivalent test
   b. test-retest
   c. split-halves
   d. a, b, and c are true
   e. a and b are true

5. The teacher who argues "It certainly is a geometry test because all the items are taken from the geometry book" is using which kind of validity?

   a. content
   b. criterion
   c. construct

6. The most troublesome problem in scoring essays is

   a. that model answers are difficult to construct
   b. the amount of time needed to grade
   c. the reliability of the grading is often low
   d. teachers cannot usually avoid grading in part on the basis of the student rather than content

7. Multiple-choice tests as compared to other objective-type tests

   a. are easier to construct
   b. do not lend themselves as easily to trivia
   c. can be used with the greatest range of subject areas
   d. are most preferred by students
   e. a and c are true

8. An intelligence test is an example of which kind of test?

   a. achievement
   b. personality
   c. aptitude
   d. diagnostic

9. The most common public school procedure for marking and grading is the

   a. letter-number system
   b. pass-fail option
   c. checklist
   d. progress letter

10. The chief difficulty in using progress letters is that

    a. teachers cannot observe enough to write a meaningful letter
    b. they need to be as diplomatic as possible
    c. the amount of time involved frequently results in the use of platitudes
    d. parents resent any move away from objective report cards

Answers

1. b (See p. 540)
2. c (See pp. 543–544)
3. e (See p. 546)
4. d (See p 547)
5. a (See p. 548)
6. c (See p. 551)
7. c (See p. 553)
8. c (See p. 556)
9. a (See p. 558)
10. c (See pp. 559, 561)

Applying Principles and Concepts

1. Which of the following statements on measurement would the text consider as valid?

_____ a. Summative and formative evaluation instruments are essentially interchangeable in terms of their objectives.

_____ b. Good instructional programs usually include remediation procedures as an integral part of the system.

_____ c. Placement and selection are acceptable measurement decisions.

_____ d. Curriculum decisions should be based on teacher experiences and knowledge rather than specific test results.

2. Categorize each of the following as either norm-referenced (N) or criterion-referenced (C).

_____ a. "My students seem to do about the same from year to year."

_____ b. "It is possible for every student to get an A."

_____ c. "Too many people get that right."

_____ d. "I rely heavily on the test to diagnose my instructional strengths."

3. Indicate whether the following measurement problems are one of reliability (R) or validity (V).

_____ a. A math teacher develops two different tests for a unit she has taught and gives both tests to her students. Scores on one test are much higher than those on the other.

_____ b. A student gets 70 percent right on his geography test on Monday. On Wednesday he gets 30 percent on the same test.

_____ c. Two instructors evaluate the same essay test using identical model answers. One instructor gives the student an A, the other an F.

_____ d. Student grades on the Econ. 1 final do not correlate at all with grades on the Econ. 2 final.

_____ e. People scoring high on a test of dominance are actually quite submissive socially.

4. The teacher has begun evaluating the results on an essay test. Correct those procedures that are in error.

a. She had students place their names on the last page.

_____

b. A model answer was prepared, listing the key points and the values assigned.

_____

c. Starting with the top paper, she graded one question at a time.

_____

d. After grading each question, she went through the pile in the same order.

_____

e. She kept comments to a minimum, asking students to "see her if they had any questions."

_____

5. The text describes four objective-item tests: short-answer (S), matching (M), true-false (T-F), and multiple-choice (M-C). From the descriptions given below, select the type of test referred to. (An answer may be used more than once.)

_____ a. Best chance for guessing
_____ b. Most compact
_____ c. Guessing is minimal
_____ d. Most versatile
_____ e. Too much trivia
_____ f. Items most difficult to construct
_____ g. Gamelike

6. A local elementary school teacher is explaining her ideas about parent-teacher conferences. Underline those passages with which the text would agree.

> I think the teacher should control the conversation from the start. For one, it will give you a chance to go through all the problems that exist. It is helpful to show samples of the child's work. Unless the parent asks for it specifically, do not plan further conferences since many parents are sensitive about coming to school.

Answers

1. b, c (See pp. 540–542)
2. a, N; b, C; c, N; d, C (See pp. 545–546)
3. a, R; b, R; c, R; d, V; e, V (See pp. 547–548)
4. c, papers should be chosen at random; d, the papers should be reshuffled after each question; e, comments should be of sufficient detail to enable students to perceive strengths and weaknesses (See p. 551)
5. a, T-F; b, M; c, S; d, M-C; e, T-F; f, M-C; g, M (See pp. 551–553)
6. Underline "It is helpful to show samples of the child's work," "many parents are sensitive about coming to school." (See pp. 563–565)

Project 1

OBJECTIVE: To have a hands-on experience building a test.

PROCEDURE: This can be done in your educational psychology course after studying this chapter. With the instructor, select at least two chapters from this text; have each student in the class develop a minimum of 10 objective-type items covering the content. The items are to be written individually on 3″ × 5″ cards, the correct answer given, and signed.

The teacher will then select what he or she considers the fifty best items covering the material. The teacher should not edit the items chosen. The test is then prepared, given, and graded.

Along with the graded exams, the teacher should return a list including the related items that were not chosen. Before the class breaks up into smaller groups the instructor ought to give his or her comments concerning how and why items were chosen. The smaller groups can then analyze the format and the content of all the test items and make suggestions for improvement to the student who prepared them. The class could meet again as a unit to disseminate the general findings of the groups.

ANALYSIS: The instructor's comments and group discussions should clarify the kinds of errors beginners make and select ways to improve the quality of the items. This project should enable you to overcome initial mistakes, not at the expense of your first students.

Project 2

OBJECTIVE: To discover the types of standards of grading teachers use.

PROCEDURE: Visit one or more teachers and ask the following questions:

1. How are grade letters assigned?
2. How are tests used to modify instruction?
3. Are test items grouped according to concepts?
4. Does the teacher derive subscores for each set of concepts?
5. Are any items omitted that everyone gets right (or fails)?
6. Are grades ever adjusted based on what previous students have done?

ANALYSIS: What you will probably discover is that most teachers use a mixture of criterion- and norm-referenced testing. See if you can discover which elements of a teacher's grading practices belong to each approach.

APPENDIX

STATISTICAL CONCEPTS AND OPERATIONS

From time to time over the course of the school year, teachers find it necessary to measure students' learning and to evaluate various measuring instruments. This requires that they organize, analyze, and interpret test scores and other numerical data. Knowledge of several simple statistical concepts and procedures will help teachers with these tasks immensely. Elementary statistics involves no more than an average knowledge of seventh-grade arithmetic, an understanding of the use of plus and minus signs, and knowledge of how to substitute numbers for letters in equations. This appendix does not aim to develop your statistical competencies to a high level but to provide you with the statistical skills generally needed by the classroom teacher.

TABULATING DATA AND FREQUENCY DISTRIBUTIONS

Table A.1 shows a record sheet of forty-nine hypothetical scores on a social science test. The raw scores are relatively meaningless unless they can be summarized in some manageable and useful fashion. The simplest way to proceed is to list the scores from high to low and tally the number of times each occurs as shown in Table A.2.

When the class is large and the scores are spread out over a substantial range, it is helpful if the scores are grouped together in broader categories.

TABLE A.1

Hypothetical Raw Scores on a Social Science Test

40	38	47	38	43	24	34	31	41	38
20	35	16	44	41	13	32	33	34	34
36	40	34	39	33	32	40	36	36	43
25	31	36	27	29	34	22	38	39	22
45	25	20	11	27	50	33	36	36	

This can be done by **class intervals** as shown in Table A.3. A number of procedures are followed in constructing this type of table:

- All intervals should be of the same size and should not overlap (for example, 42–44, 45–47, and so on).
- The intervals should be arranged in numerical order, with the highest values at the top and the lowest values at the bottom of the table.
- The most satisfactory number of class intervals is between ten and twenty. The number employed in Table A.3 is fourteen. The size of each interval in the table is three. The size interval of three was arrived at in the following fashion. The highest score is 50 and the lowest is 11. The range of scores is $50 - 11 = 39$. Dividing 39 by 14, we get 2.78. Since the nearest whole number is 3, we grouped the data by intervals of 3.
- It is desirable that the size of the class interval be an odd number (3, 5, 7) so that the midpoint of the interval is a whole number (for instance, in Table A.3, the midpoint of the interval 42–44 is 43; 45–47, 46; and so on). This facilitates graphing and some types of statistical computation.

The data contained in Table A.3 may be graphed to provide a pictorial representation. Teachers usually employ the **histogram** (bar graph) or the **frequency polygon** (line graph). Both types of graphs are presented in Figure A.1, which is based on the data in Table A.3. The scores (X) are placed along the horizontal axis (**abscissa**) and are grouped in the same intervals shown in Table A.3. The frequencies (f) are placed along the vertical axis (**ordinate**).

The histogram is sometimes referred to as "piling up the bodies" because each square represents an individual who obtained that score. Figure A.1 shows that one "body" is piled up in the interval 48–50, ten in the interval 36–38, and so on. The same data can be represented by a frequency polygon. As shown in Figure A.1, a point is plotted

TABLE A.2
Frequency Distribution of Scores from Table A.1

Scores *(X)*	*Tally*	*Frequency* *(f)*	*Scores* *(X)*	*Tally*	*Frequency* *(f)*
50	I	1	30		
49			29	I	1
48			28		
47	I	1	27	II	2
46			26		
45	I	1	25	II	2
44	I	1	24	I	1
43	II	2	23		
42			22	II	2
41	II	2	21		
40	III	3	20	II	2
39	II	2	19		
38	IIII	4	18		
37			17		
36	~~IIII~~ I	6	16	I	1
35	I	1	15		
34	~~IIII~~	5	14		
33	III	3	13	I	1
32	II	2	12		
31	II	2	11	1	1
			N = 49		

X = score
f = frequency
N = number

at the midpoint of each of the score intervals. The height of the point equals the frequency (f) of the interval. These points are then connected by a jagged line.

Over the past several decades an important graphic representation of data is the theoretical **normal curve.** As shown in Figure A.2, a normal distribution assumes the form of a bell-shaped curve (the greatest number of cases fall at the center and hence the curve is highest in the center). Considerable debate exists among psychologists as to whether human characteristics are distributed in a normal (bell-shaped) manner. Height and weight tend to be normally distributed, but it is debatable whether this also holds for psychological characteristics. Further, classes containing less than fifty students are unlikely to be normally distributed in any respect. When a distribution differs from the normal curve, it is said to be *skewed.* As shown in Figure A.2, a curve may be skewed to the right or to the left. The frequency polygon contained in Figure A.1 is skewed to the left.

TABLE A.3
Frequency Distribution of Scores from Table A.2 by Class Intervals

Class Interval	*Frequency*	*Class Interval*	*Frequency*
48–50	1	27–29	3
45–47	2	24–26	3
42–44	3	21–23	2
39–41	7	18–20	2
36–38	10	15–17	1
33–35	9	12–14	1
30–32	4	9–11	1

MEASURES OF CENTRAL TENDENCY

Teachers frequently find it useful to summarize a set of scores. A *measure of central tendency* permits

**FIGURE A.1
HISTOGRAM AND
FREQUENCY POLYGON**
The data in the graphs are
plotted from Table A.3.
The student scores (X)
are shown along the
horizontal axis; the
number of students (f)
receiving each score is
placed along the vertical
axis.

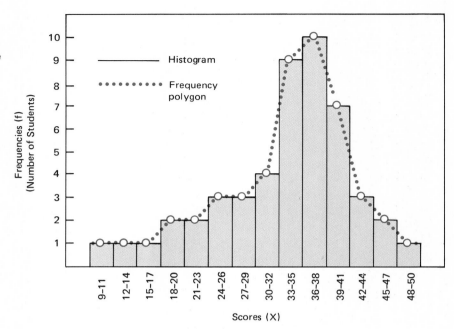

The Mean

The **mean** (represented by the symbol $\bar{X}$) is the
familiar "arithmetic average," which is derived
by adding all the scores in a set and dividing this
sum by the number of scores. It is used with
ungrouped data and can be represented by the
following formula:

$$\text{Mean} = \frac{\text{Sum of all scores}}{\text{Number of scores}} \qquad \bar{X} = \frac{\Sigma X}{N}$$

In the formula,

$\bar{X}$ = mean
Σ = the sum of
X = any score
N = number of scores

Applying this formula to the scores in Table A.1,
a mean of 33.3 is obtained:

$$\bar{X} = \frac{\Sigma X}{N} \qquad \bar{X} = \frac{1631}{49} = 33.3$$

The mean takes into account the value of each
score. As a result, one very high or very low score
could have a major effect on the mean.

The Median

The **median** (represented by the symbol Mdn
or P_{50}) is the middle number when all the numbers
in a set are arranged in increasing order by size,
from the smallest to the largest. When the number
of scores is even, the median is halfway between
the two middlemost scores (usually the teacher
simply averages the numbers on either side of the
middle). If the number of scores is odd, the mean
is the middle score. In Table A.2 the total number
of students is 49, an odd number. Hence, the

median is the middle, or 25th, number (the score being 34). It is the point that divides the set of scores into equal halves. The median is used if the teacher desires a measure of central tendency that is not affected by a few high or a few low scores.

The Mode

The **mode** is the score that occurs more often than any other score in a set of numbers. It is determined by inspection. The mode of the scores in Table A.2 is 36. The mode is the least reliable of the measures of central tendency, since it is greatly influenced by chance fluctuations.

RELATIVE POSITION: PERCENTILES

A **percentile** is a point in the distribution of test scores below which a certain percentage of the scores fall. Percentiles are widely used in educational circles in reporting the results of standardized tests. They can be viewed as ranks in a group of 100, except that with percentiles we begin counting at the bottom whereas with other ranking arrangements it is customary to start counting at the top. Accordingly, the lower the percentile, the poorer is the student's standing relative to the other test-takers. The 50th percentile (P_{50}) corresponds to the median. Percentiles above 50 constitute above-average performance; those below 50, below-average performance. Hence, if a student's score is in the 30th percentile (P_{30}), 30 percent of the test-takers did more poorly and 70 percent did better than the student in question.

To calculate a percentile rank, we count the number of scores below the score in which we are interested, divide by the total number of students (N), and multiply by 100. With reference to the scores contained in Table A.2, we can determine

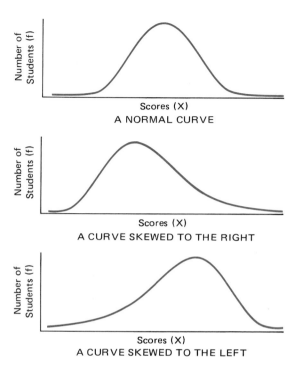

FIGURE A.2 NORMAL AND SKEWED CURVES
Skewed distributions are named by the direction in which the tail falls.

the percentile rank (PR) for a score of 29 as follows:

$$PR = \frac{cf_i}{N} \times 100$$

In the formula,

$$PR = \text{percentile rank}$$
$$cf_i = \text{the number of scores below the score in which we are interested}$$
$$N = \text{number}$$

Applying this formula to the score of 29 in Table A.2, there are 12 scores below 29. Thus:

$$PR = \frac{12}{49} \times 100 = 24$$

The percentile rank of the score is 24.

TABLE A.4
Computation of the Standard Deviation from Table A.2

X	d $(X - \bar{X} = d)$	d^2 $(d \times d)$	X	d $(X - \bar{X} = d)$	d^2 $(d \times d)$
50	50 − 33 = 17	289	32	32 − 33 = − 1	1
47	47 − 33 = 14	196	32	32 − 33 = − 1	1
45	45 − 33 = 12	144	31	31 − 33 = − 2	4
44	44 − 33 = 11	121	31	31 − 33 = − 2	4
43	43 − 33 = 10	100	29	29 − 33 = − 4	16
43	43 − 33 = 10	100	27	27 − 33 = − 6	36
41	41 − 33 = 8	64	27	27 − 33 = − 6	36
41	41 − 33 = 8	64	25	25 − 33 = − 8	64
40	40 − 33 = 7	49	25	25 − 33 = − 8	64
40	40 − 33 = 7	49	24	24 − 33 = − 9	81
40	40 − 33 = 7	49	22	22 − 33 = −11	121
39	39 − 33 = 6	36	22	22 − 33 = −11	121
39	39 − 33 = 6	36	20	20 − 33 = −13	169
38	38 − 33 = 5	25	20	20 − 33 = −13	169
38	38 − 33 = 5	25	16	16 − 33 = −17	289
38	38 − 33 = 5	25	13	13 − 33 = −20	400
38	38 − 33 = 5	25	11	11 − 33 = −22	484
36	36 − 33 = 3	9	N = 49		3520
36	36 − 33 = 3	9	$\bar{X}$ = 33		
36	36 − 33 = 3	9			
36	36 − 33 = 3	9			
36	36 − 33 = 3	9			
36	36 − 33 = 3	9			
35	35 − 33 = 2	4			
34	34 − 33 = 1	1			
34	34 − 33 = 1	1		$s = \sqrt{\dfrac{\Sigma(d)^2}{N}}$	
34	34 − 33 = 1	1			
34	34 − 33 = 1	1		$s = \sqrt{\dfrac{3520}{49}}$	
34	34 − 33 = 1	1			
33	33 − 33 = 0	0		$s = \sqrt{71.8}$	
33	33 − 33 = 0	0			
33	33 − 33 = 0	0		$s = 8.5$	

The 25th and 75th percentiles are termed the first and third *quartile* points (Q₁ and Q₃). They cut off the lowest and highest quarters of a distribution. Note that the quarter of individuals whose measures are *highest* are said to be in the *fourth* quartile (those whose measures are the lowest are in the first quartile).

Percentiles are easily understood since they appear to be like percents. However, they do have a serious limitation. Scores tend to pile up at the middle of a distribution and thus distort the distances among the scores in a set.

MEASURE OF VARIABILITY

A measure of central tendency like the mean tells us what, on the average, the group is like. Often we want to know the extent to which the scores spread out away from the average. This requires a measure of **variability.** The most commonly used measure of variability is the **standard deviation** (represented by the symbol s). It is a measure of how widely the test scores of a distribution are scattered above and below the mean of the scores.

If the scores cluster closely around the mean, the standard deviation is small and the distribution is said to have little variability. If the scores are dispersed widely from the mean, the standard deviation is large, and the distribution is said to have considerable variability. Thus, the standard deviation tells us how representative the mean is. If the variation is small, we know that the individual scores are close to it; if large, we have less assurance as to the use of the mean as a representative value.

The standard deviation for ungrouped data can be obtained with the following formula:

$$s = \sqrt{\frac{\Sigma(d)^2}{N}}$$

In the formula,

s = the standard deviation
$\sqrt{}$ = the square root
Σ = the sum of
d = the deviation of a score from the mean: $d = (X - \bar{X})$
d^2 = the deviation squared: $d^2 = d \times d$
N = number of scores

The following steps are involved in computing the standard deviation:

1. Carry out the operations for computing the mean as described earlier in the appendix. The mean of the scores in Table A.2 is 33.3; rounded to a whole number it becomes 33.

2. Prepare a table headed by the following columns: X (the score); d (deviation); and d^2. See Table A.4, which employs the data contained in Table A.2.

3. Compute the deviation of each score from the mean. Thus $d = X - \bar{X}$.

4. Square each deviation (d^2) secured in Step 3, as illustrated in Table A.4. Note that a minus times a minus is a plus. With many desk calculators we need only press the designated key to square a number.

5. Sum (add together) the squared deviations secured in Step 4: $\Sigma(d)^2$.

6. Divide the sum of the squared deviations (the value obtained in Step 5) by the total number of scores (N).

7. Find the square root of the value secured in Step 6. With many desk calculators we need only press the designated key to get the square root of a number.

Students commonly want to know what constitutes a large standard deviation and what is a small one. In truth there is no simple answer, since everything depends on what we are measuring and whether we prefer a narrow or wide spread among the scores. The standard deviation is merely a statistic that tells us about the distribution of a set of scores. Consider Table A.5. The three hypothetical classes reveal quite different score distributions. If the scores reflect academic aptitude, Class 3 would generally be more difficult to teach than Class 1 because of the considerable variability in the aptitude of the students (the standard deviation of the scores in Class 1 is 2.7; that of Class 3, 14.4).

MEASURES OF RELATIONSHIP

Teachers are often interested in the relationship between two sets of scores. By way of illustration, the teacher may want to know whether students who did well on an arithmetic test also did well on a reading test. To answer this question the teacher might begin by arranging the students according to their performance on the two tests as shown in Table A.6. The scores on the reading test are listed opposite the arithmetic scores. To facilitate interpretation, both sets of scores may be ranked from one to sixteen (N = 16) according to the position of the student with respect to each test.

TABLE A.5

Standard Deviations: Scores of Hypothetical Classes

Class 1			Class 2		
X	d	d²	X	d	d²
88	88 − 84 = 4	16	88	88 − 76 = 12	144
87	87 − 84 = 3	9	85	85 − 76 = 9	81
87	87 − 84 = 3	9	82	82 − 76 = 6	36
87	87 − 84 = 3	9	81	81 − 76 = 5	25
86	86 − 84 = 2	4	80	80 − 76 = 4	16
85	85 − 84 = 1	1	80	80 − 76 = 4	16
85	85 − 84 = 1	1	78	78 − 76 = 2	4
84	84 − 84 = 0	0	78	78 − 76 = 2	4
82	82 − 84 = −2	4	76	76 − 76 = 0	0
82	82 − 84 = −2	4	74	74 − 76 = − 2	4
82	82 − 84 = −2	4	72	72 − 76 = − 4	16
81	81 − 84 = −3	9	71	71 − 76 = − 5	25
81	81 − 84 = −3	9	68	68 − 76 = − 8	64
81	81 − 84 = −3	9	65	65 − 76 = −11	121
79	79 − 84 = −5	25	64	64 − 76 = − 12	144
N = 15		113	N = 15		700

Mean

$$\bar{X} = \frac{\Sigma X}{N} \quad \bar{X} = \frac{1257}{15} \quad \bar{X} = 84$$

Standard Deviation

$$s = \sqrt{\frac{\Sigma(d)^2}{N}} \quad s = \sqrt{\frac{113}{15}} \quad s = \sqrt{7.5} \quad s = 2.7$$

Mean

$$\bar{X} = \frac{\Sigma X}{N} \quad \bar{X} = \frac{1142}{15} \quad \bar{X} = 76$$

Standard Deviation

$$s = \sqrt{\frac{\Sigma(d)^2}{N}} \quad s = \sqrt{\frac{700}{15}} \quad s = \sqrt{46.7} \quad s = 6.8$$

Class 3		
X	d	d²
88	88 − 67 = 21	441
87	87 − 67 = 20	400
83	83 − 67 = 16	256
81	81 − 67 = 14	196
76	76 − 67 = 9	81
74	74 − 67 = 7	49
71	71 − 67 = 4	16
68	68 − 67 = 1	1
64	64 − 67 = − 3	9
61	61 − 67 = − 6	36
58	58 − 67 = − 9	81
53	53 − 67 = −14	196
51	51 − 67 = −16	256
47	47 − 67 = −20	400
41	41 − 67 = −26	676
N = 15		3094

Mean

$$\bar{X} = \frac{\Sigma X}{N} \quad \bar{X} = \frac{1003}{15} \quad \bar{X} = 67$$

Standard Deviation

$$s = \sqrt{\frac{\Sigma(d)^2}{N}} \quad s = \sqrt{\frac{3094}{15}} \quad s = \sqrt{206.2} \quad s = 14.4$$

TABLE A.6
Hypothetical Scores on an Arithmetic
and a Reading Test

Pupil's Name	Arithmetic Test		Reading Test	
	Score X	Rank R_X	Score Y	Rank R_Y
Nancy	139	1	88	2
Dave	130	2	89	1
Angelo	123	3	77	5
Bonnie	120	4	69	7
Edna	116	5	61	11
Bob	114	6	68	8
John	112	7	65	9
Cynthia	111	8	73	6
Brenda	109	9	79	4
Judy	105	10	82	3
Ron	101	11	59	12
Donna	100	12	62	10
Tim	99	13	44	14
Larry	94	14	37	15
Sandra	87	15	45	13
Mike	83	16	33	16

Based on the data contained in Table A.6, the teacher can construct a scatter diagram as in Figure A.3 to depict the data. The scores of the arithmetic test are placed along the vertical (X) axis; those of the reading test along the horizontal (Y) axis. The first student, Nancy, had a score of 139 on the arithmetic test and a score of 88 on the reading test. Plotted on the scatter diagram, 139 intersects with 88 at the upper-right-hand corner of the figure. This point is represented with a dot. In turn the scores of each of the other children are plotted in a similar fashion.

Mike, who has done poorly on both tests, falls to the lower-left-hand corner of the figure. Accordingly, students with good scores on both tests are found toward the upper-right-hand corner of the diagram; those who did poorly on both tests toward the lower-left-hand corner; and those who do about average on both tests fall toward the middle of the diagram. However, some students,

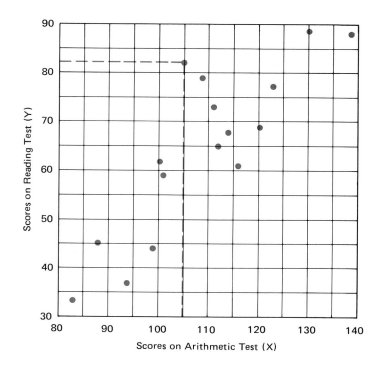

FIGURE A.3 SCATTER DIAGRAM FROM TABLE A.6
Each score in Column X intersects with a score in Row Y. For instance, Judy has a score of 105 on the arithmetic test (X) and a score of 82 on the reading test (Y). Locate 105 on the horizontal axis and 82 on the vertical axis. Her position (the dot) is represented by the intersection of the column and the row.

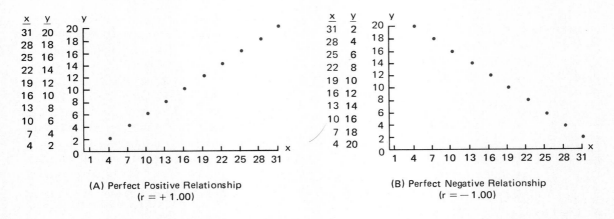

(A) Perfect Positive Relationship
(r = + 1.00)

(B) Perfect Negative Relationship
(r = − 1.00)

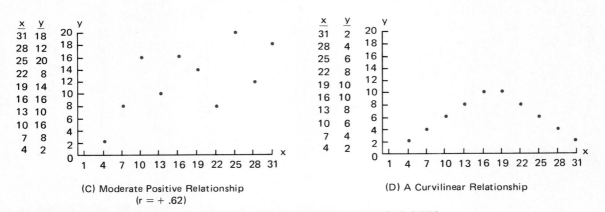

(C) Moderate Positive Relationship
(r = + .62)

(D) A Curvilinear Relationship

FIGURE A.4 SCATTER DIAGRAMS SHOWING CORRELATIONS OF VARIOUS SIZES
The value of the product-moment correlation coefficient (r) may range from + 1.00 to − 1.00. A perfect positive correlation (+ 1.00) or a perfect negative correlation (− 1.00) occurs when a change in one score is always accompanied by a commensurate change in the other score.

such as Judy, have done relatively better on one test than on the other. This is reflected in the dot representing Judy's performance that scatters toward the left of the diagram.

If there were a perfect positive relationship between each student's score on the one test and his or her score on the other test, the distribution of the dots would take the form of a straight line as reflected in Diagram A in Figure A.4. The less relationship there is between performance on one test and performance on the other test, the more scattered the dots are (see Diagram C in Figure A.4).

The **product-moment correlation coefficient** (represented by the symbol r) is the statistic most often employed to describe a relationship between two measures. It represents the degree of straight-line (linear) relationship between two sets of scores and tells us the extent to which the two groups of scores tend to covary (go together). The amount of such a relationship is indicated by the size of the correlation coefficient.

Both direct and inverse relationships are possible, since a correlation may be expressed as a continuum ranging from +1.00 to −1.00. A correlation of +1.00 indicates a perfect positive relationship between two variables; this means that as one of the variables (X) increases, the other (Y) also increases (see Diagram A in Figure A.4). For instance, the student with the highest score on one test also has the highest score on the other test; the next highest on the one test, the next highest on the other; and so on.

A correlation of −1.00 reveals a perfect inverse or negative relationship between two variables; this means that as one of the variables (X) increases, the other (Y) decreases (see Diagram B in Figure A.4). For instance, the student with the highest score on one test has the lowest score on the other test; the student with the next highest score on one test, the next lowest score on the other; and so on. If the correlation coefficient is .00, there is no relationship between the scores on the two tests.

A correlation of −.42 indicates the same magnitude of relationship as does a correlation of +.42. Hence, a correlation coeffficient indicates both the *magnitude* (high or low) and the *direction* (positive or negative) of a relationship.

The product-moment correlation coefficient can be derived for ungrouped data by using the following formula (do not be fooled by the appearance of this formula for it involves simple arithmetic):

$$r = \frac{\frac{\Sigma XY}{N} - \left(\frac{\Sigma X}{N}\right)\left(\frac{\Sigma Y}{N}\right)}{\sqrt{\frac{\Sigma X^2}{N} - \left(\frac{\Sigma X}{N}\right)^2}\sqrt{\frac{\Sigma Y^2}{N} - \left(\frac{\Sigma Y}{N}\right)^2}}$$

In the formula,

r = product-moment correlation coefficient
$\sqrt{}$ = the square root
Σ = the sum of
X = any score of one characteristic (an entry from the X column)
Y = any score of the other characteristic (an entry from the Y column)
N = number of scores

The following steps are involved in computing the product-moment correlation coefficient:

1. Prepare a worksheet like that in Table A.7 headed by the following columns: pupil's name, X, Y, X^2, Y^2, and XY.

2. Arrange the students according to their performance on one of the two tests as in Table A.6 and list the scores under column X. Next list the scores from the second test under column Y so that each student's score is paired with his or her score on the first test (the score in column X).

3. Square each of the scores in the X column and enter the result in the X^2 column.

4. Square each of the scores in the Y column and enter the result in the Y^2 column.

5. Multiply the score of each student on the test in column X by the score of the same student on the test in column Y, and enter the result in the XY column.

6. Add the entries in each column to determine the sum of each column. Thus in Table A.7:

$$\begin{aligned}\Sigma X &= 1{,}743\\ \Sigma Y &= 1{,}031\\ \Sigma X^2 &= 193{,}269\\ \Sigma Y^2 &= 71{,}163\\ \Sigma XY &= 115{,}632\end{aligned}$$

7. Divide each of the sums in Step 6 by the number of students. Thus in Table A.7, where N = 16:

$$\frac{\Sigma X}{N} = \frac{1{,}743}{16} = 108.94$$

$$\frac{\Sigma X^2}{N} = \frac{193{,}269}{16} = 12{,}079.31$$

$$\frac{\Sigma Y}{N} = \frac{1{,}031}{16} = 64.44$$

$$\frac{\Sigma Y^2}{N} = \frac{71{,}163}{16} = 4{,}447.69$$

$$\frac{\Sigma XY}{N} = \frac{115{,}632}{16} = 7{,}227$$

TABLE A.7
Computation of Product-Moment Correlation Coefficient from Table A.6

Pupil's Name	Score on Arithmetic Test X	Score on Reading Test Y	Score on Arithmetic Test Squared X^2	Score on Reading Test Squared Y^2	Score on ReadingTest Times Score on Arithmetic Test XY
Nancy	139	88	19,321	7,744	12,232
Dave	130	89	16,900	7,921	11,570
Angelo	123	77	15,129	5,929	9,471
Bonnie	120	69	14,400	4,761	8,280
Edna	116	61	13,456	3,721	7,076
Bob	114	68	12,996	4,824	7,752
John	112	65	12,544	4,225	7,280
Cynthia	111	73	12,321	5,329	8,103
Brenda	109	79	11,881	6,241	8,611
Judy	105	82	11,025	6,724	8,610
Ron	101	59	10,201	3,481	5,959
Donna	100	62	10,000	3,844	6,200
Tim	99	44	9,801	1,936	4,356
Larry	94	37	8,836	1,369	3,478
Sandra	87	45	7,569	2,025	3,915
Mike	83	33	6,889	1,089	2,739
	1,743 ΣX	1,031 ΣY	193,269 ΣX^2	71,163 ΣY^2	115,632 ΣXY

8. Substitute in the formula the values obtained in Step 7 and proceed to do the appropriate mathematical operations as below:

$$r = \frac{\dfrac{\Sigma XY}{N} - \left(\dfrac{\Sigma X}{N}\right)\left(\dfrac{\Sigma Y}{N}\right)}{\sqrt{\dfrac{\Sigma X^2}{N} - \left(\dfrac{\Sigma X}{N}\right)^2} \sqrt{\dfrac{\Sigma Y^2}{N} - \left(\dfrac{\Sigma Y}{N}\right)^2}}$$

$$= \frac{7,227 - (108.94)(64.44)}{\sqrt{12,079.31 - (108.94)^2} \sqrt{4,447.69 - (64.44)^2}}$$

$$= \frac{7,227 - 7,020.96}{\sqrt{12,079.31 - 11,867.92} \sqrt{4,447.69 - 4,152.51}}$$

$$= \frac{206.04}{\sqrt{211.39} \sqrt{1295.18}}$$

$$= \frac{206.04}{(14.54)(17.18)}$$

$$= \frac{206.04}{249.80}$$

$$= .82$$

When a teacher lacks a desk calculator and must do the computations by hand (or has a calculator but wishes to save time), a simpler method for finding the correlation coefficient involves the use of ranked scores. This is termed a **rank-correlation coefficient** (it is represented by the lower-class Greek letter rho or ρ). The rank-correlation coefficient is not an exact equivalent of the product-moment correlation coefficient (r), but rather an estimate of it. It can be derived for ungrouped data by using the following formula:

$$\rho = 1 - \left(\frac{6(\Sigma D^2)}{N(N^2 - 1)}\right)$$

In the formula,

ρ = rank-correlation coefficient
6 = the number has a constant value in the formula
Σ = the sum of
N = the number of scores
D^2 = the squared differences in rank

The following steps are involved in computing the rank-correlation coefficient:

TABLE A.8
Computation of the Rank-Correlation Coefficient from Table A.6

Pupil's Name	Score on Arithmetic Test X	Score on Reading Test Y	Rank on Arithmetic Test R_x	Rank on Reading Test R^y	Difference in Rank $(R_x - R^y = D)$ D	Difference in Rank Squared D^2
Nancy	139	88	1	2	−1	1
Dave	130	89	2	1	1	1
Angelo	123	77	3	5	−2	4
Bonnie	120	69	4	7	−3	9
Edna	116	61	5	11	−6	36
Bob	114	68	6	8	−2	4
John	112	65	7	9	−2	4
Cynthia	111	73	8	6	2	4
Brenda	109	79	9	4	5	25
Judy	105	82	10	3	7	49
Ron	101	59	11	12	−1	1
Donna	100	62	12	10	2	4
Tim	99	44	13	14	−1	1
Larry	94	37	14	15	−1	1
Sandra	87	45	15	13	2	4
Mike	83	33	16	16	0	0
						148
						ΣD^2

1. Prepare a worksheet like that in Table A.8 headed by the following columns: pupil's name, X, Y, R_x, R_y, and D^2.

2. Arrange the students according to their performance on the two tests as was done in Tables A.6 and A.7. This will provide columns X and Y.

3. Rank (R) the students in Column R_x from 1 to N (the total number in the group) according to the position of each student on one of the tests (X). Note that in Table A.8, N = 16. In the case of tied scores, an averaged rank is assigned. For instance, if four students all had scores of 103 on the test and were tied for ranks 5, 6, 7, and 8, an average rank would be derived: (5 + 6 + 7 + 8)/4 = 6.5.

4. Determine each student's rank on the second test (Y) and place this value in column R_y.

5. Determine the difference (D) in the ranks of each student by subtracting the rank in column R_y from the rank in column R_x.

6. Square each difference in rank (D) to secure the difference squared and place this value in column D^2.

7. Sum the differences in column D^2 (ΣD^2).

8. Substitute in the formula the appropriate values and proceed to do the appropriate mathematical operations as below:

$$\rho = 1 - \left(\frac{6(\Sigma D^2)}{N(N^2 - 1)} \right)$$

$$= 1 - \left(\frac{6(148)}{16(16^2 - 1)} \right)$$

$$= 1 - \left(\frac{888}{16(256 - 1)} \right)$$

$$= 1 - \left(\frac{888}{16(255)} \right)$$

$$= 1 - \left(\frac{888}{4080} \right)$$

$$= 1 - .22$$

$$= .78$$

The product-moment correlation coefficient (r) for the two sets of scores contained in Table A.6 is .82, whereas the rank-correlation coefficient (ρ) is .78. As pointed out above, ρ may be viewed as an estimate of r. When a larger number of cases are involved, ρ and r will more closely approximate each other.

The correlation coefficient has many uses. First, we may be interested in determining the reliability of a test. We can provide the same set of students with two different forms of the same test and then correlate the two sets of scores to determine the test's precision or reliability.

Second, we may wish to determine the validity of a test such as a College Board Achievement Test in Spanish. Our criterion measure might be the final exam scores of students in a first-year college Spanish course. By correlating the two sets of scores, we can acquire evidence regarding the validity of the college board test (evaluate the use of the college board test as a predictor of college performance in Spanish courses).

Third, we may be interested in the relationship between students' performance in mathematics and their verbal abilities. By administering an arithmetic test and a verbal abilities test to the students and then correlating the two sets of scores, we can gain valuable insight regarding this matter.

Although the correlation coefficient provides teachers with an exceedingly useful tool, it is one of the most widely misused procedures. First, those who use it should recognize that it measures only the strength of a straight-line (linear) relationship between two sets of data. Other statistical procedures need to be used if there is reason to believe that a nonlinear relationship holds. For instance, the procedure should not be employed with a curvilinear distribution of the sort shown in Diagram D of Figure A.4.

Second, correlation coefficients do not themselves imply any causal link between variables. For instance, the number of storks in some districts of northeastern Europe tends to be positively correlated with the birth rate in these same districts. Obviously, this does not provide confirmation to the tale that storks cause (bring) babies.

CHAPTER SUMMARY

1. Knowledge of elementary statistical concepts and procedures can help teachers analyze and interpret test scores and other numerical data. To obtain a meaningful summary picture of a set of test scores, the first step would be to construct a frequency distribution of the scores by arranging them from lowest to highest and counting the number of times each score occurs. If the set of scores is large and their range is wide, the scores can be grouped together by class intervals. Scores are then tallied for each interval. The distribution of scores at each score point or interval is often represented visually on a histogram (bar graph) or frequency polygon (line graph). The theoretical distribution that assumes the form of a symmetrical bell-shaped curve is known as the normal curve, and it has certain special statistical properties. When the shape of a distribution of data differs from that of a normal curve, it is said to be skewed.

2. While a frequency distribution depicts the range and occurrence of a set of scores, a measure of central tendency provides a summary statistic to represent a set of scores. The three common measures of central tendency are the mean, the median, and the mode. The mean is the familiar "arithmetic average," which can be obtained by adding all the scores in a set and dividing the sum by the number of scores. The *median* is the score point which divides an ordered set of scores into two. Half the scores will be below the median, and half above. The *mode* is the most frequent score in a set. It is determined by inspecting the distribution to see which score occurs most often.

3. Different measures are used to describe how one score compares to the range of scores in a distribution. A percentile is that point in the distribution of test scores at or below which a certain percentage of scores fall. A student whose score is at the 80th percentile, for example, has achieved a score as good as or better than 80 percent of the students taking the test.

4. Measures of variability reflect the degree to

which a particular set of scores varies or spreads out from the average score. The standard deviation, the most commonly used measure of variability, indicates how widely scores are distributed above and below the mean.

5. Other sets of statistics describe the degree of relationship between two sets of scores. They reflect, for example, whether the same students who did well on an arithmetic test also performed well on a reading test. The statistic most often used to represent this relationship is the product-moment correlation coefficient. It indicates the extent to which two groups of scores tend to covary. The degree, or magnitude, of the relationship is expressed by the absolute size of the correlation coefficient, while the direction (positive or negative) of the relationship is indicated by its sign. For example, a correlation of $+ .80$ indicates that as one variable or set of scores increases, the other tends to do so also.

6. The rank-correlation coefficient, which uses ranked scores, provides an estimate of the product-moment correlation coefficient and is easier to calculate by hand.

CHAPTER GLOSSARY

abscissa   The horizontal axis of a graph.

class intervals   groups of scores, preferably consisting of an odd number of scores, within a larger set of scores.

frequency polygon   A line graph.

histogram   A bar graph.

mean   A measure of central tendency, obtained by adding all the scores in a set and dividing the sum by the number of scores.

median   A measure of central tendency; the middle number when all the numbers in a set are arranged in increasing order by size, from smallest to largest.

mode   A measure of central tendency; the score that occurs more often than any other score in a set of numbers.

normal curve   A bell-shaped curve of distribution, in which the greatest number of cases falls at the center.

ordinate   The vertical axis of a graph.

percentile   A point in a distribution of scores below which a certain percentage of the scores fall.

product-moment correlation coefficient   A statistic that represents the degree of straight-line relationship between two sets of scores and tells the extent to which the two sets of scores tend to covary.

rank-correlation coefficient   A statistic that provides an estimate of the product-moment correlation coefficient, using ranking scores.

standard deviation   A measure of how widely scores of a distribution are scattered above and below the mean of the scores.

variability   The extent to which a score spreads out away from the average.

GLOSSARY

Note: The number following each definition indicates the chapter in which the term is discussed at length.

ability grouping   The practice of placing together children of a given age and grade who have nearly the same standing on measures of learning achievement or capability. (15)

abscissa   The horizontal axis of a graph. (Appendix)

accommodation   A Piagetian concept that refers to the process of changing a scheme to make it a better match to the world of reality. (6)

adjustment   The process of finding means for coping with the demands of our environment. (11)

adolescence   The phase of the life span that lies between childhood and adulthood. (3)

adolescent growth spurt   A period that begins at about the age of twelve in girls and fourteen in boys when they undergo a rapid increase in height and weight. (3)

affective domain   All those aspects of human behavior involving feelings, emotions, tastes, preferences, values, attitudes, morals, character, philosophies of life, and guiding principles. (11)

aggression   Behavior that is socially defined as injurious or destructive. (15)

anxiety   Apprehension, dread, or uneasiness. (12)

aptitude-treatment interactions (ATI)   Programs concerned with adapting instructional treatments to individual differences among student aptitudes. (14)

assimilation   A Piagetian concept that refers to the process of taking in new information and interpreting it in such a manner that the information conforms to a currently held scheme. (6)

asynchrony   Dissimilarity in the growth rates of different parts of the body; a process prevalent during adolescence. (10)

attachment   An affectional tie individuals form between themselves and another specific person that binds them together in space and endures over time. (2)

attitude   A learned and relatively enduring tendency to evaluate a person, event, or situation in a certain way and to act in accordance with that evaluation. (11)

behavior modification   An approach that applies the results of learning theory and experimental psychology to the problem of altering maladaptive behavior. (16)

behavioral objectives   Statements regarding the specific changes educators intend to produce in pupil behavior. (13)

behaviorism   The view that psychology should concern itself exclusively with external, observable events (peripheralism) and that a functional relationship exists between a particular stimulus and a particular response (associationism). (5)

brainstorming   A process by which a great many solutions to a problem are encouraged by deferring judgment and evaluation. (8)

cephalocaudal principle   A developmental pattern that proceeds from head to the feet. (10)

child abuse   A catchall term referring to physical, emotional, social, or sexual mistreatment inflicted upon a child by an adult caretaker. (2)

childhood   The period in the human life span between two years of age and puberty. (2)

classical conditioning   A process of stimulus substitution in which a new, previously neutral stimulus is substituted for the stimulus that naturally elicits the response. (5)

class intervals   Groups of scores, preferably consisting of an odd number of scores, within a larger set of scores. (Appendix)

cognition   The process of knowing; our reception of raw sensory information and our transformation, elaboration, storage, recovery, and use of this information. (6)

cognitive style   An individual's typical mode of processing information; the consistencies in an individual's ways of functioning in his or her day-to-day activities, especially when they have to do with organizing and categorizing perceptions. (4)

computer-assisted instruction (CAI) A variety of educational programs in which the student interacts with an electromechanical device that has as its purpose the dissemination of certain information or the transmission of specific skills. (14)

conditioned response (CR) A response aroused by some stimulus other than the one that naturally produces it. (5)

conditioned stimulus (CS) A previously neutral stimulus that acquires the property of eliciting a particular response through being paired during training with an unconditioned stimulus. (5)

conservation The recognition that the quantity or amount of something stays the same despite changes in shape or position. (6)

contingency contract A negotiated agreement, usually in writing, that specifies the behaviors required of a party and the reinforcements the party is to receive upon completing these requirements. (16)

contingency management The rearrangement of environmental rewards and punishments to strengthen or weaken specified behaviors. (16)

creativity The occurrence of responses that are both new and useful. (8)

criterion-referenced measure An evaluation instrument by which a student's performance is compared against some established standard. (18)

crystallized intelligence Knowledge and skills acquired through cultural experience. Tests of general information, vocabulary, abstruse word analogies, and the mechanics of language as viewed as measures of crystallized intelligence. (4)

curriculum The most comprehensive category of the instructional program. (13)

desegregation The removal of formal barriers within a society, both legal and social, that are premised upon racial or ethnic membership. (15)

diagnostic-prescriptive teaching Identifying the most effective instructional strategy for each child. (17)

discovery learning The teaching of principles, rules, and problem solving through minimal teacher guidance and maximal student exploration and trial-and-error learning. (6)

drive A mechanism that incites activity when conditions depart from some physiological or psychological optimum and sustains activity until the physiological or psychological balance again returns to normal. (12)

drug abuse The excessive or compulsive use of chemical agents to an extent that they interfere with health, social, or vocational functioning. (3)

educational goals Statements regarding the outcomes of instruction. (13)

educational psychology An academic discipline that studies the learning-teaching process. (1)

encoding The process by which information is put into the memory system. (7)

episodic memory The information we have about particular events that we experienced in the past. (7)

equilibrium A Piagetian concept that refers to a balance among the contending forces of assimilation and accommodation. (6)

evaluation The process by which qualitative or quantitative data are used to make judgments and decisions. (18)

expository learning The teaching of principles, rules, and problem solving through maximal teacher guidance and minimal student exploration and trial-and-error learning. (6)

extinction A decrease in a response that results from its repeated failure to find reinforcement. (5)

extrinsic motivation Activity undertaken for some purpose other than its own sake. (12)

feedback The information we receive about some performance or the consequences of the performance. (10)

field dependence A cognitive style characterized by the tendency to categorize a task or situation in a global way. Individuals who are field dependent focus on the whole, overlooking individual elements. (4)

field independence A cognitive style characterized by the tendency to analyze the individual elements making up a task or situation. Individuals who are field independent focus upon undertakings in an analytical manner, separating items from their backgrounds. (4)

fixed-interval (FI) schedule A specific period of time that must elapse after a reinforcer has been delivered before another can be secured. (5)

fixed-ratio (FR) schedule A specific number of responses that must occur before an individual is reinforced. (5)

fluid intelligence A factor of general brightness or abstract mental efficiency thought to be independent of schooling or cultural experience. (4)

frequency polygon A line graph. (Appendix)

gender identities The conceptions that people have of themselves as being male or female. (2)

goal The end state or condition toward which an organism is directing its activity. (12)

human development The process by which individuals change and grow while remaining in some respects the same. It encompasses the orderly and sequential changes that occur as organisms move across the life span from conception to death. (2)

humanistic psychology A psychological school of thought that stresses the uniqueness of the human condition. It maintains that human beings, unlike other organisms, actively intervene in the course of events to control their destinies and shape the world around them. (13)

hyperactivity A collection of rather vague and global symptoms including excessive restlessness, high distractibility, a short attention span, academic difficulties, and behavior problems. (17)

identity An individual's sense of placement within the world; the meaning that one attaches to oneself as reflected in the answers one provides to the questions, "Who am I?" and, "Who am I to be?" (3)

impulsive style A cognitive style in which individuals test hypotheses quickly and make many errors. (4)

incentive External stimuli employed to arouse and direct the activity of an organism toward some goal (usually through treat or promise of future reward). (12)

infancy The first two years of human life. (2)

integration The acceptance of individuals without regard to their racial or ethnic membership within informal, personal, intimate, and voluntary relationships. (15)

intelligence A person's ability to engage in new behaviors that solve problems without recourse to other people's instructions. (4)

intrinsic motivation Activity undertaken for its own sake. (12)

language A structured system of sound patterns (words and sentences) with socially standardized meanings. (9)

language acquisition device An inborn language-generating mechanism. (9)

leadership style The instructor's characteristic ways of handling information and applying sanctions. (16)

learned helplessness A generalized expectancy that events are independent of one's responses. (12)

learning A relatively permanent change in behavior that results from experience. (5)

learning disabilities An umbrella concept referring to children who encounter difficulty in school-related subject matter despite the fact that they are of normal intelligence and have no demonstrable physical, emotional, or social handicap. (17)

linguistic relativity hypothesis The idea that the language spoken by a community affects the way the people in that community think about the world. Also referred to as the "Whorfian hypothesis," after the linguist Benjamin Lee Whorf. (9)

locus of control An individual's perception regarding the source of responsibility for the outcome of events or behaviors. (12)

long-term store A fairly permanent repository for information received from the short-term store; the retention of information over an extended period of time. (7)

mainstreaming The integration of children with special needs within regular classroom programs. (17)

mastery learning The successful attainment by a student of a prespecified instructional goal. The basic premise of mastery learning is that virtually all students, rather than just a small number, can acquire most of what is now being taught in schools. (14)

maternal deprivation The notion that the absence of normal mothering can result in psychological damage and physical deterioration in infants and children. (2)

mathemagenic behaviors Behaviors that give birth to learning; activities on the part of the student that result in the achievement of specified instructional objectives. (7)

mean A measure of central tendency, obtained by adding all the scores in a set and dividing the sum by the number of scores. (Appendix)

measurement The systematic ascertainng of a characteristic, property, or attribute by means of some sort of numerical device. (18)

median A measure of central tendency; the middle number when all the numbers in a set are arranged in increasing order by size, from smallest to largest. (Appendix)

memory A loosely defined concept that describes the ability of individuals to recall, recognize, or relearn more rapidly previously practiced behaviors. (7)

metamemory The demonstrated knowledge we have about memory and activity of remembering. (7)

mnemonics Courses of action we deliberately instigate for helping us remember things better. (7)

mode A measure of central tendency; the score that occurs more often than any other score in a set of numbers. (Appendix)

moral behavior The adoption of principles that lead people to evaluate given actions as "right" and others as "wrong" and to govern their own actions in terms of these principles. (11)

morale The extent to which individuals experience a sense of general well-being and satisfaction with their job situation. (1)

morphemes The smallest units of speech that are discriminated as having meaning. (9)

motherese A simplified form of speech used by mothers, other adults, and even older children in talking to babies. (9)

motivation Those inner states and processes that prompt, direct, and sustain activity. (12)

motive Any condition that affects an organism's readiness to initiate or continue a sequence of activity. (12)

need for achievement Success in competition with some standard of excellence. (12)

needs Those things an organism requires to survive or function in a reasonably healthy manner. (12)

negative reinforcer A stimulus that, when removed following a behavior, strengthens the probability of the behavior's future occurrence. (5)

normal curve A bell-shaped curve of distribution, in which the greatest number of cases fall at the center. (Appendix)

norm-referenced measure An evaluation instrument by which a student's performance is compared with that of others on the same test. (18)

object permanence The view that an object has a reality of its own that extends beyond one's immediate perception of it. (6)

observational (social) learning By watching others, individuals learn new responses without first having the opportunity to make the response themselves. (5)

open education An umbrella concept referring to approaches that stress individual differences in learning and the informal structuring of the schooling process. (15)

operant conditioning A type of learning in which behavior is altered in strength by its consequences. (5)

ordinate The vertical axis of a graph. (Appendix)

orthography The spelling system of a language. (9)

peers Individuals of roughly the same age. (15)

percentile A point in a distribution of scores below which a certain percentage of the scores fall. (Appendix)

phonology The sound system of a language. (9)

positive reinforcer A stimulus that, when applied following a behavior, strengthens the probability of the behavior's future occurrence. (5)

practice Repetition of a procedure with the intention of improving performance and securing appropriate feedback information. (10)

pragmatics Sociolinguistic principles dealing with the relationships between the form or meaning of spoken expressions and their use for different communicative purposes. (9)

Premack principle When high-frequency behaviors are used to reinforce low-frequency behaviors. (16)

prenatal period The time elapsing between conception and birth, which normally averages about 266 days in humans. (2)

principle of punishment A decrease in the frequency of a behavior occurs when it is followed by a contingent or associated stimulus. (5)

principle of reinforcement An increase in the frequency of a behavior occurs when it is followed by a contingent or associated stimulus. (5)

problem A stimulus situation for which an organism lacks a ready response. (8)

problem solution A new combination or rearrangement of existing ideas. (8)

product-moment correlation coefficient A statistic that represents the degree of straight-line relationship between two sets of scores and tells the extent to which the two sets of scores tend to covary. (Appendix)

prosocial behavior Ways of responding to other people through sympathetic, cooperative, trusting, helpful, rescuing, comforting, and giving acts. (11)

proximodistal principle A developmental pattern that proceeds from near to far, outward from the central axis of the body toward the extremities. (10)

psychomotor skills Motor skills that require neuromuscular coordination; motor skills are learned capabilities that find expression in those processes producing expert, rapid, accurate, forceful, or smooth bodily movement. (10)

puberty The term applied to the period in the life cycle when sexual and reproductive maturation occurs. (3)

punishment Any consequence of behavior that has the effect of decreasing the probability of that response. (5)

rank-correlation coefficient A statistic that provides an estimate of the product-moment correlation coefficient, using ranking scores. (Appendix)

reflective style A cognitive style in which individuals proceed by slow deliberation and make few errors. (4)

rehearsal A process in which we repeat information to ourselves. (7)

rehearsal buffer The set of memory traces (units of information) that can be maintained in the short-term memory store. (7)

reinforcement Any event that strengthens the probability of a particular response. (5)

reliability The degree to which an instrument yields a consistent measurement of the same thing. (18)

responses Behavior segmented into units. (5)

retrieval The process by which information is recovered when it is needed. (7)

reward structure The rules under which students receive some sort of payoff for academic success. (12)

role A set of expectations that defines the appropriate behavior for a particular category of individuals. (1)

role conflict Circumstances where individuals find themselves confronted with incompatible demands that they cannot fulfill either completely or realistically. (3)

schemes The term Piaget employs for thinking structures that people evolve for dealing with specific kinds of situations in their environment. (6)

self-concept How people perceive themselves; the sum total of all the characteristics they attribute to themselves and the positive or negative judgments they attach to these characteristics. (11)

self-esteem The positive or negative judgments individuals attach to the characteristics that they attribute to themselves. (11)

semantic memory The organized store of knowledge we have about the world. (7)

semantics That aspect of a language concerned with the meaning of words and sentences. (9)

sensory register The store where incoming information initially resides; information remains for a fraction of a second, then decays and is lost. (7)

shaping When a desired behavior is broken down into successive steps that are taught one by one. (5)

short-term store Our working memory; it receives selected inputs from both the sensory register and the long-term store. In everyday language we make reference to the short-term store when we say that something is in our "consciousness." (7)

social system A configuration in which individuals are bound together within a relatively enduring network of relationships. (15)

sociogram A diagram showing the patterns of choice existing among members of a group at some point in time. (15)

sociometry A method for assessing patterns of attraction, rejection, or indifference among members of a group. (15)

stage A concept that implies that the course of development is divided into steplike levels, with clear-cut changes in behavior occurring from one phase to the next. (6)

standard deviation A measure of how widely scores of a distribution are scattered above and below the mean of the scores. (Appendix)

standardized test A measurement device that is commercially prepared by educational specialists for widespread use in a large number of schools. (18)

state anxiety A transitory condition resulting from the perception of threat. (12)

stimuli The environment segmented into units. (5)

stimulus discrimination The ability of an organism to respond to relevant information and ignore irrelevant information from the environment. (5)

stimulus generalization The ability to apply a response learned with respect to one stimulus to other similar stimuli. (5)

storage The process by which information is retained until it is needed. (7)

symbol Something that stands for something else. (6)

synectics The joining together of different and apparently unrelated or irrelevant elements; the approach is based upon metaphorical thinking. (8)

syntax The rules of a grammar for ordering the semantic units of a language (words and sentences) into meaningful patterns. (9)

system A complex arrangement or structure made up of interdependent but semiautonomous parts. (5)

task analysis The identification of the subordinate skills and knowledge that learners must acquire before they can achieve the educational goal (the terminal objective). (13)

taxonomy A device for identifying, naming, and classifying things in terms of their characteristics. (13)

teacher-expectation effects Beliefs about other people that affect the way we behave toward them. The way we behave often causes the other people to respond just as we expected they would. (15)

teaching An activity in which the aim is to induce learning or to change behavior. (13)

team teaching A type of instructional organization in which two or more persons cooperatively plan and implement a learning program for a group of students. (15)

test A type of measurement tool or instrument consisting of a group of questions or tasks to which a student is asked to respond. (18)

trace A set of information; it is the residue of an event that remains in memory after the event has vanished. (7)

trait anxiety A relatively stable personality attribute. (12)

transfer of learning The influence that prior learning has on performance in some subsequent situation. (8)

two-factor theory of intelligence An approach that views intelligence as made up of two components; (1) a general, or "g," factor that is employed for abstract reasoning and problem solving and (2) special, or "s," factors that are peculiar to given tasks. (4)

unconditioned response (UR) The unlearned, biologically preprogrammed reaction evoked by an unconditioned stimulus. (5)

unconditioned stimulus (US) The stimulus that naturally elicits a particular response. (5)

validity The extent to which an instrument serves the purpose for which it is intended. (18)

variability The extent to which a score spreads out away from the average. (Appendix)

variable-interval (VI) schedule When reinforcement occurs after a given period of time that differs from one reinforcement to the next. (5)

variable-ratio (VR) schedule When individuals receive a reinforcer after a different number of responses on different occasions (usually varying about an average). (5)

REFERENCES

Abrams, J. C. and Kaslow, F. (1977) Family systems and the learning disabled child: Intervention and treatment. *Journal of Learning Disabilities*, 10:86–90.

Abramson, L. Y., Seligman, M. E. P., and Teasdale, J. D. (1978) Learned helplessness in humans: Critique and reformulation. *Journal of Abnormal Psychology*, 87:49–74.

Achenbach, T. M. (1970) Standardization of a research instrument for identifying associative responding in children. *Developmental Psychology*, 2:283–291.

Adam, B. D. (1978) Inferiorization and "self-esteem." *Social Psychology*, 41:47–53.

Adams, G. R. and Crane, P. (1980). An assessment of parents' and teachers' expectations of preschool children's social preference for attractive or unattractive children and adults. *Child Development*, 51:224–231.

Adams, J. A. (1976) *Learning and Memory*. Homewood, Ill.: Dorsey.

Adams, J. A. (1977) Motor learning and retention. In Marx, M. H. and Bunch, M. E., eds. *Fundamentals and Applications of Learning*. New York: Macmillan.

Adams, J. R. (1971) A closed-loop theory of motor learning. *Journal of Motor Behavior*, 3:111–149.

Adams, R. S. and Biddle, B. J. (1970) *Realities of Teaching*. New York: Holt, Rinehart and Winston.

Adelman, H. S. and Compas, B. E. (1977) Stimulant drugs and learning problems. *The Journal of Special Education*, 11:377–416.

Adkison, J. A. (1981). Women in school administration: A review of the research. *Review of Educational Research*, 51:311–343.

Aiken, L. R., Jr. (1970) Attitudes towards mathematics. *Review of Educational Research*, 40:551–606.

Aiken, L. R., Jr. (1973) Ability and creativity in mathematics. *Review of Educational Research*, 43:405–430.

Aiken, L. R., Jr. (1976) Update on attitudes and other affective variables in learning mathematics. *Review of Educational Research*, 46:293–311.

Ainsworth, M. D. S. (1962) The effects of maternal deprivation: A review of findings and controversy in the context of research strategy. In *Deprivation of Maternal Care: A Reassessment of Its Effects*. Geneva: World Health Organization.

Ainsworth, M. D. S. (1967) *Infancy in Uganda: Infant Care and the Growth of Attachment*. Baltimore: Johns Hopkins University Press.

Ainsworth, M. D. S. and Bell, S. M. (1969) Some contemporary patterns of mother-infant interaction in the feeding situation. In Ambrose, A., ed. *Stimulation in Early Infancy*. New York: Academic Press.

Ainsworth, M. D. S. and Bell S. M. (1970) Attachment, exploration, and separation: Illustrated by the behavior of one-year-olds in a strange situation. *Child Development*, 41:49–67.

Ajzen, I. and Fishbein, M. (1973) Attitudinal and normative variables as predictors of specific behaviors. *Journal of Personality and Social Psychology*, 27:41–57.

Albert, R. S. (1975) Toward a behavioral definition of genius. *American Psychologist*, 30:140–151.

Aldous, J. (1973) Family background factors and originality in children. *Gifted Child Quarterly*, 17:183–190.

Alexander, L., Frankiewicz, R. G., and Williams, R. E. (1979) Facilitation of learning and retention of oral instruction using advance and post organizers. *Journal of Educational Psychology*, 71:701–707.

Algozzine, B. (1977) Perceived attractiveness and classroom interactions. *The Journal of Experimental Education*, 46:63–65.

Algozzine, B. and Sutherland, J. (1977) The "learning disabilities" label: An experimental analysis. *Contemporary Educational Psychology*, 2:292–297.

Allen, G. J., Chinsky, J. M., Larcen, S. W., Lochman, J. E., Selinger, H. V. (1976) *Community Psychology and the Schools*. Hillsdale, N.J.: Lawrence Erlbaum.

Allen, V. L., ed. (1976) *Children as Teachers: Theory and Research on Tutoring*. New York: Academic Press.

Allen, V. L. and Feldman, R. S. (1974) Learning through tutoring: Low-achievement children as tutors. *Journal of Experimental Education*, 42:1–5.

Allen, V. L. and Feldman R. S. (1976) Studies on the role of tutor. In Allen, V. L., ed. *Children as Teachers*. New York: Academic Press.

Allport, G. W. (1954) *The Nature of Prejudice*. Boston: Beacon Press.

Alpert, R. and Haber, R. (1960) Anxiety in academic achievement situations. *Journal of Abnormal and Social Psychology*, 61:207–215.

Altus, W. D. (1965) Birth order and academic primogeniture. *Journal of Personaltiy and Social Psychology*, 2:872–876.

American Demographics (1981). Who cares for the kids? (May):12.

Ames, C. (1981). Competitive versus cooperative reward structures: The influence of individual and group performance factors on achievement attributions and affect. *American Educational Research Journal*, 18:273–287.

Ames, C., Ames, R., and Felker, D. W. (1977) Effects of competitive reward structure and valence of outcome on children's achievement attributions. *Journal of Educational Psychology* 69:1–8.

Ames, C. and Felker, D. W. (1979) Effects of self-concept on children's causal attributions and self-reinforcement. *Journal of Educational Psychology*, 71:613–619.

Amir, Y. (1969) Contact hypothesis in ethnic relations. *Psychological Bulletin*, 71:319–342.

Ammons, R. B. (1956) Effects of knowledge of performance: A survey and tentative theoretical formulation. *Journal of General Psychology*, 54:279–299.

Amsel, A. (1967) Partial reinforcement effects on vigor and persistence: Advances in frustration theory derived from a variety of within-subjects experiments. In Spence, K. W. and Spence, J. T., eds. *The Psychology of Learning and Motivation: Advances in Research and Theory*. Vol. 1. New York: Academic Press.

Anastasi, A. (1958) Heredity, environment, and the question "how?" *Psychological Review*, 65:197–208.

Anastasi, A. (1973) Common fallacies about heredity, environment, and human behavior. *American College Testing Research Report*, No. 58, May 1973.

Anastasiow, N. J., Sibley, S. A., Leonhardt, T. M., Borich, G. D. (1970) A comparison of guided discovery, discovery and didactic teaching of math to kindergarten poverty children. *American Educational Research Journal*, 7:493–510.

Anderson, C. M. and Plymate, H. B. (1962) Management of the brain-damaged adolescent. *American Journal of Orthopsychiatry*, 32:492–500.

Anderson, J. R. and Bower, G. H. (1972) Recognition and retrieval processes in free recall. *Psychological Review*, 79:97–123.

Anderson, L. M., Evertson, C. M., and Brophy, J. E. (1979) An experimental study of effective teaching in first-grade reading groups. *The Elementary School Journal*, 79:193–223.

Anderson, L. W. and Block, J. H. (1977) Mastery learning. In Treffinger, D. J., Davis, J. K., and Ripple, R. E., eds. *Handbook on Teaching Educational Psychology*. New York: Academic Press.

Anderson, R. C. (1974) Concretization and sentence learning. *Journal of Educational Psychology*, 66:179–183.

Anderson, R. C. (1977) The notion of schemata and the educational enterprise. In Anderson, R. C., Spiro, R. J., and Montague, W. E., eds. *Schooling and the Acquisition of Knowledge*. Hillsdale, N.J.: Lawrence Erlbaum.

Anderson, R. C., Reynolds, R. E., Schallert, D. L., and Goetz, E. T. (1977) Frameworks for comprehending discourse. *American Educational Research Journal*, 14:367–382.

Anderson, R. C., Spiro, R. J., and Anderson, M. C. (1978) Schemata as scaffolding for the representation of information in connected discourse. *American Educational Research Journal*, 15:433–440.

Anderson, T. H. (1980) Study strategies and adjunct aids. In Spiro, R. J., Bruce, B. C., and Brewer, W. F., eds. *Theoretical Issues in Reading Comprehension*. Hillsdale, N.J.: Lawrence Erlbaum.

Anderson, T. H. and Armbruster, B. B. (1982) Reader and text-studying strategies. In Otto, W. and White, S., eds. *Reading Expository Material*. New York: Academic Press.

Andison, F. S. (1977) TV violence and viewer aggression: A cumulation of study results 1956–1976. *Public Opinion Quarterly*, 41:314–331.

Andre, M. E. D. A. and Anderson, T. H. (1978–1979) The development and evaluation of a self-questioning study technique. *Reading Research Quarterly*, 14:605–623.

Annis, L. F. (1979) Effect of cognitive style and learning passage organization on study technique effectiveness. *Journal of Educational Psychology*, 71:620–626.

Antinucci, F. and Parisi, D. (1973) Early language acquisition: A model and some data. In Ferguson, C. A. and Slobin, D. L., eds. *Studies of Child Language Development*. New York: Holt, Rinehart and Winston.

Applegate, J. R. (1969) Why don't pupils talk in class discussions? *Clearinghouse*, 44:78–81.

Argyle, M. (1976) Social skills theory. In Allen, V. L., ed. *Children as Teachers*. New York: Academic Press.

Arlin, M. (1976) Open education and pupils' attitudes. *The Elementary School Journal*, 76:219–228.

Armbruster, F. E. (1977) The more we spend, the less children learn. *The New York Times Magazine* (August 28):9 + .

Armstrong, D. G. (1977) Team teaching and academic achievement. *Review of Educational Research*, 47:65–86.

Arnold, D. J. and Brooks, P. H. (1976) Influence of contextual organizing material on children's listening comprehension. *Journal of Educational Psychology*, 68:711–716.

Arnold, M., Cranwell, N. and Spar, A. (1977) The LD movement: Brilliant star or glaring copout? In Clarizio, H. F., Craig, R. C., and Mehrens, W. A., eds. *Contemporary Issues in Educational Psychology*. 3rd ed. Boston: Allyn and Bacon.

Atkinson, J. W. (1958) *Motives in Fantasy Action*. Princeton, N. J.: Van Nostrand.

Atkinson, J. W. (1964) *An Introduction to Motivation*. Princeton, N.J.: Van Nostrand.

Atkinson, J. W. (1966) Motivational determinants of risk-taking behavior. In Atkinson, J. W. and Feather, N. T., eds. *A Theory of Achievement of Motivation*. New York: Wiley.

Atkinson, J. W. and Raynor, J. O. (1974) *Motivation and Achievement*. New York: Halsted Press.

Atkinson, R. C. (1972) Ingredients for a theory of instruction. *American Psychologist*, 27:921–931.

Atkinson, R. C. (1974) Teaching children to read using a computer. *American Psychologist*, 29:169–178.

Atkinson, R. C. and Shiffrin, R. M. (1968) Human memory: A proposed system and its control processes. In Spence, K. W. and Spence, J. T., eds. *The Psychology of Learning and Motivation*. Vol. 2. New York: Academic Press.

Atkinson, R. C. and Shiffrin, R. M. (1971) The control of short-term memory. *Scientific American*, 224:82–90.

Austin, G. R. (1979) Exemplary schools and the search for effectiveness. *Educational Leadership*, 37:10–14.

Austin, J. L. (1962) *How to Do Things with Words*. Cambridge: Oxford University Press.

Ausubel, D. P. (1963) *The Psychology of Meaningful Verbal Learning*. New York: Grune & Stratton.

Ausubel. D. P. (1968) *Educational Psychology: A Cognitive View*. New York: Holt, Rinehart and Winston.

Ausubel, D. P. (1978) In defense of advance organizers: A reply to the critics. *Review of Educational Research*, 48:251–257.

Ausubel, D. P. (1980) Schemata, cognitive structure, and advance organizers: A reply to Anderson, Spiro, and Anderson. *American Educational Research Journal*, 17:400–404.

Ausubel, D. P., Novak, J. D., and Hanesian, H. (1978) *Educational Psychology: A Cognitive View*. 2nd ed. New York: Holt, Rinehart and Winston.

Ausubel, D. P. and Robinson, F. G. (1969) *School Learning*. New York: Holt, Rinehart and Winston.

Ayllon, T. and Roberts, M. D. (1974) Eliminating discipline problems by strengthening academic performance. *Journal of Applied Behavior Analysis*. 7:71–76.

Babad, E. Y. and Budoff, M. (1974) Sensitivity and validity of learning-potential measurement in three levels of ability. *Journal of Educational Psychology*, 66:439–447.

Bach, L. (1976) Of women, school administration, and discipline. *Phi Delta Kappan*, 57:463–466.

Backman, C. W. and Secord, P. F. (1968) *A Social Psychological View of Education*. New York: Harcourt, Brace and World.

Baddeley, A. D. (1978) The trouble with levels: A reexamination of Craik and Lockhart's framework for memory research. *Psychological Review*, 85:139–152.

Bagnato, S. J. (1981) Developmental diagnostic reports: Reliable and effective alternatives to guide individualized intervention. *Journal of Special Education*, 15:65–76.

Baird, L. L. (1973) Teaching styles: An exploratory study of dimensions and effects. *Journal of Educational Psychology*, 64:15–21.

Baker, E. L., Herman, J. L., and Yeh, J. P. (1981) Fun and games: Their contribution to basic skills instruction in elementary school. *American Educational Research Journal*, 18:83–92.

Baker, F. B. (1971) Computer-based instructional management systems: A first look. *Review of Educational Research*, 41:51–70.

Ball, S. (1977) Introduction. In Ball, S., ed. *Motivation in Education*. New York: Academic Press.

Ballard, M., Corman, L., Gottlieb, J., and Kaufman, M. J. (1977) Improving the social status of mainstreamed retarded children. *Journal of Educational Psychology*, 69:605–611.

Ballew, H. (1977) The new mathematics as scapegoat. *The Elementary School Journal*, 78:107–109.

Bandura, A. (1964) The stormy decade: Fact or fiction? *Psychology in the Schools*, 1:224–31.

Bandura, A. (1965) Influence of models' reinforcement contingencies on the acquisition of imitative responses. *Journal of Personality and Social Psychology*, 1:589–595.

Bandura, A. (1967) The role of modeling processes in personality development. In Hartup, W. W. and Smothergill, N. L., eds., *The Young Child: A Review of Research*. Washington, D. C.: National Association for the Education of Young Children.

Bandura, A. (1969) *Principles of Behavior Modification*. New York: Holt, Rinehart and Winston.

Bandura, A. (1971) *Social Learning Theory*. Morristown, N. J.: General Learning Corporation.

Bandura, A. (1973a) Social learning theory of aggression. In Knutson, J. F., ed. *The Control of Aggression*. Chicago: Aldine.

Bandura, A. (1973b) *Aggression: A Social Learning Analysis*. Englewood Cliffs, N.J.: Prentice-Hall.

Bandura, A. (1977) *Social Learning Theory*. Englewood Cliffs, N.J.: Prentice-Hall.

Bandura, A. and Menlove, F. L. (1968) Factors determining vicarious extinction of avoidance behavior through symbolic modeling. *Journal of Personality and Social Psychology*, 8:99–108.

Bandura, A. and Mischel, W. (1965) Modification of self-imposed delay of reward through exposure to live and symbolic models. *Journal of Personality and Social Psychology*, 2:698–705.

Bandura, A., Ross, D., and Ross, S. (1963) Imitation of film-mediated aggressive models. *Journal of Abnormal and Social Psychology*, 63:575–582.

Banks, J. H. (1964) *Learning and Teaching Arithmetic*. 2nd ed. Boston: Allyn and Bacon.

Banks, W. C. (1976) White preference in blacks: A paradigm in search of a phenomenon. *Psychological Bulletin*, 83:1179–1186.

Banks, W. C. and Rompf, W. J. (1973) Evaluative bias and preference behavior in black and white children. *Child Development*, 44:776–783.

Banton, L. (1977) Broadening the scope of classroom questions. *Virginia Journal of Education*, 71:13–15.

Barber, P. and Holden, C. (1977) Is it possible to be a creative teacher? *Instructor*, 87 (September):76+.

Barclay, C. R. and Newell, K. M. (1980) Children's processing of information in motor skill acquisition. *Journal of Experimental Child Psychology*, 30:98–108.

Bard, B. (1975) The failure of our school drug abuse programs. *Phi Delta Kappan*, 57:251–255.

Barnard, C. (1964) *The Functions of the Executive*. Cambridge: Harvard University Press.

Barnes, B. R. and Clawson, E. U. (1975) Do advance organizers facilitate learning? Recommendations for further research based on an analysis of thirty-two studies. *Review of Educational Research*, 45:637–659.

Barnett, J. E., DiVesta, F. J., and Rogozinski, J. T. (1981) What is learned in note taking? *Journal of Educational Psychology*, 73:181–192.

Barrish, H. H., Saunders, M., and Wolf, M. M. (1969) Good behavior game: Effects of individual contingencies for group consequences on disruptive behavior in a classroom. *Journal of Applied Behavior Analysis*, 2:119–124.

Barron, F. (1969) *Creative Person and Creative Process*. New York: Holt, Rinehart and Winston.

Bar-Tal, D., Bar-Tal, Y., and Leinhardt, G. (1975) *The Environment, Locus of Control and Feelings of Satisfaction*. Pittsburgh: University of Pittsburgh, Learning Research and Development Center.

Bar-Tal, D. and Bar-Zohar, Y. (1977) The relationship between perception of locus of control and academic achievement. *Contemporary Educational Psychology*, 2:181–199.

Barth, R. S. (1977) Beyond open education. *Phi Delta Kappan*, 58:489–492.

Bartlett, F. C. (1932) *Remembering: A Study in Experimental and Social Psychology*. Cambridge: Cambridge University Press.

Bates, E. (1976) Pragmatics and sociolinguistics in child language. In Morehead, D. M. and Morehead, A. E., eds. *Normal and Deficient Child Language*. Baltimore: University Park Press.

Bates, J. A. (1979) Extrinsic reward and intrinsic motivation: A review with implications for the classroom. *Review of Educational Research*, 49:557–576.

Baumrind, D. (1980) New directions in socialization research. *American Psychologist*, 35:639–652.

Bayley, N. (1935) The development of motor abilities during the first three years. *Monographs of the Society for Research in Child Development*, 1.

Bayley, N. (1956) Individual patterns of development. *Child Development*, 27:45–74.

Beady, C. H., Jr. and Hansell, S. (1981) Teacher race and expectations for student achievement. *American Educational Research Journal*, 18:191–206.

Beane, J. A., Lipka, R. P., and Ludewig, J. W. (1980) Synthesis of research on self-concept. *Educational Leadership*, 38 (October):84–88.

Beatty, W. H. (1976) Emotions: The missing link in education. In Roweton, W. E., ed. *Revitalizing Educational Psychology*. Chicago: Nelson-Hall.

Becker, W. C. (1964) Consequences of different kinds of parental discipline. In Hoffman, M. L. and Hoffman, L. W., eds. *Review of Child Development Research*. New York: Russell Sage Foundation.

Beckerman, T. M. and Good, T. L. (1981) The classroom ratio of high- and low-aptitude students and its effect on achievement. *American Educational Research Journal*, 18:317–327.

Beers, C. S. and Beers, J. W. (1980) Early identification of learning disabilities: Facts and fallacies. *The Elementary School Journal*, 81:67–76.

Begley, S. (1981) The mystery of memory. *Newsweek* (June 1):89–90.

Behrens, M. L. (1954) Child rearing and the character structure of the mother. *Child Development*, 25:225–238.

Bell, M. E. (1958) A comparative study of mentally gifted children heterogeneously grouped. Doctoral dissertation, Indiana University.

Bell, R. Q. and Harper, L. V. (1977) *Child Effects on Adults*. New York: Halsted Press.

Bellack, A. S. and Hersen, M. (1977) *Behavior Modification*. Baltimore: Williams & Wilkins.

Bennett, W. J. and Delattre, E. J. (1978) Moral education in the schools. *The Public Interest*, 50:81–98.

Bennets, L. (1978) Beauty is found to attract some unfair advantages. *New York Times* (March 18):10.

Benowitz, M. L. and Busse, T. V. (1976) Effects of material incentives on classroom learning over a four-week period. *Journal of Educational Psychology*, 68:57–62.

Bentz, W. K., Hollister, W. G., and Edgerton, J. W. (1971) An assessment of the mental health of teachers: A comparative analysis. *Psychology in the Schools*, 8:72–76.

Bentzen, F. (1963) Sex ratios in learning and behavior disorders. *American Journal of Orthopsychiatry*, 33:92–98.

Bentzen, M. M., Williams, R. C., and Heckman, P. (1980) A study of schooling: Adult experiences in schools. *Phi Delta Kappan*, 61:394–397.

Best, D. L., Williams, J. E., Cloud, J. M., Davis, S. W., Robertson, L. S., Edwards, J. R., Giles, H., and Fowles, J. (1977) Development of sex-trait stereotypes among young children in the United States, England, and Ireland. *Child Development*, 48:1375–1384.

Biddle, B. J., Bank, B. J., and Marlin, M. M. 1980. Parental and peer influences on adolescents. *Social Forces*, 58:1057–1079.

Biehler, R. F. (1976) *Child Development: An Introduction*. Boston: Houghton Mifflin.

Bijou, S. W. and Baer, D. M. (1961) *Child Development: A Systematic and Empirical Theory*. Vol. 1. New York: Appleton-Century-Crofts.

Bilodeau, E. A. and Bilodeau, I. McD. (1961) *Annual Review of Psychology*, 12:243–280.

Bindra, D. (1976) *A Theory of Intelligent Behavior*. New York: Wiley.

Bischof, L. J. (1976) *Adult Psychology*. 2nd ed. New York: Harper & Row.

Bjorklund, D. F., Ornstein, P. A., and Haig, J. R. (1977) Developmental differences in organization and recall: Training in the use of organizational techniques. *Developmental Psychology*, 13:175–183.

Blasi, A. (1980) Bridging moral cognition and moral action: A critical review of the literature. *Psychological Bulletin*, 88:1–45.

Blatt, M. and Kohlberg, L. (1975) The effects of classroom moral discussion upon children's level of moral judgment. *Journal of Moral Education*, 4:129–161.

Blauner, R. (1969) Internal colonialism and ghetto revolt. *Social Problems*, 16:393–408.

Block, J. H. (1974a) A description and comparison of Bloom's learning for mastery strategy and Keller's personalized system of instruction. Block, J. H., ed. *Schools, Society, and Mastery Learning*. New York: Holt, Rinehart and Winston.

Block, J. H. (1974b) Mastery learning in the classroom: An overview of recent research. In Block, J. H., ed. *Schools, Society, and Mastery Learning*. New York: Holt, Rinehart and Winston.

Block, J. H. (1980) Promoting excellence through mastery learning. *Theory into Practice*, 19:66–74.

Blom, G. E. (1971) Sex differences in reading disability. In Calkins, E., ed. *Reading Forum*. Bethesda, Md.: National Institute of Neurological Disease and Stroke.

Bloom, B. S. (1956) *Taxonomy of Educational Objectives, Handbook I: The Cognitive Domain*. New York: David McKay.

Bloom, B. S. (1969) Letter to the editor. *Harvard Education Review*, 39:419–421.

Bloom, B. S. (1976) *Human Characteristics and School Learning*. New York: McGraw-Hill.

Bloom, B. S. (1977) Affective outcomes of school learning. *Phi Delta Kappan*, 59:193–198.

Bloom, B. S. (1980) The new direction in educational research: Alterable variables. *Phi Delta Kappan*, 61:382–385.

Bloom, L. (1970) *Language Development: Form and Function in Emerging Grammars*. Cambridge, Mass.: M.I.T. Press.

Bloomfield, L. and Barnhart, C. L. (1961) *Let's Read—A Linguistic Approach*. Detroit: Wayne State University Press.

Blumer, H. (1969) *Symbolic Interactionism: Perspective and Method*. Englewood Cliffs, N.J.: Prentice-Hall.

Blumer, H. (1977) Comment on Lewis' "The classic American pragmatists as forerunners to symbolic interactionism." *Sociological Quarterly*, 18:285–289.

Bodoin, J. J. and Pikunas, J. (1977) Affective learning and content achievement in grades three and four. *The Journal of Educational Research*, 70:235–237.

Bond, G. and Dykstra, R. (1967) The cooperative research

program in first-grade reading instruction. *Reading Research Quarterly*, 2:123.

Bonsall, M. and Stefflre, B. (1955) The temperament of gifted children. *California Journal of Educational Research*, 6:195–199.

Boocock, S. S. (1972) *An Introduction to the Sociology of Learning*. Boston: Houghton Mifflin.

Borland, B. L. and Heckman, H. K. (1976) Hyperactive boys and their brothers. *Archives of General Psychiatry*, 33:669–675.

Borman, K. M. (1979) Children's interactions on playgrounds. *Theory into Practice*, 18:251–257.

Bosco, J. (1975) Behavior modification drugs and the schools: The case of Ritalin. *Phi Delta Kappan*, 56:489–492.

Bossert, S. T. (1981) Understanding sex differences in children's classroom experiences. *The Elementary School Journal*, 81:256–266.

Bower, E. M. (1969) *Early Identification of Emotionally Handicapped Children in School*. 2nd ed. Springfield, Ill.: Charles C Thomas.

Bowerman, M. (1978) Semantic and syntactic development: A review of what, when, and how in language acquisition. In Schiefelbusch, R. L., ed. *Bases of Language Intervention*. Baltimore: University Park Press.

Bowers, W. J. (1964) *Student Dishonesty and Its Control in College*. New York: Columbia University, The Bureau of Applied Social Research.

Bradfield, R. H., Brown, J., Kaplan, P. P., Rickert, E., and Stannard, R. (1973) The special child in the regular classroom. *Exceptional Children*, 39:384–390.

Brainerd, C. J. (1977) Cognitive development and concept learning: An interpretative review. *Psychological Bulletin*, 84:919–939.

Brainerd, C. J. (1979) *The Origins of the Number Concept*. New York: Praeger.

Braun, C. (1976) Teacher expectation: Sociopsychological dynamics. *Review of Educational Research*, 46:185–213.

Brenton, M. (1977) What can be done about child abuse? *Today's Education*, 66:51–53.

Breslow, L. (1981) Reevaluation of the literature on the development of transitive inferences. *Psychological Bulletin*, 89:325–351.

Bretzing, B. H. and Kulhavy, R. W. (1979) Notetaking and depth processing. *Contemporary Educational Psychology*, 4:145–153.

Brick, P. (1981) Sex education belongs in school. *Educational Leadership*, 38:390–394.

Brickell, H. M. (1978) Seven key notes on minimal competency testing. *Educational Leadership*, 35:551–557.

Broadbent, D. E. (1963) Flow of information within the organism. *Journal of Verbal Learning and Verbal Behavior*, 2:34–39.

Broadbent, D. E. and Broadbent, M. H. P. (1977) Comment. *Journal of Experimental Psychology: General*, 106:330–335.

Broderick, C. B. and Rowe, G. P. (1968) A scale of preadolescent heterosexual development. *Journal of Marriage and the Family*, 30:97–101.

Brody, E. B. and Brody, N. (1976) *Intelligence: Nature, Determinants, and Consequences*. New York: Academic Press.

Brody, J. E. (1981) Male hormones tied to aggressive acts. *New York Times* (March 7):7.

Bronfenbrenner, U. (1970) *Two Worlds of Childhood: U.S. and U.S.S.R.* New York: Russell Sage Foundation.

Brookover, W., Beady, C., Flood, P., Schweitzer, J., and Wisenbaker, J. (1979) *Schools Can Make a Difference*. New York: J. F. Bergin.

Brophy, J. E. (1976) Reflections on research in elementary schools. *Journal of Teacher Education*, 27:31–34.

Brophy, J. E. (1979) Teacher behavior and student learning. *Educational Leadership*, 37:33–38.

Brophy, J. E. (1981) Teacher praise: A functional analysis. *Review of Educational Research*, 51:5–32.

Brophy, J. E. (1982) Successful teaching strategies for the inner-city child. *Phi Delta Kappan*, 63:527–553.

Brophy, J. E. and Evertson, C. M. (1976) *Learning from Teaching: A Developmental Perspective*. Boston: Allyn and Bacon.

Brophy, J. E. and Good, T. L. (1970) Teacher's communication of differential expectations for children's classroom performance: Some behavioral data. *Journal of Educational Psychology*, 61:365–374.

Brophy, J. E. and Good, T. L. (1974) *Teacher-Student Relationships: Causes and Consequences*. New York: Holt, Rinehart and Winston.

Broughton, S. F. (1974) The unwitting behavior modifier. *The Elementary School Journal*, 75:143–151.

Brown, A. L. (1975) The development of memory: Knowing, knowing about knowing, and knowing how to know. In Reese, H. W., ed. *Advances in Child Development*. Vol. 10. New York: Academic Press.

Brown, A. L. (1980) Metacognitive development and reading. In Spiro, R. J., Bruce, B., and Brewer, W. F., eds. *Theoretical Issues in Reading Comprehension*. Hillsdale, N.J.: Lawrence Erlbaum.

Brown, A. L. (1982) Learning and development: The problems of compatibility, access and induction. *Human Development*, 25:89–115.

Brown, A. L. and Smiley, S. S. (1977) Rating the importance of structural units of prose passages: A problem of metacognitive development. *Child Development*, 48:1–8.

Brown, B. F. (1980) A study of the school needs of children from one-parent families. *Phi Delta Kappan*, 61:537–540.

Brown, D. L. (1976) Faculty ratings and student grades: A universitywide multiple regression analysis. *Journal of Educational Psychology*, 68:573–578.

Brown, J., ed. (1976) *Recall and Recognition*. New York: Wiley.

Brown, R. (1973) *A First Language: The Early Stages*. Cambridge, Mass.: Harvard University Press.

Brown, R. (1977) Introduction. In Snow, C. E. and Ferguson, C. A. eds. *Talking to Children: Language Input and Acquisition*. Cambridge: Cambridge University Press.

Brozan, N. (1981) Births up in teen-agers despite contraception. *New York Times* (March 12):17, 19.

Bruner, J. S. (1960) *The Process of Education*. Cambridge: Harvard University Press.

Bruner, J. S. (1961) The act of discovery. *Harvard Educational Review*, 31:21–32.

Bruner, J. S. (1966) *Toward a Theory of Instruction*. Cambridge, Mass.: Belknap Press.

Bruner, J. S. (1970) Bad education: A conversation with Jerome Bruner. *Psychology Today*, 4 (December):51+.

Bruner, J. S., Olver, R. R., and Greenfield, P. M. (1966) *Studies in Cognitive Growth*. New York: Wiley.

Bryan, J. H. (1972) Why children help: A review. *Journal of Social Issues*, 28:87–104.

Bryan, J. H. (1977) Prosocial behavior. In Hom, H. L., Jr. and Robinson, P. A., eds. *Psychological Processes in Early Education*. New York: Academic Press.

Bryan, T., Wheeler, R., Felcan, J., and Henek, T. (1976) "Come on, Dummy": An observational study of children's communications. *Journal of Learning Disabilities*. 9:661–669.

Bryant, B. K. (1977) The effects of the interpersonal context of evaluation on self- and other-enhancement behavior. *Child Development*, 48:885–892.

Buckley, P. K. and Cooper, J. M. (1978) Classroom management: A rule establishment and enforcement model. *The Elementary School Journal*, 78:255–263.

Budd, K. S., Green, D. R., and Baer, D. M. (1976) An analysis of multiple misplaced parental social contingencies. *Journal of Applied Behavior Analysis*, 9:459–470.

Bunderson, C. V. and Faust, G. W. (1976) Programmed and computer-assisted instruction. In Gage, N. L., ed. *The Psychology of Teaching Methods*. Chicago: National Society for the Study of Education.

Bunker, R. M. (1977) Beyond inservice: Toward staff renewal. *Journal of Teacher Education*, 28:31–34.

Burchard, J. D. and Harig, P. T. (1976) Behavior modification and juvenile delinquency. In Leitenberg, H., ed. *Handbook of Behavior Modification*. New York: Prentice-Hall.

Bureau of Census (1976) *Persons of Spanish Origin in the U.S.*: March, 1976. Washington, D.C.: Government Printing Office.

Bureau of Labor Statistics (1976) *Multiple Jobholders*. Special Labor Force Report 194. Washington, D.C.: Government Printing Office.

Burton, R. V. (1976) Honesty and dishonesty. In Lickona, T., ed. *Moral Development and Behavior: Theory, Research, and Social Issues*. New York: Holt, Rinehart and Winston.

Burton, T. A. and Hirshoren, A. (1978) The focus of responsibility for education of the severely and profoundly retarded. *Psychology in the Schools*, 15:52–56.

Burtt, H. E. (1941) An experimental study of early childhood memory: Final report. *The Journal of Genetic Psychology*, 58:435–439.

Bushway, A. and Nash, W. R. (1977) School cheating behavior. *Review of Educational Research*, 47:623–632.

Butterfield, E. C., Wambold, C., and Belmont, J. M. (1973) On the theory and practice of improving short-term memory. *American Journal of Mental Deficiency*, 77:654–669.

Campbell, D. N. (1976) Open education and the open classroom: A conceptual analysis. Thibadeau, G., ed. *Opening Up Education*. Dubuque, Iowa: Kendall/Hunt.

Carithers, M. (1970) School desegregation and racial cleavage, 1954–1970: A review of the literature. *Journal of Social Issues*, 26:25–47.

Carrier, C. A. and Titus, A. (1979). The effects of notetaking: A review of studies. *Contemporary Educational Psychology*, 4:299–314.

Carroll, J. B. (1963) A model of school learning. *Teachers College Record*, 64:723–733.

Carroll, J. B. and Horn, J. L. (1981) On the scientific basis of ability testing. *American Psychologist*, 36:1012–1020.

Carson, R. B., Goldhammer, K., and Pellegrin, R. J. (1967) *Teacher Participation in the Community: Role Expectations and Behavior*. Eugene, Oregon: Center for the Advanced Study of Educational Administration, University of Oregon.

Carter, J. F. and Van Matre, N. H. (1975) Note-taking versus note having. *Journal of Educational Psychology*, 67:900–904.

Carter, T. (1968) Negative self-concept of Mexican-American students. *School and Society*, 96:217–219.

Cartledge, G. and Milburn, J. F. (1978) The case for teaching social skills in the classroom: A review. *Review of Educational Research*, 48:133–156.

Casler, L. R. (1961) Maternal deprivation: A critical review of the literature. *Monographs of the Society for Research in Child Development*, 26 (2).

Casler, L. R. (1967) Perceptual deprivation in institutional settings. In Newton, G. and Levine, S., eds. *Early Experience and Behavior*. New York: Springer.

Cattell, R. B. (1943) The measurement of adult intelligence. *Psychological Bulletin*, 40:153–193.

Cattell, R. B. (1971) *Abilities: Their Structure, Growth, and Action*. Boston: Houghton Mifflin.

Cavanaugh, J. C. and Perlmutter, M. (1982) Metamemory: A critical examination. *Child Development*, 53:11–28.

Cazden, C. B. (1970) The situation: A neglected source of social class differences in language use. *Journal of Social Issues*, 26:35–60.

Cervantes, L. (1965) *The Dropout: Causes and Cures*. Ann Arbor: University of Michigan Press.

Chalfant, J. C. and King, F. S. (1976) An approach to operationalizing the definition of learning disabilities. *Journal of Learning Disabilities*, 9:228–243.

Chall, J. S. (1967) *Learning to Read: The Great Debate*. New York: McGraw-Hill.

Chall, J. S. (1977) Review: *Human Characteristics and School Learning*. *Harvard Educational Review*, 47:447–451.

Chambers, M. (1977) Segregated classes tied to court cases. *New York Times* (November 25):B9.

Chan, K. S. (1978) Locus of control and achievement motivation—Critical factors in educational psychology. *Psychology in the Schools*, 15:104–110.

Chance, P. (1981) The remedial thinker. *Psychology Today*, 15:63–73.

Charters, W. W., Jr. (1962) The social background of teaching. In Gage, N. L., ed. *Handbook of Research on Teaching*. Chicago: Rand McNally.

Chasen, B. (1974) Sex-role stereotyping and prekindergarten teachers. *The Elementary School Journal*, 74:220–235.

Cherry, F. F. and Eaton, E. L. (1977) Physical and cognitive development in children of low-income mothers working in the child's early years. *Child Development*, 48:158–166.

Chomsky, C. (1969) *The Acquisition of Syntax in Children from 5 to 10*. Cambridge, Mass.: M.I.T. Press.

Chomsky, N. (1957) *Syntactic Structures*. The Hague: Mouton.

Chomsky, N. (1959) A review of *Verbal Behavior* by B. F. Skinner. *Language*, 35:26–58.

Chomsky, N. (1965) *Aspects of a Theory of Syntax*. Cambridge, Mass.: MIT Press.

Chomsky, N. (1968) *Language and Mind*. New York: Harcourt Brace Jovanovich.

Chomsky, N. (1972) *Language and Mind*. Enlarged ed. New York: Harcourt Brace Jovanovich.

Chomsky, N. (1975) *Reflections on Language*. New York: Pantheon.

Chomsky, N. (1980) *Rules and Representations*. New York: Columbia University Press.

Christenson, R. M. (1977) McGuffey's ghost and moral education today. *Phi Delta Kappan*, 58:737–742.

Christian, C. C., Jr. (1976) Social and psychological implications of bilingual literacy. In Simões, A., Jr., ed. *The Bilingual Child*. New York: Academic Press.

Chu, G. C. and Schramm, W. (1967) *Learning from Television: What the Research Says*. Stanford, Calif.: Institute for Communication Research.

Cicchetti, D. and Rizley, R. (1981) Developmental perspectives on the etiology, intergenerational transmission, and sequelae of child maltreatment. *New Directions for Child Development*, 11:31–56.

Clarizio, H. F. (1976) *Toward Positive Classroom Discipline*. 2nd ed. New York: Wiley.

Clarizio, H. F. (1977) Natural versus accelerated readiness. In Clarizio, H. F., Craig, R. C., and Mehrens, W. A., eds. *Contemporary Issues in Educational Psychology*. 3rd ed. Boston: Allyn and Bacon.

Clarizio, H. F., Craig, R. C., and Mehrens, W. A. (1977) *Contemporary Issues in Educational Psychology*. 3rd ed. Boston: Allyn and Bacon.

Clark, C. M., Gage, N. L., Marx, R. W., Peterson, P. L., Stayrook, N. G., and Winne, P. H. (1979) A factorial experiment on teacher structuring, soliciting, and reacting. *Journal of Educational Psychology*, 71:534–552.

Clark, D. L., Lotto, L. S., and McCarthy, M. M. (1980) Factors associated with success in urban elementary schools. *Phi Delta Kappan*, 61:467–470.

Clark, H. H. and Clark, E. V. (1977) *Psychology and Language: An Introduction to Psycholinguistics*. New York: Harcourt Brace Jovanovich.

Clark, K. B. and Clark, M. P. (1939) Development of consciousness of self and the emergence of racial identification in Negro preschool children. *Journal of Social Psychology*, 10:591–599.

Clark, K. B. and Clark, M. P. (1947) Racial identification and preference in Negro children. In Newcomb, T. M. and Hartley, E. L., eds. *Readings in Social Psychology*. New York: Holt.

Clark, K. B. and Clark, M. P. (1950) Emotional factors in racial identification and preference in Negro children. In Grossack, M., ed. *Mental Health and Segregation*. New York: Springer.

Clay, M. M. (1976) Early childhood and cultural diversity in New Zealand. *The Reading Teacher*, 29:333–342.

Clifford, M. M. and Walster, E. (1973) Research note: The effect of physical attractiveness on teacher expectations. *Sociology of Education*, 46:248–258.

Clore, G. L., Bray, R. M., Itkin, S. M., and Murphy, P. (1978) Interracial attitudes and behavior at a summer camp. *Journal of Personality and Social Psychology*, 36:107–116.

Cloward, R. D. (1976) Teenagers as tutors of academically low-achieving children: Impact on tutors and tutees. In Allen, V. L., ed. *Children as Teachers*. New York: Academic Press.

Cockerham, W. C. and Blevins, A. L., Jr. (1976) Open school vs. traditional school: Self-identification among Native American and white adolescents. *Sociology of Education*, 49:164–169.

Cohen, A. K. (1966) *Deviance and Control*. Englewood Cliffs, N.J.: Prentice-Hall.

Cohen, E. (1975) The effects of desegregation on race relations. *Law and Contemporary Problems*, 39:271–299.

Cohen, R. B. and Bradley, R. H. (1978) Simulation games, learning, and retention. *The Elementary School Journal*, 78:247–253.

Colbert, C. D. (1979) Instructional organization patterns of fourth-grade teachers. *Theory into Practice*, 18:170–173.

Cole, S. (1980) Send our children to work? *Psychology Today*, 14:44–68.

Coleman, J. C. (1978) Current contradictions in adolescent theory. *Journal of Youth and Adolescence*, 7:1–11.

Coleman, J. S. (1966) *Equality of Educational Opportunity*. Washington, D. C.: Government Printing Office.

Coleman, J. S. (1970) *The Role of Modern Technology in Relation to Simulation and Games for Learning*. ERIC: ED 039 704. Washington, D.C.: Academy for Educational Development.

Coleman, J. S., and Livingston, S., Fennessey, G., Edwards, K., and Kidder, S. (1973) The Hopkins games program: Conclusions from seven years of research. *Education Researcher*, 2:3–7.

Coles, G. S. (1978) The learning disabilities test battery: Empirical and social issues. *Harvard Educational Review*, 48:313–340.

Collinge, J. (1976) Teachers and teaching methods. *The Elementary School Journal*, 76:259–265.

Collins, B. E. and Raven, B. H. (1969) Psychological aspects of structure in the small group: Interpersonal attraction, coalitions, communication, and power. In Lindzey, G. and Aronson, E., eds. *The Handbook of Social Psychology*. 2nd ed. Vol. 4. Reading, Mass.: Addison-Wesley.

Collins, G. (1981). Schools stereotype children with one parent. *New York Times* (February 2):16.

Coltheart, M. (1979) When can children learn to read—and when should they be taught? In Waller, T. G. and MacKinnon, G. E., eds. *Reading Research: Advances in Theory and Practice*. Vol. 1. New York: Academic Press.

Columbus Dispatch (1981). ''Latchkey kids'' spiraling problem (March 25):A-10.

Combs, A. W. (1978) Humanism, education, and the future. *Educational Leadership*, 35:300–303.

Combs, A. W. (1981) Humanistic education: Too tender for a tough world? *Phi Delta Kappan* 62:446–449.

Combs, A. W., Avila, D. and Purkey, W. W. (1971) *Helping*

Relationships: Basic Concepts for the Helping Professions. Boston: Allyn and Bacon.

Condry, J. (1977) Enemies of exploration: Self-initiated versus other-initiated learning. *Journal of Personality and Social Psychology,* 35:459–477.

Condry, J. and Dyer, S. (1976) Fear of success: Attribution of cause to the victim. *Journal of Social Issues,* 32:63–83.

Conger, J. J. (1977) *Adolescence and Youth.* 2nd ed. New York: Harper & Row.

Connell, W. F. (1975) Moral education: Aims and methods in China, the USSR, the U.S., and England. *Phi Delta Kappan,* 56:702–706.

Conners, C. K. (1972a) Stimulant drugs and cortical evoked responses in learning and behavior disorders in children. In Smith, W. L., ed. *Drugs, Development, and Cerebral Function.* Springfield, Ill.: Charles C Thomas.

Conners, C. K. (1972b) Pharmacotherapy of psychopathology in children. In Quay, H. C. and Werry J. S., eds. *Psychopathological Disorders of Childhood.* New York: Wiley.

Cooke, T. P. and Cooke, S. (1975) Behavior modification: Answers to some ethical issues. *Psychology in the Schools,* 11:5–10.

Cooley, C. H. (1902) *Human Nature and the Social Order.* New York: Charles Scribner's.

Cooley, C. H. (1909) *Social Organization.* New York: Charles Scribner's.

Cooper, H. M. (1979). Pygmalion grows up: A model for teacher expectation communication and performance influence. *Review of Educational Research,* 49:389–410.

Cooper, L. A. and Shepard, R. N. (1973) Chronometric studies of the rotation of mental images. In Chase, W. G., ed. *Visual Information Processing.* New York: Academic Press.

Coopersmith, S. (1967) *Antecedents of Self-Esteem.* San Francisco: W. H. Freeman.

Corno, L. and Mitman, A. (1981). The influence of direct instruction on student self-appraisals: A hierarchical analysis of treatment and aptitude-treatment effects. *American Educational Research Journal,* 18:39–61.

Corwin, R. G. (1970) *Militant Professionalism.* New York: Meredith.

Coughlan, R. J. (1970) Dimensions of teacher morale. *American Educational Research Journal,* 7:221–234.

Covington, M. V. and Omelich, C. L. (1979). Effort: The double-edged sword in school achievement. *Journal of Educational Psychology,* 71:169–182.

Cowgill, M. L., Friedland, S., and Shapiro, R. (1973) Predicting learning disabilities from kindergarten reports. *Journal of Learning Disabilities,* 6:577–582.

Craighead, W. E., Kazdin, A. E., and Mahoney, M. J. (1976) *Behavior Modification: Principles, Issues, and Applications.* Boston: Houghton Mifflin.

Craik, F. I. M. (1976) Age differences in human memory. In Birren, J. E. and Schaie, K. W. eds. *Handbook of the Psychology of Aging.* New York: Van Nostrand Reinhold.

Craik, F. I. M. and Levy, B. A. (1976) The concept of primary memory. In Estes, W. K. ed. *Handbook of Learning and Cognitive Processes.* Vol. 4. Hillsdale, N.J.: Lawrence Erlbaum.

Craik, F. I. M. and Lockhart, R. S. (1972) Levels of processing: A framework for memory research. *Journal of Verbal Learning and Verbal Behavior,* 11:671–684.

Crandall, V. C., Katkovsky, W., and Crandall, V. J. (1965) Children's beliefs in their own control of reinforcement in intellectual-academic situations. *Child Development,* 36:91–109.

Crano, W. D. and Mellon, P. M. (1978) Causal influence of teachers' expectations on children's academic performance: A cross-lagged panel analysis. *Journal of Educational Psychology,* 70:39–49.

Crockenberg, S. B. (1972) Creativity tests: A boon or boondoggle for education? *Review of Educational Research,* 42:27–45.

Cromer, R. F. (1976) The cognitive hypothesis of language acquisition and its implications for child language deficiency. In Morehead, D. M. and Morehead, A. E., eds. *Normal and Deficient Child Language.* Baltimore: University Park Press.

Cronbach, L. J. and Snow, R. E. (1977) *Aptitudes and Instructional Methods: A Handbook for Research on Interactions* New York: Irvington.

Cross, K. P. (1976) *Accent on Learning.* San Francisco: Jossey-Bass.

Crowl, T. K. and MacGinitie, W. H. (1974) The influence of students' speech characteristics on teachers' evaluations of oral answers. *Journal of Educational Psychology,* 66:304–308.

Cruickshank, D. R. and Telfer, R. (1980). Classroom games and simulations. *Theory into Practice,* 19:75–80.

Cruickshank, W. M. (1972) Some issues facing the field of learning disability. *Journal of Learning Disabilities,* 5:380–388.

Crutchfield, R. S. (1969) Nurturing the cognitive skills of productive thinking. In Rubin, L. J., ed. *Life Skills in School and Society.* Washington, D. C.: Association for Supervision and Curriculum Development.

Cryan, J. R. and Smith, J. C. (1981). The hick'ry stick: It's time to change the tune. *Phi Delta Kappan,* 62:433–435.

Cummings, S. (1975) An appraisal of some recent evidence dealing with the mental health of black children and adolescents, and its implications for school psychologists and guidance counselors. *Psychology in the Schools,* 12:234–238.

Cummings, S. T. (1976) The impact of the child's deficiency on the father: A study of fathers of mentally retarded and chronically ill children. *American Journal of Orthopsychiatry,* 46:246–255.

Cunningham, C. E. and Barkley, R. A. (1978) The role of academic failure in hyperactive behavior. *Journal of Learning Disabilities,* 11:274–280.

Curtiss, S. (1977). *Genie: A Psycholinguistic Study of a Modern Day "Wild Child."* New York: Academic Press.

Danner, F. W. (1976) Children's understanding of intersentence organization in the recall of short descriptive passages. *Journal of Educational Psychology,* 68:174–183.

Darley, S. A. (1976) Big-time careers for the little woman: A dual-role dilemma. *Journal of Social Issues,* 32:85–98.

Davies, M. and Kandel, D. B. (1981). Parental and peer influences on adolescents' educational plans: Some further evidence. *American Journal of Sociology,* 87:363–387.

Davis, G. A. (1973) *Psychology of Problem Solving.* New York: Basic Books.

Davis, G. A. (1976) Research and development in training creative thinking. In Levin, J. R. and Allen, V. L., eds. *Cognitive Learning in Children*. New York: Academic Press.

Davis, K. (1947) Final note on a case of extreme isolation. *American Journal of Sociology*, 52:432–437.

Davis, R. H., Alexander, L. T., and Yelon, S. L. (1974) *Learning System Design*. New York: McGraw-Hill.

Day, B. and Brice, R. (1977). Academic achievement, self-concept development, and behavior patterns of six-year-old children in open classrooms. *The Elementary School Journal*, 78:133–139.

DeBlaissie, R. R. and Healy, G. W. (1970) *Self-Concept: A Comparison of Spanish-American, Negro, and Anglo Adolescents across Ethnic, Sex, and Socioeconomic Variables*. Las Cruces, N.M.: ERIC Clearinghouse on Rural Education and Small Schools.

Deci, E. L. (1975) *Intrinsic Motivation*. New York: Plenum Press.

Deci, E. L. (1980). *The Psychology of Self-Determination*. Lexington, Mass.: D.C. Heath.

Deci, E. L. and Ryan, R. M. (1980). The empirical exploration of intrinsic motivational processes. In Berkowitz, L., ed. *Advances in Experimental Social Psychology*. Vol. 13. New York: Academic Press.

Deci, E. L., Schwartz, A. J., Sheinman, L., and Ryan, R. M. (1981). An instrument to assess adults' orientations toward control versus autonomy with children: Reflections on intrinsic motivation and perceived competence. *Journal of Educational Psychology*, 73:642–650.

Deffenbacher, J. L. (1977) Relationship of worry and emotionality to performance on the Miller Analogies Test. *Journal of Educational Psychology*, 69:191–195.

Deffenbacher, J. L. (1978) Worry, emotionality, and task-generated interference in test anxiety: An empirical test of attentional theory. *Journal of Educational Psychology*, 70:248–254.

DeFleur, L. B. and Menke, B. A. (1975) Learning about the labor force: Occupational knowledge among high school males. *Sociology of Education*, 48:324–345.

Delefes, P. and Jackson, B. (1972) Teacher-pupil interaction as a function of location in the classroom. *Psychology in the Schools*, 9:119–123.

DeMeis, D. K. and Turner, R. R. (1977) The usefulness of teachers' characteristics in predicting teachers' ratings of racially and linguistically different students. *Contemporary Educational Psychology*, 2:384–392.

DeMeis, D. K. and Turner, R. R. (1978) Effects of students' race, physical attractiveness, and dialect on teachers' evaluations. *Contemporary Educational Psychology*, 3:77–86.

Dempster, F. N. (1981). Memory span: Sources of individual and developmental differences. *Psychological Bulletin*, 89:63–100.

Denham, C. H. and Keese, J. F. (1977) The victim of aggression in fifth- and sixth-grade classrooms. *Journal of Educational Research*, 70:192–194.

Dennis, W. (1973) *Children of the Crèche*. New York: Appleton-Century-Crofts.

Depue, R. A. and Monroe, S. M. (1978) Learned helplessness in the perspective of the depressive disorders: Conceptual and definitional issues. *Journal of Abnormal Psychology*, 87:3–20.

Dermer, M. and Thiel, D. L. (1975) When beauty may fail. *Journal of Personality and Social Psychology*, 31:1168–1176.

Deutsch, M. (1949) An experimental study of the effects of cooperation and competition upon group process. *Human Relations*, 2:199–231.

Deutsch, M. (1962) Cooperation and trust: Some theoretical notes. In Jones, M. R., ed. *Nebraska Symposium on Motivation*. Vol. 10. Lincoln: University of Nebraska Press.

Devin-Sheehan, L., Feldman, R. S., and Allen, V. L. (1976) Research on children tutoring children: A critical review. *Review of Educational Research*, 46:355–385.

DeVito, J. A. (1970) *The Psychology of Speech and Language*. New York: Random House.

DeVries, D. L. and Edwards, K. J. (1974) Student teams and learning games: Their effects on cross-race and cross-sex interaction. *Journal of Educational Psychology*, 66:741–749.

DeVries, D. L., Edwards K. J., and Slavin, R. E. (1978) Biracial learning teams and race relations in the classroom: Four field experiments using Teams-Games-Tournament. *Journal of Eductional Psychology*, 70:356–362.

Dewey J. (1909) The influence of Darwinism on philosophy. *Popular Science 1909*. Reprinted in John Dewey, *The Influence of Darwin on Philosophy*. Bloomington: Indiana University Press.

Dewey, J. (1910) *How We Think*. Boston: D. C. Heath.

Dewey, J. (1928) *Democracy and Education*. New York: Macmillan.

Dewey, J. (1933) *How We Think*. Lexington, Mass.: D. C. Heath.

Dewey, J. (1934) *A Common Faith*. New Haven: Yale University Press.

Diener, C. I. and Dweck, C. S. (1978) An analysis of learned helplessness: Continuous changes in performance, strategy, and achievement cognitions following failure. *Journal of Personality and Social Psychology*, 36:451–462.

Diener, C. I. and Dweck, C. S. (1980). An analysis of learned helplessness: II. The processing of success. *Journal of Personality and Social Psychology*, 39:940–952.

Dillon, J. T. (1981). Duration of response to teacher questions and statements. *Contemporary Educational Psychology*, 6:1–11.

Dineen, J. P., Clark, H. B., and Risley, T. R. (1977) Peer tutoring among elementary students: Educational benefits to the tutor. *Journal of Applied Behavior Analysis*, 10:231–238.

Dion, K., Berscheid, E., and Walster, E. (1972) What is beautiful is good. *Journal of Personality and Social Psychology*, 24:285–290.

DiStefano, J. J. (1970). Interpersonal perceptions of field independent and field dependent teachers and students. Doctoral dissertation, Cornell University.

Doleys, D. M., Wells, K. C., Hobbs, S. A., Roberts, M. W., and Cartelli, L. M. (1976) The effects of social punishment on noncompliance: A comparison with timeout and positive practice. *Journal of Applied Behavior Analysis*, 9:471–482.

Domino, G. (1971) Interactive effects of achievment orientation and teaching style on academic achievement. *Journal of Educational Psychology*, 62:427–432.

Dominowski, R. L. (1977) Problem solving. In Marx, M. H.

and Bunch, M. E., eds. *Fundamentals and Applications of Learning.* New York: Macmillan.

Doob, A. N. and Kirschenbaum, H. M. (1973) The effects on arousal of frustration and aggressive films. *Journal of Experimental Social Psychology*, 9:57–65.

Downing, J. (1973) *Comparative Reading*. New York: Macmillan.

Doyle, W. (1979). Making managerial decisions in classrooms. *Classroom Management*. Duke, D. L., ed. Chicago: The University of Chicago Press.

Drabman, R. S., Jarvie, G. J. and Archbold, J. (1976) The use and misuse of extinction in classroom behavioral programs. *Psychology in the Schools*, 13:470–476.

Dragastin, S. E. and Elder, G. H., Jr. (1975) *Adolescence in the Life Cycle*. New York: Wiley.

Dreeben, R. (1968) *On What Is Learned in School*. Reading, Mass.: Addison-Wesley.

Dressel, P. and Mayhew, L. B. (1954) *General Education: Explorations in Evaluation*. Washington, D.C.: American Council on Education.

Dubin, R. and Hedley, R. A. (1969) *The Medium May Be Related to the Message: College Instruction by TV*. Eugene: University of Oregon Press.

Dubin, R., Hedley, R. A., and Taveggia, T. C. (1976) In Dubin, R., ed. *Handbook of Work, Organization, and Society*. Chicago: Rand McNally.

Duchastel, P. C. and Brown, B. R. (1974) Incidental and relevant learning with instructional objectives. *Journal of Educational Psychology*, 66:481–485.

Duchastel, P. C. and Merrill, P. F. (1974) The effects of behavioral objectives on learning: A review of empirical studies. *Review of Educational Research*, 43:53–69.

Duckworth, E. (1964) Piaget rediscovered. In Ripple, R. E. and Rockcastle, V. N., eds. *Piaget Rediscovered*. Ithaca, New York: Cornell University Press.

Duckworth, E. (1979) Either we're too early and they can't learn it or we're too late and they know it already: The dilemma of "applying Piaget." *Harvard Educational Review*, 49:297–312.

Duke, D. L. (1978) How administrators view the crisis in school discipline. *Phi Delta Kappan*, 59:325–330.

Dullea, G. (1975) Women in classrooms, not the principal's office. *New York Times* (July 13):7.

Dunkin, M. J. and Biddle, B. J. (1974) *The Study of Teaching*. New York: Holt, Rinehart and Winston.

Dunn, L. M. (1968) Special education for the mildly retarded— Is much of it justified? *Exceptional Children*, 35:2–22.

Dunn, R. S. and Dunn, K. J. (1979) Learning styles/teaching styles: Should they . . . can they . . . be matched? *Educational Leadership*, 36:238–244.

Durkin, D. (1978–1979) Reading comprehension instruction. *Reading Research Quarterly*, 14:481–527.

Dusek, J. B. (1975) Do teachers bias children's learning? *Review of Educational Research*, 45:661–684.

Dusek, J. B. and Flaherty, J. F. (1981) The development of the self-concept during the adolescent years. *Monographs of the Society for Research in Child Development*, 46:No. 4.

Dusek, J. B., Mergler, N. L., and Kermis, M. D. (1976) Attention, encoding, and information processing in low- and high-test-anxious children. *Child Development*, 47:201–207.

Dweck, C. S. (1975) The role of expectations and attributions in the alleviation of learned helplessness. *Journal of Personality and Social Psychology*, 31:674–685.

Dweck, C. S. and Bush, E. S. (1976) Sex differences in learned helplessness: I. Differential debilitation with peer and adult evaluators. *Developmental Psychology*, 12:147–156.

Dweck, C. S., Davidson, W., Nelson, S., and Enna, B. (1978) Sex differences in learned helplessness: II. The contingencies of evaluative feedback in the classroom and III. An experimental analysis. *Developmental Psychology*, 14:268–276.

Dweck, C. S. and Gilliard, D. (1975) Expectancy statements as determinants of reactions to failure: Sex differences in persistence and expectancy change. *Journal of Personality and Social Psychology*, 32:1077–1084.

Dweck, C. S., Goetz, T. E., and Strauss, N. L. (1980) Sex differences in learned helplessness: IV. An experimental and naturalistic study of failure generalization and its mediators. *Journal of Personality and Social Psychology*, 38:441–452.

Dweck, C. S. and Reppucci, N. D. (1973) Learned helplessness and reinforcement responsibility in children. *Journal of Personality and Social Psychology*, 25:109–116.

Dykman, B. M. and Reis, H. T. (1979) Personality correlates of classroom seating position. *Journal of Educational Psychology*, 71:346–354.

Dykstra, R. (1968) First-grade reading studies follow-up. *Reading Research Quarterly*, 4:61–65, 66.

D'Zurilla, T. J. and Goldfried, M. R. (1971) Problem solving and behavior modification. *Journal of Abnormal Psychology*, 78:107–126.

Eaves, L. C., Kendall, D. C., and Crichton, J. U. (1973) The early identification of learning disabilities: A follow-up study. *Journal of Learning Disabilities*, 7:632–638.

Ebel, R. L. (1970) Behavioral objectives: A close look. *Phi Delta Kappan*, 52:171–173.

Ebel, R. L. (1974) Shall we get rid of grades? *Measurement in Education*, 5:1–5.

Ebel, R. L. (1975) Educational tests: Valid? Biased? Useful? *Phi Delta Kappan*, 57:83–89.

Edison, T. A. (1948) *The Diary and Sundry Observations of Thomas Alva Edison*. Runes, D. D., ed. New York: Philosophical Library.

Eger, M. (1981) The conflict in moral education: An informal case study. *The Public Interest*, 63:62–80.

Ehly, S. W. and Larsen, S. C. (1976) Peer tutoring to individualize instruction. *The Elementary School Journal*, 76:475–480.

Ehri, L. C. (1970) Linguistic insight: Threshold of reading acquisition. In Waller, T. G. and MacKinnon, G. E., eds. *Reading Research: Advances in Theory and Practice*. Vol. 1. New York: Academic Press.

Ehrhardt, A. A. and Meyer-Bahlburg, H. F. L. (1981) Effects of prenatal sex hormones on gender-related behavior. *Science*, 211:1312–1318.

Eisenstadt, J. M. (1978) Parental loss and genius. *American Psychologist*, 33:211–223.

Eisenstadt, S. N. (1956) *From Generation to Generation: Age Groups and Social Structure*. New York: Free Press.

Elashoff, J. D. and Snow, R. E. (1971) *Pygmalion Reconsidered*. Worthington, Ohio: Charles A. Jones.

Elias, S. F. and Elias, J. W. (1976) Curiosity and openmindedness in open and traditional classrooms. *Psychology in the Schools,* 13:226–232.

Elkind, D. (1975) Piaget. *Human Behavior,* 4 (August):25–31.

Elkind, D. (1976) *Child Development and Education.* New York: Oxford University Press.

Elkonin, D. B. (1973) U.S.S.R. In Downing, J., ed. *Comparative Reading.* New York: Macmillan.

Ellis, H. C. (1972) *Fundamentals of Human Learning and Cognition.* Dubuque, Iowa: William C. Brown.

Ellis, H. C. and Hunt, R. R. (1977) Memory: The processing of information. In Marx, M. H. and Bunch, M. E., eds. *Fundamentals and Applications of Learning.* New York: Macmillan.

Ellis, M. J., Witt, P. A., Reynolds, R., and Sprague, R. L. (1974) Methylphenidate and the activity of hyperactives in the informal setting. *Child Development,* 45:217–220.

Emmer, E. T. and Evertson, C. M. (1981) Synthesis of research on classroom management. *Educational Leadership,* 38:342–347.

Emmer, E. T., Evertson, C. M., and Anderson, L. M. (1980) Effective classroom management at the beginning of the school year. *The Elementary School Journal,* 80:219–231.

Engle, P. L. (1975) Language medium in early school years for minority language groups. *Review of Educational Research,* 45:283–325.

Epstein, Y. M., Krupat, E., and Obudho, C. (1976) Clean is beautiful: Identification and preference as a function of race and cleanliness. *Journal of Social Issues,* 32:109–118.

Erikson, M. R. and Cromack, T. (1972) Evaluating a tutoring program. *Journal of Experimental Education,* 41:27–31.

Erikson, E. H. (1968) *Identity: Youth and Crisis.* New York: Norton.

Ervin-Tripp, S. and Mitchell-Kernan, C. (1977) *Child Discourse.* New York: Academic Press.

Estes, W. K. (1976) Introduction to Volume 4. In Estes, W. K., ed. *Handbook of Learning and Cognitive Processes.* Vol. 4. Hillsdale, N.J.: Lawrence Erlbaum.

Etaugh, C. (1980) Effects of nonmaternal care on children. *American Psychologist,* 35:309–319.

Etzioni, A. (1977) Can schools teach kids values? *Today's Education,* 66 (September–October):29 + .

Evertson, C. M., Anderson, C. W., Anderson, L. M., and Brophy, J. E. (1980) Relationships between classroom behaviors and student outcomes in junior high mathematics and English classes. *American Educational Research Journal,* 17:43–60.

Faerstein, L. M. (1981) Stress and coping in families of learning disabled children: A literature review. *Journal of Learning Disabilities,* 14:420–423.

Falk, W. W., Falkowski, C., and Lyson, T. A. (1981) "Some plan to become teachers": Further elaboration and specification. *Sociology of Education,* 54:64–69.

Fanelli, G. C. (1977) Locus of control. In Ball, S., ed. *Motivation in Education.* New York: Academic Press.

Farnsworth, C. H. (1976) Taxes for Dutch highest in West. *New York Times,* June 6, 1976, 8.

Feather, N. T. and Raphelson, A. C. (1974) Fear of success in Australian and American student groups: Motive or sex-role stereotype. *Journal of Personality,* 42:190–201.

Fein, M. (1976) Motivation for work. In Dubin, R., ed. *Handbook of Work, Organization, and Society.* Chicago: Rand McNally.

Feitler, F. C. and Tokar, E. (1982) Getting a handle on teacher stress: How bad is the problem? *Educational Leadership,* 39:456–458.

Feldman, D. (1979) Toward a nonelitist conception of giftedness. *Phi Delta Kappan,* 60:660–663.

Feldman, R. S. and Prohaska, T. (1979) The student as pygmalion: Effect of student expectation on the teacher. *Journal of Educational Psychology,* 71:485–493.

Felker, D. B. and Dapra, R. A. (1975) Effects of question type and question placement on problem-solving ability from prose material. *Journal of Educational Psychology,* 67:380–384.

Ferguson, C. A. (1977) Baby talk as a simplified register. In Snow, C. E. and Ferguson, C. A., eds. *Talking to Children: Language Input and Acquisition.* Cambridge: Cambridge University Press.

Fillmore, C. J. (1968) The case for case. In Bach, E. and Harms, R. T., eds. *Universals in Linguistic Theory.* New York: Holt, Rinehart and Winston.

Fincher, J. (1978) The new idea man. *Human Behavior,* 7:28–32.

Finn, J. D. (1972) Expectations and the educational environment. *Review of Educational Research,* 42:387–410.

Fischer, B. B. and Fischer, L. (1979) Styles in teaching and learning. *Educational Leadership,* 36:245–254.

Fisher, C., Filley, N., Marliave, R., Cahen, L., Dishaw, M., Moore, J., and Berliner, D. (1978) *Teaching Behaviors, Academic Learning time and Student Achievement: Final Report of Phase III-B, Beginning Teacher Evaluation Study.* San Francisco: Far West Laboratory.

Fisher, J. L. and Harris, M. B. (1973) Effect of notetaking and review on recall. *Journal of Educational Psychology,* 65:321–325.

Fishman, J. A. (1975) Bilingual education and the future of language teaching and language learning. *ADFL Bulletin of the Association of Departments of Foreign Languages,* 6:5–8.

Fiske, E. B. (1975) What difference does class size make? *New York Times* (September 10):32.

Fiske, E. B. (1978) Small classes do not always lead to better education, a study finds. *New York Times* (July 30):1, 16.

Fitts, P. M. (1965) Factors in complex skill training. In Glaser, R. *Training Research and Education.* New York: Wiley.

Fitts, P. M. and Posner, M. I. (1967) *Human Performance.* Belmont, Calif.: Wadsworth.

Fitzsimmons, S. J., Cheever, J., Leonard, E., and Macunovich, D. (1969) School failures: Now and tomorrow. *Developmental Psychology,* 1:134–146.

Flanagan, J. C. (1973) Education: How and for what. *American Psychologist,* 28:551–556.

Flanders, N. A. (1963) Teacher influence in the classroom. Bellack, A. A., ed. *Theory and Research on Teaching.* New York: Teachers College.

Flavell, J. H. (1963) *The Developmental Psychology of Jean Piaget.* Princeton, N.J.: Van Nostrand.

Flavell, J. H. (1977) *Cognitive Development*. Englewood Cliffs, N.J.: Prentice-Hall.

Flavell, J. H. (1978) Developmental stage: Explanans or explanandum? *Behavioral and Brain Sciences*, 1:187.

Flavell, J. H. (1982) On cognitive development. *Child Development*, 53:1–10.

Flavell, J. H. and Wellman, H. M. (1977) Metamemory. In Kail, R. and Hagen, J., eds. *Perspectives on the Development of Memory and Cognition*. Hillsdale, N.J.: Lawrence Erlbaum.

Flesch, R. (1955) *Why Johnny Can't Read*. New York: Harper & Row.

Fletcher, J. D. and Atkinson, R. C. (1972) Evaluation of the Stanford CAI program in initial reading. *Journal of Educational Psychology*, 63:597–602.

Flexser, A. J. and Tulving, E. (1978) Retrieval independence in recognition and recall. *Psychological Review*, 85:153–171.

Flynn, J. R., Gacka, R. C., and Sundean, D. A. (1978) Are classroom teachers prepared for mainstreaming? *Phi Delta Kappan*, 59:562.

Ford Foundation (1972) *Drug Abuse Survey Project*. New York: Praeger.

Form, W. H. (1975) The social construction of anomie: A four-nation study of industrial workers. *American Journal of Sociology*, 80:1165–1191.

Forman, S. G. and McKinney, J. D. (1978) Creativity and achievement of second graders in open and traditional classrooms. *Journal of Educational Psychology*, 70:101–107.

Forness, S. R. (1976) Behavioristic orientation to categorical labels. *Journal of School Psychology*, 14:90–96.

Forness, S. R. (1981) Concepts of learning and behavior disorders: Implications for research and practice. *Exceptional Children*, 48:56–64.

Forness, S. R., Hall, R. J., and Guthrie, D. (1977) Eventual school placement of kindergartners observed as high-risk in the classroom. *Psychology in the Schools*, 14:315–317.

Forsyth, D. R. and McMillan, J. H. (1981) Attributions, affects, and expectations. *Journal of Educational Psychology*, 73:393–403.

Foster, G. G., Schmidt, C. R., and Sabatino, D. (1976) Teacher expectancies and the label "learning disabilities." *Journal of Learning Disabilities*, 9:111–114.

Fox, L. H. (1981) Identification of the academically gifted. *American Psychologist*, 36:1103–1111.

Francis, E. W. (1975) Grade level and task difficulty in learning by discovery and verbal reception methods. *Journal of Educational Psychology*, 67:146–150.

Franklin, B. (1969) Operant reinforcement of prayer. *Journal of Applied Behavior Analysis*, 2:247. Submitted by B. F. Skinner.

Franks, D. R. and Marolla, J. (1976) Efficacious action and social approval as interacting dimensions of self-esteem: A tentative formulation through construct validation. *Sociometry*, 39:324–341.

Frase, L. T. (1967) Learning from prose material: Length of passage, knowledge of results and position of questions. *Journal of Educational Psychology*, 58:266–272.

Frase, L. T. (1968) Effect of question location, pacing and mode upon retention of prose material. *Journal of Educational Psychology*, 59:244–249.

Freeman, J., Butcher, H. J., and Christie, T. (1971) *Creativity: A Selective Review of Research*. 2nd ed. London: Society for Research into Higher Education.

French, E. G. and Lesser, G. S. (1964) Some characteristics of achievement motive in women. *Journal of Abnormal and Social Psychology*, 68:119–128.

French, J. R. P. and Raven, B. H. (1959) The bases of social power. In Cartwright, D., ed. *Studies in Social Power*. Ann Arbor: Univ. of Michigan Press.

Freud, A. (1936) *The Ego and the Mechanisms of Defense*. New York: International Universities Press.

Freud, A. (1958) Adolescence. *Psychoanalytic Study of the Child*, 16:225–278.

Friedlander, B. Z. (1975) Some remarks on "open education." *American Educational Research Journal*, 12:465–468.

Fries, C. C. (1962) *Linguistics and Reading*. New York: Holt, Rinehart and Winston.

Fromkin, V. and Rodman, R. (1974) *An Introduction to Language*. New York: Holt, Rinehart and Winston.

Fromm, E. (1955) *The Sane Society*. New York: Holt, Rinehart and Winston.

Fuqua, R. W., Bartsch, T. W., and Phye, G. D. (1975) An investigation of the relationship between cognitive tempo and creativity in preschool-age children. *Child Development*, 46:779–782.

Furst, E. J. (1981) Bloom's taxonomy of educational objectives for the cognitive domain: Philosophical and educational issues. *Review of Educational Research*, 51:441–453.

Furth, H. G. (1977) Comments on the problem of equilibration. In Apple, M. H. and Goldberg, L. S., eds. *Topics in Cognitive Development*. Vol. 1. New York: Plenum Press.

Fyans, L. J., Jr. and Maehr, M. L. (1979) Attributional style, task selection, and achievement. *Journal of Educational Psychology*, 71:499–507.

Gaede, O. F. (1978) Reality shock: A problem among first-year teachers. *The Clearinghouse*, 51:405–409.

Gage, N. L. (1972) *Teacher Effectiveness and Teacher Education*. Palo Alto, Calif.: Pacific Books.

Gage, N. L. (1976) A factorially designed experiment on teacher structuring, soliciting, and reacting. *Journal of Teacher Education*, 27:35–38.

Gage, N. L. (1978) *The Scientific Basis of the Art of Teaching*. New York: Teacher's College, Columbia University.

Gage, N. L. (1978) The yield of research on teaching. *Phi Delta Kappan*, 60:229–235.

Gagné, E. D. and Middlebrooks, M. S. (197) Encouraging generosity: A perspective from social learning theory and research. *The Elementary School Journal*, 77:281–291.

Gagné, R. M. (1962) The acquisition of knowledge. *Psychological Review*, 69:355–365.

Gagné, R. M. (1964) Problem solving. In Melton, A. W., ed. *Categories of Human Learning*. New York: Academic Press.

Gagné, R. M. (1968) Contributions of learning to human development. *Psychological Review*, 75:177–191.

Gagné, R. M. (1968) Learning hierarchies. *Educational Psychologist*, 6:3–6, 9.

Gagné, R. M. (1977) *The Conditions of Learning*. 3rd ed. New York: Holt, Rinehart and Winston.

Gagné, R. M. (1977) Instructional programs. In Marx, M. H. and Bunch, M. E., eds. *Fundamentals and Applications of Learning.* New York: Macmillan.

Gagné, R. M. and Briggs, L. J. (1974) *Principles of Instructional Design.* New York: Holt, Rinehart and Winston.

Gagné, R. M. and White, R. T. (1978) Memory structures and learning outcomes. *Review of Educational Research,* 48:187–222.

Gall, M. D. (1970) The use of questions in teaching. *Review of Educational Research,* 40:707–720.

Gall, M. D. and Gall, J. P. (1976) The discussion method. In Gage, N. L., ed. *The Psychology of Teaching Methods.* Chicago: The National Society for the Study of Education.

Gall, M. D. and Gillett, M. (1980) The discussion method in classroom teaching. *Theory into Practice,* 19:98–103.

Gallagher, J. J. (1965) *Productive Thinking in Gifted Children.* Cooperative Research Project No. 965. Institute for Research on Exceptional Children, University of Illinois.

Gallagher, J. J. (1966) *Research Summary on Gifted Child Education.* Springfield, Ill.: Office of the Superintendent of Public Education.

Gallagher, J. J. (1970) Three studies of the classroom. In Gallagher, J. J., Nuthall, G. A., and Rosenshine, B., eds. *Classroom Observation.* Chicago: Rand McNally.

Gallagher, J. J. (1976) The gifted child in elementary school. In Dennis, W. and Dennis, M. W., eds. *The Intellectually Gifted: An Overview.* New York: Grune & Stratton.

Gallagher, J. J. (1982) A plan for catalytic support for gifted education in the 1980s. *The Elementary School Journal,* 82:180–184.

Galloway, C. M. (1977) Nonverbal: Authentic or artificial. *Theory into Practice,* 16:129–133.

Gallup, G. (1978a) Gallup youth survey: Premarital sex ok with most teens. *Columbus Dispatch* (October 11):A–4.

Gallup, G. (1978b) Birth control devices favored by teen-agers. *Columbus Dispatch* (September 27):7A.

Gallup, G. (1978c) Most teens say sex education classes helpful. *Columbus Dispatch* (October 4):A–8.

Gallup, G. (1980a) Gallup youth survey. *Columbus Dispatch* (October 29):A–12.

Gallup, G. (1980b) Gallup youth survey. *Columbus Dispatch* (May 7):A–9.

Gallup, G. (1980c) Gallup youth survey. *Columbus Dispatch* (December 31):A–5.

Gallup, G. (1980d) Teachers receive teens' high marks. *Columbus Dispatch* (May 14):A–12.

Gallup, G. (1981) The 13th annual Gallup poll of the public's attitudes toward the public schools. *Phi Delta Kappan,* 63:33–47.

Garcia, J. (1981) The logic and limits of mental aptitude testing. *American Psychologist,* 36:1172–1180.

Gardner, H. (1976) The grasp of consciousness. *The New York Times Book Review,* August, 1, 1976, 1–2.

Gardner, L. (1972) Deprivation dwarfism. *Scientific American,* 227:76–82.

Garfinkel, H. (1964) Studies of the routine grounds of everyday activities. *Social Problems,* 11:225–250.

Garfinkel, H. (1967) *Studies in Ethnomethodology.* Englewood Cliffs, N.J.: Prentice-Hall.

Garner, R. and Reis, R. (1981) Monitoring and resolving comprehension obstacles: An investigation of spontaneous text lookbacks among upper-grade good and poor comprehenders. *Reading Research Quarterly,* 16:569–582.

Gartner, A., Kohler, M., and Riessman, F. (1971) *Children Teach Children.* New York: Harper & Row.

Gast, D. L. and Nelson, C. M. (1977) Legal and ethical considerations for the use of timeout in special education settings. *The Journal of Special Education,* 11:457–467.

Gaudry, E. and Bradshaw, G. D. (1970) The differential effects of anxiety on performance in progressive and terminal school examinations. *Australian Journal of Psychology,* 22:1–4.

Gecas, V. (1971) Parental behavior and dimensions of adolescent self-evaluation. *Sociometry,* 35:332–345.

Gecas, V. (1972) Parental behavior and contextual variations in adolescent self-esteem. *Sociometry,* 35:466–482.

Gelb, I. J. (1952) *A Study of Writing.* Chicago: University of Chicago Press.

Gelman, D. (1981) Just how the sexes differ. *Newsweek* (May) 18:72–83.

Gelman, R. (1978) Cognitive development. In Rosenzweig, M. R. and Porter, L. W., eds. *Annual Review of Psychology.* Palo Alto, Calif.: Annual Reviews.

Gentry, W. D. (1974) Aggression in fairy tales: A study of three cultures. Paper presented to the meetings of the Southeastern Psychological Association, April 1974.

Gerall, A. A. (1973) Influence of perinatal androgen on reproductive capacity. In Zubin, J. and Money, J., eds. *Contemporary Sexual Behavior: Critical Issues in the 1970s.* Baltimore: Johns Hopkins University Press.

Gerard, H. B. and Miller, N. (1975) *School Desegregation.* New York: Plenum Press.

Gergen, K. J. (1965) Interaction goals and personalistic feedback as factors affecting the presentation of self. *Journal of Personality and Social Psychology,* 1:413–424.

Gergen, K. J. (1971) *The Concept of Self.* New York: Holt, Rinehart and Winston.

Gergen, K. J. (1972) Multiple identity. *Psychology Today,* 5 (May):31 + .

Gettinger, M. and White, M. A. (1980) Evaluating curriculum fit with class ability. *Journal of Educational Psychology,* 72:338–344.

Getzels, J. W. and Dillon, J. T. (1973) The nature of giftedness and the education of the gifted. In Travers, R. M. W., ed. *Second Handbook of Research on Teaching.* Chicago: Rand McNally.

Getzels, J. W. and Jackson, P. W. (1962) *Creativity and Intelligence.* New York: Wiley.

Gewirtz, J. L. and Boyd, E. F. (1976) Mother-infant interaction and its study. In Reese, H. W., ed. *Advances in Child Development and Behavior.* Vol. 11. New York: Academic Press.

Gibson, E. J. and Levin, H. (1975) *The Psychology of Reading.* Cambridge, Mass.: MIT Press.

Gickling, E. E. and Theobold, J. T. (1975) Mainstreaming: Affect or effect. *Journal of Special Education,* 9:317–328.

Gideonse, H. D. (1969) Behavioral objectives: Continuing the dialogue. *Science Teacher,* 36 (January):51–54.

Gilligan, C. F. (1963) Responses to temptation: An analysis of motives. Unpublished doctoral dissertation, Harvard University.

Ginzberg, E. (1980) Youth unemployment. *Scientific American,* 242 (May):43–49.

Glanzer, M. and Koppenaal, L. (1977) The effect of encoding tasks on free recall: Stages and levels. *Journal of Verbal Learning and Verbal Behavior*, 16:21–28.

Glaser, R. (1966) Variables in discovery learning. In Shulman, L. S. and Keislar, E. R., eds. *Learning by Discovery: A Critical Appraisal*. Chicago: Rand McNally.

Glaser, R. (1973) Educational psychology and education. *American Psychologist*, 28:557–566.

Glaser, R. (1976) Components of a psychology of instruction: Toward a science of design. *Review of Educational Research*, 46:1–24.

Glass, G. V. and Smith, M. L. (1978). *Meta-analysis of Research on the Relationship of Class Size and Achievement*. San Francisco: Far West Laboratory.

Glazer, N. and Moynihan, D. P. (1963) *Beyond the Melting Pot*. Cambridge: MIT Press and Harvard University Press.

Glick, H. M. and Schubert, M. (1981) Mainstreaming: An unmandated challenge. *Educational Leadership*, 38:326–329.

Glueck, S. and Glueck, E. (1950) *Unravelling Juvenile Delinquency*. Boston: Harvard University Press.

Glueck, S. and Glueck, E. (1957) Working mothers and delinquency. *Mental Hygiene*, 41:327–352.

Godenne, G. D. (1974) Sex and today's youth. *Adolescence*, 9:67–72.

Goetz, T. E. and Dweck, C. S. (1980). Learned helplessness in social situations. *Journal of Personality and Social Psychology*, 39:246–255.

Goff, R. (1949) *Problems and Emotional Difficulties of Negro Children*. New York: Columbia University Press.

Goffman, E. (1959) *The Presentation of Self in Everyday Life*. Garden City, N.Y.: Doubleday.

Gold, D. and Andres, D. (1978a) Comparisons of adolescent children with employed and nonemployed mothers. *Merrill-Palmer Quarterly*, 24:243–254.

Gold, D. and Andres, D. (1978b) Developmental comparisons between ten-year-old children with employed and nonemployed mothers. *Child Development*, 49:75–84.

Goldberg, F. (1974) Effects of imagery on learning incidental material in the classroom. *Journal of Educational Psychology*, 66:233–237.

Goldfarb, W. (1945) Psychological privation in infancy and subsequent adjustment. *American Journal of Orthopsychiatry*, 15:247–255.

Goldfarb, W. (1947) Variations in adolescent adjustment of institutionally reared children. *American Journal of Orthopsychiatry*, 17:449–457.

Goldfarb, W. (1949) Rorschach test differences between family-reared, institution-reared, and schizophrenic children. *American Journal of Orthopsychiatry*, 19:624–633.

Goldman, A. L. (1978) Should school teachers get professional state license? *New York Times* (February 20):20.

Goldsmid, C. A. and Wilson, E. K. (1980) *Passing on Sociology: The Teaching of a Discipline*. Belmont, Calif.: Wadsworth.

Goleman, D. (1980) 1,528 little geniuses and how they grew. *Psychology Today*, 13:28–43.

Good, T. L. (1979) Teacher effectiveness in the elementary school. *Journal of Teacher Education*, 30:52–63.

Good, T. L. (1981) Teacher expectations and student perceptions: A decade of research. *Educational Leadership*, 38:415–422.

Good, T. L., Biddle, B. J., and Brophy, J. E. (1975) *Teachers Make a Difference*. New York: Holt, Rinehart and Winston.

Good, T. L. and Brophy, J. E. (1973) *Looking in Classrooms*. New York: Harper & Row.

Good, T. L. and Brophy, J. E. (1974) Changing teacher and student behavior: An empirical investigation. *Journal of Educational Psychology*, 66:390–405.

Good, T. L., Cooper, H. M., and Blakey, S. L. (1980) Classroom interaction as a function of teacher expectations, student sex, and time of year. *Journal of Educational Psychology*, 72:378–385.

Good, T. L. and Grouws, D. A. (1979) Teaching and mathematics learning. *Educational Leadership*, 37:39–45.

Good, T. L., Sikes, J. N., and Brophy, J. E. (1973) Effects of teacher sex and student sex on classroom interaction. *Journal of Educational psychology*, 65:74–87.

Goodman, M. E. (1952) *Race Awareness in Young Children*. Reading, Mass.: Addison-Wesley.

Goodwin, W. L. and Klausmeier, H. J. (1975) *Facilitating Student Learning*. New York: Harper & Row.

Gordon, W. J. J. (1961) *Synectics*. New York: Harper & Row.

Gorfein, D. S. and Viviani, J. M. (1978) The nature of transfer in free recall. *Journal of Experimental Psychology: Human Learning and Memory*, 4:222–238.

Gorman, A. H. (1974) *Teachers and Learners*. 2nd ed. Boston: Allyn and Bacon.

Gottlieb, J., Semmel, M. I., and Veldman, D. J. (1978) Correlates of social status among mainstreamed mentally retarded children. *Journal of Educational Psychology*, 70:396–405.

Grabe, M. and Latta, R. M. (1981) Cumulative achievement in a mastery instructional system: The impact of differences in resultant achievement motivation and persistence. *American Educational Research Journal*, 18:7–13.

Granger, R. C., Mathews, M., Quay, L. C., and Verner, R. (1977) *Journal of Educational Psychology*, 69:793–796.

Green, B. F. (1981) A primer of testing. *American Psychologist*, 36:1001–1011.

Greenberg, J. (1981) Pregnant women warned on alcohol. *New York Times* (July 18):1, 7.

Greene, D. and Lepper, M. R. (1974) How to turn play into work. *Psychology Today*, 8 (September 1974):49–54.

Greene, J. C. (1980) Individual and teacher/class effects in aptitude treatment studies. *American Educational Research Journal*, 17:291–302.

Greenfield, P. M. and Smith, J. H. (1976) *The structure of communication in early language development*. New York: Academic Press.

Greenwald, A. G. (1980) The totalitarian ego. *American Psychologist*, 35:603–618.

Grice, H. P. (1973) *Logic and Conversation*. In Cole, P. and Morgan, J., eds.

Gronlund, N. E. (1959) *Sociometry in the Classroom*. New York: Harper & Row.

Gronlund, N. E. (1976) *Measurement and Evaluation in Teaching*. 3rd ed. New York: Macmillan.

Groobman, D. E., Forward, J. R., and Peterson, C. (1976) Attitudes, self-esteem, and learning in formal and informal schools. *Journal of Educational Psychology,* 68:32–35.

Gross, N. and Trask, A. E. (1976) *The Sex Factor and the Management of Schools.* New York: Wiley.

Grotevant, H. D., Scarr, S., and Weinberg, R. A. (1977) Patterns of interest similarity in adoptive and biological families. *Journal of Personality and Social Psychology,* 35:667–676.

Grotevant, H. D., Scarr, S., and Weinberg, R. A. (1978) Are career interests inheritable? *Psychology Today,* 11:88–90.

Gruber, H. (1981) Breakaway minds. *Psychology Today,* 15 (July):64–73.

Grupe, A. J. (1961) Adjustment and acceptance of mentally superior children in regular and special fifth-grade classes in a public school system. Doctoral dissertation, University of Illinois.

Guilford, J. P. (1959) Three faces of intellect. *American Psychologist,* 14:469–479.

Guilford, J. P. (1967) *The Nature of Human Intelligence.* New York: McGraw-Hill.

Guilford, J. P. (1979) *Cognitive Psychology with a Frame of Reference.* San Diego, Calif.: EDITS.

Guinagh, B. (1980) The social integration of handicapped children. *Phi Delta Kappan,* 62:27–30.

Gump, P. V. (1967) The classroom behavior setting: Its nature and relation to student behavior. *Final Report, Project No. 2453.* Lawrence, Kan.: University of Kansas.

Gumperz, J. J. (1981) Conversational inference and classroom learning. In Green, J. L. and Wallat, C., eds. *Ethnography and Language in Educational Settings.* Norwood, N.J.: Ablex.

Gurth, H. P. (1974) The monkey on the bicycle: Behavioral objectives and the teaching of English. In Gall, M. D. and Ward, B. A., eds. *Critical Issues in Educational Psychology.* Boston: Little, Brown.

Guskey, T. R. (1980) Mastery learning: Applying the theory. *Theory into Practice,* 19:104–111.

Guthrie, J. T. (1976) *Aspects of Reading Acquisition.* Baltimore: Johns Hopkins University Press.

Guttman, N. and Kalish, H. I. (1956) Discriminability and stimulus generalization. *Journal of Experimental Psychology,* 51:79–88.

Guttmann, J., Levin, J. R., and Pressley, M. (1977) Pictures, partial pictures, and young children's oral prose learning. *Journal of Educational Psychology,* 69:473–480.

Haaf, R. A. and Smith, J. A. (1976) Developmental differences in reinforcer preference value and in learning-set performance under inconsistent reward. *Child Development,* 47:375–379.

Haddon, F. A. and Lytton, H. (1971) Primary education and divergent thinking abilities—Four years on. *British Journal of Educational Psychology,* 41:136–147.

Haefele, D. L. (1978) The Teacher Perceiver Interview: How valid? *Phi Delta Kappan,* 59:683–684.

Hafner, L. E. (1977) *Developmental Reading in Middle and Secondary Schools.* New York: Macmillan.

Hall, C. S. and Lindzey, G. (1970) *Theories of Personality.* 2nd ed. New York: John Wiley.

Hall, G. S. (1904) *Adolescence.* Vols. I and II. New York: Appleton-Century-Crofts.

Hall, J. A., Rosenthal, R., Archer, D., DiMatteo, M. R., and Rogers, P. L. (1977) Nonverbal skills in the classroom. *Theory into Practice,* 16:162–166.

Hall, J. F. (1976) *Classical Conditioning and Instrumental Learning: A Contemporary Approach.* Philadelphia: Lippincott.

Hall, M. A., Ribovich, J. K., and Ramig, C. J. (1979) *Reading and the Elementary School Child.* 2nd ed. New York: D. Van Nostrand.

Hall, V. C. and Turner, R. R. (1974) The validity of the "different" language explanation for poor scholastic performance of black students. *Review of Educational Research,* 44:69–81.

Halpin, A. W. and Croft, D. B. (1963) *The Organizational Climate of Schools.* Chicago: Midwest Administration Center, University of Chicago.

Hamachek, D. E. (1977) Humanistic psychology: Theoretical-philosophical framework and implications for teaching. In Treffinger, D. J., Davis, J. K., and Ripple, R. E., eds. *Handbook on Teaching Educational Psychology.* New York: Academic Press.

Hambleton, R. K. (1974) Testing and decision-making procedures for selected individualized instructional programs. *Review of Educational Research,* 44:371–400.

Hammond, J. M. (1979) Children of divorce: A study of self-concept, academic achievement, and attitudes. *The Elementary School Journal,* 80:55–62.

Hansen, R. A. (1977) Anxiety. In Ball, S., ed. *Motivation in Education.* New York: Academic Press.

Harber, J. R. and Bryen, D. N. (1976) Black English and the task of reading. *Review of Educational Research,* 46:387–405.

Harding, C. (1983) Setting the stage for language acquisition: Communicative development in the first year. In Golinkoff, R. M., ed. *The Transition from Prelinguistic to Linguistic Communication: Issues and Implications.* Hillsdale, N.J.: Lawrence Erlbaum.

Hare, A. P. (1976) *Handbook of Small Group Research.* 2nd ed. New York: Free Press.

Hare, N. (1966) The vanishing woman principal. *National Principal,* 46:12–13.

Harlow, H. F. (1949) The formation of learning sets. *Psychological Review,* 56:51–65.

Harmer, E. W. (1979) Veteran teachers: Old myths and new realities. *Phi Delta Kappan,* 60:536–538.

Harris, M. B. (1970) Reciprocity and generosity: Some determinants of sharing in children. *Child Development,* 41:313–328.

Harris, V. W. and Sherman, J. A. (1973) Use and analysis of the "good behavior game" to reduce disruptive classroom behavior. *Journal of Applied Behavior Analysis,* 6:405–417.

Harrison, A., Jr. and Westerman, J. E. (1974) Ideal child and successful student: Are they the same? *Phi Delta Kappan,* 55:635–636.

Harrison, G. V. (1976) Structured tutoring: Antidote for low achievement. In Allen, V. L., ed. *Children as Teachers.* New York: Academic Press.

Harrow, A. J. (1972) *A taxonomy of the Psychomotor Domain.* New York: David McKay.

Hart, J. T., Guthrie, J. T., and Winfield, L. (1980) Black English phonology and learning to read. *Journal of Educational Psychology*, 72:636–646.

Hartley, J. and Davies, I. K. (1976) Preinstructional strategies: The role of pretests, behavioral objectives, overviews and advance organizers. *Review of Educational Research*, 46:239–265.

Hartshorne, H. and May, M. A. (1928) *Studies in the Nature of Character. Vol. I: Studies in Deceit.* New York: Macmillan.

Hartshorne, H., May, M. A., and Maller, J. B. (1929) *Studies in the Nature of Character. Vol. II: Studies in Self-Control.* New York: Macmillan.

Hartshorne, H., May, M. A., and Shuttleworth, F. K. (1930) *Studies in the Nature of Character. Vol. III: Studies in the Organization of Character.* New York: Macmillan.

Harvey, K. and Horton, L. (1977) Bloom's *Human Characteristics and School Learning. Phi Delta Kappan*, 59:189–193.

Hauserman, N., Walen, S. R., and Behling, M. (1973) Reinforced racial integration in the first grade: A study in generalization. *Journal of Applied Behavior Analysis*, 6:193–200.

Havighurst, R. J. (1976) *Human Characteristics and School Learning:* Essay Review. *The Elementary School Journal*, 77:101–109.

Hayes, L. A. (1976) The use of group contingencies for behavioral control: A review. *Psychological Bulletin*, 83:628–648.

Hearn, J. C. and Moos, R. H. (1978) Subject matter and classroom climate: A test of Holland's environmental propositions. *American Educational Research Journal*, 15:111–124.

Hechinger, F. M. (1981a) Nature versus nurture: Israeli urges intervention. *New York Times* (March 24):15, 17.

Hechinger, F. M. (1981b) U.S. ruling on bilingualism fuels controversy. *New York Times* (January 20):21.

Heckhausen, H. (1967) *The Anatomy of Achievement Motivation.* New York: Academic Press.

Heinstein, M. I. (1963) Behavioral correlates of breast-bottle regimes under varying parent-child relationships. *Monographs of the Society for Research in Child Development*, 28 (4).

Heiss, J. and Owens, S. (1972) Self-evaluations of blacks and whites. *American Journal of Sociology*, 78:360–370.

Helfer, R. E. and Kempe, C. H. (1977) *The Battered Child.* Chicago: University of Chicago Press.

Helton, G. B. and Oakland, T. D. (1977) Teachers' attitudinal responses to differing characteristics of elementary school students. *Journal of Educational Psychology*, 69:261–265.

Hemphill, J. K., Griffiths, D. E., and Frederikson, N. (1962) *Administrative Performance and Personality.* New York: Bureau of Publications, Teachers College, Columbia University.

Herson, P. F. (1974) Biasing effects of diagnostic labels and sex of pupil on teachers' views of pupils' mental health. *Journal of Educational Psychology*, 66:117–122.

Hess, R. D. and Camara, K. A. (1979) Post-divorce family relationships as mediating factors in the consequences of divorce on children. *Journal of Social Issues*, 35:79–96.

Hess, R. D. and Tenezakis, M. D. (1971) *Selected Findings from "The Computer as a Socializing Agent: Some Socioaffective Outcomes of CAI."* Stanford: Center for Research and Development in Teaching, Stanford University.

Hetherington, E. M., Cox, M., and Cox, R. (1976) Divorced fathers. *Family Coordinator*, 25:417–427.

Hetherington, E. M., Cox, M., and Cox, R. (1977) Divorced fathers. *Psychology Today*, 10 (April):42–46.

Hetherington, E. M. and Feldman, S. E. (1964) College cheating as a function of subject and situational variables. *Journal of Educational Psychology*, 55:212–218.

Hewett, F. M. and Blake, P. R. (1973) Teaching the emotionally disturbed. In Travers, R. M. W., ed. *Second Handbook of Research on Teaching.* Chicago: Rand McNally.

Hicks, F. R. (1934) *The Mental Health of Teachers. Contributions to Education*, 123. Nashville: George Peabody College Press.

Higbee, K. L. (1977) *Your Memory.* Englewood Cliffs, N.J.: Prentice-Hall.

Higbee, K. L. (1979) Recent research on visual mnemonics: Historical roots and educational fruits. *Review of Educational Research*, 49:611–629.

Highet, G. (1976) *The Immortal Profession.* New York: Weybright & Talley.

Hilgard, E. R. (1971) The psychological heuristics of learning. In Tickton, S. G., ed. *To Improve Learning: An Evaluation.* New York: Bowker.

Hilgard, E. R., Atkinson, R. C., and Atkinson, R. L. (1975) *Introduction to Psychology.* 6th ed. New York: Harcourt Brace Jovanovich.

Hilgard, E. R. and Bower, G. H. (1975) *Theories of Learning.* 4th ed. Englewood Cliffs, N.J.: Prentice-Hall.

Hill, J. P. and Kochendorfer, R. A. (1969) Knowledge of peer success and risk of detection as determinants of cheating. *Developmental Psychology*, 1:231–238.

Hill, K. T. (1972) Anxiety in the evaluative context. In Hartup, W. W., ed. *Young Child.* Vol. 2. Washington, D.C.: National Association for the Education of Young Children.

Hill, K. T. and Sarason, S. B. (1966) The relation of test anxiety and defensiveness to test and school performance over the elementary school years: A further longitudinal study. *Monographs of the Society for Research in Child Development*, 31 (Serial No. 104).

Hiroto, D. S. (1974) Locus of control and learned helplessness. *Journal of Experimental Psychology*, 102:187–193.

Hobbs, N. (1975) *The Futures of Children.* San Francisco: Jossey-Bass.

Hoben, M. (1980) Toward integration in the mainstream. *Exceptional Children*, 47:100–105.

Hobson, J. R. (1948) Mental age as a workable criterion for school admission. *The Elementary School Journal*, 48:312–321.

Hobson, J. R. (1956) Scholastic standing and activity participation of underage high school pupils originally admitted to kindergarten on the basis of physical and psychological examination. Presidential Address, American Psychological Association, Division 16 (September).

Hoffman, L. W. (1974) Effects of maternal employment on the child—A review of the research. *Developmental Psychology*, 10:204–228.

Hoffman, L. W. (1974) Fear of success in males and females: 1965–1972. *Journal of Consulting and Clinical Psychology*, 42:353–358.

Hoffman, L. W. and Nye F. I. (1974) *Working Mothers*. San Francisco: Jossey-Bass.

Holcomb, J. D. (1972) The many facets of self-instruction: Some pros and cons. *University College Quarterly*, 18:10–23.

Holden, C. (1977) Carl Rogers: Getting people to be themselves. *Science*, 198:31–35.

Holden, M. H. and MacGinitie, W. H. (1972) Children's conceptions of word boundaries in speech and print. *Journal of Educational Psychology*, 63:551–557.

Holinger, P. C. (1980) Violent deaths as a leading cause of mortality: An epidemiologic study of suicide, homicide, and accidents. *American Journal of Psychiatry*, 137:472–476.

Holland, J. L. and Nichols, R. C. (1964) Prediction of academic and extracurricular achievement in college. *Journal of Educational Psychology*, 55:55–65.

Holland, J. L. and Richards, J. M., Jr. (1965) Academic and nonacademic accomplishment: Correlated or uncorrelated. *Journal of Educational Psychology*, 56:165–174.

Holroyd, K. A. (1976) Cognition and desensitization in the group treatment of test anxiety. *Journal of Consulting and Clinical Psychology*, 44:991–1001.

Holt, J. (1964) *How Children Fail*. New York: Dell.

Homme, L. (1970) *How to Use Contingency Contracting in the Classroom*. Champaign, Ill.: Research Press.

Horan, J. J. (1974) Outcome difficulties in drug education. *Review of Educational Research*, 44:203–211.

Horan, J. J., Girolomo, M. A., Hill, R. L., and Shute, R. E. (1974) The effect of older-peer participant models on deficient academic performance. *Psychology in the Schools*, 11:207–212.

Horner, M. S. (1968) Sex differences in achievement motivation and performance in competitive and noncompetitive situations. Unpublished doctoral dissertation. University of Michigan.

Horner, M. S. (1970) Femininity and successful achievement: A basic inconsistency. In Bardwick, J., ed. *Feminine Personality and Conflict*. Belmont, Calif.: Brooks/Cole.

Horner, M. S. (1972) Toward an understanding of achievement-related conflicts in women. *Journal of Social Issues*, 28:157–175.

Horowitz, I. L. and Liebowitz, M. (1968) Social deviance and political marginality: Toward a definition of the relation between sociology and politics. *Social Problems*, 15:280–296.

Horton, D. L. and Turnage, T. W. (1976) *Human Learning*. Englewood Cliffs, N.J.: Prentice-Hall.

Horwitz, R. A. (1979) Psychological effects of the "open classroom." *Review of Educational Research*, 49:71–86.

Houston, J. P. (1976) *Fundamentals of Learning*. New York: Academic Press.

Howe, M. J. (1970) Using students' notes to examine the role of the individual learner in acquiring meaningful subject matter. *Journal of Educational Research*, 64:61–63.

Howsam, R. B., Corrigan, D. C., Denemark, G. W., and Nash, R. J., (1976) *Educating a Profession*. Report of the Bicentennial Commission on Education for the Profession of Teaching. Washington, D.C.: American Association of Colleges for Teacher Education.

Hoyt, K., Evans, R., Mackin, E., and Mangum, G. (1972) *Career Education: What It Is and How to Do It*. Salt Lake City: Olympus.

Huessy, H. R., Metoyer, M., and Townsend, M. (1974) Eight–ten year follow-up of 84 children treated for behavior disorder in rural Vermont. *Acta Paedopsychiatrica*, 40:230–235.

Huey, E. B. (1908/1968) *The Psychology and Pedagogy of Reading*. Cambridge, Mass.: MIT Press.

Hulse, S. H., Deese, J., and Egeth, H. (1975) *The Psychology of Learning*. New York: McGraw-Hill.

Hulse, S. H. and Dorsky, N. P. (1977) Structural complexity as a determinant of serial pattern learning. *Learning and Motivation*, 8:488–506.

Humphreys, L. G. (1939) The effect of random alternation of reinforcement on the acquisition and extinction of conditioned eyelid reactions. *Journal of Experimental Psychology*, 25:141–158.

Hunt, D. E. (1975) Person-environment interaction: A challenge found wanting before it was tried. *Review of Educational Research*, 45:209–230.

Hunter, M. (1977) A tri-dimensional approach to individualization. *Educational Leadership*, 34:351–355.

Hyde, J. S. and Rosenberg, B. G. (1976) *Half the Human Experience*, Lexington, Mass.: D. C. Heath.

Hyman, R. B. (1978) Creativity in open and traditional classrooms. *The Elementary School Journal*, 78:267–274.

Hyman, R. T. (1973) Individualization: The hidden agenda. *The Elementary School Journal*, 73:413–423.

Hymes, J. J. (1958) *Before the Child Reads*. New York: Harper & Row.

Inbau, F. and Reid, J. (1962) *Criminal Interrogation and Confessions*. Baltimore: Williams & Wilkins.

Inhelder, B. and Piaget, J. (1958) *The Growth of Logical Thinking from Childhood to Adolescence*. New York: Basic Books.

Instructor (1981) Second national teacher poll. *Instructor*, 91:18–20.

Isakson, M. B. and Isakson, R. L. (1978) Modifying impulsivity through training in analysis. *The Elementary School Journal*, 79:99–107.

Israel, J. (1971) *Alienation: From Marx to Modern Sociology*. Boston: Allyn and Bacon.

Jackson, P. W. (1968) *Life in Classrooms*. New York: Holt, Rinehart and Winston.

Jacobson, R. L. (1980) Theories of Piaget, who died this month, inspire growing band of U.S. professors. *The Chronicle of Higher Education* (September 29):5.

Jahoda, M. (1958) *Current Concepts of Positive Mental Health*. New York: Basic Books.

James, W. (1890) *The Principles of Psychology*. Vols. I and II. New York: Holt.

James, W. (1890) *Psychology*. New York: Holt, Rinehart and Winston.

Jamison, D., Suppes, P., and Wells, S. (1974) The effectiveness of alternative instructional media: A survey. *Review of Educational Research*, 44:1–67.

Jansky, J. and de Hirsch, K. (1972) *Preventing Reading Failure.* New York: Harper & Row.

Jantzen, J. M. (1947) Why college students choose to teach. *Phi Delta Kappan*, 28:333–335.

Jantzen, J. M. (1959) An opinionaire on why college students choose to teach. *Journal of Educational Research*, 53:13–17.

Jantzen, J. M. (1981) Why college students choose to teach: A longitudinal study. *Journal of Teacher Education*, 32:45–48.

Jenkins, J. G. and Dallenbach, K. M. (1924) Oblivescence during sleep and waking. *American Journal of Psychology*, 35:605–612.

Jenkins, J. R. and Deno, S. L. (1971) Influence of knowledge and type of objectives on subject-matter learning. *Journal of Educational Psychology*, 62:67–70.

Jensen, A. R. (1969a) How much can we boost IQ and scholastic achievement? *Harvard Educational Review*, 39:1–123.

Jensen, A. R. (1969b) Reducing the heredity-environment uncertainty: A reply. *Harvard Educational Review*, 39:449–483.

Jensen, A. R. (1973a) Race, intelligence and genetics: The differences are real. *Psychology Today*, 7 (December):80–86.

Jensen, A. R. (1973b) *Educability and Group Differences.* New York: Harper & Row.

Jensen, A. R. (1973c) Genetics and Education. New York: Harper & Row.

Jensen, A. R. (1980) *Bias in Mental Testing.* New York: Free Press.

Jensen, M. and Rosenfeld, L. B. (1974) Influence of mode of presentation, ethnicity, and social class on teachers' evaluations of students. *Journal of Educational Psychology*, 66:540–547.

Jessor, S. and Jessor, R. (1975) Transition from virginity to nonvirginity among youth: A social-psychological study over time. *Developmental Psychology*, 11:473–484.

Johnson, B. R. (1976) What administrators look for in teacher interviews. *Phi Delta Kappan*, 58:283–284.

Johnson, D. (1972) An investigation of sex differences in reading in four English-speaking nations. Technical Report No. 209., Research and Development Center for Cognitive Learning, University of Wisconsin.

Johnson, D. W. and Ahlgren, A. (1976) Relationship between student attitudes about cooperation and competition and attitudes toward schooling. *Journal of Educational Psychology*, 68:92–102.

Johnson, D. W. and Johnson, R. T. (1974) Instructional goal structure: Cooperative, competitive, or individualistic. *Review of Educational Research*, 44:213–240.

Johnson, D. W. and Johnson, R. T. (1975) *Learning Together and Alone: Cooperation, Competition, and Individualization.* Englewood Cliffs, N.J.: Prentice-Hall.

Johnson, D. W., Johnson, R. T., Johnson, J., and Anderson, D. (1976) Effects of cooperative versus individualized instruction on student prosocial behavior, attitudes toward learning, and achievement. *Journal of Educational Psychology*. 68:446–452.

Johnson, D. W., Maruyama, G., Johnson, R., Nelson, D., and Skon, L. (1981) Effects of cooperative, competitive, and individualistic goal structures on achievement: A meta-analysis. *Psychological Bulletin*, 89:47–62.

Johnson, G. O. (1962) Special education for the mentally retarded—A paradox. *Exceptional Children*, 29:62–66.

Johnson, J. A. (1981) The etiology of hyperactivity. *Exceptional Children*, 47:348–354.

Johnson, R. E. (1974) Abstractive processes in the remembering of prose. *Journal of Educational Psychology*, 66:772–779.

Johnson, S. W. and Morasky, R. L. (1977) *Learning Disabilities.* Boston: Allyn and Bacon.

Johnston, L., Bachman, J., and O'Malley, P. (1981) *Highlights from Student Drug Use in America*, 1975–1980. Washington, D.C.: National Institute on Drug Abuse.

Joiner, L. M., Miller, S. R., and Silverstein, B. J. (1980) Potential and limits of computers in schools. *Educational Leadership*, 37:498–501.

Jones, M. C. and Bayley, N. (1950) Physical maturing among boys as related to behavior. *Journal of Educational Psychology*, 41:129–148.

Jones, R. L., Gottlieb, J., Guskin, S., and Yoshida, R. K. (1978) Evaluating mainstreaming programs: Models, caveats, considerations and guidelines. *Exceptional Children*, 44:588–601.

Jones, R. T. and Evans, H. L. (1980) Self-reinforcement: A continuum of external cues. *Journal of Educational Psychology*, 72:625–635.

Josephson, M. (1959) *Edison, A Biography.* New York: McGraw-Hill.

Joyce, B. R. (1966) Children's verbalisms and the new curriculums. *National Elementary Principal*, 45 (April):23–25.

Judd, C. H. (1908) The relation of special training to general intelligence. *Educational Review*, 36:28–42.

Justman, J. (1953) Personal and social adjustment of intellectually gifted accelerants and nonaccelerants in junior high schools. *School Review*, 62:468–478.

Justman, J. (1954) Academic achievement of intellectually gifted accelerants and nonaccelerants in junior high school. *School Review*, 63:143–150.

Kagan, J. (1965) Reflection-impulsivity and reading ability in primary grade children. *Child Development*, 36:609–628.

Kagan, J. (1972) A conception of early adolescence. In Kagan, J. and Coles, R., eds. *Twelve to Sixteen: Early Adolescence,* New York: Norton.

Kagan, J., Kearsley, R. B., and Zelazo, P. R. (1978) *Infancy: Its Place in Human Development.* Cambridge: Harvard University Press.

Kagan, J. and Kogan, N. (1970) Individual variation in cognitive processes. In Mussen, P., ed. *Carmichael's Manual of Child Psychology*. 3rd ed. New York: Wiley.

Kagan, J., Pearson, L., and Welch, L. (1966) Conceptual impulsivity and inductive reasoning. *Child Development*, 37:583–594.

Kamii, C. and DeVries, R. (1978) *Physical Knowledge in Preschool Education: Implications of Piaget's Theory.* Englewood Cliffs, N.J.: Prentice-Hall.

Kamin, L. J. (1974) *The Science and Politics of IQ.* Potomac, Md.: Lawrence Erlbaum.

Kandel, D. B. (1974) Inter- and intragenerational influences on adolescent marijuana use. *Journal of Social Issues,* 30:107–135.

Kandel, D. B. and Lesser, G. S. (1972) *Youth in Two Worlds.* San Francisco: Jossey-Bass.

Kane, R. and Marsh, C. J. (1980) Progress toward a general theory of instruction? *Educational Leadership,* 38:253–255.

Kanfer, F. H. (1975) Self-management methods. In Kanfer, F. H. and Goldstein, A. P., eds. *Helping People Change.* New York: Pergamon Press.

Kanfer, F. H. (1976) The many faces of self-control, or behavior modification changes its focus. Paper presented at the Eighth International Banff Conference. Banff, Alberta.

Kaplan, H. R. (1977) Introduction. In Kaplan, H. R., ed. *American Minorities and Economic Opportunity.* Itasca, Ill.: F. E. Peacock.

Kaplan, H. R. and Tausky, C. (1972) Work and the welfare Cadillac: The function of and commitment to work among the hard-core unemployed. *Social Problems,* 19:469–483.

Kaplan, R. (1974) Effects of learning prose with part versus whole presentations of instructional objectives. *Journal of Educational Psychology,* 66:787–792.

Kaplan, R. and Simmons, F. G. (1974) Effects of instructional objectives used as orienting stimuli or as summary/review upon prose learning. *Journal of Educational Psychology,* 66:614–622.

Karmiloff-Smith, A. (1979) Language development after five. In Fletcher, P. and Garman, M., eds. *Language Acquisition: Studies in First Language Development.* New York: Cambridge University Press.

Karnes, M. B., Shwedel, A. M., and Linnemeyer, S. A. (1982) The young gifted/talented child: Programs at the University of Illinois. *The Elementary School Journal,* 82:195–213.

Kass, C. E., Lewis, R. B., Havertape, J. F., Maddux, C. D., Horvath, M. J., and Swift, C. A. (1982) A field test of a procedure for identifying learning disability. *Journal of Learning Disabilities,* 15:173–177.

Katz, P. A. (1973) Perception of racial cues in pre-school children: A new look. *Developmental Psychology,* 8:295–299.

Katz, P. A. (1976) The acquisition of racial attitudes in children. In Katz, P. A., ed. *Towards the Elimination of Racism.* New York: Pergamon Press.

Katz, P. A., Sohn, M., and Salk, S. R. (1975) Perceptual concomitants of racial attitudes in urban grade-school children. *Developmental Psychology,* 11:135–144.

Katz, P. A. and Zalk, S. R. (1974) Doll preferences: An index of racial attitudes? *Journal of Educational Psychology,* 66:663–668.

Kaufman, M. J., Gottlieb, J., Agard, J. A., and Kukic, M. B. (1975) Mainstreaming: Toward an explication of the construct. *Focus on Exceptional Children,* 7:1–12.

Kausler, D. H. (1974) *Psychology of Verbal Learning and Memory.* New York: Academic Press.

Kavanagh, E. (1977) A classroom teacher looks at mainstreaming. *Elementary School Journal,* 77:318–322.

Kazdin, A. E. (1977) *The Token Economy: A Review and An Evaluation.* New York: Plenum Press.

Kelley, H. H. (1973) The processes of causal attribution. *American Psychologist,* 28:107–126.

Kelly, D. H. (1975) Tracking and its impact upon self-esteem: A neglected dimension. *Education,* 96:2–9.

Kempe, R. S. and Kempe, C. H. (1978) *Child Abuse.* Cambridge, Mass.: Harvard University Press.

Kennamer, L. and Hall, G. E. (1975) *Educational Staff Development and Its Implementation.* Austin: University of Texas at Austin College of Education and University of Texas at Austin Research and Development Center for Teacher Education.

Kenny, T. J., Clemmens, R. L., Hudson, B., Lentz, G. A., Jr., Cicci, R. and Nair, P. (1971) Characteristics of children referred because of hyperactivity. *Journal of Pediatrics,* 79:618–622.

Keogh, B. K., Tchir, C., and Windeguth-Behn, A. (1974) Teachers' perceptions of educationally high-risk children. *Journal of Learning Disabilities,* 7:367–374.

Kepler, K. and Randall, J. W. (1977) Individualization: The subversion of elementary schooling. *The Elementary School Journal,* 77:358–363.

Khan, S. B. and Weiss, J. (1973) The teaching of affective responses. In Travers, R. M. W., ed. *Second Handbook of Research on Teaching.* Chicago: Rand McNally.

Kibby, M. W. (1977) The status and the attitudes of homogeneously grouped second-graders: An exploratory study. *The Elementary School Journal,* 78:13–21.

Kier, R. J., Styfco, S. J., and Zigler, E. (1977) Success expectancies and the probability learning of children of low and middle socioeconomic status. *Developmental Psychology,* 13:444–449.

Kifer, E. (1973) The effects of school achievement on the affective traits of the learner. Doctoral dissertation, University of Chicago.

Kindsvatter, R. (1978) A new view of the dynamics of discipline. *Phi Delta Kappan,* 59:322–325.

Kinsey, A. C., Pomeroy, W. B., Martin, C. E., and Gebhard, P. H. (1953) *Sexual Behavior in the Human Female.* Philadelphia: Saunders.

Kintsch, W. (1970) *Learning, Memory, and Conceptual Process.* New York: Wiley.

Kintsch, W. (1977) *Memory and Cognition.* New York: John Wiley.

Kintsch, W. and van Dijk, T. A. (1978) Toward a model of text comprehension and production. *Psychological Review,* 85:363–394.

Kirschenbaum, H., Harmin, M., Howe, L., and Simon, S. B. (1977) In defense of values clarification. *Phi Delta Kappan,* 58:743–746.

Klaff, F. R. and Docherty, E. M. (1975) Children's self-concept and attitude toward school in open and traditional classrooms. *Journal of School Psychology,* 13:97–103.

Klatzky, R. L. (1975) *Human Memory: Structures and Processes.* San Francisco: W. H. Freeman.

Klausmeier, H. J., Rossmiller, R. A., and Saily, M., eds. (1977) *Individually Guided Education: Concepts and Practices.* New York: Academic Press.

Kleiman, D. (1981) When parent meets with teacher, anxieties rise. *New York Times* (April 1):19.

Klein, R. D. (1982) An inquiry into the factors related to creativity. *The Elementary School Journal,* 82:256–265.

Klein, S. S. (1971) Student influence on teacher behavior. *American Educational Research Journal,* 8:403–421.

Klineberg, O. (1935) *Negro Intelligence and Selective Migration.* New York: Columbia University Press.

Kochanek, T. T. (1980) Early detection programs for preschool handicapped children: Some procedural recommendations. *Journal of Special Education*, 14:347–353.

Kogan, N. (1976) *Cognitive Styles in Infancy and Early Childhood*. Hillsdale, N.J.: Lawrence Erlbaum.

Kogan, N. and Pankove, E. (1974) Long-term predictive validity of divergent-thinking tests: Some negative evidence. *Journal of Educational Psychology*, 68:802–810.

Kohlberg, L. (1963) The development of children's orientations toward a moral order. I: Sequence in the development of human thought. *Vita Humana*, 6:11–33.

Kohlberg, L. (1966) A cognitive-developmental analysis of children's sex-role concepts and attitudes. In Maccoby, E. E., ed. *The Development of Sex Differences*. Stanford, Calif.: Stanford University Press.

Kohlberg, L. (1968) Early education: A cognitive-developmental view. *Child Development*, 39:1014–1062.

Kohlberg, L. (1969) Stage and sequence: The cognitive development approach to socialization. In Goslin, D., ed. *Handbook of Socialization Theory and Practice*. Chicago: Rand McNally.

Kohlberg, L. (1975) The cognitive-developmental approach to moral education. *Phi Delta Kappan*, 56:670–677.

Kohlberg, L. (1976) Moral stages and moralization. In Lickona, T., ed. *Moral Development and Behavior: Theory, Research, and Social Issues*. New York: Holt, Rinehart and Winston.

Kohlberg, L. (1978) Revisions in the theory and practice of moral development. *New Directions for Child Development*, 2:83–87.

Kohlberg, L. (1980) Moral education. *Educational Leadership*, 38:19–23.

Kohlberg, L. (1981) *The Philosophy of Moral Development*. New York: Harper & Row.

Kohlberg, L. and Gilligan, C. (1971) The adolescent as a philosopher: The discovery of the self in the postconventional world. *Daedalus*, 100:1051–1086.

Kohlberg, L. and Kramer, R. B. (1969) Continuities and discontinuities in childhood and adult moral development. *Human Development*, 12:93–120.

Kohlberg, L. and Mayer, R. (1972) Development as the aim of education. *Harvard Educational Review*, 42:449–496.

Kohlberg, L. and Ullian, D. Z. (1974) Stages in the development of psychosexual concepts and attitudes. In Friedman, R. C., Richart, R. N., and Vande Wiele, R. L., eds. *Sex Differences in Behavior*. New York: Wiley.

Köhler, W. (1927) *The Mentality of Apes*. Rev. ed. New York: Harcourt, Brace.

Kohn, M. L. and Schooler, C. (1973) Occupational experience and psychological functioning: An assessment of reciprocal effects. *American Sociological Review*, 38:97–118.

Kolata, G. B. (1978) Childhood hyperactivity: A new look at treatment and causes. *Science*, 199:515–517.

Korner, A. F. (1979) Conceptual issues in infancy research. In Osofsky, J. D., ed. *Handbook of Infant Development*. New York: Wiley.

Koslin, S., Koslin, B., Pargament, R., and Waxman, H. (1972) Classroom racial balance and students' interracial attitudes. *Sociology of Education*, 45:386–407.

Kounin, J. S. (1970) *Discipline and Group Management in Classrooms*. New York: Holt, Rinehart and Winston.

Krathwohl, D. R., Bloom, B. S., and Masia, B. B. (1964) *Taxonomy of Educational Objectives. Handbook II: The Affective Domain*. New York: David McKay.

Krebs, R. L. (1977) Girls—More moral than boys or just sneakier? In Pottker, J. and Fishel, A., eds. *Sex Bias in the Schools*. Rutherford, N.J.: Fairleigh Dickinson University Press.

Kreutzer, M. A., Leonard, C., and Flavell, J. H. (1975) An interview study of children's knowledge about memory. *Monographs of the Society for Research in Child Development*, 40: Serial No. 159.

Kronick, D. (1976) The importance of a sociological perspective towards learning disabilities. *Journal of Learning Disabilities*, 9:115–119.

Kronick, D. (1977) The pros and cons of labeling. *Academic Therapy*, 13:101–104.

Krusell, J. L. (1973) Attribution of responsibility for performance outcomes of males and females. Unpublished doctoral dissertation, University of Rochester.

Kuhn, D. (1974) Inducing development experimentally: Comments on a research paradigm. *Developmental Psychology*, 10:590–600.

Kuhn, D. (1979) The application of Piaget's theory of cognitive development to education. *Harvard Educational Review*, 49:340–360.

Kuhn, D., Nash, S. C., and Brucken, L. (1978) Sex role concepts of two- and three-year-olds. *Child Development*, 49:445–451.

Kunen, S., Cohen, R., and Solman, R. (1981) A levels-of-processing analysis of Bloom's taxonomy. *Journal of Educational Psychology*, 73:202–211.

Kunzelmann, H. D. (1970) *Precision Teaching*. Seattle: Special Child Publications.

Kurland, N. D. (1977) Review: *Human Characteristics and School Learning*. *Teachers College Record*, 79:156–159.

LaBerge, D. and Samuels, S. J. (1974) Toward a theory of automatic information processing in reading. *Cognitive Psychology*, 6:293–323.

Labov, W. (1970) *The Study of Nonstandard English*. Champaign, Ill.: National Council of Teachers of English.

Labov, W. (1972) *Language in the Inner City: Studies in the Black English Vernacular*. Philadelphia: University of Pennsylvania Press.

Ladas, H. (1973) The mathemagenic effects of factual review questions on the learning of incidental information: A critical review. *Review of Educational Research*, 43:71–82.

Lancaster, J. (1803) *Improvements in Education as It Respects the Industrious Classes of the Community*. London: Darton and Harvey.

Landreneau, E. and Halpin, G. (1978) The influence of modeling on children's creative performance. *The Journal of Educational Research*, 71:137–139.

Landsmann, L. (1978) Is teaching hazardous to your health? *Today's Education*, 67:49–50.

Lange, G. and Griffith, S. B. (1977) The locus of organization failures in children's recall. *Child Development*, 48:1498–1502.

Langman, L. (1971) Dionysus—Child of tomorrow. *Youth and Society*, 3:84–87.

Langmeier, J. and Matějček, Z. (1974) *Psychological Deprivation in Childhood*. New York: Halsted Press.

Laosa, L. M. (1975) Bilingualism in three United States Hispanic groups: Contextual use of language by children and adults in their families. *Journal of Educational Psychology,* 67:617–627.

Laosa, L. M. (1977) Socialization, education, and continuity: The importance of the sociocultural context. *Young Children,* 32:21–27.

Larkin, R. W. (1975) Social exchange in the elementary school classroom: The problem of teacher legitimation of social power. *Sociology of Education,* 48:400–410.

Larsen, S. C. (1976) The learning disabilities specialist: Role and responsibilities. *Journal of Learning Disabilities,* 9:498–508.

Larson, L. E. (1972) The influence of parents and peers during adolescence: The situation hypothesis revisited. *Journal of Marriage and the Family,* 34:67–74.

Larson, M. S. (1977) *The Rise of Professionalism: A Sociological Analysis.* Berkeley: University of California Press.

Lashley, K. S. and Ball, J. (1929) Spinal conduction and kinesthetic sensitivity in the maze habit. *Journal of Comparative Psychology,* 9:71–106.

Lawther, J. D. (1977) *The Learning and Performance of Physical Skills.* 2nd ed. Englewood Cliffs, N.J.: Prentice-Hall.

Lawton, J. T., Saunders, R. A., and Muhs, P. (1980) Theories of Piaget, Bruner, and Ausubel: Explications and implications. *Journal of Genetic Psychology,* 136:121–136.

Lawton, J. T. and Wanska, S. K. (1977) Advance organizers as a teaching strategy: A reply to Barnes and Clawson. *Review of Educational Research,* 47:233–244.

Layton, E. T. (1932) The persistence of learning in elementary algebra. *Journal of Educational Psychology,* 23:46–55.

Lazarus, R. S. (1976) *Patterns of Adjustment.* 3rd ed. New York: McGraw-Hill.

Lee, C. L. and Estes, W. K. (1977) Order and position in primary memory for letter strings. *Journal of Verbal Learning and Verbal Behavior,* 16:395–418.

Lee, E. S. (1951) Negro intelligence and selective migration: A Philadelphia test of the Klineberg hypothesis. *American Sociological Review,* 16:227–243.

Lee, R. V. (1977) Adolescent sexuality: Fact and fantasy about the ''new morality.'' *Medical Aspects of Human Sexuality,* 11:6–21.

Lefcourt, H. M. (1976) *Locus of Control: Current Trends in Theory and Research.* Hillsdale, N.J.: Lawrence Erlbaum.

Leffingwell, R. J. (1977) Misbehavior in the classroom—Anxiety, a possible cause. *Education,* 97:360–363.

Lefkowitz, M. M., Eron, L. D., Walder, L. O., and Huesman, L. R. (1977) *Growing Up to Be Violent: A Longitudinal Study of the Development of Aggression.* New York: Pergamon Press.

Leifer, A. D. (1976) Teaching with television and film. In Gage, N. L., ed. *The Psychology of Teaching Methods.* Chicago: The National Society for the Study of Education.

Leinhardt, G. (1980) Transition rooms: Promoting maturation or reducing education? *Journal of Educational Psychology,* 72:55–61.

Leming, J. S. (1978) Cheating behavior, situational influence, and moral development. *The Journal of Educational Research,* 71:214–217.

Lepper, M. R. and Greene, D. (1975) Turning play into work:

Effects of adult surveillance and extrinsic rewards on children's intrinsic motivation. *Journal of Personality and Social Psychology,* 31:479–486.

Lepper, M. R., Greene, D., and Nisbett, R. E. (1973) Undermining children's intrinsic interest with extrinsic reward. *Journal of Personality and Social Psychology,* 28:129–137.

Lerner, B. (1981) The minimum competence testing movement. *American Psychologist,* 36:1057–1066.

Lerner, R. M. (1976) *Concepts and Theories of Human Development.* Reading, Mass.: Addison-Wesley.

Lerner, R. M. (1978) Nature, nurture, and dynamic interactionism. *Human Development,* 21:1–20.

Lerner, R. M. and Lerner, J. V. (1977) Effects of age, sex, and physical attractiveness on child-peer relations, academic performance and elementary school adjustment. *Developmental Psychology,* 13:585–590.

Lesgold, A. M., Levin, J. R., Shimron, J., and Guttmann, J. (1975) Pictures and young children's learning from oral prose. *Journal of Educational Psychology,* 67:636–642.

Lester, B. M., Kotelchuck, M., Spelke, E., Sellers, M. J., and Klein, R. E. (1974) Separation protest in Guatemalan infants: Cross-cultural and cognitive findings. *Developmental Psychology,* 10:79–85.

Leveque, K. L. and Walker, R. E. (1970) Correlates of high school cheating behavior. *Psychology in the Schools,* 7:159–163.

Levin, J. R. (1973) Inducing comprehension in poor readers. *Journal of Educational Psychology,* 65:19–24.

Levin, J. R. and Divine-Hawkins, P. (1974) Visual imagery as a prose learning process. *Journal of Reading Behavior,* 6:23–30.

Levin, J. R., Ghatala, E. S., DeRose, T. M., Wilder, L., and Norton, R. W. (1975) A further comparison of imagery and vocalization strategies in children's discrimination learning. *Journal of Educational Psychology,* 67:141–145.

Levin, J. R., Yussen, S. R., DeRose, T. M., and Pressley, M. (1977) Developmental changes in assessing recall and recognition memory capacity. *Developmental Psychology,* 13:608–615.

Levine, A. and Crumrine, J. (1975) Women and the fear of success: A problem in replication. *American Journal of Sociology,* 80:964–974.

Levine, F. M., ed. (1975) *Theoretical Readings in Motivation.* Chicago: Rand McNally.

Levitt, E. E. (1955a) Punitiveness and ''causality'' in grade-school children. *Journal of Educational Psychology,* 46:494–499.

Levitt, E. E. (1955b) Effect of a ''causal'' teacher training program on authoritarianism and responsibility in grade-school children. *Psychological Reports,* 1:449–458.

Levitt, E. E. (1971) Research on psychotherapy with children. In Bergin, A. E. and Garfield, S. L., eds. *Handbook of Psychotherapy and Behavior Change.* New York: Wiley.

Lewin, K., Lippitt, R., and White, R. K. (1939) Patterns of aggressive behavior in experimentally created ''social climates.'' *Journal of Social Psychology,* 10:271–299.

Lewis, C. C. (1981) The effects of parental firm control: A reinterpretation of findings. *Psychological Bulletin,* 90:547–563.

Leyser, Y. and Gottlieb, J. (1981) Social status improvement of unpopular handicapped and nonhandicapped pupils: A review. *The Elementary School Journal*, 81:228–235.

Liebert, R. M. and Baron, R. A. (1972) Some immediate effects of televised violence on children's behavior. *Developmental Psychology*, 6:469–475.

Limber, J. (1977) Language in child and chimp. *American Psychologist*, 32:280–295.

Linn, M. C. and Kyllonen, P. (1981) The field dependence-independence construct: Some, one, or none. *Journal of Educational Psychology*, 73:261–273.

Linton, T. E. and Juul, K. R. (1980) Mainstreaming: Time for reassessment. *Educational Leadership*, 37:433–437.

Lippitt, P. (1976) Learning through cross-age helping: Why and how. In Allen, V. L., ed. *Children as Teachers*. New York: Academic Press.

Lippitt, R. K. (1939) Field theory and experiment in social psychology: Autocratic and democratic group atmospheres. *American Journal of Sociology*, 45:26–49.

Little, J. W. (1982). Norms of collegiality and experimentation: Workplace conditions of school success. *American Educational Research Journal*, 19:325–340.

Locurto, C. M., Terrace, H. S., and Gibbon, J. (1981) *Autoshaping and Conditioning Theory*. New York: Academic Press.

Loehlin, J. C., Lindzey, G., and Spuhler, J. N. (1975) *Race Differences in Intelligence*. San Francisco: W. H. Freeman.

Loehlin, J. C. and Nichols, R. C. (1976) *Heredity, Environment, and Personality: A Study of 850 Sets of Twins*. Austin: University of Texas Press.

Loftus, E. F. and Loftus, G. R. (1980) On the permanence of stored information in the human brain. *American Psychologist*, 35:409–420.

Looft, W. R. (1971) Egocentrism and social interaction in adolescence. *Adolescence*, 6:485–494.

Lortie, D. C. (1969) The balance of control and autonomy in elementary school teaching. In Etzioni, A., ed. *The Semi-Professions and Their Organizations*. New York: Free Press.

Lortie, D. C. (1975) *Schoolteacher: A Sociological Study*. Chicago: University of Chicago Press.

Lott, A. and Lott, B. (1974) The role of reward in the formation of positive interpersonal attitudes. In Houston, T. L., ed. *Foundations of Interpersonal Attraction*. New York: Academic Press.

Lovaas, O. I. and Bucher, B. D. (1974) *Perspectives in Behavior Modification with Deviant Children*. Englewood Cliffs, N.J.: Prentice-Hall.

Love, H. (1973) *The Mentally Retarded Child and His Family*. Springfield, Ill.: Charles C Thomas.

Luiten, J., Ames, W., and Ackerson, G. (1980) A meta-analysis of the effects of advance organizers on learning and retention. *American Educational Research Journal*, 17:211–218.

Lyman, K. D. and Speizer, J. J. (1980) Advancing in school administration: A pilot project for women. *Harvard Educational Review*, 50:25–35.

Lytton, H. (1980) *Parent-Child Interaction: The Socialization Process Observed in Twin and Singleton Families*. New York: Plenum Press.

McCallum, C. J. and Roark, A. E. (1974) Children's problems in team-teaching schools. *The Elementary School Journal*, 74:436–439.

McCandless, B. R. (1955) Should a bright child start school before he's five? *Education*, 77:370–375.

McCandless, B. R., Roberts, A., and Starnes, T. (1972) Teachers' marks, achievement test scores, and aptitude relations with respect to social class, race, and sex. *Journal of Educational Psychology*, 63:153–159.

McCarthy, J. D. and Yancey, W. L. (1971) Uncle Tom and Mr. Charlie: Metaphysical pathos in the study of racism and personal disorganization. *American Journal of Sociology*, 76:648–672.

McCarthy, M. M. (1977) How can I best manage my classroom? *Instructor*, 87:72–73 + .

McClelland, D. C. (1961) *The Achieving Society*. Princeton: Van Nostrand.

McClelland, D. C. (1965) Achievement and entrepreneurship: A longitudinal study. *Journal of Personality and Social Psychology*, 1:389–392.

McClelland, D. C. and Alschuler, A. S. (1971) The achievement development project. Final Report to USOE Project No. 7–1231, Bureau of Research.

McClelland, D. C., Atkinson, J. W., Clark, R. A., and Lowell, E. L. (1953) *The Achievement Motive*. New York: Appleton-Century-Crofts.

McClelland, D. C., Constantian, C. A., Regalado, D., and Stone, C. (1978) Making it to maturity. *Psychology Today*, 12 (June):42–52.

McClelland, D. C. and Winter, D. G. (1969) *Motivating Economic Achievement*. New York: Free Press.

Maccoby, E. E. and Jacklin, C. N. (1974) *The Psychology of Sex Differences*. Stanford, Calif.: Stanford University Press.

Maccoby, E. E. and Masters, J. C. (1970) Attachment and dependency. In Mussen, P. H., ed. *Carmichael's Manual of Child Psychology*. 3rd ed. New York: Wiley.

McCormick, P. D. and Swenson, A. L. (1972) Recognition memory for common and rare words. *Journal of Experimental Psychology*, 95:72–77.

McDaniel, T. R. (1977) Principles of classroom discipline: Toward a pragmatic synthesis. *The Clearinghouse*, 51:149–152.

McDaniel, T. R. (1980) Exploring alternatives to punishment: The keys to effective discipline. *Phi Delta Kappan*, 61:455–458.

McDermott, J. (1970) Divorce and its psychiatric sequelae in children. *Archives of General Psychiatry*, 23:421–428.

Macdonald, J. B. and Wolfson, B. J. (1970) A case against behavioral objectives. *The Elementary School Journal*, 71:119–128.

McDougall, R. (1904) Recognition and recall. *Journal of Philosophical Psychology and Scientific Methods*, 1:229–233.

McDowell, R. L. (1976) Parent counseling: The state of the art. *Journal of Learning Disabilities*, 9:614–619.

McGee, C. S., Kauffman, J. M., and Nussen, J. L. (1977) Children as therapeutic change agents: Reinforcement intervention paradigms. *Review of Educational Research*, 47:451–477.

McGeoch, J. A. (1932) Forgetting and the law of disuse. *Psychological Review*, 39:352–370.

McGeoch, J. A. and Irion, A. L. (1952) *The Psychology of Human Learning*. New York: Longmans.

McKeachie, W. J. (1965) *Teaching Tips: A Guide Book for the Beginning College Teacher*. 5th ed. Ann Arbor, Mich.: George Wahr.

McKeachie, W. J. (1974) Instructional psychology. In Rosenzweig, M. R. and Porter, L. W., eds. *Annual Review of Psychology*. Vol. 27. Palo Alto, Calif.: Annual Reviews.

Mackey, W. F. (1970) A Typology of bilingual education. *Foreign Language Annals* (May):596–608.

MacKinnon, D. W. (1962) The nature and nurture of creative talent. *American Psychologist*, 17:484–495.

MacKinnon, D. W. (1975) IPAR's contribution to the conceptualization and study of creativity. In Taylor, I. A. and Getzels, J. W., eds. *Perspectives in Creativity*. Chicago: Aldine.

McLaughlin, B. (1977) Second-language learning in children. *Psychological Bulletin*, 84:438–459.

McLaughlin, T. F. (1976) Self-control in the classroom. *Review of Educational Research*, 46:631–663.

McLeish, J. (1976) The lecture method. In Gage, N. L., ed. *The Psychology of Teaching Methods*. Chicago: The National Society for the Study of Education.

MacMillan, D. L. (1973) *Behavior Modification in Education*. New York: Macmillan.

McMillin, M. R. (1975) Leadership aspirations of prospective teachers—A comparison of men and women. *Journal of Teacher Education*, 26:323–325.

McNeil, J. (1971) *Toward Accountable Teachers: Their Appraisal and Improvement*. New York: Holt, Rinehart, and Winston.

MacNeill, D. (1970) *The Acquisition of Language: The Study of Developmental Psycholinguistics*. New York: Harper & Row.

Macy, D. J. and Carter, J. L. (1978) Comparison of a mainstream and self-contained special education program. *Journal of Special Education*, 12:303–313.

Madaus, G. F. (1981) NIE clarification hearing: The negative team's case. *Phi Delta Kappan*, 63:92–94.

Madsen, C. H., Jr., Becker, W. C., and Thomas, D. R. (1968) Rules, praise, and ignoring: Elements of elementary classroom control. *Journal of Applied Behavior Analysis*, 1:139–150.

Madsen, C. H., Jr., Becker, W. C., Thomas, D. R., Koser, L., and Plager, E. (1968) An analysis of the reinforcing function of "sit-down" commands. In Parker, R. K., ed. *Readings in Educational Psychology*. Boston: Allyn and Bacon.

Maeroff, G. I. (1977a) The unfavored gifted few. *The New York Times Magazine* (August 21):30 +.

Mager, R. F. (1962) *Preparing Instructional Objectives*. Palo Alto, Calif.: Fearon.

Mahoney, E. (1978) Seeking a new teaching job? *Instructor*, 87:21.

Mansfield, R. S., Busse, T. V., and Krepelka, E. J. (1978) The effectiveness of creativity training. *Review of Educational Research*, 48:517–536.

Marcus, R. F. (1975) The child as elicitor of parental sanctions for independent and dependent behavior: A simulation of parent-child interaction. *Developmental Psychology*, 11:443–452.

Margolis, H., Brannigan, G. G., and Poston, M. A. (1977) Modification of impulsivity: Implications for teaching. *The Elementary School Journal*, 77:231–237.

Marholin, D., II. and Steinman, W. M. (1977) Stimulus control in the classroom as a function of the behavior reinforced. *Journal of Applied Behavior Analysis*, 10:465–478.

Marjoribanks, K. (1976) School attitudes, cognitive ability, and academic achievement. *Journal of Educational Psychology*, 68:653–660.

Mark, J. H. and Anderson, B. D. (1978) Teacher survival rates—A current look. *American Educational Research Journal*, 15:379–383.

Markman, E. M. (1979) Realizing that you don't understand: Elementary school children's awareness of inconsistencies. *Child Development*, 50:643–655.

Marsh, H. W., Overall, J. U., and Kesler, S. P. (1979) Class size, students' evaluations, and instructional effectiveness. *American Educational Research Journal*, 16:57–69.

Marshall, H. H. (1981) Open classrooms: Has the term outlived its usefulness? *Review of Educational Research*, 51:181–192.

Martin, C. L. and Halverson, C. F., Jr. (1981) A schematic processing model of sex typing and stereotyping in children. *Child Development*, 52:1119–1134.

Martin, E. W. (1974) Some thoughts on mainstreaming. *Exceptional Children*, 41:150–153.

Martin, J. A. (1981) A longitudinal study of the consequences of early mother-infant interaction: A microanalytic approach. *Monographs of the Society for Research in Child Development*, 46:No. 3.

Martin, L. S. and Pavan, B. N. (1976) Current research on open space, nongrading, vertical grouping, and team teaching. *Phi Delta Kappan*, 57:310–315.

Martin, R. (1972) Student sex and behavior as determinants of the type and frequency of teacher-student contacts. *Journal of School Psychology*, 10:339–347.

Martin, R. and Keller, A. (1976) Teacher awareness of classroom dyadic interactions. *Journal of School Psychology*, 14:47–55.

Marusek, J. (1979) Team teaching: A survival system in teaching slow-learning. *Phi Delta Kappan*, 60:520–523.

Maslow, A. H. (1955) Deficiency motivation and growth motivation. In Jones, M. R., ed. *Nebraska Symposium on Motivation*. Lincoln: University of Nebraska Press.

Maslow, A. H. (1964) *Religions, Values, and Peak-Experiences*. Columbus, Ohio: Ohio State University Press.

Maslow, A. H. (1967) Self-actualization and beyond. In Bugental, J. F. T., ed. *Challenges of Humanistic Psychology*. New York: McGraw-Hill.

Maslow, A. H. (1968) *Toward a Psychology of Being*. 2nd ed. New York: Van Nostrand.

Maslow, A. H. (1970) *Motivation and Personality*. 2nd ed. New York: Harper & Row.

Mason, J. (1980) When do children begin to read: An exploration of four-year-old children's letter and word reading competencies. *Reading Research Quarterly*, 15:203–223.

Massari, D. J. and Rosenblum, D. C. (1972) Locus of control, interpersonal trust and academic achievement. *Psychological Reports*, 31:355–360.

Mathis, C. (1959) The relationship between salary policies and teacher morale. *Journal of Educational Psychology*, 50:275–279.

Maurer, A. (1974) Corporal punishment. *American Psychologist*, 29:614–626.

May, R. (1975) *The Courage to Create*. New York: Norton.

Mayer, R. E. (1976) Some conditions of meaningful learning for computer programming: Advance organizers and subject control of frame order. *Journal of Educational Psychology*, 68:143–150.

Mayer, R. E. (1979) Can advance organizers influence meaningful learning? *Review of Educational Research*, 49:371–383.

Mayer, R. E. (1980) Elaboration techniques that increase the meaningfulness of technical text: An experimental test of the learning strategy hypothesis. *Journal of Educational Psychology*, 72:770–784.

Meacham, J. A. (1972) The development of memory abilities in the individual and society. *Human Development*, 15:205–228.

Mead, G. H. (1932) *The Philosophy of the Present*. Chicago: Open Court.

Mead, G. H. (1934) *Mind, Self, and Other*. Chicago: University of Chicago Press.

Medland, M. B. and Stachnik, T. J. (1972) Good-behavior game: A replication and systematic analysis. *Journal of Applied Behavior Analysis*, 5:45–51.

Medway, F. J. and Baron, R. M. (1977) Locus of control and tutor's instructional style as determinants of cross-age tutoring effectiveness. *Contemporary Educational Psychology*, 2:298–310.

Medway, F. J. and Smith, R. C., Jr. (1978) An examination of contemporary elementary school affective education programs. *Psychology in the Schools*, 15:260–269.

Meeker, B. F. and Weitzel-O'Neill, P. A. (1977) Sex roles and interpersonal behavior in task-oriented groups. *American Sociological Review*, 42:91–105.

Mehan, H. (1979) *Learning lessons: Social Organization in the Classroom*. Cambridge, Mass.: Harvard University Press.

Mehan, H. and Wood, H. (1975) *The Reality of Ethnomethodology*. New York: Wiley.

Mehan, H. and Wood, H. (1976) De-secting ethnomethodology. *American Sociologist*, 11:13–21.

Mehrens, W. A. and Lehmann, I. J. (1978) *Measurement and Evaluation*. 2nd ed. New York: Holt, Rinehart and Winston.

Meichenbaum, D. H. (1972) Cognitive modification of test-anxious college students. *Journal of Consulting and Clinical Psychology*, 39:370–380.

Melaragno, R. J. (1977) Pupil tutoring: Directions for the future. *The Elementary School Journal*, 77:384–387.

Melton, A. W. and Irwin, J. M. (1940) The influence of degree of interpolated learning on retroactive inhibition and the overt transfer of specific responses. *American Journal of Psychology*, 53:175–203.

Meltzer, B. N., Petras, J. W., and Reynolds, L. T. (1975) *Symbolic Interactionism*. London: Routledge & Kegan Paul.

Mercer, B. E. and Carr, E. R. (1957) *Education and the Social Order*. New York: Holt, Rinehart and Winston.

Mercer, C. D., Forgnone, C., and Wolking, W. D. (1976) Definitions of learning disabilities used in the United States. *Journal of Learning Disabilities*, 9:376–386.

Merrill, P. F. (1974) Effects of the availability of objectives and/or rules on the learning process. *Journal of Educational Psychology*, 66:534–539.

Messer, S. B. (1976) Reflection-impulsivity: A review. *Psychological Bulletin*, 83:1026–1052.

Messick, S. (1980) Test validity and the ethics of assessment. *American Psychologist*, 35:1012–1027.

Metfessel, W. S., Michael, W. B., and Kirsner, D. A. (1969) Instrumentation of Bloom's and Krathwohl's taxonomies for the writing of educational objectives. *Psychology in the Schools*, 6:227–231.

Metz, K. E. (1978) Children's thinking and primary social studies curricula. *The Elementary School Journal*, 79:115–121.

Meyer, B. (1980) The development of girls' sex-role attitudes. *Child Development*, 51:508–514.

Meyer, B. J. F. (1975) *The Organization of Prose and Its Effect on Memory*. New York: Elsevier.

Meyer, J. and Cohen, E. (1970) *The Impact of the Open-Space School upon Teacher Influence and Autonomy: The Effects of an Organizational Innovation*. Stanford, Calif.: Stanford Center for Research and Development in Teaching.

Meyer, J. W., Rubinson, R., Ramirez, F. O., and Boli-Bennett, J. (1977) The world educational revolution, 1950–1970. *Sociology of Education*, 50:242–258.

Michaels, J. W. (1977) Classroom reward structures and academic performance. *Review of Educational Research*, 47:87–98.

Middleton, D. (1976) Army uses teaching machine to improve soldiers' training. *New York Times* (May 19):18.

Midlarsky, E., Bryan, J. H., and Brickman, P. (1973) Aversive approval: Interactive effects of modeling and reinforcement on altruistic behavior. *Child Development*, 44:321–328.

Miles, C. C. (1954) Gifted children. In Carmichael, L., ed. *Manual of Child Psychology*. New York: Wiley.

Miller, A. (1981) Conceptual matching models and interactional research in education. *Review of Educational Research*, 51:33–84.

Miller, G. A. (1956) The magical number seven, plus or minus two: Some limits on our capacity for processing information. *Psychological Review*, 63:81–97.

Miller, J. (1981) What's in a skull? *Newsweek* (November 9):106.

Miller, N. and Gerard, H. B. (1976) How busing failed in Riverside. *Psychology Today*, 10 (June):66+.

Miller, V. (1957) Academic achievement and social adjustment of children young for their grade placement. *The Elementary School Journal*, 57:257–263.

Millichap, J. G. (1973) Drugs in management of minimal brain dysfunction. *Annals of the New York Academy of Sciences*, 205:321–334.

Milofsky, C. D. (1974) Why special education isn't special. *Harvard Educational Review*, 44:437–458.

Monahan, J. E. and Hollingworth, L. S. (1927) Neuromuscular capacity of children who test above 135 IQ (Stanford-Binet). *Journal of Educational Psychology*, 18:88–96.

Money, J. (1977) The "givens" from a different point of view: Lessons from intersexuality for a theory of gender identity. In Oremland, E. K. and Oremland, J. D., eds. *The Sexual and Gender Development of Young Children: The Role of the Educator.* Cambridge, Mass.: Ballinger.

Money, J. and Ehrhardt, A. (1972) *Man & Woman; Boy & Girl.* Baltimore: Johns Hopkins University Press.

Money, J. and Tucker, P. (1975) *Sexual Signatures.* Boston: Little, Brown.

Monge, R. H. (1973) Developmental trends in factors of adolescent self-concept. *Developmental Psychology,* 8:382–393.

Montagu, A. (1964) *Life Before Birth.* New York: The New American Library.

Montague, W. E. and Carter, J. E. (1973) Vividness of imagery in recalling connected discourse. *Journal of Educational Psychology,* 64:72–75.

Moore, S. G. (1981) The unique contribution of peers to socialization in early childhood. *Theory into Practice,* 20:105–108.

Moore, W. E. (1969) Occupational socialization. In Goslin, D. A., ed. *Handbook of Socialization Theory and Research.* Chicago: Rand McNally.

Moos, R. H. (1978) A typology of junior high and high school classrooms. *American Educational Research Journal,* 15:53–66.

Morine-Dershimer, G. (1978–1979) Planning in classroom reality, an in-depth look. *Educational Research Quarterly,* 3:83–99.

Morland, J. K. (1962) Racial acceptance and preference of nursery school children in a southern city. *Merrill-Palmer Quarterly of Behavior and Development,* 8:271–280.

Morris, C. D., Bransford, J. D., and Franks, J. J. (1977) Levels of processing versus transfer appropriate processing. *Journal of Verbal Learning and Verbal Behavior,* 16:519–533.

Morris, L. W. and Fulmer, R. S. (1976) Test anxiety (worry and emotionality) changes during academic testing as a function of feedback and test importance. *Journal of Educational Psychology,* 68:817–824.

Morris, L. W. and Liebert, R. M. (1969) Effects of anxiety on timed and untimed intelligence tests: Another look. *Journal of Consulting and Clinical Psychology,* 33:240–244.

Morris, L. W. and Liebert, R. M. (1970) Relationship of cognitive and emotional components of test anxiety to physiological arousal and academic performance. *Journal of Consulting and Clinical Psychology,* 35:332–337.

Morris, L. W. and Liebert, R. M. (1973) Effects of negative feedback, threat of shock, and level of trait anxiety on the arousal of two components of anxiety. *Journal of Counseling Psychology,* 20:321–326.

Morrison, G. M. (1981) Sociometric measurement: Methodological consideration of its use with mildly learning handicapped and nonhandicapped children. *Journal of Educational Psychology,* 73:193–201.

Morrison, J. (1970) Parental divorce as a factor in childhood psychiatric illness. *Comprehensive Psychiatry,* 15:95–102.

Morse, N. C. and Weiss, R. S. (1955) The function and meaning of work and the job. *American Sociological Review,* 20:191–198.

Moses, M. and Dickens, C. (1980) Three misconceptions about humanistic education. *Educational Leadership,* 38:227–228.

Mosher, R. (1980) *Moral Education: A First Generation of Research and Development.* New York: Praeger.

Müller, G. E. (1913) Zur Analyse der Gedächtnistätigkeit und des Vorstellungsverlaufes. III. Teil. *Zeitschrift für Psychologie,* Ergänzungsband, 8.

Munz, D. C. and Smouse, A. D. (1968) Interaction effects of item-difficulty sequence and achievement-anxiety reaction on academic performance. *Journal of Educational Psychology,* 59:370–374.

Murdock, B. B., Jr. (1976) Methodology in the study of human memory. In Estes, W. K., ed. *Handbook of Learning and Cognitive Processes.* Vol. 4. New York: Wiley.

Murdock, G. P. (1935) Comparative data on the division of labor by sex. *Social Forces,* 15:551–553.

Murray, F. B. and Pikulski, J. J. (1978) *The Acquisition of Reading: Cognitive, Linguistic, and Perceptual Prerequisites.* Baltimore: University Park Press.

Murray, H. A. (1938) *Explorations in Personality.* London: Oxford University Press.

Musella, D. and Rusch, R. (1968) Student opinion on college teaching. *Improving College and University Teaching,* 16:137–140.

Musemeche, R. A. and Sauls, C. W. (1976) Policies and attitudes on corporal punishment. *Phi Delta Kappan,* 58:283.

Muson, H. (1979) Moral thinking: Can it be taught? *Psychology Today,* 12:48–68 +.

Mussen, P. H., Harris, S., Rutherford, R., and Keasey, C. B. (1970) *Developmental Psychology,* 3:169–194.

Mussen, P. H. and Jones, M. C. (1957) Self-conceptions, motivations, and interpersonal attitudes of late- and early-maturing boys. *Child Development,* 28:243–256.

Muuss, R. E. (1960) The relationship between causal orientation, anxiety and insecurity in elementary school children. *Journal of Educational Psychology,* 51:122–129.

Muuss, R. E. (1976) The implications of social learning theory for an understanding of adolescent development. *Adolescence,* 11:61–85.

Muuss, R. E. (1976) Kohlberg's cognitive-developmental approach to adolescent morality. *Adolescence,* 11:39–59.

Myers, C. R. (1970) Journal citations and scientific eminence in contemporary psychology. *American Psychologist,* 25:1041–1048.

Nash, R. (1976) Pupils' expectations of their teachers. In Stubbs, M. and Delamont, S., eds. *Explorations in Classroom Observation.* New York: Wiley.

Nash, R. J. and Ducharme, E. R. (1975) A sociologist looks at teachers: Careers, realities, and dreams. *Journal of Teacher Education,* 26:360–363.

National Advisory Committee on Handicapped Children (1968) *First Annual Report: Special Education for Handicapped Children.* Washington, D.C.: U.S. Office of Education.

National Education Association (1972) *Status of the American Public School Teacher, 1970–71.* Washington, D.C.: National Education Association.

National Institute of Education (1977) *Violent Schools—Safe Schools.* Washington, D.C.: Government Printing Office.

Nawas, M. M. (1971) Change in efficiency of ego functioning and complexity from adolescence to young adulthood. *Developmental Psychology,* 4:412–415.

NEA Research (1978) School violence. *Today's Education*, 67 (February–March):16.

Neisser, U. (1967) *Cognitive Psychology*. New York: Appleton-Century-Crofts.

Neisser, U. (1976) *Cognition and Reality*. San Francisco: W. H. Freeman.

Nelson, D. L., Reed, V. S., and McEvoy, C. L. (1977) Learning to order pictures and words: A model of sensory and semantic encoding. *Journal of Experimental Psychology: Human Learning and Memory*, 3:485–497.

Nelson, K. (1981) Social cognition in a script framework. In Flavell, J. H. and Ross, L., eds. *Social Cognitive Development: Frontiers and Possible Futures*. New York: Cambridge University Press.

Nelson, K. E. (1977) Facilitating children's syntax acquisition. *Developmental Psychology*, 13:101–107.

Nelson, T. O. (1977) Repetition and depth of processing. *Journal of Verbal Learning and Verbal Behavior*, 16:151–171.

New York Times (1977) Husband and wife work in 47.1% of marriages. March 8:21.

New York Times (1977) Violence is occurring in the best of families. March 20: 6E.

Newell, A. and Simon, H. A. (1956) The logic theory machine: A complex information-processing system. *IRE Transactions on Information Theory*, IT-2:61–69.

Newell, A. and Simon, H. A. (1961) Computer simulation of human thinking. *Science*, 134:2011–2017.

Newell, A. and Simon, H. A. (1972) *Human Problem Solving*. Englewood Cliffs, N.J.: Prentice-Hall.

Newell, K. M. and Kennedy, J. A. (1978) Knowledge of results and children's motor learning. *Developmental Psychology*, 14:531–536.

Newland, T. E. (1976) *The Gifted in Socioeducational Perspective*. Englewood Cliffs, N.J.: Prentice-Hall.

Newport, E. L. (1976) Motherese: The speech of mothers to young children. In Castellan, N., Pisoni, D. P., and Potts, G. R., eds. *Cognitive Theory*. Vol. 2. Hillsdale, N.J.: Lawrence Erlbaum.

Nicholls, J. G. (1972) Creativity in the person who will never produce anything original and useful. *American Psychologist*, 27:717–727.

Nicholls, J. G. (1975) Causal attributions and other achievement-related cognitions: Effects of task outcomes, attainment value, and sex. *Journal of Personality and Social Psychology*, 31:379–389.

Nicholls, J. G. (1979) Quality and equality in intellectual development. *American Psychologist*, 34:1071–1084.

Nilsen, A. P. (1977) Alternatives to sexist practices in the classroom. *Young Children*, 32:53–58.

Nitko, A. J. (1980) Distinguishing the many varieties of criterion-referenced tests. *Review of Educational Research*, 50:461–485.

Nixon, J. E. and Locke, L. F. (1973) Research on teaching physical education. Travers, R. M. W., ed. *Second Handbook of Research on Teaching*. Chicago: Rand McNally.

Noble, C. G. and Nolan, J. D. (1976) Effect of student verbal behavior on classroom teacher behavior. *Journal of Educational Psychology*, 68:342–346.

Norman, D. A., ed. (1972) *Memory and Attention*. 2nd ed. New York: Wiley.

Nottelmann, E. D. and Hill, K. T. (1977) Test anxiety and off-task behavior in evaluative situations. *Child Development*, 48:225–231.

Notz, W. W. (1975) Work motivation and the negative effects of extrinsic rewards. *American psychologist*, 30:884–891.

Nugent, G. C., Tipton, T. J., and Brooks, D. W. (1980) Use of introductory organizers in television instruction. *Journal of Educational Psychology*, 72:445–451.

Nussel, E. J., Inglis, J. D., and Wiersma, W. (1976) *The Teacher and Individually Guided Education*. Reading, Mass.: Addison-Wesley.

Nuthall, G. and Snook, I. (1973) Contemporary models of teaching. In Travers, R. M. W., ed. *Second Handbook of Research on Teaching*. Chicago: Rand McNally.

Nye, F. (1957) Child adjustment in broken and unhappy homes. *Marriage and Family Living*, 19:356–361.

O'Brien, T. C. (1973) Why teach mathematics? *The Elementary School Journal*, 73:258–268.

O'Connell, E., Dusek, J., and Wheeler, R. (1974) A follow-up study of teacher expectancy effects. *Journal of Educational Psychology*, 66:325–328.

O'Connell, M., Orr, A. C., and Lueck, M. (1982) The children of working mothers. *American Demographics*, 4:26–31.

Offer, D. (1969) *The Psychological World of the Teen-Ager: A Study of Normal Adolescent Boys*. New York: Basic Books.

Offer, D. and Offer, J. B. (1975) *From Teenage to Young Manhood*. New York: Basic Books.

Office of Career Education (1976) *Career Education and the Marshmallow Principle*. Washington, D.C.: U.S. Office of Education.

Offner, C. D. (1978) Back-to-basics mathematics: An educational fraud. *The Mathematics Teacher*, LXXI:211–217.

Ojemann, R. H. (1959) *Developing a Program for Education in Human Behavior*. Iowa City: State University of Iowa Press.

Ojemann, R. H. (1961) The effects of teaching behavior dynamics. In Caplan, G., ed. *Prevention of Mental Disorders in Children*. New York: Basic Books.

Ojemann, R. H. (1967) Incorporating psychological concepts in the school curriculum. *Journal of School Psychology*, 5:195–204.

Ojemann, R. H., Levitt, E. E., Lyle, W. H., and Whiteside, M. F. (1955) The effects of a causal teacher training program and certain curricular changes on grade-school children. *Journal of Experimental Education*, 24:95–114.

Oldenquist, A. (1981) "Indoctrination" and societal suicide. *The Public Interest*, 63:81–94.

O'Leary, K. D. and Drabman, R. S. (1971) Token reinforcement programs in the classroom: A review. *Psychological Bulletin*, 75:379–398.

O'Leary, S. G. and O'Leary, K. D. (1976) Behavior modification in the school. In Leitenberg, H., ed. *Handbook of Behavior Modification and Behavior Therapy*. Englewood Cliffs, N.J.: Prentice-Hall.

Olson, D. R. (1977) From utterance to text: The bias of language in speech and writing. *Harvard Educational Review*, 47:257–281.

Olson, D. W. (1977) Nonresponsive students? Check the classroom communication channels. *The Clearinghouse*, 51:160–162.

Olson, M. N. (1971) Ways to achieve quality in school classrooms: Some definitive answers. *Phi Delta Kappan,* 53:63–65.

Olweus, D. (1977) Aggression and peer acceptance in adolescent boys: Two short-term longitudinal studies of ratings. *Child Development,* 48:1301–1313.

Olweus, D. (1978) *Aggression in the Schools: Bullies and Whipping Boys.* New York: Halsted Press.

O'Neil, H. F., Jr. (1972) Effects of stress on state anxiety and performance in computer-assisted learning. *Journal of Educational Psychology,* 63:473–481.

Ornstein, A. C. (1981) The trend toward increased professionalism for teachers. *Phi Delta Kappan,* 63:196–198.

Ornstein, P. A., Naus, M. J., and Liberty, C. (1975) Rehearsal and organizational processes in children's memory. *Child Development,* 46:818–830.

Ornstein, P. A., Naus, M. J., and Stone, B. P. (1977) Rehearsal training and developmental differences in memory. *Developmental Psychology,* 13:15–24.

Osborn, A. F. (1963) *Applied Imagination.* 3rd ed. New York: Scribner's.

Osofsky, J. D. and Danzger, B. (1974) Relationships between neonatal characteristics and mother-infant interactions. *Developmental Psychology,* 10:124–130.

Overmier, J. B. and Seligman, M. E. P. (1967) Effects of inescapable shock upon subsequent escape and avoidance learning. *Journal of Comparative and Physiological Psychology,* 63:28–33.

Owen, J. A., Braggio, J. T., and Ellen, P. (1976) Individual diagnosis and remediation of educational handicaps manifested by learning disabled children. *Journal of Learning Disabilities,* 9:638–645.

Pace, A. J. and Feagans, L. (1983) Knowledge and language: Children's ability to use and communicate what they know about everyday experiences. In Feagans, L., Garvey, C., and Golinkoff, R., eds. *The Origins and Growth of Communication.* Norwood, N.J.: Ablex.

Packer, J. and Bain, J. D. (1978) Cognitive style and teacher-student compatibility. *Journal of Educational Psychology,* 70:864–871.

Paivio, A. (1969) Mental imagery in associative learning and memory. *Psychological Review,* 76:241–263.

Paivio, A. (1971) *Imagery and Verbal Processes.* New York: Holt, Rinehart and Winston.

Paivio, A. (1974) Language and knowledge of the world. *Educational Researcher,* 3:5–12.

Paolitto, D. P. (1976) The effect of cross-age tutoring on adolescence: An inquiry into theoretical assumptions. *Review of Educational Research,* 46:215–237.

Papay, J. P., Costello, R. J., Hedl, J. J., Jr., and Spielberger, C. D. (1975) Effects of trait and state anxiety on the performance of elementary school children in traditional and individualized multiage classrooms. *Journal of Educational Psychology,* 67:840–846.

Papert, S. (1981) *Mindstorms: Children, Computers, and Powerful Ideas.* New York: Basic Books.

Parelius, A. P. and Parelius, R. J. (1978) *The Sociology of Education.* Englewood Cliffs, N.J.: Prentice-Hall.

Parnes, S. J. (1967) *Creative Behaviour Guidebook.* New York: Scribner.

Parnes, S. J. (1971) Can creativity be increased? In Davis, G. A. and Scott, J. A., eds. *Training Creative Thinking.* New York: Holt, Rinehart and Winston.

Parr, F. W. (1936) The problem of student honesty. *Journal of Higher Education,* 7:318–326.

Passow, A. H. (1958) Enrichment of education for the gifted. In Henry, N. B., ed. *Education for the Gifted.* Chicago: The National Society for the Study of Education.

Patchen, M., Davidson, J. D., Hofmann, G., and Brown, W. R. (1977) Determinants of students' interracial behavior and opinion change. *Sociology of Education,* 50:55–75.

Patchen, M., Hofmann, G., and Davidson, J. D. (1976) Interracial perceptions among high school students. *Sociometry,* 39:341–354.

Paton, S. M., Walberg, H. J., and Yeh, E. G. (1973) Ethnicity, environmental control, and academic self-concept in Chicago. *American Educational Research Journal,* 10:85–99.

Patten, B. M. (1973) Visually mediated thinking: A report of the case of Albert Einstein. *Journal of Learning Disabilities,* 6:415–420.

Payne, D. A. (1974) *The Assessment of Learning: Cognitive and Affective.* Lexington, Mass.: D. C. Heath.

Pearce, D. (1980) *Breaking Down Barriers: New Evidence on the Impact of Metropolitan School Desegregation on Housing Patterns.* Washington, D.C.: Center for National Policy Review, Catholic University.

Pedersen, E., Faucher, T. A., and Eaton, W. W. (1978) A new perspective on the effects of first-grade teachers on children's subsequent adult status. *Harvard Educational Review,* 48:1–31.

Pellegrin, R. J. (1976) Schools as work settings. In Dubin, R., ed. *Handbook of Work, Organization, and Society.* Chicago: Rand McNally.

Penk, W. E. (1969) Age changes and correlates of internal-external locus of control scale. *Psychological Reports,* 25:857.

Perry, D. G. and Bussey, K. (1977) Self-reinforcement in high- and low-aggressive boys following acts of aggression. *Child Development,* 48:653–657.

Perry, D. G. and Perry, L. C. (1974) Denial of suffering in the victim as a stimulus to violence in aggressive boys. *Child Development,* 45:55–62.

Peters, N. A. (1977) An interdisciplinary approach to the assessment and management of severe language-learning problems. In Otto, W. and Peters, N. A., eds. *Reading Problems.* Reading, Mass.: Addison-Wesley.

Peters, R. S. (1975) A reply to Kohlberg. *Phi Delta Kappan,* 56:678.

Peters, W. A. (1971) *A Class Divided.* New York: Doubleday.

Peterson, P. L., Marx, R. W., and Clark, C. M. (1978) Teacher planning, teacher behavior, and student achievement. *American Education Research Journal,* 15:417–432.

Peterson, W. F., Morese, K. N., and Kaltreider, D. F. (1965) Smoking and prematurity: A preliminary report based on study of 7740 Caucasians. *Obstetrics and Gynecology,* 26:775–779.

Phares, E. J. (1976) *Locus of Control in Personality.* Morristown, N.J.: General Learning Press.

Pharis, W. and Zachariya, S. (1979) *The Elementary School Principal in 1978: A Research Study.* Washington, D.C.: National Association of Elementary School Principals.

Phillips, R. B. (1973) Teacher attitude as related to student attitude and achievement in elementary school mathematics. *School Science and Mathematics*, 73:501–507.

Phipps, P. M. (1982) The merging categories: Appropriate education or administrative convenience? *Journal of Learning Disabilities*, 15:153–154.

Piaget, J. (1932) *The Moral Judgment of the Child*. Trans. Gabain, M. London: Kegan Paul, Trench, Trubner.

Piaget, J. (1952) *The Origins of Intelligence in Children*. New York: International Universities Press.

Piaget, J. (1963) *Psychology of Intelligence*. New Jersey: Littlefield, Adams.

Piaget, J. (1964) Development and learning. In Ripple, R. E. and Rockcastle, V. N., eds. *Piaget Rediscovered*. Ithaca, N.Y.: Cornell University Press.

Piaget, J. (1970a) A conversation with Jean Piaget. *Psychology Today*, 3 (May):25 +.

Piaget, J. (1970b) *Science of Education and the Psychology of the child*. New York: Viking.

Piaget, J. (1977) Problems of equilibration. In Appel, M. H. and Goldberg, L. S., eds. *Topics in Cognitive Development*. Vol. 1. New York: Plenum Press.

Pines, M. (1981) The civilizing of Genie. *Psychology Today*, 15 (September):28–34.

Pines, M. (1982) What produces great skills? Specific pattern is discerned. *New York Times* (March 30):21–22.

Pinneau, S. R. (1955) The infantile disorders of hospitalism and anaclitic depression. *Psychological Bulletin*, 52:429–452.

Pipho, C. (1978) Minimum competency testing in 1978: A look at state standards. *Phi Delta Kappan*, 59:585–587.

Plomin, R., DeFries, J. C., and Loehlin, J. C. (1977) Genotype-environment interaction and correlation in the analysis of human behavior. *Psychological Bulletin*, 84:309–322.

Plummer, S., Baer, D. M., and LeBlanc, J. M. (1977) Functional considerations in the use of procedural timeout and an effective alternative. *Journal of Applied Behavior Analysis*, 10:689–705.

Polirstok, S. R. and Greer, R. D. (1977) Remediation of mutually aversive interactions between a problem student and four teachers by training the student in reinforcement techniques. *Journal of Applied Behavior Analysis*, 10:707–716.

Popham, W. J. (1976) Normative data for criterion-referenced tests? *Phi Delta Kappan*, 57:593–594.

Popham, W. J. (1978) *Criterion-Referenced Measurement*. Englewood Cliffs, N.J.: Prentice-Hall.

Popham, W. J. (1980a) Educational measurement for the improvement of instruction. *Phi Delta Kappan*, 61:531–534.

Popham, W. J. (1980b) Well-crafted criterion-referenced tests. *Educational Leadership*, 36:91–95.

Popham, W. J. (1981) The case for minimum competency testing. *Phi Delta Kappan*, 63:89–91.

Porter, J. (1971) *Black Child, White Child: The Development of Racial Attitudes*. Cambridge: Harvard University Press.

Posner, M. I. (1967) Short-term memory systems in human memory. *Acta Psychologica*, 27:267–284.

Posner, M. I. and Keele, S. W. (1973) Skill learning. In Travers, R. M. W., ed. *Second Handbook of Research on Teaching*. Chicago: Rand McNally.

Postman, L. and Underwood, B. J. (1973) Critical issues in interference theory. *Memory and Cognition*, 1:19–40.

Postman, N. and Weingartner, C. (1969) *Teaching as a Subversive Activity*. New York: Delacorte Press.

Powledge, T. M. (1977) What schools teach of sex is still controversial. *New York Times* (February 27):18E.

Prawat, R. S. and Jarvis, R. (1980) Gender difference as a factor in teachers' perceptions of students. *Journal of Educational Psychology*, 72:743–749.

Prawat, R. S., Jones, H., and Hampton, J. (1979) Longitudinal study of attitude development in pre-, early, and later adolescent samples. *Journal of Educational Psychology*, 71:363–369.

Premack, D. (1959) Toward empirical behavior laws: I. Positive reinforcement. *Psychological Review*, 66:219–233.

Prescott, D. (1971) Efficacy-related imagery, education, and politics. Unpublished honors thesis, Harvard University.

Pressey, S. L. (1949) *Educational Acceleration: Appraisals and Basic Problems*. Bureau of Educational Research Monographs, No. 31. Columbus, Ohio: Ohio State University.

Pressey, S. L., Robinson, F. P., and Horrocks, J. E. (1959) *Psychology in Education*. New York: Harper & Row.

Pressley, G. M. (1976) Mental imagery helps eight-year-olds remember what they read. *Journal of Educational Psychology*, 68:355–359.

Pressley, M. (1977) Imagery and children's learning: Putting the picture in developmental perspective. *Review of Educational Research*, 47:585–622.

Pressley, M. (1979) Increasing children's self-control through cognitive interventions. *Review of Educational Research*, 49:319–370.

Preston, R. (1962) Reading achievement of German and American children. *School and Society*, 90:350–354.

Primack, R. and Aspy, D. (1980) The roots of humanism. *Educational Leadership*, 38:224–226.

Prince-Bonham, S. and Addison, S. (1978) Families and mentally retarded children: Emphasis on the father. *The Family Coordinator*, 27:221–230.

Pullin, D. (1981) Minimum competency testing and the demand for accountability. *Phi Delta Kappan*, 63:20–22.

Quadagno, D. M., Briscoe, R., and Quadagno, J. S. (1977) Effect of perinatal gonadal hormones on selected nonsexual behavior patterns: A critical assessment of the nonhuman and human literature. *Psychological Bulletin*, 84:62–80.

Quarantelli, E. L. and Cooper, J. (1966) Self-conceptions and others: A further test of Meadian hypothesis. *The Sociological Quarterly*, 7:281–297.

Rabbitt, J. A. (1978) The parent/teacher conference: Trauma or teamwork? *Phi Delta Kappan*, 59:471–472.

Rabinowitz, J. C., Mandler, G., and Patterson, K. E. (1977) Determinants of recognition and recall: Accessibility and generation. *Journal of Experimental Psychology: General*, 106:302–329.

Radloff, B. (1975) The tot in the gray flannel suit. *New York Times* (May 4):8E.

Ragsdale, C. E. (1950) How children learn motor types of activities. Learning and instruction. *Washington: Forty-ninth Yearbook of the National Society for the Study of Education*: 69–91.

Raschke, H. J. and Raschke, V. J. (1979) Family conflict and children's self-concepts: A comparison of intact and single-parent families. *Journal of Marriage and the Family,* 41:367–374.

Raths, L. E., Harmin, M., and Simon, S. B. (1966) *Values and Teaching.* Columbus, Ohio: Charles E. Merrill.

Raven, B. H. (1974) The comparative analysis of power and power preference. In Tedeschi, J. T., ed. *Perspectives on Social Power.* Chicago: Aldine.

Ravitz, M. (1963) The role of the school in the urban setting. In Passov, A. R., ed. *Education in Depressed Settings.* New York: Teachers College Bureau of Publications.

Reed, E. W. and Reed, S. C. (1965) *Mental Retardation: A Family Study.* Philadelphia: Saunders.

Reese, H. W. and Overton, W. F. (1970) Models of development and theories of development. In Goulet, L. R. and Baltes, P. B., eds. *Life-Span Developmental Psychology: Research and Theory.* New York: Academic Press.

Reimer, J. (1981) Moral education: The just community approach. *Phi Delta Kappan,* 62:485–487.

Reinhold, R. (1982) Student abuse of drugs reported to decline. *New York Times* (February 25):1, 12.

Reiss, I. L. (1976) *Family Systems in America.* 2nd ed. Hinsdale, Ill.: Dryden Press.

Reitman, J. S. (1971) Mechanisms of forgetting in short-term memory. *Cognitive Psychology,* 2:185–195.

Renzulli, J. S. (1978) What makes giftedness? Reexamining a definition. *Phi Delta Kappan,* 60:180–184.

Renzulli, J. S., Smith, L. H., and Reis, S. M. (1982) Curriculum compacting: An essential strategy for working with gifted students. *The Elementary School Journal,* 82:185–194.

Rest, J., Turiel, E., and Kohlberg, L. (1969) Level of moral development as a determinant of preference and comprehension of moral judgments made by others. *Journal of Personality,* 37:225–252.

Rheingold, H. L. (1961) The effect of environmental stimulation upon social and exploratory behavior in the human infant. In Foss, B. M., ed. *Determinants of Infant Behavior.* Vol. 1. New York: Wiley.

Rheingold, H. L. (1969) The social and socializing infant. In Goslin, D. A., ed. *Handbook of Socialization Theory and Research.* Chicago: Rand McNally.

Richards, P. N. and Bolton, N. (1971) Type of mathematics teaching, mathematical ability and divergent thinking in junior school children. *British Journal of Educational Psychology,* 41:32–37.

Rickards, J. P. (1977) On inserting questions before or after segments of text. *Contemporary Educational Psychology,* 2:200–206.

Rickards, J. P. (1979) Adjunct postquestions in text: A critical review of methods and processes. *Review of Educational Research,* 49:181–196.

Rickards, J. P. and DiVesta, F. J. (1974) Type and frequency of questions in processing textual material. *Journal of Educational Psychology,* 66:354–362.

Rie, H. E. and Rie, E. D. (1980) *Handbook of Minimal Brain Dysfunctions: A Critical View.* New York: Wiley.

Rienzo, B. A. (1981) The status of sex education: An overview and recommendations. *Phi Delta Kappan,* 63:192–193.

Riley, J. W., Ryan, B. F., and Lifshitz, M. (1950) *The Student Looks at His Teacher.* New Brunswick, N.J.: Rutgers University Press.

Ringness, T. A. (1967) Identification patterns, motivation, and school achievement of bright junior high school boys. *Journal of Educational Psychology,* 58:93–102.

Ringness, T. A. (1975) *The Affective Domain in Education.* Boston: Little, Brown.

Ringness, T. A. (1976) Whatever happened to the study of classical conditioning? *Phi Delta Kappan,* 57:447–455.

Ripple, R. E. (1965) Affective factors influence classroom learning. *Educational Leadership,* 22:476–480.

Robin, S. S. and Bosco, J. J. (1973) Ritalin for school children: The teacher's perspective. *Journal of School Health,* 43:624–628.

Roe, A. (1953) *The Making of a Scientist.* New York: Dodd, Mead.

Rogers, C. R. (1947) *Casebook of Non-Directive Counseling.* Boston: Houghton Mifflin.

Rogers, C. R. (1959) Toward a theory of creativity. In Anderson, H. H., ed. *Creativity and Its Cultivation.* New York: Harper & Row.

Rogers, C. R. (1963) Learning to be free. *NEA Journal,* 52:28–30.

Rogers, C. R. (1967) The facilitation of significant learning. In Siegel, L., ed. *Instruction: Some Contemporary Viewpoints.* San Francisco: Chandler.

Rogers, C. R. (1970) *On Becoming a Person: A Therapist's View of Psychotherapy.* Boston: Houghton Mifflin-Sentry Edition.

Rogers, C. R. (1977) Beyond education's watershed. *Educational Leadership,* 34:623–631.

Rogers, V. R. (1971) *Teaching in the British Primary School.* New York: Macmillan.

Rogers, V. R. (1976) Answering your questions on open education. Thibadeau, G., ed. *Opening Up Education.* Dubuque, Iowa: Kendall/Hunt.

Rohwer, W. D., Jr., and Harris, W. J. (1975) Media effects on prose learning in two populations of children. *Journal of Educational Psychology,* 67:651–657.

Rohwer, W. D., Jr., and Matz, R. (1975) Improving aural comprehension in white and black children: Pictures versus print. *Journal of Experimental Child Psychology,* 19:23–26.

Rollins, H. A., Jr. and Genser, L. (1977) Role of cognitive style in a cognitive task: A case favoring the impulsive approach to problem solving. *Journal of Educational Psychology,* 69:281–287.

Rosch, E. (1973) On the internal structure of perceptual and semantic categories. In Moore, T. E., ed. *Cognitive Development and the Acquisition of Language.* New York: Academic Press.

Rosch, E. (1977) Human categorization. In Warren, N., ed. *Advances in Cross-Cultural Psychology,* Vol. 1. London: Academic Press.

Rosch, E., Mervis, C. B., Gray, W., Johnson, D., and Boyes-Braem, P. (1976) Basic objects in natural categories. *Cognitive Psychology,* 8:382–439.

Rosen, B. C. (1959) Race, ethnicity and achievement syndrome. *American Sociological Review,* 24:47–60.

Rosenbaum, J. E. (1976) *Making Inequality.* New York: Wiley.

Rosenberg, M. and Simmons, R. G. (1972) Black and white self-esteem: The urban school child. Washington, D. C.: American Sociological Association.

Rosenhan, D. (1972) Prosocial behavior in children. In Hartup,

W. W., ed. *The Young Child*. Vol. 2. Washington: National Association for the Education of Young Children.

Rosenhan, D., Moore, B. S., and Underwood, B. (1976) The social psychology of moral behavior. In Lickona, T., ed. *Moral Development and Behavior*. New York: Holt, Rinehart and Winston.

Rosenshine, B. (1979) Content, time, and direct instruction. In Peterson, P. and Walberg, H., eds. *Research on Teaching: Concepts, Findings, and Implications*. Berkeley, Calif.: McCutchan.

Rosenthal, J. H. (1973) Self-esteem in dyslexic children. *Academic Therapy*, 9:27–39.

Rosenthal, R. and Jacobson, L. (1968) *Pygmalion in the Classroom*. New York: Holt, Rinehart and Winston.

Rosenthal, R. H. and Allen, T. W. (1978) An examination of attention, arousal, and learning dysfunctions of hyperkinetic children. *Psychological Bulletin*, 85:689–715.

Rosenthal, T. L. and Zimmerman, B. J. (1973) Organization, observation, and guided practice in concept attainment and generalization. *Child Development*, 44:606–613.

Ross, A. O. (1976) *Psychological Aspects of Learning Disabilities and Reading Disorders*. New York: McGraw-Hill.

Ross, D. M. and Ross, S. A. (1976) *Hyperactivity: Research, Theory, and Action*. New York: Wiley.

Ross, M. and Salvia, J. (1975) Attractiveness as a biasing factor in teacher judgments. *American Journal of Mental Deficiency*, 80:96–98.

Rothkopf, E. Z. (1970) The concept of mathemagenic activities. *Review of Educational Research*, 40:325–336.

Rothkopf, E. Z. (1976) Writing to teach and reading to learn. In Gage, N. L., ed. *The Psychology of Teaching Methods*. Chicago: University of Chicago Press.

Rothkopf, E. Z. and Bisbicos, E. (1967) Selective facilitative effects of interspersed questions on learning from written material. *Journal of Educational Psychology*, 57:56–61.

Rotter, J. B. (1966) Generalized expectancies for internal versus external control of reinforcement. *Psychological Monographs*, 80:No. 1 (Whole No. 609).

Royer, J. M. and Cable, G. W. (1976) Illustrations, analogies, and facilitative transfer in prose learning. *Journal of Educational Psychology*, 68:205–209.

Rubin, R. T., Reinisch, J. M., and Haskett, R. F. (1981) Postnatal gonadal steroid effects on human behavior. *Science*, 211:1318–1324.

Rubovits, P. C. and Maehr, M. L. (1971) Pygmalion analyzed: Toward an explanation of the Rosenthal-Jacobson findings. *Journal of Personality and Social Psychology*, 19:197–203.

Rubovits, P. C. and Maehr, M. L. (1973) Pygmalion black and white. *Journal of Personality and Social Psychology*, 25:210–218.

Ruedi, J. and West, C. K. (1973) Pupil self-concept in an "open" school and in a "traditional" school. *Journal of School Psychology*, 10:48–53.

Rumberger, R. W. (1981) *Why Kids Drop Out of High School*. Washington, D.C.: U.S. Department of Labor.

Rumelhart, D. E. and Ortony, A. (1977) The representation of knowledge in memory. In Anderson, R. C., Spiro, R. J., and Montague, W. E., eds. *Schooling and the Acquisition of Knowledge*. Hillsdale, N.J.: Lawrence Erlbaum.

Rushton, J. P. (1976) Socialization and the altruistic behavior of children. *Psychological Bulletin*, 83:898–913.

Rutherford, W. L. (1975) *Team Teaching—How Do Teachers Use It?* Austin: University of Texas at Austin Research and Development Center.

Rutter, M. (1974) *The Qualities of Mothering*. New York: Jason Aronson.

Rutter, M. (1979) *Fifteen Thousand Hours: Secondary Schools and Their Effects on Children*. Cambridge, Mass.: Harvard University Press.

Ryan, W. (1972) *Blaming the Victim*. New York: Vintage.

Sachs, J. and Devin, J. (1976) Young children's knowledge of age-appropriate speech styles. *Journal of Child Language*, 3:81–98.

Sadker, D., Sadker, M., and Cooper, J. M. (1973) Elementary school—Through children's eyes. *The Elementary School Journal*, 73:289–296.

Sadker, M. (1975) Sexism in schools. *Journal of Teacher Education*, 26:317–322.

Saenger, G. and Gilbert, E. (1950) Customer reactions to the integration of Negro sales personnel. *International Journal of Opinion and Attitude Research*, 4:57–76.

Safer, D. J. and Allen, R. P. (1976) *Hyperactive Children: Diagnosis and Management*. Baltimore: University Park Press.

Sage, G. H. (1971) *Introduction to Motor Behavior*. Reading, Mass.: Addison-Wesley.

St. John, N. (1975) *School Desegregation: Outcomes for Children*. New York: Wiley.

St. John, N. and Lewis, R. G. (1975) Race and the social structure of the elementary classroom. *Sociology of Education*, 48:346–368.

Salmon-Cox, L. (1981) Teachers and standardized achievement tests: What's really happening? *Phi Delta Kappan*, 62:631–634.

Salomon, G. (1971) Heuristic models for the generation of aptitude-treatment interaction hypotheses. *Review of Educational Research*, 42:327–343.

Saltz, R. (1973) Effects of part-time "mothering" on IQ and SQ of young institutionalized children. *Child Development*, 44:166–170.

Sameroff, A. J. (1975) Transactional models in early social relations. *Human Development*, 18:65–79.

Samuels, S. J. (1981) Characteristics of exemplary reading programs. In Guthrie, J. T., ed. *Comprehension and Teaching: Research Reviews*. Newark, Del.: International Reading Association.

Samuels, S. J. and Terry, P. (1977) Future trends and issues in educational psychology. In Treffinger, D. J., Davis, J. K., and Ripple, R. E., eds. *Handbook on Teaching Educational Psychology*, New York: Academic Press.

Sanders, N. M. (1966) *Classroom Questions: What Kinds?* New York: Harper & Row.

Sandoval, J. (1977) The measurement of the hyperactive syndrome in children. *Review of Educational Research*, 47:293–318.

Sandoval, J., Lambert, N. M., and Sassone, D. M. (1981) The comprehensive treatment of hyperactive children: A continuing problem. *Journal of Learning Disabilities*, 14:117–118.

Sandoval, J., Lambert, N. M., and Yandell, G. W. (1976)

Current medical practice with hyperactive children. *American Journal of Orthopsychiatry,* 46:323–334.

Santogrossi, D. A., O'Leary, K. D., Romanczyk, R. G., and Kaufman, K. F. (1973) Self-evaluation by adolescents in a psychiatric hospital school token program. *Journal of Applied Behavior Analysis,* 6:277–287.

Santrock, J. W. and Warshak, R. A. (1979) Father custody and social development in boys and girls. *Journal of Social Issues,* 35:112–125.

Sapon-Shevin, M. (1978) Another look at mainstreaming: Exceptionality, normality, and the nature of difference. *Phi Delta Kappan,* 60:119–121.

Saracho, O. N. and Dayton, C. M. (1980) Relationship of teachers' cognitive styles to pupils' academic achievement gains. *Journal of Educational Psychology,* 72:544–549.

Sarason, I. G. (1960) Empirical findings and theoretical problems in the use of anxiety scales. *Psychological Bulletin,* 57:403–415.

Sarason, I. G. (1961) The effect of anxiety and threat on the solution of a difficult task. *Journal of Abnormal and Social Psychology,* 62:165–168.

Sarason, I. G. (1972) Experimental approaches to test anxiety: Attention and the uses of information. In Spielberger, C. D., ed. *Anxiety: Current Trends in Theory and Research.* New York: Academic Press.

Sarason, I. G. (1973) Test anxiety and cognitive modeling. *Journal of Personality and Social Psychology,* 28:58–61.

Sartain, H. W. (1976) Instruction of disabled learners: A reading perspective. *Journal of Learning Disabilities,* 9:489–497.

Sassen, G. (1980) Success anxiety in women: A constructivist interpretation of its source and its significance. *Harvard Educational Review,* 50:13–24.

Saudargas, R. W., Madsen, C. H., Jr., and Scott, J. W. (1977) Differential effects of fixed- and variable-time feedback on production rates of elementary school children. *Journal of Applied Behavior Analysis,* 10:673–678.

Scandura, J. M. (1977) Structural approach to instructional problems. *American Psychologist,* 32:33–53.

Scarr, S., Webber, P. L., Weinberg, R. A., and Wittig, M. A. (1981) Personality resemblance among adolescents and their parents in biologically related and adoptive families. *Journal of Personality and Social Psychology,* 40:885–898.

Scarr, S. and Weinberg, R. A. (1975) When black children grow up in white homes. . . . *Psychology Today,* 9 (December, 1975), 80–82.

Scarr, S. and Weinberg, R. A. (1976) IQ test performance of black children adopted by white families. *American Psychologist,* 31:726–739.

Scarr, S. and Weinberg, R. A. (1980) Calling all camps! The war is over. *American Sociological Review,* 45:859–864.

Schachter, F. F. (1981) Toddlers with employed mothers. *Child Development,* 52:958–964.

Schaefer, C. E. (1969) The self-concept of creative adolescents. *Journal of Psychology,* 72:233–242.

Schaeffer, D. T. (1969) An investigation into the differences between male and female elementary teachers in their perceptions of problem pupils. Doctoral dissertation. College Park, Md.: University of Maryland.

Schaer, H. F. and Crump, W. D. (1976) Teacher involvement

and early identification of children with learning disabilities. *Journal of Learning Disabilities,* 9:91–95.

Schaffer, H. R. and Emerson, P. E. (1946a) The development of social attachments in infancy. *Monographs of the Society for Research in Child Development,* 29 (3).

Schaffer, H. R. and Emerson, P. E. (1964b) Patterns of response to physical contact in early human development. *Journal of Child Psychology and Psychiatry,* 5:1–13.

Scharf, M. (1976) *Body, Mind, Behavior.* Washington, D.C.: The New Republic Book Company.

Schank, R. C. and Abelson, R. (1977) *Scripts, Plans, Goals, and Understanding.* Hillsdale, N.J.: Lawrence Erlbaum.

Schlechty, P. C. and Atwood, H. E. (1977) The student-teacher relationship. *Theory into Practice,* 16:285–289.

Schlesinger, I. M. (1971) Production of utterances and language acquisition. In Slobin, D. I., ed. *The Ontogenesis of Grammar: A Theoretical Symposium.* New York: Academic Press.

Schmuck, R. A. (1977) Peer groups as settings for learning. *Theory into Practice* 16:272–279.

Schofield, J. W., and Sagar, H. A. (1977) Peer interaction patterns in an integrated middle school. *Sociometry,* 40:130–138.

Schott, A. (1957) New tools, methods for their use, and a new curriculum. *The Arithmetic Teacher,* 5:204.

Schramm, W. (1977) *Big Media, Little Media.* Beverly Hills, Calif.: Sage Publications.

Schulman, A. I. and Lovelace, E. A. (1970) Recognition memory for words presented at a slow or rapid rate. *Psychonomic Science,* 21:99–100.

Schulman, J. L., Ford, R. C., Busk, P. L., and Kaspar, J. C. (1973) Mental health in the schools. *The Elementary School Journal,* 74:48–56.

Schwartz, B. (1981) Autoshaping: Driving toward a psychology of learning. *Contemporary Psychology,* 26:823–825.

Scott, K. P. (1980) Sexist and nonsexist materials: What impact do they have? *The Elementary School Journal,* 81:47–52.

Searle, J. (1969) *Speech Acts.* Cambridge: Cambridge University Press.

Sears, R. R. (1970) Relation of early socialization experience to self-concepts and gender role in middle childhood. *Child Development,* 41:267–289.

Sears, R. R., Maccoby, E. E., and Levin, H. (1957) *Patterns of Child Rearing.* New York: Harper & Row.

Sebald, H. (1977) *Adolescence: A Social Psychological Analysis.* 2nd ed. Englewood Cliffs, N.J.: Prentice-Hall.

Seddon, G. M. (1978) The properties of Bloom's taxonomy of educational objectives for the cognitive domain. *Review of Educational Research,* 48:303–323.

Sefkow, S. B. and Myers, J. L. (1980) Review effects of inserted questions on learning from prose. *American Educational Research Journal,* 17:435–447.

Segal, J. and Yahraes, H. (1978) Bringing up mother. *Psychology Today* 12 (November):90–96.

Seidner, C. J. (1976) Teaching with simulations and games. In Gage, N. L., ed. *The Psychology of Teaching Methods.* Chicago: The National Society for the Study of Education.

Seidner, C. J., Lewis, S. C., Sherwin, N. V., and Troll, E. W. (1978) Cognitive and affective outcomes for pupils in an open-space elementary school: A comparative study. *The Elementary School Journal,* 78:208–219.

Selfridge, O. G. and Neisser, U. (1960) Pattern recognition by machine. *Scientific American*, 203:60–68.

Seligman, M. E. P. (1975) *Helplessness*. San Francisco: W. H. Freeman.

Seligman, M. E. P. (1978) Comment and integration. *Journal of Abnormal Psychology*, 87:165–179.

Seligman, M. E. P. and Maier, S. F. (1967) Failure to escape traumatic shock. *Journal of Experimental Psychology*, 74:1–9.

Sewall, G. and Lee, E. D. (1980) Jensen's rebuttal. *Newsweek* (January 14):59.

Sewell, W. H. and Mussen, P. H. (1952) The effects of feeding, weaning, and scheduling procedures on childhood adjustment and the formation of oral symptoms. *Child Development*, 23:185–191.

Sexton, P. C. (1969) *The Feminized Male: Classrooms, White Collars, and the Decline of Manliness*. New York: Random House.

Shapero, S. and Forbes, C. B. (1981) A review of involvement programs for parents of learning disabled children. *Journal of Learning Disabilities*, 14:499–504.

Shapson, S. M., Wright, E. N., Eason, G., and Fitzgerald, J. (1980) An experimental study of the effects of class size. *American Educational Research Journal*, 17:141–152.

Shatz, M. and Gelman, R. (1973) The development of communication skills: Modifications in the speech of young children as a function of listener. *Monographs of the Society for Research in Child Development*, 38:No. 152.

Shavelson, R. J. and Bolus, R. (1982) Self-concept: The interplay of theory and methods. *Journal of Educational Psychology*, 74:3–17.

Shavelson, R. J. and Stern, P. (1981) Research on teachers' pedagogical thoughts, judgments, decisions, and behavior. *Review of Educational Research*, 51:455–498.

Shepard, R. N. (1967) Recognition memory for words, sentences, and pictures. *Journal of Verbal Learning and Verbal Behavior*, 6:156–163.

Sherif, M., Harvey, O. J., White, B. J., Hood, W. R., and Sherif, C. W. (1961) *Intergroup Conflict and Cooperation: The Robbers Cave Experiment*. Norman, Okla.: University of Oklahoma Book Exchange.

Shiffrin, R. M. and Atkinson, R. C. (1969) Storage and retrieval processes in long-term memory. *Psychological Review*, 76:179–193.

Shimron, J. (1975) Imagery and comprehension of prose by elementary school children. Doctoral dissertation, University of Pittsburgh.

Shoemaker, J. and Fraser, H. W. (1981) What principals can do: Some implications from studies of effective schooling. *Phi Delta Kappan*, 63:178–182.

Shore, M. F., Milgram, N. A., and Malasky, C. (1971) The effectiveness of an enrichment program for disadvantaged young children. *American Journal of Orthopsychiatry*, 41:442–449.

Shotel, J. R., Iano, R. P., and McGettigan, J. F. (1972) Teacher attitudes associated with the integration of handicapped children. *Exceptional Children*, 38:677–683.

Shulman, L. S. (1968) Psychological controversies in the teaching of science and mathematics. *Science Teacher*, 35:34–38 + .

Siegel, A. W., Kirasic, K. C., and Kilburg, R. R. (1973) Recognition memory in reflective and impulsive preschool children. *Child Development*, 44:651–656.

Siegelman, M. (1973) Parent behavior correlates of personality traits related to creativity in sons and daughters. *Journal of Consulting and Clinical Psychology*, 40:139–147.

Silberman, C. E. (1970) *Crisis in the Classroom*. New York: Random House.

Silberman, M. L. (1969) Behavioral expression of teachers' attitudes toward elementary school students. *Journal of Educational Psychology*, 60:402–407.

Silberman, M. L. (1971) Teachers' attitudes and actions toward their students. In Silberman, M. L., ed. *The Experience of Schooling*. New York: Holt, Rinehart and Winston.

Simmons, R. G., Brown, L., Bush, D. M., and Blyth, D. A. (1978) Self-esteem and achievement of black and white adolescents. *Social Problems*, 26:86–96.

Simon, S. B., Howe, L. W., and Kirschenbaum, H. (1972) *Values Clarification: Handbook of Practical Strategies for Teachers and Students*. New York: Hart Publishing.

Simons, H. D. (1973) Behavioral objectives: A false hope for education. *The Elementary School Journal*, 73:173–181.

Simpson, R. L. (1969) The school teacher: Social values, community role, and professional self-image. *Final Report, Cooperative Research Project No. 5-0451*. Washington, D.C.: Bureau of Research, Office of Education, U.S. Department of Health, Education and Welfare.

Simpson, W. J. (1957) A preliminary report on cigarette smoking and the incidence of prematurity. *American Journal of Obstetrics and Gynecology*, 73:808–815.

Singleton, L. C. and Asher, S. R. (1977) Peer preferences and social interaction among third-grade children in an integrated school district. *Journal of Educational Psychology*, 69:330–336.

Sisk, D. A. (1977) What if your child is gifted? *American Education*, 13:23–26.

Skeels, H. M. (1966) Adult status of children with contrasting early life experiences. *Monographs of the Society for Research in Child Development*, 31(3).

Skinner, B. F. (1948) *Walden II*. New York: Macmillan.

Skinner, B. F. (1953) *Science and Human Behavior*. New York: Free Press.

Skinner, B. F. (1957) *Verbal Behavior*. Englewood Cliffs, N.J.: Prentice-Hall.

Skinner, B. F. (1968) *The Technology of Teaching*. New York: Appleton-Century-Crofts.

Skinner, B. F. (1971) *Beyond Freedom and Dignity*. New York: Knopf.

Skinner, B. F. (1974) *About Behaviorism*. New York: Knopf.

Skolnick, A. (1978) The myth of the vulnerable child. *Psychology Today*, 11 (February):56–65.

Skon, L., Johnson, D. W., and Johnson, R. T. (1981) Cooperative peer interaction versus individual competition and individualistic efforts: Effects on the acquisition of cognitive reasoning strategies. *Journal of Educational Psychology*, 73:83–92.

Slavin, R. E. (1977) Classroom reward structure: An analytical and practical review. *Review of Educational Research*, 47:633–650.

Slobin, D. I. (1979) *Psycholinguistics*. 2nd ed. Glenview, Ill.: Scott, Foresman.

Smedslund, J. (1961) The acquisition of conservation of substance and weight in children. *Scandinavian Journal of Psychology*, 2:71–84, 85–87; 153–155; 156–160; and 203–210.

Smirnov, A. A. and Zinchenko, P. I. (1969) Problems in the psychology of memory. In Cole, M. and Maltzman, I., eds. *A Handbook of Contemporary Soviet Psychology*. New York: Basic Books.

Smith, F. (1973) *Psycholinguistics and Reading*. New York: Holt, Rinehart and Winston.

Smith, F. (1975) *Comprehension and Learning*. New York: Holt, Rinehart and Winston.

Smith, H. A. (1979) Nonverbal communication in teaching. *Review of Educational Research*, 49:631–672.

Smith, I. D. (1973) Impact of computer-assisted instruction on student attitudes. *Journal of Educational Psychology*, 64:366–372.

Smith, M. L. and Glass, G. V. (1980) Meta-analysis of research on class size and its relationship to attitudes and instruction. *American Educational Research Journal*, 17:419–433.

Smithers, A. (1970) What do students expect of lectures? *Universities Quarterly*, 24:330–336.

Snow, C. E. (1977) Mothers' speech research: From input to interaction. In Snow, C. E., and Ferguson, C. A., eds. *Talking to Children: Language Input and Acquisition*. Cambridge: Cambridge University Press.

Snow, C. E. and Ferguson, C. A., eds. (1977) *Talking to Children: Language Input and Acquisition*. Cambridge: Cambridge University Press.

Snow, R. E. (1969) Unfinished Pygmalion. *Contemporary Psychology*, 14:197–199.

Soeffing, M. (1975) Abused children are exceptional children. *Exceptional Children*, 42:126–133.

Solnick, J. V., Rincover, A., and Peterson, C. R. (1977) Some determinants of the reinforcing and punishing effects of timeout. *Journal of Applied Behavior Analysis*, 10:415–424.

Solomon, D. and Kendall, A. J. (1976) Individual characteristics and children's performance in "open" and "traditional" classroom settings. *Journal of Educational Psychology*, 68:613–625.

Solomon, D. and Kendall, A. J. (1976) *Individual Characteristics and Children's Performance in Varied Educational Settings*. Rockville, Md.: Montgomery County Public Schools.

Sommer, R. (1977) Classroom layout. *Theory into Practice*, 16:174–175.

Sorensen, R. C. (1973) *Adolescent Sexuality in Contemporary America*. New York: Harry N. Abrams.

Spearman, C. (1904) "General intelligence" objectively determined and measured. *American Journal of Psychology*, 15:201–293.

Spearman, C. (1927) *The Abilities of Man*. New York: Macmillan.

Spencer, R. E. and Semb, G. (1977) The Personalized System of Instruction—A new idea in higher education. In Treffinger, D. J., Davis, J. K., and Ripple, R. E., ed. *Handbook on Teaching Educational Psychology*. New York: Academic Press.

Spielberger, C. D. (1966) Theory and research on anxiety. In Spielberger, C. D., ed. *Anxiety and Behavior*. New York: Academic Press.

Spielberger, C. D. (1972) Anxiety as an emotional state. In Spielberger, C. D., ed. *Anxiety: Current Trends in Theory and Research*. Vol. 1. New York: Academic Press.

Spielberger, C. D., O'Neil, H. F., Jr., and Hansen, D. N. (1972) Anxiety, drive theory, and computer-assisted learning. In Maher, B. A., ed. *Progress in Experimental Personality Research*. Vol. 6. New York: Academic Press.

Spinetta, J. J. and Rigler, D. (1975) The child-abusing parent: A psychological review. *Psychological Bulletin*, 77:296–304.

Spitz, R. A. (1945) Hospitalism: An inquiry into the genesis of psychiatric conditions in early childhood. *Psychoanalytic Study of the Child*, 1:53–74.

Spitz, R. A. (1946) Hospitalism: A follow-up report., *Psychoanalytic Study of the Child*, 2:113–117.

Sprinthall, N. A. (1972) Humanism: A new bag of virtues for guidance? *Personnel and Guidance Journal*, 50:349–356.

Spoull, L. and Zubrow, D. (1981) Standardized testing from the administrative perspective. *Phi Delta Kappan*, 62:628–631.

Stallings, J. A. (1976) How instructional processes relate to child outcomes in a national study of follow through. *Journal of Teacher Education*, 27:43–47.

Stallings, J. and Hentzell, S. (1978) Effective teaching and learning in urban schools. Paper presented at the National Conference on Urban Education, July 10–14, St. Louis.

Stallings, L. M. (1973) *Motor Skills: Development and Learning*. Dubuque, Iowa: William C. Brown.

Standing, Conezio, J. and Haber, R. (1970) Perception and memory for pictures: Single-trial learning of 2500 visual stimuli. *Psychonomic Science*, 19:73–74.

Stanley, J. C. (1976) Identifying and nurturing the intellectually gifted. *Phi Delta Kappan*, 58:234–237.

Stanton, H. E. (1977) Dyadic discussion as a teaching method. *Contemporary Educational Psychology*, 2:99–107.

Staub, E. (1973) To rear a prosocial child: Reasoning, learning by doing, and learning to teach others. Paper presented at the Conference on Contemporary Issues in Moral Development.

Staub, E. (1978) *Positive Social Behavior and Morality: Social and Personal Influence*. New York: Academic Press.

Staub, E. and Sherk, L. (1970) Need for approval, children's sharing behavior, and reciprocity in sharing. *Child Development*, 41:243–252.

Steel, B. F. and Pollock, C. B. (1977) A psychiatric study of parents who abuse infants and small children. In Helfer, R. E. and Hempe, C. H., eds. *The Battered Child*. Chicago: The University of Chicago Press.

Steelman, L. C. and Mercy, J. A. (1980) Unconfounding the confluence model. *American Sociological Review*, 45:571–582.

Stein, A. H. (1971) The effects of sex-role standards for achievement and sex-role preference on three determinants of achievement motivation. *Developmental Psychology*, 4:219–231.

Stein, B. S. (1978) Depth of processing reexamined: The effects of the precision of encoding and test appropriateness. *Journal of Verbal Learning and Verbal Behavior*, 17:165–174.

Stein, M. I. (1975) *Stimulating Creativity*. Vol. 2. New York: Academic Press.

Stein, N. L. and Glenn, C. G. (1979) An analysis of story comprehension in elementary school children. In Freedle, R., ed. *New Directions in Discourse Processing*. Norwood, N.J.: Ablex.

Steinberg, L. D., Catalano, R., and Dooley, D. (1981) Economic antecedents of child abuse and neglect. *Child Development*, 52:975–985.

Stenner, A. J. and Katzenmeyer, W. G. (1976) Self-concept development in young children. *Phi Delta Kappan*, 58:356–357.

Stephan, W. G. (1978) School desegregation: An evaluation of predictions made in *Brown* v. *Board of Education*. *Psychological Bulletin*, 85:217–238.

Stephan, W. G. and Rosenfield, D. (1979) Black self-rejection: Another look. *Journal of Educational Psychology*, 71:708–716.

Sternberg, R. J. (1981a) Intelligence and nonentrenchment. *Journal of Educational Psychology*, 73:1–16.

Sternberg, R. J. (1981b) Intelligence as thinking and learning skills. *Educational Leadership*, 39:18–21.

Stevens, G. and Boyd, M. (1980) The importance of mother: Labor force participation and intergenerational mobility of women. *Social Forces*, 59:186–199.

Stevenson, H. W. and Steward, E. C. (1958) A developmental study of race awareness in young children. *Child Development*, 29:399–409.

Steward, M. A., Pitts, F. N., Craig, A. G., and Dieruf, W. (1966) The hyperactive child syndrome. *American Journal of Orthopsychiatry*, 36:861–867.

Stewart, J. S. (1975) Clarifying values clarification: A critique. *Phi Delta Kappan*, 56:684–688.

Stinard, T. A. and Dolphin, W. D. (1981) Which students benefit from self-paced mastery instruction and why. *Journal of Educational Psychology*, 73:754–763.

Stotz, S. B., Wienckowski, L. A., and Brown, B. S. (1975) Behavior modification: A perspective on critical issues. *American Psychologist*, 30:1027–1048.

Strike, K. A. (1975) The logic of learning by discovery. *Review of Educational Research*, 45:461–483.

Stringer, L. A. (1973) Children at risk 2. The teacher as change agent. *The Elementary School Journal*, 73:425–433.

Strodtbeck, F. L., Ronchi, D., and Hansell, S. (1976) Tutoring and psychological growth. In Allen, V. L., ed. *Children as Teachers*. New York: Academic Press.

Stuart, R. B. (1974) Teaching facts about drugs: Pushing or preventing. *Journal of Educational Psychology*, 66:189–201.

Suits, B. (1967) What is a game? *Philosophy of Science*, 34:148–156.

Suler, J. R. (1980) Primary process thinking and creativity. *Psychological Bulletin*, 88:144–165.

Sullivan, H. S. (1947) *Conceptions of Modern Psychiatry*. Washington, D.C.: William A. White Psychiatric Foundation.

Sullivan, H. S. (1953) *The Interpersonal Theory of Psychiatry*. New York: Norton.

Sulzbacher, S. I. and Houser, J. E. (1970) A tactic to eliminate disruptive behaviors in the classroom: Group contingent consequences. In Ulrich, R., Stachnik, T., and Mabry, J.,

eds. *Control of Human Behavior*. Vol. 2. Glenview, Ill.: Scott, Foresman.

Sumby, W. H. (1963) Word frequency and the serial position effect. *Journal of Verbal Learning and Verbal Behavior*, 1:443–450.

Sutherland, A. and Goldschmid, M. (1974) Negative teacher expectation and IQ change in children with superior intellectual potential. *Child Development*, 45:852–856.

Sutherland, N. S. (1968) Outlines of a theory of visual pattern recognition in animals and man. *Proceedings of the Royal Society*, Series B, 171:297–317.

Swann, W. B., Jr. and Pittman, T. S. (1977) Initiating play activity of children: The moderating influence of verbal cues on intrinsic motivation. *Child Development*, 48:1128–1132.

Swanson, J. M. and Kinsbourne, M. (1976) Stimulant-related state-dependent learning in hyperactive children. *Science*, 192:1354–1357.

Swift, D. W. (1974) Situations and stereotypes: Variations in the school administrator's role. *The Elementary School Journal*, 75:69–78.

Tanner, J. M. (1970) Physical growth. In Mussen, P. H., ed. *Carmichael's Manual of Child Psychology*. 3rd ed. New York: Wiley.

Tanner, J. M. (1972) Sequence, tempo, and individual variation in growth and development of boys and girls aged twelve to sixteen. In Kagan, J., and Coles, R., eds. *Twelve to Sixteen, Early Adolescence*. New York: Norton.

Tanner, J. M. (1978) *Foetus into Man*. Cambridge, Mass.: Harvard University Press.

Tanner, L. N. and Lindgren, H. C. (1971) *Classroom Teaching and Learning*. New York: Holt, Rinehart and Winston.

Tausky, C. (1969) Meanings of work among blue collar men. *Pacific Sociological Review*, 12:49–55.

Taylor, C. W. and Barron, F. (1963) *Scientific Creativity: Its Recognition and Development*. New York: Wiley.

Taylor, I. A. (1975) An emerging view of creative actions. In Taylor, I. A. and Getzels, J. W., eds. *Perspectives in Creativity*. Chicago: Aldine.

Taylor, S. P. and Lewit, D. W. (1966) Social comparison and deception regarding ability. *Journal of Personality*, 34:94–104.

Telford, C. W. and Sawrey, J. M. (1977) *The Exceptional Individual*. 3rd ed. Englewood Cliffs, N.J.: Prentice-Hall.

Tennyson, R. D. and Part, O. (1980) The teaching of concepts: A review of instructional design research literature. *Review of Educational Research*, 50:55–70.

Terman, L. M. (1925) *Mental and Physical Traits of a Thousand Gifted Children*. Stanford: Stanford University Press.

Terman, L. M. (1954) The discovery and encouragement of exceptional talent. *American Psychologist*, 9:221–230.

Tharp, R. G. and Wetzel, R. J. (1969) *Behavior Modification in the Natural Environment*. New York: Academic Press.

Thomas, A. and Chess, S. (1977) *Temperament and Development*. New York: Brunner/Mazel.

Thomas, A., Chess, S., Birch, H. G., Hertzig, M. E., and Korn, S. (1963) *Behavioral Individuality in Early Childhood*. New York: New York University Press.

Thomas, C. W., Petersen, D. M., Zingraff, M. T. (1975) Student drug use: A re-examination of the ''hang-loose ethic'' hypothesis. *Journal of Health and Social Behavior*, 16:63–73.

Thomas, D. R. (1975) Cooperation and competition among Polynesian and European children. *Child Development*, 46:948–953.

Thomas, D. R., Becker, W. C., and Armstrong, M. (1968) Production and elimination of disruptive classroom behavior by systematically varying teacher's behavior. *Journal of Applied Behavior Analysis*, 1:35–45.

Thompson, L. J. (1971) Language disabilities in men of eminence. *Journal of Learning Disabilities*, 4:34–45.

Thompson, R. F. (1976) The search for the engram. *American Psychologist*, 31:209–227.

Thompson, S. K. (1975) Gender labels and early sex role development. *Child Development*, 46:339–347.

Thorndike, E. L. and Woodworth, R. S. (1901a) The influence of improvement in one mental function upon the efficiency of other functions. I. *Psychological Review*, 8:247–261.

Thorndike, E. L. and Woodworth, R. S. (1901b) The influence of improvement in one mental function upon the efficiency of other functions. II. The stimulation of magnitudes. *Psychological Review*, 8:384–395.

Thorndike, E. L. and Woodworth, R. S. (1901c) The influence of improvement in one mental function upon the efficiency of other functions. III. Functions involving attention, observation, and discrimination. *Psychological Review*, 8:553–564.

Thorndike, R. L. (1968) Review of *Pygmalion in the Classroom*. *American Educational Research Journal*, 5:708–711.

Thorndike, R. L. and Hagen, E. P. (1977) *Measurement and Evaluation in Psychology and Education*. 4th ed. New York: Wiley.

Throne, J. M. (1973) Learning disabilities: A radical behaviorist point of view. *Journal of Learning Disabilities*, 6:543–546.

Thurstone, L. L. (1938) *Primary Mental Abilities*. Chicago: University of Chicago Press.

Thurstone, L. L. (1947) *Multiple Factor Analysis: A Development and Expansion of "The Vectors of the Mind."* Chicago: University of Chicago Press.

Tittle, C. R. and Rowe, A. R. (1973) Moral appeal, sanction threat, and deviance: An experimental test. *Social Problems*, 20:488–497.

Toffler, A. (1970) *Future Shock*. New York: Random House.

Torrance, E. P. (1962) Developing creative thinking through school experiences. In Parnes, S. and Harding, G., eds. *A Sourcebook for Creative Thinking*. New York: Scribner's.

Torrance, E. P. (1968) Creative abilities of elementary school children. In Michael, W. B., ed. *Teaching for Creative Endeavor*. Bloomington, Ind.: University of Indiana Press.

Torrance, E. P. (1970) *Encouraging Creativity in the Classroom*. Dubuque, Iowa: William C. Brown.

Torrance, E. P. (1972) Creative kids. Today's Education: *NEA Journal*, 61:25–28.

Torrance, E. P. (1975) Motivation and creativity. In Torrance, E. P. and White, W. F., eds. *Issues and Advances in Educational Psychology*. Itasca, Ill.: F. E. Peacock.

Torrance, E. P. and Myers, R. E. (1972) *Creative Learning and Teaching*. New York: Dodd, Mead.

Torrey, J. W. (1979) Reading that comes naturally: The early reader. In Waller, T. G., and MacKinnon, G. E., eds.

Reading Research: Advances in Theory and Practice. Vol. 1. New York: Academic Press.

Travis, C. B. (1977) Social behavior of children in a classroom setting. *Contemporary Educational Psychology*, 2:373–383.

Treiman, D. J. (1977) *Occupational Prestige in Comparative Perspective*. New York: Academic Press.

Treisman, A. (1964) A monitoring and storage of irrelevant messages in selective attention. *Journal of Verbal Learning and Verbal Behavior*, 3:449–459.

Trelease, J. (1982) *The Read-Aloud Handbook*. New York: Penguin.

Trezise, R. L. (1976) The gifted child: Back in the limelight. *Phi Delta Kappan*, 58:241–243.

Trosky, O. S. and Wood, C. C. (1973) Discussion: Intuitive or learned? *The Elementary School Journal*, 73:328–332.

Trosky, O. S. and Wood, C. C. (1976) Discussion: A chance for everyone. *The Elementary School Journal*, 76:296–301.

Trow, M. (1968) Research and the racial revolution in American education. Paper read at the Sixteenth Congress of the International Association of Applied Psychology, Amsterdam, Holland.

Tuddenham, R. D. (1948) Soldier intelligence in World Wars I and II. *American Psychologist*, 3:54–56.

Tuddenham, R. D., Brooks, J., Milkovich, L. (1974) Mothers' reports of behavior of ten-year-olds: Relationships with sex, ethnicity, and mother's education. *Developmental Psychology*, 10:959–995.

Tulving, E. (1968) Theoretical issues in free recall. In Dixon, T. R. and Horton, D. L., eds. *Verbal Behavior and General Behavior Theory*. Englewood Cliffs, N.J.: Prentice-Hall.

Tulving, E. (1972) Episodic and semantic memory. In Tulving, E. and Donaldson, W., eds. *Organization of Memory*. New York: Academic Press.

Tulving, E. (1974) Cue-dependent forgetting. *American Scientist*, 62:74–82.

Tulving, E. (1976) Ecphoric processes in recall and recognition. In Brown, J., ed. *Recall and Recognition*. New York: Wiley.

Tulving, E. and Pearlstone, Z. (1966) Availability versus accessibility of information in memory for words. *Journal of Verbal Learning and Verbal Behavior*, 5:381–391.

Tulving, E. and Psotka, J. (1971) Retroactive inhibition in free recall: Inaccessibility of information available in the memory store. *Journal of Experimental Psychology*, 87:1–8.

Tulving, E. and Thomson, D. M. (1973) Encoding specificity and retrieval processes in episodic memory. *Psychological Review*, 80:352–373.

Tumblin, A. and Gholson, B. (1981) Hypothesis theory and the development of conceptual learning. *Psychological Bulletin*, 90:102–124.

Turiel, E. (1973) Stage transition in moral development. In Travers, R. M. W., ed. *Second Handbook of Research on Teaching*. Chicago: Rand McNally.

Turner, R. H. (1962) Role-taking: Process versus conformity. In Rose, A., ed. *Human Behavior and Social Processes*. Boston: Houghton Mifflin.

Turner, R. L. (1979) The value of variety in teaching styles. *Educational Leadership*, 36:257–258.

Ullmann, L. P. and Krasner, L. (1965) *Case Studies in Behavior Modification*. New York: Holt, Rinehart and Winston.

Underwood, B. J. (1957) Interference and forgetting. *Psychological Review,* 64:49–60.

Underwood, B. J. (1972) Are we overloading memory? In Melton, A. W. and Martin, E., eds. *Coding Processes in Human Memory.* New York: Wiley.

U.S. Department of Labor (1970) Career Thresholds: A longitudinal study of the educational and labor market experience of male youth. *Research Monograph No. 16,* Vol. 1–3. Washington, D.C.: Government Printing Office.

Urevick, S. J. (1974) Ability grouping: Why is it undemocratic? In Gall, M. D. and Ward, B. A., eds. *Critical Issues in Educational Psychology.* Boston: Little, Brown.

Vacc, N. A. and Kirst, N. (1977) Emotionally disturbed children and regular classroom teachers. *The Elementary School Journal,* 77:309–317.

Vander Zanden, J. W. (1983) *American Minority Relations.* New York: Knopf.

Vander Zanden, J. W. (1984) *Social Psychology.* 2nd ed. New York: Random House.

Venezky, R. L. (1970a) Nonstandard language and reading. *Elementary English,* 47:334–345.

Venezky, R. L. (1970b) *Regularity in Reading and Spelling.* In Levin, H. and Williams, J. P., eds. *Basic Studies in Reading.* New York: Basic Books.

Venezky, R. L. (1970c) *The Structure of English Orthography.* The Hague: Mouton.

Venezky, R. L. (1978) Reading acquisition: The occult and the obscure. In Murray, F. B., and Pikulski, J. J., eds. *The Acquisition of Reading: Cognitive, Linguistic, and Perceptual Prerequisites.* Baltimore: University Park Press.

Venezky, R. L. and Winfield, L. (1979) Schools that succeed beyond expectations in teaching reading. Technical Report No. 1, University of Delaware Studies on Education.

Veroff, J., Wilcox, S., and Atkinson, J. W. (1953) The achievement motive in high school and college-age women. *Journal of Abnormal and Social Psychology,* 48:103–109.

Vetter, B. and Babco, E. (1975) *Professional Women and Minorities: A Manpower Resource Service.* Washington, D.C.: Scientific Manpower Commission.

Vittetoe, J. O. (1977) Why first-year teachers fail. *Phi Delta Kappan,* 58:429–430.

Voysey, M. (1975) *A Constant Burden: The Reconstruction of Family Life.* Boston: Routledge & Kegan Paul.

Vroegh, K. (1976) Sex of teacher and academic achievement: A review of research. *The Elementary School Journal,* 76:389–405.

Vygotsky, L. S. (1962) *Thought and Language.* Cambridge, Mass.: MIT Press. First published in 1934.

Wagner, P. (1978) Elusive notion of creativity and pedagogical practice. *The Clearinghouse,* 51:204–205.

Waks, L. J. (1969) Philosophy, education, and the doomsday threat. *Review of Educational Research,* 39:607–622.

Walberg, H. J. and Thomas, S. C. (1972) Open education: An operational definition and validation in Great Britain and United States. *American Education Research Journal,* 9:197–209.

Walden, E. L. and Thompson, S. A. (1981) A review of some alternative approaches to drug management of hyperactivity in children. *Journal of Learning Disabilities,* 14:213–218.

Wallach, M. A. (1970) Creativity. In Mussen, P. H., ed. *Carmichael's Manual of Child Psychology.* 3rd ed. Vol. 1. New York: Wiley.

Wallach, M. A. (1971) *The Intelligence/Creativity Distinction.* New York: General Learning Press.

Wallach, M. A. and Kogan, N. (1965) *Modes of Thinking in Young Children: A Study of the Creativity-Intelligence Distinction.* New York: Holt, Rinehart and Winston.

Wallas, A. (1926) *The Art of Thinking.* London: Watts.

Waller, W. (1932) *The Sociology of Teaching.* New York: Wiley.

Wallerstein, J. S. and Kelly, J. B. (1980) California's children of divorce. *Psychology Today,* 13:67–76.

Walters, G. C. and Grusec, J. E. (1977) *Punishment.* San Francisco: W. H. Freeman.

Ward, W. D. and Barcher, P. R. (1975) Reading achievement and creativity as related to open classroom experience. *Journal of Educational Psychology,* 67:683–691.

Warner, L. G. and DeFleur, M. L. (1969) Attitude as an interactional concept: Social constraint and social distance as intervening variables between attitudes and actions. *American Sociological Review,* 34:153–169.

Warner, S. P., Miller, F. D., and Cohen, M. W. (1977) Relative effectiveness of teacher attention and the ''good behavior game'' in modifying disruptive classroom behavior. *Journal of Applied Behavior Analysis,* 10:737.

Waterman, A. S., Geary, P. S., and Waterman, C. K. (1974) Longitudinal study of changes in ego identity status from the freshman to the senior year at college. *Developmental Psychology,* 10:387–392.

Watkins, O. C. and Watkins, M. J. (1975) Buildup of proactive inhibition as a cue-overload effect. *Journal of Experimental Psychology: Human Learning and Memory,* 104:442–452.

Watson, J. B. (1924) *Behaviorism,* New York: Norton.

Watson, J. B. and Rayner, R. (1920) Conditioned emotional reactions. *Journal of Experimental Psychology,* 3:1–14.

Watts, G. H. and Anderson, R. C. (1971) Effects of three types of inserted questions on learning from prose. *Journal of Educational Psychology,* 62:387–394.

Weatherley, D. (1964) Self-perceived rate of physical maturation and personality in late adolescence. *Child Development,* 35:1197–1210.

Webb, P. K. (1980) Piaget: Implications for teaching. *Theory into Practice,* 19:93–97.

Weber, L. (1971) *The English Infant School and Informal Education.* Englewood Cliffs, N.J.: Prentice-Hall.

Weber, M. B., Feldman, J. R., and Poling, E. C. (1981) Why women are underrepresented in educational administration. *Educational Leadership,* 38:320–322.

Weber, R. (1970) Some observations on the significance of dialect in the acquisition of reading. In Figurel, J. A., ed. *Reading Goals for the Disadvantaged.* Newark, Del.: International Reading Association.

Wegmann, R. G. (1976) Classroom discipline: An exercise in the maintenance of social reality. *Sociology of Education,* 49:71–79.

Weiner, B. (1972) *Theories of Motivation.* Chicago: Markham.

Weiner, B. (1979) A theory of motivation for some classroom experiences. *Journal of Educational Psychology,* 71:3–25.

Weiner, M. and Samuel, W. (1975) The effect of attributing internal arousal to an external source upon test anxiety and performance. *Journal of Social Psychology,* 96:255–265.

Weiss, G. and Hechtman, L. (1979) The hyperactive child syndrome. *Science,* 205:1348–1354.

Weisz, J. (1981) Learned helplessness in black and white children identified by their schools as retarded and nonretarded: Performance deterioration in response to failure. *Developmental Psychology,* 17:499–508.

Wellman, H. M. (1977) Tip of the tongue and feeling of knowing experiences: A developmental study of memory monitoring. *Child Development,* 48:13–21.

Wellman, H. M. (1978) Knowledge of the interaction of memory variables: A developmental study of metamemory. *Developmental Psychology,* 14:24–29.

Westerhoff, J. H., III (1978) *McGuffey and His Readers.* Nashville: Abingdon.

Whalen, C. K. and Henker, B. (1976) Psychostimulants and children: A review and analysis. *Psychological Bulletin,* 83:1113–1130:

White, B. L. (1969) Child development research: An edifice without a foundation. *Merrill-Palmer Quarterly,* 15:49–79.

White, B. L. and Watts, J. C. (1973) *Experience and Environment.* Englewood Cliffs, N.J.: Prentice-Hall.

White, G. M. (1967) The elicitation and durability of altruistic behavior in children. *Research Bulletin.* Princeton: Educational Testing Service.

White, L. A. (1949) *The Science of Culture: A Study of Man and Civilization,* New York: Farrar, Straus.

White, L. K. and Brinkerhoff, D. B. (1981) The sexual division of labor: Evidence from childhood. *Social Forces,* 60:170–181.

White, M. A. (1975) Natural rates of teacher approval and disapproval in the classroom. *Journal of Applied Behavior Analysis,* 8:367–372.

White, R. K. and Lippitt, R. (1960) *Autocracy and Democracy.* New York: Harper & Row.

White, R. T. (1973) Research into learning hierarchies. *Review of Educational Research,* 43:361–365.

White, R. T. and Gagné, R. M. (1976) Retention of related and unrelated sentences. *Journal of Educational Psychology,* 68:843–852.

White, R. T. and Gagné, R. M. (1978) Formative evaluation applied to a learning hierarchy. *Contemporary Psychology,* 3:87–94.

White, R. W. (1959) Motivation reconsidered: The concept of competence. *Psychological Review,* 66:297–333.

Whitehead, A. N. and Russell, B. (1925) *Principia Mathematica.* 2nd ed. Cambridge: Cambridge University Press.

Whitely, J. D. (1970) Effects of practice distribution on learning a fine motor task. *Research Quarterly,* 48:576–593.

Whitmore, J. R. (1982) Recognizing and developing hidden giftedness. *Elementary School Journal,* 82:274–283.

Whorf, B. L. (1956) Science and linguistics. In Carroll, J. B., ed. *Language, Thought and Reality: Selected Writings of Benjamin Lee Whorf.* Cambridge, Mass.: M.I.T. Press.

Wicker, A. W. (1969) Attitudes versus actions: The relationship of verbal and overt behavioral responses to attitude objects. *Journal of Social Issues,* 25:41–78.

Wiemann, J. M. and Backlund, P. (1980) Current theory and research in communicative competence. *Review of Educational Research,* 50:185–199.

Wikler, L. (1981) Chronic stresses of families of mentally retarded children. *Family Relations,* 30:281–288.

Wilder, G. (1977) Five exemplary reading programs. In Guthrie, J. T., ed. *Cognition, Curriculum, and Comprehension.* Newark, Del.: International Reading Association.

Willenberg, E. P. (1977) Foreward. In Gearheart, B. R., ed. *Learning Disabilities: Educational strategies.* Saint Louis: C. V. Mosby.

Williams, C. R., Neff, A. R., and Finkelstein, J. H. (1981) Theory into practice: Reconsidering the preposition. *Theory into Practice,* 20:93–96.

Williams, F., Whitehead, J. L., and Miller, L. (1972) Relations between language attitudes and teacher expectancy. *American Education Research Journal,* 9:263–277.

Williams, J. E., Bennett, S. M., and Best, D. L. (1975) Awareness and expression of sex stereotypes in young children. *Developmental Psychology,* 11:635–642.

Williams, J. E. and Morland, J. K. (1976) *Race, Color, and the Young Child.* Chapel Hill: University of North Carolina Press.

Williams, J. E. and Stabler, J. R. (1973) If white means good then black . . .'' *Psychology Today,* 7 (July, 1973):51–54.

Willis, S. and Brophy, J. (1974) Origins of teachers' attitudes toward young children. *Journal of Educational Psychology,* 66:520–529.

Wine, J. (1971) Test anxiety and the direction of attention. *Psychological Bulletin,* 76:92–104.

Winett, R. A. and Winkler, R. C. (1972) Current behavior modification in the classroom: Be still, be quiet, be docile. *Journal of Applied Behavior Analysis,* 5:499–504.

Winne, P. H. (1979) Experiments relating teachers' use of higher cognitive questions to student achievement. *Review of Educational Research,* 49:13–50.

Winokur, S. (1976) *A Primer of Verbal Behavior: An Operant View.* Englewood Cliffs, N.J.: Prentice-Hall.

Wirtenberg, J., Klein, S., Richardson, B., and Thomas, V. (1981) Sex equity in American education. *Educational Leadership,* 38:311–319.

Wiseman, S. and Tulving, E. (1976) Encoding specificity: Relation between recall superiority and recognition failure. *Journal of Experimental Psychology: Human Learning and Memory,* 2:349–361.

Wispé, L. G. (1972) Positive forms of social behavior: An overview. *Journal of Social Issues,* 28:1–19.

Withey, S. B. and Abeles, R. P. (1980) *Television and Social Behavior: Beyond Violence and Children.* Hillsdale, N.J.: Lawrence Erlbaum.

Witkin, H. A. (1973) A cognitive-style perspective on evaluation and guidance. *Proceedings of the 1973 Invitational Conference on Testing Problems-Measurement for Self-Understanding and Personal Development.*

Witkin, H. A. and Goodenough, D. R. (1977) Field dependence and interpersonal behavior. *Psychological Bulletin,* 84:661–689.

Witkin, H. A., Moore, C. A., Goodenough, D. R., and Cox, P. W. (1977) Field-dependent and field-independent cognitive styles and their educational implications. *Review of Educational Research*, 47:1–64.

Witkin, H. A., Moore, C. A., Oltman, P. K., Goodenough, D. R., Friedman, F., Owen, D. R., and Raskin, E. (1977) Role of the field-dependent and field-independent cognitive styles in academic evolution: A longitudinal study. *Journal of Educational Psychology*, 69:197–211.

Wittmaier, B. C. (1974) Test anxiety, mood, and performance. *Journal of Personality and Social Psychology*, 29:664–669.

Wittrock, M. C. (1966) The learning by discovery hypothesis. In Shulman, L. S. and Keislar, E. R., eds. *Learning by Discovery: A Critical Appraisal*. Chicago: Rand McNally.

Wittrock, M. C. and Lumsdaine, A. A. (1977) Instructional psychology. In Rosenzweig, M. R. and Porter, L. W., eds. *Annual Review of Psychology*. Vol. 28. Palo Alto, Callif.: Annual Reviews, Inc.

Witty, P. A. (1930) A study of one hundred gifted children. *University of Kansas Bulletin of Education*, State Teachers College Studies in Education: 1 (13).

Wohlwill, J. F. (1973) The concept of experience: S or R? *Human Development*, 16:90–107.

Wolff, P. H. and Hurwitz, I. (1973) Functional implications of the minimal brain damage syndrome. In Walzer, S. and Wolff, P. H., eds. *Minimal Cerebral Dysfunction in Children*. New York: Grune & Stratton.

Wood, F. H. and Zabel, R. H. (1978) Making sense of reports on the incidence of behavior disorders/emotional disturbance in school-aged populations. *Psychology in the Schools*, 15:45–51.

Woodward, J. E. (1980) Peer acceptance for the handicapped: Myth or reality? *Phi Delta Kappan*, 61:715.

Woolfolk, A. E. (1978) Student learning and performance under varying conditions of teacher verbal and nonverbal evaluative communication. *Journal of Educational Psychology*, 70:87–94.

Worcester, D. A. (1956) *The Education of Children of Above-Average Ability*. Lincoln: University of Nebraska Press.

Worden, P. E. (1975) Effects of sorting on subsequent recall of unrelated items: A developmental study. *Child Development*, 46:687–695.

Wright, A. R. (1976) Beyond behavioral objectives. In Mehrens, W. A., ed. *Readings in Measurement and Evaluation in Education and Psychology*. New York: Holt, Rinehart and Winston.

Wright, P. H. and Keple, T. W. (1981) Friends and parents of a sample of high-school juniors: An exploratory study of relationship intensity and interpersonal rewards. *Journal of Marriage and the Family*, 43:559–570.

Wright, R. J. (1975) The affective and cognitive consequences of an open elementary school. *American Educational Research Journal*, 12:449–468.

Wrong, D. (1961) The oversocialized conception of man in modern sociology. *American Sociological Review*, 26:183–193.

Wylie, R. (1979) *The Self-Concept*. Lincoln: University of Nebraska Press.

Wynne, E. A. (1981) Looking at good schools. *Phi Delta Kappan*, 62:377–381.

Yancey, W. L., Rigsby, L., and McCarthy, J. D. (1972) Social position and self-evaluation: The relative importance of race. *American Journal of Sociology*, 78:338–359.

Yarborough, B. H. and Johnson, R. A. (1980) Research that questions the traditional elementary school marking system. *Phi Delta Kappan*, 61:527–528.

Yarrow, M. R. and Waxler, C. Z. (1976) Dimensions and correlates of prosocial behavior in young children. *Child Development*, 47:118–125.

Yarrow, M. R., Waxler, C. Z., and Scott, P. M. (1971) Child effects on adult behavior. *Developmental Psychology*, 5:300–311.

Yates, F. A. (1966) *The Art of Memory*. Chicago: University of Chicago Press.

Yinger, R. (1979) Routines in teacher planning. *Theory into Practice*, 18:163–169.

Yinger, R. J. (1980) A study of teacher planning. *The Elementary School Journal*, 80:107–127.

Young, M. N. and Gibson, W. B. (1966) *How to Develop an Exceptional Memory*. Hollywood: Wilshire Press.

Ysseldyke, J. E, (1977) Aptitude-treatment interaction research with first-grade children. *Contemporary Educational Psychology*, 2:1–9.

Ysseldyke, J. E. and Salvia, J. (1974) Diagnostic-prescriptive teaching: Two models. *Exceptional Children*, 41:181–185.

Yuille, J. C. and Paivio, A. (1969) Abstractness and recall of connected discourse. *Journal and Experimental Psychology*, 82:467–471.

Zahorik, J. A. (1970) The effect of planning on teaching. *The Elementary School Journal*, 71:143–151.

Zahorik, J. A. (1976a) The virtue of vagueness in instructional objectives. *The Elementary School Journal*, 76:411–419.

Zahorik, J. A. (1976b) Learning activities: The objectives-seeking function. *The Elementary School Journal*, 77:50–56.

Zajonc, R. B. (1976) Family configuration and intelligence. *Science*, 192:227–236.

Zelnik, M. and Kantner, J. S. (1980) Report. *Family Planning Perspectives*, 12:230.

Zigler, E. and Muenchow, S. (1979) Mainstreaming. *American Psychologist*, 34:993–996.

Zigler, E. and Trickett, P. K. (1978) IQ, social competence, and evaluation of early childhood intervention programs. *American Psychologist*, 33:789–798.

Zimmerman, B. J. (1977) Modeling. In Hom, H. L., Jr. and Robinson, P. A., eds. *Psychological Processes in Early Education*. New York: Academic Press.

Zimmerman, B. J. (1978) A social learning explanation for age-related changes in children's conceptual behavior. *Contemporary Educational Psychology*, 3:11–19.

Zimmerman, B. J. and Ghozeil, F. S. (1974) Modeling as a teaching technique. *The Elementary School Journal*, 74:440–446.

Zimmerman, B. J. and Kleefeld, C. F. (1977) Toward a theory of teaching. A social learning view. *Contemporary Educational Psychology*, 2:158–171.

Zimmerman, B. J. and Koussa, R. (1979) Social influences on children's toy preferences: Effects of model rewardingness and affect. *Contemporary Educational Psychology*, 4:55–66.

Zimmerman, B. J. and Rosenthal, T. L. (1972) Concept attainment, transfer, and retention observation and rule provision. *Journal of Experimental Child Psychology*, 14:139–150.

Zimmerman, D. H. and Wieder, D. L. (1970) Ethnomethodology and the problem of order. In Douglas, J. D., ed. *Understanding Everyday Life*. Chicago: Aldine.

Zimmerman, E. H. and Zimmerman, J. (1962) The alteration of behavior in a special classroom situation. *Journal of the Experimental Analysis of Behavior*, 5:59–60.

Zirkel, P. A. (1971) Self-concept and the "disadvantage" of ethnic group membership and mixture. *Review of Educational Research*, 41:211–225.

Zirkel, P. A. (1976) The why's and ways of testing bilinguality before teaching bilingually. *The Elementary School Journal*, 76:323–330.

Zirkel, P. A. (1977) The legal vicissitudes of bilingual education. *Phi Delta Kappan*, 58:409–411.

Zoll, E. J. (1969) Research in programmed instruction in mathematics. *The Mathematics Teacher*, 62:103–110.

Zuckerman, M. and Wheeler, L. (1975) To dispel fantasies about the fantasy-based measure of fear of success. *Psychological Bulletin*, 82:932–946.

AUTHOR INDEX

Abeles, R. P., 153
Abelson, R., 271–272
Abrams, J. C., 524
Abramson, L. Y., 349
Achenbach, T. M., 350
Adam, B. D., 310
Adams, G. R., 447
Adams, J. A., 201, 291–292
Adams, R. S., 436
Addison, S., 524–525
Adelman, H. S., 513
Adkison, J. A., 20, 22
Adler, A., 237
Ahlgren, A., 353, 357
Aiken, L. R., Jr., 238, 306
Ainsworth, M. D. S., 43–45, 49
Ajzen, I., 304
Albert, R. S., 526
Alexander, L. T., 143, 177, 211, 382–383, 405
Algonzzine, B., 447, 511
Allen, G. J., 311
Allen, R. P., 512–513
Allen, T. W., 512
Allen, V. L., 410–411
Allport, G. W., 388, 457
Alpert, R., 352
Alson, M. L., 516
Altus, W. D., 51, 239
Ames, C., 307, 353, 356
Amir, Y., 457
Ammons, R. B., 296
Amsel, A., 146
Anastasi, A., 100, 102
Anastasiow, N. J., 179
Anderson, B. D., 19
Anderson, C. M., 513
Anderson, J. R., 193
Anderson, L. M., 445, 482
Anderson, L. W., 407, 414–415
Anderson, M. C., 272
Anderson, R. C., 198, 210, 271–273
Anderson, T., 272, 273
Andison, F. S., 153
Andre, M. A., 273
Andres, D., 57
Annis, L. F., 115
Antinucci, F., 261

Applegate, J. R., 403
Archbold, J., 146
Argyle, M., 411
Arlin, M., 441, 443
Armbruster, F. E., 179
Armstrong, D. G., 442
Armstrong, M., 485
Arnold, D. J., 210
Arnold, M., 508
Asher, S. R., 456
Aspy, D., 388
Atkinson, J. W., 358–360, 362
Atkinson, R. C., 146, 189, 195–197, 200, 211, 419
Atkinson, R. L., 147
Atwood, H. E., 454
Austin, G. R., 444
Austin, J. L., 263
Ausubel, D. P., 163, 174, 179, 181, 210
Avila, D., 304
Ayllon, T., 478
Azzi, R., 421

Babad, E. Y., 114
Babco, E., 20
Bach, L., 20
Backlund, P., 434
Bacon, F., 231
Baddeley, A. D., 200
Baer, D. M., 138, 142, 145
Bagnato, S. J., 510
Bain, J. D., 118
Baird, L. L., 472
Baker, F. B., 418
Ball, J., 292
Ball, S., 344
Ballard, M., 518
Ballew, H., 179
Bandura, A., 62, 77, 149–150, 152–153, 320, 372, 461, 492
Bank, B. J., 78
Banks, J. H., 306
Banks, W. C., 310
Banton, L., 401
Barcher, P. R., 441
Barclay, C. R., 291, 297
Bard, B., 86
Barkley, R. A., 513

633

SUBJECT INDEX

ABOUT THE AUTHORS

James W. Vander Zanden is a professor in the College of Social and Behavioral Sciences at the Ohio State University and previously taught at Duke University. His Ph.D. degree is from the University of North Carolina. Professor Vander Zanden's published works include more than twenty professional articles, primarily in the area of race relations, and six other books.

Ann J. Pace is an assistant professor of educational psychology at the University of Missouri - Kansas City. She received her Ph.D. degree from the University of Delaware, and she has taught at the University of Delaware and the University of North Carolina at Greensboro. Her areas of specialization are reading comprehension and school learning. She has published in the *Journal of Educational Psychology* and in the volume *The Origins and Growth of Communications,* and has contributed frequently to the professional meetings of the American Educational Research Association.